FUCHSIAS
OF THE 19th AND
EARLY 20th CENTURY

by
Eric A. Johns

A B.F.S. Publication

AN HISTORICAL CHECKLIST OF FUCHSIA SPECIES & CULTIVARS, PRE-1939

First published in 1997 by
The British Fuchsia Society
15 Summerfield Lane
Summerfield
Kidderminster
Worcs DY11 7SA

ISBN 0 901774 15 4

The author wishes to express thanks to the
Royal Botanical Garden Library in Edinburgh for
permission to reproduce the colour plates taken by
the author from various journals held.

Output from disc by Avonset, Palace Yard Mews, Bath
Printed and bound in Great Britain by
Redwood Books, Trowbridge, Wiltshire

In memory of my Father,
and
for his Grandchildren,
Michael and Andrew,
who only knew him for a
few precious years.

FOREWORD

On 17 September 1995 my father suffered a huge heart attack and died. It was a terrible shock and tragic loss for our family. Accompanying the personal tragedy of losing a very special father, was the awful realisation that he would never be able to complete fully his painstaking research into the fuchsias of the 19th and early 20th centuries, a task which had occupied the last eight years of his life.

My father, in keeping with his passion for fuchsias, his enquiring mind and ceaseless thirst for knowledge, had read widely on the subject of Fuchsias and their history and was struck by several glaring inconsistencies given on the origins of various cultivars. Resolved to investigate further, he commenced checking back through the literature of the period to determine for himself the correct origins. There began this book, which is essentially a checklist of all the fuchsias of the times, with descriptions of the flowers, the names of the growers, or raisers, the dates of introduction and any other information he could come across in contemporary literature. It is based almost entirely on primary sources, and he records faithfully any discrepancies which may occur between different contemporary sources. If he could find no contemporary record attributing a certain cultivar to an accepted hybridiser, he has not done so; omissions therefore may prove significant. Shortly before he died, he told me that the work was just about complete, although further primary source materials particularly for European horticulturists were just coming to light. He appeared, for example, to be working through the research of Bruno Fournier on the nurserymen Rozain-Boucharlat recorded in "Fuchsiaphiles" at the time of his death.

I was naturally determined that all the knowledge he had acquired through hours of research would not die with him. With the assistance of the British Fuchsia Society, I have been able to publish this, his catalogue of fuchsias in existence before the Second World War. What follows is the findings of his research as it stood in September 1995, preserved on the database of his beloved computer, merely formatted, indexed and edited by myself and with the inclusion of my father's own slides taken from various Journals in the possession of the Royal Botanical Garden Library in Edinburgh. I am very grateful to them for granting permission for these slides to be reproduced to illustrate this book.

Retrieving the work from the depths of my fathers database has proved a long and frustratingly difficult task and I would like to thank Keith Winton for the computer expertise he so gladly lent to the project. I have spent much time attempting to clarify the origin of the abbreviations used and double check some references and inconsistencies, the help and support of John Porter in this regard has been invaluable. John even undertook to proof read the text, for which I am very grateful. Above all, John along with Kathleen & Jim Muncaster, held a strong belief in my father and the value of his work, which has proved very inspiring. My thanks must also go to my mother who has shared my determination to see this work through and encouraged me throughout.

We will never know how my father would have eventually finished his work, but I hope this book is sufficiently complete to be of lasting value. I am sure, moreover, that he would have wished to share the results of his research with others, and for the benefit of future scholarship into fuchsias. I am therefore doubly grateful to the British Fuchsia Society who has agreed that any profits from the sale of this book will be used to fund further research.

Alison Connelly, September 1996

CONTENTS

Index of Major Hybridizers of the Period

LIST OF ABBREVIATIONS

Adv	Advertised
App to	Appendix to
B cat	W J Bull catalogue
Bot	Botanical
BSW cat	B S Williams catalogue
C G & J H	Cottage Garden & Journal of Horticulture
C of M	Certificate of Merit
Cat	Catalogue
Cert	Certificate
Col Pl	Colour Plate
Ed	Edition
F & P	Florist & Pomologist
F de S	Flore des Serres
FC	Floricultural Cabinet
FJ	Florists Journal
FCC	Floral Committee Commended
FW & GG	Floral World & Gardeners Gazette
G	The Garden
GC	Gardeners Chronicle
GB	Great Britain
GM	Gardeners Magazine
GO	Gardeners Oracle
GO "select"	Gardeners Oracle " Selection"
Gr	Gardener
HC cat	H. Cannell catalogue
HS	Horticultural Society
Hort	Horticultural
Imp	Improved
Intro	Introduced
J	Journal
JF cat	John Forbes catalogue
JH (or J of H)	Journal of Horticulture
J of RHS	Journal of Royal Horticultural Society
Jr	Junior
L cat	V Lemoine catalogue
LHS	London Horticultural Society
ND	Not defined
NFS	National Floral Society
NK	Not Known
P	Page
RB cat	Rozain & Boucharlet Catalogue
RBS	Royal Botanical Society
RH	Revue Horticole
RH Scty	Royal Horticultural Society
SG	Scottish Gardener
V & A	Vilmorin & Andrieux
Vol	Volume
X	cross

LIST OF ILLUSTRATIONS

NOTE ON TEXT

Information on the Fuchsias which follows is listed in abbreviated form in the same unified format. First is given the name of Fuchsia, its type (e.g. single or double), its colour combination, description of its tube, sepals and corolla. Then follows details of sources of information, any interesting observations/references, the fuchsias parentage, the introducer, the raiser/hybridiser, the town, country and year.

A. BERTHOUD. Double. Red/Purple. Tube. Dull red. Sepals. Dull red. Twisted. Corolla. Marine blue. Broad. Well open. L. Cat. 1906. *Rozain. Lyons. France. 1905.*

ABEL CARRIÈRE (a). Single. Red/Red. Tube. Brilliant Red. Sepals. Brilliant red. Open. Corolla. Dark red shading to violet at extremities. Very short. RH. P60/61 1883. Coloured plate. Named after the Departmental head of the Nurseries, National History Musuem, Paris. GO. "Select" 1888. HC. Cat. 1885. Grown largely for the Paris market. Globosa x Corymbiflora. *Aubin, R. Bagnolet. France. 1883.*

ABEL CARRIÈRE (b). Single. Red/Red. Tube. Brilliant Scarlet. Sepals. Brilliant Scarlet. Elegantly reflexed. Corolla. Amaranth changing to violet purple. Vigorous. Compact. B. Cat. 1870. *Lemoine. Nancy. France. 1868.*

ABBÉ DAVID. Double. Red/Purple. Tube. Dark red. Sepals. Dark red. Corolla. Violet. Very full. Regular. Large leaves. L. Cat. 1901. *Lemoine. Nancy. France. 1901.*

ABBÉ FARGES. Double. Red/Purple. Tube Blood Red. Sepals. Blood red. Curled back. Corolla. Reddish violet. Full. Compact. L. Cat. 1901. *Lemoine. Nancy. France. 1901.*

ABBÉ GARNIER. Double. Red/Purple. Tube. Bright rose pink. Sepals. Bright rose pink. Corolla. Violet blue. Palmate. (Listed as a single GO. "Select" 1891). L. Cat. 1890. *Rozain. Lyons. France. 1889.*

ABBÉ GOURDON. Double. Red/Purple. Tube. Red. Sepals. Red. Corolla. Slate blue, petals red in centre. L. Cat. 1901. *Rozain. Lyons. France. 1899.*

ABBÉ LEMIRE. Single. Red/White. Tube. Clear red. Sepals. Clear red. Corolla. White. Large. L. Cat. 1896. *Rozain. Lyons. France. 1896.*

ABD EL KADIR (a). Single. ND/ND. Tube. ND. Sepals. ND. Corolla. ND. P84 2nd Ed by Porcher 1848. Resembles "Exoniensis". App. to RH. 1851 by Porcher "Mediocre". *Souchet. Fontainbleu. France. 1850.*

ABD EL KADIR (b). Double. Red/Purple. Tube. Red. (Rosy carmine). Sepals. Red. (Rosy Carmine). Corolla. Purple. (Violet). Large. Well produced. Show variety. Named after an Algerian Resistance leader (1807-83). HC. Cat. 1882-1885. BSW. Cat. 1888. *Lemoine. Nancy. France. 1880.*

ABELINE FABRE. Double. Red/White. Tube. Coral. Sepals. Coral. Large. Corolla. Milky white. Enormous. L. Cat. 1901. *Rozain. Lyons. France. 1899.*

ABONDANCE (a). Single. Pink/Red. Tube. Light flesh. 25mm long. Stout. Short. Sepals. Light flesh. Horizontal. Corolla. Pale red. (Vermilion red). P136 3rd. Ed by Porcher 1858 Large flowers. Floriferous. Similar but superior to "Minerva Superba". App. to RH. 1851 by Porcher. Perfection on "Empress" by Hally. *De Jonghe, Brussels. Belgium. 1850.*

ABONDANCE (b). ND. ND/ND. Tube. ND. Sepals. ND. Corolla. ND. LB. Cat. 1883. *Boucharlet. Lyons. France. NK.*

ABUNDANCE. Single. Red/Purple. Tube. Bright red. Sepals. Bright red. Corolla. Rich dark purple, shaded maroon. G. Vol 36. P277 21/9/1889 Exhibited by J. Lye at Bath Floral Fete 9 pot class (Third). GC. P138 1888 "Recommended". JF. Cat. 1888 New in 1887. HC. Cat. 1890. GO. "Select" 1890. *Lye, J. Market Lavington. GB. 1887.*

ACANTHA. Single. White/Red. Tube. Waxy white. Sepals. Waxy white. Tipped green. Corolla. Bright scarlet. Opens well. GC. P423 1851 Exhibited at RBS Show June 1851. GC. P517 1/8/1846 "Stands at the head of the whites". GC. P140 27/2/1847 & P250 17/4/1847 Listed by W.Miller, Ramsgate. P57 2nd Ed. by Porcher 1848 Tube and Sepals White tinged pink. 45 mm. Sepals Raised up. Corolla Vermilion cerise. P137 3rd Ed. by Porcher 1858. GC. P216 27/3/1847 & P232 1/4/1848 & P256 21/4/1849 Listed by R. Cooper, Croydon. GC. P203 25/3/1848 Listed by W. Rumley, Richmond. GC. P259 28/4/1849 & P241 20/4/1850 Listed by W. Rendle, Plymouth. GC. P226 13/4/1850 Listed by Poole Nurseries. GC. P869 27/12/1845 Intro. by F & J. Dickson. Chester. *Dickson F & J. Chester. GB. 1846.*

ACHIEVEMENT. Single. Red/Purple. Tube. Red. Sepals. Red. Corolla. Rich purple, shading to crimson at base. Dicksons, Chester Cat. 1907. NK. NK. *GB. NK.*

ACHILLES (a). Single. ND/ND. Tube. ND. Sepals. ND. Corolla. ND. GC. P375 4/6/1844 Exhibited by J. Smith. Vol XIV P12 Floricultural Cabinet. 1846. *Smith, J. Dalston. GB. 1844.*

ACHILLES (b). Double. Red/Purple. Tube. Dark red. Short. Sepals. Dark red. Corolla. Rich plum. Petals much waved. B. Cat. 1898-1901. L. Cat. 1901. *Bull, W. Chelsea. GB. 1898.*

ACIDALIE. ND. White/ND. Tube. White. Sepals. White. Corolla. ND. P120 4th. Ed. by Porcher 1874. Good, but not first class. *Demay, H. Arras. Belgium. 1865.*

ACIS. Single. Red/Purple. Tube. Deep crimson. Sepals. Deep crimson. Broad. Slightly reflexed. Corolla. Purple. Large. B. Cat. 1880-1881. Intro. by W. Bull. *Bull, W. Chelsea. GB. 1880.*

ACMON. Double. Red/Purple. Tube. Deep rosy pink. Sepals. Deep rosy pink. Large. Corolla. Slate Blue. Large. B. Cat. 1880-1881. Intro. by W. Bull. *Bull, W. Chelsea. GB. 1880.*

ACTAEON (a). Single. Red/Purple. Tube. Rich crimson. Sepals. Rich crimson. 4" across. Corolla. Bright purple. GC. P240 13/4/1850 Listed by W. Gregory, Cirencester. GC. P465 27/7/1850 Listed by W. Rumley, Richmond. GC. P465 27/7/1850 Listed by G. Smith. Islington. GC. P689 3/11/1849 Intro. by Gregory, Cirencester. *Gregory. Cirencester GB. 1849.*

ACTAEON (b). Double. Red/White. Tube. Red. Sepals. Red. Corolla. White. Large. Very full. Short petals. P131 4th. Ed. by Porcher 1874. *Demay, H. Arras. Belgium. 1872.*

ADA BRIGHT. Single. White/ND. Tube. White. Sepals. White. Corolla. ND. G. Vol36 1889 P277 21/9/1889 Exhibited at Bath Floral Fete by J. Lye (Third) Light. *Lye, J. Market Lavington. GB. 1889.*

ADAIR. Double. Red/Purple. Tube. Bright crimson. Short. Sepals. Bright crimson. Well reflexed. Corolla. Bluish Purple occasionally flaked rose. Short. B. Cat. 1889-1893. *Bull, W. Chelsea. GB. 1888.*

ADAM KOCK. Double. Red/Purple. Tube. Clear crimson red. Long. 15mm. Sepals. Clear crimson red. Horizontal. Corolla. Violet streaked and striped red. Short petals. Pleated and spiralled. P121 4th Ed. by Porcher 1874. *Weinrich, H. Germany. 1863.*

ADDINGTON. Single. Red/Red. Tube. Rosy scarlet. (Deep rose). Sepals. Rosy scarlet. (Deep rose). Corolla. Rosy scarlet (Deep rose). GO. P121 1898 AM. RHS 13/4/1897. GC. Vol 21 P257 17/4/1897. Exhibited at RHS by Cannell. HC. Cat. 1898 Intro. by H. Cannell. B. Cat. 1898-1899. F. fulgens x F. cordifolia splendens. *Fry, P. GB. 1897.*

ADDISON. Single. Red/Purple. Tube. Crimson. Sepals. Crimson. Broad. Horizontal. Corolla. Deep purple, striped and flaked rose. Large. B. Cat. 1881-1883. Intro. by W. Bull, Chelsea. *Bland, E. Fordham. GB. 1881.*

ADELA. Single. Red/Purple. Tube. Bright crimson. Sepals. Bright crimson, Completely reflexed. Corolla. Rich purple with distinct red base. Beautifully formed. B. Cat. 1870-1873. Intro. by W. Bull. *Bull, W. Chelsea. GB. 1869.*

ADELAIDE. Single. White/Red. Tube. White. Sepals. White. Reflex to tube. Corolla. Bright rose. Raised by W. Knight, Gr. to Duchess of Kent. GC. P126 20/2/1858 Intro. by W. Rollinson Tooting. *Knight, W. GB. 1858.*

A. DE LEAU. Double. Red/Purple. Tube. Dark red. Sepals. Dark red. Large. Corolla. Amaranth violet palmate red. L. Cat. 1888. *Rozain, Lyons. France. 1887.*

ADELINE. Double. Red/Purple. Tube. Red. Sepals. Red. Reflexed and of unusual length. Corolla. Purple. Irregular. Some petals long, others short. GC. P952 11/10/1862 Intro. by W. Bull. *Bull, W. Chelsea. GB. 1862.*

ADINE. Single. White/Purple. Tube. White. Sepals. White. Completely reflexed. Corolla. Rich deep rosy magenta, B. Cat. 1878-1883. Intro. by W. Bull. *Bland, E. Fordham GB. 1878.*

ADINE AVENAL. Double. ND/ND. Tube. ND. Sepals. ND. Corolla. ND. L. Cat. 1886. *Deles France. 1885.*

ADMIRABLE (a). Single. Red/Red. Tube. Light rosy crimson. Sepals. Light rosy crimson. Corolla. Purplish rose. Harrison Cat. 1845. GC. P241 15/4/1843 Listed by F & A Smith, Hackney. GC. P112 17/2/1844 Listed by W. Miller, Ramsgate. *Harrison. Dereham. GB. 1842.*

ADMIRABLE (b). Single. Red/Red. Tube. Red. Sepals. Red. Horizontal. Corolla. Crimson shaded vermilion. P31 2nd Ed. by Porcher 1848 Dwarf. Small foliage. Very multiflowered. Flowers small 2cms long. GC.P216 27/3/1847 & P 252 1/4/1848 Listed by R. Cooper, Croydon. GC. P259 28/4/1849 & P241 20/4/1850 Listed by W. Rendle, Plymouth. *Knight. GB. 1846.*

ADMIRABLE (c). Single. Red/Red. Tube. Light vermilion. Thick. 25 mm long. Sepals. Light vermilion. Large. Spreading. Bent. Corolla. Carmine vermilion. (Purple). Petals pleated. Medium size. App. to RH. 1851 by Porcher. GC. P497 11/8/1849 Listed by G. Smith, Tollington Nurseries. *Keynes. GB. 1848.*

2

ADMIRABLE (d). Single. Red/Purple. Tube. Purple red. Sepals. Purple red. Corolla. Amarinth. App. to RH. 1851 by Porcher. *Racine. France. 1850.*

ADMIRABLE (e). Single. ND/ND. Tube. ND. Sepals. ND. Corolla. ND. GC. P545 30/8/1851. Listed by G. Smith, Islington. *Meillez. Lille. France. 1851.*

ADMIRABLE. See "Wonderful". P136 3rd. Ed. by Porcher 1858. *Epps. Maidstone. GB. 1856.*

ADMIRAL (a). Single. Red/Red. Tube. Light crimson. 12mm long. Sepals. Light crimson. Spreading. Bent. Corolla. Light crimson. (Violet carmine). Free bloomer. P139 3rd Ed. by Porcher 1858 Tube and Sepals Flesh pink shaded bright pink. This variety by its form and colouring recalls "Elise Meillez". GC. P213 8/4/1854 Listed by H. Low. GC. P401 24/6/1854 Listed by H. Walton, Burnley. GC. P466 22/7/1854 Listed by Bass & Brown Sudbury GC. P83 11/2/1854. Intro. by T. Batten, Clapton. *Batten, T. Clapton. GB.1854.*

ADMIRAL BOXER. Single. Red/Purple. Tube. Scarlet. (Reddish purple). Short 10 mm. Sepals. Scarlet. (Reddish purple). Well reflexed. Long. Finely formed. Very large. Twice as long as the tube. (Totally reflexed). Corolla. Deep violet blue fading violet purple. P139 3rd Ed. by Porcher 1858. Resembles "Prince Albert". It is descended from "Corallina". GC. P451 5/7/1856 Listed by H. Walton, Burnley. GC. P146 7/3/1856 Listed by W. Rumley, Richmond. GC. P251 1/4/1857 Listed by W. Masters, Canterbury. GC. P82 9/2/1856 Intro. by G. Smith. *Smith, G. Islington. GB. 1856.*

ADMIRATION (a). Single. Red/Red. Tube. Flesh flushed orange. 25 mm long. Thick. Sepals. Flesh flushed rose. Spreading. White tips, turned down. Corolla. Orange vermillion. "Selected from 2,500 seedlings". App. to RH. 1851 by Porcher. P137 3rd Ed. by Porcher 1858. *Meillez. Lille. France. 1851.*

ADMIRATION (b). Single. Red/Purple. Tube. Rich crimson. Sepals. Rich crimson. Completely recurved. Corolla. Purplish crimson. Well expanded. GC. P427 3/4/1875. B. Cat. 1875-1882. Intro. by W. Bull. *Bull, W. Chelsea. GB. 1875.*

A. DE.NEUVILLE. Double. Red/Purple. Tube. Bright rose. Sepals. Bright rose. Reflexed. Corolla. Reddish Violet. Large. Open Dedicated to a French war artist and book illustrator (1836-85). L. Cat. 1892. B. Cat. 1888-1893. *Lemoine. Nancy. France. 1888.*

ADOLPHE LEGEUR. Single. ND/ND. Tube. ND. Sepals. ND. Corolla. ND. L. Cat. 1892. *Aubin, Bagnolet. France. 1885.*

ADOLPHE WEICK. Single. White/Purple. Tube. White veined pink. Thick. Short. Bulbous at top. Sepals. White veined pink. Horizontal. Large Points turned up. Corolla. Violet carmine. P35 & P137 3rd. Ed. by Porcher 1858 Product of Germany which is not without merit. *Schule, Stuttgart. Germany. 1855.*

ADOLPHE WELCH. Double. Red/Purple. Tube. Crimson. Short. Sepals. Crimson. Reflexed. Corolla. Bluish violet, stained with red at base. Full. Large foliage. P121 4th Ed. by Porcher 1874. *Lemoine. Nancy. France. 1868.*

ADOLPHINA. Single. Red/Purple. Tube. Red. Sepals. Red. Corolla. Purple. Prostrate. Creeps along the ground, and is pretty when grafted upon the top of the stem of one of taller kinds. GC. P630 25/9/1841. Floral Cabinet Vol II P177 1834 NK. NK. *GB. 1833.*

ADONIS (a). Single. ND/ND. Tube. ND. Sepals. ND. Corolla. ND. GC. P551 17/8/1844 Listed by T. Cripps. GC. P66 1/2/1845 Listed by W.Miller, Ramsgate. GC. P250 17/4/1847 Listed by J. Hally, Blackheath. GC. P177 23/3/1844 Intro. by Pullen, Midhurst. *Pullen, Midhurst. GB. 1844.*

ADONIS (b) Single. Red/Purple. Tube. Red. Sepals. Red. Corolla. Purple. Well open. GC. P515 25/7/1857 Listed by H. Walton, Burnley. GC. P357 7/4/1858 & P418 22/5/1858 Listed by C.E. Allen, Stoke Newington. P38 & P138 3rd Ed. by Porcher 1858. *Smith, G. Islington. GB. 1857.*

ADRIA. Single. Red/Red. Tube. Red. Sepals. Red. Corolla. Red. Almost a self. Basket variety. GC. P442 1/10/1881. *Lowe, Nottingham GB. NK.*

ADRIAN BERGER. Single. Pink/Red. Tube. Blush. Sepals. Blush. Corolla. Rosy carmine. Named after the raiser's son. JF. Cat. 1898. *Berger, L. Bagnolet. France. 1895.*

ADRIEN MARIE. Double. Red/Pink. Tube. Scarlet. Sepals. Scarlet. (Red). Completely recurved. Short. Broad. Corolla. Salmon White. (Salmon). Large. JF. Cat. 1895. B. Cat. 1894-1895. L. Cat. 1894. *Lemoine. Nancy. France. 1894.*

ADRIENNE DE CARDOVILLE. Single. Red/Red. Tube. Vermilion. Sepals. Vermilion. Corolla. Salmon red. App. to RH. 1851 by Porcher. *Racine. France. 1848?*

ADRIEN SENECLAUSE. Double. Red/Purple. Tube. Bright carmine. Sepals. Bright carmine. Slightly reflexed. Corolla. Blue. Remarkable for the peculiar blue corolla. B. Cat. 1870. NK. NK. *France.* NK.

AENEAS. Single. Red/Red. Tube. Light rose. (Carmine rose).Sepals. Light rose. (Carmine rose). Corolla. Rose Lake. (Violet red).Named after a Trojan Warrior, hero of Virgil's poem Aeneid. RH. P23 1846. P57 2nd Ed. by Porcher 1848. *Salter, J. Versailles. France. 1845.*

AERIEL. Single. White/Purple. Tube. Cream. Sepals. Cream. Corolla. Crimson purple. GC. P184 13/3/1847 Listed by W. Miller Ramsgate (red). GC. P164 8/3/1845 Intro. by E. Tiley, Bath. *Tiley, E. Bath. GB. 1847.*

AÉROSTAT. Single. Red/Purple. Tube. Wine red. Sepals. Wine red. Recurved. Corolla. Bluish violet. Long. Trumpet shaped. B. Cat. 1889-1893. L. Cat. 1892. *Lemoine. Nancy. France. 1889.*

AGATHA. Single. Red/Red. Tube. Soft vermilion pink. 5mm long. Large. Sepals. Vermillion pink. Arched. Uplifted. Green tips. Corolla. Vermilion red. P57 2nd Ed. by Porcher 1848. *Salter,J. Versailles. France. 1845.*

AGEMEMNON. Double. Red/Purple. Tube. Rich scarlet. (Dark red) (Clear red). Swollen at top. Sepals. Rich Scarlet. Large. Reflexed. Rounded. Corolla. Dark plum flaked crimson at base. (Dark purple). (Bluish violet). Freest bloomer of all the doubles. Petals pleated and extended. P56 F&P 3/1866. P121 4th. Ed. by Porcher 1874. GC. P287 1/4/1865 Intro. by B.& S. Williams. *Williams B & S. Holloway. GB. 1865.*

AGNES (a). Single. Red/Purple. Tube. Bright pink. Sepals. Bright Pink. Corolla. Bright rosy purple. Globular form. P84 2nd Ed. by Porcher 1848. Short flower. GC. 7/2/1846 Intro. by Youell, Gt. Yarmouth. *Youell. Gt. Yarmouth. GB. 1846.*

AGNES (b). Double. Red/Purple. Tube. Crimson. Sepals. Crimson. Slightly reflexed. Corolla. Dark purple, almost black. Changing deep brown. Two layers of petals. Pleated. Dark violet shading to red at base. RH. P170 1857. P138 3rd Ed. by Porcher 1858. GC. P449 17/7/1852 Listed by H. Walton, Burnley. GC. P593 20/9/1851 & P143 6/3/1853. Intro. by J. Dobson, Isleworth. *Story, W.H. Newton Abbott. GB. 1852.*

AGNES (c). Single. Red/Purple. Tube. Red. Sepals. Red. Corolla. Purple. Expanded. Small. Dwarf. Free.

Vol P3 J of RHS P88 1863. Fuchsia trials at Chiswick 1862. Sent by E. Smith. NK. NK. GB. 1862.

AGNES (d). Single. White/Red. Tube. White. Sepals. White. Corolla. Pink/scarlet. GC. P55 19/1/1867 Review by H. Cannell. NK. *GB. 1866.*

AGNES SOREL. Single. White/Purple. Tube. White. Sepals. White. Corolla. Purplish to carmine at base. RH. P95 1859. GC. P308 9/4/1859 Intro. by Epps, Maidstone. *Demouveaux. Lille. France. 1858*

AGRA. Single. Red/Pink. Tube. Deep coral pink. (Scarlet). Sepals. Deep coral Pink. Completely recurving. Corolla. Pale pink, veined magenta rose. (Pink). Very long. JF. Cat. 1903. B. Cat. 1899 Intro. by W. Bull. *Bull, W. Chelsea. GB. 1899.*

AHKBAR KHAN. Single. ND/ND. Tube. ND. Sepals. ND. Corolla. ND. GC. P369 1/6/1844 Intro. by T. Cripps. Maidstone. NK. *GB. 1844.*

AIMÉ MILLET. Single. Pink/Red. Tube. Pale salmon. Sepals. Pale salmon. Fiery salmon on reverse. Long. Bent. Corolla. Orange copper. (Red). Long. Large. Free. JF. Cat.1892-1895. B. Cat. 1892. L. Cat. 1892. *Lemoine. Nancy. France. 1891.*

AJAX. Single. Red/Purple. Tube. Red. Sepals. Red. Corolla. Purple. GC. P279 30/4/1853 "Dark wooded stem". GC. P454 16/7/1853 Exhibited at Hort. Scty Show, London by Mr. Bousie Gr. to Rt. Hon Labouchere 19/7/1853 1st prize for a pyramid. GC. P209 5/4/1851 Intro. by C. Turner, Slough. *Hocken. GB. 1851.*

ALABASTER. Double. Red/White. Tube. ND. Sepals. ND. Corolla. ND. *Twrdy, Brno. Austria. NK.*

ALARIC. Single. Red/Purple. Tube. Dull crimson. Sepals. Dull crimson. Expanded. Short. Very broad. Corolla. Deep purple. Free flowering. Dwarf. Angular globular buds. P59 Vol. P1 J of RHS 1859 28/7/1859. Exhibited at HS. Show. *Smith, G. Islington. GB. 1859.*

ALARM. Single. Red/Purple. Tube. Rich scarlet. Sepals. Rich scarlet. Well reflexed. Corolla. Violet plum. Immensely expanded. Spreads like a parasol. GC. P771 24/8/1861 Listed by H. Walton, Burnley. GC. P594 29/6/1861 Listed by Godwin & Padman, Sheffield. GC. P140 16/2/1861 Intro. by F&A Smith. *Smith F&A, Dulwich. GB. 1861.*

ALATA. Single. Red/Purple. Tube. Red. (Bright cherry red). Thin. Sepals. Red. Long. Almost horizontal. Corolla. Light Purple. P31 2nd. Ed. by Porcher Resembles "Brockmanii". Large leaves. Harrisons List 1845. RH. P166 1857. GC. P98 17/2/1844 Listed by Youell,Gt. Yarmouth. GC. P112 17/2/1844 & P66 1/2/1845 Listed by W. Miller. Ramsgate. GC. P264 24/4/1847 Listed by W. Rendle. Plymouth. *Smith. J. Dalston GB. 1843.*

ALBA COCCINEA. Single. White/Red. Tube. Red. Sepals. White. Green tips. Corolla. Red. (Pale rose shaded with lake carmine and crimson). (Violet mottled rose). 4th. Ed. by Porcher 1874. P67 J of RHS 1877. Fuchsia trials. No Award. Bad habit. GC.P825 27/6/1885 Fuchsia trials. Best. HC. Cat. 1882-1885. *Henderson, E.G., St Johns Wood. GB. 1867.*

ALBA MULTIFLORA. Single. ND/ND. Tube. ND. Sepals. ND. Corolla. ND. GC. P248 15/4/1854 "1853 fuchsias" offered by Mitchell & Co, Kempston, Brighton. NK. NK. *GB. 1853.*

ALBANO. Single. White/Purple. Tube. White. Long. Sepals. White. (Pale pink). Corolla. Crimson Purple. (Rose edged carmine). App. to RH. 1851 by Porcher. GC. P537 12/8/1848 Listed by G. Smith, Islington. GC.P161 17/3/1849 Listed by W. Rumley, Richmond. GC. P224 14/4/1849 Listed by R. Whibley, Kennington. GC. P265 23/4/1848 Intro. by J. Schofield, Leeds. *Schofield, J. Leeds. GB. 1848.*

ALBA REFLEX. Single. White/Red. Tube. Pure white. Sepals. Pure white. Beautifully reflexing. Corolla. Dark scarlet. Like "Goldfinch". A great improvement on "Delicata". GC. P183 13/3/1847 Intro. by W. Miller, Ramsgate. *Miller, W. Ramsgate. GB. 1847.*

ALBA ROSEA. Single. White/Red. Tube. White. Sepals. White. Corolla. Pale red. GC. P112 17/2/1844 Listed by W. Miller, Ramsgate. NK. NK. *GB. 1843.*

ALBERTA. Double. Red/Purple. Tube. Bright crimson. Thick. Short. Sepals. Bright crimson. Corolla. Bluish purple. Dwarf. Free. Small Leaves. Fine for the table. GC. P55 19/1/1869 Review by H. Cannell. GC. P330 13/3/1875 Listed by T. Fletcher, Chesterfield. B. Cat. 1870-1873. HC. Cat. 1882. *Bull, W. Chelsea. GB. 1868.*

ALBERT DELPIT. Double. Red/Pink. Tube. Scarlet. Sepals. Scarlet. Recurved. Corolla. Flesh Coloured. Immense. B. Cat. 1893-1895. *Lemoine. Nancy. France. 1893.*

ALBERTI. ND. ND/ND. Tube. ND. Sepals. ND. Corolla. ND. RH. P311 1889 "Select" by E.A. Carrière. NK. NK. NK. NK.

ALBERT MEMORIAL. Double. Red/Purple. Tube. Scarlet. Small. Sepals. Scarlet. Well reflexed. (Arched and Raised up). Corolla. Purple. (Two shades of violet washed red). (Violet changing to reddish violet). Its foliage, leaves something to be desired. GC. P1554 2/12/1871. P67 J of RHS 1877 Fuchsia Trials at Chiswick. GC. P510 22/4/1871 Intro. by H. Cannell. *Bland, E. Fordham. GB. 1871.*

ALBERT SMITH. Single. Red/ND. Tube. Scarlet. Short, almost non existant. Sepals. Scarlet. Large. Reflexed. Tips turned down. Corolla. Bright violet blue. Large size. Spiralled. Porcher P 138 3rd. Ed. 1858. GC. P515 25/7/1857 Listed by H. Walton, Burnley. GC. P357 7/8/1857 Listed by C.E. Allen, Stoke Newington. GC. P210 28/3/1857 & P283 25/4/1857 Intro. by E. G. Henderson, St. Johns Wood. *Banks, E. Deal. GB. 1857.*

ALBERT VICTOR. Single. Red/Purple. Tube. Crimson. Sepals. Crimson. Corolla. Very black. Large. Perfect shape. GO. P109 "Select" 1880. HC. Cat. 1882. BSW. Cat. 1878 Intro. by B.S Williams, Holloway. *Banks, E. Deal. GB. 1878.*

ALBION (a). Single. Pink/Red. Tube. Pale peach. Sepals. Pale peach. Corolla. Crimson. Free Bloomer. Dwarf habit. Lax. FJ. P95 May 1845, "Recommended". GC. P66 1/2/1845 Listed by W. Miller, Ramsgate. P146 8/3/1845 Listed by Youells, Gt. Yarmouth. GC. P193 30/3/1844 Intro. by J. Smith, Dalston. *Smith, J. Dalston. GB. 1844*

ALBION (b). Single. Red/Purple. Tube. Rosy carmine. Sepals. Rosy carmine. Corolla. Purplish crimson. J. Harrison List 1845. GC. P66 1/2/1845 Listed by W. Miller, Ramsgate. *Miller, W. Ramsgate. GB. 1844.*

ALBION (c). GC. P249 27/4/1847 Intro. by W. Rendle Plymouth. Correct name should be APOLLO. *Passingham, Truro. GB. 1847.*

ALBION (d). Double. Red/White. Tube. Cherry red. Sepals. Cherry red. Uplifted. Corolla. White. Large. Full. L. Cat. 1890. *Lemoine. Nancy. France. 1890.*

ALBINOS. Single. Pink/Red. Tube. Soft pink. Long. Sepals. Soft pink. Green tips. Pendant. Corolla. Vermilion. Very floriferous. Leaves 7cms x 4 cms. Elegant. P32 2nd Ed. by Porcher 1848. *Salter, J. Versailles. France. 1844.*

5

ALBO COCCINEA. Single. Red/Purple. Tube. Red. Sepals. White. Spreading. Corolla. Purple. Spreading. Distinct in character. P218 Vol. 4 J of RHS 1877 Chiswick trials. 2nd Class Cert. GC. P17 7/7/1877. GC. P311 8/9/1877 Exhibited by J. Matthews at Trowbridge Hort. Scty. Show. NK. NK. NK. *1876.*

ALBONI. Single. Pink/Red. Tube. Pale blush. Sepals. Pale blush, tipped green. Reflexed. Corolla. Rosy Pink, margined bright rosy scarlet on a pale blush ground. Named after an Italian contralto singer (1826-94). GC. P210 6/4/1850 Listed by H. Marsden, Burnley. GC. P610 Intro. by A. Laing. Oct 1849. *Atkinson, Beverley. GB. 1849.*

ALDÉGONDE. Single. ND/Purple. Tube. ND. Long. Sepals. ND. Corolla. Rosy Violet. App. to RH. 1851 by Porcher. *De Jonghe, Brussels. Belgium. 1851.*

ALEXANDRE DUMAS FILS. Single. Red/Purple. Tube. Brilliant Rose. Sepals. Brilliant rose. Prettily recurved. Corolla. Plum. Terminal bunches of large and long flowers. Named after a French novelist 1824-95. (Son of Alexandre Dumas). L. Cat. 1895. B. Cat. 1895. *Lemoine. Nancy. France. 1895.*

ALEXANDER DUMAS. JF. Cat. 1898. See Alexandre Dumas Fils.

ALEXANDRIA. Single. Red/White. Tube. Red. Long. Sepals. Red. Corolla. White. Free Bloomer. Branching habit. G. Vol36 P384 1889. JF. Cat. 1885. NK. NK. *GB. 1884?*

ALEXANDRINA. Single. Red/White. Tube. Brilliant glossy scarlet. Short. 10mm. Sepals. Pure white. Finely reflexed. 22mm. Corolla.Pure white. Medium (Veined and flushed rose at base) 16mm. Pcxiv J of RHS 1872 Fuchsia trials at Chiswick. Slender, drooping, free. P216 Vol 4 J of RHS 1877 FCC. B. Cat. 1870. GC. P382 28/9/1866 Intro. by E.G. Henderson, St. Johns Wood. *Banks, E. Deal. GB. 1866.*

ALFONSO. Single. Red/Purple. Tube. Coral Red. (Rich crimson). Sepals. Coral red. (Bright crimson). Reflexed. Corolla. Dark Purple. (Deep violet). Fine flower. GO. "Select" 1886-1887. HC. Cat. 1885. Named after Alfonso XII King of Spain (1857-85). B. Cat. 1877-1879. *Bull, W. Chelsea. GB. 1875.*

ALFONSO DAUDET. Double. Red/Purple. B. Cat. 1883. See ALPHONSE DAUDET.

ALFRED BUMESNIL. Double. Red/Purple. Tube. Crimson Red. Thick. Sepals. Crimson red. Short. Reflexed. Rounded. Corolla. Violet blue variegated at base. Full. 4th Ed. by Porcher 1874 Globular. Low. Floriferous. Vigorous. Pedicel 30 mms. *Chater. France. 1872.*

ALFRED DUMESNIL. Double. Red/Purple. Tube. Bright crimson. Sepals. Bright crimson. Well recurved. Corolla. Pale Violet. Long. Very free.. GO. "Select" 1887-1889. BSW. Cat. 1888-1897. HC. Cat. 1885. *Lemoine. Nancy. France. 1882.*

ALFRED FOUILLÉE. Double. Red/Purple. Tube. Brilliant red. Sepals. Brilliant red. Corolla. Violet. Large. L. Cat. 1898. JF. Cat. 1899. *Lemoine. Nancy. France. 1898.*

ALFREDI. Single. Red/Purple. Tube. Dark crimson. Sepals. Dark crimson. Corolla. Purple. J. Harrison, Dereham, List of 1845. *Salter, J. Versailles. France. 1844.*

ALFRED NEYMARCK. Double. Red/Purple. Tube. Coral. Sepals. Coral. Very broad. Corolla. Mauve lilac fading soft mauve pink. Large petals. Full. L. Cat. 1907. *Lemoine. Nancy. France. 1907.*

ALFRED PICARD. Double. Red/Purple. Tube. Blood red. Sepals. Blood red. Short. Uplifted. Corolla. Reddish Violet. Floriferous. Full. JF. Cat. 1907. L. Cat. 1906. *Lemoine. Nancy. France. 1906.*

ALFRED RAMBAUD. Double. Red/Purple. Tube. Crimson. (Scarlet). Sepals. Crimson. (Scarlet). Reflexed. Corolla. Rich violet. (Purple). Very large. G. P198 11/9/1887 Seen at Bull's Nursery. Named after a French historian (1842-1905). B. Cat. 1898-1899. *Lemoine. Nancy. France. 1896.*

ALFRED SALTER. Single. Red/Red. Tube. Pale lilac rose. Thick. 22 mm long. Sepals. Pale lilac rose. Long. Horizontal. Corolla. Bright carmine pink.Bell shaped. P138 3rd Ed. by Porcher 1858. Possiby same as Alfredi. P138 3rd. Ed. by Porcher 1858. (Salter left Versailles in 1849 and returned to England). Gartenflora Vol. 2 P351. *Salter, J. Versailles. France. 1851.*

ALFRED THE GREAT. Single. Red/Red. Tube. Deep red. Sepals. Deep red. Reflex. Corolla. Crimson. Long. Cupped. GC. P162 14/3/1846 & P147 13/3/1847 Listed by W. Miller, Ramsgate. GC. P216 27/3/1847 & P232 1/4/1848 Listed by R. Cooper, Croydon. GC. P201 28/3/1846. Intro. by Standish, Bagshot. *Standish, Bagshot. GB. 1846.*

ALGESIRAS. Double. Red/Purple. Tube. Carmine red. Sepals. Carmine red. Corolla. Plum ruby rose. L. Cat. 1908. *Rozain, Lyons. France. 1907.*

ALICE. Single. White/Red. Tube. White. 20mm long. Sepals. White tinged rose. Long. Pointed. Well reflexed. Horizontal. Corolla. Bright rosy scarlet occasionally edged with a deeper shade. (Light violet rose margined vermilion). 4th Ed. by Porcher 1874. Yellow green foliage. B. Cat. 1873-1882. *Bull, W. Chelsea. GB. 1873.*

ALICE HOFFMAN. S/Double. Red/White. Tube. Brilliant Carmine. Sepals. Brilliant carmine. Corolla. White. Low growing. Very floriferous. L. Cat. 1903. *Keise. Germany. 1902.*

ALICE MAUD (MARY). Single. Pink/Red. Tube. Pale flesh. Sepals. Pale flesh, tipped green. Corolla. Rose. Singularly quilled. Petals long, separated and quilled. Each is furnished with an anther also 4 perfect stamens. GC. P417 17/6/1843 & P420 12/1844 "Recommended". Harrison's List 1845. GC. P553 12/8/1843. Intro. by W. Bell. *Bell, W. Thirsk.?*

ALICE MAUD. Single. White/ND. Tube. White. Sepals. White. Corolla. ND. RHS. Vol 3 1848, Exhibited at LHS by Mr. Wrench of London Bridge, GC. P808 11/1846 "Recommended". *Smith, J. Dalston. GB. 1844?*

ALICE (MARY) PEARSON. Single. White/Red. Tube. White. Sepals. White. Corolla. Crimson. Excellent habit and grower. Very free. Laings Cat. circa 1890. B. Cat. 1888-1889. GO."Select" 1890-1891. JF. Cat. 1888. New in 1887. *Lye, J. Market Lavington. GB. 1887.*

ALICIA. Single. Pink/Red. Tube. Nearly white. (Pink). Sepals. White, tipped green. Corolla. Deep blood crimson. Flower is 5" long. GC. P820 12/1844 "Recommended". GC. P46 8/3/1845 Intro. by Youells, Gt. Yarmouth. *Youell, Gt. Yarmouth GB. 1845.*

ALLIANCE. Double. Red/Purple. Tube. Carmine. 10mm long. Sepals. Carmine. Reflexed. 25mm long. Corolla. Purple. (Reddish Violet with a red base). Full. Very neat flower. 22mm long. P cxv Vol 3 J of RHS 1872 Chiswick Trial 1872 Habit neat and dwarf. Large. Awarded **. GO. "Select" 1880. B. Cat. 1870-1873. *Bull, W. Chelsea. GB. 1869.*

ALMA (a) Single. Red/Purple. Tube. Scarlet. Sepals. Scarlet. Well reflexed. Corolla. Bright purple, striped and shaded bright vermilion to the edge, which is often edged with white. Long bold flower 6 to 7" long. Commemorates a victory over the Russians in the Crimea 1854. GC. P319 10/5/1856 Intro. by Turville, Chelmsford. *Turville, T. Chelmsford. GB. 1856*

ALMA (b). Double. Red/Purple. Tube. Scarlet. Sepals. Scarlet. Tipped green. Broad. Well reflexed. Corolla. Dark plum, striped rose scarlet. Large. Very double. GC. P450 17/5/1862. Intro. by B. W. Knight. *Knight, B.W. Battle. GB. 1862.*

ALMA (c). Single. Red/Purple. Tube. Reddish purple. 20 mm long. Large. Sepals. Reddish purple. Arched. Spreading. Points downturned. Corolla. Reddish purple. Petals are much shorter than the sepals. P36 & P138 3rd Ed. by Porcher 1858. *Dender, Coblenz Germany. 1856.*

ALPHA (a). Single. Red/Purple. Tube. Red. Short. Thin. 10mm long .Sepals. Red. Large. Horizontal. Corolla. Purple. (Violet purple). P138 3rd Ed. by Porcher 1858 Foliage dull green. Veined purple. Very dentate. Similar to "Don Juan" but proportionally better. More florifereous. GC.P375 31/5/1856 Exhibited at Crystal Palace by Mr. Bousie as a pyramid 7' High. GC. P177 20/3/1852 Listed by W. Rumley, Richmond. GC. P201 27/3/1852 Listed by H. Walton, Burnley. GC. P83 8/2/1851 Intro. by G. Smith. *Smith, G. Islington. GB. 1851.*

ALPHA (b). Double. Red/Purple. Tube. Crimson red. (Coral red). Thick. 15 mm long. Sepals. Crimson red. (Coral red).Very large. Reflexed.Corolla. Bluish violet variegated crimson at base. (Purple). P121 4th Ed. by Porcher 1874 Resembles "President Humann", but superior. Foliage greenish yellow. Pedicel 50mm. Vol. 4 J of RHS P66 Chiswick fuchsia trials 1873, "Best" Habit free and good. Very free flowering. FCC. HC. Cat. 1882. GO. Select 1881-1885. B. Cat. 1872. GC. P500 13/4/1872 Intro. by G. Smith. *Smith, G. Islington. GB. 1872.*

ALPHAND. Double. Red/Purple. Tube. Dark red. Sepals. Dark red. Reflexed. Corolla. Light violet. Good habit. Compact. Full. JF. Cat. 1901. L. Cat. 1901. *Lemoine. Nancy. France. 1900.*

ALPHONSE DAUDET. Double. Red/Purple. Tube. Bright red. (Claret). Sepals. Bright red. (Claret). Recurved. Corolla. Bluish violet. (Deep violet). GO. "Select" 1885-1888. B. Cat. 1888-1893. BSW. Cat. 1888. JF. Cat. 1899 (New for 1899) L. Cat. 1901. Named after a French author and writer 1840-1897 (? re-introduced) HC. Cat. 1885 *Lemoine. Nancy. France. 1883?*

7

ALPHONSE FILLOT. Double. Red/White. Tube. Red. Sepals. Red. Spreading. Horizontal. Corolla. White. Revue D'Horticultuer Belge P505 15/9/1876. *Coene, Ghent. Belgium. 1875.*

ALPHONSE KARR. Double. Red/Purple. Tube. Rose red. Sepals. Rose red. Enormous. Raised up. Corolla. Bishops violet with a coppery tint. (Metallic violet). Very large. Fine form. Named after a French writer (1808-90). B. Cat. 1892-1893. L. Cat. 1892. *Lemoine. Nancy. France. 1891.*

ALSACE. Double. Red/White. Tube. Rose. Sepals. Rose, tipped yellow. Corolla. Pinkish white. RB. Cat. 1926. *Rozain Jr. Lyons. France. 1921.*

ALSACIEN LORRAIN. Double. Red/White. Tube. Carmine (Clear red) Sepals. Carmine. Reflexed. Reddish violet underneath. Corolla. Matt white. Very full. Dwarf but vigourous. Very free flowering. One of the best. Named after the two French provinces ceeded to Germany after the Franco Prussian war of 1870/1. 4th Ed. by Porcher 1874. BSW. Cat. 1878. HC. Cat. 1882. *Lemoine. Nancy. France. 1874.*

ALTAIR. Double. Red/Purple. Tube. Bright coral red. Short. Sepals. Bright coral red. Corolla. Bluish violet. Very shallow and much expanded. Large. JF. Cat. 1903. B. Cat. 1901. Intro. by W. Bull. *Bull, W. Chelsea. GB. 1900.*

ALWAYS READY. Single. Red/Purple. Tube. Deep red. Very short. Sepals. Deep red. Broad. Waxy. Reflexed. Corolla. Purple. Much expanded. Distinct. Vol P3 J of RHS 1863. Chiswick trials. Habit Stiff. Erect. Dark coloured stems. GC. P594 29/6/1861 Listed by Godwin and Padman, Sheffield. GC. P771 24/8/1861 Listed by H. Walton, Burnley. *Henderson, E.G. St. Johns Wood. GB. 1861.*

AMADEO. Single. Red/Purple. Tube. Bright rosy pink. Very short. Sepals. Bright rosy pink. Corolla. Pale Bluish. B. Cat. 1880-1889. Intro by W. Bull, Chelsea. *Bull, W. Chelsea.GB. 1879.*

AMALIA. Double. Red/Purple. Tube. Red. Sepals. Red. Corolla. Purple. P126 4th Ed. by Porcher 1874. Not in the first selection. *Twrdy.Brno. Austria 1870.*

AMADIS. Single. Pink/Red. Tube. Salmon pink. 55mm long. Thick. Sepals. Salmon pink. Very short. Green tips. Corolla. Vermilion red. Small. P57 2nd Ed. by Porcher 1848. P33 3rd Ed. by Porcher 1858. *Salter, J. Versailles. France. 1848.*

AMANDA. Single. Pink/Purple. Tube. Rosy peach. Sepals. Rosy peach. Horizontal. Corolla. Rosy lilac. P32 2nd Ed. by Porcher 1848. Harrison's List 1845. *Harrison, Dereham. GB. 1843.*

AMATO. Single. Red/Red. Tube. Lake. (Scarlet). Slender. Sepals. Lake. (Scarlet). Corolla. Deep carmine. (Bright cherry red). P32 2nd Ed by Porcher 1848. GC. P241 15/4/1843 Listed by F & A. Smith, Hackney. Harrison's List 1845. *Harrison, Dereham. GB. 1842.*

AMBASSADOR (a). Double. Red/Purple. Tube. Red. Sepals. Red. Long. Straight. Narrow. Corolla. Reddish Purple. A poor flower. Vol P3 J of RHS 1863 Fuchsia Trials 1862. Submitted by Bull. GC. P771 24/8/1861 Listed by H. Walton, Burnley. Intro. by Bull, Chelsea. *Bull, W. Chelsea. GB. 1861*

AMBASSADOR (b). Single. Red/Purple. Tube. Red. Medium. 12mm long. Sepals. Crimson. Reflexed. 1" long. Narrow. Corolla. Deep violet purple. Pcxvii Vol 3 J of RHS 1872 Fuchsia trials. Rather expanded. Tendancy to come double, and then resembles "Sir Colin Campbell". Discarded. B. Cat. 1872-1875. *Bull, W. Chelsea. GB. 1871.*

AMBIORIX. Single. Red/Red. Tube. Red. Thin. Sepals. Red. Large. Corolla. Red. Large. App. to RH 1851 by Porcher. *De Jonghe, Brussels. Belgium. 1850.*

AMBROISE. ND. ND/ND. Tube. ND. Sepals. ND. Corolla. ND. Mentioned in Catalogues but flower not seen or description given. App. to RH. 1851 by Porcher. *Verschaffelt. Belgium. 1851.*

AMBROISE LAUGIER. Single. Red/Purple. Tube. Red. Sepals. Red. Corolla. Slate veined clear red. (Violet veined crimson). Large. L. Cat. 1906. JF. Cat. 1907. Bruant, Poitiers. Cat.1911. *Rozain, Lyons. France. 1906.*

AMBROISE VERSCHAFFELT.
Double. Red/Purple. Tube. Red. Sepals. Red. Corolla. Purple. "Not in the first selection" P126 4th. Edition by Porcher 1874. *Cornelissen, Arras. Belgium. 1866.*

AMBROSIA. Single. Red/Purple. Tube. Bright crimson. Short. Thick. Sepals. Bright crimson. Broad. Nicely reflexed. Corolla. Purplish plum, rosy crimson at base. GC. P647 22/5/1880. Intro. by W. Bull. B. Cat. 1880-1883. *Bull, W. Chelsea. GB. 1880.*

AMÉDÉE DASSY. Single. Red/Purple. Tube. Dullish purplish red. 35mm long. Very thick. Sepals. Dullish red. Large. Reflexed. Corolla. Crimson with brown shading. Flower almost globular. P57 2nd. Ed. by Porcher 1848 & P139 3rd Ed. by Porcher 1858. Colour is nearly unique amongst fuchsias. Short style. Filaments bright pink. Named after his employer. *Baudinet, J. Meaux. France. 1848.*

AMELIA. Single. Pink/Red. Tube. Pink. Sepals. Pink. Corolla. Rosy red. Small. Girling, Stowmarket List 1845. NK. NK. *GB. 1844.*

AMELIE AUBIN. Single. White/Red. Tube. White. Long. Stout. Waxy. Sepals. White. Green tips. Corolla. Pinkish red, shaded white at base. Brilliant Green foliage. Lax. Requires frequent pinching. P311 RH. 1889 "Select" by E. A. Carriere. Rozain Boucharlet Cat. 1885. *Aubin, R. Bagnolet. France 1883.*

AMELIE BOTTERI. ND.ND/ND. Tube. ND. Sepals. ND. Corolla. ND. LB. Cat. 1883. *Boucharlet, Lyons. France. 1881.*

AMETHYST. Single. Red/Purple. Tube. Brilliant Scarlet. Long. Sepals. Brilliant Scarlet. Much expanded. Corolla. Deep violet purple. Similar to "Formosa Elegans", but larger. GC. P162 14/3/1846 & P147 13/3/1847 Listed by W. Miller, Ramsgate. GC. P82 6/2/1845 Intro by Bass & Brown. *Bass & Brown, Sudbury. GB. 1845.*

AMI. Single. White/Purple. Tube. White. 25mm long. Large. Sepals. White. Reflexed. A little longer than the tube. Corolla. Violet pink, bordered carmine, Bell shaped. P139 3rd. Ed. by Porcher 1858. *Turner, C. Slough. GB. 1853.*

AMIE. Single. Red/Purple. Tube. Crimson. Sepals. Crimson. Very long 63 mm long. Corolla. Very rich dark purple. HC. Cat. 1890 Illustration No. 3. L. Cat 1891. JF. Cat. 1888. *Sankey. GB. 1888.*

AMI HOSTE. Double. Red/Purple. Tube. Crimson. Very short, almost nil. Sepals. Crimson. Large. Reflexed. Corolla. Two shades of violet, variegated reddish crimson. Upright grower. P131 4th. Ed. by Porcher. P67 J of RHS Vol 4 1877. Fuchsia trials at Chiswick 1873. Habit compact Free flowering. Small tube. Sepals short and broad. Well reflexed. Bright Scarlet. Corolla. Very Double. Large, Heavily streaked and blotched with red. Sent by F&A Smith. No Award. *Lemoine. Nancy. France. 1866.*

AMIRAL AUBE. Double. Red/Purple. Tube. Light red. (Dark red). Sepals. Light red. (Dark red). Reflexed. Corolla. Mauve pink. (Rosy mauve). New colour. Very floriferous. Large. B. Cat. 1892-1893. L. Cat. 1892. *Lemoine. Nancy. France. 1891.*

AMIRAL COURBET. Double. Red/Purple. Tube. Dark red. (Bright coral). Sepals. Dark red. (Bright coral). Corolla. Dark violet. (Red veined violet). Robust. Immense. Dobbies Cat. 1893-4. B. Cat. 1888-1893. BSW. Cat. 1888. *Lemoine. Nancy. France. 1887.*

AMIRAL EVANS. Single. Pale Pink/Lilac. Tube. Pale Pink. Sepals. Pale Pink. Reflexed Corolla. Silvery lilac. Small plant. L. Cat. 1908. *Lemoine. Nancy. France. 1908.*

AMIRAL GERVAIS. Single. Red/Red. Tube. Red. Sepals. Red. Corolla. Bright carmine red. Almost a self. JF. Cat. 1893. L. Cat 1892. *Rozain, Lyons France. 1892.*

AMIRAL MIOT. Double. Red/Purple. Tube. Bright red. Sepals. Bright red. Corolla. Plum. (Bright plum). BSW. Cat. 1888. B. Cat. 1888-1889. *Lemoine. Nancy. France. 1886.*

AMIRAL OLRY. Double. Red/Purple. Tube. Red. Sepals. Red. Extremely long and curl back to tube in a circle. Corolla. Reddish violet. (Violet red). B. Cat. 1892. L. Cat.1892. *Lemoine. Nancy. France. 1891.*

AMIRAL REINIER. Double. Red/White. Tube. Bright red. Sepals. Bright red. Corolla. White, marked rose at base. Enormous. B. Cat. 1893-1895. *Rozain, Lyons. France. 1893.*

AMOENA. Double. Red/Purple. Tube. Crimson red. Short. Sepals. Crimson red. Large. Reflexed. Corolla. Blue violet splashed red. Trailer, P121 4th Ed. by Porcher 1874. Improves with pinching. Pedicel 50 mm. *Twrdy. Brno. Austria. 1866.*

AMORETTE. Single. Pink/Red. Tube. Clear pink. Sepals. Clear Pink. Corolla. Carmine tinted magenta. L. Cat. 1908. *Bornemann, Germany. 1907.*

AMPHION. Single. Red/Purple. Tube. Rich deep crimson. Short. Sepals. Rich deep crimson. Well reflexed. Right back to tube. Corolla. Very dark purple. (Violet washed red). Bell shaped. Much expanded. 4th. Ed. by Porcher 1874. B. Cat. 1872-1876. Intro. by W. Bull. GC. P502 13/4/1872. *Bull, W. Chelsea. GB. 1872.*

AMULET. Single. Pink/Red. Tube. Pale flesh salmon. Sepals. Rich crimson with green tips. Corolla. Crimson red. (Violet red).P58 2nd Ed by

Porcher 1848 Sepals reflex like a Chinese hat. GC. P234 11/4/1846 Listed by A.J. Stewart, Windsor. Girling, Stowmarket List 1845. J. Harrison's List 1845. *Harrison, J. Dereham GB. 1844.*

AMY. Single. Single. White/Purple. Tube. White. 25 mm long. Sepals. White. Large. Reflexed. A little longer than the tube. Corolla. Violet rose bordered carmine. P139 3rd Ed. by Porcher 1858 Bell shaped. GC. P279 30/4/1853 "Light green stemmed". *Turner, C. Slough. GB. 1853*

AMY LYE. Single. White/Red. Tube. White. Sepals. White. Corolla. Salmon. JF. Cat. 1901. *Lye, J. Market Lavington. GB. 1901.*

ANDRÉ CARNEGIE. Double. Red/Pink. Tube. Scarlet. Sepals. Scarlet. Corolla. Rosy Salmon pink. (Salmon). Named after a Scottish American philanthropist (1835-1918). JF. Cat. 1907. L. Cat. 1906. *Lemoine. Nancy. France. 1906.*

ANASTASIUS GRÜN. Double. Red/White. Tube. Red. Sepals. Red. Horizontal. Corolla. White with rose and carmine streaks. Opens out wide. *Twrdy, J.W. Brno. Austria. 1878.*

ANDRÉ LENOSTRE. Double. Red/Red. Tube. Carmine. Sepals. Carmine. Corolla. Carmine Lake. Almost a self. Globular. Full. Probably named after A. Lenotre, (1613-1700). Creator of French landscape gardening. Laid out St. James Park, London. L. Cat 1909. *Lemoine. Nancy. France. 1909.*

ANDROMEDA. Single. Pink/Red. Tube. Soft pink. (Red). Sepals. Red. Expanded. Shorter than the tube. Green tips. Corolla. Crimson Red. (Coral). Floriferous. P58 2nd Ed. by Porcher 1848. P23 RH 1845/6 GC. P184 13/3/1847 Listed by W. Miller, Ramsgate. *Salter, J. Versailles. France. 1846.*

ANDROMEDA NOVA. Single. Pink/Pink. Tube. Salmon rose. 55mm long. Thick. Strong. Sepals. Salmon rose. Long. Reflexed. Green tips. Corolla. Capucine pink. P58 2nd Ed. by Porcher 1848. *Salter, J. Versailles. France. 1848.*

ANGELIC. Single. White/Purple. Tube. Pure white. Sepals. Pure white. Beautifully reflexed. Corolla. Violet rose. Large. Long. B. Cat. 1870-1873. *Bull, W. Chelsea. GB. 1869.*

ANGELINA BRAEMT. Double. Red/White. Tube. Bright carmine. Sepals. Bright carmine. Broad. Well reflexed. Horizontal. Corolla. White striped rose. (Blush white, each petal marked with a large carmine band). P127 4th. Ed. by Porcher 1874. B. Cat. 1870. *Cornelissen, Arras. Belgium. 1868.*

ANGELO FERRARIO. Double. Red/White. Tube. Carmine pink. Sepals. Carmine Pink. Reflexed. Corolla. Alabaster white. Vigorous. Enormous. L. Cat. 1911. *Rozain, Lyons. France. 1911.*

ANITA. Double. ND/ND. Tube. ND. Sepals. ND. Corolla. ND. L. Cat. 1886. *Bull. W. Chelsea. GB. 1885.*

ANNA. Single. Red/Red. Tube. Vermilion Pink. Thick. 20mm long. Large. Sepals. Vermilion Pink. Horizontal. Points bent. Corolla. Brilliant vermilion. Pleated petals. Green foliage 7cms x 5cms. Very dentate. Not in the first selection. P36 & P139 3rd Ed. by Porcher 1858. *Boucharlet. Lyons. 1856.*

ANNA BULLEYN. Single. Red/Purple. Tube. Carmine scarlet. Sepals. Carmine scarlet. Broad. Recurving. Corolla. Rosy Lavender. Cup Shaped. GC. P983 15/10/1864 Intro. by E.G. Henderson. GC. P1 7/1/1865. *Banks, E. Deal. GB. 1864.*

ANNA MARIE. Double. ND/ND. Tube. ND. Sepals. ND. Corolla. ND. L. Cat. 1892. *Twrdy, J. Brno. Austria. 1884.*

ANNE BOLEYN. Single. White/Red. Tube. White. Very thick and bulged at base. 16mm long. Sepals. Blush, green at tips. Spreading. Corolla. Deep carmine with paler flame at base. 22mm. Dwarf habit. Free flowering. Drooping. Medium size. Very elegant. Vol P3 Pcxii J of RHS 1872 Fuchsia trials at Chiswick 1872 Awarded ***. NK. NK. NK. NK.

ANNIE. Single. White/Red. Tube. White. Thick. 16mm. Sepals. Blush pink. Reflexed round. Corolla. Vermilion. (Carmine red). (Deep rosy carmine paler at base). (Scarlet). Vol. P3 P91 J of RHS 1863 Fuchsia trials Awarded ***. Pcxii Vol 3 Jof RHS 1872 . Resembles "Anne Boleyn" but not as good. P215 Vol 4 J of RHS 1873. P116 4th. Ed. by Porcher 1874. Intro. by E.G.Henderson. *Henderson, E.G. St. Johns Wood. GB. 1861.*

ANNIE EARLE. Single. White/Red. Tube. White. Waxy. Sepals. White. Corolla. Bright Carmine. GC. P307 15/9/1887 Exhibited at Bath Floral fete 7/8 Sept by J. Lye. 1st 9 pot class. JF. Cat. 1888. B. Cat. 1888. *Lye, J. Market Lavington. GB. 1887.*

ANNIE HOSTE. Double. Red/Purple. See AMI HOSTE.

ANNIE LUSTRE. Single. White/Red. Tube. Pure white. Very long. Sepals. Pure white. Beautifully reflexed. Broad. Corolla. Vivid crimson. Fine flower. Intro. by W. Bull. Cat. 1877-1883. *Bull, W. Chelsea. GB. 1876.*

ANOMIA. Single. Red/Purple. Tube. Rich bright crimson. Short. Sepals. Rich bright crimson. Broad. Thick. Recurved. Corolla. Dark purple. Large. Long. B. Cat. 1876-1877. *Bull, W. Chelsea. GB. 1875.*

ANTAGONIST (a). Single. Red/Purple. Tube. Scarlet. Sepals. Scarlet. Corolla. Violet. GC. P66 1/2/1845 Listed by W. Miller, Ramsgate. GC. P146 8/3/1845 Listed by Youells, Gt. Yarmouth. GC. P821 25/11/1843 & P401 22/6/1844 & P559 17/8/1844 Intro. by Standish, Bagshot. *Standish, Bagshot. GB. 1843.*

ANTAGONIST (b). Single. White/Red. Tube. White. Very strong. Sepals. Rose pink. Horizontal. Corolla. Vermilion shaded Violet. Spiral shaped. 4th. Ed. by Porcher 1874. GC. P515 25/7/1857 & P418 22/5/1858 Listed by H. Walton, Burnley. *Brittle. GB. 1857.*

ANTIGONE. Single. White/Red. Tube. White, veined pink.. Long. Thick.Sepals. White. Corolla. Soft orange red. (Pink vermilion). L. Cat. 1886. HC. Cat. 1890. *Aubin, Bagnolet. France. 1886.*

ANTONA. Single. Red/Purple. Tube. Bright crimson. Sepals. Bright crimson. Corolla. Dark purple. B. Cat. 1881-1883. *Bull, W. Chelsea. GB. 1881.*

APOLLO (a). Single. ND/ND. Tube. ND. Sepals. ND. Corolla. ND. J. Harrison's List 1845. P32 2nd Ed. by Porcher 1848. *Smith, J. Dalston. GB. 1843.*

APOLLO (b). Single. Red/Purple. Tube. Red. Sepals. Red. Corolla. Purple. GC. P256 16/4/1848 Listed by G. Rogers, Uttoxeter. GC. P224 14/4/1849 Listed by R. Whibley, Kennington. GC. P249 27/4/1847 Sent out by W. Rendle of Plymouth as Albion in error. Subsequently corrected see GC. P30 15/5/1847. *Passingham, Truro. GB. 1847.*

APOLLO (c). Single. Red/Purple. Tube. Rosy. (Carmine) rose/. 15mm long. Bulged at base. Sepals. Rosy. (Carmine rose). Well reflexed. (Horizontal). Corolla. Purplish lilac. (Violet carmine bordered purple). P140 3rd Ed. by Porcher 1858 Multiflowered. GC. P353 5/6/1852 to be sent out 5/7/1852. *Luccombe & Pince, Exeter. GB. 1852.*

APOLLO (d). Single. Red/Red. Tube. Reddish purple. 40 mm long. Sepals. Reddish purple. Half open. Green tips. Corolla. Crimson. P58 2nd Ed. by Porcher 1848. P32 3rd Ed. by Porcher 1858. *Verscheffelt. Belgium. 1844.*

APOLLON. Single. Red/Red. Tube. Red. Sepals. Red. Corolla. Red. P84 2nd Ed. by Porcher 1848, Flowers resemble those of "Madame Thibault". P30 3rd Ed. by Porcher 1858. *Souchet, Fontainbleu France. 1848.*

A.P. VIDAL. Double. Red/Purple. Tube. Carmine. Sepals. Carmine. Corolla. Dark plum. Very full. JF. Cat. 1904. L. Cat. 1903. *Rozain. Lyons. France. 1903.*

ARAB. Double. Red/Purple. Tube. Bright crimson. Short. Sepals. Bright crimson. Well reflexed. Corolla. Deep bluish Purple. Large. B. Cat. 1888-1895. L. Cat. 1886. JF. Cat. 1886. NK. NK. *1886.*

ARABELLA. Single. White/Red. Tube. White. 1" long. Sepals. White. Long. Well reflexed. 29mm long. Corolla. Rich rose. (Deep rosy carmine) Superior to "Arabella Improved", which is coarse in habit. Similar to "Mrs. Marshall" and "Attraction". An improvement on "Annie". Pcxii Vol 3 J of RHS 1872 Report of Fuchsia Trials at Chiswick. GC. P120 4th Ed. by Porcher 1874. Not in the first selection. GC. P211 17/2/1877 Line drawing. BSW Cat. 1878. G. 6/9/1886 Exhibited at Trowbridge Hort. Scty Show by J.Lye, G. Tucker, H. Pocock. GC. Vol.18 1882 Report on Devizes Hort. Scty. Show Exhibited by T. Chandler & W. Hitch. GC. Vol 20 1883 Report of Trowbridge Hort. Scty. Show, Exhibited by G. Tucker & H. Pocock. GC. P382 29/4/1866 Intro. by E.G. Henderson, St. Johns Wood. *Banks, E. Deal. GB. 1866.*

ARABELLA IMPROVED. Single. White/Red. Tube. White. Very long. Thick. 29mm long. Sepals. White. Points lifted. Large. 29mm. Fleshy. Corolla. Red. (Bright rose margined carmine). (Bright lake flushed carmine). Spiral shaped. P116 4th Ed. by Porcher 1874. Improvement on "Arabella". Flower same colour but larger. Habit similar. B. Cat. 1872-1873. Pcxi Vol. 3 J of RHS 1872 Fuchsia trials at Chiswick. Habit coarse. Flowers very large. In the way of "Mrs. Marshall" but a month later. GC. P510 22/4/1871 Intro. by H. Cannell. GC. P1554 2/12/1874 Review. Resembles "Arabella" in conjunction with "Annie". J. Lye x Arabella. *Lye, J. Market Lavington. GB. 1871.*

A. RAMBAUD. Double. Red/Purple. See ALFRED RAMBAUD. (JF Cat 1898).

ARAGO. Single. Red/ND. Tube. Bright cherry red. Slender. 4 cms long. Sepals. Bright cherry red. Held down. Corolla. ND. Small foliage. Bushy. P32 Review by Porcher. *Harrison, J. Dereham. GB. NK.*

ARAYSS. Single. ND/ND. Tube. ND. Sepals. ND. Corolla. ND. GC. P112 17/2/1844 & P66 1/2/1845 Listed by W. Miller, Ramsgate. NK. NK. NK. NK.

ARBOREA. Single. White/Red. Tube. Yellow. (Flesh). Short. Sepals. Yellow. Green tips. (Flesh). (Clear pink). Reflexed. Horizontal. Corolla. Bright red. (Salmon red). (Vermilion). P32 2nd Ed. by Porcher 1848 Very profuse. Similar to "Chanderii" and "Conspicua Arborea", "Blanda", "Dalstonii", "Chandlerii", "Compacta". GC. P668 11/10/1841 Exhibited at RHS of Ireland show by Mr. Keefe. P13 Floral Cabinet Vol IX 1841. P32 2nd Ed. by Porcher 1848. Medium foliage. Oval. Pointed leaves. J. Harrison, Dereham list 1845. Girlings List 1845. GC. P393 6/1842 Listed by Youell, Gt. Yarmouth. X Fulgens. *Smith, J. Dalston. GB. 1841.*

ARBOREA CONSPICUA. Single. Red/Red. Tube. Rose. Sepals. Rose. Corolla. Scarlet. Girlings, Stowmarket List 1845. NK. NK. NK. NK.

ARBOREA NEVA. Single. ND/ND. Tube. ND. Sepals. ND. Corolla. ND. GC. P495 23/7/1842. Exhibited by W.M. Tweedy at RHS of Cornwall show. NK. NK. NK

ARC EN CIEL. Single. Red/Purple. Tube. Light carmine. Sepals. Light carmine. Turned up. Corolla. White veined rose, shading to blue. Large round petals. Name in English is Rainbow. JF. Cat. 1892. L. Cat. 1892. *Rozain. Lyons. France. 1891.*

ARCHETTE. Single. Red/Purple. Tube. Scarlet crimson. Short. Sepals. Scarlet crimson. Beautifully reflexed. Corolla. Dark bluish purple. Small flower. B. Cat. 1872-1876. *Bull, W. Chelsea. GB. 1872.*

ARCHIDUCHESSE MARIE THERESE. Double. Red/Purple. Tube. Red. Sepals. Red. Corolla. Purple. Not in the first selection. 4th Ed. by Porcher, 1874. *Twrdy, Brno. GB. 1874.*

ARG. Single. ND/ND. Tube. ND. Sepals. ND. Corolla. ND. GC. P241 15/4/1843 Listed by F&A Smith, Hackney. *Harrison, J. Dereham. GB. NK.*

ARIA. Single. Red/Purple. Tube. Rosy crimson. Sepals. Rosy crimson. Corolla. Deep purple. B. Cat. 1883. *Bull, W. Chelsea. GB. 1883.*

ARIEL. Single. White/Red. Tube. White. (Pale flesh). Thick. Short. Sepals. White. (Pale flesh). Broad. Stout. Horizontal. Reflexed. Corolla. Vermillion Scarlet. (Bright carmine). P140 3rd Ed. by Porcher 1858 Bell shaped. Perfect flower. GC. P449 17/7/1852 Listed by H. Walton, Burnley. GC. P279 30/4/1853 "Light green stemmed". GC. P221 26/3/1853 Listed by W. Rumley, Richmond. P307 14/5/1853 Listed by B. Cant, Colchester. GC. P241 27/4/1852 Intro. by G.Smith, Islington. *Banks, E. Deal. GB. 1852.*

ARLEQUIN (a). Single. Red/Purple. Tube. Red. Sepals. Red. Corolla. Violet blue striped red. (Rosy carmine edged violet). L. Cat. 1894. JF. Cat. 1898. HC. Cat. 1890. *Rozain, Lyons. France. 1894.*

ARLEQUIN (b). ND. Red/Purple. Tube. Red. Sepals. Red. Corolla. Violet ribbed red. RB. Cat. 1926. *Rozain Jr, Lyons. 1923.*

ARMAND GAUTIER. Double. Red/Purple. Tube. Bright red. Sepals. Bright red. Horizontal. Corolla. Violet red. Very full. Exceptional dimensions. Petals close set. Short and Compact. L. Cat. 1906. Bruant, Poitiers Cat. 1911. *Lemoine. Nancy. France. 1904.*

ARMEDE. Single. ND/ND. Tube. ND. Sepals. ND. Corolla. ND. P30 3rd Ed by Porcher 1858. GC. P154 4/3/1848 Listed by Conways, Old Brompton. *Demouveaux. Lille. France. 1858.*

ARMIDE. Single. Red/Purple. Tube. Vermilion pink. Good size. Sepals. Vermilion pink. Spreading. Green tips. Corolla. Violet vermilion red. P58 2nd Ed. by Porcher 1848. Upright habit. Large pale green foliage. *Meillez. Lille. France. 1848.*

ARPA. Double. Red/Purple. Tube. Bright Carmine. Sepals. Bright carmine. Broad. Horizontally reflexed. Corolla. Violet Red. B. Cat. 1883. *Bull, W. Chelsea. GB. 1883.*

ARTABAN. Double. Red/White. Tube. Bright rose. Sepals. Bright rose. Corolla. White, slightly veined rose. GC. P824 27/6/1885 Report of RHS Trials at Chiswick. "Best in its class". HC. Cat. 1885. NK. NK. NK. 1883?

ARTAGNAN. Single. Red/Purple. Tube. Dull red. Sepals. Dull red. Corolla. Red, tinted blue. P84 2nd Ed. by Porcher 1848. Exhibited 7/11/1847 Societe Horticulture de Auvergne. *De Bar. France. 1847.*

ARTÉMISE. Single. Red/Purple. Tube. Pale rose. (Pink). Sepals. Pale rose. (Pink). Corolla. Purple. Similar to "Venus Victrix". Numerous branches absolutely covered with small flowers. JF. Cat.1892. L. Cat. 1892. Hybrid of F. Macrostemma. *Lemoine. Nancy. France. 1892.*

ARTEMISIA. Single. Pink/Purple. Tube. Flesh pink. Sepals. Flesh pink. Corolla. Violet Pink. P58 2nd Ed. by Porcher 1848. *Salter, J. Versailles. France. 1847.*

ARTHUR DE LA FERTÉ. Single. Red/Red. Tube. Soft vermilion pink. Very bulged. 20 mm. Sepals. Soft vermilion pink. Long. Horizontal. Points Up. Corolla. Dull vermilion. Petals pleated. Nice variety. P 35 & P140 3rd Ed. by Porcher 1858. *Narcis, Evry. France. 1855.*

ARTISTIC. Single. ND/ND. Tube. ND. Sepals. ND. Corolla. ND. GC. P478 26/5/1866 Intro. by G. Fry, Manor Rd., Lee SE5. *Fry, G. Lee. GB. 1866.*

ASHFORDIENSIS. Single. ND/ND. Tube. ND. Sepals. ND. Corolla. ND. GC. P530 11/8/1855 Listed by Bainbridge & Hewison, York. NK. NK. *GB. NK.*

ASPASIA (a). Single. Red/Purple. Tube. Scarlet. Sepals. Scarlet. Corolla. Beautiful blue. GC. P211 26/3/1853 Listed by W. Rumley, Richmond. GC. P353 5/6/1852 Intro. by Luccombe and Pince. *Luccombe & Pince, Exeter. GB. 1852.*

ASPASIA (b). Single. Red/Purple. Tube. Light red. Short. Sepals. Light red. Completely reflexed. Corolla. Bluish shaded violet. Bell shaped. B. Cat. 1901. Intro. by Wm. Bull. *Bull, W. Chelsea. GB. 1900.*

ASPIRATION. Single. Red/Purple. Tube. Clear scarlet. Sepals. Clear scarlet. Corolla. Rose purple, shaded salmon at base. Erect flowers. JF. Cat. 1893. L. Cat. 1892. *Rozain, Lyons. France. 1892.*

ASSEMBLY. Double. Red/Purple. Tube. Crimson red. (Coral). Sepals. Crimson red. (Coral). Large. Raised right up. Corolla. Violet blue, splashed red at base. Pedicel 35 mm. 4th Ed. by Porcher 1874. B. Cat. 1870-1873. Intro. by W. Bull. *Bull, W. Chelsea. GB. 1869.*

ASTARTE. Single. White/Purple. Tube. Pure white. Sepals. Pure white, tipped green. Corolla. Dark crimson purple. (Rosy vermilion). GC. P183 13/3/1847 Intro. by W. Miller, Ramsgate. *Hocking GB. 1847.*

ATALA. Single. Red/Pink. Tube. Bright coral red. Sepals. Bright coral red. Corolla. Rose veined

carmine. Dicksons, Chester Cat. 1907. *Dickson, Chester GB. 1907.*

ATALANTA. Single. Red/Purple. Tube. Crimson Sepals. Crimson. Completely reflexed. Corolla. Purplish crimson. B. Cat. 1875-1882. *Bull, W. Chelsea. GB. 1874.*

ATHALIE. Single. Red/Purple. Tube. Bright crimson. Sepals. Bright crimson. Broad. Elegantly recurved. Corolla. Rich satiny purple. B. Cat. 1878-1880 Intro. by W. Bull. *Bull, W. Chelsea. GB. 1878.*

ATHENES. Double. Red/Purple. Tube. Blood red. Sepals. Blood red. Broad. Reflexed. Corolla. Blue violet. Expanded. Enormous. Full. Very vigourous. Bruant, Poitiers Cat. 1915. L. Cat. 1911. *Lemoine. Nancy. France. 1911.*

ATHLETE. Single. ND/ND. Tube. ND. Sepals. ND. Corolla. ND. App. to RH. 1851 by Porcher. Mentioned in catalogues, but flower not seen or description given. *Dubus, Lille. France. NK.*

ATKINSONIA. ND. ND/ND. Tube. ND. Sepals. ND. Corolla. ND. P32 2nd Ed. 1848 by Porcher 1848. *Atkinson. GB. 1841?*

ATLAS (a). Single. Red/Purple. Tube. Carmine. Sepals. Carmine. Corolla. Light lilac purple. P32 2nd Ed. by Porcher 1844. J. Harrison's List 1845. *Thew. GB. NK.*

ATLAS (b). Single. ND/ND. Tube. ND. Sepals. ND. Corolla. ND. GC. P254 19/4/1845 New Seedling. GC. P216 27/3/1847 Listed by R. Cooper, Croydon. *Smith. J. Dalston. GB. 1845.*

ATLAS (c). ND. ND/ND. Tube. ND. Sepals. ND. Corolla. ND. GC. P314 10/5/1856 Listed by W. Rumley, Richmond. NK. NK. *GB. 1855.*

ATROPURPUREA FLORE PLENO. Double. ND/ND. Tube. ND. Sepals. ND. Corolla. ND. P211 3rd Ed. by Porcher 1858. *Lemoine. Nancy. France. 1858.*

ATROSANGUINEA. Single. Red/Red. Tube. Very dull red. Thin. Short.Sepals. Very dull red. Narrow. Horizontal. Corolla. Crimson. P59 2nd Ed.by Porcher 1848 The tube is too thin for perfection. GC. P153 4/3/1848 Listed by R. Cooper, Croydon. GC. P256 8/4/1848 Listed by G. Rogers, Uttoxeter. P274 5/5/1849 Listed by H. Walton, Burnley. P241 20/4/1850 Listed by W. Rendle, Plymouth. GC. P505 21/7/1847 Intro. by G. Smith, Islington. *Salter, J. Versailles. France. 1847.*

13

ATTILA. Single. ND/ND. Tube. ND. Sepals. ND. Corolla. ND. P86 2nd Ed. by Porcher 1848 Mentioned in catalogues but not yet seen. NK. NK. NK. *1848.*

ATTRACTION. Florists Journal Apl 1845 Gives description but wrongly named. Should be Attractor.

ATTRACTION (a). Single. ND/ND. Tube. ND. Sepals. ND. Corolla. ND. GC. P241 20/4/1850 Listed by W. Rendle, Plymouth. NK. NK. *GB.* NK.

ATTRACTION (b). Single. Red/Purple. Tube. Vermilion. Sepals. Vermilion. Corolla. Purple. GC. P274 30/8/1851 Listed by G. Smith, Islington. GC. P274 3/5/1851 Intro. by Veitch, Exeter. *Story, W.H. Newton Abbot. GB. 1851.*

ATTRACTION (c). Single. White/Red. Tube. White. Sepals. White. Corolla. Rosy Carmine. Pcxii Vol 3 J of RHS 1872. Fuchsia trials at Chiswick. Considered to be identical with "Arabella". (Synonymous with Arabella).NK. NK. *GB.* NK.

ATTRACTION (d). Single. Red/Purple. Tube. Rich crimson. Sepals. Rich crimson. Broad. Well reflexed. Corolla. Deep maroon. Margins scalloped. P97 GO. 1882. GO. "Select" 1885. GC. Vol 17 20/5/1882 New fuchsias from B. S. Williams. BSW. Cat. 1881. Intro. by B. S. Williams, Holloway. *Bland, E. Fordham. GB. 1881.*

ATTRACTOR. Single. Red/Purple. Tube. Deep crimson. (Bright red) Sepals. Deep crimson. (Bright red). Corolla. Crimsony purple. (Violet red). In 1841 Thomsons "Formosa Elegans" was crossed with "F. Corymbiflora" . The progeny were then selfed, which resulted in a very much larger bloom. In all 3 cultivars were sent out "Colossus", "President" and "Attractor". GC. P574 19/8/1843 Exhibited at Hort. Scty Show by Standish. GC. P401 22/6/1844 Largest yet sent out. P59 2nd Ed. by Porcher 1848. GC. Good engraving in Paxton's magazine of Botany March 1844. GC. P66 1/2/1845 Listed by W. Miller, Ramsgate. GC. P146 8/3/1845 Listed by Youells, Gt. Yarmouth & Harrisons, Dereham 1845. Listed by Girlings, Stowmarket, 1845. Formosa Elegans x F. Corymbiflora. *Standish, Bagshot. GB. 1843.*

AUCUBAEFOLIA. Single. Red/Purple. Tube. Dull red. Long. Sepals. Dull red. Not reflexed. Corolla. Purplish red. Foliage pale green, thickly blotched with white. Very distinct. Worth growing but requires to be grown freely to bring out its character. Leaves have a central creamy white blotch. P68 & P217 Vol.4 Jof RHS 1877. NK. NK. NK. NK.

AUDOTI. Single. Red/Red. Tube. Carmine red. (Deep rose). Slender. Long. Sepals. Carmine red. (Deep rose). Divergent. Corolla. Lake. (Rosy crimson). (Violet red). GC. P694 7/10/1843 Exhibited by raiser at Cercle Generale D'Horticulture de Paris 19/8/1843. P32 2nd.Ed. by Porcher 1848. GC. P369 8/6/1844 Listed by T Cripps. RH. P23 1846. Harrisons Dereham List 1845. *Salter, J. Versailles. France. 1843.*

AUGUSTA. Single. Red/Red. Tube. Rose. (Light carmine). Sepals. Rose. (Light carmine tipped green). Corolla. Carmine Lake. (Crimson red).RH. P23 1845/6. Harrison's, Dereham List 1845. GC. P112 17/2/1844 & P66 1/2/1845 & P147 13/3/1847 Listed by W.Miller, Ramsgate. *Rickard. GB. 1844.*

AUGUSTA HOLMES. Double. Red/White. Tube. Bright red. Sepals. Bright red. Corolla. White. Full. Extra Large. L. Cat. 1903. *Lemoine. Nancy. France. 1903.*

AUGUSTE FLEMENG. Double. Red/Purple. Tube. Rosy carmine. Sepals. Rosy carmine. Large. Reflexed. Corolla. Lilac. Large. Good habit. B. Cat. 1888. *Lemoine. Nancy. France. 1884.*

AUGUSTE GEVAERT. Double. Red/Purple. Tube. Red. Sepals. Red. Corolla. Purple. Illustration in Flor Des Serres Vol. 8 1858 Plate 85. *Coene. Ghent. Belgium. NK.*

AUGUSTE HARDY. Double. Red/Purple. Tube. Brilliant red. Sepals. Brilliant red. Horizontal. Corolla. Violet Pink. (Violet rose). Large. Full. Very floriferous. Branching from the base. B. Cat. 1892-1893. JF. Cat. 1892. L. Cat. 1892. *Lemoine. Nancy. France. 1892.*

AUGUSTE LEMARCHAND. Double. Red/White. Tube. Bright crimson. Thin. Swollen at the top. Sepals. Bright crimson. Large. Reflexed. Rounded. Corolla. White striped carmine at the base. Very full. P127 4th. Ed. by Porcher 1874. *Crousse. France. 1864.*

AUGUSTÉ RENOULT. Double. Red/Purple. Tube. Very dull red. Short. Very thick. 15mm. Sepals. Very dull red. Almost horizontal. Twice length of tube. Corolla. Purple violet. P 37 & 141 3rd Ed by Porcher 1858 Flower contains 12/15 petals. Spreading. Resembles "Don Giovanni". *Renoult. France. 1857.*

AUGUSTE ZAUBITZ. Double. Red/White. Tube. Crimson. Short. Sepals. Crimson. Very large. Uplifted. Corolla. White striped carmine red.

Globular. Full. P127 4th. Ed. by Porcher 1874. *L'Huiller. France. 1864.*

AUGUSTINA. Single. Red/ND. Tube. Crimson red. Sepals. Crimson red. Divergent. Corolla. ND. P32 1st Ed. by Porcher 1844.The only quality of this variety is the brilliant colours of the flowers. Erect. Non Branching. Leaves are oblong oval. Reddish stems. NK. NK. NK. NK.

AUGUSTIN THIERRY. S/Double. Red/Red. Tube. Bright red. Sepals. Bright red. Corolla. Bright rose. Good market variety. Named after a French historian (1795-1856). B. Cat 1889-1893. L. Cat. 1891. *Lemoine. Nancy. France. 1889.*

AURANTIA (a). Single. Pink/Red. Tube. Light pink. (Flesh). Sepals. Light pink. (Flesh). Corolla. Vermilion. (Light orange). Flowers 45 mm long. Greenish yellow foliage. GC. P393 6/1842 Listed by Youells, Gt. Yarmouth. GC. P112 17/2/1844 & P66 1/2/1845 Listed by W. Miller, Ramsgate. GC. P345 28/5/1842 Intro. by J. Smith. *Smith, J. Dalston. GB. 1842.*

AURANTIA (b). Single. Red/Purple. Tube. ND. Sepals. ND. Corolla. ND. Similar to "Eclipse", but with more gloss. New seedling fuchsia. GC. P66 1/2/1845. Intro. by W. Miller, Ramsgate. *Miller, W. Ramsgate GB. 1845.*

AURANTIA (c). Single. Red/Red. Tube. Orange. Sepals. Orange. Corolla. Rich vermilion. GC. P22908 8/5/1847 Foliage resembles polished copper. Metallic hue. P59 2nd Ed. by Porcher 1848 Very curious variety Tube and sepals are coppery orange with a vermillion corolla.GC. P153 4/3/1848 & P256 21/4/1849 Listed by R. Cooper, Croydon. GC. P298 8/5/1847 Intro. by Tiley, Bath. *Tiley, Bath. GB. 1847.*

AURANTIACA. Single. Red/Red. Tube. Vermilion. Thin. Sepals. Vermilion. Green points. Open. Corolla. Orange red shaded brown and crimson. P59 2nd Ed. by Porcher 1848. Mediocre. *Meillez. Lille. France. 1847.*

AURITA. Single. ND/ND. Tube. ND. Sepals. ND. Corolla. ND. GC. P200 28/3/1846. Listed by J & S Shilling, Odiham. NK. NK. NK. NK.

AURORA (a). Single. ND/ND. Tube. ND. Sepals. ND. Corolla. ND. GC. P98 17/2/1844 Listed by Youells, Gt. Yarmouth. GC. P66 1/2/1845 Listed by W. Miller, Ramsgate. *Bell, Thirsk. GB. 1843?*

AURORA (b). Single. Red/Purple. Tube. Dull crimson. (Cherry). Thick. Sepals. Dull Crimson. (Cherry red). Large. Very open. Corolla. Violet. (Purple). GC. P112 17/2/1844 Listed by W. Miller, Ramsgate. P167 RH. 1857. Harrison, Dereham List of 1845. P32 2nd Ed. by Porcher 1848 Large leaves 7cms x 5cms. Large open sepals longer than tube. Flowers 5cms long. *Standish, Bagshot. GB. 1843?*

AURORA (c). Single. ND/ND. Tube. ND. Sepals. ND. Corolla. ND. GC. P66 1/2/1845 & P147 13/3/1847 Listed by Millers, Ramsgate. *Miller, W. Ramsgate. GB. 1844?*

AURORA (d). Single. Red/Purple. Tube. Carmine. Long. Sepals. Carmine. Long. Corolla. Deep purple. GC. P143 6/3/1853 Listed by J. Dobson. GC. P449 17/7/1852 & P209 26/3/1853 Listed by H. Walton, Burnley. GC. P595 20/9/1851 Intro. by J. Dobson, Isleworth who purchased entire stock of 1850 seedlings. *Story, W.H. Newton Abbot. GB. 1852.*

AURORA (e). ND. Red/Purple. Tube. Red. Sepals. Red. Corolla. Purple. GC. P55 19/1/1867 Review by H. Cannell. NK. NK. *GB. 1866.*

AURORA (f). Single. Red/Purple. Tube. Scarlet. Waxy. Sepals. Scarlet. Broad. Waxy. Corolla. Warm rosy plum. JF. Cat. 1885. *Lye. J. Market Lavington. GB. 1885.*

AURORA (g). Single. Red/Red. Tube. Soft vermilion pink. 20mm. Sepals. Soft vermilion pink. Short. Horizontal. Points down. Corolla. Carmine vermilion. Bell shaped. P35 & P140 3rd Ed. by Porcher 1858. Clear green foliage. 7cm x 5cm. Very dentate. Large calyx. *Dender, Coblenz. Germany. 1855.*

AURORA SUPERBA. Single. Pink/Red. Tube. Rich salmon. Sepals. Rich salmon, tinged yellow at tips. Broad. Reflexed. Corolla. Scarlet (Orange red), (Orange scarlet). Large. Spreading. Very even. BSW. Cat. 1878. HC. Cat. 1882-1885. BSW. Cat. 1897. GO. "Select" 1880-1890. GC. Vol. 26 1886 RHS. Fuchsia trials at Chiswick 1886 "Best". NK. NK. NK. NK.

AUSTERLITZ. Double. Red/Purple. Tube. Crimson red. Sepals. Crimson red. Reflexed. Corolla. Blue with undertones of violet and red. Multiflowered. Pedicel 30 mm. P121 4th. Ed. by Porcher 1874. *Demay, H. Arras. France. 1869.*

AUTOCRAT (a). Single. Red/Purple. Tube. Crimson. Thin. 15mm longSepals. Crimson. Reflex back to tube. Twice as long as tube.Corolla. Deep

Purple. (Dull purplish violet). P141 3rd Ed. by Porcher 1858 Intense green foliage. GC. P375 31/5/1856 Exhibited as a fine pyramid 7' high by Mr. Bousie at Crystal Palace. GC. P401 24/6/1854 Listed by H.Walton, Burnley & B. Cant Colchester. GC. P466 22/7/1854 Listed by Bass & Brown, Sudbury. GC. P194 1/4/1854 Intro. by C. Turner, Slough. *Banks, E. Deal. GB. 1854.*

AUTOCRAT (b). Single. Red/Purple. Tube. Bright crimson. Short. Sepals. Bright crimson. Completely recurved. Corolla. Satiny plum marked crimson at base. B. Cat. 1872-1875. GC. P476 15/4/1871 Intro. by W. Bull. *Bull, W. Chelsea. GB. 1871.*

AUTUMNALE see METEOR (b).

AVALANCHE (a). Double. Red/Purple. Tube. Red. (Brilliant crimson). (Bright carmine). Slender. 10mm long. Sepals. Red. (Brilliant Crimson).(Bright carmine). Reflexed. Large. Round. 22mm" long. 13mm across. Corolla. Purple. (Bluish violet washed red). Even. P121 4th Ed. by Porcher 1874.Petals folded and extended. 19mm . Deep yellowish green foliage. Pedicel 30 mm. Vol.3 J of RHS 1873. Fuchsia Trials at Chiswick FCC. Vol 4 J of RHS 1873 FCC. GC. P824 27/6/1885 RHS Trials "Best". GC. Vol 26 1886 RHS Trials 31/7/1886 "Good". HC. Cat. 1882. BSW. Cat. 1878. GO. "Select" 1880-1888. GC. P778 7/6/1873. Intro. by E.G. Henderson. *Henderson, E.G. St. Johns Wood. GB. 1869.*

AVALANCHE (b). Double. Red/White. Tube. Carmine Scarlet. Sepals. Carmine Scarlet. Short. Well recurved. Corolla. Pure white. 25 petals in a bloom.(Pure white, striped rose pink). Exceedingly double. Fine form GC. P1554 2/12/1871 Review by H. Cannell. P127 43th Ed by Porcher 1874 Wood thin and wiry. Profuse bloomer.Pedicel 35 mm. GO. "Select" 1880-1891. RH. P311 "Select" by E.A. Carrière. B. Cat. 1870-1873. BSW. Cat. 1878-1888. Carmine filaments. Vol. 4 J of RHS 1873. Fuchsia trials at Chiswick. Habit rather sparse. Not very free. FCC. F&P 1870 March Coloured plate. GC. P294 26/2/1870 Intro. by G. Smith. *Smith, G. Islington. GB. 1870*

AVANTE GARDE. Double. Red/Purple. Tube. Red. Sepals. Red. Corolla. Plum. Enormous globular flower. RB. Cat. 1926. *Rozain (Jr.) Lyons. France. 1920.*

AYRSHIRE. S/Double. Red/Purple. Tube. Bright coral. (Red). Sepals. Bright coral. (Red). Corolla. Rich blue. A decided advance in the way of a blue coralla. JF. Cat. 1889-1890. B. Cat. 1889-1893. *Lye, J. Market Lavington. GB. 1889.*

AZUREA. Single. Red/Purple. Tube. Clear red. Sepals. Clear red. Corolla. Dull sky blue. Large. Well open. L. Cat. 1888. *Rozain, Lyons. France. 1888.*

AZUREA SUPERBA. Double. Red/Purple. Tube. Bright reddish coral. Sepals. Bright reddish coral. Recurved. Corolla. Azure Violet. Very large petals. B. Cat. 1879-1893. Intro. by W. Bull. *Bull, W. Chelsea. GB. 1879.*

BACCHUS (a).Single. Red/Purple. Tube. Red. Slender. 9mm. Sepals. Red. 25mm. Spreading. Corolla. Reddish Purple,darker at edges. 19mm. Prominent. GC. P55 19/1/1867 Review by H. Cannell "Best in small pots". Pcxvii Vol. 3 J of RHS 1872. P115 4th.Ed.by Porcher 1874. *Banks E., Deal. GB. 1863.*

BACCHUS (b). ND. ND/ND. Tube. ND. Sepals. ND. Corolla. ND. RB cat. *Rozain(Jr), Lyons. France. 1924.*

BAHIA. Double. Red/Purple. Tube. Red. Sepals. Red. Corolla. Blackish Violet, striped carmine. L. Cat. 1910. *Rozain, Lyons. France 1910.*

BALAKLAVA. Double. Red/Purple. Tube. Carmine Scarlet. Sepals. Carmine Scarlet. Corolla. Violet. Large. Finely folded. HC. Cat. 1882. NK. NK. NK.*1882.*

BALDUIN. ND. ND/ND. Tube. ND. Sepals. ND. Corolla. ND. P37 & P141 3rd. Ed. by Porcher 1858. *Erber. Germany 1857.*

BALLET GIRL. Double. Red/White. Tube. Scarlet. Sepals. Scarlet. Corolla. White. Dwarf. AM. RHS 24/7/1894. Spent blooms hang from the style. GO. P151 1895. JF.Cat. 1895. BSW.Cat. 1897. *Veitch, R. London. GB. 1894.*

BALLOONII. Single. Red/Purple. Tube. Crimsol. Sepals. Crimson. Corolla. Purple. Globular Form. Dark foliage. P33 2nd. Ed by Porcher 1848. GC. P112 17/2/1844 & P66 1/2/1845 & P146 8/3/1846 Listed by W. Miller, Ramsgate. GC. P98 17/2/1844. Listed by Youells, Gt.Yarmouth. Harrisons, Dereham List 1845. Girlings Stowmarket List 1845. GC P114 25/2/1843 Intro. by Wm. May. *May,W. Bedale GB. 1843.*

BALLOONII SUPERBA. Single. Red/Purple. Tube. Red. Sepals. Rich Red. Short. Corolla. Purple. Small. Colour of "Meteor". P59 2nd Ed. by Porcher 1848. Mediocre. GC.P66 1/2/1845 & P162 14/3/1846 & P184 13/3/1847. Listed by W.Miller, Ramsgate. *Miller, W. Ramsgate. GB. 1845.*

BALTIC. Single. Red/Purple. Tube. Crimson. Sepals. Crimson. Reflexed. Corolla. Light Purple, veined crimson at base. B. Cat. 1898-1901. L. Cat. 1901. GC. 1/5/1897 Intro. by W. Bull. *Bull W.,Chelsea. GB. 1897.*

BARAMO. Single. Red/Purple. Tube. Deep rose. Sepals. Deep rose. Reflexed. Corolla. Rich purplish crimson. B. Cat. 1881. NK. NK. NK.*1881.*

BARCELONA. Single. Red/Purple. Tube. Scarlet. 15mm long. Sepals. Scarlet. Recurved.(Rosy Carmine).(Purplish red). Corolla. Rich dark marine blue. Large and of great depth. (Violet splashed red). P106 4th Ed. by Porcher 1874. Bell shaped. Floriferous. Sepals. Large. Reflexed and rounded. HC. Cat. 1882. GC. P430 29/3/1873. Intro. by E.G. Henderson. St. Johns Wood. *Banks E, Deal? GB. 1873.*

BARON DE KETTELER. Double. Red/Purple. Tube. Blood red. Sepals. Blood Red. Reflexed. Corolla. Intense Plum Violet. Full. Enormous. Large Petals. L.Cat. 1901. *Lemoine. Nancy. France. 1901.*

BARONESS. Single. White/Purple. Tube. White. Long. Sepals. White. Well reflexed. Corolla. Violet Rose. Distinct colour. Pretty and attractive flower. B. Cat. 1875-1882. *Bull, W. Chelsea. GB. 1875.*

BARONESS BURDETT COUTTS. Single. White/Red. Tube. Pure White. Thick. Long 15mms, Sepals. Pure White. Large. Reflexed. Corolla. Orange Scarlet (Vermillion). Spiral shaped. Nice shade. Similiar to "Virgo Maria". Named after an English philanthropist (1814-1906). Commemorates granting Freedom of London to her in 1872. P116 4th Ed. by Porcher 1874. Pedicel 50mms. Strong Growth. Yellowish Green Foliage. GO. "Select" 1880-1890. B. Cat. 1876. HC. Cat. 1882. *Banks, E. Deal. GB. 1872.*

BARONET. Single. Red/Purple. Tube. Bright rose. Sepals. Bright Rose. Completely reflexed. Corolla. Violet Purple marked rose. B. Cat.1870. NK. NK. *GB. 1867?*

BARONNE BLANCHE EZPELTA. Double. Red/Purple. Tube. Coral Red. Sepals. Coral Red. Well reflexed. Corolla. Azure Violet shaded scarlet. Large. Well expanded. B. Cat. 1877-1880. *Bull, W. Chelsea. GB. 1875.*

BARTHOLDII. Double. Red/Purple. Tube. Brilliant carmine. Sepals. Brilliant carmine. Corolla. Plum Violet. Expanded. Named after a French sculptor, (1834-1904)who designed the Statue of Libery in New York, and was awarded the Legion of Honour in 1877. Gartenflora 1888. L. Cat 1887. *Lemoine. Nancy. France. 1887.*

BASILISK. Single. White/Red. Tube. White. Long. Thick. Sepals. Blush White. Broad. Horizontally reflexed. Corolla. Bright Light Scarlet. Sepals tipped green. B. Cat. 1875-1883. *Bull,W. Chelsea. GB. 1873?*

BATESII. Single. ND/ND. Tube. ND. Sepals. ND. Corolla. ND. Shown by W.M. Tweedy. RHS of Cornwall Show. GC P495 23/7/1842. NK.NK. *GB. NK.*

BAUCIS. Double. Pink/Purple. Tube. Clear Pink. Sepals. Clear Pink. Reflexed. Corolla. Dark Lilac. P149 L. Cat. 1901. *Lemoine. Nancy. France. 1901.*

BAUDUIN. Single. Red/Red. Tube. Rose Carmine. Thin. Sepals. Rose Carmine. Horizontal. Corolla. Lake. (Harrisons List 1845 T/S Pale crimson. Corolla Rosy Purple). (Girlings List 1845 Large Red). P33 2nd Ed. by Porcher 1848. Foliage 6 x 4 cm. Dedicated to a French horticulturalist. RH. P23 1846. *Salter, J. Versailles. France. 1844.*

BAYARD. Single. Red/Purple. Tube. Rose pink. Sepals. Rose Pink. Corolla. Mauve. Long Pedicel. Bruant, Poitiers Cat. 1914. NK. NK. *France. 1914.*

BEACON. Single. Red/Purple. Tube. Deep rose. Sepals. Deep rose. Lighter at tips. Horizontal. Corolla. Bright carmine shaded Violet, marked rose at base. Immense size. P115 4th Ed. by Porcher 1874 "Not in the first selection". B. Cat. 1872-1875. GC. P476 15/4/1871 Intro. by W. Bull. *Bull,W. Chelsea. GB. 1871.*

BEATRICE (a). Single. White/Red. Tube. White. Sepals. White. Moderately reflexed. Corolla. Red. Lovely shade. Named after the youngest daughter of Queen Victoria (1857-1944). GC. P539 10/7/1858 Listed by F. Godwin, Sheffield, GC. P238 19/3/1859. Listed by W. Rumley, Richmond. GC. P126 20/2/1845 Raised by W. Knight Gr. to Duchess of Kent. Intro. by W. Rollinson, Tooting. *Knight, W. GB. 1858.*

BEATRICE (b). Single. White/Purple. Tube. Pure white. Sepals. Pure White. Reflexed. Corolla. Rich violet rose margined with Scarlet. White at base. Large. Full. GC. P74 24/1/1863. Intro. by W. Bull, Chelsea. *Bull, W. Chelsea. GB. 1863.*

BEATRICE (c). Single. Red/Purple. Tube. Deep Crimson. Short. Stout. Sepals. Deep Crimson.

17

Corolla. Reddish Purple. Good shaped flowers. BSW. Cat. 1878-1888. GC. P521 28/4/1877 Intro. by B&S Williams. *Bland, E. Fordham. GB. 1877.*

BEATRIX. Double. Red/White. Tube. Dull red. Short. Sepals. Dull red. Uplifted. Corolla. Cream veined rose. RB. Cat. 1885. *Aubin, Bagnolet. France. 1884.*

BEAUMARCHAIS. Double. Red/Purple. Tube. Red. Sepals. Red. Corolla. Purple. (Dark violet with red bands). Named after a French playwright (1732-1799). Kelways Cat. 1899. Hardy. Not a true F.Coccinea x, but a F.Magellanica variant. L. Cat. 1901. F. Coccinea x. *Lemoine. Nancy. France. 1897.*

BEAUTÉ. ND. ND/ND.Tube. ND. Sepals. ND. Corolla. ND. RB. Cat. 1883. *Boucharlet. Lyons. France. 1880.*

BEAUTÉ PARFAIT. Single. White/Purple. Tube. White. Sepals. White. Corolla. Purple? GC. P184 13/3/1847 Listed by W.Miller, Ramsgate. *Harrison, Dereham. GB. 1847.*

BEAUTÉ PARFAITE. Single. White/Purple. Tube. White, tinted pink. Short. Sepals. White, tinted pink. Divergent. Large. Corolla. Lilac rose. Similar to "Candidissima", "Delicata", "Diana", "Lady Julia" & "Sans Pareil". P59 2nd Ed. by Porcher 1848. *Salter, J. Versailles. France. 1846.*

BEAUTÉ SANS PAREILLE. Single. Red/Purple. Tube. Vermilion veined greenish white. 25mm long. Sepals. Vermilion veined greenish white. Long, Horizontal. Corolla. Violet red. P442 3rd Ed. by Porcher 1858. *Crousse, Nancy. France. 1854.*

BEAUTY (a). Single. ND/ND. Tube. ND. Sepals. ND. Corolla. ND. P33 2nd Ed. by Porcher 1848. GC. P112. 17/2/1844. & P66 1/2/1845. Listed by W. Miller, Ramsgate. *Standish. Bagshot. GB. 1843.*

BEAUTY (b). Single. Red/Purple. Tube. Red. Sepals.Red. Corolla. Purple. GC. P98 17/2/1844 & P146 8/3/1845 Intro. by Youells. Gt Yarmouth. *Youell. Gt.Yarmouth GB. 1844.*

BEAUTY (c). Single. White/Purple. Tube. Blush white. Sepals. Blush white. Horizontal. Corolla. Violet Purple. P141 3rd. Ed. by Porcher 1858. GC. P385 18/6/1853 Listed by W. Rumley, Richmond. GC. P248 18/4/1854 Listed by Mitchell & Co. Brighton. GC. P483 30/7/1853 & P162 18/3/1854 Listed by H.Walton, Burnley. GC. P98 11/2/1853 Intro. by G. Smith,Tollington Nurseries. *Smith,G.*

Islington. GB. 1853.

BEAUTY (d). Single. Red/Purple. Tube. Rosy Carmine. Sepals. Rosy Carmine. Gracefully recurved. Corolla. Rosy Lilac edged carmine. Beautifully expanded. GC. P450 17/5/1862 Intro. by B.W. Knight, Battle. *Knight,B.W., Battle GB. 1862.*

BEAUTY (e). Single. Red/Purple. Tube. Carmine. (Scarlet carmine). (Crimson red). Sepals. Carmine. (Scarlet carmine). Broad. Gracefully recurved. Corolla. Pure Lavender. (Lilac Violet washed red and stained white). Cup Shaped. F&P P56. 1866. GC P55 19/1/1867 Review by H. Cannell. Vigourous bush. P103 4th Ed. Porcher 1874. GC. P982 26/10/1865 Intro. by E.G. Henderson, St. Johns Wood. *Banks, E. Deal. GB. 1865.*

BEAUTY (f). Double. Red/Purple. Tube. Crimson. Sepals. Crimson. Corolla. Purple, margined crimson. JF. Cat. 1912. New. NK. NK. *1912.*

BEAUTY OF CHELMSFORD. Single. White/Pink. Tube. White. Sepals. White. Corolla. Shaded rose. Small. Elegant. App. to RH. 1851 by Porcher. GC. P537 12/8/1848. Listed by G.Smith, Islington. GC. P161 17/3/1849 Listed by W.Rumley, Richmond. GC. P224 14/4/1849 & P274 4/5/1850. Listed by Bass & Brown, Sudbury. GC. P224 14/4/1849 Listed by R.Whibley, Kennington. GC. P274 5/5/1849 Listed by H. Walton, Burnley. *Turville, Chelmsford. GB. 1848.*

BEAUTY OF CLAPHAM. Single. White/Red. Tube. Blush. Sepals. Blush white. Spreading. Corolla. Lake with white feather at base. 1". P115 4th. Ed. by Porcher 1874. "Not in the first selection". Pcxi Vol 3 P of RHS. Fuchsia trial at Chiswick 1872. Submitted by E.G.Henderson. NK. NK. *GB. 1871?*

BEAUTY OF CLAPTON. ND. ND/ND. Tube ND. Sepals. ND. Corolla. ND. GC. P213 8/4/1854 Listed by C.H. Gardiner, Maidstone. NK. NK. *GB. NK.*

BEAUTY OF CLYFFE HALL. Single. White/Red. Tube. Blush White. Sepals. Blush White. Corolla. Rich carmine pink. Free Bloomer. Vigourous Grower. Good habit. GC. Vol 20 P243 25/8/1883. GC. P153 29/1/1887. GO. "Select" 1886-1889. JF. Cat. 1885. Dobbies Cat. 1892-1894. B.Cat. 1883. HC. Cat. 1885. *Lye,J. Market Lavington. GB. 1883.*

BEAUTY OF DALSTON. Single. White/Red. Tube. Whitish Pink. Swollen. Sepals. Whitish Pink. Large. Spreading. Corolla. Orange/Red/Carmine. Small. App.to RH.1851 by Porcher. GC. P184 13/3/1847 Listed by W. Miller, Ramsgate. GC. P249

18

18/4/1846. Intro. by J. Smith, Dalston. *Smith,J. Dalston. GB. 1846.*

BEAUTY OF DEAL. Single. White/Red. Tube. White. Sepals. White. Corolla. Bright Vermillion. Opens well. GC. P279 30/4/1853 "Light green stemmed". GC. P454 16/7/1853 Exhibited at H.S. Show on 9/7/1853, as a 7' pyramid, by Mr. Bousie Gr. to Rt. Hon. Labouchere. GC. P211 26/3/1853. Listed by W. Rumley, Richmond. GC. P248 15/4/1854 Listed by Mitchell & Co. Brighton. GC. P2283 21/4/1854 Listed by Hart & Nickling, Guildford. GC. P223 10/4/1852. Intro. by C.Turner, Slough. *Banks,E. Deal. GB. 1852.*

BEAUTY OF DEVONSHIRE. ND. ND/ND. GC. P162 18/3/1854 Listed as a new variety of 1853, by H.Walton, Burnley. NK.NK. *GB. 1853.*

BEAUTY OF EXETER. S/Double. Pink/Red. Tube. Pink. Sepals. Pink. Corolla. Reddish Bronze. Not bright. Complete cross between the light and dark tubed varieties. Illustrated. HC. Cat. 1891. L. Cat. 1892. JF.Cat. 1892. Dobbies. Cat. 1892-4. *Letheren, W. Exeter. GB. 1891.*

BEAUTY OF HIGH BEECHES. Single. Red/Red. Tube. Dark Crimson. Sepals. Dark Crimson. Well Reflexed. Corolla. Variegated Crimson, White and Lake. Large. Expanded like "La Crinoline". GC. P264 21/3/1863. Intro. by J. Crawford, Loughton. *Crawford,J. Loughton. GB. 1863.*

BEAUTY OF KENT. Single. Red/Purple. Tube. Scarlet. Sepals. Scarlet. Reflex right round to form a perfect ring. Corolla. Dark Plum Blue. Large. (Fine Purple). GC. P1554 2/12/1871 Review by H. Cannell. FW & GG P4 Jan.1870. GO. "Select" 1883-1889. G. P317 July 1874 Better than "Incomparible". B. Cat. 1870. HC. Cat. 1882-1885 "One of the prettiest". *Banks, E. Deal. GB. 1870.*

BEAUTY OF LAVINGTON. Single. White/Red. Tube. White. Sepals. White. Corolla. Rosy Carmine shaded Violet. GC. Vol 24 P277 1885 FCC at Bath. 2/9/1885. GO."Select" 1890-1891. JF.Cat. 1886. B. Cat. 1888. *Lye,J. Market Lavington. GB. 1886.*

BEAUTY OF LEEDS. Single. White/Red. Tube. Flesh. Thick. Sepals. Flesh. Tipped green. Corolla. Deep red. (Vermilion bordered crimson). P59 & P142 3rd Ed. by Porcher 1858 Reintroduced into commerce as "As you Like it" in 1852. App. to RH. 1851 by Porcher "First Class Variety". GC. P153 4/3/1847 Listed by R. Cooper, Croydon. GC. P169 11/3/1847 Intro. by G. Nicholls. *Nicholls,G. Leeds. GB. 1847.*

BEAUTY OF RICHMOND. Single. White/Purple. Tube. White. Sepals. White stained pale purple. Corolla. Deep Violet. GC. P658 20/10/1849 For release in May 1850, a large sized "Venus Victrix", by W. Rumley. GC. P387 15/6/1850 Listed by H Walton, Burnley. GC.P465 27/7/1850 Listed by W. Rumley, Richmond & G. Smith, Islington. App. to RH. 1851 by Porcher. First class variety. Venus Victrix X. *Rumley, W. Richmond. GB. 1850.*

BEAUTY OF SHOLDEN. Single. Red/Purple. Tube. Red. (Carmine red). Sepals. Red. (Carmine red). Corolla. Lavender. (Violet Rose splashed red and striped at base of petals). P106 4th Ed. by Porcher 1874. P4 FW & GG Jan 1870. *Banks,E. Deal. GB. 1868.*

BEAUTY OF ST. LEONARDS. Single. White/Purple. Tube. White. Sepals. Waxy white. Well extended. Corolla. Purple. GC. P153 4/3/1848 & P232 1/4/1848 & P256 21/4/1849 Listed by R. Cooper, Croydon. GC. P216 27/3/1847 Listed by W. Miller, Ramsgate. GC. P224 14/4/1848 Listed by R. Whibley, Kennington. GC.P338 22/5/1847 Intro. by Knight. *Knight,B.W. St. Leonards on Sea. GB. 1847.*

BEAUTY OF STORTFORD. Single. White/Purple. Tube. White. Sepals. White. Corolla. Bluish. App. to RH. 1851 by Porcher. GC. P647 11/10/1851 Exhibited by F.H. Earle of Falmouth at RHS of Cornwall Show on 9/9/1851. GC P417 6/7/1850 & P706 9/11/1850 Listed by H.Walton Burnley, GC. P465 27/7/1850 & P144 8/3/1851 Listed by W. Rumley, Richmond.GC. P465 27/7/1850 Listed by G. Smith, Islington. 27/7/1850 *Glasscock. GB. 1850.*

BEAUTY OF SWANLEY. Single. White/Pink. Tube. White. Sepals. White. Well Reflexed. Corolla. Bright Rose. (Bright Pink). (Pink). HC. Cat. 1882-1885. GC P206 17/2/1877 Growers of the West Country - Varieties. BSW. Cat. 1878-1897. *Lye,J. Market Lavington. GB. 1875.*

BEAUTY OF THE BOWER. Single. Red/Purple. Tube. Red. Sepals. Red. Reflex over tube. Corolla. Dark Purple. GC. P467 14/7/1855 Listed by Bass & Brown, Sudbury & H.Walton, Burnley. GC. P530 11/8/1850 Listed by Bainbridge & Hewson, York. GC. P314 10/5/1856 Listed by W.Rumley, Richmond & Youells, Gt Yarmouth. GC. P34 20/1/1855 Intro. by W.J. Epps, Maidstone. *Banks, E. Deal. GB. 1855.*

BEAUTY OF THE WEST. Single. White/Red. Tube. White. Sepals. White. Corolla. Vermillion Scarlet. B. Cat. 1880-1882. JF. Cat. 1885. G.

6/9/1884 Exhibited at Trowbridge by J. Lye 20/8/1884. GC. P450 10/4/1880 J.Lye advert. *Lye,J. Market Lavington. GB 1880.*

BEAUTY OF TROWBRIDGE. Sepals. White/Pink. Tube. White. Sepals. White. Corolla. Orange Pink. Similar to "Mrs. Marshall". Attributed to J. Lye, but refuted by H.Cannell. GC 1879. GO. "Select" 1883-1891. HC.Cat. 1882-1885. *Smith,G. Trowbridge. GB. 1879.*

BEAUTY OF WEST KENT. Double. Red/Pink. Tube. Deep reddish purple. Sepals. Reddish Purple. (Purple red.). Corolla. Deep flesh. (Warm flesh. Bright carmine lines). (Soft carmine). L.Cat. 1892. Dobbies Cat. 1892. B. Cat. 1892-1895. *Fry,G. Lee. GB. 1890.*

BEAUTY OF WILTS. Single. White/Pink. Tube. Creamy white. Long. Sepals. Delicate flesh. Elegantly recurved. Corolla. Violet Rose. (Rich rosy carmine margined carmine red). GC Vol 18 P215 1882. B. Cat. 1878-1882. BSW. Cat. 1878. GO "Select" 1880-1891. Dobbies Cat. 1892-1894. GC. Vol 24 P722 9/6/1877. P342 J of RHS 1900. Arabella Imp.x J.Lye. *Lye,J., Market Lavington. GB. 1877.*

BEAUTY'S BLOOM. Single. Red/Purple. Tube. Glossy Scarlet Carmine. Sepals. Glossy Scarlet Carmine. Corolla. Dark Violet tinted plum black. Long. Oblong or cup shaped. P106 4th Edition by Porcher 1874. GC. P382 28/4/1866 Intro. by E.G.Henderson, St Johns Wood. *Banks,E. Deal. GB. 1866.*

BEAUTY SUPREME (a). ND. ND/ND. Tube. ND. Sepals. ND Corolla. ND. Vol xii P224 Floral Cabinet. GC. P541 10/8/1844 HS Meeting. New Seedling exhibited by Low & Co. Low,H. NK NK. *GB. 1844.*

BEAUTY SUPREME (b). Single. White/Red. Tube. Waxy White. Sepals. Waxy White, tinted rose. Horizontal. Corolla. Cerise red. FC. Mar 1849. P142 3rd Ed. by Porcher 1858.GC. P537 12/8/1848 Listed by G. Smith, Islington. P161 17/3/1849. Listed by W. Rumley, Richmond. GC. P274 5/5/1849 Listed by H. Walton, Burnley. GC. P241 20/4/1850 Listed by W. Rendle, Plymouth. App. to RH. 1851 by Porcher gives Proctor as raiser. CG. Vol. 6 P326 1853 "Recommended" GC. P153 4/3/1848 Intro. by Kendall, Stoke Newington. *Proctor. GB. 1848.*

BÉBÉ. Single. White/Red. Tube. Flesh. Sepals. Flesh. Long. Outspread. Corolla. Vermillion red. Free flowering. App. to RH 1851 by Porcher. *Meillez. Lille. France. 1849*

BEESWING. Single. Red/Purple. Tube. Red. Sepals. Red. Corolla. Purple. GC. P404 1848 Listed as "Good". GC. P241. 20/4/1850 Listed by W.Rendle, Plymouth. *Kendall, Stoke Newington. GB. 1847?*

BELGIQUE. ND. ND/ND. Tube. ND. Sepals. ND. Corolla. ND. RB cat. *Rozain, Lyons. France. 1915.*

BELLA. Double. Red/Purple. Tube. Deep rose. Sepals. Deep rose. Broad. Reflexed into a concave form. Corolla. Bright Bluish Purple striped rose at base. (Violet Blue striped red). Vigorous bush. P122. 4th. Ed. by Porcher 1874. Buds are bell shaped buttons. B.Cat. 1872-1876. *Bull,W. Chelsea GB. 1872.*

BELLADONNA. Single. White/Purple. Tube. White. Short. Thick. Sepals. Whiter, Open. Points down. Corolla. Lilac Rose. Pleated petals. P142 3rd Ed. by Porcher 1858. Mediocre. Yellow green foliage. GC. P211 26/3/1853. Listed by W. Rumley, Richmond. *Hocking. GB. 1852.*

BELLA FORBES. Double. Red/White. Tube. Clear Carmine. Sepals. Clear Carmine. Corolla. White. Large. Full. JF. Cat. 1912. Intro by J. Forbes. *Forbes, J. Hawick. Scotland 1912.*

BELLADIFOLIATA. See "Rosea Alba"

BELLE DE DORK. Single. Red/Purple. Tube. Red. Sepals. Red. Corolla. Purple. GC. P184 13/3/1847 & P250 17/4/1847 Listed by W.Miller, Ramsgate. NK. NK. *1846.*

BELLE ÉTOILE (a). Single. Red/Red. Tube. Pale vermilion pink. 15 mm long. Sepals. Vermilion pink. Large. Spreading. Shorter than the tube. Corolla. Vermilion. Petals pleated. Lax. Bushy. P143 3rd Ed. by Porcher 1858. *Smith, G. Islington. GB. 1851.*

BELLE ÉTOILE (b). Single. ND/ND. Tube. ND. Sepals. ND. Corolla. ND. P35 3rd. Ed. by Porcher 1858. *Baudinet, Meaux. France. 1853.*

BELLE HÉLÈNE. Double. Red/Purple. Tube. Carmine. Sepals. Carmine. Downturned. Corolla. Purple striped. P80 Witte 1882. Laings Cat. circa 1890. *Weinrich. Germany. 1879.*

BELLE HÒVRAISE. ND ND/ND. Tube. ND. Sepals. ND. Corolla. ND. 1888 Gartenflora. *Avenal, E. NK NK.*

BELLIANA. Single. See "Rosea Alba" GC. P202 26/3/1842. GC. P146 8/3/1845

BELLIDI FLORA FLORE PLENA. Double. Red/Purple. Tube. Rose Lilac. Sepals. Rose Lilac. Corolla. Bluish Violet shaded crimson. Very full.(Violet Blue shaded Carmine). Good habit and foliage. A large and finely shaped bloom. RH. P170 1857. GC. P285 25/4/1857. Intro. by H. Low. *Dubus. France. 1856.*

BELLIDIFOLIATA. Single. White/Red. Tube. Pale Pink. Sepals. Pale Pink. Corolla. Crimson. Girlings List 1845. NK. NK NK.

BELLISSIMA. Single. White/Pink. Tube. Light Pink. Sepals. Light Pink, tipped green. Corolla. Deep rose. GC. P161 16/3/1844 Intro. by A.J. Jones. *Jones,A.J. Ackworth. GB. 1844.*

BELL OF BARTON. Single. ND/ND. Tube. ND. Sepals. ND. Corolla. ND. GC P248 15/4/1854 "Fuchsias of 1853". Listed by Mitchell & Co, Brighton. NK NK. *1853.*

BELLONA (a). Single. Red/Red. Tube. Red. Large. Short. Sepals. Red. Corolla. Deep crimson. Large. P33 2nd Ed. by Porcher 1848 Foliage clear green. Their form resembles "Globosa". Similar to "Syrius" and "Edwardsii". Harrisons, Dereham List 1845. Girlings, Stowmarket List 1845. *Salter. Versailles. France. 1844?*

BELLONA (b). Double. Red/White. Tube. Rosy Carmine. Short. Sepals. Rosy carmine. Completely reflexed. Corolla. White. Long. B. Cat. 1896-1898. HC. Cat. 1896. GC. P128 1/2/1896 Intro. by W. Bull. *Bull,W. Chelsea. GB. 1896.*

BEN E GLOE. Single. Red/Purple. Tube. Carmine. Sepals. Carmine. Recurved. Corolla. Lavender, marked carmine. Cup shaped. GC. P55 19/1/1867 Review by H. Cannell. Distinct and very dwarf. One of the prettiest little fuchsias ever seen. GC. P382 28/4/1866 Intro. by E.G. Henderson, St.John's Wood. *Banks, E. Deal. GB. 1866.*

BENGALI. Double. White/Purple. Tube. Greenish white. Sepals. Greenish White. Corolla. Dark purple plum. Full. Good habit. L. Cat. 1911. *Rozain. Lyons. France. 1911.*

BENJAMIN PEARSON. Single. Red/Purple. Tube. Scarlet. Sepals. Scarlet. Corolla. Carmine. (Purple). GC. Vol 26 18/9/1986 Exhibited at Bath Floral Fete by J. Lye, 1st. 9" pot class. GC.Vol 2 1887 1st 9" pot class. G. P277 21/9/1889. 3rd. JF. Cat. 1888. Laings Cat. circa 1890. *Lye, J. Market Lavington. GB. 1887.*

BENMANII. ND. White/Pink. Tube. White. Sepals. White. Elegantly recurved. Corolla. Rich Rose. BSW. Cat. 1878. NK. NK. *1877.*

BÉRANGER (a). Single. Red/Red. Tube. Red. Sepals. Red. Sepals just curl. Corolla. Rosy Red. Coloured Plate 87 F de S. Vol 8 1859. *Coene, Ghent. Belgium 1858?*

BÉRANGER (b). Double. Red/Purple.Tube. Reddish purple. Sepals. Reddish purple.Corolla. Violet blue. Not the true F. Coccinea, but a F.Magellanica Variant. L. Cat. 1901. Hardy. F.Coccinea X. *Lemoine. Nancy. France. 1897*

BÉRANGER (c). Double. Red/Purple. Tube. Red. Sepals. Red. Corolla. Purple. P126. 4th. Edition by Porcher 1874. Not in the first selection. *Lemoine. Nancy. France. 1865.*

BÉRANGER (d). Double. Red/Purple. Tube. Red. Sepals. Red. Reflexed. Corolla. Violet Purple, red at base. Small flowers. Bruant, Potiers Cat. No. 290 1911. NK. NK. NK. *1910.*

BERCERA. Double. Red/Purple. Tube. Bright crimson. Short. Sepals. Bright crimson. Corolla. Purplish Violet. Irregular. Spreading. B. Cat. 1898. *Bull, W. Chelsea. GB. 1897.*

BERENICE. Double. Red/Purple. Tube. Rich crimson. Sepals. Rich crimson. Broad. Beautifully reflexed. Corolla. Rich Deep Purple, marked rosy crimson at base. B. Cat. 1880-1882. *Bull, W. Chelsea. GB. 1880.*

BERLINER KIND. Double. Red/White. Tube. Red. Sepals. Red.(Coral red. well reflexed.) Corolla. White. GC. P824 27/6/1885 RHS Trials at Chiswick "Best in its class". GO. "Select" 1890. Dobbies Cat. 1893-1894 Similar to "Miss Lucy Finnis". Laings Cat. circa 1890. BSW Cat. 1897. *Eggbrecht. Germany. NK.*

BERLIOZ. Double. ND. Tube. ND. Sepals. ND. Corolla. ND. L. Cat. 1892. NK. NK. *1890.*

BERQUIN. Single. Red/Red. Tube. Reddish Orange. Long. Sepals. Reddish Orange. Corolla. Bright rosy lake. Dobbies Cat. 1892-1894. HC. Cat. 1885-1890. *Gabriel. GB. 1885.*

BERRYER. Single. Red/Purple. Tube. Reddish Purple. Short. Sepals. Reddish purple. Horizontal. Corolla. Violet red. P143 3rd Ed. by Porcher 1858. Corallina X. *Gaines. Battersea. GB. 1851.*

21

BERTHENAY. Double. Red/Purple. Tube. Red. Sepals. Red. Corolla. Violet, shaded blue. (Violet tinted marine blue, splashed bright red). Enormous. JF. Cat. 1907. L. Cat. 1906. *Rozain. Lyons. France.1906.*

BERTHOLDI Double. Red/Purple. Tube. Deep red. Sepals. Deep red. Recurved. Corolla. Deep Violet Blue. Laings Cat. circa 1890. NK. NK. NK.

BERTRADE. Double. Red/White. Tube. Crimson. Sepals. Wine Red. Corolla. White. Dwarf. Free. Small plant forming open button type flowers. JF. Cat. 1907. L. Cat. 1906. *Lemoine. Nancy. France. 1906.*

BESSIE CALLOUN. ND. ND/ND. Tube. ND. Sepals. ND. Corolla. ND. GC. P338 15/4/1865 Listed by H. Walton, Burnley. NK. NK. NK.

BETA. Single. Red/Purple. Tube. Bright Crimson. Sepals. Bright Crimson. Recurved. Corolla. Rich Plum. Good shape. B. Cat. 1901. NK NK. NK.

BIANCA MARGINATA. ND. White/Purple. Tube. White. Sepals. White. Corolla. Purple. GC. P55 19/1/1867 Review by H. Cannell. P120 4th Ed. by Porcher 1874. GC. P806 30/8/1862 & P72 21/1/1863 Intro. by E. G. Henderson. *Banks, E. Deal. GB. 1862.*

BIANCA (a). Single. Red/Purple. Tube. Pale rose vermilion. Sepals. Pale rose vermillion. Open a little. Corolla. Violet vermilion. P59 2nd Ed 1848 & P143 3rd Ed. 1858 by Porcher. P250 17/4/1847 Listed by J.Hally, Blackheath. GC. P455 8/7/1847 Shown by Gaines at RBS Show London. GC. P226 13/4/1850. Listed by Poole Nurseries. *Salter, J. Versailles. France. 1844.*

BIANCA (b). ND. ND/ND. Tube. ND. Sepals. ND. Corolla. ND. GC. P771 24/8/1861. Listed by H. Walton, Burnley. NK. NK. *1861.*

BIANCA (c). Double. Red/White. Tube. Rosy Carmine. Sepals. Rosy Carmine. Corolla. Pure white. JF. Cat. 1898. NK. NK. *1897.*

BIANCA (d). Double. Red/White. Tube. Deep red. Short. Sepals. Deep red. Recurved. Corolla. White, suffused and veined bright red at base. Excellent shape. Being sent out for the first time 1907. Dicksons, Chester, Cat 1907. NK. NK. *GB. 1907.*

BIANCA MARGINATA. ND. White/Purple. Tube. White. Sepals. White. Corolla. ND. GC. P55 19/1/1867 Review by H. Cannell. P120 4th Ed. by Porcher 1874 Meritorous variety but not in the first class. GC. P806 30/8/1862 and P72 24/1/1863 Intro. by E.G.Henderson. *Banks, E. Deal. GB. 1862.*

BICOLOUR. Single. Red/Purple. Tube. Cerise red. Thin. Sepals. Cerise red. Long. Green tips. Corolla. Violet. P33 2nd Ed. by Porcher 1848. Leaves 6cm by 4cm. GC. P481 10/7/1843 Exhibited at Bath Hort. & Bot. Show by Sclater & Son. GC. P393 June 1842 & P98 17/2/1844 Listed by Youells, Gt. Yarmouth. GC. P241 15/4/1843. Listed by F & A Smith, Hackney. *Tansley. GB. 1842.*

BIG BEN. Single. Red/Purple. Tube. Scarlet. Sepals. Scarlet. Broad. Gracefully reflexed. Corolla. Deep Purple, shaded blue. Large. Review in CG & JH. P406 20/8/1863. Wonderful expansion. Named after the bell in the Clock Tower of the Houses of Parliament. Named after Sir Benjamin Hall who was Commissioner of Works during the building. GC. P18 14/1/1860. Intro. by Wm. Rollinson. *Rollinson, W. Tooting. GB. 1860.*

BIRD OF PARADISE. Single. Red/Pink. Tube. Red. Sepals. Scarlet. Well reflexed. Corolla. Delicate rose. GC. P486 9/4/1870 Intro. by B S. Williams, London. GB. 1870. Intro. by B S Williams. *Bland, E. Fordham. GB. 1870.*

BIRD OF PASSAGE. Double. Red/Purple. Tube. Red. ½". Medium. Bulged. Sepals. Red. Concave. Deflexed. Corolla. Reddish Purple. Loose. Pcxv. Vol.3 J.RHS 1872 Chiswick Trial 1872. Too dull in colour. NK. NK. NK,

BLACK PRINCE (a). Single. Red/Red. Tube. Red. Sepals. Red. Long. Reflex rather gracefully. Corolla. Red. Branches to be horizontal for flowers to hang free. CG. Vol 6 P272 31/7/1853. Intro. by C. Turner, Slough. *GB. NK.*

BLACK PRINCE (b). Single. Red/Purple. Tube. Dark carmine sepals. Dark carmine. Broad. Spreading. Corolla. Dark almost black corolla. Well cupped. JH & CG. P406 20/8/1864. GC. P771 24/8/1861 Listed by H. Walton, Burnley. GC. P594 29/6/1861 Listed by Godwin & Padman. Sheffield. Intro. by E.G. Henderson, St. John's Wood. *Banks,E. Deal. GB. 1861.*

BLACK PRINCE (c). Single. Red/Pink. Tube. Waxy Carmine. Sepals. Waxy Carmine. Large. Broad. Pale green tips. Corolla. Pale Pink margined deep rose. Large. Open. GC. P406 28/9/1877 Noted at H. Cannells Nursery. B. Cat. 1877-1879. *Bull, W. Chelsea. GB. 1876.*

BLACK PRINCE (d) ND. Red/Purple. Tube. Red. Sepals. Red. Corolla. Purple. Laings Cat. circa 1890 NK. NK. NK.

BLACK PRINCE (e). Single. Red/Purple. Tube. Bright coral. Sepals. Bright coral. Uplifted. Corolla. Solferino red with violet reflections. Brilliant colouration. Distinct. Compact. Very abundant flowering. Bell shaped. Good plant for pots and vases. Bruant,Poitier. Cat. No. 209, 1911. NK. NK. NK. NK.

BLANCHE. Single. Pink/Red. Tube. Deep Flesh. Sepals. Deep Flesh. Corolla. Red. (Violet red). Profuse and early bloomer. P33 2nd. Ed. by Porcher 1848. Dwarf GC. P241 15/4/1843 Listed by F&A Smith. GC. P112 17/2/1844 Listed by W. Miller, Ramsgate. Harrison, Dereham List 1845. *Harrison, Dereham. GB. 1842*

BLANCHE DE CASTILLE (a). ND. ND/ND. RH. P311 1889 "Select" by E.A. Carrière. NK. NK. NK.

BLANCHE DE CASTILLE (b). Double. Red/White. Tube.Scarlet. (Gooseberry red). Sepals. Scarlet. (Gooseberry red). Corolla. Pure White. Full. Enormous. Good habit. P148 L. Cat. 1901. JF. Cat. 1901. Kelways Cat. 1905. *Lemoine. Nancy. France. 1900.*

BLANCHETTE (a). Single. White/Red. Tube. Pure White. Glossy. Sepals. Pure white. Gracefully recurved. Corolla. Scarlet tinted rose. Large. Cup shaped. Long. Good Texture. P120 4th. Ed. by Porcher 1874. "Not in the first selection". GC. P382 28/4/1866 Intro. by E.G. Henderson. *Banks,E. Deal. GB. 1866.*

BLANCHETTE (b), Double. Red/White. Tube. Carmine. Sepals. Carmine. Elegant. Corolla. Snow white. L. Cat. 1906. *Lemoine. Nancy. France. 1904.*

BLANDA. Single. Pink/Red. Tube. Pale rosy flesh pink. Sepals. Pale rosy flesh, tipped green. Waxy. Corolla. Bright ruby. (Bright carmine). P33 2nd Ed. by Porcher 1848 by its habit, foliage and the formation of the flowers, this variety is very similar to "Carnea". Small flowers. FC. Vol IX P13 1841. GC. P97/98 17/2/1844 Listed by Youells, Gt.Yarmouth. GC. P241 Listed by F&A Smith, Hackney. Harrisons, Dereham List 1845. F.Fulgens X. *Smith, J. Dalston. GB. 1842.*

BLANDS FLORIBUNDA NK. NK. NK. GC. 1894. Vol. I p.146. Intro. by H Cannell. *Bland, E. Fordham. GB. 1867.*

BLANDS NEW STRIPED. Single. Red/Purple. Tube. Dark Scarlet. Very Short. Sepals. Dark Scarlet. Corolla. Rich Plum regularly and distinctly striped red and rose. Strong habit. BSW. Cat. 1897. HC. Cat. 1885-1891 Intro. by H. Cannell. *Bland,E. Fordham. GB. 1873.*

BLONDIN. Single. Red/Purple. Tube. Rich crimson. Sepals. Rich crimson. Well reflexed. 4" across. Corolla. Dark Violet. Long. Named after a French tightrope walker, (1824-97), who walked across Niagara Falls. GC. P87 1/2/1862 Intro. by R. Rea, Ipswich. *Rea,R. Ipswich. GB. 1862.*

BLOOD ROYAL. Single. White/Red. Tube. Creamy white. Sepals. Creamy white. Corolla. Dark crimson. GC. P161 17/3/1849 Listed by W. Rumley, Richmond. GC. P201 25/3/1848. Intro. by W. Rumley, Richmond. GB. 1848.

BLUE BEAUTY. Double. Red/Blue. Tube. Red. (Crimson red). Short. Sepals. Red. (Crimson red). Large. Horizontal. Corolla. Blue. (Violet Blue). Spreading. Short petals. Pleated and extended, and look like violets. Vol. 2 J of RHS 1870 Fuchsia trials at Chiswick "Passed over". Vol. 4 J of RHS 1877 Fuchsia trials at Chiswick 1873 2nd.Class Cert. Habit good, compact, free flowering. Light red. Corolla very large double clear Purple. GC. P338 15/4/1865 Listed by W. Rumley, Richmond. GC. P55. 19/1/1867 Review by H.Cannell. 4th Edition by Porcher 1874. *Banks,E. Deal. GB. 1864.*

BLUE BONNET. ND. ND/ND. Tube. ND. Sepals. ND. Corolla. ND. SG. P459 1866. Recommended dark variety. NK. NK. NK.

BLUE BOY. Double. Red/Blue. Tube. Red. Sepals. Red. Corolla. Dark Blue. FW & GG. 1869 & P4 Jan 1870. A true cobalt blue. *Turner, C. Slough. GB. 1869.*

BLUE KING. Single. Red/Blue. Tube. Bright crimson. Sepals. Bright Crimson. Corolla. Beautiful blue. Cup shaped. B. Cat. 1877-1899. *Bull, W. Chelsea GB. 1877.*

BLUSHING BRIDE. Single. White/Red. Tube. Blush White. Sepals. Blush white. (Delicate flesh). Corolla. Dark Carmine shaded Violet. (Scarlet Lake). (Rich Scarlet). B. Cat. 1878. BSW. Cat. 1878-1897 An improved "Lustre". Dobbies Cat. 1892-1894. HC. Cat. 1885-1892 one of the strongest growing light varieties. JF. Cat. 1885. GO. "Select" 1880-1888. GC. P722 9/6/1877. GC. P773 15/6/1878 Refers to Coloured Plate T291 in F.M. *Lye,J. Market Lavington. GB. 1877.*

BOADICEA. Double. Red/Purple. Tube. Red. Sepals. Red. Corolla. Purple. A coarse looking variety, balloon shaped in bud. Vol. 3 J of RHS 1863 Report of fuchsias grown for trial at Chiswick 1862. Sent by Laxton. NK NK. NK.

BOLIVIANA. Single. Red.Tube. Red, long funnel shape. Sepels reflex. Corolla, Red. From Bolivia, where discovered by M. Rozel in 1873. Description by E A Carrière and illustration RH 1876.

BOLIVIANA IGNEA. Sepals. Red/Red. Tube. Bright Red. Sepals. Bright Red. Recurved. Corolla. Dazzling Orange Vermillion. Large. Expanded bunches of drooping flowers. Hybrid from Boliviana. B. Cat. 1878. F. Boliviana X. NK. NK. *1878.*

BOQUET. Single. Red/Purple. Tube. Red. (Coral). Sepals. Red. (Coral). Reflex to a half circle. Reflexed.Corolla. Purple. (Mauve shaded violet).(Blue). Dwarf. Hybrid of F.Myrtifolia. L. Cat. 1893. Bruant, Poitiers Cat. 1911. F. Myrtifolia X. *Lemoine. Nancy. France. 1893.*

BOREATTON. Double. Red/Purple. Tube. Crimson. Sepals. Crimson. Corolla. Deep Purple. Full. Smooth. Regular Petals. The finest double yet introduced. L. Cat. 1891. HC. Cat. 1890 Illustration in HC. Floral Guide 1890. JF. Cat. 1888. Dobbies Cat. 1892-4. *Sankey. GB. 1888.*

BORUSSIA. Single. Red/Purple. Tube. Violet rose. 15mm long. Sepals. Violet rose. Large. Almost horizontal. Corolla. Violet. P144 3rd Ed. by Porcher 1858. One of those plants which should not have appeared in commerce. *Dender. NK. 1851.*

BOSSUET. Single. Red/Red. Tube. Bright Scarlet. Sepals. Bright Scarlet. Reflexed. Corolla. Dark Carmine veined red. ((Dull blue).HF. Cat. 1899. L. Cat 1899. *Rozain. Lyons. France 1898.*

BOU-DENIB. Double. Red/White. Tube. Bright Carmine. Sepals. Bright Carmine. Reflexed. Corolla. White. Very Full. Large. Very floriferous. L. Cat. 1909. *Rozain. Lyons. France. 1909.*

BOUCHARLAT. ND. ND/ND. Tube. ND. Sepals. ND. Corolla. ND. RH. P311 1889. "Select" by E.A. Carrière. NK. NK. NK.

BOUNTIFUL. Single. Red/Purple. Tube. Red. Sepals. Red. Corolla. Purple. GC. Vol. 18 P215 Exhibited at Devizes 7/8/1882 by J. Lye(1st). GC. P280 1/9/1883. Exhibited at Trowbridge by J. Lye (1st), G.Tucker (2nd). GC. Vol 23 P209 14/2/1885

Illustrated. Arabella Imp. x J.Lye. *Lye.J. Market Lavington. GB. 1883.*

BOYDII. Single. Red/Red. Tube. Scarlet. (Carmine rose). Green tips. Large. Hood corolla. Corolla. Bright crimson. (Lake). P63 2nd. Ed. by Porcher 1848. GC. P369. 8/6/1844 Listed by T.Cripps. GC. P146 8/3/1845 Listed by Youells, Gt.Yarmouth. GC. P473 20/7/1844 Listed by W. Wood, Uckfield. GC. P162 16/3/1844 Intro. by Hally, Blackheath. *Hally. Blackheath. GB. 1844.*

BRANLY. Single. White/Purple. Tube. Gooseberry. Sepals. Gooseberry. Corolla. Dark Plum bordered blue. L. Cat. 1913. *Rozain. Lyons. France. 1913.*

BRAVO. Double. Red/Purple. Tube. Crimson. Sepals. Crimson. Short. Corolla. Plum. Full. GC. P406 2/5/1863 Listed by W. Hussey, Norwich. Vol. P3 J of RHS 1863. Fuchsias grown for trial at Chiswick 1862. A full but confused looking flower. Sepals converge over the coralla. GC. P960 26/10/1861 Intro. by W. Bull, Chelsea. *Bull, W. Chelsea. GB. 1862.*

BRENDA. Double. Red/Purple. Tube. Rosy red. Sepals. Rosy red. Corolla. Bluish Plum. Spreading. B Cat. 1901. *Bull, W. Chelsea. GB. 1900?*

BRENNUS (a). Single. Red/Red. Tube. Crimson red. Sepals. Crimson red. Green tips. Corolla. Bright crimson. P33 2nd Ed. by Porcher 1848. Harrisons, Dereham List 1845. *Salter. Versailles. France. 1844.*

BRENNUS (b). Single. Red/Purple. Tube. Red. Sepals. Red. Corolla. Purple. P115 4th Ed. by Porcher 1874. "Not in the first selection". *Lemoine. Nancy. France. 1867.*

BRETAGNE. ND. ND/ND. Tube. ND. Sepals. ND. Corolla. ND. P311 RH. 1889 "Select" by E.A. Carrière. NK. NK. NK.

BREWSTERII (BRUESTERII). Single. Red/Purple. Tube. Light red. Sepals. Light Red. Reflexed. (Divergent). Corolla. Blue Purple. (Nice shade of blue). Short. Small flowers. Long pedicel. P34 2nd Ed. by Porcher 1848. GC. P112 17/2/1844 & P66 1/2/1845. Listed by W. Miller, Ramsgate. GC. P630 25/9/1841 One of the best of the Chilean varieties. Harrisons, Dereham List 1845. *Brewster. GB. NK.*

BRIDAL BOQUET. Single. White/Pink. Tube. Blush white.Sepals. Blush White. Recurved. Corolla. Deepest Blush. Stiff shrubby habit. Free. Vol. P3 J of RHS. Fuchsias grown for trial at

Chiswick 1862. Submitted by E.G. Henderson. *Banks,E. Deal.? GB. 1862?*

BRIDE. Single. White/Red. Tube. White. 25 mm. Sepals. White. (Pink). Horizontal. Corolla. Coral vermilion. P144 3rd. Ed. by Porcher 1858. D. GC.P207 27/3/1852, Listed by H. Walton, Burnley. GC. P151 5/3/1853 Light. Good for exhibition. *Mayle. Birmingham. GB. 1850.*

BRIDEGROOM. Single. Pink/Red. Tube. Pink. Sepals. Pink. (Very pale crimson). (Light pink). Corolla. Light Red. (Crimson). (Vermillion). FJ. May P995 1845 "Recommended". P69 2nd Ed. by Porcher 1848.GC. P112 17/2/1844 & P66 1/2/1845. Listed by W.Miller Ramsgate. Harrisons, Dereham List 1845. Girlings, Stowmarket List 1845. *Epps,W.J. Maidstone. GB. 1844.*

BRIDESMAID (a). Single. White/ND. Tube. White. Sepals. White. Corolla. ND. GC. P184 23/3/1847 & P250 27/4/1847 Listed by W.Miller, Ramsgate. *Fairbeard GB. 1846.*

BRIDESMAID (b). ND. ND/ND. Tube. ND. Sepals. ND. Corolla. ND.GC. P207 27/3/1852 Listed by H. Walton, Burnley NK. NK. NK.

BRIDESMAID (c). Single. White/Purple. Tube. White. Sepals. White. Well reflexed. Corolla. Rosy Violet. GC. P344. 11/4/1864. GC. P122 7/2/1863 Intro. by G. Smith. *Smith,G. Islington. GB. 1863.*

BRIGADE. Single. Red/Purple. Tube. Deep rose. Sepals. Deep Rose. Tipped Green. Reflexed. Corolla. Bright rose, shaded violet. Large flower. Stiff. P115 4th Ed. by Porcher 1874. "Not in the first selection." B. Cat. 1872-1873. GC. P476 15/4/1871 Intro. by W. Bull. *Bull, W. Chelsea. GB. 1871.*

BRIGAND. ND. Red/Purple. Tube. ND. Sepals. ND. Corolla. ND. Habit loose. Flowers large in size, form and colour simliar to "Monarch" but the sepals are of a somewhat more rosy tint. Report on Fuchsias grown for Trial at Chiswick. Pcxvii Vol. 3 P of RHS. MOST LIKELY CONFUSED WITH BRIGADE.

BRIGHTNESS. Double. Red/Purple. Tube. Red. Sepals. Crimson. (Red). Long. Moderately reflexed. Corolla. Dark Purple. Loose. P90. Vol 3 P of RHS 1863 Fuchsias grown for trial at Chiswick. GC. P108 1/2/1862. GC. P960 26/10/1861 Intro. by W. Bull. *Bull, W. Chelsea. GB.1861.*

BRILLIANT (a). Single. ND/ND. Tube. ND. Sepals. ND. Corolla. ND. GC. P161 17/3/1849

Listed by W.Rumley, Richmond. GC. P224 14/4/1849 Listed by Bass & Brown Sudbury, & R. Whibley, Kennington Cross. GC P241 20/4/1850 Listed by W.Rendle, Plymouth. App. to RH. 1851 by Porcher. "Mediocre". *Barkway, London. GB. 1848.*

BRILLIANT (b). Single. Red/Purple. Tube. Red. Sepals. Red. Corolla. Purple. GC. P545 30/8/1851 Listed by G. Smith. GC. P207 27/3/1851 Listed by H. Walton, Burnley. GC. P209 5/4/1851. Intro. by C.Turner, Slough. *Banks, E. Deal. GB. 1851.*

BRILLIANT (c). Single. Red/Purple. Tube. Red. Almost globular.Sepals. Red. Corolla. Rosy Purple. (Carmine red). P144 3rd Ed. by Porcher 1858. Bell shaped. Petals pleated. GC. P385 18/6/1853 & P147 11/3/1854 Listed by W. Rumley, Richmond. GC. P483 30/7/1853 & P162 18/3/1854. Listed by H. Walton, Burnley. GC. P98 12/2/1853 Intro. by G. Smith, Islington. *Patterson, GB. 1853.*

BRILLIANT (d). Single. Red/Purple. Tube. Red. Thick. Short. Sepals. Red. Large reflexed. Corolla. Dark blue splashed Violet red. P106 4th Ed. by Porcher 1874. *Bull, W. Chelsea. GB. 1865.*

BRILLIANT (e). Single. White/Red. Tube. White. Thick. Swollen in the middle. Sepals. White. Long 15mms. Large. Reflexed round tube. Corolla. Vermillion shaded to white. Good variety. P116 4th Ed.by Porcher 1874. Pedicel 50mms long. Intro. by E.G. Henderson. *Banks, E. Deal.? GB. 1867.*

BRILLIANT (f). S/Double. Red/Purple. Tube. Rich red. Sepals. Rich red. Well reflexed. (Recurved Carmine red). Corolla. Violet, well reflexed. (Reddish Purple). GC. P198 31/8/1911. B. Cat. 1901. JF. Cat. 1901. *Lye,J. Market Lavington. GB. 1901*

BRILLIANTE. Single. Red/Purple. Tube. Bright Carmine. Sepals. Bright Carmine. Corolla. Purple. Harrisons, Dereham List 1845. *Kyle. GB. 1842?*

BRILLIANTISSIMA. Single. White/Red. Tube. Greenish White. Sepals. Greenish white. Reflexed. Corolla. Dark crimson. Vol 4 J of RHS 1877 P68 & P215. Fuchsia trial at Chiswick in 1873. Sent by Downie & Co. In the way of "Lustre" but superior. Fine in colour, but small. No award. NK. NK. NK.

BRITANNIA. Single. Red/Purple. Tube. Pale Crimson. (Light Pink). Short.Sepals. Pale Crimson. (Light Pink). Divergent. P34 2nd Ed. by Porcher 1848. Corolla. Violet Purple. Good. Distinct. Leaves dull green. Very dentate. GC. P441 1/7/1843 Listed by Marnock and Manby. GC. P481 15/7/1843

Shown at HS.Show by Catleugh. GC. P98 17/2/1844 Listed by Youells. Gt. Yarmouth. GC. P112 17/2/1844 & P66 1/2/1845 Listed by W. Miller, Ramsgate. GC. P184 27/3/1847 Listed by R. Smith, Croydon. Harrisons, Dereham List 1845. Girlings, Stowmarket List 1845. *Smith, J. Dalston. GB. 1842.*

BRITISH QUEEN (a). Single. Pink/Red. Tube. Pale Rose. Sepals. Pale Rose. Corolla. Bright Red. GC. P184 13/3/1847 Listed by W. Miller Ramsgate. FJ. P253 1845 Awarded FCC at Royal South London Floricultural Show. GC. P114 1/2/1846 Intro. by F.Jennings. *Jennings, F. GB. 1846.*

BRITISH QUEEN (b). ND ND/ND. Tube. ND. Sepals. ND. Corolla. ND. GC. P515 25/7/1857. Listed By H. Walton, Burnley. NK. NK. *1857.*

BRITISH SAILOR. Single. Red/Purple. Tube. Red. Sepals. Red. Corolla. Purple. GC. P539 10/8/1858 Listed by F. Godwin, Sheffield. GC. P571 24/7/1858 Listed by H. Walton, Burnley. GC. P238 19/3/1859 Listed by W.Rumley, Richmond. GC. P260 24/3/1860 Listed by W. Hussey, Norwich. SG P459 1866 "Recommended". Intro. by E.G.Henderson. *Banks, E. Deal. GB. 1858.*

BRITON. S/Double. Red/Purple. Tube. Reddish Scarlet. Sepals. Reddish Scarlet. Long. Nicely recurved. Broad. Corolla, Reddish Purple. Large. B.Cat. 1901. *Bull, W. Chelsea. GB. 1901.*

BRIXTONIENSIS. Single. Red/Red. Tube. Crimson. Sepals. Crimson. Corolla. Crimson. Extra Large Size. Abundant bloomer. Recommended cultivar. FJ. P95 May 1845. NK. NK. NK.

BROCKMANII (BROOKMANII), Single. Red/Purple. Tube. Red. Sepals. Red. Corolla. Purplish crimson. Good. GC. P98 17/2/1844 & P146 8/3/1845. Listed by Youells, Gt. Yarmouth. GC. P112 17/2/1844 & P66 1/2/1845 Listed by W,. Miller, Ramsgate. GC. P33 21/1/1843 Raised by P.Padden Gr. to Rev. W.Brockman. *Padden, P. Beachborough. GB. 1843.*

BROMESTERII. Single. ND. Tube. ND. Sepals. ND. Corolla. ND. GC. P668 11/10/1841 Exhibited by Mr. Rickard at RHS of Cornwall show 26/9/1841. NK. NK. NK.

BRUCEIANA. (BRUCEANA). Single. Red/Purple. Tube. Dark Vermillion. Short (Crimson). Sepals. Dark Vermillion. (Crimson). Corolla. Deep Purple. GC. P393, 1843 & P97 17/2/1844 & P146 8/3/1845 Listed by Youells. Gt. Yarmouth. Harrisons, Dereham, List 1845. *Bruce. GB. 1842.*

BRUNA. Double. Red/White. Tube. Red. Sepals. Red. Raised up. Corolla. White. P131. 4th Edition by Porcher 1874. Not in the first selection. *Twrdy. Brno. Austria. 1872.*

BRUTUS (a). Single. Pink/Red. Tube. Light Pink. Green tips. Sepals. Light Pink. Corolla. Crimson. (Lilac cerise). P69 2nd Ed by Porcher. Named after a French horticulturalist. Habit like "Brockmanii". Large and Stout. GC. P162 14/3/1846 & P184 13/3/1847 & GC. P66 1/2/1845 Listed by W.Miller, Ramsgate. *Miller, W. Ramsgate. GB. 1845,*

BRUTUS (b). Single. Red/Purple. Tube. Crimson scarlet. Short. Sepals. Crimson Scarlet. Long. Narrow. Reflexed. Corolla. Bright Purplish Crimson. Good shape. B. Cat. 1901. P149 L. Cat. 1901. Intro. by W. Bull. *Bull, W. Chelsea. GB. 1901.*

BUDGET. S/Double. Red/Purple. Tube. Red. Very short. Sepals. Red. Large. Broad. Completely recurved. Corolla. Rich Purple. Large. Expanded. B.Cat. 1901. L.Cat. 1901. *Bull, W. Chelsea. GB. 1901.*

BUFFON. Double. Red/Pink. Tube. Red. Sepals. Red. Reflexed. Corolla. Rose. Very large. (Rosy white). G. 11/2/1903 Noteworthy for the peculiar pinkish tinged corolla. GO. P141 1891. L.Cat. 1892. B. Cat. 1892-1893. NK. NK. NK. *1890.*

BUISSON BLANC. Double. Red/White. Tube. Rose pink. Sepals. Rose pink. Corolla. White, carmine at base. L. Cat. 1907. *Rozain, Lyons. France 1907.*

BUISTII. Single. Red/Purple. Tube. Rosy Carmine. Sepals. Rosy Carmine. Reflexed. Corolla. Violet Profuse. A very near "Formosa Elegans". Small flowered. GC. P473 16/7/1842 & P431 24/6/1843. Exhibited at HS. Show, London by Catleugh. GC. P242 Listed by A.J.Stewart,Windsor. Fl.Cab.P213 Vol IX 1841. Intro by Catleugh, Chelsea. *Buist. GB. 1840.*

BULGARIE. Single. Red/Purple. Tube. Brilliant red. (Deep crimson). Sepals. Brilliant red. (Deep crimson). Well shaped. Corolla. Violet Plum. Gartenflora P149 1888 "New". B. Cat. 1888-1893. BSW. Cat. 1888. *Lemoine, Nancy. France. 1886.*

BULRUSH. Single. Red/Purple. Tube. Light crimson. Long. Sepals. Light crimson. Horizontal. Corolla. Light rosy purple. B.Cat. 1880-1893. *Bull, W. Chelsea. GB. 1880.*

BURNOUF. Double. Red/Blue. Tube. Red. Sepals. Red. Reflexed. Blue. Dedicated to a family of French philologists and orientalists BSW. Cat. 1878. NK. NK. NK.

BUSSIERE. Double. Red/Purple. Tube. Crimson red. Sepals. Crimson red. Very Broad. Corolla. Purple Violet. Petals pleated and spread horizontal. Full. L. Cat. 1903. *Lemoine. Nancy. France. 1903.*

BUTCHERII. Single. Red/ND. Tube. Light crimson. Sepals. Light crimson. Corolla. ND. P34 2nd Ed. by Porcher 1848. Harrisons, Dereham List 1845. *Butcher. GB. 1845.*

BUTTERFLY. Single. Red/White. Tube. Bright crimson. Short. Stout. Sepals. Bright crimson, tipped white. Broad. Reflexed. Corolla. Pure White. Good size and form. GC. P594 30/6/1860 Listed by F.Godwin, Sheffield. GC. P93 4/2/1860 Intro. by G. Smith. *Smith,G., Islington. GB. 1860.*

BUZENVAL. Double. Red/Blue. Tube. Red. Sepals. Red. Corolla. Blue. Gartenflora. P149 1888 New from Lemoine. Laing. Cat. circa 1890. L. Cat. 1888. *Lemoine. Nancy. France. 1887.*

BYZANCE Semidouble. Red/Pink. Tube. Carmine rose. Sepals. Carmine Rose. Broad. Turned up. Corolla. Soft rose mauve. (Mauve Blue) Average sized flowers. L. Cat. 1911. *Lemoine. Nancy. France. 1911.*

CADMUS. Single. Red/White. Tube. Brilliant carmine. Sepals. Brilliant carmine. Much reflexed. Corolla. White veined red at base. Bruant, Poitiers Cat. 1911. NK. NK. NK. NK.

CAISSIER-HOCHSTETTER. Single. Red/Purple. Tube. Carmine rose. Thin. 25mm long. Sepals. Carmine rose. Large. Tips bent. Corolla. Violet. Petals fold inwards at edge. Mediocre, P143 3rd. Ed. by Porcher 1858. *Schüle. Stuttgart. Germany. 1855.*

CALCHAS. Double. Red/Purple. Tube. Carmine. Sepals. Carmine. Broad. Corolla. Plum Purple streaked pink. Full. L. Cat. 1911. *Lemoine, Nancy. France. 1911.*

CALEDONIA. Single. Red/Purple. Tube. Red. Sepals. Red. Corolla. Rosy Purple. Vol. 2 J.of RHS 1870 Fuchsia Trials at Chiswick."Passed Over" GC.P220 1/10/1904 Awarded FCC. Royal Caledonian H.S. Show 14/9/1904. Raised at the nurseries of Cunningham Fraser, Comley Bank, Edinburgh. JF. Cat 1905. First exhibited as "Profusion". Riccartonii X. *Cunningham, Edinburgh. Scotland. 1869.*

CALLAO. Double. Red/Purple. Tube. Carmine. Short. Thick. Sepals. Carmine. Well Reflexed. Corolla. Deep Bluish Purple, flaked Red. B. Cat. 1876-1877. *Bull,W. Chelsea. GB. 1876.*

CALLIOPE. Double. Red/Purple. Tube. Dark red. Short. Sepals. Dark red. Corolla. Rich Violet Purple. B. Cat. 1898-1901. GC. Vol 19. P596 1896 Intro. by W. Bull. *Bull, W. Chelsea. GB. 1896.*

CALYPSO. Single. Red/Purple. Tube. Rich crimson. Sepals. Rich crimson. Completely reflexed. Corolla. Rich crimson purple. Expanded. Bell shaped. Large well formed flowers. GC. P427 3/4/1875 Intro. by W. Bull. B. Cat.1875-1882 *Bull,W. Chelsea. GB. 1875.*

CAMBODA. Double. Red/White. Tube. Red. Sepals. Red. Completely reflexed. Long. White. Very suitable for growing against a pillar. B. Cat. 1901. NK. NK. *1900?*

CAMÉLÉON. Single. White/Red. Tube. Greenish white. Thin. 20mm long. Sepals. Greenish white. Narrow. Aligned to tube. Green Tips. Corolla. Vermilion red. Petals narrow. Divided by a white line. Same length as tube. P145 3rd Ed. by Porcher 1858. *Demouveaux. Lille. France. 1856.*

CAMELIA. Double. Red/White. Tube. Red. Sepals. Red. Corolla. White. RB. Cat. 1934. *Rozain Jr. Lyons. France. 1928.*

CAMEO. S/Double. Red/Purple. Tube. Crimson. Sepals. Crimson. Large. Recurved. (Very Broad). Corolla. Lavender Purple. Long. B. Cat. 1901. L. Cat. P149 1901. *Bull,W. Chelsea. GB. 1901.*

CAMERON. Single. Red/Blue. Tube. Crimson. Sepals. Crimson. Wide. Corolla, Rich deep blue. Very floriferous. Good compact habit. B. Cat. 1872-1876. GC. P502 13/4/1872 Intro. by W. Bull. *Bull,W. Chelsea. GB. 1872.*

CAMILLE FLAMMARION. Single. Red/Purple. Tube. Rosy Red. Sepals. Rosy red. Corolla. Reddish Violet. Large. Well formed. B. Cat. 1879-1893. NK. NK. *1879?*

CAMPANULE. Double. Red/Purple. Tube. Bright carmine rose. Sepals. Bright carmine rose. Corolla. Bright indigo blue. Enormous. RB,Lyons. Cat. 1926. *Rozain Jr, Lyons. France. 1926.*

CANARY BIRD. Single. Red/Purple. Tube. Scarlet. Sepals. Scarlet. Broad. Finely reflexed. Corolla. Dark Purple. Golden yellow foliage, veined crimson. 4th. Ed. by Porcher 1874 "Not in first selection". B. Cat. 1873-1889. *Bull,W. Chelsea. GB. 1873.*

CANDIDATE (a). Single. Red/Purple. Tube. Carmine. Sepals. Carmine. Corolla. Deep bluish carmine. Largest yet sent out. GC. P574 19/8/1843 Hort.Scty Show 15/8/1843. See also "Colossus", "President", "Attractor". GC. P401 22/6/1844 Now being sent out. *Standish, Bagshot. GB. 1843.*

CANDIDATE (b). Single. Red/Purple. Tube. Crimson. Sepals. Crimson. Reflexed. Corolla. Bright Violet Purple. GC. P97. 17/2/1844 Listed by Youell, Gt. Yarmouth. GC. P112 17/2/1844 & P98 1/2/1845 Listed by W. Miller, Ramsgate. Harrisons, Dereham List 1845. Girlings, Stowmarket List 1845. GC. P177 23/3/1844. Intro. by Girling. *Girling, Stowmarket. GB. 1844.*

CANDIDISSIMA. Single. White/Purple. Tube. White. Sepals. White. Corolla. Rose. GC. P216 27/3/1845 Listed by R. Cooper, Croydon. GC. P201 27/3/1847 Listed by Hart & Nickling, Guildford. Twice the size of "Venus Victrix". GC. P820 Dec 1844. Recommended. GC. P34 17/1/1846 Intro. by Hallys, Blackheath. Venus Victrix X. *Hally, Blackheath GB. 1846.*

CANNELS FAVOURITE. Single. White/ND. Tube. White. Sepals. White. Corolla. ND. P120 4th Ed. by Porcher 1874 Not in the first selection. *Doel GB. 1873.*

CANNELS GEM. Single. Red/White. Tube. Glowing red. Sepals. Glowing red. Reflexed. Corolla. White. Cup Shaped. Large. P135 4th Ed. by Porcher. GO. "Select" 1880-1888. GC P406 29/9/1877 Seen at Cannels. BSW. Cat. 1897. Laings Cat. circa 1890. HC. Cat. 1882-1898. Intro. by H. Cannell. *Bland,E. Fordham. GB. 1873.*

CAPITAINE BINGER. Double. Red/Blue. Tube. Rosy Carmine. Sepals. Rosy Carmine. Corolla. Violet Blue. Large. B. Cat. 1894-1895. *Lemoine. Nancy. France. 1894.*

CAPITAINE BOYTON. Double. Red/Purple. Tube. Brilliant Red. Short. Sepals. Brilliant red. Recurved. Corolla. Metallic Violet. Dwarf. Full. Essigs Check list gives parentage as Dominiana x Serratifolia (Most unlikely). HC.Cat. 1st Class variety. B. Cat. 1878-1879. *Lemoine, Nancy. France. 1878.*

CAPITAINE TILHO. Double. Red/Red. Tube. Clear Coral. Short. Sepals. Clear Coral. Broad. Twisted. Corolla. Rose Lake. Full. Large. L. Cat. 1907. *Lemoine, Nancy. France. 1907.*

CAPTAIN NARES. Double. Red/Purple. Tube. Bright crimson. Sepals. Bright crimson. Corolla. Dark Violet. BSW. Cat. 1878. NK. NK. NK.

CAPTIVATION (a). Single. Pink/Pink. Tube. Pink. Sepals. Pink. Corolla. Rose. Very free bloomer. GC. P162 14/3/1846 & P184 13/3/1847 Listed by W. Miller, Ramsgate. GC. P66 1/2/1845 Intro by W. Miller, Ramsgate. *Miller, W. Ramsgate. GB. 1845.*

CAPTIVATION (b). Single. ND/ND. Tube. ND. Sepals. ND. Corolla. ND. GC. P265 22/4/1848 Intro. by J. Smith. *Smith, J. Dalston . GB. 1848.*

CAPTIVATION (c). Single. Red/Purple. Tube. Deep Red. Sepals. Deep red. Sepals curve over. Corolla. Violet Purple. GC. P353 8/6/1850 Intro. by E. Tiley. *Tiley,E. Bath. GB. 1850.*

CARACAS. Double. Red/Pink. Tube. Clear Crimson. Sepals. Clear Crimson. Long. Corolla. Flesh Pink veined carmine. Full. L. Cat. 1910. *Rozain. Lyons. France. 1910.*

CARACTUS. Single. Red/Purple. Tube. Rosy vermillion. Sepals. Rosy vermillion. Bent Divergent. Corolla. Reddish violet margined carmine. GC. P210 6/4/1850 Listed by H. Walton, Burnley. GC. P225 14/4/1849 Intro. by T Sorrell, Chelmsford. *Sorrell,T. Chelmsford. GB. 1849.*

CARBEAU. Double. ND/ND. Tube. ND. Sepals. ND. Corolla. ND. Haage & Schmidt, Erfurt. Cat. 1880.NK. NK. NK. NK.

CARDINAL. ND. ND/ND. Tube. ND. Sepals. ND. Corolla. ND. GC. P112 17/2/1844 Listed by W. Miller, Ramsgate. NK. NK. NK.

CARDINALIS ND, ND/ND. Tube . ND. Sepals. ND. Corolla. ND. HC. Floral Guide 1882 P79. Species of Fuchsia. Violet Rose. NK. NK. NK.

CARILLON (a). Double. Red/Purple. Tube. Red. Sepals. Red. Corolla. Dark Plum marked carmine. Large. L. Cat. 1913. *Rozain, Lyons. France. 1913.*

CARILLON (b). ND. Red/Purple. Tube. Red. Sepals. Red. Corolla. Purple veined carmine. RB,Lyons.,Cat. 1926. *Rozain Jr. Lyons. France. 1926.*

28

CARL HALT. ND. ND/ND. Tube. ND. Sepals. ND. Corolla. ND. P133 4th Ed. by Porcher 1874. "Not in the first selection". "Identical with "Striata Perfecta" by B.S. Williams. *Hoppe. Germany.* NK.

CARLO DOLCI. Single. ND/ND. Tube. ND. Sepals. ND. Corolla. ND. Haage & Schmidt, Erfurt. Cat 1881. NK. NK. NK. NK.

CARLOTA. ND. Red/White. Tube. Red. Sepals. Red. Corolla. White striped carmine. RB. Cat. 1937. NK. NK. NK. NK.

CARMEN. ND. Red/Purple. Tube. Red. Sepals. Red. Corolla. Violet. Dwarf. L. Cat. 1901. F.Myrtifolia X. *Lemoine, Nancy. France. 1893.*

CARMEN SYLVA. Double. Red/White. Tube. Bright red. Sepals. Bright red. Corolla. Greenish white. Full.L. Cat.1898-1901. *Lemoine, Nancy. France. 1898*

CARMINATA. ND. Red/Purple. Tube. Bright carmine. Sepals. Bright Carmine. Very broad and well reflexed. Corolla. Deep Violet Petals round and smooth. GC. P521 28/4/1877. BSW. Cat. 1878. Intro. by B S Williams. *Bland, E. Fordham. GB. 1877.*

CARMINATA ROSEA. Single. Red/Red. Tube. Flesh or carmine colour. 3" to 4" long. Sepals. Pale scarlet. Trumpet shaped terminal clusters of flowers. Intermediate between both parents. GC. P430 29/3/1873. Intro. by E.G. Henderson. Fulgens Rubre Grandiflora X F. Serratifolia. *Henderson E.G. St. Johns Wood. GB. 1873.*

CARNEA. Single. Red/Red. Tube. Bright rosy carmine. Sepals. Greenish Yellow. Corolla. Bright Carmine. Most profuse. (Rose flesh) (Very Pretty) P34 2nd Ed. by Porcher 1848 Resembles "Blanda". Harrisons Dereham List. 1845. GC. P393 June 1842 Listed by Youells,Gt Yarmouth. FC. P13 Vol IX 1841. F. Fulgens X. *Smith, J. Dalston. GB. 1841.*

CARPEAUX. Double. Red/Blue. Tube. Carmine. (Bright red). Sepals. Carmine. Reflexed. (Bright Red). (Well recurved). Corolla. Clear Violet Blue. Well opened. Compact B. Cat. 1877. BSW. Cat. 1878. NK. NK. NK.

CAROLA. Double. ND/ND. Tube. ND Sepals. ND. Corolla. ND. Haage & Schmidt Cat. 1885. NK. NK. NK. NK.

CAROLUS DURAN. Single Red/Red. Tube. Clear red. Sepals. Clear red. Corolla. Madder. Shown as

double on same page. R.B. Laird Murrayfield Cat. NK. NK. NK. NK.

CARRY SYMES. Double. Red/White. Tube. Red. Sepals. Red. Corolla. White. GC. P102 1/2/1868 Review by H. Cannell. The undivided petals are 1¼" in length, almost the same in breadth. Requires early pinching. GO. Select 1880-1881. Floral World & GG P4.Jan 1870. NK. NK. *1867*

CASCADE FLEURIE. ND. ND/ND. Tube. ND. Sepals. ND. Corolla. ND. RB. Cat. 1938. *Rozain. Lyons. France. 1938.*

CASILDA. Double. Red/White. Tube. Rich rosy carmine. Sepals. Rich rosy carmine, broad and completely reflexed. Corolla. White. Exterior petals suffused to half their length from the central vein with rosy carmine. L. Cat. P149 1901. Intro. by W. Bull. *Bull, W. Chelsea. GB. 1901.*

CASINO. Single. Red/Purple. Tube. Crimson. Very short. Sepals. Crimson. Broad. Corolla. Rich purple. Petals spreading. B. Cat. 1898. *Bull, W. Chelsea. GB. 1897.*

CASSANDRA (a). Single. Pink/Purple. Tube. Delicate Pink. Sepals. Delicate Pink, tipped green. Corolla. Peculiar rosy colour, tinged violet. GC. P820 Dec 1844 Recommended light variety. RBS Show 2/7/1845. Exhibited by Gaines. GC. P66 1/2/1845. Listed by W. Miller, Ramsgate. GC. P354 1/6/1844. Intro. by Pawley, White Hart Hotel,Bromley. *Pawley, Bromley. GB. 1844.*

CASSANDRA (b). Single. Red/Purple. Tube. Red. Sepals. Red. Corolla. Purple. FC. Vol. xiv P 204 1846. Exhibited by Kendall at RBS. Show 20/5/1846. GC. P820 Dec 1844 Recommended Dark Variety. *Barnes, London. GB. 1844?*

CASSIA. Single. Red/Purple. Tube. Rich rosy crimson. Sepals. Rich rosy crimson. Symmetrically Reflexed. Corolla. Dark Violet Plum. B. Cat. 1875-1879. Intro by W. Bull. *Bull, W. Chelsea. GB. 1875.*

CASTELAR. Single. Red/Lilac. Tube. Scarlet. Sepals. Scarlet. Finely reflexed. Corolla. Mauve Lilac. Large. Well open. L. Cat. 1901. JF. Cat. 1900. *Lemoine. Nancy. France. 1899.*

CATHERINE HAYES. Single. Red/Purple. Tube. Scarlet. Short. 10 mm long. Sepals. Scarlet. Smallish. Recurved. Corolla. Purple. (Clear lilac voilet). Much expanded. Bell shaped. P145 3rd. Ed. by Porcher 1858 The same type as the "Duke of Wellington". Vol. P3 J of RHS 1863. Fuchsias

Grown for trial at Chiswick. GC. P515 25/7/1857, & P418 22/5/1858 Listed by H. Walton Burnley. GC P210 28/3/1857 Intro. by E.G. Henderson. *Banks, E. Deal. GB. 1857.*

CATHERINE PARR. Single. White/Red. Tube. White. Sepals. White, Recurved. Broad. (Tinged Green). Corolla. Rich red scarlet tinted rose. In the style of "Reine Blanche". GC. P55 29/1/1867 Review by H. Cannell. Pcxii Vol. 3 J of RHS 1872 Fuchsia trials at Chiswick 1872. Drooping. Small very pretty. GC. P382 28/4/1866. Possibly named after 6th wife of King Henry VIII. Intro. by E.G. Henderson. *Banks, E. Deal. GB. 1866.*

C.D. HUGHES. Double. Red/Red. Tube. Clear carmine. Sepals. Clear Carmine. Long. Corolla. Scarlet veined bright rose. JF. Cat. 1898. NK. NK. *1898.*

CECIL GLASS. Single. White/Carmine. Tube. White. Sepals. White. Corolla. Carmine. (Pink). (Pale magenta pink margined carmine). Fine form. JF. Cat. 1888 "New fuchsias in 1887(Lye's)". B. Cat. 1888. Laings Cat. circa 1890. *Lye,J. Mkt.Lavington. GB. 1887.*

CECIL. Single. Red/Purple. Tube.Coral Red. Short. Sepals. Coral Red. Corolla. Purplish Red. B. Cat. 1898-1901. *Bull, W. Chelsea. GB. 1898.*

CEDO NULLI (a). Single. White/ND. Tube, White. Sepals. White. Corolla. ND. "Best light variety ever offered". GC. P515 25/7/1857 & P418 22/5/1858 Listed by H. Walton, Burnley. GC. P231 4/4/1857. Intro. by J. Keynes, Salisbury. *Pond. GB. 1857.*

CEDO NULLI (b). Double. Red/Purple. Tube. Crimson. Sepals. Crimson. Corolla. Dark Violet. GC. P87 1/2/1862. Intro by R. Rea. *Rea,R. Ipswich. GB. 1862.*

CEDO NULLI (c). ND. Red/Purple. Tube. Bright Scarlet. Sepals. Bright Scarlet. Corolla. Violet soon changing to reddish violet. Free blooming. Good habit, but not a very desirable variety. Sent by Veitch. P68 Vol 4 J of RHS Chiswick trials 1873. NK. NK. NK.

CELESTINUM. Double. Red/Purple. Tube. Red. Sepals. Red. Corolla. Sky blue. RB. Cat 1898. *Rozain. Lyons. France. 1898.*

CELINE MONTALAND. Double. Red/White. Tube. Carmine. Sepals. Carmine. A little reflexed. Corolla. Pinkish white veined red. Very full. Extremely large. Expanded. Vigourous. JF. Cat.

1892. B. Cat. 1892. L. Cat 1892. *Lemoine. Nancy. France. 1891.*

CERASIFORMIS. Single. Red/Purple. Tube. Carmine red. Almost non existant. Sepals. Carmine red. Large. Points bent. Corolla. Violet red. Short pedicel. Globular. Flower has little grace. P145 3rd Ed. by Porcher 1858. *Meillez. Lille. France. 1851.*

CERBÉRE. Double. ND/ND. Tube. ND. Sepals. ND. Corolla. ND. Haage & Schmidt Cat. 1895. NK. NK. NK. NK.

CERBERUS. Single. Red/Purple. Tube. Bright crimson. Short. Sepals. Bright crimson. Broad. Thick. Completely reflexed. Corolla. Deep rich satiny purple. B. Cat. 1875-1878. *Bull, W. Chelsea. GB. 1874?*

CERES (a). Single. White/Violet. Tube. White, tinged red. Thick. Sepals. White. Horizontal, points lifted. Corolla. Violet margined bright rose. Spotted white at base. Spiralled. Pedicel 40mms. Similar to "Rose of Castille", but flowers are bigger. P116. 4th Edition by Porcher. 1874. *Demay, H. France. 1872?*

CERES (b) Double. Red/Pink. Tube. Crimson. Short. Sepals. Crimson. Well reflexed. Corolla. Pale blush veined pink. Spreading. GC. Vol 19 5/1896 P579. Intro. by W. Bull. 1898. *Bull, W. Chelsea. GB. 1896.*

CERVANTES. Double. Red/Purple. Tube. Rose. Sepals. Rose. Corolla. Rosy mauve bordered with blue. B. Cat. 1889-1893. L. Cat. 1901. *Lemoine. Nancy. France. 1889.*

CHALLENGER. ND. ND/ND. Tube. ND. Sepals. ND. Corolla. ND. GC. P145 9/8/1859, Listed by W. Rumley, Richmond. NK. NK. *GB. 1859.*

CHAMELEON. Single. White/Red. Tube. White, spotted rose. Sepals. White spotted rose. Tipped green. Corolla. Orange striped with white. GC. P286 21/4/1857 Intro. by H. Low. *Dubus. France. 1856.*

CHAMPION (a). Single. Red/Purple. Tube. Light Carmine. Sepals. Light carmine. Half open. Corolla. Crimson purple. P34 2nd Ed. by Porcher 1848. GC. P481 15/7/1843 Exhibited by Catleugh. GC. P375 4/6/1844 Exhibited by Cole. HS Show. GC. P441 1/7/1843 Listed by Marnock & Manby. GC. P97 17/2/1844 & P146 18/3/1845 Listed by Youell, Gt. Yarmouth and J. Hancock, Durham. GC. P66 1/2/1845 & P112 17/2/1844 Listed by W. Miller, Ramsgate. Harrisons, Dereham and Girlings, Stowmarket Lists. 1845. *Smith, J. Dalston. GB. 1842.*

30

CHAMPION (b). Single. Red/Purple. Tube. Crimson. Sepals. Crimson. Thick. Broad. Symmetrically reflexed. Corolla. Dark Violet Plum. Immense. Perfect form. Ages to crimson. RH. P311. 1889 "Select by E.A. Carriere". B. Cat. 1870-1875. Intro. by W. Bull. *Bull,W. Chelsea. GB. 1870.*

CHAMPION (c) Single. Red/Purple. Tube. Bright red. Sepals. Bright red. Completely reflexed. Corolla. Reddish Violet. Immense size. B. Cat. 1895-1899. *Bull,W. Chelsea. GB. 1895.*

CHAMPION OF ENGLAND. Single. Red/Purple. Tube. Red. Sepals. Red. Corolla. Purple. App. to RH. 1851 by Porcher. Seedling from "Corallina". Surpasses all the other hybrids. GC P289 11/5/1850 & P706 9/11/1850 Listed by H. Walton, Burnley. GC P183 20/3/1852 "Select", P151 5/3/1853 "1st Rate". Corollina X. *Mayle. Birmingham. GB. 1850.*

CHAMPION OF THE WORLD. Double. Red/Purple. Tube. Coral red. Short.15mms long. Sepals. Coral red. Large. Reflexed. Spotted white. Corolla. Immense Dark Purple. Immense Size expands to 2/3rds. of a perfect ball. 4th Ed. by Porcher 1874 Washed red. Petals pleated and expanded. FCC Chiswick 1875 & 1877 GC. P488 9/4/1870 New 2" Double. Intro. by H. Cannell. *Bland, E. Fordham. GB. 1870.*

CHANCELLOR. Single. Red/Purple. Tube. Scarlet Crimson. Short. Sepals. Scarlet crimson. (Bright red). Recurved. Corolla. Violet Purple. Moderately expanded. Vol.P3 J of RHS 1863 Chiswick trials 1862. GC. P569 24/7/1858 Cert.of Merit NFS. GC P260 24/3/1860 Listed by W. Hussey, Norwich etc. GC. P90 5/2/1859. Intro by G. Smith. *Smith,G. Islington. GB. 1859.*

CHANDLERII. Single. White/Red. Tube. Light rose.(Pale flesh). Sepals. Light rose. Green tips. (Pale flesh).(Soft pink) Open. Corolla. Vermilion red. Globular. Bushy. Dwarf. Leaves Yellowish green. P34 2nd Ed. 1848 & P146 3rd Ed. 1858 by Porcher. FC P185 Vol ix 1841 "The flowers are generally produced in some kind of raceme". The first cross between F. Fulgens and one of the Magallenica type. GC. P299 29/6/1841. F.Fulgens X. *Chandler. Vauxhall. GB. 1840.*

CHARLEMANGE. Single. Red/Purple. Tube. Scarlet. Thin. 112 mm long.Sepals. Rich scarlet. Well reflexed. Twice as long as the tube.Corolla. Violet Purple. Large. Barrel shaped. Dwarf habit. Free. Petals turn in. Descended from "Corallina".Free Bloomer. P146 3rd Ed. by Porcher 1858. Pedicel purplish. 3/4 cm long.GC. P419

21/6/1856. Listed by Bainbridge & Hewison, York. GC. P451 5/7/1856 Listed by H. Walton, Burnley. GC.P114 23/2/1856 Intro. by E.G. Henderson, St. Johns Wood. *Banks,E. Deal GB. 1856.*

CHARLES GARNIER. Double. Red/Purple. Tube. Red. Sepals. Wine red. Corolla. Bishops Violet. Very large. Full and free. JF. Cat. 1901. L. Cat. 1901 (P148). *Lemoine, Nancy. France 1900.*

CHARLES HOOTON. Single. Red/Red. Tube. Rich pink. Sepals. Rich Pink. Well expanded. Corolla. Delicate red. Large. Purchased from Mr. Brown, Gr. to Alfred Lowe, Highfield House, Nottingham. Midland Florist. P195 1847. GC. P281 1/5/1847 Introduced by W, Miller, Ramsgate. *Brown. Nottingham. GB. 1847.*

CHARLES LAMOUREUX. Double. Red/Purple. Tube. Carmine. Sepals. Carmine. Large. Corolla. Plum Violet. Enormous. Full. L. Cat. P149 1901. *Lemoine. Nancy. France. 1900.*

CHARLES MIEG. Single. Red/Red. Tube. Clear rose vermilion. Thick. 25mm long. Sepals. Clear rose vermilion. Large. Short. Almost horizontal. Points bent. Corolla. Vermilion. Nice variety, but the corolla is not in proportion to the other parts of the flower. P146 3rd. Ed by Porcher 1858. *Narcis. Evry France. 1855.*

CHARLES PALMER. Single. Red/Red. Tube. Soft vermilion pink. Thick. 25 mm long. Sepals. Soft vermilion pink. Large. Narrow. Tips bent. Corolla. Vermilion shaded brown. P146 3rd Ed. by Porcher 1858. 2nd Class. Resembles "Duchess of Bordeaux" but the flowers of this variety are better. *Batten, Clapton. GB. 1855.*

CHARLES SECRÉTAN. Double. Red/White. Tube. Bright pink. Sepals. Bright pink. Corolla. Creamy white. Very full. Enormous. Long petals. L. Cat. 1893 B. Cat. 1893-1895. *Lemoine. Nancy. France. 1893.*

CHARLOTTE SALLIER. Single. Pink/Pink. Tube. Pink. Sepals. Pink. Corolla. Clear pink. (Rose). Small leaves. Pendant branches. L. Cat. 1895. JF. Cat. 1898. *Berger, Bagnolet. France. 1895.*

CHARM. Single. Red/Purple. Tube. Carmine. Sepals. Carmine. Corolla. Violet. RB. Cat. 1937. NK. NK. NK. *1937.*

CHARMER (a) Single. White/Purple. Tube. White. 15 mm long.Points bent. Sepals. White. (greenish white with a pinkish tint.Corolla. Purple. P146 3rd.

31

Ed by Porcher 1858 Similar to "Euterpe". GC. P401 24/6/1854. Listed by H. Walton, Burnley. GC.P466 23/7/1854. Listed by Bass & Brown, Sudbury.GC. P353 26/5/1855. Listed by Hart & Nicklin, Guildford. GC. P194 1/4/1854. Intro. by C. Turner, Slough. *Banks, E. Deal. GB. 1854.*

CHARMER (b). Single. Red/Purple. Tube. Bright reddish crimson. Short. Sepals. Bright reddish crimson. Broad. Well reflexed. Corolla. Rich Purple Plum. Large fine flowers. B. Cat. 1875-1882. *Bull, W. Chelsea. GB. 1875.*

CHARMER (c). Single. White/Rose. Tube. White. Sepals. White. Corolla. Light rose. JF. Cat. 1885. NK. NK. NK.

CHARMING (a). Single. Red/Purple. Tube. Red. Sepals. Red. Corolla. Purple. GC P55. 19/1/1867. Corolla distinct from any other-Review by H. Cannell. CG. P257 1865 "Best of 1864 varieties" & P492. GC. P338 15/4/1865 Listed by W. Rumley, Richmond. NK. NK. *1864.*

CHARMING (b). Single. Red/Purple. Tube. Scarlet. Sepals. Scarlet . Corolla. Purple. Excellent habit. GC. P206 17/2/1877. GC. P722 9/6/1877. New seedling. GC. P311 8/9/1877 Exhibited at Trowbridge by J. Lye. J of RHS Vol 24 P342 1900. BSW. Cat. 1878. 1897. Arabella Improved X J. Lye. *Lye, J. Market Lavington. GB. 1877.*

CHARTER. Double. Red/Purple. Tube. Rose. Sepals. Rose. Completely reflexed. Corolla. Violet Plum, striped and blotched orange scarlet. Large. Full. B. Cat. 1870-1872. NK. NK. NK.

CHASTITY. Double. Red/White. Tube. Rosy carmine red. Sepals. Rosy Carmine. Reflexed. Corolla. Pure White. GC. Vol 17 1882 New fuchsias from B. S. Williams. *Bland, E.Fordham. GB. 1882*

CHATEAUBRIAND. Single. Red/Red. Tube. Rose. Swollen. Sepals. Rose tipped yellow. Wide. Short. Only half up. Corolla. Orange Scarlet. (Salmon red. petals edged carmine). App. to RH. 1851 by Porcher. GC.P497 11/8/1849 Listed by G. Smith. GC. P145 9/3/1850 Listed by W. Rumley, Richmond. GC P210 6/4/1850 Listed by H. Walton, Burnley. GC P427 7/7/1849 Intro. by Youell, Gt. Yarmouth. *Meillez. Lille. France. 1849.*

CHAUCER. Single. Red/Purple. Tube. Red. Short. Sepals. Red. Broad. Completely recurved. Corolla. Lavender Purple. Veined and shaded crimson at base. B. Cat. 1901. NK. NK. *1900?*

CHAUVIERII. Single. Red/Purple. Tube. Dark crimson. Sepals. Dark crimson (Carmine). Half open. Corolla. Purplish crimson. (Chocolate). P34 2nd Ed. by Porcher 1848 Large leaves. Very dentate. P23 RH. 1845. GC. P479 20/7/1844. Possibly named after contemporary fellow french horticulturist M. Chauviere. Exhibited by A. Henderson at HS Show London. Harrisons, Dereham List 1845. Girlings, Stowmarket List 1845. *Salter,J. Versailles. France. 1843.*

CHEIRANTHIFLORA FLORE PLENO. Double? Red/Red. Tube. Rose. Sepals. Rose. Corolla. Carmine red. Very full. Vigourous. RH. P95. 1859. GC. P308. 9/4/1859. Listed by W. J. Epps, Maidstone. *Dubus. Lille. France. 1858.*

CHERUB. Single. White/Red. Tube. Pure white. Very long. Sepals. Pure white. Well reflexed. 1". (Pale blush). Spreading. Corolla. Bright carmine. Vol.3 J of RHS Pcxii. 1872 Chiswick Trials. Habit good. Free blooming. Medium size. Compact. Bright Red. Awarded **. Laings Cat. circa 1890. B. Cat.1870. NK. NK. *1868?*

CHEVALERII. See Chauvierii. GC. P66 1/2/1845 Listed by Millers Ramsgate.

CHICAGO. Double. Red/White. Tube. Carmine rose. Long. 20mms. Thin. Swollen at top. Sepals. Carmine rose. Large. Hang down to cover the petals. Corolla. White striped carmine at the top. P127 4th Ed. by Porcher 1874 Form is not perfect but it is different to others. Almost identical with "Lohengrin". HC. Cat. 1882. GC. P430 29/3/1873 Intro. by E.G.Henderson. *Henderson, E.G. St. Johns Wood. GB. 1873.*

CHIEFTAIN. Single. Red/Purple. Tube. Bright crimson. Short. Sepals. Bright crimson. Well reflexed. Corolla. Rich plum. shaded rosy crimson at base. Large. Well formed. P115 4th Ed. by Porcher 1874 Not in the first selection. B. Cat. 1872-1876. *Bull, W. Chelsea. GB. 1872.*

CHOPIN. Single. ND/ND. Tube. ND. Sepals. ND. Corolla. ND. GC. P481 15/7/1843 Exhibited at RBS Show by Catleugh. NK. NK. NK.

CHRISTOPE COLOMBE (a) Single. Red/Red. Tube. Soft vermilion rose. Thick. 15 mm long. Corolla. Soft vermilion pink. Large. Short. Horizontal. Tips bent. Corolla. Vermilion. Pleated petals. This fuchsia is similar to "Anna" by Boucharlet.L cat? *Crousse. France. 1853.*

CHRISTOPHE COLOMB (b). Double. Red/Purple. Tube. Red. Scarlet. Sepals. Scarlet. Large. Corolla. Rosy Carmine. This is one of the most beautiful fuchsias. The brilliant colouring of the flowers make it exceptionally distinct. B. Cat. 1893-1895 L. Cat 1901. *Lemoine. Nancy. France. 1893.*

CHROGANIANA. Single. Red/Red. Tube. Pale salmon. Long. Sepals. Pale salmon. Green tips. Corolla. Salmon Orange. P35 2nd Ed. by Porcher 1848. Harrisons, Dereham List 1845. *Chrogan. GB. NK.*

CHUBBY BOY. Single. Red/Red. Tube. Bright scarlet red. Stout. Sepals. Bright scarlet red. Corolla. Red. Habit similar to Smiths "Robusta". Editor of Gardeners Gazette speaks of it as a curiosity. GC. P162 14/3/1846 & P184 13/3/1847 Listed by W. Miller, Ramsgate. GC. P216 27/3/1847 Listed by R. Cooper, Croydon. GC. P66 1/2/1845 Intro. by W. Miller. *Miller, W. Ramsgate GB. 1845.*

CICESTRIA. Single. ND/ND. Tube. ND. Sepals. ND. Corolla. ND. GC. P216 27/3/1847 Listed by R. Cooper, Croydon. *Silverlock. GB. 1846.*

CIEL D'AZUR. ND ND/ND. Tube. ND. Sepals. ND. Corolla. ND. RB Cat. *Boucharlet, Lyons France. 1883.*

CISSIE. Single. Red/Purple. Tube. Bright crimson. Sepals. Bright crimson. Recurved. Corolla. Rich dark purple. B.Cat. 1880-1889. *Bull,W. Chelsea. GB. 1879.*

CLAIR DE LUNE. Single. Red/Red. Tube. Orange salmon. Sepals. Salmon. Coralla. Orange salmon.L. Cat. 1891. *Aubin. France 1888.*

CLAPTON HERO. Single. Red/Purple. Tube. Red. 20 mm long.Sepals. Red.Large. Long. Corolla. Purple. Open. P147 3rd Ed. by Porcher 1858. Very similar to "Don Juan", and needs a good examination to find the difference. Clapton Hero has a longer tube The corolla has a brighter tone. GC. P279 30/4/1853. Dark Wooded stem. GC P535 23/8/1851 Exhibited at Vauxhall Garden Show. GC. P545 30/8/1851 Listed by G. Smith, Islington. GC. P337 24/5/1851 Intro. by Batten. *Batten. Clapton. GB. 1851.*

CLARA ZIEGLEAR. ND. ND/ND. Tube. ND. Sepals. ND. Corolla. ND. RH. P311 1889 Select by E.A. Carrière. NK. NK. NK.

CLARA (a). Single. Red/Red. Tube. Light rosy flesh. Long. Sepals. Light rosy flesh. Short. Corolla.

Deep Carmine. GC. P234 11/4/1846 Listed by A.J. Steward, Windsor. Harrison's, Dereham List 1845. Girling's List, Stowmarket. 1845. *Harrison. Dereham. GB. 1844.*

CLARA (b) Single. Red/Purple. Tube. Scarlet Crimson. Sepals. Scarlet Crimson. Corolla. Blue Violet. GC. P594 29/6/1861 Listed by Godwin & Padman Sheffield. GC. P771 24/8/1861 Listed by H. Walton, Burnley. GC. P140 16/2/1861. Intro. by F&A. Smith, Dulwich. *Smith, F&A. Dulwich. GB. 1861.*

CLARINDA. Double. Red/White. Tube. Rich crimson. Short. Sepals. Rich crimson. Broad. Corolla. White. Loose. Spreading. Huge. See "Edelweise" GC. P647 21/1/1880. JF. Cat. 1885. B. Cat. 1880-1893. Intro. by W. Bull. *Bland, E. Fordham. GB. 1880.*

CLARISSA. Single. White/Violet. Tube. Pure white. Sepals. Pure white. Tipped Green. Horizontal. Corolla. Soft Violet rose, shaded white at base. Margined rosy crimson. 4th Ed. by Porcher 1874 Not in the first selection. B. Cat. 1870-1875, *Bull,W. Chelsea. GB. 1870.*

CLARICE. Double. Red/White. Tube. Scarlet. Sepals. Scarlet. Corolla. White. Little veining. L. Cat. 1906. *Bull, W. Chelsea. GB. 1905.*

CLAUD DE LORRAIN. Double. Red/Purple. Tube. Carmine red. Thick and Swollen. Sepals. Carmine red. Large. Corolla. Lilac Violet or mauve, striped and splashed with red. P106 4th Ed. by Porcher 1874 edges of petals involcrute. Petals spiralled. Long pedicel 6.5 cms. *Lemoine. Nancy. France. 1872.*

CLAUDIA. Double. Red/Pink. Tube. Bright red. Short. Sepals. Bright red. Broad. Completely reflexed. Corolla. Blush pink. Very full. B. Cat. 1901. *Bull,W. Chelsea. GB. 1900.*

CLEOPATRA (a). Single. White/ND. Tube. White. Sepals. White. Corolla. ND. GC. P820 12/1844 "Recommended". GC.P808 Dec 1846 Good light variety. GC. 216 27/3/1847 & P232 1/4/1848 Listed by R. Cooper, Croydon. GC. P264 24/4/1847 & P259 28/4/1849 & P241 20/4/1850 Listed by W. Rendle, Plymouth. GC. P254 19/4/1845 Intro. by J. Smith. *Smith, J. Dalston. GB. 1845.*

CLEOPATRA (b). ND. Red/White. Tube. Deep red. Sepals. Deep red. Fully reflexed. Corolla. White. JF. Cat. 1885. NK. NK. NK.

CLÉOPÂTRE Single. ND/ND. Tube. ND. Sepals. ND. Corolla. ND. P30 3rd. Ed. by Porcher 1858. *Oudin, Liseaux. France. 1848.*

CLÉOPÂTRE. ND. Red/Purple. Tube. Carmine. Sepals. Carmine. Corolla. Clear mauve shaded carmine. V&A, Paris Cat, 1914. *Boucharlet, Lyons. France. 1884.*

CLIMAX (a). Single. White/Red. Tube. Creamy white. Sepals. Creamy white. Corolla. Rosy crimson. GC. P185 20/3/1847. Intro. by Gaines. Battersea. *Gaines. Battersea. GB. 1847.*

CLIMAX (b). Single. Red/Purple. Tube. Crimson. Stout. A little bulged. Short. 10 mm long. Sepals. Crimson. Broad. Very large. Reflex with a pretty curve or half circle so the points touch the seed vessel. Corolla. Violet. Involocrute. (Dull blue fading to purple violet) P147 3rd. Ed by Porcher 1858. Seedling from "Corallina". Named by Mr. Banks. GC. P34 20/1/1855 Intro. by W.J.Epps, Maidstone. *Banks, E. Deal. GB. 1855.*

CLINTONIA. Single. Red/Purple. GC. P89 11/2/1843 recommended for open ground without protection. GC. P66 1/2/1845 & P112 17/2/1844. Listed by W. Miller, Ramsgate. GC. P289 29/5/1841 Listed by Hugh Low, Clapton. *Clinton. GB. NK.*

CLIO (a). Single. Red/Purple. Tube. Bright crimson. Sepals. Bright crimson. Large. Short. Green tips. Corolla. Deep purple tinged crimson. Large flowers. Free. GC. P35 2nd. Ed by Porcher 1848. Leaves 8cm x 5cm. By its habit, foliage and the colouration of the flowers, this variety very much resembles "Excelsa" and "Macnabiana". GC. P241 15/4/1843. Listed by F&A Smith, Hackney. Harrisons list 1845. *Harrison. Dereham. GB. 1842.*

CLIO (b). Single. White/Red. Tube. White. (Flesh) 15mm long.Sepals. White. (Pink).Spreading. Corolla. Deep Red. (Vermilion purple).Large petals. GC. P401 24/6/1854. Listed by Benj. R.Cant, Colchester & H. Walton, Burnley. GC. P466 22/7/1854 Listed by Bass & Brown, Sudbury. GC. P238 14/4/1855 Listed by J. Hoads, Addlestone. GC. P530 11/8/1855 Listed by Bainbridge & Hewison, York. GC. P314 10/5/1856 Listed by Youell, Gt. Yarmouth. Vol P3 J of RHS 1863 P92. Fuchsia trials of 1862. Not a free bloomer GC. P194 1/4/1854 Intro. by C. Turner, Slough. *Banks, E. Deal. GB. 1854.*

CLIO (c). Single. Pink/Red. Tube. Bright Pink. Sepals. Bright Pink. Corolla. Red. Leaves green. Long flowers in panicles. L. Cat 1907, 1908. *Bonstedt. Germany. 1906.*

CLIPPER (a). Single. Red/Purple. Tube. Crimson Scarlet. Sepals. Crimson red. Broad. Well reflexed. Corolla. Deep purple shaded violet. BSW. Cat. 1878. GC. P521 28/4/1877. Intro. by B.S. Williams. *Bland, E. Fordham. GB. 1877.*

CLIPPER (b) ND. Red/White. Tube. Scarlet. Sepals. Scarlet. Corolla. Pure white. Good exhibition variety. JF. Cat. 1885.NK. NK. NK.

CLIPPER (c). Single. Red/Red. Tube. Scarlet. Sepals. Scarlet. Well reflexed. Corolla. Rich claret. (Deep red). Vol. 24 J of RHS P342. GC. Vol 22 P295 1897. New. JF. Cat. 1901. New for 1901. *Lye, J. Market Lavington. GB. 1901.*

CLOCHE BLUE. Double. Red/Purple. Tube. Red. Sepals. Red. Corolla. Clear purple shaded blue. RB. Cat. 1934. *Rozain Jr.,Lyons. France. 1934.*

CLOSIOT. ND. ND/ND. Misnamed. See "Gloriot" GC. P479 20/7/1844 Exhibited by A. Henderson, Pine Apple Place, London at RHS. Show London.

CLOTH OF GOLD. Single. Red/Purple. Tube. Red. Sepals. Red. Corolla. Purple. New variegated leaved sport of "Souvenir de Chiswick". introduced by S.Stafford, Hyde at RHS Show. "White edged leaves" CG 19/7/1864 A golden variegated sport. GC. P262 19/3/1864. Variegated sport. *Stafford, Hyde. GB. 1864.*

CLUMBERII. Single. ND/ND. Tube. ND. Sepals. ND. Corolla. ND. GC. P482 15/7/1843 Exhibited by Mr. Pearson. Notts Flower & Horticultural Show. NK. NK. GB. NK.

C.N. MAY. Single. Red/Purple. Tube. Scarlet. Sepals. Scarlet. Stout and brilliant in colour. Corolla. Very dark plum. GC. Vol. 18 P215 Exhibited at Devizes Hort. Scty. Show, by W.C. Hitch 7/8/1882. GC. Vol 18 P215.B. Cat. 1888. BSW.Cat. 1888. JF. Cat. 1888. *Lye,J. Market Lavington. GB. 1888.*

COCCINEA VERA. Single. Red/Red. Tube. Deep bright crimson. Sepals. Deep rich crimson. Corolla. Vermillion Scarlet. Thick and Fleshy. FC.. Vol XI 1843 P200 RBS Seedling Show. A slight improvement on "Cormackii". P35 2nd Ed. by Porcher In the presence of F. coccinea, the pretence that it is different is far from the truth. Harrisons, Dereham List 1845. RH. P23 1846. Carmine Red. GC. P193 30/3/1844. Intro. by J. Smith. *Smith,J. Dalston. GB. 1844.*

COELESTINA. Double. Red/Blue. Tube. Bright pink. Sepals. Bright Pink. Corolla. Sky blue tinted lilac in the centre. L. Cat. 1892. *Rozain, Lyons. France. 1891.*

COERULEA. Single. Red/Purple. Tube. Red. Sepals. Red. Corolla. Violet. Vol. P1 J of RHS. 1860. P262/3 Proceedings of the floral committee. NK. NK. NK.

COEUR DE LION. Single. Red/Purple. Tube. Scarlet. Thin. Short.Sepals. Scarlet. Entirely reflexed. Corolla. Purple. Open. GC. P515 25/7/1857 Listed by H. .Walton, Burnley & C. E. Allen, Stoke Newington. GC. P357 7/4/1858 & GC. P210 28/3/1857. Intro. by E.G. Henderson. *Banks,E. Deal. GB. 1857.*

COLBERT. Single. Red/Purple. Tube. Orange red. Sepals. Orange pink. Corolla. Dull bluish pink. Very multiflowered. Named after a Minister of Louis XIV. L. Cat. 1886. *Aubin. Bagnolet. France. 1886.*

COLEEN BAWN. Single. Red/Purple. Tube. Red. Sepals. Red. Curled back to tube. Corolla. Violet Blue, splashed red. Bell shaped. GC. P594 29/6/1861. Listed by Godwin & Padham. Sheffield. GC. P771 24/8/1861 Listed by H. Walton, Burnley. P105 4th Ed. by Porcher 1874. *Rollinson. London GB. 1861.*

COLERIDGE. Single. Red/Purple. Tube. Rose. Sepals. Rose. Corolla. Clear Violet, white at base. BSW. Cat. 1878. NK. NK. NK.

COLIBRI. Single. Red/Purple. Tube. Scarlet. Sepals. Scarlet. Reflexed. Corolla. Violet red. Forms a bush about 40 cms high and covered with flowers all summer.Hardy. L. Cat. 1899. F. Coccinea x. *Lemoine. Nancy. France. 1898.*

COLLEGIAN. Single. Red/Purple. Tube. Reddish purple. Thin. Short. Sepals. Reddish purple. Reflexed. Corolla. Violet blue. P147 3rd Ed. by Porcher . This variety with small flowers is so near many other varieties which are of superior merit, and will not last long. GC P483 30/7/1853 and P162 18/3/1854 Listed by H. Walton, Burnley. GC. P438 6/7/1854 Listed by Mitchell & Co. Kemptown, Brighton. GC. P439 6/7/1854 Exhibited as a 7' high pyramid by Mr. Bray at RB. Show, Regents Park. *Banks, E. Deal. GB. 1853.*

COLONEL ARCHINARD. Single. Red/Blue. Tube. Red. Sepals. Red. Corolla. Blue, lighter at base. Large. B. Cat. 1893-1895. *Rozain. Lyons. France. 1893.*

COLONEL BORGNIS-DESBORDES. Single. Red/Purple. Tube. Rosy Red.(Salmoin pink) . Sepals. Rosy Red.(Salmon pink) Corolla. Purple. (Clear violet) Very free. Squat. Very large. Globular. Good for market. HC. Cat. 1890. L. Cat 1887 *Lemoine. Nancy. France.1886.*

COLONEL BRANLIERES. Double. Red/Purple. Tube. Carmine red. Short. Sepals. Carmine Red. Broad. Corolla. Wine Violet. Full. L. Cat. 1908. *Lemoine. Nancy. France. 1908.*

COLONEL DE TRENTIAN. Double. Red/Pink. Tube. Bright red. Sepals. Bright red. Very large. Recurved. Corolla. Pinkish White, veined carmine. Enormous. JF. Cat 1900. L. Cat. 1901. *Lemoine. Nancy. France 1899.*

COLONEL DOMINIÉ. Double. Red/White. Clear Red. (Rosy Lake). Sepals. Clear red. (Rosy lake). Large. Reflexed. White, Lightly suffused rose. Imbricated (Petals overlap one another). GC. P518 28/4/1888 Listed by Daniels, Norwich. L. Cat. 1886. Laings Cat. circa 1890. BSW. Cat. 1897. B. Cat. 1888-1899. *Lemoine. Nancy. France. 1886.*

COLONEL G. DE CONSEIL. ND. ND/ND. Tube. ND. Sepals. ND. Corolla. ND. P148 3rd Ed. by Porcher. This variety appeared illustrated in Baudry's Spring 1857 catalogue without description. *Baudry, Avranches. France. 1857.*

COLONEL HARCOURT. Single. Red/Purple. Tube. Scarlet. Sepals. Light Scarlet. Well reflexed. Corolla. Rose suffused with purple. B. Cat. 1876-1878. HC. Cat. 1882. *Banks, E. Deal. GB. 1876.*

COLONEL LAWRENCE. Single. Red/Purple. Tube. Crimson. Sepals. Crimson. Well reflexed. Corolla. Dark Purple. Selected from 3000 seedlings. GC. P611 15/9/1856 Intro. by Stewart & Nielsen, Liscard. *Stewart & Nielsen. Liscard GB. 1857.*

COLONEL POUGET. Double. Red/Purple. Tube. Crimson. Sepals. Crimson. Corolla. Bluish Purple. GC. P426 10/5/1862 Intro. by Veitch & Co. *Mollen,H. GB. 1862.*

COLOSSUS (a). Single. Red/Purple. Tube. Carmine. Stout. Sepals. Carmine. Corolla. Purplish Crimson. Florists Journal P78 4/1845. In 1841 a cross between "Formosa Elegans X Corymbiflora" was achieved. Seedlings pretty and free but not much different from hybrids of F.Fulgens. Selfed and resultant seedlings flowers are much larger. Sister seedlings are "President" ,"Attractor", and

"Candidate". Ilustrated in Paxton's Magazine of Botany March 1844. GC. P66 1/2/1845 & P250 17/4/1847 Listed by W. Miller, Ramsgate. GC. P216 27/3/1847 & P232 1/4/1848 Listed by R. Cooper, Croydon. GC. P146 8/3/1845 Listed by Youell, Gt. Yarmouth. *Standish J. Bagshot. GB. 1843.*

COLOSSUS (b). ND. ND/ND Tube. ND. Sepals. ND. Corolla. ND. GC. P184 13/3/1847 Listed By W. Miller, Ramsgate. *Fowles, London GB. 1846.*

COLOSSUS (c). Double. Red/Purple. Tube. Red. Sepals. Red. Corolla. Purple. 4th Ed. by Porcher 1874. Not in the first selection. GC. P376 26/4/1862 Possess entire stock. Intro. by F&A Smith. *Smith F&A, Dulwich. GB. 1862.*

COLOSSUS (d). Single. Red/Purple. Tube. Bright glossy crimson. Sepals. Crimson, Broad. Thick. Horizontally recurved. Corolla. Deep purplish plum. Well expanded. Immense. JF. Cat. 1887. B. Cat. 1883-1889. Intro. by W. Bull. *Bland, E. Fordham GB. 1883.*

COLOSSUS (e). Single. Red/Purple. Tube. Brilliant red. Sepals. Brilliant red. Long. Stout. Well reflexed. Corolla. Violet. Very large. GC. P344 4/4/1868 Intro. by B.W. Knight, Battle. *Knight, B.W. Battle. GB. 1868.*

COLUMBINE. ND. White/Purple. Tube. Blush. Sepals. Blush. Corolla. Rosy Purple. Laings Cat. circa. 1890. NK. NK. NK.

COMA. Single. Red/Purple. Tube. Deep crimson. Sepals. Deep crimson. Elegantly recurved. Corolla. Blue shaded rose at base of petals. P115 4th. Ed. by Porcher 1874. Not in the first selection. B. Cat. 1873-1876. *Bull,W. Chelsea. GB. 1873.*

COMET. Single. Red/Purple. Tube. Red. Sepals. Red. Reflexed. Corolla. Blue Violet. P106 4th. Ed. by Porcher. Vol 2 J of RHS 1870 Chiswick trials. Free. GC. P905 12/10/1861 Intro. by E.G. Henderson. *Banks,E. Deal GB. 1862.*

COMMANDANT BARATIER. Double. Red/Blue. Tube. Red. Sepals. Red. Corolla. Dark blue, exterior bright rose. Large. Well open. L. Cat. P149 1901. *Rozain. Lyons. France. 1900.*

COMMANDANT MARCHAND. Double. Red/Purple. Tube. Blood red. (Scarlet). Sepals. Blood red. (Scarlet). Corolla. Dark Violet with rose marbling on the exterior petals. Very large. Full. L. Cat. 1901. JF. Cat. 1900. *Lemoine, Nancy. France. 1899.*

COMMANDANT TAILLANT. Double. Red/ White. Tube. Carmine red. Sepals. Carmine red. Corolla. White. Fully double. This fuchsia because of its habit and foliage resembles "Globosa". Vigourous. Floriferous. HC. Cat. 1882. P128 4th. Ed. by Porcher 1874. *Lemoine, Nancy. France. 1874.*

COMMANDER. Single. Red/Purple. Tube. Dark red. Sepals. Dark red. Partially reflexed. 1?" long. Corolla. Purplish crimson. P216 Vol 4 J of RHS. Pcxvii Vol 3 P of RH, awarded ***. Flowers large 1" long, conical. A bold handsome flower and showy as a pot plant. B. Cat. 1872-1873. *Bull,W. Chelsea. GB. 1871*

COMMANDEUR. Single. ND. ND/ND. Tube. ND. Sepals. ND. Corolla. ND. See "Commanduer Nouveau". *Racine. France. 1850.*

COMMANDEUR NOUVEAU. Single. Red/Purple. Tube. Soft rose 20mm long. Sepals. Soft rose. Long. Arched. Violet rose. P148 3rd Ed. by Porcher 1858. In 1850 Racine introduced a fuchsia named Commandeur, which on propogation was found to vary in colour. I determined to replace it with a more stable variety, which I did. *Porcher, New Orleans France. 1853.*

COMMANDORE. Single. Red/Purple. Tube. Bright carmine. Sepals. Bright carmine. Broad. Corolla. Rich Plum. Raised by either J. Smith of Whalleys nursery, Liverpool or a celebrated amateur from the North of England. GC. P130 21/2/1852. GC. P449 17/7/1852 & P209 26/3/1853 Listed by H. Walton, Burnley. GC. P213 8/4/1854 Listed by C.H. Gardiner, Maidstone. GC. P283 22/4/1854 & P353 26/5/1855 Listed by Hart & Nicklin, Guildford. GC. P130 21/2/1852 Intro. by E.G. Henderson. St. Johns Wood. NK. *GB. 1852.*

COMPACT. Single. Red/White. Tube. Bright crimson. Short. Sepals. Bright crimson. Long and elegantly reflexed. Corolla. White, veined bright rosy crimson. Long. B. Cat. 1875-1876. *Bull,W. Chelsea. GB. 1874.*

COMPACTA (a). Single. Pink/Red Tube. Salmon. Sepals. Salmon. Spreading. Corolla. Purple red. Good. Leaves oblong. GC. P97 18/2/1843 Listed by Youell, Gt. Yarmouth. GC. P241 15/4/1843 Listed by F&A Smith. GC P66 1/2/1845. Listed by W. Miller, Ramsgate. Harrison, Dereham List 1845. *Smith, J. Dalston. GB. 1842.*

COMPACTA (b). Single. Pink/Purple. Tube. Flesh. Sepals. Flesh coloured. Corolla. Rosy Purple. Bell shaped. GC. P232 1/4/1848. Listed by R. Cooper,

Croydon. GC. P256 16/4/1845 Listed by G. Rogers, Uttoxeter. GC. P298 8/5/1847 Intro. by Barkway. *Barkway, London. GB. 1847.*

COMPACTA (c) Single. Red/Purple. Tube. Red. Short. Thick. Sepals. Red. Corolla. Violet Purple. Very floriferous and holds itself better than "Corallina". App. to RH. 1851 by Porcher. Corallina X . *Malou. France. 1850.*

COMPACTA (d) Double. Red/Purple. Tube. Red. Sepals. Red. Corolla. Purple. P126 4th Ed. by Porcher 1874 Not in the first selection. *Smith,F&A. Hackney. GB. 1866.*

COMPACTA NOVA. Single. Red/Purple. Tube. Lilac pink. Sepals.Lilac pink. Corolla. Violet lilac. Bell shaped. Yellowish Green foliage. Flowers held on short pedicels. P148 3rd. Ed. by Porcher. Twice in recent years fuchsias bearing the name "Compacta" have appeared and twice have found to be mediocre. *Porcher, New Orleans, France. 1853.*

COMPACTA FLORIBUNDA. ND. ND/ND. Tube. ND. Sepals. ND. Corolla. ND. L Boucharlet cat 1883. *Boucharlet,L Lyons. France. 1880?*

COMPACTA SUPERBA. ND. ND/ND. Tube. ND. Sepals. ND. Corolla. ND. L Bouchlaret cat 1883. *Boucharlet,L Lyons, France. 1880?*

COMTE CAVOUR. See COUNT CAVOUR.

COMTE DE BEAULIEU. Single. Red/Purple. Tube. Red. Sepals. Red. Corolla. Purple. App. to RH. 1851 by Porcher "1st. Class Variety". GC. P184 13/3/1847 Listed by Millers, Ramsgate. GC. P153 4/3/1848 & P232 1/4/1848 & P256 21/4/1849 Listed by R, Cooper Croydon. GC. P224 18/4/1849 Listed by R. Whibley, Kennington Cross. GC. P241 20/4/1850 Listed by W. Rendle, Plymouth. GC. P454 16/7/1853 Exhibited at H.S. Show by Salter. *Salter. Versailles France. 1846.*

COMTE DE FLANDRE. Double. Red/Purple. Tube. Dark carmine. Sepals. Dark carmine. Gracefully reflexed. Corolla. Dark indigo at extremity, bright carmine at base. Large. Full. P126 4th Ed. by Porcher 1874. Not in the first selection. B. Cat. 1870. *Cornelissen, Arras. Belgium. 1868.*

COMTE DE HAINAUT. Double. Red/Purple. Tube. Red. Sepals. Red. Long. Reflexed. Corolla. Purple. Loose. Vol P3 J of RHS 1863, Chiswick trials 1862. Submitted by A. Lowe. Poor sort. GC. P771 24/8/1861 Listed by H. Walton, Burnley. NK. NK. *1860?*

COMTE D'HUGUES. Double. Red/Pink. Tube. Clear carmine. Sepals. Clear carmine. Corolla. Flesh pink veined bright rose. Large. L. Cat 1898. *Rozain, Lyons. France. 1897.*

COMTE DE LOPINAU. Double. Red/Purple. Tube. Red. Sepals. Red. Corolla. Purple. P126 4th Ed. by Porcher 1874 Not in the first selection, *Crousse. NK. 1866.*

COMTE DE MEDICI SPADA. Double. Red/Purple. Tube. Crimson red. Short. Thin. Sepals. Crimson red. Raised and Rounded. Corolla. Bluish Violet, washed with red. P122 4th Ed. by Porcher 1874. This is a first class double, and not without merit, and worth keeping for comparitive purpose. Small flower. Good do-er. *Lemoine, Nancy. France. 1859.*

COMTE DE MUN. Double. Red/Purple. Tube. Red. Sepals. Red. Corolla. Violet striated with rose at the base. B. Cat. 1893-1895. *Rozain, Lyons. France. 1893.*

COMTE DE PRESTON. Double. Red/Purple. Tube. Rosy Red. Sepals. Rosy red. Reflexed. Corolla. Rosy purple. Large. Coarse. Vol P3 J of RHS P90 1863. Fuchsias grown for trial at Chiswick. GC. P771 24/8/1861. Listed by H. Walton, Burnley. NK. NK. NK.*1860.*

COMTE DE VERTAMONT. Double. Red/White. Tube. Bright red. Sepals. Bright red. Corolla. Milk white. L. Cat. 1906. *Rozain. Lyons. France. 1904.*

COMTE LÉON TOLSTOI. Double. Red/Blue. Tube. Dark scarlet. Sepals. Dark scarlet. Corolla. Dark blue.(deep blush purple without markings of any kind. Habit is good.) Compact. G. 11/2/1903. Similar to "Solferino".Named after a Russian writer, who wrote War and Peace (1828-1910). B. Cat. 1888-1892. L. Cat 1892. *Lemoine, Nancy. France. 1888.*

COMTE LÉONTIEFF. Double. Red/Pink. Tube. Flesh pink.(Dark Scarlet). Sepals. Flesh pink.(Dark Scarlet). Corolla. Rose veined carmine. Large. JF. Cat. 1899. L. Cat. 1899. *Rozain, Lyons. France. 1898.*

COMTE SANNOY. ND. ND/ND. Tube. ND. Sepals. ND. Corolla. ND. GC. P406 2/5/1863 Listed by Wm. Hussey, Norwich NK. NK. NK.

COMTESSE DE NIEWERKERKE. Single. White/Pink. Tube. Whitish pink. Thin. Tube 25mm. Sepals. Whitish pink. Sepals slightly larger than tube. Corolla. Crimson red. Open. Pleated petals. P149 3rd Ed. by Porcher. Not in the elite class, the tube is too thin. *Narcis, Evry. France. 1854.*

COMTESSE DE FLANDRE Double. Red/White. Tube. Red, Sepals. Red. Corolla. White. Not in the first selection. P131. 4th. Edition by Porcher 1878.. *Cornelissen. Belgium. 1868.*

COMTE WITTE. Double. Red/Purple. Tube. Scarlet. Sepals. Scarlet. Broad. Corolla. Violet Purple. Enormous. Very full. JF. Cat. 1906. L. Cat. 1906. *Lemoine, Nancy. France. 1906.*

CONCILE. Single. White/Violet. Tube. White. Sepals. White. Corolla. Violet. P120 4th. Ed. by Porcher 1874. Not in the first selection. *Lemoine, Nancy. France. 1870.*

CONCILIATION. Single. White/Red. Tube. White. (Soft pink). 18 mm long. Sepals. White, (Soft pink).tipped green. Open. Points bent. Well open. Horizontal. Corolla. Cerise red. Short pedicel. Bushy. P149 3rd Ed. by Porcher 1858. P168 RH. 1857. App, to RH, 1851 by Porcher. *Meillez. France. 1850*

CONDORCET. Single. White/Red. Tube. White. Long. Stout. Sepals. White, shaded rose. Uplifted. Green tips. Corolla. Orange red. HC. Cat. 1890 L. Cat. 1886. *Aubin, Bagnolet. France. 1886.*

CONDUCTOR. Single. Red/Purple. Tube. Red. Sepals. Red. Corolla. Purple. GC. P146 8/3/1845 Listed by Youell, Gt Yarmouth. GC. P265 24/4/1847 Listed by W, Rendle, Plymouth. GC. P401 22/6/1844 Being sent out. GC P820 12/44 Recommended. GC. P821 25/11/1843. Intro. by Standish. *Standish, Bagshot. GB. 1843*

CONFIDENCE. Single. Red/Purple. Tube. Red. Sepals. Red. Corolla. Purple. GC. P465 27/7/1850 & P144 8/3/1851 Listed by W. Rumley, Richmond. GC. P242 20/4/1850 Intro. by E.G. Henderson, St. Johns Wood. *Henderson E.G. St. Johns Wood. GB. 1850.*

CONQUEROR (a). Single. Red/Red. Tube, Scarlet. Long. Sepals. Scarlet. Corolla. Salmon. GC. P225 13/4/1844. *Jackson, Bedale. GB. 1844*

CONQUEROR (b). Single. Red/Purple. Tube. Dark rich crimson red. Sepals. Dark rich crimson red. Corolla. Violet crimson. Harrisons, Dereham List 1845. *Salter, Versailles. France. 1844*

CONQUEROR (c). Single. Red/Purple. Tube. Bright vermillion. Sepals. Bright vermillion. Expanding well. Corolla. Deep purple. Long. GC. 7/2/1846 Intro. by Youell, Gt. Yarmouth. *Youell, Gt. Yarmouth. GB. 1846.*

CONQUEROR (d). Single. Red/Purple. Tube. Bright red. Sepals. Bright red. Finely reflexed. Corolla. GC. P224 14/4/1849 Listed by R. Whibley, Kennington Cross. GC. P259 28/4/1849 & P241 20/4/1850 Listed by W. Rendle, Plymouth. Midland Florist. P195 1847. Deep Lake. Cupped. GC.P249 27/4/1847 Introduced by W. Rendle, Plymouth GB. 1847 *Passingham, Truro. GB. 1847.*

CONQUEROR (e). Single. Red/Purple. Tube. Crimson. Sepals. Crimson. Broad. Well reflexed. Corolla. Purple. Very long and circular. NFS Commended. Vol P3 J of RHS 1863 Fuchsia trials at Chiswick 1862. Dwarf, free, bushy. Brightly coloured.GC. P419 21/6/1856 Listed by Bainbrige & Hewitson York. GC. P451 5/7/1856 & P642 27/9/1856 Listed by H. Walton, Burnley. GC.P690 18/10/56 & P146 7/3/1857 Listed by W. Rumley, Richmond. GC.P251 11/4/1857 Listed by W. Masters, Canterbury. GC. P283 25/4/1857 Listed by W. Cutbush, Highgate. GC. P260 24/3/1860 Listed by Wm. Hussey, Norwich. GC. P82 9/2/1856 Intro. by G. Smith, Islington. *Smith,G. Islington. GB. 1856.*

CONQUEROR (f). Single. Red/Purple. Tube. Bright crimson. Sepals. Bright crimson. Beautifully reflexed. Large. Corolla. Blue. Long. Smooth. Perfect form. CG & JH P406 20/8/61. GC. P459 1866 Recommended. GC P594 30/6/1860 Listed by F. Godwin, Sheffield. GC. P18 14/1/1860 Intro. by W. Rollinson. *Rollinson W, Tooting. GB. 1860.*

CONQUEROR (g). Double. Red/Purple. Tube. Light crimson. Short. Sepals. Bright crimson. Long. Broad. Elegantly reflexed. Corolla. Dark purple, flamed crimson. GC. P320 20/3/1869 Intro. by Felton & Son, Birmingham. *Felton, Birmingham. GB. 1869.*

CONQUEST (a). Single. Red/Purple. Tube. Red. Sepals. Scarlet. Broad. Reflex gracefully. Corolla. Violet Plum. Expanded. GC. P87 1/2/1862. *Rea, R. Ipswich. GB. 1862.*

CONQUEST (b). Single. Red/Purple. Tube. Carmine Scarlet. Sepals. Carmine Scarlet. Recurved. Corolla. Lavender marked carmine. P55 19/1/1867 Review by H. Cannell Cup shaped. Rather dwarf. Beautifully shaped flower. P115. 4th Ed. by Porcher 1874. Not in the first selection. GC.

P382 28/4/1866 Intro. by E.G. Henderson, St. Johns Wood. *Banks,E. Deal GB. 1866.*

CONSERVATIVE (a). Single. Red/Purple. Tube. Red. Sepals. Red. Corolla. Purple. GC. P98. 17/2/1844 Intro. by Youells, Gt. Yarmouth. *Youell. Gt.Yarmouth GB. 1844.*

CONSERVATIVE (b). Single. ND/ND. Tube. ND. Sepals. ND. Corolla. ND. Light Variety. GC. P146 8/3/1845 Intro. by Foxton. *Foxton. GB. 1844.*

CONSOLATION (a). Single. Red/Red. Tube. Soft vermilion. 20 mm long. Thick. Sepals. Soft vermilion. Horizontal. Tips bent. Corolla. Carmine vermilion. Expanded. GC. P149 3rd Ed. by Porcher 1858. 2nd Class. GC. P177 20/3/1852. Listed by W. Rumley, Richmond. *Turville, Chelmsford. GB.. 1851.*

CONSOLATION (b). Single. Red/Purple. Tube. Light carmine. Short. Sepals. Light carmine. Large. Reflexed. Rounded. Corolla. Bluish Lavender fades to plum when fully open. (Violet, red at base.). Very splayed out. GC.P55 19/1/1867 Review by H. Cannell. P106 4th Ed. by Porcher 1874. GC. P382 29/4/1865. Intro, by E.G. Henderson, St. Johns Wood. *Banks, E. Deal GB. 1865.*

CONSPICUA (a). Single. Red/Red. Tube. Bright carmine. Sepals. Bright carmine outside, rosy carmine inside. Corolla. Crimson red. GC. P668 11/10/1841 Exhibited at RHS of Ireland show. P13. Vol IX Floricultural Cabinet. Harrison, Dereham List 1845. GC. P393 June 1842. Listed by Youell, Gt. Yarmouth. GC.P66 1/2/1845 Listed by Millers, Ramsgate. X F. Fulgens. *Smith J. Dalston. GB. 1840.*

CONSPICUA (b). Single. White/Red. Tube orange. Sepals. Orange. Corolla. Purple, GC. P183 13/3/1847. *Miller,W. Ramsgate. GB. 1847.*

CONSPICUA (c). Single. White/Red. Tube. White. (Pinkish white.). Horizontal. Very bulged. 20mm long. Sepals. White. (Pinkish white) Corolla. Vermillion. Foliage yellowish green. Very dentate GC. P545 30/8/1851 Listed by G. Smith, Islington. GC. P177 20/3/1852 Listed by W. Rumley, Richmond. GC. P207 27/3/1852 Listed by H. Walton, Burnley. GC. P199 19/3/1853 Recommended. GC. P209 5/4/1851 Intro. C. Turner, Slough. *Banks, E. Deal GB. 1851*

CONSPICUA (d). Single. Red/White. Tube. Scarlet. Bulged. Sepals. Scarlet. Well reflexed. 1?" Spreading. Corolla. Pure White, feathered carmine. 12-18 flowers at each joint from May to Nov. GC.

P763 16/8/1861 RHS. Floral Committee. 2nd Class Cert. Pcxiii Vol 3 J of RHS Fuchsia Trials Awarded ***. GC. P344 11/4/1863. Intro. by G. Smith. *Smith. G. Islington. GB. 1863.*

CONSPICUA ARBOREA. Single. White/Red. Tube. Pale flesh. Sepals. Pale flesh. Tipped green. Corolla. Bright Scarlet. PP35 2nd. Ed. by Porcher 1848. GC P431 24/6/1842 HS Show. Resembles "Chandlerii", but has a more erect habit. Harrison's, Dereham List 1845. GC. P201 26/3/1842 Intro. by W. Catleugh, Chelsea. "The blooms are always axilliary". *Prouse, S.R. GB. 1842.*

CONSTANCE. Single. White/Rose. Tube. White. Sepals. White. Corolla. Rose. Vol P1 J of RHS P262/3 1860. Floral Committee report. *Banks, E. Deal GB. 1860.*

CONSTANCY. Single. White/Red. Tube. Flesh. Sepals. Flesh. Well reflexed. Corolla. Rich carmine. Extra fine. B. Cat. 1889-1893. JF. Cat. 1890. *Lye,J. Market Lavington. GB. 1889.*

CONSTELLATION (a). Single. Pink/Red. Tube. Delicate pale pink. Long. Slender 3½" long. Sepals. Tipped greenish primrose. Corolla. Bright red. Flowers in racemes, 150 flowers in each bunch. GC. P633 1843. GC. P112 17/2/1844 Listed by W. Miller,Ramsgate. GC, P98 17/2/1844 Listed by Youells, Gt. Yarmouth. Not sent out in 1844. Harrisons, Dereham List 1845. See GC. P66 1/2/1845. Col pl in Floricultural Cabinet April 1844. P 73. Fulgens X Corymbiflora. Intro. by Miller, W. Ramsgate. GB. *Miller, W. Ramsgate 1845.*

CONSTELLATION (b). Single. White/Purple. Tube. Flesh. Sepals. Flesh, Expanded sepals. Corolla. Crimson Purple. GC. P232 & P256 21/4/1849 Listed by R. Cooper, Croydon. GC. P256 16/4/1848 Listed by G. Rogers, Uttoxeter. GC. P298 8/5/1847 Intro by Barkway. *Barkway, London. GB. 1847.*

CONSTELLATION (c). Double. Red/Purple. Tube. Light red. Sepals. Light red. Corolla. Light Violet tinted lilac. Immense size and substance. GC. P287 31/3/1860 Intro. by W. Windebank, Southampton. *Windebank, Southampton GB. 1860.*

CONSTELLATION (d). Single. Red/Purple. Tube. Red. Sepals. Red. Corolla. Pale Violet (lavender). Expanded. Finely shaped Erect Habit. Convolvulous like flowers. Vol 2 J of RHS 1870 Fuchsia trials 1st class. GC. P55 19/1/1867 Review by H. Cannell. GC P338 15/4/1865 Listed by W. Rumley. NK. *NK. 1864.*

CONSTITUTIONAL. Single. Red/Purple. Tube. Crimson. Sepals. Crimson. Completely reflexed. Corolla. Violet, red at base. B. Cat. 1870. NK. NK. NK.

CONTRASTE. Double. Red/Purple. Tube. Dark red. Sepals. Dark Red. Reflexed. Corolla. Blue. Very fine. L. Cat 1901. JF. Cat. 1898. *Rozain, Lyons. France. 1897*

CONVENTINO. Single. ND/ND. Tube. ND. Sepals. ND. Corolla. ND. GC. P162 14/3/1846 Listed by Millers, Ramsgate. NK, NK, NK.

COOPERII. Single. Red/Purple. Tube. Dull cerise red. Thin. Sepals. Dull cerise red. Long. Half open. Corolla. Violet. P36 2nd Ed. by Porcher 1848. GC. P97 18/2/1843 & P98 17/2/1844 Listed by Youell, Gt. Yarmouth. NK. NK. NK. NK.

COQUETTE. Double. Red/Purple. Tube. Light carmine. Sepals. Waxy white tinged rose pink. Well reflexed. Corolla. Delicate light mauve, one or two petals stained cinammon red. P115 4th Edition by Porcher ? wrongly identified. HC. Cat 1882. GC. P396 22/3/1873 Intro. by B&S Williams. *Bland E. Fordham GB. 1873.*

COQUELIN. Double. Red/Purple. Tube. Red. Sepals. Red. Aorolla. Sky blue exterior lavender. L. Cat. 1906. *Rozain. Lyons. France 1904.*

CORA. ND, ND/ND. Tube. ND. Sepals. ND. Corolla. ND. RH. P295 1887 Fuchsia grown as standards at Twickel,Holland. Raiser given as *E.G. Henderson. GB* NK.

CORALLE. Single Red/Red. Tube. Coral Red. Sepals. Coral Red. Corolla Red. Very floriferous. L.Cat 1906. F.Triphylla X. *Bonstedt, Gottingen. Germany. 1905.*

CORALLINA. Single. Red/Purple. Tube. Scarlet. ½" long. Sepals. Scarlet. 1" Narrow. Deflexed (bend down). Corolla. Dark purple.?" small. Fine. Hardy. Good for covering walls. Exhibited by Luccombe & Pince RBS Show 1845 GC. P545 15/8/1846 to be sent out in Sept.1846. P150 3rd Ed. by Porcher 1858. A hybrid between Radicans and a variety arising from Macrostema. It retains almost all, the characteristics of the first with the exception of some modifications of the flower. It has taken an interesting role in the development of the fuchsia, it has brought about an amelioration on its type which is not very floriferous, into numerous remarkable hybrids. Its habit is upright, often spindly. Foliage is dull green, Braches and veins purple. The tube and sepal;s are a clear purplish red. Tube thin and short,,15 mm long. Large sepals 35mm, Only open a little Bent tips. Corolla is a dull violet blue with involocrute petals. The sepals are sometimes reflexed to the horizontal, with bent tips like "Radicans". Stated by HC to be synonomous with Exoniensis. Disputed. Exoniensis X F.montana. *Luccombe & Pince. Exeter. GB. 1846.*

CORDATA SUPERBA. Single. ND/ND. Tube. ND. Sepals. ND. Corolla. ND. GC. P393 June 1842 Listed by Youell, Gt. Yarmouth. GC. P289 29/5/1841 listed by Hugh Lowe, Clapton. NK. NK. NK.

CORENTINI. Single. Red/Red. Tube. Coral. Very long. Sepals. Coral. Corolla. Lake. GC. P162 14/3/1846 & P184 13/3/1847 Listed by W. Miller, Ramsgate. RH. P 24 1846. *Salter. Versailles GB. 1845.*

CORINIUM. Single. Red/Purple. Tube. Rich crimson. Short. Thin. 15 mm long. Sepals. Rich crimson. Large. Points bent. Corolla. Rich purple. (Violet blue) Petals involocrute. Open. Dwarf habit. P150 3rd Ed. by Porcher 1858. GC. P240 13/4/1850 Listed by W. Gregory, Cirencester. GC. P465 27/7/1850 & P144 8/3/1851 Listed by W. Rumley, Richmond. GC. P465 27/7/1850 Listed by G. Smith, Islington. GC. P689 3/11/1849 Intro. by W. Gregory, Cirencester. Out Nov 1849. *Gregory W. Cirencester. GB.1849.*

CORINNE. Single. ND/ND. Tube. ND. Sepals. ND. Corolla. ND. P31 3rd Ed. by Porcher 1858. *Harrison, Dereham GB. 1846.*

CORINTH. Single. Red/Purple. Tube. Rosy carmine. Sepals. Rosy crimson. Corolla. Rosy crimson. Large. B. Cat. 1872-1876. *Bull, W. Chelsea. GB. 1872.*

CORINTHE. Double. Red/Purple. Tube. Carmine. Sepals. Carmine. Corolla. Violet Blue fading to magenta. Enormous. Full. Fimbriated. L. Cat 1911. *Lemoine, Nancy France. 1911.*

CORMACKII. Single. Red/Red. Tube. Red. Long and thick. Sepals. Red. Light green tips. Corolla. Red. GC P481 15/7/1843 "A short and broad and peculiarly rich flowered variation of Fulgens". P36 2nd Ed. by Porcher 1848.Exhibited by Catleugh. HS Show 12/7/1842. GC. P375 4/6/1844. Again exhibited by Catleugh.GC. P98 17/2/1844 & P146 8/3/1845 Listed by Youell, Gt. Yarmouth. GC. P66 1/2/1845 & P112 17/2/1844 Listed by W. Miller, Ramsgate. Harrison, Dereham List 1845. F.Fulgens X. GC. P242 15/4/1843. Intro. by Cormack, New Cross. *Cormack. New Cross. GB. 1843.*

CORMORANT. Semi Double. Red/Purple. Tube. Crimson. Short. Sepals. Rosy Crimson. Long. Corolla. Bluish Purple. Large. JF. Cat. 1886. B. Cat. 1888-1895. NK. NK. NK.

CORNE D' ABONDANCE. Single. Red/Red. Tube. Bright carmine rose. Sepals. Carmine rose. Corolla. Nasturtian orange. Large and long. See also "Gerbe de Corail" L. Cat 1901. Venusta x Boliviana. *Lemoine, Nancy. France. 1894?*

CORNEILLE. Single. Red/Purple. Tube. Scarlet. Long. Sepals. Scarlet. Long. Recurved. Twisted. Corolla. Bluish Violet. Large. JF. Cat. 1898. L. Cat. 1901. B. Cat. 1898-1899. *Lemoine. Nancy. France. 1897*

CORNELIA. Single. White/ND. Tube. White. Sepals. White. Corolla. ND. GC. P184 13/3/1847. Listed by W Miller, Ramsgate. *Harrison, Dereham GB. 1846*

CORNELISSEN. Double. Red/Purple. Tube. Red. 20mm. Sepals. Red. Large. Reflexed. Corolla. Dull violet blue. Ribboned with purple. P151 3rd Ed. by Porcher 1858. Superior to "Hendersonii". Coloration is better, tube longer, Sepals larger and more reflexed. *Cornelissen. Brussel. Belgium. 1857.*

CORONAL. Single. Red/Purple. Tube. Vermillion. Sepals. Vermillion. elegantly curved. Corolla. Rich violet purple. GC.P594 29/6/1861 Listed by Godwin & Padham, Sheffield. GC. P771 24/8/1861 Listed by H. Walton, Burnley. GC. P140 16/2/1861.Intro by *Smith F&A, Dulwich. GB. 1861.*

CORONATA FLORE PLENO. Double. Red/Purple. Tube. Reddish purple. Short. 10mm. Sepals. Reddish purple. Large. 25mm long., Points bent. Corolla. Violet purple. Very double and contains a very large number of petals. A feature is a second corolla which is superimposed on the first in the centre. P151 3rd Ed. by Porcher 1858. RH. P170 1857. *Dubus, Lille. France. 1857.*

CORONATION (a). ND. ND/ND. Tube. ND. Sepals. ND. Corolla. ND. GC. P259 28/4/1849 Listed by W. Rendle, Plymouth. NK. NK. NK.

CORONATION (b). Single. Red/Purple. Tube. Bright Scarlet. Sepals. Bright red. Broad. Recurving forming a perfect crown. Corolla. Violet Purple. Long. GC. P450 17/5/1862 Intro. by B. W. Knight. *Knight, B.W. Battle. GB. 1862.*

CORONET (a). Single. White/Red. Tube. Buff. (Flesh). Sepals. Buff. (Flesh). (Bright green tips).

Corolla. Carmine. Medium size. Free. Vigourous. Lax. (Vermillion red). GC. P820 Dec.1844 "Recommended". GC. P375 4/6/1844 Exhibited by J. Smith HS Show. GC. P193 30/3/1844. P24 RH.1846. Harrison, Dereham List 1845. Florists Journal P95 5/1845 "Recommended". GC. P66 1/2/1845 & P184 13/3/1847 Listed by W. Miller,Ramsgate. GC. P146 8/3/1845 Listed by Youell, Gt. Yarmouth. GC. P216 27/3/1847 & P232 1/4/1848 Listed by R. Cooper,Croydon. GC. P193 30/3/1844 Intro. by J. Smith. *Smith, J. Dalston. GB. 1844.*

CORONET(b) Single. White/Purple. Tube. White. Sepals. White. Corolla. Violet. GC. P531 11/8/1855 Listed by J. Courcha. GC. P218 7/4/1855 Intro. by G. Smith. *Smith G. Islington. GB. 1855.*

CORSAIR. Double. Red/Purple. Tube. Bright crimson. Sepals. Bright crimson. Well reflexed. Corolla. Bright Purple marked crimson. Compact. P126 4th Ed. by Porcher 1874 Not in the first selection. Only semi double. The form is not perfect. B. Cat. 1872-1875. *Bull, W. Chelsea GB. 1870.*

CORTONA. Single. Red/Purple. Tube. Rich crimson. Thin. Short. Sepals. Rich crimson. Reflex well. Corolla. Almost black. (Dull blue) P145 3rd Ed. by Porcher 1858 (recorded as Cartoni). GC. P454 16/7/1853 Exhibited as a pyramid by Bousie. GC. P449 17/7/1852 Listed by H. Walton, Burnley. GC. P211 26/3/1853 Listed by W. Rumley, Richmond. GC. P248 15/4/1854 Listed by Mitchell & Co. Brighton. GC. P283 20/4/1854 Listed by Hart & Nicklin, Guildford. GC. P223 10/4/1852 Introduced by C. Turner, Slough. *Banks, E. Deal. GB. 1852.*

COTE D'AZUR. Double. Red/Purple. Tube. Brilliant red. Sepals. Brilliant red. Corolla. Bluish purple. L. Cat. 1913. *Rozain, Lyons. France. 1912.*

COUNT CAVOUR. Single. Red/Purple. Tube. Red. Thick. Sepals. Clear red. Well reflexed. Corolla. Lilac Lavender Mauve. (Nice shade of violet rose). Large open. (Bell shaped). P106 4th Edition by Porcher 1874. J of RHS Vol 1 P184 Commended. Vol 2 1870 Passed over. Vol p3 1863 Awarded **. A dwarf free blooming sort. Bushy growth with very pretty and distinct flowers . Corolla is large and much expanded. Light bluish or slaty purple. Desirable for its distinctness. GC. P215 10/3/1860 Intro. by E.G. Henderson. *Banks, E. Deal GB. 1860*

COUNTESS OF ABERDEEN. Single. White/Pink. Tube. White, Sepals. White. Corolla. Palest Pink. GC. Vol 4 P641 1/12/88 Seen at gardens of Castle

Neve, Strathdon, Mr. Pirie Gr. Vol 3 P323. G. 6/10/1888 Only sent out this year. JF. Cat. 1888. B. Cat. 1889-1895. L. Cat. 1901. BSW Cat.1897. Intro. by *Cocker, Aberdeen, GB. 1888.*

COUNTESS OF BACTIVE. Single. ND/ND. Tube. ND. Sepals. ND. Corolla. ND. GC. P250 17/4/1847 Listed by J. Hally, Blackheath. NK. NK. NK.

COUNTESS OF BURLINGTON, Single. Red/White. Tube. Scarlet. Sepals. Scarlet. Elegantly reflexed. Corolla. Pure white. GC. P451 5/7/1856 & P642 27/9/1856 Listed by H. Walton, Burnley. GC. P497 26/6/1856 Listed by Fowle, Brixton. GC. P690 18/10/1856 Listed by W. Rumley, Richmond. GC. P283 25/4/1857 Listed by W. Cutbuish, Highgate. GC. P114. 23/2/1856 Intro. by E.G. Henderson. *Story, W.H. Newton Abbott. GB. 1856.*

COUNTESS OF CORNWALLIS. Single. White/Red. Tube. Light striped pink. Sepals. Light pink. Expanded. Corolla. Rosy crimson. GC. P140 27/2/1847 Good light variety. GC. P184 13/3/1847 & P200 27/3/1847 Listed By W. Miller, Ramsgate. GC. P250 17/4/1847 Listed by W.J. Epps. Maidstone. GC. P216 27/3/1847 & P232 1/4/1848 Listed by R. Cooper, Croydon.GC. P113 14/2/1846. Intro by W.J. Epps. *Epps, W.J. Maidstone. GB. 1846.*

COUNTESS OF TYRECONNEL. Single. Red/Purple. Tube. Red. Sepals. Red. Corolla. Purple. GC. P820 Dec 1844 "Recommended". GC. P989 17/2/1844 and P25 11/1/1845 Listed by Youell, Gt. Yarmouth. *Youell, Gt.Yarmouth. GB. 1844.*

COUNTESS OF WARWICK. Double. Red/White. Tube. Rosy crimson. Short. Sepals. Rosy Crimson. Broad. Corolla. Blush White, tinged pink, deeper at the base of the petals. B. Cat. 1895-1898. *Bull, W. Chelsea. GB. 1895.*

COUNTESS OF ZETLAND. Single. Red/Purple. Listed by Youells, Gt. Yarmouth. GC. P98 17/2/1844 and P146 8/3/1845. NK. NK. NK.

COUNTESS. Single White/Purple. Tube. White. Sepals. White. Reflexed. Corolla. Light Violet. Listed by F. Godwin, Sheffield. GC P539 10/7/1858. Raised by W. Knight Gr. to Duke of Kent. GC. P126 20/2/1858 Introduced by W. Rollinson. *Knight, W. GB. 1858*

COVENT GARDEN SCARLET. Single. Red/Purple. Tube. Brilliant dark red. Sepals. Brilliant dark red. Corolla. Purple Blue. Wide.P76 Witte 1882. NK. NK. *GB. 1875.*

COVENT GARDEN WHITE. Single. White/Red. Tube. White. Sepals. White. Corolla. Scarlet. HC. Cat 1882-1885.Superceeds "Arabella" and "Mrs. Lye" See GC. Vol 7 1877 P206. GC. P406 29/9/1877 Noted at HC. Swanley. GO. "Select 1880 - 1891" JF. Cat 1884. Dobbies Cat. 1892-4. *Doel GB. 1877.*

CRAIGIEANNA. Single. Red/Purple. Tube. Red. Sepals. Red. Corolla. Purple. GC. p299 26/6/1841 Exhibited at Bot.Scty. Show, Edinburgh 1841. Raised by Mr. P. Thomson, Gr to Lord Advocate Rutherford. P36 2nd. Ed. by Porcher 1848. GC P97 18/2/1843. Listed by Youells. *Thomson, P. Edinburgh. GB. 1841.*

CRAMOISI PARFAIT. ND ND/ND. Tube. ND. Sepals/ ND. Corolla. ND. App. to RH 1851 by Porcher. *Meillez. France. 1850.*

CRENULATA. ND. ND/ND. Tube. ND. Sepals. ND. Corolla. ND. P152 3rd Ed. by Porcher 1858. *Erben, Germany. 1857.*

CREPUSCULE. Double. Red/Purple. Tube. Red.(Dark red) Sepals. Red. (Dark red) Corolla. Violet tipped rose.(distinctly striped red).Fine Grower. HC.Cat. 1885-1898. GO "Select" 1886-1891. Dobbies. Cat. 1893-1894. *Boucharlet. Lyons. France 1883.*

CREUSA. Single. Red/Purple. Tube. Crimson. Short. Sepals. Crimson. Completely reflexed. Corolla. Rich dark purple plum, shaded crimson at base. JF. Cat. 1885. GC. P647 24/5/1880. Intro by W, Bull. B. Cat. 1880-1892. *Bland,E. Fordham. GB. 1880.*

C. RICKMAN. ND. ND/ND. Tube. ND. Sepals. ND. Corolla. ND. Vol 36 The Garden P277. A Trowbridge seedling grown and raised by G. Tucker. Exhibited at Bath Floral Fete. *Tucker, G. Trowbridge. GB. 1889.*

CRIMSON BEDDER. Single. Red/ND. Tube. Red. Sepals. Red. Corolla. ND. Distinct foliaged variety with bronze crimson leaves, flowers pale red. Young leaves are bright red, change on maturity to bronzy crimson. G. Vol 33 P414 1887. JF. Cat 1885. B. Cat 1888-1889. *Eckford. GB. 1884?*

CRIMSON EXPANSA. ND ND/ND. Tube. ND. Sepals. ND. Corolla. ND. GC. P647 11/10/1851 Exhibited at RHS of Cornwall Show 8/8/1851 by Mr. Friend. NK. NK. NK. NK.

CRIMSON GEM. ND ND/ND. Tube. ND. Sepals. ND. Corolla. ND. JF. Cat.1898 Crimson foliage. NK. NK. NK.

CRIMSON GLOBE. Single. Red/Purple. Tube. Bright coral red. Sepals. Bright coral red. Reflexed. Corolla. Violet Purple. GC. P684 29/11/1879 Colour Plate T371 Floral Magazine. GC. P824 27/6/1885 Fuchsia Trials "Best in Class". JF. Cat. 1885, Laings Cat. circa 1890. *Lye,J. Market Lavington. GB. 1879.*

CRIMSON KING. Single. Red/Purple. GC. P404 1848 "Choice kind". GC. P537 12/8/1848. Listed by G. Smith, Islington. GC. P161 17/3/1849 Listed by W. Rumley, Richmond. GC. P256 21/4/1849 Listed by R. Cooper, Croydon. GC P274 5/5/1849 Listed by H. Walton, Burnley. GC. P241 20/4/1850 Listed by W. Rendle, Plymouth. CG Vol III P272 1850 For exhibition. GC P153 4/3/1848 Intro. by Kendall. *Kendall, Stoke Newington. GB. 1848.*

CRINOLINE. Single. Red/Purple. Tube. Bright crimson. Sepals. Bright crimson. Waxy. Finely reflexed. Corolla. Violet crimson. Has an enormous skirt or petticoat. Vol. P1 J of RHS 1860 Floral Committee. "Sepals reflexed dark coral red. Corolla Purple. Crinoline type". GC. P450 19/5/1860 Intro. by J & C Lee, Hammersmith. NK. *France? 1860*

CRINOLINEFORMIS. Single. Red/Purple. Tube. Carmine red. Sepals. Carmine red. Reflexed. Corolla. Clear violet. Petals shaded rose pink at base. Bell shaped. Open. Very floriferous. P152 3rd Ed. by Porcher 1858. The name given is bizarre. The flower does not expand sufficiently to have this name. *Kock. Germany 1857.*

CRISTAL. Double. Red/White. Tube. Carmine. Sepals. Carmine. Corolla. White. RB. Cat. 1926. *Rozain Jr., Lyons. France. 1925.*

CRITERION (a). Single. Red/Purple. Tube. Rosy crimson. Short. Sepals. Rosy crimson. Long. Reflex to tube. Waxy. Corolla.Intense Purple. GC. P120 23/2/1850 "Select". App to RH. by Porcher 1851 "Small flowers". GC. P274 4/5/1850 Listed by Bass & Brown, Sudbury. GC. P109 11/12/1847 Intro. by H. Pope, Gib Heath B'ham. Corallina X. *Pope, H.J. Birmingham GB. 1848.*

CRITERION (b). Single. Red/Purple. Tube. Coral red. Sepals. Coral Red. Corolla. Violet Purple. Stout. Well expanded. GC. P595 30/6/1860. Listed by F. Godwin, Sheffield. CG & JH. P406 1861. SG. P459 1866 Prolific flowering. Dwarf. Compact. GC. P93 4/2/1860 Intro by G. Smith. *Smith, G. Islington. GB. 1860*

CRITERION (c). Double. Red/Purple. Tube. Crimson Scarlet. Sepals. Crimson Scarlet. Corolla. Pale rose striped deep mauve. GC. Vol 17 20/5/1882

Intro by B.S. Williams. GO P97 1882. BSW. Cat 1888. HC. Cat. 1885. *Bland, E. Fordham. GB. 1882*

CROCE SPINELLI. Single. Red/Purple. Tube. Scarlet. Sepals. Scarlet. Recurved. Corolla. Dark mauve, veined rose. Finely formed flowers. B. Cat. 1877-1878. BSW. Cat. 1878. NK. NK. NK.

CROGGIANNA. Single. ND/ND. Tube. ND. Sepals. ND. Corolla ND. GC. P112 17/2/1844. Listed by W. Miller, Ramsgate. NK. NK. NK.

CROWN JEWEL. Single. Red/Purple. Tube. Rich crimson. Sepals. Rich crimson. Long. Narrow. Recurved. Corolla. Darkest Black Violet. Small corolla. Vol. P3 J of RHS Fuchsia trials of 1862. GC. P260 24/3/1860 Listed by Wm. Hussey, Norwich. GC. P165 26/2/1859 Intro. by E.G. Henderson. *Banks, E. Deal GB. 1859.*

CROWN OF JEWELS. ND. ND/ND. Tube. ND. Sepals. ND. Corolla. ND. Foliage cultivar. Clear golden yellow tipped rich red crimson. P134 4th Ed. by Porcher 1874 Not in the first selection. GC. P375 19/3/1870 Introduced by E.G. Henderson. NK. *GB. 1870.*

CROWN PRINCE OF PRUSSIA. Single. Red/Purple. Tube. Dark Red. Bulged. Sepals. Intense scarlet. Broad. Thick. Reflexed. Corolla. Violet blue. Floriferous. P106 4th. Edition by Porcher 1874. Vol 3 Pcxvi.JofRHS Trials.Awarded ** 1872. Sepals broad. Prominent, Vol 4 J of RHS 1877 Fuchsia Trials FCC. GO. Select 1880-1890. GC. P1554 2/12/1871. Intro. By E.G.Henderson. NK. GB. 1871.

CRYSTAL. Single. White/Red. Tube. Greenish white. Thin. 20 mm long. Sepals. Greenish white. Arched. Narrow. Tips bent. Corolla. Carmine red. Open. P152 3rd Ed. by Porcher. Nice variety, but the tube is too bulged. *Fountain. GB. 1852.* "(Most likely the same as Crystal Fountain)".

CRYSTAL FOUNTAIN. Single. White/Red. Tube. Waxy white. Sepals. Waxy white. Corolla. Scarlet. GC. P211 26/3/1853 "Largest and best light variety offered". W. Rumley, Richmond. GC. P199 10/3/1853 Recommended. GC. P2488 15/4/1854 Listed by Mitchell & Co. Brighton. GC. P283 22/4/1854 Listed by Hart & Nicklin, Guildford. GC. P274 1/5/1852. Intro. by E. Perkins, Leamington. *Perkins, E. Leamington. GB. 1852.*

CUPID. Single. Red/Pink. Tube. Carmine. Sepals. Carmine. Corolla. Soft rose. Abundant of flowers. H.J. Jones, Sydenham Cat. 1901. NK. NK. NK. NK.

CUPIDON. Single. Red/Purple. Tube. Carmine. Sepals. Carmine. Corolla. Clear voilet. Bushy. Compact. Well branched. Small foliage. Covered with flowers all summer. Semi erect. Bush never exceeds 30/40 cms in height. Brant, Poitiers Cat. 1911. L. Cat 1886. *Hoste. Germany. 1885.*

CURIOSA. ND. ND/ND. Tube. ND. Sepals. ND. Corolla. ND. GC. P66 1/2/1845 & P114 22/2/1845 Listed by W. Miller, Ramsgate. P176 Vol XIV Floricultural Cabinet "Which, if not the same, is very similar to F. Cordifolia". P152 3rd. Ed. by Porcher 1858. NK. NK. NK. NK.

CURIOSITY. S/Double. Pink/Purple. Tube. Blush. Small. Sepals. Pink. Very large (Pale red) Corolla. Violet Blue.(Bright purple shaded red at base). P67 Vol. 4 J of RHS Trials 1873 No award. P126 4th Ed. by Porcher 1874. Not in the first selection. JF. Cat 1885. GC. P452 6/4/1872 Intro. by E.G. Henderson, St. Johns Wood. NK. *GB. 1872.*

CURTISII. Single. Red/Purple. Tube. Red. Sepals. Red. Corolla. Purple. p36 2nd Ed. by Porcher 1848. GC. P825 18/12/1841. Listed by Youells, Gt. Yarmouth. GC. P98 18/2/1844 & P112 17/2/1844 & P66 1/2/1845. Listed by Miller, Ramsgate. GC. P375 4/6/1844 Exhibited at HS by Mr. Cole. Girlings, Stowmarket List 1845. NK. NK. NK.

CUSPITATA. Single. ND/ND. Tube. ND. Sepals. ND. Corolla. ND. P152 3rd Ed. by Porcher 1858. *Erben. Germany. 1857.*

CUSTOZZA. Double. Red/White. Tube. Crimson. Thin. Short. Sepals. Crimson. Large. Reflexed round. Corolla. Pure white. Large. Very full. P295 RH. 1887 Fuchsias grown as Standards at Twickel. P128 4th Ed. by Porcher 1874. *Twrdy, Brno. Austria. 1867.*

CYLINDRICA SUPERBA. Single. Red/ND. Tube. Scarlet. Sepals. Vivid Scarlet. Corolla. ND. GC. P66 1/2/1845 Listed by W. Miller, Ramsgate. GC. P146 8/3/1845 Listed by Youell, Gt. Yarmouth. Harrisons, Dereham List 1845. GC. P177 23/3/1844 Intro. by G. Smith, Islington. *Smith, G. Islington. GB. 1844.*

CYNTHIA. Double. Red/Pink. Tube. Crimson cerise. Short. Sepals. Cerise crimson. Completely reflexed. Broad. Corolla. Greyish rose veined crimson at base. Irregular. Dicksons Seed Warehouse, Chester. Cat. 1907. *Dickson, Chester. GB. 1907.*

CYPRIS. S/Double. Red/Purple. Tube. Carmine Pink. Short. Sepals. Carmine Pink. Reflexed.

Corolla. Bluish purple. L. Cat. 1906. *Bull, W. Chelsea. GB. 1905.*

CYRUS. ND. ND/ND. Tube. ND. Sepals. ND. Corolla. ND. GC. P66 1/2/1845 Listed by Millers, Ramsgate. NK. NK. NK.

DACIA Single. Red/Purple. Tube. Crimson. Short. Sepals. Crimson. Broad. Corolla. Purple veined crimson. Can come Semi Double. B. Cat. 1901. *Bull, W. Chelsea GB. 1901.*

DAISY. Double. Red/Purple. Tube. Scarlet. Sepals. Scarlet. Corolla. Violet Purple. Very Large. JF. Cat. 1912. NK. *GB. 1912.*

DALSTONII. Single. Cream/Red. Tube. Rose buff. Sepals. Yellow, green tips. Corolla. Rosy Carmine. Floral Cabinet Vol 9 P13 1841. GC. P393 Jun 1842 & P98 17/2/1844 Listed by Youell. Gt. Yarmouth. GC. P241 15/4/1843 Listed by F&A Smith, Hackney. GC. P112 17/2/1844 & P66 17/2/1845 Listed by W. Miller, Ramsgate. X Fulgens. *Smith J. Dalston. GB. 1841.*

DAMON. Single. Red/White. Tube. Bright Carmine. Sepals. Bright Carmine. Recurved. Corolla. White. Bell shaped. Petals marked at base with rosy carmine. B. Cat. 1898. *Bull, W. Chelsea. GB. 1898.*

DANDIE DINMOUNT. Single. Red/Purple. Tube. Scarlet. Stout. (Thin). Short. 10mm long.Sepals. Scarlet. 25mm long. Well reflexed. Corolla. Deep Violet. 3rd Ed. by Porcher 1858 Petals folded in and much enveloped by the sepals. GC. P51 26/1/1856. To be sent out in May by W. Fuller, Florist, Newton Bushel former Gardener to W.H. Story. *Story W.H. Newton Abbott, GB. 1856.*

DANDY. Double. Red/Red. Tube. Crimson. Sepals. Crimson. Corolla. Carmine Salmon. Very double. GC. P643 12/7/1862 Awarded FCC at RBS. Exhibition 9/7/1862. GC. P344 11/4/1863 Dwarf 9 to 12 inches high. Constant free flowering. Intro. by G. Smith. *Smith, G. Islington. GB. 1863.*

DANIEL DEFOE. ND. ND/ND. Tube. ND. Sepals. ND. Corolla. ND. GC. P201 27/3/1847 Listed by Hart & Nickling, Guildford. GC.P250 17/4/1847 Listed by J. Hally, Blackheath. NK. *GB. 1846.*

DANIEL LAMBERT. Single. Red/Purple. Tube. Crimson. Sepals. Crimson. Slightly reflexed. Corolla. Rich Purple. Vol P3 J of RHS. 1863. Chiswick Trial 1862. A poor coarse sort, light red, green tipped sepals. Reddish Purple Corolla. P459

44

SG. Dwarf compact habit. P115 4th Ed. by Porcher 1874. GC.P280. 18/4/1857 Intro.by J&C Lee. *Lee J&C, Hammersmith. GB. 1857.*

DANTE. ND. ND/ND. Tube. ND. Sepals. ND. Corolla. ND. GC. P406 2/5/1863 Listed by Wm. Hussy, Norwich. NK. NK. NK.

DANTON. Single. Pink/Purple. Tube. Pale pink. Short. Sepals. Pale pink tinted red at extremities. Corolla. Azure violet. Named after a Minister of Justice during the French Revolution, who was guillotined. L. Cat. 1886. *Aubin, Bagnolet. France. 1884.*

DANUBE BLEU. Double. Red/Purple. Tube. Red. Sepals. Red. Corolla. Dark blue. RB. Cat. 1934. *Rozain, Jr.. Lyons. France. 1929.*

DARING. Single. Red/Purple. Tube. Carmine. Sepals. Carmine. Long and Broad. Reflexing. Corolla. Bluish Plum, tinted rose at base. B. Cat. 1905. *Bull, W. Chelsea. GB. 1905.*

DARLING. Double. Red/Purple. Tube. Bright crimson. Sepals. Bright crimson. Corolla. Violet Purple. Dwarf. Bushy. Bedder.GC. P449 17/7/1852 & P209 26/3/1853 Listed by H. Walton. Burnley. GCX. P211 26/3/185553 Listed by W. Rumley, Richmond. GC. P130 21/2/1853 Raised by J. Smith, Manager to T. Whalley Nurseries, Liverpool. Intro. by E.G.Henderson. *Smith, J. Liverpool GB. 1852.*

D'ARTAGNAN. Single. ND/ND. Tube. ND. Sepals. ND. Corolla. ND. App. to RH. 1851 by Porcher. Vicomte de Bar France. NK. NK. NK.

DAUBENTON. S/Double. Red/Purple. Tube. Brilliant scarlet. Sepals. Brilliant Scarlet. Corolla. Clear Violet. Dwarf compact habit. B. Cat. 1888-1889. *Lemoine, Nancy. France. 1888*

DAUNTLESS. Double. Red/Purple. Tube. Light rosy carmine. Sepals. Light rosy crimson. Corolla. Dark Violet. Short. Dumpy. Very full. B. Cat. 1872. NK. NK. *1872?*

DAVID ALSTON. Double. Red/White. Tube. Carmine. Sepals. Carmine. Corolla. White, suffused rose. JF. Cat. 1921. *Forbes, J. Hawick. GB 1921.*

DAYDAWN. Single. Red/Purple. Tube. Carmine. Sepals. Carmine. Corolla. Pinkish Violet. Laings Cat. circa 1890 NK. NK. NK.

DAY DREAM. Single. Red/Purple. Tube. Crimson. Thick. Short. Sepals. Crimson. Reflexed. Lavender

with crimson base. (Violet Blue). Cup shaped. (Petals very open) P107 4th Edition by Porcher 1874. HC. Cat. P73 1882. GC. P506 18/7/1865. X Beauty. *Banks, E. Deal. GB. 1865?*

DEADÉMONE. Double. Red/White. Tube. Red. Sepals. Red. Corolla. White veined rose. Bushy. Compact. NK. NK. *France. 1893.*

DEANSII Single. Red/Purple. Tube. Crimson. Thick Sepals. Crimson. Corolla. Rosy Purple. Much of the character of Globosa, lacks globular shaped blossoms. GC P509 30/7/1842. Exhibited at Newcastle on Tyne Hort Scty. Listed by Millers Ramsgate P441 1/7/1843. Adv. W. Deans, Jedburgh. GC P82 11/2/1843 Globosa x Fulgens *Deans, W. Newcastle GB. 1842.*

DE CHERVILLE. Double. Red/Pink. Tube. Dark red. Sepals. Dark red. (Rose).Well reflexed. Large. Twisted. Corolla. Dark red. B. Cat. 1898-1899. JF. Cat. 1898. *Lemoine. Nancy. France. 1896.*

DECIMA. Single. Red/Purple. Tube. Rose. Sepals. Rose. Corolla. Violet purple. B. Cat. 1880-1883. *Bull, W. Chelsea. GB. 1880.*

DECORA. Single. Red/Red. Tube. Carmine. Sepals. Carmine. Corolla. Crimson. GC. P112 17/2/1844 & P66 1/2/1845 Listed by W.Miller, Ramsgate. P146 8/3/1845 Listed by Youells, Gt. Yarmouth. GC. P375 4/6/1844 Exhibited by Catleugh HS Show 1844. RH. P24. 1846. GC. P193 30/3/1844. Intro. by J. Smith. *Smith, J. Dalston. GB. 1844.*

DÉESSE. Single. Red/White. Tube. Wine red. Sepals. Wine red. Raised up.. Corolla. White. Cloche shaped. L. Cat. 1890. NK. *France. NK.*

DEFIANCE (a). Single. Red/Purple. Tube. Red. Sepals. Red. Corolla. Purple. GC. P151 5/3/1853 First rate for exhibition. GC. P207 5/3/1852 and P275 1/5/1852 Listed by H.Walton, Burnley. *Mayle. Birmingham. GB.1851?*

DEFIANCE (b). Double. Red/Purple. Tube. Bright scarlet. Sepals. Bright scarlet. Reflexed. Corolla. Dark Violet. Barrel shaped. GC. P144 14/2/1863 Intro. by R. Rea. *Rea, R. Ipswich. GB. 1863.*

DEFIANCE (c). Single. Red/Purple. Tube. Red. Sepals. Red. Corolla. Purple? GC. P375 4/6/1844 Exhibited by J. Smith and Mr.Cole HS Show London. GC.P610 2/9/1843 Practical Floral and Hort Scty of Ireland exhibited by T. Farrell. GC. P441 1/7/1843 Listed by Marnock & Manby. GC.

P98 17/2/1844 Listed by Youell, Gt. Yarmouth. GC. P112 17/2/1844 & P66 1/2/1845 Listed by W. Miller, Ramsgate. GC. P705 1843 Listed by J. Whiteley. Sulcoates, Wakefield. *Smith, J. Dalston GB. 1843.*

DEFIANCE (d). Single. Red/Purple. Tube. Crimson Red. Sepals. Crimson Red. Corolla. Azure violet veined carmine. GO. P141 1891. L. Cat. 1890. *Rozain, Lyons. France. 1890.*

DE GONCOURT. Single. Red/White. Tube. Rosy carmine. (Carmine red). Sepals. Rosy Carmine. (Carmine red). Corolla. Creamy white. Good habit. JF. Cat. 1898. B. Cat. 1898-1899. *Lemoine, Nancy. France. 1896.*

DE JUSSIEUX. Double. ND/ND. Tube. ND. Sepals. ND. Corolla. ND. L. Cat. 1901. *Rozain, Lyons. France. 1898.*

DELACROIX. Double. Red/Red. Tube. Crimson. Sepals. Crimson. Corolla. Wine red. Sombre colouring. L. Cat. 1892. NK. NK. *France. 1890.*

DELICATA (a). Single. Pink/Red. Tube. Pale rose. Sepals.Pale rose. Corolla. Deep red, shaded scarlet. Stiff erect habit. P37 2nd Ed. by Porcher 1848. Small pale green foliage. GC. P97 18/2/1843 & P98 17/2/1844 & P146 8/3/1845 Listed by Youell, Gt. Yarmouth. GC. P641 2/10/1841 Intro. by Standish. *Standish,J. Bagshot. GB. 1841.*

DELICATA (b). Single. Pink/Purple. Tube. Flesh pink. Sepals. Flesh Pink. Green tips. Corolla. Crimson Purple. GC. P184 13/3/1847 Listed by W. Miller, Ramsgate. P216 27/3/1847.GC. P216 27/3/1847 Listed by R. Cooper, Croydon. GC. P161 14/3/1846. Intro. by J Barkway. *Barkway,J. East Dereham. GB. 1846.*

DELICATA (c). Single. White/Purple. Tube. White. Sepals. White. Corolla. Purple. 3 to 4 times the size of "Venus Victrix" GC. P80 6/2/1847 & P216 27/3/1847 & P232 1/4/1848 Listed by R. Cooper, Croydon. GC.P184 13/3/1847 & P250 17/4/1847 Listed by W. Miller, Ramsgate. GCX. P250 17/4/1847 Listed by J. Halley, Blackheath. GC. P97 7/2/1846 Intro. by Newberry. *Newberry, Dorchester. GB. 1846.*

DELICATA (d). Single. White/Red. Tube. White. Sepals. White. Expanded. Corolla. Rose, edged carmine. GC. P450 17/5/1862. Intro. by B.W. Knight, Battle. *Knight, B.W. Battle. GB. 1862.*

DELICATA (e). Single. White/Purple. Tube. White. Sepals. White. Corolla. Pale Pinkish Violet,

margined brilliant carmine. GC. P311 8/9/1877 Exhibited at Trowbridge Hort. Scty.(2nd). GC.P211 17/2/1877. P722 9/6/1877. HC.Cat. 1882 Similar to "Beauty of Wilts". BSW Cat. 1878. GO Select 1880-1888. *Lye, J. Market Lavington. GB. 1877.*

DELICATA (f). Single. ND/ND. Tube. ND. Sepals. ND. Corolla. ND. P30 3rd Ed. by Porcher 1858. *Bell, Thirsk. GB. 1845.*

DELICATA (g). Single. White/Red. Tube. White tinged pink.18mm long. Sepals. White tinged pink. Horizontal. Corolla. Carmine red. P35 and P153 3rd. Ed. by Porcher 1858. *Smith, G. Islington. GB. 1854.*

DELICATISSIMI. Single. White/Purple. Tube. Pale. Short. Sepals. Pale. Tipped Green. Corolla. Purple Crimson. GC. P162 14/3/1846 & P184 13/3/1847 Listed by W. Miller, Ramsgate.GC. P265 24/4/1847 Listed by W. Rendle, Plymouth. App. to RH. 1851 by Porcher 1st Class. GC. P2 8/1/1845 Intro. by Girling. *Girling. Stowmarket. GB. 1845*

DELIGHT (a). ND. ND/ND. Tube. ND. Sepals. ND. Corolla. ND. GC. P154 27/2/1847 Listed by Youells, Gt. Yarmouth. NK. NK. NK.

DELIGHT (b). Single. White/Purple. Tube. Pure white. Half inch long. Bulged. Sepals. Pure white. Reflexed. Spreading 1½". Corolla. Violet Lake. Conical. Deep Lake with whitish base. Drooping. Free Medium size. Pcxi.Vol III J of RHS 1872 Chiswick trials Awarded *** (an improvement on "Duchess of Lancaster"). B. Cat. 1870. *Bull,W. Chelsea? GB. 1870?*

DELIGHT (c). Single. Red/White. Tube. Bright crimson. Sepals. bright crimson. Corolla. Pure white. Few rosy streaks at base. Very Large. Bell shaped. 8 to 10 blooms per joint. Like "Roderic Dhu". Pcxi Vol 3 J of RHS 1872. Vol 4 1877 1st Class Merit. GO "Select". 1880-1886. B. Cat. 1873-1876. GC. P181 7/2/1880 Good market variety. HC. Cat. 1885-1898. P311 RH. 1889 "Select" by E.A. Carrière. GC. P462 5/4/873 Intr. by G. Smith. *Smith G. Isleworth GB. 1873*

DELIGHT (d). Single. White/Red. Tube. Pure White. Sepals. Pure White. Corolla. Pink and Carmine, slightly shaded violet. JF. Cat. 1889. B. Cat. 1889. L. Cat. 1892. *Lye, J. Market Lavington. GB. 1889.*

DÉLOS. Double. Red/White. Tube. Carmine. Sepals. Carmine. Laid on Corolla. Broad. Long. Corolla. Creamy white. Petals fall in tiers. Enormous. L. Cat. 1911. *Lemoine. Nancy. France. 1911.*

DE MERIBEL. ND. Red/Purple. Tube. Bright red. Sepals. Bright red. Well reflexed. Corolla. Rose and Violet. RB. Cat 1885. HC. Cat. 1890. NK. NK. NK.

DÉMOSTHÈNE (a). Single. Red/White. Tube. Red. Sepals. Red. Corolla. White. Very large. Very much expanded. Appx. to 4th Ed. by Porcher 1874. New variety by Lemoine for 1875. (Different to 1878 cultivar) ? error by Porcher. *Lemoine. Nancy. France. 1875.*

DÉMOSTHÈNE(b), Double. Red/Purple. Tube. Red. Sepals. Red. Corolla. Mauve (Deep violet mauve) GO. "Select" 1880-1886. HC. Cat. 1882 JF. Cat. 1885. BSW. Cat. 1878. *Lemoine. Nancy. France. 1878.*

DE MONTALIVET. Double. Red/Purple. Tube. Rose. Sepals. Outer yellowish rose, inner rosy carmine. Reflexed. Short. Corolla. Clear Violet flaked rose. Outer petals dark rose. (Deep blue marked carmine). HC. Cat. 1882-1898. Small flowers very double. B. Cat. 1879-1880. *Lemoine, Nancy. France. 1879.*

DENNISIANA. Single. White/Red. Tube. White. Sepals. Whitish pink. Corolla. Cerise shaded vermilion. P37 2nd Ed. by Porcher 1848. GC. P112 17/2/1844 and P66 1/2/1845 Listed by W. Miller, Ramsgate. *Dennis. GB. 1843.*

DÉPUTÉ BERLET. Double. Red/Purple. Tube. Red. Sepals. Red. Corolla Reddish Violet. Globular. Full. Free. GO. "Select" 1883-1891. HC. Cat. 1882. Laings cat. circa 1890. *Lemoine. Nancy. France. 1881.*

DÉPUTÉ TEUTSCH. Single. Red/Red. Tube. Vermillion red. Long 5cms. Sepals. Vermillion red. Sepals bent in. Corolla. Amarinth red. Best outside. P107 4th Ed. by Porcher 1874. *Lemoine. Nancy. France. 1874.*

DE QUATREFAGES. Double. Red/Purple. Tube. Clear red. Sepals. Clear red. Uplifted. Reflexed. Large. Corolla. Violet marbled pink. (Violet marbled rose). Very large. Very full. JF. Cat. 1893. B. Cat. 1892. L. Cat. 1892. *Lemoine. Nancy. France. 1892.*

DE SAINT-HILAIRE. Double. Red/White. Tube. Carmine. Sepals. Carmine. Corolla. White, veined carmine. L. Cat. 1909. *Rozain. Lyons. France. 1909*

DES FRANCAISE. Single. ND/ND. Tube. ND. Sepals. ND. Corolla. ND. GC. P201 27/3/1847 Listed by Hart & Nicklin, Guildford. NK. NK. NK.

DESDEMONA. Single. Pink/Red. Tube. Pale peachy flesh. (Light rose). Sepals. Pale peachy flesh. (Light rose). Corolla. Light ruby. GC. P423 7/7/1849. Exhibited at Australian Bot and Hort Scty. 1/3/1849. GC. P66 1/2/1845 & P184 13/3/1847 Listed by Millers, Ramsgate. Harrisons, Dereham List 1845. *Harrison, Dereham. GB. 1844.*

DESIDERATA. Double. Red/Purple. Tube. Scarlet. Sepals. Scarlet. Well reflexed. Corolla. Bright blue shaded mauve. Round flower buds. GC. Vol 26 1886 RHS Trials at Chiswick 31/7/1886. HC. Cat. 1882-1885. Illustrated page 68(1882). *Henderson, E.G.St. Johns Wood. GB. NK.*

DESIDERATUM. Double. Red/White. Tube. Deep scarlet. Sepals. Deep scarlet. Well reflexed. Corolla. Deep blush white. Edges of petals frilled. Very Double. P136 4th Ed. Porcher 1874 Appendix new for 1874. GC. P363 31/3/1874 B&S Williams. *Bland, E. Fordham. GB.1874.*

DE TOLLENAÈRE. ND. ND/ND. Tube. ND. Sepals. ND. Corolla. ND. GC. P406 2/5/1863 Listed by Wm. Hussey, Norwich. NK. NK. NK.

DEUIL DE L'AMIRAL COURBET. Double. Red/Purple. Tube. Bright coral. Short. Sepals. Bright coral. Large. Long. Corolla. Violet flamed red. Expanded. L. Cat. 1886. *Rozain, Lyons. France. 1886.*

DEUTSCHER KAISER. Double. Red/Red. Tube. Bright red. Sepals. Bright red. Partially reflexed. Corolla. Rosy crimson. (Purplish red). Very large. Habit strong, drooping and straggling. P69 J of RHS 1877 Vol 4. No award. Flowers produced in huge bunches. HC. Cat. 1882-1890. GC. P505 15/4/1876 Germania X. NK. *Germany. 1875.*

DEVONIANA. Single. ND/ND. Tube. ND. Sepal. ND. Corolla. ND. P97 18/2/1843. Listed by Youell, Gt. Yarmouth. GC. P112 17/2/1844 &P66 1/2/1845 Listed byv W. Miller, Ramsgate. GC. P289 29/5/1841 Listed by Hugh Low, Upper Clapton. NK. NK. NK.

DEVONIENSIS. Single. Red/Purple. Tube. Scarlet. Short. Sepals. Scarlet. Corolla. Light Violet. GC. P545 30/8/1851 Listed by G. Smith. GC P274 3/5/1851 Intro. by Veitch, Exeter. *Story W.H. Newton Abbot. GB. 1851.*

DE WITTE. Single. Red/White. Tube. Scarlet. Sepals. Scarlet. Well reflexed. Twisted. (Bright red). Corolla. White veined carmine. Long. JF. Cat. 1907. L. Cat. 1906. *Rozain, Lyons. France 1906.*

D. FOURNIER. Double. Pink/Pink. Tube. Pink. Sepals. Silvery pink. Short. Broad. Horizontal. Corolla. Silvery pink. Voluminous. L. Cat. 1906. *Lemoine, Nancy. France. 1905.*

DIADEM (a). Single. Red/Purple. Tube. Rich crimson. Sepals. Rich crimson. Corolla. Dark purple. Fine shape. CG. Vol 6 P272 Mr. Turner showed this variety, an improvement on the reds. Sepals reflex like a Martagen lily. GC. P727 Nov. 1851 Awarded Certificate by National Floral Committee, Nov 1851. GC. P449 17/7/1852 Listed by H. Walton, Burnley. GC. P223 10/4/1852 Intro. by C. Turner, Slough. *Banks, E. Deal. GB. 1852.*

DIADEM (b). Double. Red/Purple. Tube. Crimson red. Short. Thick Sepals. Crimson red. Large. Well reflexed. Turned up points. Corolla. Dark Violet with vermillion feather. Petals expanded but a "little short". Very full. P122 4th Ed. by Porcher 1874. Vol 2 J of RHS 1870 Trials. Passed over. GC. P289 1/4/1865 Intro. by G. Smith. *Smith G. Islington. GB. 1865.*

DIADEM (c). Single. White/Purple. Tube. Blush. Sepals. Blush. Corolla. Pale Magenta broadly edged brilliant carmine. GC. Vol 24 P277 1885 "New for 1886". B. Cat. 1888-1893. Laings Cat. circa 1890. JF. Cat. 1886. (Seedling no 3). *Lye, J. Market Lavington. GB. 1886.*

DIADEM OF FLORA. Single. White/Red. Tube. White. Thin. 25mm long. Sepals. White. Large. Open. Points turned up. Corolla. Vermilion Carmine. Very long style. PP153 3rd Ed. by Porcher 1858. GC. P706 9/11/1850 & P207 27/3/1852 Listed by H. Walton, Burnley. GC.P647 11/10/1851 Exhibited at RHS of Cornwall Show 8/9/1851 by F.H. Earle of Falmouth. GC P144 8/3/1851 Listed by W. Rumley Plymouth. GC. P289 11/5/1850. Intro. by Mayle. *Mayle. Birmingham. GB. 1850*

DIADÈME (a). Double. Red/White. Tube. Carmine rose. Thin. Long 12 mms. Sepals. Carmine rose. Large. Reflexing. Corolla. White, striped carmine at base. Full. P128 4th Ed. by Porcher 1874. *Demay, H. Arras. France. 1873.*

DIADÈME (b). Double. Red/White. Tube. Red. Sepals. Red. Horizontal. Corolla. Milk white. Large. Fully double. L. Cat. 1892. *Rozain, Lyons. France. 1891.*

DIAMANT. Double. Red/White. Tube. Bright pink. Sepals. Bright pink. Corolla White. Broad petals. JF. Cat. 1904. L. Cat. 1902. *Rozain, Lyons. France. 1902.*

DIAMOND JUBILEE. Single. Red/Purple Tube. Red. Sepals. Red. Corolla. Purple. Exhibited at Bath 1898 by G. Tucker, 1st 9 pot class. G. Vol 55 28/1/1899. GC. Vol 23 P170 27/8/1898 Trowbridge Hort. Scty Show 17/8/1898. Exhibited by G. Tucker, 1st 6 pot class. *Tucker, G. GB. 1897*

DIAMOND. Single. White/Purple. Tube. White. Sepals. White. Reflexed. Corolla. Rosy lilac. Introduced after the death of W. Miller by his successor. GC. P161. 17/3/1849 Listed by W. Rumley, Richmond. GC. P281 29/4/1848 Intro. by J.G. Hine. Ramsgate. *Miller, W. Ramsgate GB. 1848*

DIANA (a). Single. White/Red. Tube. White. Sepals. White. Corolla. Scarlet flushed crimson. GC. P535 23/8/1851 Exhibited at Vauxhall Garden Show. App. to RH. 1851 by Porcher. GC. P689 3/11/1849 Intro. by W. Gregory. *Gregory, W. Cirencester. GB. 1849.*

DIANA (b). Single. Pink/Purple. Tube. Pink. Sepals. Pink. Long. Horizontally extended. Corolla. Plum, marked rose pink at base. B. Cat. 1901. *Bull W., Chelsea. GB. 1901*

DICKENS. Single. Red/Purple. Tube. Carmine. Sepals. Carmine. Corolla. Dark violet. In the form of "Formosa Elegans", but excels it, in form and colour. Listed by W. Miller, Ramsgate GC P 66 1/2/1845 & P184 13/3/1847. RH. P23 1846 GC. P241 20/4/1844, Intro. by J. Ingram. *Ingram J., Southampton. GB. 1844.*

DICKSONII Single. ND/ND. Tube. ND. Sepals. ND. Corolla. ND. GC. P393 16/6/1842 & GC.P98 17/2/1844 Listed by Youell, Gt. Yarmouth. P29 3rd Ed. by Porcher 1858. *Dickson, Edinburgh. GB. 1843.*

DICTATOR (a). Single. Red/Purple. Tube. Crimson. Sepals. Crimson. Corolla. Violet Purple. "Largest and finest single ever offered" GC. P402 3/5/1862 Not being sent out as plant has wintered badly. GC P65 25/1/1862 *Smith, G. Isleworth. GB. 1862.*

DICTATOR (b). Single. Red/Purple. Tube. Bright red. Sepals. Bright red. Completely reflexed tipped green. Corolla. Bright Violet plum, marked rose base. Large. P115 4th Ed. by Porcher 1874 "Not in first selection". Vigourous. Likes sun. GC. P476 15/4/1871. B. Cat. 1872-1876. *Bull, W. Chelsea, GB. 1871.*

DIDO. Single. Pink/Red. Tube. Flesh. Sepals. Flesh. Corolla. Orange crimson. RH. P24 1846. *Salter, Versailles. France. 1845.*

DIDON. Double. Red/Purple. Tube. Cerise. Sepals. Cerise. Corolla. Dark Blue. Laings Cat. circa 1890. L. Cat. 1885. *Rozain, Lyons. France.1885.*

DIE JUNGFRAU. Double. ND/ND. Tube. ND. Sepals. ND. Corolla. ND. Haage & Schmidt, Erfurt. Cat. 1880. NK. NK. *Germany.* NK.

DIOMEDE. Single. Red/Purple. Tube. Red. Sepals. Red. Corolla. Purple. GC. P146 8/3/1845 listed by Youells, Gt. Yarmouth NK. NK. NK.

DIONE. Single. Red/Purple. Tube. Rosy crimson. Short. Sepals. Rosy crimson. Horizontal. Corolla. Bluish purple marked rose at base. Fully expanded B. Cat. 1873-1876. *Bull, W. Chelsea. GB. 1873.*

DIRECTEUR POYARD. ND. Red/White. Tube. Reddish Purple. Sepals. Reddish purple. Corolla. Pure white, veined rose at base. Large. L. Cat. 1906. JF. Cat. 1907. *Rozain, Lyons. France. 1906.*

DISPLAY (a). Single. Red/Red. Tube. Scarlet. Sepals. Scarlet. Corolla. Deep rose. Free. Laings Cat. circa 1890. HC. Cat. 1882-1885. NK. NK. NK.

DISPLAY (b). Double. Red/Purple. Tube. Rose. Sepals. Rose. Corolla. Lavender Blue. Very full double. Large and flat. B. Cat. 1870-1872. *Bull, W. Chelsea. GB. 1869.*

DISTINCTION (a). Single. Red/Purple. Tube. Coral. Short. Sepals. Coral. Broad. Expanded. Corolla. Purple. Widely expanded. RHS Journal P78 22/9/1859 Floral Committee. *Ivery. Dorking. GB. 1859.*

DISTINCTION (b). Double. Red/Purple. Tube. Lake red. Sepals. Lake red. Corolla. Purple Violet with lavender stripes. P79 Witte 1882. *Demay, H. Arras. Belgium. 1878.*

DISTINCTUS. Single. Red/Purple. Tube. Rosy red. Small. Sepals. Rosy red. Long. Reflexed. Corolla. Deep violet blue. Short. GC.P465 27/7/1850 Listed by G. Smith, Islington. GC. 465 27/7/1850 & P144 8/3/1851 by W. Rumley, Richmond.. GC. P658 20/10/1849 Intro by W. Rumley to be released May 1850. *Rumley, W. Richmond. GB. 1850.*

DOCTEUR BOISDUVAL. Single. Red/Purple. Tube. Reddish purple. Thick. 18/20 mm long. Sepals. Reddish purple. Horizontal. Corolla. ND. Petals 20mm long. Bell shaped. Expanded. P153 3rd. Ed. by Porcher 1858. Introduced into commerce in 1857 by M. Buril of Paris. *Duru, Ville D'Avry. France. 1857.*

DOCTEUR COMPIN. ND. ND/ND. Tube. ND. Sepals. ND. Corolla. ND. Boucharlet Cat. 1883. *Boucharlet, Lyons. France. 1883.*

DOCTEUR LACROZE. Single. Red/Purple. Tube. Carmine red. Strong. 15/20 mm long. Sepals. Carmine red. Horizontal. Short. Corolla. Purple. P154 3rd Ed. by Porcher 1858 Tube and sepals are of the same colour as "Comte de Beaulieu" *Narcis, Evry. France. 1855.*

DOCTEUR KERNER. ND. ND/ND. Tube. ND. Sepals. ND. Corolla. ND. RH. P295 1887 "Fuchsias grown as standards at Twickel". NK. NK. NK.

DOCTOR FENZL. Double. Red/Purple. Tube. Red. Sepals. Red. Corolla. Purple P126 4th. Ed. by Porcher 1874. Not in the first selection. NK. NK. NK.

DOCTOR JEPHSON. Single. White/Red. Tube. White. Sepals White. Corolla. Rich rose. Coloured plate in Maunds Botanic Garden P1037 Vol 11. GC. P423 7/7/1849 Exhibited at Australian Bot. & Hort.Scty. Show, Sydney. 1/3/1849. GC. P808 Nov 1846 "Recommended". GC. P140 27/2/1847 Good light variety. GC. P184 13/3/1847 & P250 17/4/1847 Listed by W. Miller, Ramsgate. GC. P216 27/3/1847 & P232 1/4/1848 & P256 21/4/1849 Listed by R. Cooper, Croydon. GC. P265 24/4/1847 & P259 28/4/1849 & P241 20/4/1850 Listed by W. Rendle, Plymouth. GC. P249 18/4/1846 Raised by the gardener to Dr. Jephson and introduced by J. Cullis, Leamington. NK. *Leamington. GB. 1846.*

DOCTEUR WIRTGEN. Single. Red/Purple. Tube. Reddish Purple. Thick. 15mm long. Sepals. Reddish purple. Large. Horizontal. Corolla. Violet purple. Foliage is clear green 8cm x 6cm. P154 3rd. Ed. by Porcher 1858. *Dender, Coblenz. Germany. 1856.*

DOEL'S FAVOURITE. Single. Red/Purple. Tube. Red. Sepals. Red. Corolla. Purple. GC. P280 1/9/1883 Exhibited by J. Lye, Pocock, and G. Tucker at Trowbridge. G. 6/9/1884 ditto. GC. Vol 26 P375 18/9/1886 Exhibited at Bath. by J. Lye and G. Tucker. *Doel. GB. 1860?.*

DOLLAR PRINZESSIN. Double. Red/Purple. Tube. Carmine Red. Sepals. Carmine Red. Corolla. Dark violet. Medium Size. Market variety. Bruiant, Poitiers Cat. 1911. L. Cat. 1912. *Kroger. Germany. 1910.*

DOMINGO. Double. Red/Purple. Tube. Deep crimson. (Crimson red). Sepals. Deep crimson. Completely reflexed round. Corolla. Purplish crimson, striped rose.(Violet blue washed rose). Long pedicel 60 mms. 4th Ed. by Porcher 1874. B. Cat. 1872-1876. Troubador X. GC. P502 13/4/1872 Intro. by Wm. Bull. *Bull, W. Chelsea. GB. 1872.*

DOMINIANA. Single. Red/Red. Tube. Red. Long. Sepals. Red. Corolla. Red. GC. P370 12/6/1854 Raised by Mr. Dominy, foreman at Veitch's Exeter Nurseries. Winter flowering. Intro. by Veitch. GC.P315 12/5/1855 Listed by Veitch. GC. P3688 26/5/1855 Listed by E.G. Henderson. GC. P547 11/8/1855 & P208 22/3/1856 Listed by Bainbridge & Hewison, York. GC. P314 10//5/1856 Listed by W. Rumley, Richmond. GC. P824 8/9/1860 Listed by F. Goodwin, Sheffield. P68 Vol 4 J of RHS 1877 Fuchsia trials 1873. No award. A vigorous growing hybrid, not well known. It is very distinct and handsome, and best adapted for planting out in a cool conservatory. HC. Cat 1882. For cultivation for winter blooms see Vol 33 The Garden 1888. Jf. Cat 1885. F.Serratifolia x F. Spectablis. *Dominy, Exeter. GB. 1854.*

DON GIOVANNI (a). Single. Red/Purple. Tube. Crimson. Short. Fat. Sepals. Crimson. Reflexed. Corolla. Violet Purple. App. to RH. 1851 by Porcher. Style red. Large Foliage. GC. P465 27/7/1850 & P144 8/3/1851 Listed by W. Rumley, Richmond. GC. P241 20/4/1859 Intro. by E.G. Henderson. *Henderson E.G. St.Johns Wood. GB. 1850*

DON GIOVANNI (b). Single. Red/Purple. Tube. Red. Sepals. Red. Straight back. Corolla. Rose Lavender. (Violet rose). Bell Shaped. GC. P55 19/1/1867 Review by Cannell. One of the best for small pots. PP152 3rd Ed. by Porcher 1858 Resembles "Clapton Hero". CG P492 1865. P107 4th Ed. by Porcher 1874. *Banks, E. Deal GB. 1864.*

DON PEDRO. Double. Red/Purple. Tube red. Sepals. Red. Twisted in a spiral and adhere to corolla. Corolla. Purple. P126 4th. Edition by Porcher 1874. Not in the first selection. The flower has little grace. *Twrdy, Brno. Austria. 1872.*

DONNA JOAQUINA, Single. Red/Purple. Tube. Scarlet crimson. Short and Thick. Sepals. Scarlet crimson. Reflexed. Corolla. Violet Blue. P155 3rd Ed. by Porcher 1858. Colour of corolla is the same shade as "Omega" and "Duke of Wellington" GC. P451 5/7/1856 & P642 27/9/1856 Listed by H. Walton, Burnley. GC. P497 26/7/1856 Listed by Fowle & Son, Brixton. GC. P251 11/4/1857 Listed by W. Masters, Canterbury. GC. P283 25/4/1857 Listed by W. Cutbush, Highgate. GC. P114 23/2/1856 Intro. by E.G. Henderson, St. Johns Wood. *Banks, E. Deal. GB. 1856.*

D'ORBIGNY. Double. Red/Purple. Tube. Bright carmine. Sepals. Bright carmine. Reflexed. Corolla. Amaranth Violet. R.B. Laird ,Murrayfield Cat. NK. NK. *France. NK.*

DORCAS. Single. Red/Purple. Tube. Rosy carmine. Short. Sepals. Rosy carmine. Corolla. Soft Bluish Purple. Veined and shaded rose. B. Cat. 1888-1893. *Bull, W. Chelsea. GB. 1887?*

DORIS. Double. Red/Purple. Tube. Coral Red. Sepals. Coral Red. Horizontal. Corolla. Reddish Violet margined blue. Immense. B. Cat. 1898-1901. GC. Vol 19 P579 5/1896.Intro. by W. Bull. *Bull, W. Chelsea. GB. 1896.*

DOROTHY FRY. S/Double. Red/White. Tube. Carmine red. Sepals. Carmine red. Recurved. Corolla. Pure white. Very large. Described as both single and double. G. Vol 35 P567 15/6/1889 FCC. RHS. GO.1890 "New fuchsias of 1889". Laings Cat. circa 1890. L. Cat 1892. Dobbies Cat. 1892-1894. B. Cat. 1892. *Fry G.B. Lee. GB. 1889.*

DRAME. S/Double. Red/Purple. Tube. Bright Red. Sepals. Bright Red. Reflexed. Corolla. Clear Violet. (Purple). P149 Gartenflora 1888 New from Lemoine. Riccartonii X. *Lemoine, Nancy. France. 1887.*

DR. A. WATELLE. ND. Pink/Purple, Tube. Pink. Sepals. Pink. Corolla. Rosy lilac. Fine habit. Free blooming. Dobbies Cat 1893-1894. NK. NK. NK.

DR. BEHRING. Double. Red/Red. Tube. Wine red. (Rose). Sepals. Wine red. (Rose). Turned back. Corolla. Puce. (Red). Large and Full. Named after a German Bacteriologist who discovered the diptheria and tetanus antitoxins',and was awarded the first Nobel peace prize in medicine in 1901. (1854-1917). L. Cat. 1902. JF. Cat. 1904. *Lemoine, Nancy. France. 1902.*

DR. BORNET. Double. Red/Purple. Tube. Carmine rose. Sepals. Carmine Rose. Broad. Long. Horizontal. Corolla. Plum mingled with pinkish mauve. Spreading. Full. L. Cat 1912. *Lemoine, Nancy. France. 1912.*

DR. CREVAUX. Double. Red/Purple. Tube. Dark red. Sepals. Dark red. Corolla. Reddish violet. (Coppery violet). BSW. Cat. 1888. Laings Cat. circa 1890. (Possibly incorrectly named, should be Dr. Cremanieux of Nancy). *Lemoine, Nancy. France. 1880.*

DREAM. Single. Red/Red. Tube. Red. Sepals. Red. Corolla. Rose pink. RB. Cat. 1937. NK. NK. NK. NK.

DR. FOURNIER. Double. Red/Pink. Tube. Red. Sepals. Red.Short. Large. Horizontal. Corolla. Silvery rose. Voluminous. Kelways, Langport Cat. 1906/7. Bruant, Poitieres Cat.1911. NK. NK. *France.* NK.

DR. GODRON. Single. Red/Red. Tube. Brilliant purplish rose. 4 inches long. Sepals. Orange. Yellow tipped. Corolla. Rich orange vermillion. Drooping flowers. Name sometimes given as Dr. Gordon. Dr. Godson. B. Cat. 1878-1881. HC. Cat. P78.1880. Dominiana x Serratifolia. *Lemoine, Nancy. France. 1878.*

DR. GROSSE. Single. Pink/Red. Tube. Pale flesh. Long. Sepals. Pale flesh. Reflexed. Corolla. Carmine red. Bell shaped. Style whitish. App. to RH. 1851 by Porcher. GC. P423 6/1851 Exhibited RBS Show by H. Low. GC. P279 30/4/1853 Light green stemmed. GC. P465 27/8/1850. Listed by G. Smith, Islington. *Kendall, GB. 1850.*

DR. HESSLE. Single. Red/Purple. Tube. Deep carmine. Sepals. Deep carmine. Well refexed. Corolla. Rich purple violet. (Dark violet blue shaded red at base) Expanded. P107 4th Ed. by Porcher 1874. HC. Cat. 1882. GC. P396 22/3/1873 Intro. by B.S. Williams. *Bland E, Fordham. GB. 1873.*

DR. JOHANNSEN. Double. Red/Purple. Tube. Carmine red. Sepals. Carmine red. Rise up. Corolla. Plum Violet. Large. Full. L. Cat. 1906. *Lemoine, Nancy. France. 1904.*

DR. KITTO GIDDINGS. Single. Red/Purple. Tube. Red. Sepals. Red. Corolla. Satiny Purple. Exceeds "Lord Warden" in beauty. GO.1880-1884 "Select". HC. Cat. 1882. GC. Vol 26 P403 1/5/1886 Good kind. BSW. Cat. 1878. *Banks, E. Deal. GB. 1878?*

DR. LINDLEY. Single. Red/Purple. Tube. Deep crimson. Sepals. Deep crimson. Broad and expanded. Corolla. Deep purple. Florist Sept 1852. FCC. Nat Flor. Scty. GC P824 27/6/1885 RHS Trials "Best in class". GC. P535 20/8/1853 Seen at C. Turners Nursery, Slough - of the darks this was the best, being robust with well contrasted colours, the corolla retaining its rich violet hue for a much longep time than is usual. GC. P385 18/6/1843 Listed by W.Rumley, Richmond. GC. P465 23/7/1853 Listed by J. Harrison, Darlington. GC. P483 30/7/1853 & P162 18/3/1854 Listed by H. Walton, Burnley. GC.

P627 1/10/1853 Listed by S. Fenney, Gateshead. GC. P213 8//4/1854 Listed by H. Gardiner, Maidstone. GC. P293 21/4/1854 Listed by Hart & Nicklen, Guildford. GC. P337 28/5/1853 Intro. by Bass & Brown, Sudbury. *Banks E. Deal. GB. 1853*

DR. LIVINGSTONE. Single. White/Purple. Tube. Clear delicate blush white. Sepals. Blush white. White on underside. Recurved. Corolla. Violet rose shading blush at base. Habit of "Silver Swan". Free. Requires pinching. CG & JH P361 1961 "Select 12". GC. P360 30/6/1860. Listed by F. Godwin, Sheffield. GC. P215 10/3/1860 Intro. by E.G. Henderson. *Banks,E. Deal. GB. 1860.*

DR. NOBLE. ND. ND/ND. Tube. ND. Sepals. ND. Corolla. ND. GC. P389 8/6/1844 Listed by T. Cripps, Maidstone. NK. NK. NK.

DR. NOEL-MARTIN. Double. Red/Pink. Tube. Red. (Flesh pink). Sepals. Red. (Flesh pink). Corolla. Rose veined carmine. (Flesh pink. Exterior veined pink at edges). JF. Cat. 1900. *Rozain. Lyons. France. 1899.*

DR. PRILLIEUX. Double. Red/Purple. Tube. Bright Scarlet. Sepals. Bright scarlet. Recurved. Corolla. Dark Violet. Uniform.GO. P141 1891. L. Cat. 1892. B. Cat. 1892. *Lemoine. Nancy. France. 1890.*

DR. SANKEY. Single. Red/White. Tube. Bright red. Sepals. Bright red. Corolla. White. Similar but distinct to "Madame Thibaut". Long pendulous blooms. GC. Vol 26 RHS Trials Chiswick 26/7/1886. GC P152 29/1/1887 Good sort. JF. Cat 1885. *Eckford. GB. 1883?*

DR. SMITH. Single. Red/Purple. Tube. Red. Short. Thin. Sepals. Red. Long. Reflexed. Corolla. Violet Purple. (Violet blue). App. to RH. 1851 by Porcher. 1st. class variety. GC. P161 17/3/1849 Listed by W. Rumley, Richmond. GC. P224 14/4/1849 Listed by Bass & Brown,Sudbury. GC. P224 14/4/1849 Listed by R. Whibley, Kennington Cross.GC. P 256 21/4/1849 Listed by R. Cooper, Croydon. GC. P274 5/5/1849 Listed by H. Walton, Burnley. GC.P112 12/2/1848 Purchased from a Mr. Michie and intro. by G. Smith, Islington. X Corallina. *Michie. GB. 1848.*

DR. TOPINARD. Single. Red/White. Tube. Cerise red. Sepals. Cerise red. Corolla. White veined with rose at base.. Petals evenly extended. B. Cat. 1892-1893. L. Cat. 1892. *Lemoine, Nancy. GB. 1890.*

DR. WOLF. ND. Red/ND. Tube. Red. Sepals. Red. Corolla. ND. GC. P184 13/3/1847. Listed by W. Miller, Ramsgate. *Nicholls GB. 1846.*

DREADNOUGHT (a). Single. Red/Purple. Tube. Red. Sepals. Red. Long. Horizontal. Corolla. Reddish crimson. GC. P537 12/8/1848 Listed by G. Smith.. GC. P224 14/4/1849 Listed by R. Whibley, Kennington. GC. P274 5/5/1849 Listed by H.Walton,Burnley. GC. P241 20/4/19850 Listed by W. Rendle, Plymouth. App. to RH. 1851 by Porcher. P156 3rd Ed. by Porcher 1858. GC. P153 4/3/1848. Named after revolutionary battleship of times. Intro. by Kendall, Stoke Newington. *Proctor. GB. 1848.*

DREADNOUGHT (b). Double. Red/Purple. Tube. Red. Bulged.½" long. Sepals. Red. Broad, waxy and reflexed. Corolla. Rich violet. (Reddish Purple). P115 4th Ed. by Porcher 1874 Not in the first selection. Pcvv Vol 3 J of RHS 1872 A coarse and inferior variety. GC. P122 10/2/1866 Intro. by G. Smith. *Smith,G. Isleworth GB. 1866.*

DREADNOUGHT (c). Double. Red/Purple. Tube. Bright crimson. Sepals. Bright crimson. Corolla. Purple. (Blush violet washed red). P122 4th. Ed. by Porcher 1874. B. Cat 1870-1872. GC. P451 2/4/1870 Intro by Felton & Son, Birmingham. *Felton, Birmingham GB. 1870.*

D.T. FISH. Single. Red/Purple. Tube. Red. Sepals. Red. Corolla. Purple. GO. 1880. "Select" NK. NK. NK.

DUC D' AUMALE. Double. Red/White. Tube. Bright red. Sepals. Bright red. Large. Corolla. White suffused salmon. G. Vol.52 P198 11/9/1887. JF. Cat. 1898. B. Cat. 1898-1899. L. Cat. 1901. *Lemoine, Nancy. France. 1896.*

DUC D'ARENBURG. ND. ND/ND. Tube. ND. Sepals. ND. Corolla. ND. P311 RH 1889. "Select" by E. A. Carrière. NK. NK. NK.

DUC DE BRABANT. ND. Red/Purple. Tube. Red. Sepals. Red. Recurved. Corolla. Purple. Small. Vol P3 J of RHS 1863 Fuchsia Trial 1862. RH. P295 1887 Grown as a standard at Twickel(Nr. Arnhem). Intro. by H. Low. *Cornelissen,Arras, Belgium. NK.*

DUC DE CRILLON. Double. Red/Purple. Tube. Red. Sepals. Red. Corolla. Purple. P126 4th Ed. by Porcher 1874. *Cornelissen, Arras. Belgium. 1866.*

DUC DE TREVISE. Double. Red/Purple. Tube. Red. Sepals. Red. Reflexed. Corolla. Purple striped red. Rather small. Compact. Vol P3 J of RHS 1863 P90.

Free blooming. GC. P824 8/9/1860 Listed by F. Godwin, Sheffield. *Cornelissen, Arras, Belgium. 1859.*

DUCHESSE DE GEROLSTEIN. ND. White/ND. Tube. White. Sepals. White. P120 4th Ed. by Porcher 1874. Not in the first selection. *Lemoine, Nancy. France. 1868.*

DUCHESSE OF MONTPENSIER. Single. Pink/Purple. Tube. Pale pink. Large. Sepals. Pale pink. Large. Only spread a little. Green tips. Corolla. Violet edged carmine. App. to RH. 1851 by Porcher. *Racine. France. NK.*

DUCHESS OF ALBANY. Single. White/Red. Tube. White. Sepals. White. Corolla. Rosy red. Fine shape. GC. Vol 1 29/1/1887 Good. JF. Cat. 1885. *Lye, J. Market Lavington. GB. 1885.*

DUCHESS OF BORDEAUX. Single. White/Red. Tube. White. Sepals. Rose. Reflexed. Corolla. Scarlet. Flowers until January. Similar to "Blanche Perfection" but it carries its flowers better, and has brigher colours. P168 RH. 1857. App. to RH. 1851 by Porcher.LGC. P 144 8/3/1851 Listed by W. Rumley, Richmond. GC. P465 27/7/1850. Intro. by G. Smith, Islington. *Meillez. France 1850.*

DUCHESS OF EDINBURGH. Double. Red/White. Tube. Carmine. Sepals. Carmine. Broad. Completely reflexed. Corolla. White, suffused and marked rose at base. B. Cat. 1892-1893. BSW. Cat. 1897. Dobbies Cat. 1893. Mrs. E. G. Hill X Molesworth. *Rundle, G. Molesworth. GB. 1892.*

DUCHESS OF FIFE. S/Double. Red/White. Tube. Light red. Sepals. Light red. Small. Reflexed. Corolla. White, slightly shaded red. Very free. Dobbies Cat. 1893-1894. *Lye, J. Market Lavington. GB. 1892.*

DUCHESS OF GLOUCESTER. Single. ND/ND. Tube. ND. Sepals. ND. Corolla. ND. GC. P98 17/2/1844 Listed by Youells, Gt. Yarmouth. GC P112 17/2/1844 Listed by W. Miller, Ramsgate. *Standish, J Bagshot. GB. 1843?*

DUCHESS OF KENT (a). ND. ND/ND. Tube. ND. Sepals. ND. Corolla. ND. G. P151 13/8/1892 Mentioned in G. Fry's lecture to the RHS. Mr. Bunyars, the Chairman, stated his grandfather raised the above, many years ago. It was a chance seedling, and was tended by his gardener, who is still in his employ 45 years later. GC. P250 27/4/1847 Listed by Millers, Ramsgate. GC. P259 28/4/1849 & P241 20/4/1850 Listed by W. Rendle, Plymouth. P34 3rd Ed. by Porcher 1858. *Ivery. GB. NK.*

52

DUCHESS OF KENT (b). Single. White/Red. Tube. Blush. Sepals. Blush, tipped green. Corolla. Vermillion. GC. P545 30/8/1851 Listed by G. Smith. GC. P177 20/3/1852 Listed by W. Rumley, Richmond. GC. P209 5/4/1851 Listed by C. Turner, Slough. *Knight, B.W., Battle.? GB. 1850.*

DUCHESS OF KENT (c). Single. White/Purple. Tube. Pure white. Sepals. Pure white. Gracefully recurved. Corolla. Dark rosy purple. GC. P450 17/3/1862. Intro. by B. W. Knight. *Knight, B W. Battle. GB. 1862.*

DUCHESS OF LANCASTER. Single. White/Purple. Tube. Pure white. 1" long. Sepals. Pure white. Reflexed round. Corolla. Deep rose, shaded violet. Vol P3 J of RHS 1863 P91 Chiswick trials. Awarded *. A useful variety. P156 3rd Ed. by Porcher 1858 Superceeds "Englands Glory". P116 4th Ed. by Porcher 1874. Yellowish green foliage GC. P385 18/6/1853 & P147 11/3/1854 Listed by Wm. Rumley, Richmond. GC. P483 30/7/1853 & P162 18/3/1854 Listed by H. Walton, Burnley. GC. P529 30/7/1853 Listed by Youell, Gt. Yarmouth. GC. P627 1/10/1853 Listed by S. Fenney, Gateshead. GC. P213 8/4/1854 Listed by C.H. Gardiner, Maidstone. GC. P240 15/4/1854 Listed by Mitchell & Co. Brighton. GC. P249 21/4/1854 Listed by Hart & Nicklin Guildford. Raised in Lancaster. GC. P226 9/4/1853 Intro. E.G. Henderson. NK, *Lancaster. GB. 1853.*

DUCHESS OF NORTHUMBERLAND. Single. ND ND/ND. Tube. ND. Sepals. ND. Corolla. ND. GC P177 20/3/1852 Listed by Wm. Rumley, Richmond.NK. NK. NK.

DUCHESS OF SUTHERLAND. Single. White/Purple. Tube. Flesh. Sepals. Flesh. Corolla. Rosy Purple. GC. P820 Dec 1844 Recommended. GC. P162 14/3/1846 & P184 13/3/1847 Listed by W. Miller, Ramsgate. GC. P250 17/4/1847 Listed by J. Hally, Blackheath. GC. P216 27/3/1847 & P232 1/4/1848 Listed by R. Cooper, Croydon. GC.P224 14/4/1849 Listed by R. Whibley, Kennington. GC. P259 28/4/1849 & P241 20/4/1850 Listed by W. Rendle, Plymouth. GC. P270 26/4/1845 Intro. by Gaines, Battersea. *Gaines, Battersea. GB. 1844.*

DUCHESS. Single. White/Purple. Tube. Blush white. Sepals. Blush white. Corolla. Violet Purple, merging with magenta crimson. Flower trusses long, terminal, and freely produced. P120 4th Ed. by Porcher 1874. Not in the first selection. GC. P375 19/3/1870 Intro. by E.G. Henderson. *Carter GB. 1870.*

DUKE OF ALBANY. Single. Red/Purple. Tube. Red. Sepals. Red. Corolla. Rich purplish red. Free. Bushy. GO. "Select" 1887-1891. JF. Cat. 1885. *Lye, J. Market Lavington. GB. 1885.*

DUKE OF CAMBRIDGE. Single. ND. GC. P505 31/7/1847 Listed by G. Smith, Islington. *Rendle, W. Plymouth GB 1847.*

DUKE OF CONNAUGHT. ND. Red/Purple. Tube. Scarlet. Sepals. Scarlet. Well reflexed. Corolla. Violet Purple, veined red. Long. Good shape. JF. Cat. 1895-1898. HC. Cat. 1896. B. Cat. 1894-1895. *Banks, E. Deal. GB. 1894.*

DUKE OF CORNWALL. Single. Pink/Red. Tube. Flesh. 2" long. Sepals. Delicate flesh. Corolla. Deep salmon. App. to RH. 1851 by Porcher. Midland Florist P195 1847.GC. P256 16/4/1848 Listed by G. Rogers, Uttoxeter. GC. P 224 14/4/1849. Listed by R. Whibley, Kennington. GC. P259 28/4/1849 & P241 20/4/1850 Listed by W. Rendle, Plymouth. GC. P219 3/4/1847 Introduced by W. Rendle, Plymouth. *Passingham, Truro. GB. 1847*

DUKE OF EDINBURGH (a). Single. Red/Purple. Tube. Brilliant dark red. Short. Sepals. Brilliant Dark red. Reflexed. Corolla. Clear lilac rose or mauve. Bell shaped. Charming colours. P107 4th Edition by Porcher 1874. P311 RH. 1889 "Select" by E.A. Carrière. *Banks, E. Deal. GB. 1872.*

DUKE OF EDINBURGH (b). Single. Red/Purple. Tube. Red. Sepals. Red. Corolla. Dark Plum. Large. Globular. (Purple). Free. JF. Cat. 1895. HC. Cat. 1896. B. Cat. 1894-1895. *Banks, E. Deal. GB. 1894.*

DUKE OF FIFE. Single. Red/Purple. Tube. Fiery red. Sepals. Fiery red. Corolla. Magenta Purple. (Purple distinctly striped rose). HC. Cat. 1896. JF. Cat. 1898. B. Cat. 1894-1895. *Banks, E. Deal GB. 1894*

DUKE OF LEEDS. ND. ND/ND. Tube. ND. Sepals. ND. Corolla. GC.P201 25/8/1848. Listed by Hart & Nicklin, Guildford. NK. NK. NK.

DUKE OF NORFOLK. Single. White/Purple. Tube. White. Sepals. White tipped green. Corolla, Dark rosy pink corolla. GC. P216 27/3/18437 & P231 1/4/1848 Listed by R. Cooper, Croydon. GC. P201 27/3/1847 Listed by Hart & Nicklin, Guildford. GC. P250 17/4/1847 Listed by W. Miller, Ramsgate. GC. P161 14/3/1846 Intro. by J. Barkway. *Barkway, J. East Dereham. GB. 1846.*

DUKE OF WELLINGTON (a). Single. Red/Red. Tube. Rich rosy pink. Sepals. Rich rosy Pink. Almost reflex. Tipped Green. Corolla. Rich rosy crimson. (Lake). GC. P686 12/10/1844 Exhibted at RHS of Cornwall Show. GC. P112 17/2/1844 & P66 1/2/1845 Listed by W. Miller, Ramsgate. GC.P146 8/3/1844 Listed by Youell, Gt. Yarmouth. P24 RH. 1846. GC. P97 17/2/1844 Intro. by W.J. Epps. *Epps, W.J. Maidstone GB. 1844.*

DUKE OF WELLINGTON (b). Single. NK/NK. Tube. ND. Sepals. ND. Corolla. ND. GC. P627 1/10/1853 Flowers available. GC. P81 11/2/1854 Out on 20/4/1854. GC. P192 25/3/1854. Illustrated, Raiser shown as Stokes. GC. P401 244/6/1854 Listed by B. Cant, Colchester GC. P401 24/6/1854 Listed by H.Walton, Burnley. GC. P466 22/7/1854 Listed by Bass 7 Brown, Sudbury. GC P238 21/4/1855 Listed by J. Hoade, Addlestone. GC. P529 11/8/1855 Listed by Bainbridge & Hewison, York. Intro. by J. Moore, Birmingham. *Stokes. GB. 1854.*

DUKE OF YORK (a). Single. Red/Purple. Tube. Carmine. Sepals. Carmine. Corolla. Purple. Largest yet offered to the public. GC. P216 27/3/1847 & P232 1/4/1848 & P256 21/4/1849 Listed by R. Cooper, Croydon. GC. P162 14/3/1846 & P184 13/3/1847 Listed by W. Miller, Ramsgate. GC. P265 24/4/1847 Listed by. W. Rendle, Plymouth. GC. P66 1/2/1845 Intro. by W. Miller, Ramsgate. *Miller, W. Ramsgate GB. 1845.*

DUKE OF YORK (b). Single. Red/Purple. Tube. Crimson Scarlet. Sepals. Crimson Scarlet. Well reflexed. Corolla. Purple, tinged Violet. (Rosy violet occasionally striped). JF. Cat. 1895. HC. Cat. 1896. B. Cat. 1894. *Banks, E. Deal GB. 1894.*

DUKE. Double. Red/Purple. Tube. Rose. Sepals. Rose. Corolla. Rosy Violet. Compact. Globular. B Cat. 1870-1872. NK. NK. NK.

DUNOIS. Single. Red/Purple. Tube. Bright reddish crimson. Sepals. Bright reddish crimson. Well reflexed. Corolla. Rich Purple. Each petal is distinctly serrated on the edge. B. Cat. 1876-1881. *Bull, W. Chelsea.GB. 1876.*

DUNROBIN BEDDER Single. Red/Purple. Tube. Coral Red. Sepals. Coral Red. Corolla. Purple. Compact. 1 foot high. Floriferous. JF. Cat. 1894. L. Cat. 1901. BSW Cat.1897. GC. P680 27/5/1893 Listed by Veitch, 10/6d each. *Melville. Scotland. 1893.*

DUNROBIN CASTLE. Single. Red/Purple. Tube. Coral Red. Sepals. Coral red. HC. Cat. 1896 an old

favourite re-introduced. distinct. Bedder. Small dark foliage. *Melville, Scotland. NK.*

DUPLEX. Double. Red/Purple. Tube. Bright red.Short. Sepals. Bright red. Broad. Well reflexed. Corolla. Deep rich Purple. Dwarf grower, Abundant bloomer. GC. P568 8/9/1849 Adv. by Veitch. New. Flowers available. Seedling No 3/48. Figured in the Florist 1850. GC. P387 15/6/1850 Listed by H. Walton, Burnley. GC. P465 27/7/1850 Listed by G. Smith. GC. P568 8/9/1849 Advance notice, by Veitch of Exeter, of a double flowered fuchsia raised by W.H. Story. GC. P226 13/4/1850 Intro. By Veitch, Exeter. *Story W.H. Newton Abbott. GB. 1850*

EARL OF BEACONSFIELD. Single. Red/Red. Tube. Light rosy carmine. (Rich orange 1¼" long). Sepals. Light rosy carmine. (Rich orange). Pointed. Corolla. Deep Carmine. (Crimson Scarlet). Flowers in clusters. GC. P73 17/7/1875 Leaves ovate. Red petioles. Flowers large but not as large as Fulgens. GC. P153 4/8/1877 FCC. RHS. by Floral Committee. GC. P304 6/3/1880 Raised some 7 or 8 years ago at the Forest Hill Nurseries of J. Laing. Mr. Laing fertilised the flowers of F. Fulgens with the pollen of some of the best florists varieties of the day. In due time some 100 seedlings, amongst which were some curious things, which were subsequently thrown away. Awarded Certificate of the RBS on 21/6/1876 under the name of Laing's Hybrid, and again the following year by the Floral Committee of the RHS, under the name it now bears. (Also listed as Lord Beaconsfield). Its fault, a very curious one, it will not bear seed. GC. Vol 26 1886. RHS Trials at Chiswick 31/7/1886 Orange yellow flowers produced in clusters. Flowers not handsome. Named after B. Disraeli, a former Conservative Prime Minister (1804-81). P311 RH. 1889 "Select" by E.A. Carrière. G. Vol 33 20/7/1889 Being grown in Regents Park. JF. Cat. 1885. Laings Cat. 1890. HC. Cat. 1882-1885. Blooms nearly all the year round, if allowed plenty of root room. BSW. Cat. 1878-1897. Fulgens X. *Laing J. Forest Hill. GB. 1873.*

EARL OF DEVON. Single. Red/Purple. Tube. Coral Red. (Dark bright red). Thin. Very Long. Sepals. Coral Red. (Dark red). Broad. Stout. Reflexed. Corolla. Rich velvet purple. Stained crimson at base. Cup shaped. Overlapping. P107 4th Ed. by Porcher 1874. GC. P335 11/4/1863 Intro. by Luccombe & Pince. *Luccombe & Pince. Exeter GB. 1863.*

EASTERN BEAUTY. Single. White/Purple. Tube. Whitish. Sepals. White. Corolla. Bluish. Dwarf. Small flowers. GC. P145 9/3/1850 Listed by W. Rumley, Richmond. GC. P274 4/5/1850 Listed by

Bass & Brown, Sudbury. App. to RH. 1851 by Porcher. *Smith, G. Islington. GB. 1849.*

EBOREANA. Single. Red/Purple. Tube. Red. Sepals. Red. Corolla. Purple. Colour Plate 4. Page 61. Floricultural Magazine. 1836. *Backhouse. York. GB. 1836.*

E.CHAPOTON. Double. Red/Purple. Tube. Clear red. Sepals. Clear red. Corolla. Clear Red bordered marine blue. (Purple red). Full. L. Cat. 1896. Kelways Cat. 1903. RB. Cat. 1906. *Rozain. Lyons. France. 1895.*

ECLAT. Single. Red/White. Tube. Scarlet. Sepals. Scarlet. Inside rose. Corolla. White (as "Princess of Prussia"). GC. P90 5/2/1859. FCC of National Floral Committee. Florist P33 Feb 1858 Colour Plate No.148. GC. P426 12/5/1860. Listed by F. Godwin, Sheffield. *Smith, G. Islington. GB. 1859.*

ECLIPSE (a). Single. Red/Purple. Tube. Bright Red. (Coral Red). Sepals. Bright Red. (Coral Red). Broad. Recurved. Corolla. Deep Purple. (Deep rich violet purple). Good habit. Free flowering. Large. GO. "Select" 1881-1888. B. Cat. 1880-1883. GO. 1879 New in 1878. *Smith, G. Islington. GB. 1878.*

ECLIPSE (b). Single. Red/Purple. Tube. Red. Sepals. Red. Corolla. Purple. GC. P820 12/1844 "Recommended". GC. P610 2/9/1843 Exhibited by T. Farrell at Practical Floral & Hort Scty of Ireland Show 25/8/1843. GC. P375 4/6/1844 Exhibited by J. Smith, Hort Scty Show. P38 2nd Ed. by Porcher 1848. The foliage resembles that of Globosa Speciosa, Flower 5cm long. Sepals large, half down brilliant dark red. Glossy like those of "Smithii". Superb variety. Similar to "Noblissima" but the latter is more round and the colours are less bright. GC. P441 1/7/1843 Listed by Marnock & Manby. GC. P66 1/2/1845 & P112 17/2/1844 Listed by W. Miller, Ramsgate. GC. P146 8/3/1845 Listed by Youell, Gt. Yarmouth. *Smith, J. Dalston. GB. 1842.*

ECLIPSE (c). Single. White/Red. Tube. White. Sepals. White. Corolla. Cerise red. Massive. GC. P295. Vol 22. 1897. *Lye, J. Market Lavington. GB. 1897.*

ECLIPSE (d). Single. Red/Purple. Tube. Carmine rose. A little thin. 20mm long. Sepals. Carmine rose. Horizontal. Corolla. Violet red. Mediocre. Clear green foliage. P157 3rd Ed. by Porcher 1858. *Meillez, Lille. France. 1853.*

ED.ANDRÉ. Single. Red/Red. Tube. Carmine. Long. Sepals. Carmine, tipped yellow. Corolla. Pale

Orange. Very large. Open. Resembles Serratifolia in foliage and flowers. (See also "Dr. Godron" and "H. Lecoq"). G. Vol 19 P249 1881. B. Cat. 1879-1881. Dominiana˜üX Serratifolia. *Lemoine. Nancy. France. 1878.*

ED. DE CARVALA LUPI. Double. Red/Purple. Tube. Crimson. Sepals. Crimson. Corolla. Reddish Violet striped carmine. Very large. JF. Cat. 1893 (shown as E.C. Lupi). L. Cat. 1892. *Rozain. Lyons. France. 1892.*

EDELSTEIN. ND. ND. Tube. ND. Sepals. ND. Corolla. ND. A white Rademacher(Essig). *Grosse, G. GB. NK.*

EDELWEIS. Double. Red/White. Tube. Carmine Scarlet. ½" long. Sepals. Carmine Scarlet. (Crimson). Broad. 1¼" long. Reflexed. Corolla. Clear white, streaked rose at base. GC. P599 5/11/1881 Globose buds. 4/6 flowers at each joint. Never out of bloom. Superior to "Grand Duchess", "Clarinda", "Miss Lucy Finnis", "Snowcloud". GO. P97 1882 "Finest of the class". JF. Cat. 1885. B. Cat. 1882-1888. BSW. Cat. 1888. *Hender,W. Plymouth. GB. 1881.*

ED. FARINA. Double. Red/Pink. Tube. Carmine Pink. Sepals. Carmine Pink. Twisted. Green tips. Corolla. Pinkish Mauve. (Mauve shaded rose) L. Cat. 1903. JF. Cat. 1904. *Rozain, Lyons. France. 1903.*

EDINA. Single. Red/Purple. Tube. Red. Sepals. Red. Corolla. Purple. GC. P409 22/6/1844 Exhibited at Royal Caledonian Show 17/5/1844 and 27/6/1845. Listed by A.J. Stewart, Windsor. GC. P234 11/4/1846. GC. P714 1844 Intro. in 1845 by Dickson. *Dickson J. Inverleith. GB. 1845.*

EDITH. Single. Red/Purple. Tube. Bright red. Sepals. Bright red. Short. Spreading. Reflexed with age. Corolla. Violet Blue. (Purple). Much expanded. Vol P3 J of RHS 1863. Chiswick Trials 1862 Awarded ** Showy. Erect bushy habit. Globose buds. Very large expanded corolla. P107 4th. Ed. by Porcher 1874. Vol 12 Scottish Gardener. *Banks, E. Deal. GB. 1862.*

EDMOND ABOUT. Double. Red/White. Tube. Vermillion Carmine. Sepals. Vermillion Carmine. Reflexed. Corolla. White. (Blush white). Suffused rose. Very floriferous. Enormous. Named after a French author (1828-85). B. Cat. 1888-1893. Laings Cat. (circa 1890). *Lemoine, Nancy. France. 1888.*

EDMOND PERRIER (a). Double. Pink/White. Tube. Clear Pink. Sepals. Clear Pink. Green tips. Sepals rise up, Corolla. Pure white. L. Cat. 1906. *Lemoine, Nancy. France. 1904.*

EDMOND PERRIER (b). Double. Red/White. Tube. Crimson. Sepals. Crimson. Broad. Short. Corolla. Cream veined carmine, bordered pale rose. Spreading. L. Cat. 1912. *Lemoine. Nancy. France. 1912.*

EDOUARD DE PERRODIL. Double. Red/Purple. Tube. Turkey red. Sepals. Turkey red. Corolla. Slate blue, flamed scarlet. Enormous. L. Cat. 1910. *Rozain, Lyons, France. 1910.*

EDWARDSII. Single. Red/Purple. Tube. Crimson purple. Thick. Sepals. Crimson Purple. Half down. Corolla. Violet red. Foliage 8cms x 5cms. P38 2nd Ed. by Porcher 1848. GC. P66 1/2/1845 Listed by W.Miller, Ramsgate. GC. P369 8/6/1844 Listed by T. Cripps, Tunbridge Wells. *Salter. Versailles. France. 1843.*

EFFECTIVE. Single. Red/Purple. Tube. Carmine scarlet. Sepals. Carmine scarlet. Well reflexed. Corolla. Crimson purple. Expanded a la Crinoline. GC. P344 4/4/1868 Intro. by B.W. Knight, Battle. *Knight, B.W. Battle. GB. 1868.*

EFFUSA FASCICULATA. Single. Red/Purple. Tube. Carmine, Sepals. Carmine. Green tips. Corolla. Rosy purple. Some of the joints producing 30 blooms. Same size as "Standishi" but thicker in the tube. GC. P112 17/2/1844. Listed by W. Miller, Ramsgate. GC. P82 11/2/1843 Intro. by W. Deans. *Deans W. Jedburgh. GB. 1843.*

EGERIA. Single. Red/Purple. Tube. Rich crimson. Short. Sepals. Rich crimson. Well recurved. Corolla. Purple. Long. Stout. B. Cat. 1875-1882. *Bull, W. Chelsea. GB. 1875.*

E.G. HENDERSON. ND. ND/ND. Tube. ND. Sepals. ND. Corolla. ND. RH. P295 1887 Standards grown at Twickel, Nr. Arnheim. *Cornelissen, Arras. Belgium. NK.*

E. JOUBERT. Double. Red/Pink. Tube. Dull red. Sepals. Dull red. Corolla. Flesh pink, veined carmine. Large. L. Cat. 1906. *Rozain, Lyons. France. 1904.*

ELAINE. Double. Red/White. Tube. Crimson. Short. Sepals. Crimson. Corolla. White veined at base with bright rose. B. Cat. 1901. *Bull, W. Chelsea. GB. 1901.*

ELBA. Double. Red/White. Tube. Dark rose. Sepals. Dark rose. Well reflexed. Corolla. White marked deep rose at base. Irregular. B. Cat. 1898. *Bull, W. Chelsea. GB. 1897.*

ELDORADO. Single. Pink/Orange. Tube. Dawn Pink. Elongated. Sepals. Dawn Pink. Corolla. Bright Orange. Good habit. L. Cat. 1888. *Rozain. Lyons. France. 1888.*

ELECT. Single. Red/Purple. Tube. Rosy carmine. Sepals. Rosy carmine. Corolla. Purple. GC. P545 30/8/1851 Listed by G. Smith, Islington. GC. P207 27/3/1852 Listed by H. Walton, Burnley. GC. P209 5/4/1851 Intro. by C. Turner, Slough. *Banks, E. Deal GB. 1851.*

ELECTRIC LIGHT. Single. White/Red. Tube. Pure white. Sepals. Pure white. Corolla. Rose. P84 Witte 1882. *Todman. GB. 1879.*

ELEGANCE (a). Single. Red/Purple. Tube. Scarlet. Sepals. Scarlet. Corolla. Light Blue. GC. P722 9/6/1877 New seedling. GC. P206 17/2/1877. Floral Magazine P773 15/6/1878 Colour Plate T291. GC. P183 1888 "Recommended" GC. Vol 18 1882 P215 Exhibited at Devizes Hort Scty Show by J. Lye (1st) also by T. Chandler & W.C. Hitch. GC. Vol 20 P280 1/9/1883 Exhibited at Trowbridge Hort Scty Show by G. Tucker. G. 6/9/1884 Exhibited at Trowbridge Hort Scty Show by H. Pocock (2nd). HC. Cat. P80 1882 Similar to James Lye. Immense grower. GC. Vol 23 1885 Illustrated Fig. 39. BSW. Cat. 1878-1897. Arabella Imp. x James Lye. *Lye, J. Market Lavington. GB. 1877.*

ELEGANCE (b). Single. White/Red. Tube. Clear White. Sepals. Clear White. Horizontal. Corolla. Rosy Vermillion. (Bright rosy purple). 6" to 8" long. GC. P280 5/5/1849. GC. P120 23/2/1850 "Select" App. to RH. 1851 by Porcher Long pedicel 6.5cms long. 1st class variety. GC. P497 11/8/1849 Listed by G. Smith, Islington. GC. P145 9/3/1850 Listed by W. Rumley, Richmond. GC. P210 6/4/1850 Listed by H. Walton, Burnley. GC. P241 20/4/1850 Listed by W. Rendle, Plymouth. GC. P274 4/5/1850 Listed by Bass & Brown, Sudbury. GC. P226 14/4/1849 Intro. by Turville, Chelmsford. *Turville. Chelmsford GB. 1849.*

ELEGANCE (c). Single. White/Red. Tube. White. ½" long. Enlarged at base. Tapers downwards. Sepals. White. Reflexed. 1¼" long. Green at tips. Corolla. Rose shaded carmine. (Lake). rather spreading. Large. Pcxi Vol III J. of RHS 1872. Fuchsia trial at Chiswick. Habit loose. B. Cat. 1870. NK. *GB. 1868?*

56

ELEGANCE (d). Single. Red/Purple. Tube. Crimson. Sepals. Crimson. Twisted or Contorted. Corolla. Deep Purple broadly striped pale red. HC. Cat. 1890. Illustration no 5. JF. Cat. 1888. *Sankey GB. 1888.*

ELEGANCE (e). Single. White/Pink. Tube. White. Sepals. White. Broad. Elegantly recurved. Corolla. Blush pink, each petal margined bright blue. B. Cat. 1899-1901. L. Cat. 1901. JF. Cat. 1899. *Bull, W. Chelsea. GB. 1898.*

ELEGANCE (f). ND. White/Red. Tube. White. Sepals. White. Corolla. Carmine. JF. Cat. 1921. NK NK. 1921.

ELEGANCE (g). ND. ND/ND. Tube. ND. Sepals. ND. Corolla. ND. Essig 1936. F. fulgens x Sultan. *Lowe. GB. 1875.*

ELEGANS (a). Single. Red/Red. Tube. Brilliant Scarlet. Sepals. Brilliant Scarlet. Corolla. Dark Vermillion. Flowers larger than "Formosa Elegans". GC. P820 12/1844 "Recommended". GC. P663 18/10/1851 Exhibited York Hort Scty Show on 24/9/1851 by Mrs. Staplyton. CG. Vol 3 P272 "For exhibition". GC. P146 8/3/1845 Intro. by Youell, Gt. Yarmouth. Formosa Elegans X. *Youell. Gt. Yarmouth GB. 1844.*

ELEGANS (b). Single. Red/Purple. Tube. Red. Short. Thin. Sepals. Red. Reflexed. Corolla. Purple. (very dull violet blue fading to purple violet) P157 3rd. Ed. by Porcher 1858. Long petals. GC. P401 24/6/1854 Listed by B.R. Cant, Colchester & H. Walton, Burnley. GC. P466 22/7/1854 Listed by Bass & Brown, Sudbury. GC. P258 21/4/1855 Listed by H. Walton, Burnley. GC. P530 1/8/1855 Listed by Bainbridge & Hewison, York. GC. P194 1/4/1854 Intro. by C. Turner, Slough. *Banks, E. Deal. GB. 1854.*

ELEGANS (c). Single. White/Red. Tube. White. Thick. 15mms long. Sepals. White tinged rose. Very long. Reflexed round. Corolla. Rose Carmine, margined bright carmine, shaded white at base. Expanded. P116 4th Ed. by Porcher 1874 Early flowering. Floriferous. Lax grower, needs regular pinching. Pedicel 60mm. *Bull, W. Chelsea. GB. 1866.*

ELEGANS (d). Single. Red/Purple. Tube. Red. Sepals. Red. Corolla. Purple. Laings Cat. circa 1890. NK. GB. NK.

ELEGANS (e). Single. White/Red. Tube. White shaded pink. Sepals. White shaded pink. Horizontal.

Corolla. Carmine red. Open. Long pedicel. Pendant flowers. P157 3rd. Ed. by Porcher 1858. In all probability identical to "Elegance (b)". *Turville, Chelmsford GB. 1849.*

ELEGANS SUPERBA. Single. Red/ND. Tube.Crimson. Sepals. Crimson.Large. Only half open. Corolla. Yellowish green foliage. P38 2nd Ed. by Porcher 1848. GC. P299 1841 Exhibited by J. Downie, gardener to Count Elohault at Bot. Scty of Edinburgh Show. GC. P393 6/11/1842 Listed by Youells, Gt. Yarmouth. NK. GB. NK.

ELEGANT (a). Double. Red/Purple. Tube. Bright red. Short. Sepals. Bright red. Recurved. Waxy. Corolla. Bright Purple flamed carmine at base. Beautiful corolla but delicate growth. P126 4th Ed. by Porcher 1874 Not in the first selection. B. Cat. 1870-1873. GC. P451 2/4/1870 Intro. by Felton, Birmingham. *Felton, Birmingham. GB. 1870.*

ELÉGANT (b). Double. Red/Purple. Tube. Red. Sepals. Red. Corolla. Purple. L. Cat. 1893. F. myrtifolia X. *Lemoine, Nancy. France. 1893.*

ELEGANTISSIMA (a). Single. Red/Purple. Tube. Crimson Scarlet. (Bright Scarlet) Thin. Sepals. Crimson Scarlet. Reflex and recurve to tube. Corolla. Purple. (Deep Violet). GC. P455 8/7/1847 Exhibited at RBS Show. GC. P241 21/4/1848 FCC June 1848. CG. Vol 6 1853. Sepals reflex like a Martagon Lily. GC. P120 23/2/1850 "Select" GC. P647 11/10/1851 Exhibited at Cornwall R.H.S. Show 9/9/1851 by F. H. Earle of Falmouth. App. to RH. 1851 by Porcher 2nd class. GC. P650 30/9/1848 Advance notice by Veitch. GC. P497 11/8/1849 Listed by G. Smith, Islington. GC. P145 9/3/1850 & P241 20/4/1850 Listed by W. Rendle, Plymouth. GC. P210 6/4/1850 Listed by H. Walton, Burnley GC. P274 4/5/1850 Listed by Bass & Brown, Sudbury. GC. P226 14/4/1849 Intro. by Veitch & Co. Exeter. Corollina X. *Story,W.H. Newton Abbot. GB. 1847.*

ELEGANTISSIMA (b). Single. White/Purple. Tube. White. Sepals. White. Recurved. Corolla. Purplish rose. Very dwarf. Slow growing Profuse Bloomer. Small flowers. Vol P3 J of RHS 1863. Most elegant as its name, indicates the plant is very dwarf and small growing, of free flowering habit and provided with small neat foliage. Flowers white with recurved sepals and a broad purplish rose corolla. Awarded ***. P120 4th. Ed. by Porcher 1874 Not in the first selection. GC. P856 8/9/1866 "Select". HC. Cat. 1882. *Banks, E. Deal. GB. 1862.*

57

ELEGANTISSIMA (c). Single. Red/Purple. Tube. Rich scarlet crimson. Sepals. Rich scarlet crimson. Broad. Elegant. Reflexing. Corolla. Violet purple. Quite circular and expanded. 1½" across. Very free and of fine habit. (The most elegant fuchsia in cultivation). CG &JH 20/8/1861. GC. P594 30/6/1860 Listed by F. Godwin, Sheffield. GC. P93 4/2/1860 Intro.by G. Smith, Islington. *Smith,G. Islington. GB. 1860.*

ELFIN. Double. Red/Purple. Tube. Light crimson. Sepals. Light crimson. Reflexed well. Corolla. Rich purple flaked rose. B. Cat. 1875-1883. *Bull, W. Chelsea. GB. 1875.*

ELFRIDA. Double. Red/Purple. Tube. Bright crimson. Short. Sepals. Bright crimson. Broad. Well reflexed. Corolla. Violet plum marked rose. P126 4th. Ed. by Porcher 1874. Not in the first selection. Flowers average and ordinary. B. Cat. 1872-1875. *Bull, W. Chelsea. GB. 1871.*

ELIANE. Double. Pink/White. Tube. Pink. Sepals. Pink. Laid on Corolla. Corolla. White. L. Cat. 1913. *Lemoine, Nancy. France. 1913.*

ELISE. Single. White/Red. Tube. White tinged flesh or soft rose. Very thin 20mm long. Sepals. White. Narrow. Points bent. Corolla. Bright carmine red. Small. Dwarf. Bushy. Small foliage. Mediocre. P158 3rd. Ed. by Porcher 1858. *Schule. Germany. 1855.*

ELIZABETH. Single. White/Red. Tube. Whitish rose. (Light pink). A little thin. Sepals. Whitish rose. (Light pink). Large. Horizontal. Corolla. Crimson. (Deep crimson). Medium sized. App. to RH. 1851 by Porcher Good contrast with calyx. 1st Class variety. P157 3rd Ed. by Porcher 1858. P374 Midland Florist 1849. GC. P423 6/1851 Exhibited at RBS Show by H. Low, Clapton. GC. P438 6/7/1854 Exhibited at RBS Show, Regents Park as a 7' pyramid by Mr. Bray. GC. P224 18/4/1849 Listed by R. Whibley, Kennington Cross. GC P256 21/4/1849 Listed by R. Cooper, Croydon. GC. P226 13/4/1850 Listed by Poole Nurseries. GC. P241 20/4/1850 Listed by W. Rendle, Plymouth. GC. P274 4/5/1850 Listed by Bass & Brown, Sudbury. GC. P153 4/3/1848 Intro. by Kendall. *Kendall. Stoke Newington. GB. 1848.*

ELIZABETH MARSHALL. Double. Red/White. Tube. Red. Sepals. Red. Corolla. White. Good for market. Free Bloomer. GC. Vol 26 1886 Fuchsia Trials at Chiswick. GO. "Select" 1891. HC. Cat. 1882-1898. Laings Cat. circa 1890. BSW. Cat. 1898. *Simmonds. GB. NK.*

ELISE MEILLEZ. Single. Pink/Red. Tube. Pale Pink. Long. 18mm.Sepals. Pale Pink, veined pink Horizontal. Corolla. Reddish Cerise. (Carmine Red) Pleated petals. App. to RH 1851 by Porcher Firs class variety. P157 3rd Ed. by Porcher 1858. (Firs name spelt Eliza in U.K.). GC. P465 27/7/185(Listed by G. Smith, Islington. *Meillez, Lille. France 1850.*

ELIZA SAUVAGE. Single. ND/ND. Tube. Light Sepals. Light. Corolla. ND. GC. P184 13/3/1847 an(P250 17/4/1847. Listed by W. Miller, Ramsgate. NK NK. *1846.*

ELLEN. Single. White/Red. Tube. Greenish white tinted pink. Very long. 4cms. Sepals. White tinge(pink. Reflexed. Corolla. Rosy vermillion. (Reddish cerise). App. to RH. 1851 by Porcher. GC. P15: 4/3/1848 & P256 21/4/1849 Listed by R. Cooper Croydon. GC. P259 28/4/1849 & P241 20/4/185(Listed by W. Rendle, Plymouth. GC. P22(13/4/1850 Listed by Poole Nurseries. GC. P234 10/4/1847 Intro. by Cripps, Tunbridge Wells *Cripps,T. Tunbridge Wells. GB. 1847*

ELLEN LYE. Single. White/Red. Tube. White Sepals. White. Corolla. Scarlet. Neat. Compact Flowers of great purity. GC. Vol 18 P215 Exhibite(at Devizes Hort Scty Show on 7/8/1882 by J.Lye 1st. GC. Vol 20 P280 1/9/1883 Trowbridge Hort Scty 1st by Lye. GC P824 27/6/1885 RHS trials a Chiswick Best in its class. JF. Cat. 1885. *Lye,J Market Lavington. GB. 1882.*

ELM. Single. ND/ND. Tube. ND. Sepals. ND Corolla. ND. GC. P354 27/5/1843. Intro. by Ivery *Peckham. Ivery. Peckham. GB. 1843.*

ELSA. Single. Red/Purple. Tube. Whitish. Short Sepals. Rose Pink, whitish at base. Long. Very Broad. Corolla. Rosy Purple. Shortish. (purplish rose) L. Cat. P149 1901. B. Cat. 1901. *Bull W. Chelsea. GB. 1901.*

ELSIE VERT. Double. Red/Purple. Tube. Crimson Sepals. Crimson. Corolla. Purple. Large. Full. JF. Cat 1912.NK. GB. 1912.

ELTERSFEE. Single. White/Purple. Tube. White Thick. Short. Sepals. White tinged rose. Reflexed round. Corolla. Violet red tinged white, margined with fire red. Spiral form. 4th. Ed. by Porcher 1874. *Deegin. NK. 1868.*

ELVIRA. Single. NK/NK. See "Insignis" and "Magnifica" P38 2nd. Ed. by Porcher. 1848.

ELYSÉE. ND/ND. Tube. ND. Sepals. ND. Corolla. ND. Gartenflora P149 1888. L. Cat. 1892. Riccartonii X. *Lemoine. Nancy. France. 1887.*

EMBLEM. Double. Red/White. Tube. Crimson. Sepals. Crimson. Corolla. White, carmine at base. Full. B. Cat. 1870-1873. *Bull W. Chelsea. GB. 1869?*

EMBLEMATIC. Single. Red/Purple. Tube. Scarlet. Sepals. Scarlet. Corolla. Rosy Lavender. (Purple) Very large. Immense blooms. GC P55 19/1/1867. 4th Ed. by Porcher 1874 Not in the first selection. HC. Cat. 1882. *Banks, E. Deal. GB. 1863.*

EMELINE. Single. Red/Red. Tube. Dark red. Thick. Sepals. Clear red. Raised up. Corolla. Violet red. Floriferous. Leaves 6 x 4cm. P38 2nd Ed. by Porcher 1848 . NK/NK. NK. NK.

EMILE. Single. ND/ND. Tube. ND. Sepals. ND. Corolla. ND. GC. P112 17/2/1844 Listed by W. Miller, Ramsgate. *Standish. Bagshot. GB. 1843.*

ÉMILE BAYARDE. Double. Red/Pink. Tube. Pinkish red. Sepals. Pinkish red. (Rosy red). Corolla. Rose pink in centre bordered lilac. (Rosy white edged lilac). JF. Cat. 1893. B. Cat. 1892. L. Cat. 1892. *Lemoine. Nancy. GB. 1892.*

ÉMILE DAVID. Double. Red/Purple. Tube. Red. Sepals. Red. Corolla. Violet slate with many petals flesh pink. L. Cat 1907. *Rozain. Lyons. France. 1907.*

ÉMILE DE WILDEMAN. Double. Red/Pink. Tube. Carmine pink. Sepals. Carmine Pink, Reflexed. Corolla. Pink. Very full. Very broad. Known as "Fascination" in the U.K. L. Cat. 1906. *Lemoine. Nancy. France. 1905*

EMILE ERCKMANN. Double. Red/Purple. Tube. Crimson red. Sepals. Crimson red. Short. Very broad. Corolla. Violet. Very full. New elegant form. Horizontal petals pansy violet. Named after a French Author (1822-1899). L. Cat. 1903. JF. Cat. 1904. *Lemoine. Nancy. France. 1903*

ÉMILE LAURENT. Double. Pink/White Tube. Bright clear pink. Sepals. Bright clear pink. Green tips. Corolla. White with a little pink. Full. L. Cat. 1906. *Lemoine. Nancy. France. 1904.*

EMILE LEMOINE NK. NK/NK. Tube. NK. Sepals. NK. Corolla. NK. Essig 1936. *Lemoine. Nancy. France. 1863.*

ÉMILE RICHEBOURG. Double. Red/Purple. Tube. Bright red. Sepals. Bright red. Short Broad. Corolla. Metallic violet. enormous. B. Cat. 1894-1895. *Lemoine. Nancy. France. 1894.*

ÉMILE SALLE. Double. Red/White. Tube. Red. Sepals. Red. Large. Corolla. White veined violet carmine. B. Cat. 1893-1895. *Rozain. Lyons. France. 1893.*

ÉMILE ZOLA. Double. ND. Tube. ND. Sepals. ND. Corolla. ND. Named after a French novelist who fled to England as a result of the Dreyfus affair (1840-1902). JF. Cat. 1898 New. NK. NK. *1898.*

EMILIE. Single. Red/Red. Tube. Crimson. Sepals. Crimson. Corolla. Crimson. Small flowers and foliage. Sepals raised up and more larger than the tube. P38. 2nd Ed. by Porcher 1848. NK. NK. NK. NK.

EMILY BRIGHT. Single. White/Red. Tube. Creamy white. Sepals. Creamy white. Corolla. Bright carmine. An improvement on "Mr. Bright". GC. Vol 24 P277 1885. GC. P375 1886 Exhibited at Bath 1st. FCC Bath 2/9/1885. JF. Cat. 1886. B. Cat. 1888-1893. BSW. Cat. 1888. Laings Cat. circa 1890. *Lye, J. Market Lavington. GB. 1886.*

EMILY DOEL. Single. White/Red. Tube. White. Sepals. White. Corolla. Rose. G. 6/9/1884 Exhibited at Trowbridge 20/8/1884 by G. Tucker. Laings Cat. circa 1890. HC. Cat. P78 1882. *Lye,J. Market Lavington. GB. 1882.*

EMILY LYE. Single. White/Purple. Tube. White. Sepals. White. Corolla. Shaded Purple. Free. Showy. G. 6/9/1884 Exhibited at Trowbridge 20/8/1884 by J. Lye. GC. Vol. 20 1883 Exhibited at Trowbridge 22/8/1883. JF. Cat. 1885. BSW. Cat. 1888. B. Cat. 1878-1883. *Lye, J. Market Lavington. GB. 1878.*

EMINENT. Single. ND/ND. Tube. ND. Sepals. ND. Corolla. ND. GC.P162 14/3/1846 & P184 13/3/1847 Listed by W. Miller, Ramsgate. GC. P199 27/3/1847 Listed by H. Walton Burnley. GC. P216 27/3/1847 Listed by R. Cooper, Croydon. GC. P265 24/4/1847 Listed by W. Rendle, Plymouth. GC. P254 19/4/1845 Intro by J. Smith. *Smith, J. Dalston. GB. 1845.*

EMMA. Single. Pink/Red. Tube. Flesh coloured. Sepals. Flesh Coloured. Sepals not held out. Corolla. Red. App. to RH. 1851 by Porcher. *De Jonghe. NK. 1850.*

59

EMMA CALVÉ. Double. Red/White. Tube. Coral Red. Sepals. Coral Red. Corolla. Pure white. Expanded. Full. Named after a French opera singer (1866-1942). L. Cat. 1912. *Lemoine, Nancy. France. 1912.*

EMMA TOPFER. See. Frau Emma Topfer.

EMPEROR (a). Single. ND/ND. Tube. ND. Sepals. ND. Corolla. ND. GC. P250 17/4/1847 Listed by J.Hally, Blackheath. *Kendall, Stoke Newington. GB. 1846.*

EMPEROR (b). Single. Red/Purple. Tube. Dark crimson. Very short, almost non existant. Sepals. Dark crimson. Reflexed. Corolla. Bright violet, red at base. Large. Long. 4th. Ed. by Porcher 1874. Small foliage. Vigorous. Pedicel 3 cms. B. Cat. 1872-1873. *Bull, W. Chelsea. GB. 1867.*

EMPEROR (c). Single. Red/Purple. Tube. Bright red. Sepals. Bright red. Long. Broad. Corolla. Maroon shaded purple. Fine. Bold. Distinct. Drooping habit. Good for pillars, trellis and baskets. FCC. Bath 2/9/1885. GC. Vol 24 P277 1885. B. Cat. 1888-1889. HC. Cat. 1890. JF. Cat. 1886. Known as seedling No. 1. *Lye, J. Market Lavington. GB. 1886.*

EMPEROR (d). Single. Red/Purple. Tube. Brilliant. cerise. Thin. Sepals. Brilliant carmine. Horizontal. Corolla. Violet. Little open. Old variety with small foliage. P38 2nd Ed. by Porcher 1848. NK. NK. NK. NK.

EMPEREUR DES FUCHSIAS. Double. Red/White. Tube. Scarlet. Sepals. Scarlet. Corolla. White. Floral World & GG. Vol 5 P4 Most beautiful and elegant. GC. P1015 24/10/1863 Out in 1864. GC. P57 18/7/1865. "Recommended". SG. P459 1866 "Recommended". F&P. Mar.1866 Large fine flower, habit bad when young, improves with age. GC. P55 19/1/1867 Review by H. Cannell. P131 4th Ed. by Porcher 1874 Not in the first selection. GC. P1008 24/10/1863 & P1 2/1/1864 Intro. by E.G. Henderson. *Cornelissen. Arras. Belgium. 1863.*

EMPEROR NAPOLEON. Single. Red/Purple. Tube. Scarlet Crimson. Short. 10mm. Sepals. Scarlet Crimson. Extra wide. Beautifully reflexed. Lie against the tube. Corolla. Deep Violet. Bright Violet blue fading to purple. Short. Colour Plate No. 111 P65 Florist 1856. Vol 3 1856 L'Illustration Horticole Colour Plate. P161 Vol XIV Journal d'horticulture de Belgium Colour plate. P169 RH.1857. GC. P497 26/7/1856 Listed by Fowle, Brixton. GC. P283 25/4/1857. Listed by W. Cutbush, Highgate. GC. P114 23/2/1856 Intro by E.G. Henderson, St. Johns

Wood. The largest and finest that has ever been sent out. *Banks, E. Deal. GB. 1856.*

EMPEROR NICOLAS II. Double. Red/White. Tube. Red. Sepals. Rosy carmine. Corolla. White. Very large. Good habit. L. Cat. 1899, 1901. Named after the Russian Tsar 1894-1918. JF. Cat. 1899. *Rozain, Lyons. France. 1898.*

EMPEROR OF BRAZIL. Double. Red/Purple. Tube. Reddish crimson. (Carmine red). Thin. Short. Sepals. Redddish Crimson. Raised up. Corolla. Violet Purple streaked carmine. (Pale violet). Full. Short. Open and well expanded. Resembles a parma violet. Vigorous bush. P122 4th Ed. by Porcher 1874. BSW Cat. 1878. GC. P419 30/3/1872 Intro. by B&S Williams. *Bland, E. Fordham. GB. 1872.*

EMPEROR OF CHINA. Single. ND/ND. Tube. ND. Sepals. ND. Corolla. ND. GC P112 17/2/1844 & P66 1/2/1845 Listed by W. Miller, Ramsgate. GC. P146 8/3/1845 Listed by Youells, Gt. Yarmouth. GC. P97 17/2/1844 Raised by H. Busby, Gr to T.L. Hodge, Hemstead. Intro. by W.J. Epps, Maidstone. *Busby, H. Hemstead. GB. 1844*

EMPRESS (a). Single. Red/Red. Tube. Bright Scarlet. Sepals. Bright Scarlet. Much expanded. Corolla. Crimson. Spreading. GC. P184 13/3/1847 & P250 27/4/1847 Listed by W. Miller, Ramsgate. GC. P82 6/2/1845 Intro. by Bass & Brown, Sudbury. *Bass & Brown, Sudbury. GB. 1845.*

EMPRESS (b). Single. White/ND. Tube. White. Sepals. White. Corolla. ND. GC. P279 30/4/1853 Light green stemmed. GC. P184 13/3/1847 & P250 17/4/1847 Listed by W. Miller, Ramsgate. GC. P250 17/4/1847 Listed by J. Hally, Blackheath. GC. P216 27/3/1847 & P232 1/4/1848 Listed by R. Cooper, Croydon, GC. P34 17/1/1846 Intro. by J. Hally, Blackheath. *Hally, J. Blackheath. GB. 1846.*

EMPRESS (c). Single. Red/White. Tube. Crimson. Sepals. Crimson. Reflexed. Corolla. White. Large. Long. Each petal fluted. B. Cat. 1870-1873. *Bull, W. Chelsea. GB. 1868?*

EMPRESS (d). Double. Red/White. Tube. Scarlet. Waxy. Sepals. Scarlet. Waxy. Broad. Well reflexed. Corolla. White with scarlet feather. 10/6d. GC. P120 8/2/1868 Intro. by G. Smith, Tollington, Nurseries. *Smith, G. Islington. GB. 1868.*

EMPRESS EUGENIE (a). Single. Red/White. Tube. Rosy crimson. Sepals. Rosy crimson. Inside shaded Violet. Corolla. White. Named after the wife of Napoleon III of France, who were married in

60

1853. GC. P467 14/7/1855 Listed by Bass & Brown, Sudbury & H Walton, Burnley. GC. P529 11/8/1855 Listed by W.J. Epps, Maidstone. GC. P530 11/8/1855 & P208 22/3/1856 Listed by Bainbridge & Hewison, York. GC. P531 11/8/1855 Listed by Joseph Courcha. GC. P314 10/5/1856 Listed by W. Rumley, Richmond & Youell, Gt. Yarmouth. GC. P451 5/7/1856 Listed by J. Clarke, Cheltenham. GC. P18 13/1/1855 Intro. by E.G. Henderson. *Story, W.H. Newton Abbot. GB. 1855.*

EMPRESS EUGENIE (b) Single. White/Purple. Tube. White. Sepals. White. Well reflexing. Corolla. Rosy Purple. Selected from 3000 seedlings. GC. P611 15/9/1855. To be sent out on 1/4/1856 by Stewart & Neilson, Liscard. Ches. (See Empress Eugenie (a)). *Stewart & Neilson, Liscard. GB. 1856*

EMPRESS OF GERMANY (a). Double. Red/White. Tube. Carmine. Sepals. Carmine. Well reflexed. Corolla. Pure white. HC. Cat. 1882 Light double. GC. P510 22/4/1871 Intro. by B. S. Williams. *Bland, E. Fordham. GB. 1871.*

EMPRESS OF GERMANY (b). Single. Red/Red. Tube. Red. Sepals. Red. Sepals spreading or reflexed. Corolla. Dull lake red. In shape between conical and expanded. Not a desirable variety. J of RHS Vol 3 Pcxvii. Report on fuchsias grown for trial at Chiswick 1872. NK. NK. NK.

EMPRESS OF GERMANY (c). Single. Red/Purple. Tube. Coral Red. Short. Sepals. Coral red. Reflexed. Corolla. Purple. Large. Spreading. Dwarf bushy habit. Dense. Free flowering. P216 Vol 4 J of RHS 1877. Report on fuchsias grown for trial at Chiswick 1875. FCC. awarded to E.G. Henderson. NK NK NK.

EMPRESS OF INDIA. Double. Red/White. Tube. Rosy carmine. Sepals. Rosy carmine. Well reflexed. Corolla. Pure white. An unusual quantity of petals. JF. Cat. 1885. B. Cat. 1877. *Bull,W. Chelsea. GB. 1877.*

ENCHANTRESS (a). Single. Pink/Red. Tube. Flushed pink. Sepals. Flushed pink. Corolla. Scarlet/Crimson. Floral Cabinet Vol X P169 1842 Illustration. P38 2nd Ed. by Porcher Well branching. Multiflowered. Foliage Greenish Yellow 6cm x 3cm. Flowers have a beautiful shade of vermillion rose. Sepals a shade longer than the tube. Green tips. Corolla Vermillion Cerise. GC. P242 15/4/1843 Listed by A.J. Stewart, Windsor. GC. P98 17/2/1844 & P146 8/3/1845 Listed by Youell, Gt. Yarmouth. GC. P112 17/2/1844 & P66 1/2/1845 Listed by W. Miller, Ramsgate. *Harrison, Dereham. GB. 1842.*

ENCHANTRESS (b). ND. ND/ND. Tube. ND. Sepals. ND. Corolla. ND. GC. P112 17/2/1844 Listed by Millers, Ramsgate, as from Standish. *Standish, Bagshot. GB. 1843?*

ENCHANTRESS (c). Single. Red/Purple. Tube. Crimson. Sepals. Crimson. Corolla. Purple. New Seedling. Very beautiful growth. GC. P184 13/3/1847 Intro. by W. Miller, Ramsgate. *Miller, W. Ramsgate. GB. 1845.*

ENCHANTRESS (d). Single. White/Red. Tube. White. Sepals. White. Large. Held out well. Corolla. Rosy vermillion. (Rosy carmine). App. to RH. 1851 by Porcher. First class variety. GC. P537 12/8/1848 Listed by G. Smith, Islington. GC P224 14/4/1849 Listed by Bass & Brown, Sudbury & R. Whibley, Kennington. GC. P256 21/4/1849 Listed by R. Cooper, Croydon. GC. P274 5/5/1849 Listed by H. Walton, Burnley. GC. P809 11/12/1847 Intro. by H. Pope, B'Ham. *Mayle. Birmingham. GB. 1847.*

ENCHANTRESS (e) Double. Red/White. Tube. Red. (Crimson). ½" long. Slender. Sepals. Red. (Crimson). Broad. Reflexed. Rounded. Corolla. Pure white, tinted violet crimson. P128 4th Edition by Porcher. Full. Large. Short pedicel. Vol 3 J of RHS pcxiii 1872 P216 Awarded ***. B. Cat. 1870. GC P567 23/4/1870 Intro. by W. Bull. *Bland, E. Fordham. GB. 1870*

ENCHANTRESS (f). Single. Red/Purple. Tube. Cherry red. Thin. Sepals. Cherry red. Upright. Narrow. Corolla. Violet. Very mediocre. P39 2nd.Ed. by Porcher 1848. *Smith, J. Dalston. GB. 1846.*

ENCOUNTER. Double. Red/Purple. Tube. Rose. Sepals. Rose. Corolla. Violet Blue. Very full. B. Cat. 1870-1873. *Bull, W. Chelsea. GB. 1868?*

ENFANTE PRODIGUE. S/Double. Red/Purple. Tube. Crimson. Sepals. Crimson. Corolla. Bluish purple. Medium size flowers. P149 1887 Gartenflora. L. Cat. 1892. Riccartonii X. *Lemoine. Nancy. France. 1887.*

ENGLAND'S GLORY. Single. White/Purple. Tube. Greenish white. Sepals. Greenish white, Long. Reflexed. Corolla. Violet Red. Bell shaped. Challenge of £25 by Harrison, if bettered. P118 4th. Ed. by Porcher 1874. Fine blooms. Great substance. RH. P168 1857 Enormous flowers. GC. P337 28/5/1867 Listed by Bass & Brown, Sudbury & H. Walton, Burnley (Glory of England). GC. P465 23/7/1853 Offered by Harrison as Pyramids 12"-18" high 15/-. GC. P627 1/10/1853 Listed by S. Fenney, Gateshead. GC. P147 11/3/1854 Listed by W.

Rumley, Richmond. GC. P162 18/3/1854 Listed by H. Walton, Burnley. GC. P213 8/4/1854 Listed by C.H. Gardner, Maidstsone. GC. P248 15/4/1854 Listed by Mitchell & Co, Brighton, GC. P561 4/9/1852 Intro. by J. Harrison, Darlington (Out April 1854). *Harrison, J. Darlington. GB. 1854.*

ENID. Double. NK/NK. Tube. NK. Sepals. NK. Corolla. NK. Bruant Poitiers Cat. 1911. NK. NK. NK. NK.

ENOCH ARDEN. Single. Red/Purple. Tube. Scarlet. Short. Thick. Sepals. Scarlet. Large. Horizontal. Corolla. Indigo Blue. (Blue Violet). (Violet Purple). Large. Widespread. Largest corolla and more substance of any fuchsia yet in cultivation. GC. P55 19/1/1867 Review by H. Cannell. P83 J of RHS 1867 FCC. 5/7/1865 & GC. P624 8/7/1865. 4th. Ed by Porcher 1874 Bell shaped corolla. Vol 2 J of RHS 1870 Fine elegant habit with reflexed red sepals and large moderately deep blue expanded corolla. F&P P56 3/1865 Largest corolla yet raised. B. Cat. 1870. BSW. Cat. 1878. HC. Cat. 1882-1885. GC. P382 29/4/1865 Intro.by E.G.Henderson. *Banks, E. Deal GB. 1865.*

ENSIGN (a). Single. ND/ND. Tube. ND. Sepals. ND. Corolla. ND. GC. P376 26/4/1862. Fine and distinct. Intro by F&A Smith. *Smith F & A. Dulwich GB. 1862.*

ENSIGN (b). Double. Red/Purple. Tube. Bright red. Short. Sepals. Bright red. Well reflexed. Corolla. Bright blue. Some petals blotched bright rose. B. Cat. 1873. *Bull, W. Chelsea. GB. 1871?*

EPPSII. Single. Red/Purple. Tube. Deep waxy rose. Sepals. Deep waxy rose. Corolla. Rosy magenta. Vigorous. Free flowering. P39 2nd Ed. by Porcher Superb variety. Leaves 6cms x 4 cms. Flowers 5cms long. Sepals. Violet cerise. Large tube. Sepals large and well open. Corolla. Violet.GC. P375 4/6/1844 Exhibited by Mr. Cole HS Show. GC. P535 28/3/1851 Exhibited at Vauxhall Garden Show. GC. P98 17/2/1844 & P146 8/3/1845. Listed by Youell, Gt. Yarmouth. GC. P112 17/2/1844 & P66 1/2/1845 Listed by W. Miller, Ramsgate. GC. P216 27/3/1847 Listed by R. Cooper, Croydon. GC. P154 11/3/1843. Stock purchased and Intro. by W. Pawley, Bromley. *Epps. Maidstone. GB. 1843.*

ERECTA. Single. Red/Purple. Tube. Dark crimson purple. Sepals. Dark crimson purple. Corolla. Violet red. Multiflowered and of merit. Small. P39. 2nd Ed. by Porcher 1848. Insists that as fuchsia is feminine the correct name is as given, not Erectum as below. NK. NK. NK. NK.

ERECTA COMPACTA. ND. ND/ND. Tube. ND. Sepals. ND. Corolla. ND. L. Cat. 1892. *Comte. France. 1890.*

ERECTA ELEGANS. Single. Red/Purple. Tube. Bright carmine. Sepals. Bright carmine. Corolla. Purple. GC. P480 20/7/1844 Exhibited at HS Show by Kendall. Awarded certificate. GC. P820 Dec 1844 & GC. P808 Nov 1846 "Recommended". GC P66 1/2/1845 & P184 13/3/1847 Listed by W. Miller, Ramsgate. GC. P266 25/4/1846 & P265 24/4/1847 Listed by W. Rendle, Plymouth. GC. P480 20/7/1844 & Vol J2 RHS 1847 Pxxiii Awarded Banksian Silver Medal. *Kendall, Stoke Newington. GB. 1844.*

ERECTA NOVELTY. Single. White/Pink. Tube. White. Sepals. White. Cordate gracefully recurved. Corolla. Soft rose shading to a white base. (Light pink margined with rose). Habit strong. Flowers held erect. Raised by Wyness who was the Gr. to Queen Victoria at Buckingham Palace. GC. P643 12/7/1862 Awarded FCC by Royal Botanical Society. GC. P287 1/4/1865. Intro. by BSW. Leaves marbled and veined. Entire new race. P824 27/6/1885 Report on RHS Trials "Best in its class". RH. P407 1868. RH. P464/5 1886. HC. Cat. 1882-1898. *Wyness, London. GB. 1862.*

ERECTA TRICOLOUR. Single. ND/ND. Tube. ND. Sepals. ND. Corolla. ND. GC. P393 June 1842. Listed by Youells Gt. Yarmouth. GC. P241 15/4/1843. Listed by F&A Smith. Hackney. NK. NK. NK.

ERECTUM. Single. ND/ND. Tube. ND. Sepals. ND. Corolla. ND. P39 2nd Ed. by Porcher Insists correct name is Erecta because fuchsia is feminine. GC. P98 17/2/1844 Listed by Youells, Gt. Yarmouth. GC. P112 17/2/1844 & P66 1/2/1845 Listed by W. Miller, Ramsgate. *Day. GB. NK.*

ERICA Double. Red/White. Tube. Red. Sepals. Red. Corolla. White. Veined Carmine, RB. Cat 1926. *Rozain-Boucharlet, B. (Rozain Jr) France. 1922.*

ERMAN. Double. Red/Purple. Tube. Scarlet. Short. Sepals. Scarlet. Well reflexed. Corolla. Violet Purple, shaded red. Irregular. B. Cat. 1901. *Bull, W. Chelsea. GB. 1900.*

ERNEST. Double. Red/Purple. Tube. Crimson. Sepals. Crimson. Completely reflexed. Corolla. Dark Violet, marked rose at base. B. Cat. 1872-1873. *Bull W. Chelsea. GB. 1872.*

ERNEST BENARY. NK. NK/NK. Tube. NK. Sepals. NK. Corolla. NK. Essig 1936. *Hopfe. Germany. 1868.*

ERNEST D'EVRY. Single. White/Red. Tube. Pure white, Thick. Long. 30mm. Sepals. White. Large. Expanded. Points turned down. Corolla. Vermillion carmine red. Good foliage yellowish green Similar to "Princess of Prussia.". P159 3rd Ed. by Porcher 1858. *Narcis. Evry le Chat. France. 1856.*

ERNEST d'IVRAY. ND. ND/ND. Tube. ND. Sepals. ND. Corolla. ND. GC. P418 22/5/1858 Listed by H. Walton, Burnley. Most likely Ernest D'Evry. NK. NK. NK.

ERNEST RENAN. Single. Red/Red. Tube. Rose. Short. Sepals. Rose. Reflexed. Corolla. Rose. Pyramidical habit. Named after a French philologist and historian 1823-1892. B. Cat. 1888-1893. *Lemoine. Nancy. France. 1888.*

EROS. Single. Pink/Red Tube. Pink. Sepals. Pink with white tips. Corolla. Pinkish red. Purple foliage. Flowers in clusters. Triphylla hybrid. L. Cat. 1907-1908. Triphylla X. *Bonstedt, Gottingen. Germany. 1906.*

ESMERALDA (a). Single. ND/ND. Tube. ND. Sepals. ND. Corolla. ND. GC. P455 8/7/1847 Exhibited at RBS Show by Mr Robinson. GC. P201 27/3/1847 Listed by Hart & Nickling, Guildford. GC. P216 27/3/1847 Listed by R. Cooper, Croydon. GC. P455 8/7/1847 Exhibited RBS Show by Mr. Robinson. *Meillez. Lille. France. 1846?*

ESMERALDA (b). Single. Pink/Lilac. Tube. Soft Pink. Thick. Short. Sepals. Soft Pink. Horizontal. Corolla. Lilac Rose. This variety along with "Napoleon" and "Scaramouche" were the result of Epsii x Venus Victrix. Raised by Demouveaux Gr. to Dubus. Put into commerce by Meillex of Lille. P159 3rd Ed. by Porcher. In all probability identical with one one above. *Demouveaux. France. 1845.*

ESMERALDA (c). ND. Red/Purple. Tube. Red. Sepals. Red. Corolla. Violet. Dobbies, Rothesay. Cat. 1893. NK. NK. NK.

ESMERALDA (d). NK. NK/NK. Tube. NK. Sepals. NK. Corolla. NK. *Boucharlet. France. 1884.*

ESMERALDA (e). Double. Red/Purple. Tube. Red. Sepals. Red. Corolla. Plum violet. RB. Cat. 1926. *Rozain-Boucharlet,B (Rozain Jr), Lyons. France. 1922.*

ESPARTERO.(a) Single. Red/Purple. Tube. Scarlet. Long. Large. Sepals. Scarlet. Short. Expanded well. Corolla. Rich rosy purple. Large. Twice the size of "Chandlerii". GC. P66 1/2/1845 & P112 17/2/1844 Listed by W. Miller, Ramsgate. GC. P146 8/3/1845 Listed by Youells, Gt. Yarmouth. GC. P821 25/11/1843. Intro. by Epps. As large as "Eppsii". *Epps. Maidstone. GB. 1843.*

ESPARTERO (b). Single. ND/ND. Tube. ND. Sepals. ND. Corolla. ND. GC. P66 1/2/1845 Listed by W. Miller, Ramsgate. *Bell. GB. 1844?*

ESPARTERO (c). Single. ND/ND. Tube. ND. Sepals. ND. Corolla. ND. GC. P66 1/2/1845 Listed by W.Miller, Ramsgate. *Knight. GB. 1843?*

ESPARTERO (d). Single. ND. Tube. ND. Sepals. ND. Corolla. ND. GC. P66 1/2/1845 Listed by W. Miller, Ramsgate. *Miller, Ramsgate. GB. 1844.*

ESPÉRANCE (a). Single. Pink/Purple. Tube. Flesh pink. Sepals. Flesh Pink. Corolla. Dark blue. Good foliage. Good habit. RH. P169 1857. *Demoreaux. France. 1857.*

ESPÉRANCE (b). Double. Red/Purple. Tube. Red. Sepals. Red. Corolla. Purple. L. Cat. 1889-1892. F. Riccartonii X. *Lemoine, Nancy. France. 1887.*

ESPÉRANCE.(c). Single. White/Pink. Tube. Pure White. Short. Sepals. Pure white. Corolla. Rose with a white base. Witte. 1882. Dugourd. NK. NK. *1876.*

ESTEEM. Single. Red/Purple. Tube. Crimson. Sepals. Crimson. Corolla. Rosy Purple. GC. P161 17/3/1849 Listed by W. Rumley, Richmond. GC. P112 12/2/1848 Intro. by G. Smith, Islington. *Michie. GB. 1848*

ESTELLA. ND. ND/ND. Tube. ND. Sepals. ND. Corolla. ND. RH. 1846 P270 M. Chauviere has bought the entire stock. NK. *France. 1846.*

ESTELLE. Single. White/Red. Tube. White. Sepals. White. Reflexed. Corolla. Rose shaded Violet. Raised by W. Knight Gr. to the Duke of Kent. GC. P539 10/7/1858 Listed by F. Godwin Sheffield. GC. P238 19/3/1858 Listed by W. Rumley, Richmond. GC. P126 20/2/1858 Intro. By W. Rollinson, Tooting. *Knight, W. GB. 1858.*

ESTELLE D'EVRY. Single. Pink/Violet. Tube. Soft rose. 12mm long. Sepals. Soft rose. Large. Pointed. Reflexed. Bright rose underneath. Corolla. Soft lilac violet. similiar in length to tube. Small foliage, Denticulate. 4cm x 3cm. Reddish Petioles

P159 3rd. Ed by Porcher 1858. Venus Victrix X. *Narcis, Evry le Chat. France. 1856.*

ETHEL. Single. White/Red. Tube. White. 45mms long. (2 inches). Sepals. Tinted rose. Large. Green points. Horizontal. Corolla. Violet rose fading to clear red. Spiral shape. Delicate like "Leah". Flowers from leaf joints not in terminal clusters. Query parentage "Geant of Versailles" or "Reine de France" 4th Ed by Porcher 1874. B.Cat.1872-1875. *Bull, W. Chelsea. GB. 1872.*

ETHEL FRY. Double. Red/White. Tube. Crimson Scarlet. Sepals. Crimson Scarlet. Corolla. White. Laings Cat. circa 1890. *Fry G. Lea. GB* NK.

ÉTIENNE LAMY. Double. Red/Purple. Tube. Scarlet. Sepals. Scarlet. Corolla. Violet marbled rose. Very Large. L. Cat. 1906. JF. Cat. 1907. *Lemoine, Nancy. France. 1906.*

ÉTOILE DE VERSAILLES. Single. ND. Tube. ND. Sepals. ND. Corolla. ND. GC. P224 14/4/1849. Listed by R. Whibley, Kennington. GC. P226 13/4/1850 Listed by Poole Nurseries. *Salter, J. Versailles. France. 1848*

ÉTOILE DU NORD (a). Single. Red/Purple. Tube. Scarlet. Sepals. Scarlet. Corolla. Violet Black. RH.P295 1887 grown as a standard at Twickel. GC. P515 25/7/1857 & P418 22/5/1858 Listed by H. Walton, Burnley. GC. P357 7/4/858 C. Allen, Stoke Newington. GC. P210 28/3/1857 Intro. by E.G. Henderson. *Banks, E. Deal. GB. 1857.*

ÉTOILE DU NORD (b). Single. White/Red. Tube. White. Sepals. White, tipped green. Reflexed well. Corolla. Bright rose. Dwarf compact habit. Prolific flowering. RH. P168, 1857. NK. *France.* NK.

ÉTOILE DU NORD (c). Sepals. Red/Purple. Tube. Reddish purple. 15mm long. Sepals. Reddish purple. Large. reflexed. Corolla. Bright violet purple. 3rd. Order. P159 3rd. Ed. by Porcher 1858. *Baudinet, Meaux. France. 1855.*

ÉTOILE FILANT. Double. Red/Purple. Rosy purple. Sepals. Rosy purple. Corolla. Violet. Large. JF. Cat. 1898. NK. NK. *1897.*

ETRURIA. Single. Red/Purple. Tube. Bright rose. Short. Sepals. Bright rose. Broad. Well Reflexed. Corolla. Light bluish purple, sprayed with rose at base of sepals. B. Cat. 1875-1876. *Bull, W. Chelsea. GB. 1874.*

ETTIE. Single. Red/Purple. Tube. Bright rose. Sepals. Bright rose. Large. Long. Reflexed. Corolla. Purple with red at base. Large. GC. P74 21/1/1863 Intro. by W. Bull. *Bull, W. Chelsea. GB. 1863.*

EUGÈNE DELAPLANCHE. Double. Red/Purple. Tube. Bright red. Sepals. Bright red. Reflexed. Corolla. Clear Violet. Large. Flowers are like that of "Nancy". (Very dark). B. Cat. 1892. L. Cat. 1892. *Lemoine, Nancy. France. 1891.*

EUGÈNE FOURNIERE. Double. Red/Purple. Tube. Red. Sepals. Red. Rolled up. Corolla. Amaranth Violet. Short Pedicel. P149 L. Cat. 1901. *Compere. France. 1900.*

EUGENE TURNER. NK. NK/NK. Tube. NK. Sepals. NK. Corolla. NK. Novelty of 1857 Details not known. P160 3rd Ed. by Porcher. 1858. *Turner, C. Slough. GB. 1857.*

EUGÈNE VERCONSIN. Double. Red/White. Tube. Clear red. Sepals. Clear Red. Short. Corolla. Pinky white at centre and bluish at extremity.(Petals shading from rosy white at base to lavender blue at extremity). B. Cat. 1892. L. Cat. 1892. *Lemoine, Nancy. France. 1892.*

EUGENIA. Single. Red/White. Tube. Bright red. Sepals. Bright red. Reflexed. Corolla White, veined carmine. Sometimes can come semi- double. Large. B. Cat. 1901. *Bull, W. Chelsea. GB. 1900.*

EULALIE. Single. White/Purple. Tube. Greenish white. Long. 45mm. Thick. Sepals. White, Well open. Large. Corolla. Lilac. P160 3rd Ed. by Porcher 1858. GC. P537 12/8/1848 Listed by G. Smith, Islington. GC. P161 17/3/1849 Listed by W. Rumley, Richmond. GC P256 21/4/1849. Listed by R. Cooper, Croydon. GC. P274 5/5/1849 Listed by H. Walton, Burnley. *Salter. Versailles. France. 1848.*

EUPHONIA. Single. NK/NK. Tube. NK. Sepals. Corolla. NK, Haage & Schmidt Cat. 1885. NK. NK. NK. NK.

EUREKA. Double. Red/Purple. Tube. Bright rose. Sepals. Bright rose. Corolla. Deep purple flushed magenta. Laings Cat. circa 1890. HC. Cat. 1890. NK. NK. NK.

EUROPA. Double. Red/White. Tube. Carmine. Sepals. Carmine. Large. Reflexed. Corolla. White striped bright rose. Very large and full. 4th. Ed. by Porcher 1874 Floriferous but inferior to "Madame Lemoine". Pedicel 40 mms. RH. P311 1889. *Twrdy, Brno. Austria. 1872.*

EURYDICE. Single. White/Purple. Tube. White suffused rose. Sepals. White suffused rose pink. Long. Broad. Corolla. Purplish rose. Long. Name is from Greek mythology, the wife of Orpheus. L. Cat. 1901. B. Cat. 1901. *Bull, W. Chelsea. GB. 1901.*

EUSTACE. Single. Red/Purple. Tube. Bright crimson. Sepals. Bright crimson. Corolla. Rich purple. Short thick flowers. Free bloomer. B. Cat.1872-1875. *Bull, W. Chelsea. GB. 1872.*

EUTERPE (a). Single. ND. Tube. ND. Sepals. ND. Corolla. Named after the Muse of music. ND. GC. P200 28/3/1846. Listed by J. & S. Shilling, Odiham. *Gaines. GB. NK.*

EUTERPE (b). Single. White/Purple. Tube. Greenish White. Long. Thin. 18/20mm.Sepals. Greenish white, Horizontal. Points reflexed. Corolla. Nice shade of violet, margined purple. Pleated. P160 3rd. Ed. by Porcher. 1858. Charmer x Sydonie. *Banks, E. Deal. GB. 1854.*

EVA. Double. Red/White. Tube. Scarlet. Sepals. Scarlet. Well Reflexed. Corolla. White. F&P. P57 March 1866. GC. P55 19/1/1865 Review by H. Cannell. *Bull, W. Chelsea. GB. 1864.*

ÉVELINA. Single. Lilac/Lilac. Tube. Soft lilac. Thick. Short. Sepals. Large. Spreading Points turned down. Corolla. Lilac. P160 3rd. Ed by Porcher. *Salter, J. Versailles. France. 1847.*

EVENING STAR (a). ND. White/ND. Tube. White. Sepals. White. Corolla. ND. SG. P459 1866. NK. NK. NK.

EVENING STAR (b). Single. White/Purple. Tube. White. Thick. Long 20mms. Swelling at the top. Sepals. White. Reflexed. Corolla. Violet tinged with white and bordered bright rose. Long. Spiralled. P117 4th. Edition by Porcher 1874. Intro. by E.G.Henderson. *Banks, E. Deal? GB. 1868.*

EXCELLENT (a). Single. Red/Purple. Tube. Scarlet. Sepals. Scarlet. Moderately reflexed. Corolla. Dark Bluish Violet. Well Expanded. Distinct Globose characteristics. GC. P94 30/6/1860 Listed by F. Godwin, Sheffield. GC. P18 14/1/1860 Intro. by W. Rollinson, Tooting. *Rollinson, W. Tooting. GB. 1860.*

EXCELLENT (b). Double. Red/Purple. Tube. Crimson. Sepals. Crimson. Corolla. Magenta (new colour) P126 4th. Edition by Porcher 1874. Not in the first selection. GC. P289 1/4/1865 Raised by G. Smith. *Smith G. Islington. GB. 1865.*

EXCELSEA. Single. Red/Purple. Tube. Cerise. Sepals. Cerise. Large. Open. Corolla. Violet red. P39 2nd. Ed. of Porcher 1848 Leaves 7cm x 4cm. Nice variety. Floriferous. This fuchsia resembles "Clio" and "Macnabiana". GC. P481 15/7/1843 Exhibited at H.S. Show on 12/7/1843 by Gaines, Battersea. GC. P375 4/6/1844 Exhibited at H.S. Show by Mr. Cole. GC. P393 6/1842 & P98 12/2/1844 & P146 8/3/1845 Listed by Youells. Gt. Yarmouth. GC. P241 15/4/1843 Listed by F & A Smith, Hackney. GC. P242 15/4/1842 Listed by A & J. Stewart, Windsor. GC. P345 28/5/1842 Intro. by J. Smith. *Smith, J. Dalston. GB. 1842.*

EXCELSIOR (a). ND. ND/ND. Tube. ND. Sepals. ND. Corolla. ND. GC. P238 19/3/1859. Listed by W. Rumley, Richmond. NK. NK. NK.

EXCELSIOR (b). ND. ND/ND. Tube. ND. Sepals. ND. Corolla. ND. Vol P1 J of RHS P291 1859. Submitted to Floral C'tee. GC. P594 29/6/1861. Listed by Godwin & Padnam, Sheffield. "New plants of the Season". *Smith F&A. GB. 1861.*

EXCELSIOR (c). Double. Red/Purple. Tube. Bright crimson. Sepals. Bright crimson. Completely reflexed. Corolla. Light Blue. Well formed. L. Cat. 1901. B. Cat. 1895- 1898. *Bull, W. Chelsea. GB. 1895.*

EXHIBITOR. Single. Red/Purple. Tube. Lively carmine. Short. Sepals. Lively carmine. Broad. Well reflexed. Corolla. Reddish Purple. (Indigo blue). Cup shaped. Expanded petals thick and overlapping. Spiral petals. GC. P55 19/1/1867 Review by HC. P107 4th Ed. by Porcher. Floriferous. Pedicel 30mms. Sepals rounded to tube. GC. P335 11/4/1864 Intro. by Luccombe & Pince, Exeter. *Pince, Exeter. GB. 1863.*

EXIMIA (a). Single. ND/ND. Tube. ND. Sepals. ND. Corolla. ND. GC. 23/1/1841 "Best new Plants" GC. P630 25/9/18411 "F fulgens" hybrid. GC. P833 18/12/1841 "Recommended" GC. 1/5/1841. Listed by Woodland Nurseries, Uckfield. GC. P97 18/2/1843 & P98 17/2/1844 Listed by Youell, Gt. Yarmouth. F.fulgens X. NK. *GB. 1840.*

EXIMIA (b). Single. Red/Purple. Tube. Bright Pink. Sepals. Bright Pink. Corolla. Crimson Violet. GC. P2 4/1/1845 Intro. by Girling. *Girling, Stowmarket. GB. 1845.*

EXIMIA (c). Single. Red/Purple. Tube. Crimson. Sepals. Crimson. Reflex back. Globe shaped flower. Corolla. Dark violet purple. Margined crimson. 5/6 flowers at each leaf axil. GC. P525 2/8/1845 Intro by Whale. *Whale, Kintbury. GB. 1845.*

EXIMIA (d). Single. Red/Purple. Tube. Red. Sepals. Red. Corolla. Purple. GC. P808 Nov 1846 "Recommended". GC.P140 27/2/1847 "Good". GC. P184 13/3/1847 Listed by W. Miller, Ramsgate. GC. P216 27/3/1847 Listed by R. Cooper, Croydon. GC. P265 24/4/1847 & P259 28/4/1849 & P241 20/4/1850 Listed by W. Rendle, Plymouth. GC. P224 14/4/1849 Listed by R. Whibley, Kennington. GC. P249 18/4/1846. Intro by J. Smith. *Smith, J. Dalston. GB. 1846.*

EXIMIUM. Single. Red/Red. Tube. Crimson red. Sepals. Crimson red. Corolla. Crimson red. Vol IX P13 Floricultural Cabinet 1841.The flowers are in the form of Globosa Major and produced in terminal clusters of 20 upwards in each. 1841. NK. *GB.* NK.

EXONIENSIS. Single. Red/Purple. Tube. Crimson. Short. Sepals. Crimson. Twice as long as the tube. Fall below the horizontal like a Chinese hat. Corolla. Purple. (Violet blue). Medium size. Lax.Colour Plate in Floricultural Cabinet P145 1/7/1843. Colour plate in Paxtons Magazine of Botany August 1843. GC. P369 3/6/1843 To be sent out 10/8/1843. Raised in 1842, out of many hundreds of seedlings. GC. P431 24/6/1843 Exhibited at H.S. Show by Lane, Berkhampstead. GC. P455 8/7/1847 Exhibited by Mr. Bray (and Mr. Robinson) at RBS Show. Noted that sepals fail to expand. Explained away as being forced for show. GC. GC. P375 4/6/1844 Exhibited at H.S. Show by Catleugh. GC. P820 12/1844 "Recommended". GC. P808 11/1846 "Recommended". GC. P140 27/2/1847 "Good". P39 "2nd Ed. by Porcher 1848 Upright habit. Wood, petioles and veins of foliage are violet. Foliage is 7cm x 4 cm. GC. P216 27/3/1847 & P232 1/4/1848 & P256 21/4/1849 Listed by R. Cooper, Croydon. GC. P98 17/2/1844 & P146 8/3/1845 Listed by Youell, Gt. Yarmouth. GC. P112 17/2/1844 & P66 1/2/1845 Listed by W. Miller, Ramsgate. GC. P259 28/4/1849 Listed by W. Rendle, Plymouth. H. Cannell in his catalogue states the plant is the same as "Corallina". Disputed. GC. P632 17/11/1883. Cordifolia x Globosa. Intro. by Luccombe & Pince, Exeter. *Pince. Exeter. GB. 1843.*

EXPANSA. Single. Red/Purple. Tube. Bright rose. Sepals. Bright rose. Horizontal. Corolla. Lilac. (Purple). (Rosy purple). Large. Expanded. Floricultal Cabinet Vol IX. P200 1843 RBS Show Selected for a prize. Smaller and shorter flowers with the sepals standing out horizontally. RH. P24 1844 Corolla Large and expanded. P39 2nd Ed. by Porcher 1847. FJ.P85 1845 "Recommended". GC. P146 8/3/1845 Listed by Youells, Gt. Yarmouth. GC. P216 27/3/1847 Listed by R. Cooper, Croydon. GC. P193 30/3/1844. Intro. by J. Smith. *Smith, J. Dalston. GB. 1844.*

EXPANSIA. Single. Red/Red. Tube. Rose. Sepals. Rose. Corolla. Crimson. Like "Gigantea" with much larger corolla. GC P142 14/3/1846 & P184 13/3/1847 Listed by W. Miller, Ramsgate. GC. P66 1/2/1845 Intro. by W. Miller, Ramsgate. *Miller, W. Ramsgate. GB 1845.*

EXPANSION (a). Single. White/Red. Tube. White. 15mm long. Sepals. White. Marked carmine. Horizontal. Corolla. Bright rose. P160 3rd. Ed. by Porcher 1858. Variety of the second rank. Greenish yellow foliage.GC. P183 20/3/1852 "Select" GC. P279 30/4/1853 "Light green stemmed". GC. P454 16/7/1853 Exhibited at Hort. Scty Show 9/7/1853 as a 7' pyramid by Mr. Bousie gr. to Rt. Hon. Labouchere. GC. P545 30/8/1851 Listed by G. Smith, Islington. GC.P177 20/3/1852 Listed by W. Rumley, Richmond. GC. P209 5/4/1851 Intro. by C. Turner, Slough. *Banks, E. Deal. GB. 1851.*

EXPANSION (b). Single. Red/Purple. Tube. Bright rose. Sepals. Bright rose. Completely reflexed. Corolla. Light bluish purple, widely expanded to become flat. JF. Cat. 1885. B. Cat. 1882-1883. Intro. by W. Bull, Chelsea. *Eckford. GB. 1882.*

EXPLOSION. Double. Red/Purple. Tube. Red. Sepals. Red. Corolla. Reddish Purple. Enormous. Very open. RB. Cat 1897. *Rozain. Lyons. France. 1894.*

EXQUISITA. Double. Red/White. Tube. Carmine red. Sepals. Carmine red. Corolla. White variegated pink. P82 Witte. 1882. *Twrdy, Brno. Austria. 1878.*

EXQUISITE (a). ND. ND/ND. Tube. ND. Sepals. ND. Corolla. ND. Listed by Youells, Gt. Yarmouth GC. P98 17/2/1844 & P146 8/3/1845. Intro. by Youell.Gt. Yarmouth. *Youell, Gt. Yarmouth. GB. 1843.*

EXQUISITE (b). Single. White/Red. Tube. White. Short. Very thick. Sepals. White. Horizontal. Corolla. Red. (Violet red) Crimson at petal edges. P160 3rd Ed. by Porcher 1858. Almost Globular.GC. P423 7/7/1849 Exhibited at Australian Bot. & Hort. Scty. Sydney 1/3/1849. GC. P120 23/2/1850 "Select". App. to RH.1851 by Porcher 1st class variety. GC. P423 1851 Exhibited at RBS Show, by H. Low of Clapton. GC. P535 23/8/1851 Exhibited at Vauxhall Garden Show. GC. P184 13/3/1847 & P250 17/4/1847 Listed by W. Miller, Ramsgate. GC. P216 27/3/1847 & P232 1/4/1848 & P256 21/4/1849 Listed by R. Cooper, Croydon. GC. P241 20/4/1850 Listed by W. Rendle, Plymouth. *Fowles. GB. 1846.*

EXQUISITE(c). Single. Red/Purple. Tube. Bright scarlet. Very short. 10mm. Sepals. Bright scarlet.

Fall gracefully backwards. Reflexed. Corolla Violet Purple. P160 3rd. Ed. by Porcher. Style well extended. Similiar to "Resplendent" but that is less good. Raised by either J. Smith or a celebrated amateur from the North of England. GC. P449 17/7/1852 & P209 26/3/1853. Listed by H. Walton, Burnley. GC. P130 21/2/1852 Introduced by E. G. Henderson. Corallina X. *Smith, J. Liverpool. GB. 1852.*

EXQUISITE (d). Double. Red/Purple. Tube. Bright crimson. Sepals. Bright crimson. Reflexed. Corolla. Purple and rose. Flamed and shaded rose. Large. Full. GC. P320 20/3/1869 Intro. by Felton & Son, Birmingham. *Felton, Birmingham. GB. 1869.*

EXTRAORDINARY. Double. Red/Purple. Tube. Carmine scarlet. Tapered. Sepals. Carmine Scarlet. Close. Concave. Reflexed. Corolla. Deep violet purple. ½" compact. Like a double form of "Globosa". Vol.3. J of RHS 1872. Pcxv. Fuchsia Trials at Chiswick Awarded **. HC. Cat 1882. The reflex is perfectly distinct from any other fuchsia. Gardening Illustrated 3/1/1885. *Jeffries. GB. 1871?*

EYNSFORD GEM. Single. White/Red. Tube. Waxy ivory white. Sepals. Ivory white. Stout, Broad. Leathery texture. Corolla. Fiery rose lake. Petals stout and well expanded. Loveliest reflexed fuchsia in cultivation. Illustrated in HC. Cat. 1890. GO."Select" 1889-1892. L. Cat. 1892. JF. Cat. 1888. *Weston. GB. 1888.*

FABIUS. Double. Red/Purple. Tube. Bright crimson. Sepals. Bright Crimson. Recurved. Corolla. Rich purple marked rose at base. Large. B. Cat. 1882-1888. *Bull, W. Chelsea. GB. 1882.*

FAGUS. Single. Red/White. Tube. Light Carmine. Sepals. Light carmine. Broad. Corolla. Whitish Pink veined carmine rose. L. Cat. 1906. *Bull, W. Chelsea. GB. 1905.*

FAIR HELEN. Single. White/Red. Tube. White. (Flesh). Sepals. White. (Flesh). Corolla. Scarlet. GC. P369 6/6/844 Listed by T. Cripps, Maidstone. GC P146 8/3/1845 Listed by Youells, Gt. Yarmouth. GC. P162 16/3/1844. Intro. by Hally, Blackheath. *Hally, Blackheath. GB. 1844.*

FAIR MAID (a). Single. White/Purple. Tube. Waxy White. Sepals. Waxy White. Corolla. Violet Purple. GC. P184 13/3/1847 Listed by W. Miller, Ramsgate. GC. P250 7/4/1847 Intro. by Rogers, Uttoxeter. *Rogers, Uttoxeter GB. 1847.*

FAIR MAID (b). Single. White/Red. Tube. Creamy White. Sepals. Creamy White, tinted blush. Corolla. Deep carmine flushed with magenta. Stout. Very fine. B. Cat. 1889-1892. L. Cat. 1892. JF. Cat. 1889. *Lye, J. Market Lavington. GB. 1889.*

FAIR ORIANA. Single. White/Red. Tube. White. Thick. Long. 15 mm. Sepals. White. Large. Horizontal. Points upturned. Corolla. Pure Scarlet. (Clear violet red). (Carmine). Dwarf bush. Multiflowered. Small, but nice. P117 4th Ed. by Porcher 1874. Vol 2 Jof RHS 1870. GC P283 25/4/1857 Intro. by E.G. Henderson. *Banks, E. Deal. GB. 1857.*

FAIR ROSAMOND. Single.White/Red. Tube. White. (Waxy White). Short. Swollen. Sepals. White. (White tinged pink). Spreading. Corolla. Crimson. (Cerise red). App. to RH. 1851 by Porcher. GC. 14/7/1849 H.S. Show 11/7/1849. In the way of Beauty Supreme, but larger. GC. P465 27/7/1850 Listed by W. Rumley, Richmond. GC. P242 20/4/1850 Intro. by E.G. Henderson. *E.G. Henderson, St. Johns Wood. GB. 1850.*

FAIR ROSAMUNDE. Single. ND/ND. Tube. ND. Sepals. ND. Corolla. ND. GC. P241 20/4/1850. Listed by W. Rendle, Plymouth. GC. P283 11/4/1846 & P250 17/4/1847. Intro. By Epps. *Epps, Maidstone. GB. 1846.*

FAIREST OF THE FAIR. Single. White/Red. Tube. White. Bulged. Sepals. White. ?" long.Recurved. Green at tip. Corolla. Crimson. (Clear rosy purple paler at base). ?" long. (Moderately expanded). J of RHS P3 1863 P91 & Vol III 1872. HC. Cat. 1882. GC.P515 25/7/1857 Listed by H. Walton, Burnley. GC. P210 28/3/1857 & P283 25/4/1857. Intro. by E.G. Henderson. *Banks, E. Deal. GB. 1857.*

FAIRY (a) Single. ND/ND. Tube. ND. Sepals. ND. Corolla. ND. GC. P241 15/4/1843 Listed by F&A Smith, Hackney. GC. P242 15/4/1843 Listed by A.J. Stewart, Windsor. GC. P112 17/2/1844 & P66 1/2/1845 Listed by W. Miller, Ramsgate. *Harrison, Dereham. GB. 1842.*

FAIRY (b). Single. Red/White. Tube. Dark crimson. Sepals. Dark crimson. Broad. Completely reflexed. Corollla. Pure White, red at base. GC. P74 24/1/1863 Intro. by W. Bull. *Bull, W. Chelsea. GB. 1863.*

FAIRY (c). Single. ND/ND. Tube. ND. Sepals. ND. Corolla. ND. Miniatured flowered fuchsia. GC. P382 29/4/1865. Intro. by E.G. Henderson. NK. *GB. 1865.*

FAIRY QUEEN (a). Single. Red/Red. Tube. Carmine. Long. Rough. Rich coloured. Sepals. Carmine. Corolla. Lake. Petals stout, without purple. GC. P417 17/6/1843 Assessed. GC. P112 17/2/1844 & P66 1/2/1845 GC. P201 27/3/1847 Listed by Hart & Nickling, Guildford. RH. P23 1846 Very long tube. GC. P553 28/8/1843 Intro. By W. Bell, Thirsk. *Bell, W. Thirsk. GB. 1843.*

FAIRY QUEEN (b). Single. White/Purple. Tube. Waxy White. Sepals. Waxy White, tinged lemon. Corolla. Rich plum puce. Large. GC. P530 11/8/1855 & P208 22/3/1856 Listed by Bainbridge & Hewison, York. GC. P34 20/1/1855. Intro. by Epps. *Banks, E. Deal. GB. 1855.*

FAIRY QUEEN (c). Single. White/Purple. Tube. White. Sepals. White. Finely recurved. Corolla. Magenta Pink (Rosy carmine). Select GO 1880-1886. BSW. Cat. 1878. Plate 426 Floral Magazine 1880. *Lye, J. Market Lavington. GB. 1878*

FAIRY QUEEN. Single. White/Red. Tube. Yellowish white. Sepals. Yellowish white. Corolla. Carmine rose. P83 Witte 1882. *Henderson, E.G. St Johns Wood. GB. 1875.*

FALCON. Single. Red/Purple. Tube. Crimson. Short. Sepals. Crimson. Globular Buds. Corolla. Bluish Purple. B. Cat. 1901. *Bull, W. Chelsea GB. 1900.*

FALLSCHIRM. ND. Red/Purple. Tube. Carmine rose. Sepals. Carmine rose. Corolla. Violet red. Haag & Schmidt, Erfurt Cat. 1891. NK. NK. *Germany. 1891.*

FALSTAFFE. Single. ND/ND. Tube. ND. Sepals. ND. Corolla. ND. Intro. by C. Turner, Slough. RBS Exhibition 20/6/1849 awarded C. of M. NK NK. *GB. 1849.*

FAME (a). Single. ND/ND. Tube. ND. Sepals. ND. Corolla. ND. GC. P455 8/7/1847. Exhibited at RBS. by Mr. Bray, Gr to Mr. Goldsmith. NK. NK. *GB. 1847.*

FAME (b). Single. Red/Purple. Tube. Red. (Clear red). Sepals. Red. (Clear red). Reflexed. Rounded to tube. Corolla. Purple. Bell shaped. Good habit. Good form. 4th. Ed. by Porcher 1874. GC. P55 19/1/1867 Review by H. Cannell. NK. NK. *GB. 1866.*

FANE. Double. Red/Purple. Tube. Crimson. Short. Sepals. Crimson. Recurved. Corolla. Blue splashed at base with carmine. Full. B. Cat. 1898-1899. *Bull, W. Chelsea. GB. 1897.*

FANNY ESSLER. ND. ND/ND. Tube. ND. Sepals. ND. Corolla. ND. *Meillez. France. 1867.*

FANNY WEBB. Single. ND/ND. Tube. ND. Sepals. ND. Corolla. ND. GC. P258 20/4/1855 Listed by H. Walton, Burnley. GC. P249 15/4/1854 Intro. by Cole & Sharpe, Aston. *Cole & Sharpe, Aston. GB. 1854.*

FANNY. Single. ND/ND. Tube. ND. Sepals. ND. Corolla. ND. GC. P426 12/5/1860 & GC. P824 8/9/1860 Listed by F. Godwin, Sheffield. NK. NK. *GB. 1859.*

FANTASTIC. Double. Red/Purple. Tube. Crimson. Sepals. Crimson. Well reflexed. Corolla. Mauve. 8 petals in flower, 4 expanded like "La Crinoline". Other 4 form a ring round the filaments. Floral Magazine Feb 1865. GC. P289 1/4/1865. GC. P158 26/2/1865. Intro. by G. Smith. *Smith, G. Islington. GB. 1865.*

FANTOME. Double. Red/Purple. Tube. Bright crimson. Waxy. Sepals. Bright crimson. Corolla. Violet Purple. GC. P593 20/9/1851. J. Dobson, Woodlands Nurseries, Isleworth, purchased entire stock. Raised in 1850. GC. P143 6/3/1852. Intro. by J. Dobson. *Story, W.H. Newton Abbot. GB. 1851.*

FARA. Double. Red/Red. Tube. Rich crimson. Short. Sepals. Rich crimson. Corolla. Dark crimson. Fluted petals. Large. B. Cat. 1883. *Bull, W. Chelsea. GB. 1883.*

FASCINATION (a). Single. Red/White. Tube. Red. Short. Sepals. Red. Long. Reflexed .Corolla. White. GC. P426 12/5/1860 Listed by F. Godwin, Sheffield. Vol P3 J of RHS 1863 P91. Report on Fuchsias grown for Trial at Chiswick 1862. GC. P90 5/2/1859. Intro. by G. Smith, Tollington Nurseries. *Smith, G. Islington. GB. 1859.*

FASCINATION (b). Single. White/Pink. Tube. White. Long. Sepals. White. Broad and prettily recurved. Corolla. Rose Pink. JF. Cat. 1899. L. Cat. 1901. B. Cat. 1898-1901. *Bull, W. Chelsea. GB. 1898.*

FASCINATION (c). Double Red/Pink. Renamed in England. See Emile de Wildeman.

FATHER IGNATUS. Single. Red/Purple. Tube. Scarlet. Sepals. Scarlet. Reflexed. Bushy habit. Short jointed. Corolla. Violet Purple. (Indigo blue sometimes striped with rose, mostly in the first lot of blooms). Small foliage. Free bloomer. Corolla has the finest outline of any. GC. P55 19/1/1867 Review by H. Cannell. GC P382 29/4/1865 Intro. by E.G.Henderson. *Banks, E. Deal. GB. 1865.*

FATMA. Double. Red/Purple. Tube. Bright crimson. Sepals. Bright crimson. Reflexed. Corolla. Bluish Purple. B. Cat. 1888-1895. *Bull, W. Chelsea, GB. 1886.*

FAUST. Single. Red/Purple. Tube. Red. Sepals. Red. Corolla. Purple. P115 4th Ed. by Porcher 1874. Not in the first selection. *Demay, H. France. 1866.*

FAVOURITE (a). Single. White/Purple. Tube. White. Sepals. White. Points 2?." x 2" across. Corolla. Violet. Floricultural Cabinet P220 Vol 13 1845.Larger flower than Venus Victrix. Exhibited RBS. June 1845. GC. P270 20/4/1845 Intro by Gaines. *Gaines, Battersea GB. 1845.*

FAVOURITE (b). Single. Red/Purple. Tube. Scarlet. Sepals. Scarlet. Finely reflexed. Corolla. Blue Violet. GC. P314 10/5/1856 Listed by Youell, Gt. Yarmouth. GC. P451 5/7/1856 Listed by J. Clark, Cheltenham. GC.P451 5/7/1856 & P642 27/9/1856 Listed by H. Walton, Burnley. GC. P690 18/10/1856 & P146 7/3/1857 Listed by W. Rumley, Richmond. GC. P251 11/4/1857 Listed by W. Masters, Canterbury. GC. P260 14/3/1860 Listed by Wm. Hussey, Norwich. GC. P34 20/1/1855 Intro. by E.G. Henderson. St. Johns Wood. *Banks, E. Deal. GB. 1855.*

FAVOURITE (c). Single. White/Red. Tube. Pure White. Sepals. Pure White. Corolla. Rich Orange Scarlet. B. Cat. 1875. *Bland, E. Fordham. GB. 1868.*

FAVOURITE (d). Single. Red/Purple. Tube. Red. Sepals. Red. Corolla. Purple. GC. P311 8/9/1877 Exhibited at Trowbridge by Matthews (1st), Lye (2nd). GC. P211 17/2/1877 West Country varieties and Growers. *Doel. GB. NK.*

FAVOURITE (e). Double. Red/White. Tube. Bright crimson. Sepals. Bright crimson. Completely reflexed. Corolla. Blush White, marked rose at base. B. Cat. 1895-1899. Intro. by W. Bull. *Bull, W. Chelsea. GB. 1895.*

FAVOURITE OF FORTUNE. Single. Red/Purple. Tube. Red. Sepals. Red. Corolla. Purple. Best dark dwarf. GC. P102 1/2/1868 Review by H. Cannell. NK. NK. *GB. 1867.*

F.C. HEINEMANN. ND. ND/ND. Tube. ND. Sepals. ND. Corolla. ND. RH. P295 1887 Fuchsias grown as standards at Twickel. *Cornelissen, Arras Belgium. NK.*

FÉLICIEN DAVID. Double. Red/Purple. Tube, Clear Red. Sepals. Clear Red. Well reflexed.

Corolla. Pansy Violet. (Violet). Enormous. Vigorous. Full. Well open. JF. Cat. 1904 L. Cat. 1903. *Lemoine, Nancy. France. 1903.*

FELIX DUBOIS. Double. Red/Purple. Tube. Scarlet. Sepals. Scarlet. (Cerise Red). Large. Recurved. (Reflexed). Corolla. Rosy Mauve. Dwarf. RB. Cat. 1897. JF. Cat. 1895. B. Cat. 1894. *Lemoine, Nancy. France. 1894.*

FEMINA. Single. Pink/White. Tube. White suffused salmon pink. Sepals. White, suffused salmon pink. Reflexed. Corolla. Pure white. Perfect. Plant forms a small low bush, covered with flowers. L. Cat. 1913. *Rozain, Lyons. France 1913.*

FERDINAND. Single. Red/Purple. Tube. Crimson Red. Sepals. Crimson Red. Held well out. Large. Open well. Corolla. Violet Purple. App. to RH. 1851 by Porcher. *Baudinet. France. 1850.*

FERNAND MAHNKE. Single. Red/White. Tube. Red. Sepals. Red. Corolla. Pure white. Bruant, Poitiers Cat. 1915. Identical with "Flocon de Neige" Essig 1936. NK. NK. NK. *1912.*

FESTINA. Double. Red/White. Tube. Rich crimson. Sepals. Rich crimson. Corolla. Pure white. B. Cat. 1875-1878. *Bull, W. Chelsea. GB. 1874.*

FIGARO (a). Single. ND/ND. Tube. ND. Sepals. ND. Corolla. ND. GC. P251 11/4/1857 "New fuchsias of 1856" Listed by W. Masters, Exotic Nurseries, Maidstone. NK. *GB. 1856.*

FIGARO (b). Single. ND/ND. Tube. ND. Sepals. ND. Corolla. ND. GC. P594 29/6/1861 Listed by Godwin & Padman, Sheffield. GC. P771 24/8/1861 Listed by H. Walton, Burnley. GC. P358 20/4/1861 Intro. by G. Smith, Tollington Nursery. *Smith, G. Islington. GB. 1861.*

FIGARO (c) Double. Red/Purple. Tube. Lavender red. Sepals. Lavender red. Corolla. Light violet. Very much expanded. P79 Witte 1882. *Demay, H. Arras. Belgium. 1876.*

FILLE DE L'AIR. Single. Red/White. Tube. Red. Sepals. Red. Corolla. Pure white. Essig 1936. *Lemoine, Nancy. France. 1862.*

FILLE DES CHAMPS. Single. ND/ND. Tube. ND. Sepals. ND. Corolla. ND. L. Cat. 1887. *Lemoine, Nancy. France. 1887.*

FINAL. Single. Red/Purple. Tube. Red. Sepals. Red. Corolla. Purple. GC. P183 1888 "Recommended". G. 6/9/1884 Exhibited by J Lye at Trowbridge on 20/8/1884 GC. Vol 22 P310 6/9/1884, GC. Vol 26 P375 18/9/1886, GC.Vol 2 1887.Exhibited at Bath Floral Fete by J. Lye, 1st 9 pot class 1884, 1886, 1887, The Garden Vol 36 P277 1889 Third. *Lye, J. Market Lavington. GB. 1881?*

FINSBURY VOLUNTEER. Single. Red/Purple. Tube. Red.(Bright red). Sepals. Red. (Bright red). Closely reflexed. Corolla. Lavender or Rose (Violet Rose red at base). Reflexed right out. (Widely expanded). P108 4th Ed. by Porcher 1874. Vol P3 J of RHS 1863. Report on Fuchias grown for trial at Chiswick. Shy bloomer. GC. P55 19/1/1867 Review by H. Cannell A good showy kind. *Banks, E. Deal. GB. 1861?*

FIRE KING. Single. Pink/Red. Tube. Light Pink. Sepals. Light Pink. (Light Salmon Pink). (Only out a little). Corolla. Scarlet. (Clear red). App. to RH. 1851 by Porcher. 1st class variety. GC. P497 11/8/1849 Listed by G. Smith. GC. P145 9/3/1850 Listed by W. Rumley, Richmond. GC. P210 6/4/1850 Listed by H. Walton, Burnley. GC. P274 4/5/1850 Listed by Bass & Brown, Sudbury. GC. P226 14/4/1849 & P280 5/5/1849 Intro. by Turville. *Turville, Chelmsford GB. 1849.*

FIREBALL. Single. Red/Purple. Tube. Red. Sepals. Red. Reflexed. Corolla. Purple. Moderately expanded. Vol P3 J of RHS. 1863 Fuchsias grown for Trial 1862. NK. NK. NK.

FIREWORKS. ND. Red/ND. Tube. Red. Sepals. Dark Ruby Red. Speckled all over. Corolla. ND. Trailer. HC. Cat. 1882. Illustrated P86 HC. Cat. 1885. NK. *GB. 1882.*

FIRMIN GÉMIER. Single. Red/Purple. Tube. Carmine Red. Sepals. Carmine Red. Broad. Horizontal. Reflexed. Corolla. Plum. Long. Perfectly shaped. Fades to carmine violet. L. Cat. Page 2 1914. *Lemoine, Nancy. France. 1914.*

FIRST OF THE DAY. Single. Red/Purple. Tube. Red. (Carmine red). (Crimson).(Coral Red). Short. Sepals. Red. (Carmine red).(Crimson). (Coral Red). Reflex back. Corolla. Lavender. (Dark Lilac Rose). (Purple). Very spread out. Dense pedicels. Dense bushy, free flowering. P108 4th Ed. by Porcher 1874. P216 Vol 4 1877 Fuchsia Trials Chiswick FCC.The corolla often measures nearly 3" across. Pcxxii Vol 3 P of RHS Fuchsia trials 1872. Awarded **. A good variety for growing in small pots. J of RHS Vol 13 Pcxxxviii Awarded H.C. Floral World and Garden Guide P4 Jan 1870 Now known as Swanley Gem. *Banks, E. Deal. GB. 1870.*

FLAMBEAU. Double. Red/Purple. Tube. Crimson. Short. Sepals. Crimson. Well reflexed. Corolla. Dark Violet shaded azure. Striped and spotted scarlet. Very large and full. B. Cat. 1879-1883. *Bull, W. Chelsea. GB. 1879.*

FLAMBOYANT Double Red/Purple. Tube. Crimson. Sepals. Crimson. Corolla. Purple, scarlet in centre. L. Cat. 1906. *Rozain, Lyons. France. 1906.*

FLAMINGO. Single. Pink/Red. Tube. Pale rose. Sepals. Pale rose. Corolla. Brilliant carmine. Medium size. Abundant bloomer. Recommended. Florists Journal P95. 1845. NK *GB. 1843?*

FLASH. Single. White/ND. Tube. White. Sepals. White. Corolla. ND. GC. P66 1/2/1846 & P184 13/3/1847 Listed by Millers, Ramsgate. GC. P282 29/4/1848 Listed by W. Rumley, Richmond. *Bell, Thirsk.GB. 1844?*

FLAVESCENS SUPERBA. ND. ND/ND. Tube. ND.Sepals. ND. Corolla. ND. RH. P170 1857 New fuchsia. NK *France. 1857.*

FLAVESCENS. Single. White/Red. Tube. Whitish tinged yellow. Thick and short. Sepals. Whitish tinged yellow. Large. Open well. Corolla. Cerise red. (Vermillion). Small. Sepals turn down. Grown in a peat soil in a grass border among camellias in a cold greenhouse. App. to RH. 1851 & 4th Ed. by Porcher 1874. GC P224 14/4/1849 Listed by Bass & Brown, Sudbury. GC. P274 5/5/1849 Listed by H. Walton, Burnley. Vol 11 P96 1849 Midland Florist Decided novelty. *Meillez, Lille. France. 1848.*

FLAVIA. ND. ND/ND. Tube. ND. Sepals. ND. Corolla. ND. GC. P282 25/4/1857. Listed by Youells, Gt. Yarmouth. NK. NK. *GB. NK.*

F. LEMON. Double. Red/Purple. Tube. Dark Coral. Sepals. Dark Coral. Broad. Corolla. Plum Violet, fades to Fuchsia Purple. Enormous. Bruant, Poitiers Cat. 1911. L. Cat. 1906. *Rozain, Lyons. France. 1905.*

FLEUR DE MARIE. Single. ND/ND. Tube. ND. Sepals. ND. Coralla. ND. App. to RH 1851 by Porcher. 1st Class Variety. *Dubus. France 1850?*

FLEURE ROUGE. Single. Red/Purple. Tube. Bright Scarlet. Sepals. Bright Scarlet. Recurved. Corolla. Violet. Very free. Good bedder. GC. Vol 23 P213 14/2/1885 New from Lemoine. Laings Cat. 1890. BSW. Cat. 1888. *Lemoine, Nancy France. 1885.*

FLEUVE BLEU. Single. Red/Purple. Tube. Bright red. Sepals. Bright red. Contorted. Corolla. Violet Blue. Large. L. Cat. No. 149 1901. *Lemoine, Nancy. France. 1901.*

FLOCON DE NEIGE. Single. Red/White. Tube. Carmine. Sepals. Carmine. Well reflexed. Corolla. Creamy White. GC P824 27/6/1885 RHS Trials at Chiswick "Best in its class". GO. "Select" 1887-1891. B. Cat. 1888-1889.BSW. Cat. 1897. Dobbies Cat. 1892-1894. *Lemoine, Nancy. France. 1884.*

FLORA (a). Single. Red/Red. Tube. Red. (Carmine). Sepals. Red. (Carmine tipped green). Corolla. Rosy Red. (Rosy purple). Many of the flowers have 6 to 8 sepals and a double portion of petals. Colour Plate Floricultural Cabinet P74 1/4/1843. GC. P241 15/4/1843 Listed by F&A Smith. GC. P242 15/4/1843 Listed by A.J. Stewart, Windsor. GC. P112 17/2/1844 Listed by W. Miller, Ramsgate. *Harrison, Dereham. GB. 1842.*

FLORA (b). Double. Red/Purple. Tube. Bright rosy crimson. Very Short. Sepals. Bright rosy crimson. Large. Fully reflexed. Corolla. Bright purple flaked at base with rosy carmine. Large. B. Cat. 1888. *Bull, W. Chelsea. GB. 1887*

FLORA'S BOUQUET. ND. ND/ND. Tube. ND. Sepals. ND. Corolla. ND. GC. P338 15/4/1865. Listed by W. Rumley, Richmond. NK. NK. NK. *1864.*

FLORADA. Single. ND/ND. Tube. ND. Sepals. ND. Corolla. ND. GC. P66 1/2/1845 & P112 11/2/1846 Listed by W. Miller. Ramsgate. *May, Bedale. GB. 1842.*

FLORENCE. Single. Red/Purple. Tube. Rose. Smooth.(Soft rose). Sepals. Rose. Spreading. Corolla. Rosy Purple. (Rose Lake). RH. P24 1846. GC. P112 17/2/1846 & P66 1/2/1845 Listed by W.Miller, Ramsgate. GC. P146 8/3/1845 Listed by Youells. Gt. Yarmouth. GC. P97 17/2/1844 Intro. by Epps. *Epps, Maidstone. GB. 1844.*

FLORENCE NIGHTINGALE. Single. Red/White. Tube. Red. Sepals. Red. Corolla. White (Stolen from W.H. Story by a gardener and purchased by Luccombe & Pince). See adverts in GC. from E.G. Henderson 1855. GC P467 14/7/1855 Listed by Bass & Brown Sudbury. GC. P529 11/8/1855 Listed by W. J. Epps, Maidstone. GC. P314 10/5/1856 Listed by W, Rumley, Richmond. GC. P786 9/12/1854 Intro. by Luccombe & Pince, Exeter. *Story, W.H. Newton Abbot. GB. 1855.*

FLORETTA. Single. Red/White. Tube. Crimson. Sepals. Scarlet. Corolla. Pure White. GC. P144 14/2/1863. Intro by W. Bull. *Bull, W. Chelsea. GB. 1863.*

FLORIAN. Single. Red/Purple. Tube. Red. Sepals. Red. Corollla. Violet. L. Cat. 1901. x F. coccinea. *Lemoine, Nancy. France 1897.*

FLORIBUNDA (a). Single. ND/ND. Tube. ND. Sepals. ND Corolla. ND. GC. P393 June 1842 Listed by Youells, Gt. Yarmouth. *Dicksons. GB. NK.*

FLORIBUNDA (b). Single. ND/ND. Tube. ND. Sepals. ND. Corolla. ND. GC. P98 17/2/1844 Listed by Youells. GC. P375 4/6/1844 Exhibited by J. Smith, Dalston at H.S. Show. GC. P66 1/2/1845 & P112 17/2/1844 Listed by Millers, Ramsgate. *Standish, Bagshot. GB. 1843.*

FLORIBUNDA (c). Single. ND/ND. Tube. ND. Sepals. ND. Corolla. ND. GC. P66 1/2/1845 & P184 13/3/1847 Listed by W. Miller, Ramsgate. *Day, W. Oxford. GB. 1844?*

FLORIBUNDA (d). Single. Pink/Pink. Tube. Pink. Sepals. Pink. Corolla. Deep pink. Bunches of 12 to 22 flowers at each leaf joint. GC. P338 22/5/1847. Intro. by Turville, Chelmsford. *Turville, Chelmsford GB. 1847.*

FLORIBUNDA (e) Single. Red/White. Tube. Rosy Scarlet. Sepals. Rosy Scarlet. Corolla. White. Moderately expanded. Free Bloomer. Floriferous. Upright. P131 4th Ed. by Porcher 1874. Vol 2 of RHS Fuchsia Trials 1870. Commended for beds etc. GC. P55 19/1/1867 Review by H. Cannell. Intro. by H. Cannell. *Bland, E. Fordham GB. 1867.*

FLORIBUNDA MAGNA. Single. Red/ND. Tube. Red. Sepals. Red. Corolla. ND. GC. P609 1841 Listed by T. Ansell, Camden. GC. P657 9/10/1841 Listed by Rogers, Uttoxeter. GC. P97 10/2/1843 & P98 17/2/1844 & P146 8/3/1845 Listed by Youells, Gt Yarmouth. GC. P241 15/4/1843 Listed by F&A Smith, Hackney. GC. P66 1/2/1845 & P112 17/2/1844 Listed by W. Miller, Ramsgate.8/3/1845 Lisated by Youell, Gt. Yarmouth. GC. 8/5/1841. Intro. by J. May, Edmonton. *May, W. Bedale. GB. 1841.*

FLORIBUNDA MAXIMA. Single. Red/Red. Tube. Bright crimson red. Sepals. Bright crimson red. Corolla. Violet red. (Parentage Fulgens & Grandiflora Maxima, a seedling from Fulgens (1839)). Fl. Cab Vol IX P13 1841. Retailed by J. May, Edmonton. GC. P193 27/3/1841 Intro. by Wm. May, Bedale. *May, W. Bedale. GB. 1841.*

71

FLORIBUNDA PUMILA. Single. ND/ND. Tube. ND. Sepals. ND. Corolla. ND. GC. P299 1841 Exhibited at Royal Botanical Society of Edinburgh. Raised by P. Thomson, Gr to the Lord Advocate Rutherford. GC. P518 7/8/1841. Exhibited at the Royal Caledonian Show. *Thomson, P. Edinburgh. GB. 1841.*

FLORIBUNDUS (a). Single. White/ND. Tube. White. Sepals. White. Corolla. ND. GC. P250 27/4/1846 and P184 13/3/1847 Listed by W. Miller, Ramsgate. NK. NK. *1845.*

FLORIBUNDUS (b). Single. ND/ND. Tube. ND. Sepals. ND. Corolla. ND. GC. P281 29/4/1848 New fuchsia introduced by J.G. Hine. Successor to W. Miller (Deceased). *Miller, W. Ramsgate. GB. 1848*

FLOSSIE FOWLE. Single. ND/ND. Tube. ND. Sepals. ND. Corolla. ND. GC. P338 15/4/1865 Listed by W. Rumley, Richmond. NK. NK. *GB. 1864.*

FLOWER OF FRANCE. Single. White/Purple. Tube. White. Sepals. White. Corolla. Violet tinted blue. GC. P260 24/3/1860 Listed by Wm. Hussey, Norwich. GC. P426 12/5/1860 Listed by F. Godwin Sheffield. CG. & JH P361 1861 "Select 12". GC. P165 26/2/1859 Intro. by E.G. Henderson St. Johns Wood. *Banks, E. Deal. GB. 1859.*

FLOWER OF THE FLOCK. ND. ND/ND. Tube. ND. Sepals. ND. Corolla. ND. GC. Vol 20 280 1/9/1883 Exhibited at Trowbridge Hort. Scty, Show by Pocock (3rd in 6 pot class). NK. NK. *GB. 1881?*

FOIGH A BALLAGH. Single. ND/ND. Tube. ND. Sepals. ND. Corolla. ND. GC. P265 24/4/1847 Listed by W. Rendle, Plymouth. GC. P234 11/4/1846 & P250 17/4/1847 Listed by Epps, Maidstone. NK. NK. *GB. 1845.*

FORGET ME NOT. Single. Red/Purple. Tube. Carmine. Sepals. Carmine. Corolla. Rich blue striped crimson. Well cupped. Emblem of the British Fuchsia Society. P406 CG & JH Vol V 1864. GC. P594 29/6/1861. Listed by Godwin & Padman, Sheffield. GC P771 24/8/1861 Listed by H. Walton, Burnley. Intro. by E.G. Henderson, St Johns Wood. *Banks, E. Deal GB, 1861*

FORMOSA (a). Single. ND/ND. Tube. ND. Sepals. ND. Corolla. ND. GC. P112 17/2/1844 & P66 1/2/1845. Listed by W. Miller, Ramsgate. *Harrison, Dereham. GB. NK.*

FORMOSA (b). Double. Red/Purple. Tube. Bright Scarlet. Sepals. Bright Scarlet. Slender. Corolla. Deep Violet. Outer petals, rosy red and elegantly flaked light violet. GC. P486 9/4/1870 Intro. by B&S. Williams. *Bland, E. Fordham GB. 1870.*

FORMOSA (c) Single. Red/Red. Tube. Rich magenta rose. Very long. Sepals. Rich Magenta rose, tipped green. Horizontal. Corolla. Crimson Lake. Flowers in terminal bunches. Species hybrid. Introduced by W. Bull. B. Cat. 1882. *Bland, E. Fordham. GB. 1882.*

FORMOSA ELEGANS. Single. Red/Purple. Tube. Carmine. Sepals. Carmine.(Bright red). (Rosy Carmine) Recurve at ends. Corolla. Blue. (Deep Violet striped crimson) (Deep Purple). Medium Size. Free bloomer, Dwarf Habit. Stiff lateral branches. FC P13 Vol IX 1841. FJ. P95 5/1845 "Recommended" GC P630 25/9/1841 One of the best Chilean varieties. Raised by Thompson Gr. to Lady Gambier of Iver House. GC. 17/7/1841 Exhibited at H.S. Show July 1841 by W.H. Story of Isleworth. Floricultural Cabinet Vol IX P185 1841. GC. P416 21/6/1841 Listed by Masters, Canterbury. Globosa X. *Thompson, Iver. GB. 1839.*

FORMOSE (a). Double. Red/Purple. Tube. Rosy Carmine. Sepals. Rosy Carmine. Sepals recurved in half a circle. Corolla. Bluish Violet. Large. GC. Vol 23 P213 14/2/1885 New from Lemoine. BSW. Cat. 1888. *Lemoine, Nancy France. 1885.*

FORMOSE (b). Double. Red/Pink. Tube. Bright rose pink. Sepals. Bright rose pink. Large. Short. Corolla. Pale Salmon. Full. L. Cat. 1901. *Lemoine, Nancy. France. 1901.*

FORMOSISSIMA (a). Single. Pink/Purple. Tube. Flesh. Long. Sepals. Flesh, Green tips. Corolla. Purple, goes off to orange crimson. GC. P 162 14/3/1846 & P184 13/3/1847 Listed by W. Miller, Ramsgate. GC. P2 4/1/1845 Introduced by Girling. Stowmarket. *Girling, Stowmarket. GB. 1845.*

FORMOSISSIMA (b). ND. White/Pink. Tube. White. Sepals. White. Corolla. Blush. Laings Cat. about 1890. NK. NK. NK

FORTUNA. Double. Red/White. Tube. Red. Short. Sepals. Red. Reflexed. Corolla. White. Rose crimson at base. B. Cat. 1896. *Bull, W. Chelsea. GB. 1896*

FORTUNÉE GRARDS. Double. Red/Purple. Tube. Red. Sepals. Red. Corolla. Violet. Foliage margined bright yellow. Bruant, Poitiers Cat. 1911-1915.NK. NK. NK. *1911.*

FOSTERII. Single. ND/ND. Tube. ND. Sepals. ND. Corolla. ND. GC. P200 28/3/1846 Listed by J&S Schilling, Odiham. GC. Exhibited at RBS. Show 2/7/1846 by Gaines, Battersea. NK. NK. *GB. 1845.*

FOUNTAIN. Single. Red/Purple. Tube. Dark red. Sepals. Dark Red. Large. Well Open. Corolla. Purple. Globular. GC. P537 12/8/1848, Listed by G. Smith, Islington. GC. P224 14/4/1847 Listed by Bass & Brown Sudbury and R. Whibley, Kennington Cross. GC. P256 21/4/1849 Listed by R. Cooper, Croydon. App. to RH. 1851 by Porcher. *Turville, Chelmsford GB. 1848.*

FRANCIS MAGNARD. Double. Red/Purple. Tube. Scarlet. Sepals. Scarlet. Reflexed. Corolla. Violet mottled rose pink and red. Very Large Very full. L. Cat. 1895. Kelways, Langport Cat. 1898. Bruant, Poitiers Cat. 1897. NK. NK. NK. 1895.

FRANC-NOHAIN. Double. Red/Purple. Tube. Red. Sepals. Red. Corolla. Marine blue marked rose. L. Cat. 1907. *Rozain, Lyons. France. 1907.*

FRANCISQUE SARCEY. Double. Red/Purple. Tube. Dark Rose. Sepals. Dark rose, bright red on inside. Large. Reflexed. Corolla. Bluish Violet. Very free blooming. Dwarf habit. Very full. B. Cat. 1879 - 1889. *Lemoine, Nancy. France. 1879*

FRANÇOIS BOUCHER. Double. Red/Purple. Tube. Carmine Coral. Sepals. Carmine Coral. Broad. Long. Horizontal. Corolla. Bluish Violet Plum. Enormous. Full. L. Cat. 1910. *Lemoine, Nancy. France. 1910.*

FRANÇOIS COPPÉE. Double. Red/Red. Tube. Bright red. Sepals. Bright red. Reverse Scarlet. Corolla. Wine red, veined bright pink and red. (Rose). Dwarf. Floriferous. Large. Named after a French Poet(1842-1908). JF. Cat. 1904. L. Cat. 1903. *Rozain, Lyons. France. 1903.*

FRANCOISE DESBOIS. Double. Red/Purple. Tube. Crimson. (Pink). Sepals. Crimson. Reflexed.(Pink Reflexed). Corolla. Violet stained and streaked ruby red. Very large.(Red at base. Blue at tips. Inner petals deep blue) GC. P330 13/3/1875 Listed by T. Fletcher, Chesterfield. P131 4th. Ed. by Porcher. RH.,P311 1889 "Select" by E.A. Carrière. GC. P505 15/4/1876 *Coene.Ghent. 1869.*

FRANÇOIS HAVRY. Double. Red/Purple. Tube. Red. ½" long. Sepals. Red. Slender. 1" long tipped green. Corolla. Reddish Purple. Loose, Irregular Inferior. Large flower. Pcxv Vol 3 J of RHS.

Fuchsias grown for trial at Chiswick 1872. NK, NK. NK. *1870?*

FRANK VINE. Single. Red/Purple. Tube. Red. Sepals. Red. Corolla. Dark Violet. P1 J of RHS 1860 P262/3 Report of Floral Committee. Similar to "Garibaldi", but less expanded corolla. No Award. *Banks, E. Deal. GB. 1860?*

FRANKLIN. Double. Red/Purple. Tube. Red. Sepals. Red. Corolla. Purple. P126 4th Ed. by Porcher 1874 Good variety but the flowers are small and the corolla is too short. *Demay, Arras. Belgium. 1872.*

FRANTZ WILLIAM SCHLEGEL. Single. Red/Purple. Tube. Red. Sepals Red. Corolla. Purple. P115 4th. Ed. by Porcher 1874. Not in the first selection. *Meet. Germany 1863.*

FRAU ANNA STUMPE. Double. ND/ND. Tube. ND. Sepals. ND. Corolla. ND. Bruant, Poitiers Cat. 1911. NK. NK. NK. NK.

FRAU EMMA TOPFER. Double. Red/White. Tube. Red. (Rosy coral).(Rosy magenta). Sepals. Red. (Rosy Coral). Well reflexed. Broad. Corolla. White. (Rosy blush). (White suffused and veined rose). GC. Vol 25 P389 27/3/1886 Listed by Daniel Bros, Ipswich. B. Cat. 1888-1893. BSW.Cat. 1888-1897. GC. P528 25/4/1885 Intro. by H. Cannell. JF.Cat. 1886. NK. NK. NK *1884.*

FRAU HENRIETTE ERNST. Single. Red/Purple. Tube. Bright crimson. Sepals. Bright crimson. Corolla. Violet red. Bruant, Poitiers Cat. 1911. *Teupel. Germany. 1910.*

FRAU HILDA RADEMACHER. ND. ND/ND. Tube. ND. Sepals. ND. Corolla. ND. Essig 1936. *Rademacher. Germany NK.*

FRÉDÉRIC PASSY. Single. Red/White. Tube. Scarlet. Sepals. Scarlet. Reflexed. Corolla. White veined rose. Funnel shaped. L. Cat. 1902. *Rozain, Lyons. France. 1902.*

FRÉDÉRIC. ND. ND/ND. Tube. ND. Sepals. ND. Corolla. ND. RH. P311 1889 "Select" by E.A. Carrieré. NK. NK. NK.

FREEDOM. S/Double. Red/White. Tube. Reddish crimson. Sepals. Reddish crimson. Long. Broad. Completely reflexed. Corolla. White veined crimson. Much expanded. B. Cat. 1901. *Bull, W. Chelsea. GB. 1900.*

FRÈRE HILDEGRIN. Double. Red/White. Tube. Bright red. Sepals. Bright red. Beautifully reflexed. Corolla. Pure white, pink at base. Enormous. Elongated. Full. JF. Cat. 1893. L. Cat. 1892. *Rozain, Lyons. France. 1892.*

FRÈRE MARIE-PIERRE. Single. Red/Purple. Tube. Red. Sepals. Red. Corolla. Blue veined rose. L. Cat. 1890. *Rozain, Lyons. France. 1886.*

FRÈRE MICHEL (a). Double. Red/Purple. Tube. Brilliant Red. Sepals. brilliant red. Corolla. Violet Blue. RH. P295 1887 Grown as a standard at Twickel P80 Witte 1882. *Boucharlet. France. 1881.*

FRÈRE MICHEL (b). Double. Red/White. Tube. Carmine. Sepals. Carmine. Corolla. Pure white. GO. P141 1891 "New continental fuchsias of 1890". L. Cat. 1892. *Rozain, Lyons. France. 1890.*

FRÈRE ORBAN. Double. Red/Purple. Tube. Bright red. Sepals. Bright red. Well reflexed. Corolla. Violet. (Bluish White Violet). JF. Cat. 1898-1899. NK NK. NK.

FREUND J. DURR. Double. Red/Purple. Tube. Scarlet red. Sepals. Scarlet red. Corolla. Dark blue. Flaked and shaded carmine. Long. 4 Petaloids of a similar colour. B. Cat. 1870-1873. Intro. by W. Bull, Chelsea. NK. NK. NK. *1870*

FRIED HARMS. ND. White/ND. Tube. White. Sepals. White. Corolla. ND. P120 4th Ed. by Porcher 1874 Not meritorious enough to be included in the first selection. RH. P295 1887 Grown as a standard at Twickel. *Weinrich. Germany 1870.*

FRITZ. Double. ND/ND. Tube. ND. Sepals. ND. Corolla. ND. See Colour Plate in L'Illustration Horticole. G. P503 15/12/1883. *Mahon, J. Belgium. 1883.*

FROSTII. Single. ND/ND. Tube. ND. Sepals. ND. Corolla. ND. GC. P431 4/6/1843 Shown at H.S. Show, London by Lanes, Berkhampstead. Large Flower, somewhat lacking in colour. GC. P686 12/10/1844 Exhibited at RHS of Cornwall show. GC. P112 17/2/1844 & P66 1/2/1845. Listed by W. Miller, Ramsgate. NK. NK. *GB. 1843.*

FULGENS CARMINATA ROSEA. Single. Red/Red. Tube. Clear Carmine rose. Sepals. ND. Corolla. Vermillion. Nice colour. Dwarf plant, Floriferous. Hopefully not a variation. Hybrid between Fulgens and Serratifolia. 4th. Edition by Porcher 1874. F.fulgens x F.serratifolia. Intro. by E.G. Henderson. *Henderson E.G. St. Johns Wood. GB. 1873.*

FULGENS CORYMBIFLORA. Single. Red/Red. Tube. Vermillion. 7cms long. Sepals. Vermillion. Held well out. Corolla. Vermillion. Small. On a young plant the floriferousness of this hybrid is mediocre. Perhaps it will prove a better effect on a older plant. App. to RH. 1851 by Porcher. NK. NK. *France. 1849.*

FULGENS D'ARCK. Single. Red/Red. Tube. Red. Sepals. Red. Corolla. Reddish Vermillion. Similar to Fulgens in habit, flowers and formation of flowers. Differs in having purple veins in leaf. Leaves are violet in colour. App. to RH. 1851 & 4th Ed. by Porcher 1874. Fulgens hybrid. NK. NK. *France. 1844?*

FULGENS GESNERIANA. Single. Red/Red. Tube. Red. Sepals. Red. Corolla. Red. Another variety of fulgens with the same characteristics. Dwarf Bush. The shade of the corolla is more alive. 4th Ed. by Porcher 1874. *Barbet. France. 1864.*

FULGENS LONGIFLORA. Single. Red/Red. Tube. ND. Sepals. ND. Corolla. ND. GC. P112 17/2/1844 and P66 1/2/1845 Listed by W. Miller, Ramsgate. NK. NK. *GB. 1843*

FULGENS MULTIFLORA PUMILA. Single. Red/Red. Tube. Carmine Scarlet. Sepals. Carmine Scarlet. Corolla. Carmine Scarlet. Dwarf and freeblooming form of the original fuchsia type. Short jointed growth, each branch terminating in a truss of flowers. FCC. RHS. HC. Cat. 1882. GC. P431 12/5/1866. Intro. by E.G. Henderson. NK. NK. *GB. 1866.*

FULGENS MULTIFLORA. Single. ND. Tube. ND. Sepals. ND. Corolla. ND. GC. P97 18/2/1843, P98 17/2/1844 & P146 8/3/1845 Listed by Youell, Gt. Yarmounth. GC. P112 17/2/1844 Listed by Millers, Ramsgate. NK. NK. *GB. 1842?*

FULGENS RUBRA GRANDIFLORA. Single. Red/Red. Tube. Red. Sepals. Red. Corolla. Red. H. Cannell. 1882. NK. NK. NK. NK.

FULGENS SUPERBA. Single. ND/ND. Tube. ND. Sepals. ND. Corolla. ND. GC. P112 17/2/1844 & P66 1/2/1845. Listed by W. Miller, Ramsgate. NK. NK. *GB. 1844.*

FULGIDA SUPERBA. Single. ND/ND. Tube. ND. Sepals. ND. Corolla. ND. *May. GB. 1841.*

FUNCK-BRENTANO. Double. Red/Purple. Tube. Crimson red. Sepals. Crimson Red. Broad. Corolla. Plum margined marine blue. Very large. L. Cat. 1909. *Rozain. Lyons. France. 1909.*

FURST OTTO VON WERNIGERODE. Single. Pink/Red. Tube. Crimson (Clear Pink). Sepals. Crimson. Corolla. Pink, Small. (Rose carmine). Bronze foliage. Novel and pretty. Name sometimes shortened to Furst Otto. Intro. by G. Borneman. Gartenflora 1900. JF. Cat. 1904. L. Cat. 1906. Triphylla X Surprise. *Rehder. Germany. 1900.*

GABRIEL BONVALOT. Double. Red/Blue. Tube. Red. Sepals. Red. Corolla. Sky Blue fading to reddish violet. Named after a French explorer (1853-1933), who travelled extensively in Central Asia. L. Cat. 1899. *Lemoine, Nancy. France. 1899.*

GABRIELLE D'ESTREES. Single. Pink/Red. Tube. Pink. Sepals. Pink. Large. Only open slightly. Corolla. Crimson shaded vermillion. Oval foliage, only a little denticulated. Pistil short and red. Floriferous. Named after a mistress of Henry IV of France.(1570-1599) App. to RH. 1851 by Porcher. *Racine, France. 1850.*

GAIETY (a). Single. Pink/Purple. Tube. Blush. Sepals. Blush. Corolla. Lilac Purple. Very dissimilar and novel. Listed by H. Walton, Burnley GC. P449 17/7/1852 & P209 26/3/1853. GC. P223 10/4/1852. Intro. by C. Turner, Slough. *Banks, E., Deal. GB. 1852.*

GAIETY (b). ND. Red/Purple. Tube. Rich red. Sepals. Rich red. Corolla. Blackish satiny purple. HC. Cat 1890. *Sankey. GB. 1890.*

GALANTHIFLORA PLENA. Double. Red/White. Tube. Scarlet. Sepals. Scarlet. Corolla. White. GC. P114 24/2/1855 Stolen from W.H. Story by a jobbing gardener. Vol. 4 1857 L'Illustration Horticole Pl 119 1857. GC. P786 9/12/1854. Intro by Luccombe and Pince. Exeter. *Story W.H. Newton Abbot. GB. 1855.*

GALATEA. Single. Red/Purple. Tube. Rosy Carmine. Sepals. Rosy Carmine. Long and Broad. Horizontal. Corolla. Bright bluish purple. Stout. Well formed. JF. Cat. 1885. Intro by W. Bull. Cat 1878-1883. *Bland, E. Fordham. GB. 1878.*

GAMBETTA. Single. Red/Red. Tube. Bright Carmine. Sepals. Bright carmine. Well recurved. Corolla. Rose. (Rose carmine tinted slate BSW. Cat 1878). Named after a French Politician (1832-1882). P79 Witte 1882. B. Cat 1877. *Lemoine, Nancy. France. 1876.*

GAMEBOY. Single. Red/Purple. Tube. ND. Sepals. ND. Corolla. ND. GC. P359 3/6/1852 Exhibited at Grand National Tulip Exhibition B'ham. GC. P275 1/5/1852 Listed by H. Walton Burnley. GC. P199

19/3/1853 recommended dark variety. *Mayle, Birmingham. GB. 1851.*

GANNET. Single. Red/Purple. Tube. Bright Crimson. Short. Sepals. Bright crimson. Long. Corolla. Bluish purple, shaded rosy crimson at base. B. Cat. 1888-1893. Intro. by W. Bull, Chelsea. *Bull, W. Chelsea. GB. 1887.*

GARIBALDI (a). Single. Red/Purple. Tube. Light Scarlet. Sepals. Light Scarlet. Recurved.Corolla. Dark violet tinted black. Vol P3 JofRHS 1863 Fuchsias grown for trial at Chiswick 1862. (much confusion on this cultivar, see other entries). GC. P215 10/3/1860. Intro. by E.G. Henderson. St. Johns Wood. *Banks, E. Deal. GB. 1860.*

GARIBALDI (b). Single. Red/Purple.Tube. Scarlet. Sepals. Scarlet tipped rose. Well reflexed.Corolla. Violet shaded blue. Very open expanded. GC. P 560 30/6/1860 Listed by F. Godwin, Sheffield. GC. P18 4/1/1860 Intro. by Wm. Rollinson, Tooting. *Rollinson, W. Tooting GB. 1860.*

GARIBALDI (c) Single. Red/Purple. Tube. Red. Short. Sepals. Red. Broad Recurved. Corolla. Pale Reddish Slate P1. Jof RHS 1860 Commended. NK. NK. *GB. 1860.*

GARIBALDI (d). S/Double. Red/Purple. Tube. Red. Sepals. Red. Corolla. Purple. P1 J of RHS Oct 11, 1860 P293 Submitted to Floral C'tee. "Inferior to Sir Colin Campbell". *Veitch. GB. 1861?*

GARIBALDI.(e) Single. Red/Purple. Tube. Crimson red. Sepals. Crimson. Large. Uplifted. Corolla. Clear Blue striped and streaked crimson red. (Lavender blue veined carmine) Large. Bell shaped. Named after an Italian patriot, who fought for Italian liberation, (1807-82). GC. P314 28/3/1868 Intro. by E.G. Henderson. P131 4th Ed. by Porcher 1874. *E.G. Henderson, St. Johns Wood. GB. 1868.*

GARLAND. Single. ND/ND. Tube. ND. Sepals. ND. Corolla. ND. GC. P184 13/3/1847 Listed by W. Miller, Ramsgate. *Harrison, Dereham. GB. 1846.*

GARNIER PAGES. Single. Red/Purple. Tube. Clear Red. Sepals. Clear red. Corolla. Rosy violet. Well formed. Erect. Extremely floriferous. Named after a French politician 1803-78. L Cat. *Lemoine, Nancy France. 1879.*

GARTENMEISTER BONSTEDT. Single. Red/Red. Tube Red. Orange scarlet. Sepals. Orange scarlet. Corolla. Orange scarlet. Long tubed. Similar to Thalia but has a pronouced bulge halfway down the tube. Purple foliage. Hybrid from F. Triphylla. Flowers in clusters JF. Cat 1907. L. Cat 1906. *Bonstedt, Gottingen. Germany. 1905.*

GASPAR. Single. Red/Purple. Tube. Bright coral red. Sepals. Bright coral red. Very broad. Overlaps corolla. Corolla. Violet purple striped and flaked rose. Large. GO. "Select" 1883-1888. Intro. by W. Bull, Chelsea. B. Cat 1880-1883. *Bland, E. Fordham. GB. 1880.*

GASTON CAZALIS. Double. Red/White. Tube. Carmine rose. Sepals. Carmine rose. Reflexed. Corolla. Flesh White marked carmine rose. L. Cat. 1911. *Rozain, Lyons. France. 1911.*

GAY LAD. Single. White/Pink. Tube. Whitish pink. Large. Sepals. Whitish pink. Large and spreading. Corolla. Reddish pink. Small. Very floriferous. 1st class variety. App. to RH 1851 by Porcher. *Keynes. GB. 1849.*

GAY-LUSSAC. Double. Red/Purple. Tube. Red. Sepals. Red. Corolla. Violet Purple veined red. Large. Spreading. Named after a French chemist, who invented the centesimal alcoholometer, (1778-1850). B. Cat. 1893-1896. *Rozain, Lyons. France. 1893.*

GAZELLE (a). Single. Pink/Purple. Tube. Rosy lilac. Short and thick. Sepals. Blush white, inside rosy lilac. Only open a little. Corolla. Lilac. (lilac pink) Small flowers. Long style is bright rose. Distinguished by the freshness of its colouring. App. to RH 1851 by Porcher. GC. P427 7/7/1849 Intro. by Youells, Gt. Yarmouth. *Meillez. Lille. France. 1849*

GAZELLE (b). Single. Red/Purple. Tube. Bright scarlet. Sepals. Bright scarlet. Large. Boldly reflexed. Corolla. Violet blue. GC. P1554 2/12/1871 Review by Cannell. HC. Cat 1882. one of the best for exhibition. GC. P206 1877 Growers of the West Country. GC. P375 19/3/1870 Intro. by E.G. Henderson. St Johns Wood. *Henderson, E.G. St. Johns Wood GB. 1870.*

GAZELLE (c). Single. Red/Purple. Tube. Bright crimson. Sepals. Bright crimson . Recurved. Corolla. Dark Purple. Very long. Laings Cat. circa 1890. B. Cat. 1883-1888. *Bull, W. Chelsea. GB. 1883.*

GEORGES. Single. Red/Red. Tube. Reddish Purple. Short tube. 35mms. Sepals. Reddish purple. Large. Horizontal. Corolla. Carmine red. Bell shaped. 1st class variety. App. to RH. 1851 by Porcher. *Chauviere. France. 1849?*

GEANT DE THIELT. Single. Red/Red. Tube. Rose vermillion. Long. Sepals. Rose vermillion. Large. Not spreading much. Corolla. Vermillion red. Medium size. Similiar to" Duke of Cornwall" and "Jenny Lind". App. to RH. 1851 by Porcher. NK. NK. *France. 1849.*

GEANT DES BATAILLES. Double. Red/Red. Tube. Red. Sepals. Red. Corolla. Rose. Laings Cat. circa 1890. *Boucharlat L. Lyons. France. 1881?*

GEANT OF VERSAILLES. Single. Pink/Red. Tube. Bright pink. Thin 10/11 cms long. Sepals. Bright pink. Good size. Corolla. Crimson. Good size. P.205 RH. 1847. GC. P210 25/3/1848 Listed by W. Rumley, Richmond. Crosses between Fulgens, Corymbiflora and Macrostemma. 4th. E. by Porcher P117 1874. *Salter, J. Versailles. France. 1844.*

GEM (a) Single. Red/Purple. Tube. Red. Sepals. Red. Corolla. Purple. GC. P242 15/4/1843 Listed by A.J. Stewart, Windsor. P98 17/2/1844 Youells, Gt. Yarmouth. P112 17/2/1844 P66 1/2/1845 Millers, Ramsgate, Exhibited HS Show GC. P375 4/6/1844. GC. P820 Dec 1844 Recommended. *Harrison, J. Dereham GB. 1842.*

GEM (b). Single. Red/Purple. Tube. Light rosy vermillion. Short. Thick. Sepals. Light Rosy vermillion. Corolla. Crimson purple. GC. P112 17/2/1844 & P66 1/2/1845 Listed by Millers, Ramsgate. GC. P146 8/4/1845 Listed by Youells, Gt. Yarmouth. GC. P201. 1/4/18434. Intro. by Ivery, Peckham. *Ivery, Peckham. GB. 1843.*

GEM (c). Single. White/Purple. Tube. White (Tube too short). Sepals. White. Horizontal. tipped Green. Corolla. Violet (rosy purple) 8" long. Listed by GC. P497 11/8/1849 G. Smith, Tollington Nurseries. P145 9/3/1850 W. Rumley, Richmond. P210 9/3/1850 H. Walton, Burnley. etc. App to RH 1851 by Porcher. GC P226 14/4/1849 Intro. by *Turville, Chelmsford. GB. 1849.*

GEM (d). Single. Red/White. Tube. Glowing red. Sepals. Glowing red. Corolla. Pure White. Long, Beautful form. B. Cat 1875-1876. *Bull, W. Chelsea. GB. 1874*

GEM OF IPSWICH. Double. Red/Purple. Tube. Coral red. Sepals. Coral Red. Corolla. Purple distinctly striped. HC. Cat 1882-1890. GO "Select" 1888-1891. RH. 1887. P295 Standards grown at Twickel, Nr. Arnhem. *Stokes. GB. 1881?*

GEM OF LAVINGTON. Single. White/Red. Tube. White tinted pink. Sepals. White tinted pink.

Corolla. Carmine, flushed soft violet. Very stout. Extra fine form. Robust and very free. GO. 1889 HC. Cat. 1890. JF, Cat 1888. GO. Select 1891. Intro. by B.S. Williams. *Lye, J. Market Lavington. GB. 1888.*

GEM OF MERRIOTT. ND. ND/ND. Tube. ND. Sepals. ND. Corolla. ND. GC. P756 20/7/1867 Exhibited by D.T. Fish, RHS Show at Bury St. Edmunds. GC. P571 24/7/1858 Listed by H. Walton, Burnley. NK. NK. NK. *1858.*

GEM OF THE NORTH. Single. Red/Purple. Tube. Crimson. Sepals. Crimson. Wide. Well reflexed. Corolla. Deep purple shaded violet."From a well known raiser in the North of England". Intro. by B.S. Williams. GC. P191 27/2/1864. NK. NK. *GB. 1864.*

GEM OF THE SEASON (a). Single. Red/Purple. Tube. Rich Crimson. Sepals. Rich crimson. Corolla. Deep purple. Raised by either J. Smith, Manager of T. Whalley's nursery Liverpool or a celebrated amateur from the North of England. GC. P449 17/7/1852 Listed by H.Walton, Burnley etc. GC. P130 21/2/1852 Intro. by E.G. Henderson. see above. *GB. 1852.*

GEM OF THE SEASON (b) Double. Red/Purple. Tube. Crimson. Sepals. Crimson. Short. Elegantly reflexed. Corolla. Bright purple. Free bloomer. Compact. GC. P960 20/10/1861 to be introduced in 1862. GC. P108 1/2/1862 Intro. by W. Bull. *Bull. W. Chelsea. GB. 1862.*

GEM OF THE SOUTH. Single. ND/ND. Tube. ND. Sepals. ND. Corolla. ND. GC. P647 1/10/1851 Exhibited at RHS of Cornwall Show by Mr. Friend on 9/9/1851. NK. NK. *GB.* NK.

GEM OF THE WEST (a). Single. White/Purple. Tube. White Very Thin. Sepals. Greenish white.tinged rose. Reflexed. Corolla. Violet. Purchased from Mr. Heben Gr. to Mr. Danbury of Truro. GC. P497 11/8/1849 Listed by G. Smith, Tollington Nursery. GC. P647 Exhibited at RHS of Cornwall Show 9/9/51. GC. P241 21/4/1849 Intro. by Veitch, Exeter. *Heben, Truro. GB. 1849.*

GEM OF THE WEST (b) Single. Red/Purple. Tube. Bright crimson. Short. Sepals. Bright crimson. Short. Recurved. (Bright coral red) Corolla. Purple crimson fades reddish crimson. Large. Expanded.(Dark plum). HC. Cat. 1882 Very pretty little fuchsia. One of the strongest growers. BSW. Cat. 1878. B. Cat. 1878-1882. Floral Mag. T291 1878. *Lye, J. Market Lavington. GB. 1877.*

GEM OF THE WHITES. ND. ND/ND. Tube. ND. Sepals. ND. Corolla. ND. GC. P177 20/3/1856. Listed by W. Rumley, Richmond. NK. NK. *GB. 1850?*

GEM OF WHITEHILL. Single? Red/Purple. Tube. Carmine. Sepals. Carmine. Long. Reflexed. Corolla. Deep Violet. Sent out by W. Fuller, Florist of Newton Bushel, formerly gardener to W. H. Story. GC. P51 26/1/1856 & P433 28/6/1856 Courtney Nursery, Newton Abbot. GC. P690 18/10/1856 Listed by W. Rumley, Richmond. *Story W.H., Newton Abbot. GB. 1856.*

GENERAL (a). Double. Red/Purple. Tube. Dark red. Sepals. Dark red. Recurved back to tube. Corolla. Bright light purple, flamed rose. Close. Compact.B. Cat. 1870, 1872, 1873. GC. 451 2/4/1870 Intro. by Felton & Son, Birmingham. *Felton, Birmingham. GB. 1870.*

GENERAL (b). Double. Red/Purple. Tube. Deep rose. Sepals. Deep rose. Large. Reflexed. Corolla. Rich violet flaked rose. Expanded. B. Cat. 1882-1883. Intro. by W. Bull, Chelsea. *Eckford. GB. 1882.*

GÉNÉRAL BORREMANS. Double. Red/Purple. Tube. Red. Sepals. Red. Spreading. Corolla Purple. Tolerably full. Vol. P3 JofRHS 1863 P90. Fuchsia trials at Chiswick. GC. P594 29/6/1861 listed by Godwin & Padman, Sheffield. GC. P771 24/8/1861 Listed by H. Walton, Burnley. *Cornelissen. Belgium. 1860*

GÉNÉRAL CHANGARNIER. Single. Red/Purple. Tube. Rose. Strong 45mms long. Sepals. Rose. Well reflexed (Reflex to tube). Corolla. Vermillion Purple. Foliage green tinted purple. Good variety for winter flowering. App to RH 1851 and 4th. Ed. 1874 by Porcher. GC. P465 27/7/1850 Listed by W. Rumley, Richmond and G. Smith, Tollington Nurseries. *Meiltez, Lille. France. 1850.*

GÉNÉRAL CHANZY. Double. Red/Blue. Tube. Bright crimson red. Thick and Short. Sepals. Bright crimson red. Large. Reflexed. Corolla. Indigo blue. Full. Globular (Dark Violet) Dark Green foliage. Pedicel 30 mms. P123 4th Ed by Porcher 1874. Named after a French General (1823-83). BSW. Cat. 1878. HC. Cat. 1882. GO. Select 1880. RH. P295 1887 Grown as a standard at Twickel. *Lemoine, Nancy. France. 1874*

GÉNÉRAL CHAZEL Single. Red/Purple. Tube. Light red. Sepals. Light red. Green tips. Corolla. Reddish Purple. Small. Poor looking but free blooming. Vol. P3 J of RHS 1863. 1862 Fuchsia trials at Chiswick. Submitted by E. G. Henderson. NK. NK. *France 1861?*

GÉNÉRAL D'AMADE. Double. Red/Purple. Tube. Carmine. Sepals. Carmine. Corolla. Clear violet streaked pink. Compact. L. Cat. 1908. *Lemoine, Nancy. France. 1908*

GÉNÉRAL DODDS. Double. Red/Purple. Tube. Rosy red.. Sepals. Rosy red. Large. Corolla. Bluish lilac. Named after a French general (1842-1922) B. Cat. 1893-1895. *Lemoine, Nancy. France. 1893.*

GÉNÉRAL DRUDE. Double. Red/Pink. Tube. Carmine red. Sepals. Carmine red. Short. Reflexed. Corolla. Very pale pink. Large. L. Cat 1908 *Lemoine, Nancy. France. 1908.*

GÉNÉRAL FORGEMOL. Single. Red/Purple. Tube. Wine Red. Sepals. Wine red. Corolla. Reddish Violet. BSW. Cat 1888. *Lemoine, Nancy. France. 1882.*

GÉNÉRAL GALLIENI. Double. Red/Purple. Tube. Clear red (Light scarlet). Sepals. Clear red (Light scarlet). Short. Reflexed. Corolla. Bluish red. Fine compact habit. Opens well. Very full. Named after a Marshall of France (1849-1916) JF. Cat 1900. L. Cat. 1901. *Lemoine, Nancy. France. 1899.*

GENERAL GARFIELD. Double. Red/Purple. Tube. Rich crimson Sepals. Rich crimson. Very broad. Well reflexed. Corolla. Carmine shaded blue. GO, P97 1882. BSW. Cat. 1888. HC. Cat. 1885. Named after the 20th President of the USA (1831-81). GC. Vol 17 1882 25/5/1882 Intro. by B.S. Williams. *Bland, E. Fordham GB. 1882.*

GENERAL GORDON. Single. Red/Purple. Tube. Scarlet. (Red). Sepals. Scarlet. 2 ½" long. Corolla. Plum veined scarlet. (Rich purple) Spreading. Named after British General, killed at Khartoum (1833-1885). GC. P686 30/5/1885. GO. 1886. GC. Vol 25 1886 P389 listed by Daniel Bros, Norwich. Intro by R. Owen, Maidenhead. *Owen, R. Maidenhead. GB. 1885*

GENERAL GRANT. Double. Red/Red. Tube. Red. (Carmine red). Short and Thick. Sepals. Pinkish red. Reflexed. ⅞" spread . Tips green. Corolla. Violet washed red. (Deep lake red) ¾" deep. Full. Spreading. Only fault, sepals and petals are same colour. P108 4th Ed. by Porcher 1874. Pcxvii Vol 3 P of RHS 1872. Fuchsia trials at Chiswick 1872. Named after 18th President of the USA. *Lemoine, Nancy. France. 1869.*

GENERAL GRENFELL. Single. Red/Purple. Tube. Coral Red. Sepals. Coral red. Recurved. Corolla. Blue shaded carmine. BSW. Cat 1897. Laings Cat. after 1890. NK. NK. *GB.* NK.

GENERAL HAVELOCK. ND. ND/ND. Tube. ND. Sepals. ND. Corolla. ND. GC. P238 19/8/1859 Listed by W. Rumley, Richmond. Named after a British General who distinguished himself during the Indian Mutiny. (1795-1857) NK. NK. *GB. 1858.*

GÉNÉRAL LAPASSET. Single. Red/Purple. Tube. Bright coral. Short. Sepals. Bright coral. Large. Broad. Recurved. Corolla. Violet rose. BSW. Cat. 1888. HC. Cat. 1885. *Lemoine, Nancy. France. 1883.*

GENERAL LEE. Double. Red/Purple. Tube. Red. (Rosy red). Sepals. Red. (Rosy red). Corolla. Violet purple..Very double. Vol. 2 J of RHS 1860 Fuchsias grown for trial at Chiswick. Free blooming. GC. P289 1/4/1865. Intro. by G. Smith, Tollington Nurseries Named after a Confederate General (1807-70). *Smith G, Isleworth. GB. 1865.*

GÉNÉRAL LEWAL (LEVAL). Double. Red/Purple. Tube. Red. Sepals. Bright Red. Large. Corolla. Plum. Vigourous. GC, Vol 23 1885 P213. BSW Cat 1889. *Lemoine, Nancy. France. 1885.*

GÉNÉRAL LYAUTEY. Double. Red/White. Tube. Bright pink. Sepals. Bright pink. Long. Corolla. Off white tinged pink. Petals irregular. Very open in every way. Very big. Named after a Marshal of France, born at Nancy (1854-1934). L. Cat. 1908. *Lemoine, Nancy. France. 1908.*

GÉNÉRAL MERCIER. Double. Red/White. Tube. Carmine red. Sepals. Carmine red. Corolla. Pure white. Large. Good habit and vigour. JF. Cat. 1901. L. Cat. 1901. *Rozain, Lyons. France. 1900.*

GÉNÉRAL NANSOUTY. Single. Red/Purple. Tube.Bright rose. (Scarlet). Sepals. Bright rose. (Scarlet). Corolla. Violet purple (blue) striped rose. BSW. Cat. 1878. B. Cat. 1877. NK. NK. *France. 1876?*

GÉNÉRAL NEGRIER (a). Single. Red/Red. Tube. Rose pink. Sepals. Rose pink edged white. Inside orange. Corolla. Flesh Pink. (Rosy Scarlet) App. to RH. 1851 by Porcher. GC. P497 11/8/1849 Listed by G. Smith. GC. P145 9/3/1850 Listed by W. Rumley, Richmond. etc. GC. P427 7/7/1849 Intro. by Youells, Gt. Yarmouth. *Meillez. France. 1849.*

GÉNÉRAL NEGRIER (b). Double. Red/Purple. Tube. Bright rose (Bright pink). Sepals. Bright rose (Bright pink). Reflexed. Corolla. Bluish Lavender (Magenta edged lavender blue). JF. Cat. 1901. L. Cat. 1901 (no.149). *Rozain, Lyons. France. 1900.*

GÉNÉRAL OUDINOT. Single. Red/Red.. Tube. Bright pink. Very large, 50mms long. Sepals. Bright pink shaded white. Carmine red on inside. Corolla. Reddish crimson, shaded purple. Good size. Named after a Marshal of France (1767-1847). App. to RH. 1851 by Porcher. GC. P465 27/7/1850 Listed by G. Smith, Tollington Nursery. *Meillez. France. 1850.*

GENERAL ROBERTS. Single. Red/Purple. Tube. Rosy carmine. (Crimson). Sepals. Rosy carmine. (Crimson). Well reflexed. Corolla. Rich purple shaded violet. Blooms 4" in length in large clusters. Valuable as a late flowerer) GC. P685 30/5/1885. Vol 30 GC 30/10/1886 Vol 38 1890 P438 by Cannell. L. Cat. 1892. JF. Cat. 1888. Dobbies Cat. 1892-4. BSW. Cat. 1897. *Vanden Rees, J. GB. 1885.*

GÉNÉRAL SAUSSIER. Double. Red/Purple. Tube. Dark crimson. Sepals. Dark crimson. Corolla. Violet. Laings Cat. circa 1890. BSW. Cat. 1888. *Lemoine, Nancy. France. 1882.*

GENERAL SIMPSON. Single. Red/Purple. Tube. Crimson. Sepals. Crimson. Well reflexed. Corolla. Purple brown. Selected from over 3,000 seedlings. Out on 1/4/1856. GC. P611 15/9/1855 Intro. by Stewart & Nielsen, Liscard. *Stewart & Nielsen. GB. 1856.*

GENERAL TOM THUMB. Single. Red/Purple. Tube. Red. Sepals. Red. Corolla. Purple. Very dwarf, neat growth, colour and shape of "Formosa Elegans". Well adapted for edgings. GC. P309 10/5/1845. Introduced by W. May. *May, W. Bedale. GB. 1845*

GÉNÉRAL VOYRON. Double. Red/Purple. Tube. Wine red. Sepals. Wine red. Horizontal. Corolla. Purple. Full. Large petals like a rosette. L. Cat 1901 (no. 149). *Lemoine, Nancy. France. 1901.*

GENERAL WERDER. ND. Red/Purple. Tube. Red. Sepals. Red. Corolla. Pale Violet. "Thin and not good" No Award. P68 Vol. 4 J of RHS 1877, Plants grown for trial at Chiswick. 1873. Sent by Downie NK. NK. *GB. 1872?*

GENERAL WILLIAMS. Single. Red/Purple. Tube. Bright crimson scarlet. Short. Sepals. Bright crimson scarlet. Long. Broad. Well reflexed. Corolla. Violet purple. GC. 580 9/7/1859 Exhibited

by H. Cannell, Gr to E. Groves, Tulse Hill at RBS Show 6/7/1859. GC. P456 5/7/1856 Listed by H. Walton etc, etc. GC. P82 9/2/1856. Intro. by G. Smith. *Smith, G. Isleworth GB. 1856.*

GENEROUS. Single. Red/Purple. Tube. Rose. Sepals. Rose. reflexed. Corolla. Deep pink shaded violet. B. Cat 1870. GC. P414 17/4/1869 Intro. by W. Bull. *Bull, W. Chelsea. GB. 1870.*

GEORGE BELLAIR. NK. NK/Purple. Tube. ND. Sepals. ND. Corolla Rosy violet. Well formed. Good habit. Very free. JF. Cat. 1898. NK. NK. NK. *1895?*

GEORGE BRUNNING. Single. Red/Purple. Tube. Crimson red. Very short. Sepals. Crimson red. Large, reflexed and round. Corolla Indigo Blue marked crimson, Bell shaped. Multiflowered. Raiser given as Bland by Porcher. 4th Ed. 1874.Bland, himself does not record it as one of hee, see GC 1894 Vol 1 P146. *Banks, E. Deal. GB. 1872.*

GEORGE FELTON. Double. Red/Purple. Tube. Brilliant red. Short. Thick. Sepals. Brilliant red. Elegantly recurved. Corolla. Violet variegated with red. (Bright purple). Large, full and expanded. Dwarf. Floriferous. Semi vigourous without being delicate. Family of "Ami Hoste". P131 4th Ed. by Porcher 1874. GC. P451 2/4/1870 Intro. by Felton, B'ham. *Felton, G. Birmingham GB. 1870.*

GEORGES FEYDEAU. Double. Red/Purple. Tube. Vinous red. (Scarlet). Sepals. Vinous red. (Scarlet). Large. Corolla. Lilac blue. (Bluish lilac).JF. Cat. 1895. B. Cat. 1894-1895. L. Cat. 1894. *Lemoine, Nancy. France. 1894.*

GEORGE FREDERICK. Single. Red/Purple. Tube. Rich scarlet crimson. Short. Sepals. Rich scarlet crimson. Broad. Thick. Reflexed. Corolla Rich purple crimson, Large, beautifully formed. B. Cat. 1876-1883. *Bull, W. Chelsea. GB. 1875.*

GEORGE FRY. Single Red/Purple. Tube. Scarlet (Red). Sepals. Scarlet. (Red). Corolla Violet veined and suffused. (Violet veined scarlet at base) Large fine flower. L. Cat. 1892. B. Cat. 1892. Laings cat circa 1890. *Fry, G. GB. 1890.*

GEORGE GORDON. Single. Red/Purple. Tube. Rose. Sepals. Rose. Recurved. Corolla. A lovely shade of blue with a violet tint. Elongated but well formed. Laings Cat. circa 1890. NK. NK. *GB. 1889?*

GEORGE PEABODY. Double. Red/White. Tube. Crimson. Sepals. Crimson. Corolla. White. Large.

GC. P639 20/5/1871. Raised and intro. by A. Henderson. *Henderson A. Maida Vale.GB. 1871.*

GEORGES LYON. Double. Red/Purple. Tube. Clear Carmine. Sepals. Clear carmine. Corolla. Cobalt blue fading to rosy rose. L. Cat. 1907. *Lemoine, Nancy. France. 1907.*

GERALD. Single. Red/Purple. Tube. Crimson. Sepals. Crimson, Completely reflexed. Corolla. Rich purplish crimson. Expanded. B. Cat 1882-1893. *Bland, E. Fordham GB. 1882.*

GERARD CORNELISSEN. Double. Red/Purple. Tube. Bright red. Sepals. Bright red. Corolla. Blue flaked white and rose. B. Cat 1870. *Cornelissen Belgium. 1869.*

GERARD. Single. Red/Purple. Tube. Crimson. Sepals. Crimson. Corolla. Bluish purple, deep rose at base. Large. B. Cat. 1901. *Bull, W. GB. 1900?*

GERBE DE CORAIL. Single. Red/Red. Tube. Red. Sepals. Red. Corolla. Red. Translated as "Sheaf of Coral" New novelty superior to Corne D'Abundance, in the way it carries its flowers, which are better and more brightly coloured. L. Cat 1901. F. venusta X. *Lemoine. Nancy. France 1901.*

GERBERT. Double. Red/Purple. Tube. Bright red. Sepals. Bright red. Twisted. Corolla. Reddish purple, splashed cardinal red. L. Cat. 1907. *Rozain, Lyons. France. 1907.*

GERMANIA. Single. Red/Purple. Tube. Red. Sepals. Red. Corolla. Purple. Not in the first selection. 4th Ed. by Porcher 1874. Parent of Deutscher Kaiser. *Weinrich. Germany. 1868.*

GERTRUDE (a). Double. Red/Purple. Tube. Dark crimson. Sepals. Dark crimson. Well reflexed. Corolla. Dark purple plum. Laings Cat. circa 1890. B. Cat 1872, 1873. *Bull, W. Chelsea. GB. 1870.*

GERTRUDE (b). Single. Red/White. Tube. Bright rose carmine. Sepals. Bright rose carmine. Large. Completely reflexed. Corolla. White veined carmine. Large. B. Cat. 1892-1894. *Bull, W. Chelsea. GB. 1891.*

GIANT. Double. Red/Purple. Tube. Bright rose (brilliant crimson) Slender ½" long. Sepals. Bright rose. Reflex Round. 1½" long, ½" broad. Corolla. Purple. (Violet washed red), (reddish plum passing to coral red at base). Irregular. Coarse. Full. 4th. Ed. P123 by Porcher 1874. Vol 3 J of RHS 1872 Pcxiv. B. Cat. 1870, 1872, 1873. *Bull, W. Chelsea. GB. 1869.*

GIANTESS. Single. Pink/Red. Tube. Light pink. Sepals. Light pink. Corolla. Dark rose. Large. GC. 6/2/1847 Listed by R. Cooper, Croydon. P184 18/3/1847 Millers, Ramsgate. GC. P114 21/2/1846 Intro. by F. Jennings. *Jennings, F. GB. 1846.*

GIANTESSA. Single. ND/ND. Tube. ND. Sepals. ND. Corolla. ND. GC. P369 8/6/1844. Listed by T. Cripps. NK. NK. *GB. 1844.*

GIDOUR. Double. Red/Purple. Tube. Crimson. Short. Sepals. Crimson. Very broad. Corolla. Rich plum purple. Very large. JF. Cat. 1900. L. Cat 1901. B. Cat 1899. Intro. by W. Bull, Chelsea. *Bull, W. Chelsea. GB. 1899.*

GIGANTEA REFLEXA. Single. ND/ND. Tube. ND. Sepals. ND. Corolla. ND. GC. P279 30/4/1853 "Light green stemmed". NK. NK. NK.

GIGANTEA. Single. Red/Red. Tube. Deep rose. Sepals. Deep rose. (Dark vermillion) Corolla. Crimson. (Purplish crimson). Colour plate Florists Journal Plate 1352 1843. App to RH 1851 by Porcher. P24 RH 1846. GC. P112 17/2/1844 Listed by Millers Ramsgate etc. GC. P193 30/3/1844 Intro by J. Smith, Dalston. *Smith, J. Dalston. GB. 1843.*

GIPSY QUEEN. Double. Red/Purple. Tube. Brilliant crimson. Thick and short. Sepals. Brilliant crimson. Reflexed. Corolla. Bluish violet splashed and stained red. On occasions the variegation dominates. Huge. P125 4th Ed. by Porcher 1874. J of RHS 1865 "Commended" 22/8/1865 B. Cat 1870 *Bull, W. Chelsea. GB. 1865.*

GIRALDA. ND. White/ND. Tube. White. Sepals. White. Corolla. ND. P120 4th. Ed. by Porcher 1874. Not in the first selection. *Demay, H. Arras. France. 1869.*

GLABRA MULTIFLORA. Single. ND/ND. Tube. ND. Sepals. ND. Corolla. ND. GC. P97 18/2/1843 Listed by Youells, Gt. Yarmouth. GC. P138 26/2/1842 Intro. by Marnock & Manby, Hackney. *Marnock & Manby, Hackney. GB. 1842.*

GLADIATOR (a). Double. ND/ND. Tube. ND. Sepals. ND. Corolla. ND. GC. P376 26/4/1862. Intro by F & A. Smith."Possess entire stock". NK. NK. *GB. 1862.*

GLADIATOR (b). Single. ND/ND. Tube. ND. Sepals. ND. Corolla. ND. GC. P465 27/7/1850 Listed by W. Rumley, Richmond. NK. NK. *GB. 1850.*

GLOBE CELESTE. Single. Red/Purple. Tube. Red. Sepals. Red. Corolla. Purple. GC. P184 13/3/1847 Listed by Millers, Ramsgate. *Miller, Ramsgate. GB. 1846.*

GLOBE PERFECTION. Single. ND/ND. Tube. ND. Sepals. ND. Corolla. ND. Listed in catalogues, but flowers not seen, or description obtained. App. to RH. 1851 by Porcher. *Kimberley. GB. 1850?*

GLOBE TERRESTE. Single. Red/Purple. Tube. Red. Sepals. Red. Corolla. Purple. GC. P184 13/3/1847 Listed by Millers, Ramsgate. *Miller, Ramsgate GB. 1846.*

GLOBOSA. Single. Red/Purple. Tube. Red. Sepals. Red. Corolla. Purple. GC. P518 7/8/1841 Exhibited at Royal Caledonian Show by J. Downie, Gr. to General Robertson. GC. P537 21/71841. will survive in open border. GC. P630 25/9/1841. One of the best of the Chilean varieties. *Bunney, W. Stratford. GB. 1832.*

GLOBOSA ALBA GRANDIFLORA. Single. White/Red. Tube. Whitish rose. Thin. 25mms long. Sepals. Whitish rose. Large. Reflexed. Corolla. Carmine red. Petals pleated. Globular buds. 1st Class variety. GC P465 27/7/1850 Listed by W. Rumley, Richmond. GC. P199 19/8/1853 "Recommended". GC. P535 23/8/1851 Exhibited at Vauxhall. App. to RH 1851 by Porcher. *Kendall, Stoke Newington. GB. 1850.*

GLOBOSA CARNEA. Single. Pink/Crimson. Tube. Pink. Sepals. Pink. Corolla. Crimson. Form resembles Globosa. GC. P585 4/9/1847 Intro. by R. Westmacott, Chelsea. *Westmacott, R. Chelsea. GB. 1847.*

GLOBOSA COCCINEA. Single. Red/Purple. Tube. Dark vermillion. Sepals. Dark vermillion. Corolla. Violet. GC. P112 17/2/1844 & P66 1/2/1845 Listed by Wm Miller, Ramsgate. GC. P177 23/3/1844. Intro. by Girlings, Stowmarket. *Girling, Stowmarket GB. 1844.*

GLOBOSA ELEGANS. Single. Red/Purple. Tube. Red. Sepals. Red. Corolla. Purple. GM. Vol 13. P268. Raised by Mr. Silverlock of Chichester from F. Globosa. GC. P241 15/4/1843 Listed by F&A Smith, and P242 Listed by A.J. Stewart. *Silverlock, Chichester. GB. 1836.*

GLOBOSA GRANDIFLORA. Single. Red/Purple. Tube. Red. Sepals. Red. Corolla. Purple. "Large and superior to Globosa Major" GC. P769 1843. GC. P177 23/3/1844 Intro. by G. Smith, Hornsey. *Smith, G. Hornsey. GB. 1844.*

GLOBOSA MAGNIFICA. Single. Red/Purple. Tube. Red. Sepals. Red. Corolla. Purple. GC. P275 1/5/1852 Listed by H. Walton Burnley. NK. NK. *GB. 1851.*

GLOBOSA MAJOR. Single. Red/Purple. Tube. Red. Sepals. Red. Corolla. Purple. GC. P668 11/10/1841 Exhibited by Mr. Rickard at RHS of Cornwall Show. GC. P273 23/4/1842 "Recommended" GC.P89 11/2/1843 Recommended for open ground. Colour Plate. Paxtons Mag. of Botany Pl 75. 1837. NK.NK. *GB.* NK.

GLOBOSA MULTIFLORA. Single. Red/Purple. Tube. Red. Sepals. Red. Corolla. Purple. GC. P241 15/4/1843 Listed by F&A Smith of Hackney. NK. NK. *GB.* NK.

GLOBOSA PALLIDA. Single. Pink/Purple. Tube. Flesh. Sepals. Flesh. Green tips. Corolla. Deep chocolate. Light globe kind. GC. P184 13/3/1847 Listed by Millers, Ramsgate. GC. P216 27/3/1847 Listed by R. Cooper, Croydon. GC. P2 4/1/1845 Intro. by Girlings, Stowmarket. *Girling, Stowmarket GB. 1845.*

GLOBOSA PERFECTA. Double. Red/Purple. Tube. Rich crimson. Small. Slender. Sepals. Rich crimson. Corolla. Purple. Bedding variety. Perfect globe. Blooms large and numerous hang long on the plant before they expand. Dwarf and bushy habit. Raised by J. Smith Liverpool. Selected from 1800 seedlings. GC. P130 21/2/1852 Intro. by E.G. Henderson. *Smith, J. Liverpool. GB. 1852.*

GLOBOSA PLENISSIMA. Double. ND/ND. Tube. ND. Sepals. ND. Corolla. ND. Originally called Ranunciflorae. RH. P170 1857. RH. P295 1887. Grown as a standard at Twickel, Nr. Arnhem. NK. NK. NK.

GLOBOSA PURPUREA. Single. ND/ND.Tube. ND. Sepals. ND. Corolla. ND. GC P66 1/2/1845 & P184 11/3/1847 Listed by Millers, Ramsgate. NK. NK. *GB. 1844.*

GLOBOSA RANUNCIFLORA PLENA. Double. Red/Purple. Tube. Red. Sepals. Red. Corolla. Dark Purple. J. Van Houtte renamed and released as Globosa Plenissima RH. P170 1857. Gartenflora Vol 6 1857. *Coene, H. Ghent. Belgium 1856.*

GLOBOSA ROSEA ELEGANS. Single. ND/ND. Tube. ND. Sepals. ND. Corolla. ND. GC. P241 15/4/1843 Listed by F&A Smith of Hackney. GC. P242 15/4/1843 Listed by A. J. Stewart, Windsor. NK. NK. *GB. 1842.*

81

GLOBOSA SMITHII. ND. Red/ND. Tube. Red. Sepals. Red. Corolla. ND. RH. P167 1857. Forms a Good bush. Globular flowers. Shiny red. Abundantly flowered until December. NK. NK. NK.

GLOBOSA SPLENDENS (a). Single. ND/ND. Tube. Red. Sepals. ND. Corolla. ND. GC. P502 22/7/1843 Royal Botanic Scty. Show London. New Fuchsia exhibited by F. Cox. *Cox, F. NK GB. 1843.*

GLOBOSA SPLENDENS (b). Single. Red/Purple. Tube. Bright vermillion. Sepals. Bright vermillion. Corolla. Richest purple. A fine large globular shaped flower. Profuse bloomer. GC. P146 8/3/1845 Intro. by Youells. Gt. Yarmouth. *Youell, Gt. Yarmouth GB. 1845.*

GLOBOSA SPLENDENS (c) Single. Red/Purple. Tube. Rich crimson. Sepals. Rich crimson. Corolla. Deep Purple. Largest and best globe fuchsia ever raised. GC. P401 24/6/1854 Listed by H. Walton Burnley. P466 22/7/1854 Bass & Brown, Sudbury. GC. P194 1/4/1854 Intro by Kimberley, Stoke Nursery. *Kimberley. Coventry. GB. 1854.*

GLOBOSA VARIEGATA. Single. Red/Purple. Tube. Red. Sepals. Red. Corolla. Purple. Advance notice. Ready first week in June. Exact habit of Globosa but foliage is finely variegated. Listed by Youells, Gt. Yarmouth GC P393 June 1842 & P98 17/2/1844 GC. May 8 1841 Intro. by *J. Smith. Nurseryman, Westerham. GB. 1841.*

GLOIRE DE NEISSE. Single. Pink/Red. Tube. Flesh pink. Sepals. Flesh Pink. Corolla. Rose, striped white. RH. P169 1857. GC. P419 21/6/1856 Intro. by E. G. Henderson, St. Johns Wood. *Rother. NK. 1855.*

GLOIRE DES BLANCS. Double. Red/White. Tube. Red. Sepals. Red. Corolla. White. P 131 4th Ed. By Porcher 1874. Not in the first selection. *Crousse. France. 1864.*

GLOIRE DES MARCHES. Double. Red/White. Tube. Bright scarlet. Sepals. Bright scarlet. Corolla. Pure white. Large. Splendid habit. JF. Cat. 1895. *Rozain, Lyons. France. 1894.*

GLORIOSA SUPERBA. Single. Red/Purple. Tube. Scarlet. Sepals. Scarlet. Reflexed in shape of a Turks Cap lily. Corolla. Deep Violet. GC. P51 26/1/1856 to be sent out by W. Fuller, Florist, Newton Bushel. Gardener to W.H. Story of Whitehill. *Story, W.H. Newton Abbot. GB. 1856.*

GLORIOSA. ND. ND/ND. Tube. ND. Sepals. ND. Corolla. ND.GC. P259 28/4/1849. Listed by W. Rendle, Plymouth. NK. NK. NK.

GLORIOT. Single. Pink/Red. Tube. Salmon. Sepals. Salmon. Corolla. Orange red. RH. P24 1846. *Salter, J. Versailles. France. 1846.*

GLORY (a). Single. Red/Purple. Tube. Red. Sepals. Red. Well reflexed. Corolla. Purple. Expanded. Florist P203 Sept. 1852 1st. Class Certificate. GC. P337 28/5/1853 Listed By H. Walton. GC. P385 11/6/1853 Listed by W. Rumley, Richmond. etc. etc. GC. P98 12/2/1853 Intro. by G. Smith, Tollington Nursery. *Banks, E. Deal. GB. 1853.*

GLORY (b). Single. Red/Violet. Tube. Red. Sepals. Red. Completely reflexed. Corolla. Violet. Large. Beautifully form, widely expanded. G.Vol 36 20/7/1889. Being grown in Regents Park. B. Cat 1888-1893. Intro. by W. Bull, Chelsea. *Eckford. GB. 1885.*

GLORY OF STOKE. Single. Red/Purple. Tube. Red. Sepals. Red. Stout. Broad. Nicely reflexed. Corolla. Purple. GC. P829 30/9/1860 Listed by F. Godwin, Sheffield. GC. P378 30/4/1859. Intro. by Kimberley. Stoke Nursery. *Kimberley, C. Coventry. GB. 1859.*

GLORY OF THE DAY. Single. White/Red. Tube. White. Sepals. White. Corolla. Carmine. GC. P153 29/1/1887 "Good sort". JF. Cat 1885. *Lye, J. Market Lavington. GB. 1885.*

GOLDEN CHAINS. ND. ND/ND. Tube. ND. Sepals. ND. Corolla. ND. Not in the first selection. Golden foliage. P49 4th. Ed. by Porcher 1874. NK. NK. *GB. 1865.*

GOLDEN FLEECE. ND. ND/ND. Tube. ND. Sepals. ND. Corolla. ND. Golden foliage. Good bedder. Dwarf. Compact. GC. P102 1/2/1868 Review by H. Cannell. Makes a hedge 6" to 10" high like a yellow ribbon. P134 4th Ed. by Porcher 1874. B. Cat. 1870-1873. F & P. April 1868. GC. P143 1867 Intro. by E. G. Henderson. etc. Enoch Arden X. *Henderson, E.G. St.Johns Wood GB. 1867*

GOLDEN MANTLE. ND. ND/ND. Tube. ND. Sepals. ND. Corolla. ND. Golden Leaf. Erect. Vigourous. P134 4th. Ed. by Porcher. Not in the first selection. P68 4th Ed. J of RHS. Fuchsia trials at Chiswick. "No award" HC. Cat. 1882. GC. P378 19/3/1870 Intro. by E.G. Henderson. *Henderson, E.G. St.Johns Wood. GB. 1870.*

GOLDEN PLOVER. Single. Red/Purple. Tube. Red. Sepals. Red. Reflexed. Corolla. Purple. Flower form and colour of "Souvenir de Chiswick". Golden green foliage veined purple. ? a sport. Vol P3 J.of RHS. Report on Fuchsia Trial at Chiswick 1862. GC. P90 5/2/1859. Intro. by G. Smith. Tollington Nursery. *Smith, G. Hornsey. GB. 1859.*

GOLDEN QUEEN (a). Single. Red/White. Tube. Red. Sepals. Red. Corolla. White.GC. P102 1/2/1868 Review by H. Cannell. Tricoloured leaves F&P April 1868. "It is very similar in the colour of its leaves to Mrs Pollock (Pelargonium). It is a good grower but blooms very sparingly The most attractive feature is its large tricolour leaves. Unique. HC. NK. NK. *GB. 1867.*

GOLDEN QUEEN (b). Single. Red/White. Tube. Carmine. Sepals. Carmine. Corolla. White. Beautifuly golden yellow foliage flushed crimson. JF. Cat. 1908 "New". NK. NK. *GB. 1908.*

GOLDEN TREASURE. ND. ND/ND. Tube. ND. Sepals. ND. Corolla. ND. Leaves pure gold, tinted bronze in the young growth. Compact habit. Vol. 4 J of RHS 1877 "Worthless as a flowering plant". P134 4th. Ed. by Porcher 1874. HC. Cat. 1882. BSW. Cat 1897. GC.P375 19/3/1870 Intro. by E.G. Henderson. *Henderson E.G. St. Johns Wood. GB. 1870.*

GOLDFINCH. Single. White/Red. Tube. Yellow white. (Salmon) Sepals. White. (Salmon) Tipped. Green. Horizontal. Corolla. Red. (Orangy red) Coloured Plate Flor. Cab. Vol XI. P225. GC. P686 12/10/1844 Shown at RHS of Cornwall Show. GC. P114 22/2/1845 Listed by Millers, Ramsgate. RH. P24 1846. *Harrison, J. Dereham. GB. 1844.*

GOLIAH (a). Single. ND/ND. Tube. ND. Sepals. ND. Corolla. ND. GC. P66 1/2/1845 Listed by Millers, Ramsgate. *Day. GB. NK.*

GOLIAH (b) Single. Red/Purple. Tube. Red. Sepals. Red. Corolla Rosy purple. 9" from tip of calyx to the pistil. GC. P153 4/3/1848 & P256 21/4/1849 Listed by R. Cooper, Croydon. GC. P226 13/4/1850 Listed by Poole Nurseries. GC. P338 22/5/1847 Intro. by Turville Chelmsford. *Turville, Chelmsford GB. 1847.*

GOLIATH (a). Single. Pink/Red. Tube. Flesh Colour. Large. Sepals. Flesh. Corolla. Bright Scarlet. Twice the size of "Norfolk Hero". GC. P153 4/3/1848 Listed by R. Cooper, Croydon. GC. P259 23/4/1849 & P241 30/4/1850 Listed by W. Rendle, Plymouth. GC. P298 8/5/1847 Intro. by Barkways. *Barkways. GB. 1847.*

GOLIATH (b). Single. Red/ND. Tube. Coral Red. Sepals. Coral Red. Corolla. ND. Long flowers. Good habit. GC. P594 29/6/1861 Listed by Godwin & Padman, Sheffield. GC. P77 24/8/1861 Listed by H. Walton, Burnley. GC. P140 16/2/1861 Intro. by F&A Smith, Dulwich. *F&A Smith, Dulwich. GB. 1861.*

GOLIATH (c) Double. Red/Purple. Tube. Red. Sepals. Red. Corolla. Purple. Sepals fused to Corolla. Not in the 1st Selection. 4th E. by Porcher 1874. *Twrdy. Brno. Austria. 1866.*

GOTTINGEN. Single. Red/Red. Tube. Red. Sepals. Red. Corolla. Cinnabar Red. Good bunches of flowers. Bronze foliage. L. Cat 1906. *Bonstedt, C. Gottingen. Germany. 1905.*

GOUNOD. ND. ND/ND. Tube. ND. Sepals. ND. Corolla. ND. L. Cat 1892. NK. NK. *France. 1890?*

GOVERNEUR BACKER. Single. Red/Purple. Tube. Red. Sepals. Red. Corolla. Purple. Not in the 1st selection. 4th. Ed. by Porcher, 1874. Gartenflora P40 1877. *Crousse. France. 1866.*

GOVERNOR GENERAL. Double. Red/Purple. Tube. Coral Red. Sepals. Coral red. Broad. Well reflexed. Corolla. Bold rich purple. Confused. Vol. P3 J of RHS 1863 Grown for trial at Chiswick. GC. P475 3/6/1858 "Best of the Season". GC. P571 24/7/1858 Listed by H. Walton, Burnley. GC. P85 6/2/1858 Intro by G. Smith. Tollington Nursery. *Smith, G. Hornsey. GB. 1858.*

GRACIEUX. ND. Red/Purple. Tube. Scarlet. Sepals. Scarlet. Corolla. Mauve Lavender. Free. HC. Cat. 1885. *Lemoine, Nancy. France. 1881.*

GRACILIS SUPERBA. Single. Red/Purple. Tube. Red. Sepals. Red. Corolla. Purple. The form of the flower is similar to the old flower but much larger and a fine colour. Floral Cabinet P13 Vol. IX 1841. NK. NK. *GB. 1840.*

GRACILIS VARIEGATA, Single. Red/Purple. Tube. Red. Sepals. Red. Corolla. Purple. Small leaves margined with white. Good habit. B. Cat. 1872-1888. NK. NK. *GB. NK.*

GRANADA. ND. ND/ND. Tube. ND. Sepals. ND. Corolla. ND. Exhibited by A. Lowe, Nottingham Scty. Show. Florists Journal P210 1843. NK. NK. *GB. NK.*

GRAND ADMIRAL. Double. Red/Purple. Tube. Crimson Scarlet. Sepals. Crimson Scarlet.. Broad.

Well reflexed. Corolla. Deep Violet Purple. Large and Full. GC. P55 19/1/1867. Review by H.Cannelll. GC. P382 25/4/1863 Intro. by G. Wheeler, Warminster. *Wheeler, G. Warminster. GB. 1863.*

GRAND CROSS. Double. Red/Purple. Tube. Scarlet. Sepals. Scarlet. Corolla. Purple with rosy lake shading. GC. P120 8/2/1868 Intro by G. Smith. Tollington Nurseries. *Smith, G. Islington. GB. 1868*

GRAND DUCHESS MARIE. Single. White/Red. Tube. White. Sepals. White. Recurved. Curl up at tips. Deep rose. G. Sept 1875 P435 "Good" Tube and sepals Waxy white. Sepals extra broad short and gracefully reflex Corolla pure rose pink. Superior to most others of its form. Illustration in Cannells Cat. P68 1882 P86 1885. P136 Appendix 4th. Edition by Porcher. 1874. GO. Select 1888-1891. BSW. Cat 1878. GC. P363 21/3/1874 Introduced by B.S. Williams. *Bland, E. Fordham GB. 1874.*

GRAND DUCHESS. Double. Red/White. Tube. Brilliant Carmine. Sepals. Brilliant carmine. Broad. Well reflexed. Corolla. Pure White. Fine Form. Large. GO. Select 1880-1884. B. Cat 1880-1882, HC. Cat 1882. B. Cat. 1880-1882. *Smith, G. GB. 1880.*

GRAND DUKE (a). Single. Red/Purple. Tube. Red. Sepals. Red. Corolla. Purple. GC. P328 13/5/1848. Intro by E. Mitchell, Brighton. *Mitchell, E. Brighton. GB. 1848*

GRAND DUKE (b). Double. Red/Purple. Tube. Crimson. Sepals. Crimson. Well reflexed. Corolla. Violet Purple. GC. P296 26/3/1864 Intro. by G. Smith, Tollington Nursery. *Smith, G. GB. 1864.*

GRAND DUKE (c). Double. Red/Purple. Tube. Red. (Crimson). Sepals. Red.(Crimson) Reflexed. Corolla. Purple. (Bluish violet splashed red). Distinguished by its colouring and size. P123 4th. Ed. by Porcher 1874. GC. P55 19/1/1867 Review by H. Cannell. Largest and closest corolla to date. P57 F&P 1866. *Smith, F&A, Dulwich GB. 1865.*

GRAND MASTER. Single. Red/Purple. Tube. Crimson. (Crimson red). Sepals. Crimson. (Crimson red). Corolla. Violet purple. (Purple). Petals open, coolie hat shape. A large "Rajah" 1st Class variety. App. to RH. 1851 by Porcher. GC. P465 27/7/1850 Listed by W. Rumley, Richmond. GC. P242 20/4/1840 Intro. by E.G. Henderson. St Johns Wood. *Henderson, E.G. St.Johns Wood. GB. 1850.*

GRAND SULTAN. Single. Red/Purple. Tube. Crimson. Sepals. Crimson. Reflex similar to a turn

cup lily. Corolla. Dark violet purple. GC. P467 14/7/1855 Listed by H. Walton, Burnley. P530 11/8/1855 by Bainbridge and Hewison, York. P513 by Joseph Courcha. GC. P314 10/5/1856 by Youells, Gt. Yarmouth. GC. P34 20/1/1855 Intro. by W.J. Epps Maidstone. *Banks, E. Deal. GB. 1855.*

GRANDIDENS. Double. Red/Purple. Tube. Crimson. (Waxy carmine). Sepals Crimson. (Waxy carmine) Large. Well reflexed. Corolla. Bright clear purple. (Dark Violet) Appx to 4th Edition by Porcher 1874. Very Large. G. P435 Sept 1875 Tube and sepals coral red. Corolla deep plum. GC. P363 21/3/1874 Intro. by B. S. Williams. HC. Cat. 1882. *Bland, E. Fordham GB. 1874.*

GRANDIFLORA ELEGANS. ND. ND/ND. Tube. ND. Sepals. ND. Corolla. ND. GC. P112 17/2/1844 NK. NK. NK. NK.

GRANDIFLORA MAXIMA Single. Red/Red. Tube Purplish red. Sepals. Purplish red. Corolla. Purplish red. GC. P630 25/9/841. GCP168 11/10/1841. Exhibited at RHS of Cornwall Show. Colour Plate Floral Cabinet Vol IX P13 1841. GC. 8/5/1841 Advert by James May, Edmonton. F. fulgens X. *May, W. Bedale. GB. 1840.*

GRANDIFLORA SUPERBA. Single. Red/Purple. Tube. Red. Sepals. Red. Not reflexed. Corolla. Purple. Vol. 3 P192 1835 Floral Cabinet. GC. P630 25/9/1841. One of the best of the Chilean varieties. GC.P833 18/12/1841 "Recommended 6 next best" NK. NK. *GB. 1834?*

GRANDIFLORA. ND. ND/ND. Tube. ND. Sepals. ND. Corolla. ND. GC. P260 24/3/1860 Listed by Wm. Hussey, Norwich. NK. NK. NK. NK.

GRANDIS. Single. Red/Purple. Tube. Crimson. Sepals. Crimson. Corolla. Rosy violet. 1" long. Very visible. Free Bloomer.GC. P481 15/7/1843 Shown at HS Show. Dark Flowers, ribbed leaves like Corymbiflora. GC. P393 6/1842 P98 17/2/1844 Listed by Youells. P13 F.C. Vol IX 1841. etc. *Smith, J. Dalston. GB. 1841.*

GRANDISSIMA. Single. White/Red. Tube. White.Long. Sepals. White. Corolla. Light crimson, to deep claret. Good habit. GC.P213 8/4/1854 Listed by H. Low. GC 401 24/6/1854 Listed by H. Walton, Burnley. GC. P466 22/7/1854 Bass & Brown Sudbury. GC. P83 11/2/1854 Intro. by T. Batten, Clapham. *Batten, T. Clapham. GB. 1854.*

GRAPHIE. Double. Red/Purple. Tube. Crimson. Short. Sepals. Crimson. Short. Well extended.

Plate 1 - Jean Sisley

Plate 2 - Solferino

Plate 3 - Galanthiflora

Plate 4 - Stylosa Conspicua

Plate 5 - Mrs Hooper Taylor,
Mr Hooper Taylor & Fairy Queen

Plate 6 - Emperor Napoleon &
Venus de Medicis

Plate 7 - Lye's Favourite

Plate 8 - Venus Victrix &
Enchantress

Corolla. Lavender Blue, shaded red at base. Very Large. Loose. L. Cat 1901. B. Cat. 1901. *Bull, W. Chelsea. GB. 1901.*

GREAT BRITAIN (a). Single. Red/Purple. Tube. Red. Sepals. Red. Corolla. Purple .GC. P184 13/3/1847. P281 29/4/1848 by W. Miller (J.G. Hine Successors) GC. P274 5/5/1849 H. Walton Burnley. *Miller, W. Ramsgate. GB. 1846.*

GREAT BRITIAN (b) Single. ND/ND. Tube. ND. Sepals. ND. Corolla. ND. Described as red. Listed by W. Miller GC. P184 13/3/1847. *Kendall, Stoke Newington. GB. 1846.*

GREAT EASTERN. Single. Red/Purple. Tube. Bright crimson. Sepals. Bright crimson. Broad. Well reflexed. Corolla. Dark Purple. Extra Large (By far the largest fuchsia ever offered). Loosely expanded. Vol. P3 J of RHS 1863. Fuchsia grown for trial at Chiswick. . GC. P93 4/2/1860 Intro. by G. Smith, Tollington Nursery. *Smith, G. Hornsey. GB. 1860.*

GREAT EXHIBITION. ND. Red/Purple. Tube. Crimson. Sepals. Crimson. Well reflexed. Corolla. Rich plum. Flower 1 ½" to 2" in diameter. Short jointed. GC. P374 26/4/1862 Intro. by J. Harrison, Dereham. *Harrison, J. Dereham GB. 1862.*

GREAT WESTERN (a). Single. Red/Red. Tube. Dark Vermillion. Sepals. Dark Vermillion. Corolla. Crimson. Exhibited at RBS Show by Betteridge of Abingdon. *Betteridge, Abingdon. GB. 1843.*

GREAT WESTERN (b). Single. ND/ND. Tube. ND. Sepals. ND. Corolla. ND. Exhibited at Oxford. New Fuchsia. Largest in cultivation. Raised by Mr. Patterson, Gr. to Baroness Wenman. CG. Vol. VII P30 16/10/1851. Fulgens x Beauty of Leeds. *Patterson. GB. 1851.*

GRENADIER. Double. Red/Purple. Tube. Rich crimson. Short. Thick. Sepals. Rich crimson. Broad. Elegantly reflexed Corolla. Violet Blue with pink markings. Monstrously large. 4th. Ed. by Porcher 1874. Not in 1st. selection. B. Cat. 1872-1876. *Bull, W. Chelsea. GB. 1871.*

GRENVILLII. Single. Red/Purple. Tube. Red. Sepals. Red. Corollla. Purple. Similiar to Laneii, with a wider tube and a more purple corolla. Exhibited at HS London show. GC. P431 24/6/1844. GC. P66 1/2/1845 P112 17/2/1844 Listed by Millers, Ramsgate. *Lane, Berkhampstead. GB. 1844.*

GREYIANA. ND. ND/ND. Tube. ND. Sepals. ND. Corolla. ND. GC. P518 7/8/1841 Exhibited at Royal Caledonian Show 20/7/1841 by G. Young. NK. NK. GB. NK.

GROOMII. Single. ND/ND. Tube. ND. Sepals. ND. Corolla. ND. GC. P273 23/4/1842. NK. NK. NK.

GROVEHILLII ND. ND/ND. Tube. ND. Sepals. ND. Corolla. ND. GC. P668 11/10/1841, P686 12/10/1841 Exhibited by Mr. Rickard at RHS of Cornwall Show. GC. P436 HS Show London 21/6/1845 A beautiful light variety. F.C. P12 Vol XIV 1846. Exhibited by Lane, Berkhampstead. NK. NK. NK.

GUARDSMAN. Single. Red/Purple. Tube. Thick. Bright crimson. Sepals. Bright crimson. Large. Reflexed. Corolla. Indigo blue, washed red. Spiraled. Pedicel 70 mm. Buds shaped like large bells. Similar to "Lord Derby". P108 4th. Ed. by Porcher 1874. GC.P452 6/4/1872 Intro. by E.G. Henderson, St. Johns Wood. *Henderson, E.G. St. Johns Wood. GB. 1872.*

GUIDING STAR. Single. White/Purple. Tube. White. Long. Sepals. White Reflexed. Corolla. Purple, changing to rose. G. Vol 19 P223 27/8/1881. Vol. P3 J of RHS 1863 P91. Fuchsias grown for trial at Chiswick. Graceful habit etc. GO Select 1880-1889. GC. P580 9/7/1859 Exhibited by H. Cannell at RBS Show. Intro. by E.G. Henderson, St. Johns Wood. *Banks, E. Deal. GB. 1856.*

GUILLAUME GRANDIDIER Double. Red/Purple. Tube. Blood red. Sepals. Blood red. Horizontal. Corolla. Reddish violet. Good form. L. Cat. 1906 *Lemoine, Nancy. France. 1904.*

GUILLAUME LE CONQUÉRANT. Double. Red/Purple. Tube. Red. Sepals. Red. Corolla. Purple. Not in the first selection. P126 4th. Ed. by Porcher 1874. *Baudry. France. NK.*

GUNDREDA. Single. Red/Purple. Tube. Red. Sepals. Red. Spreading. Corolla. Purple. Small. Vol. P3 JofRHS 1863 P90 Report on fuchsias grown from trial at Chiswick, 1862. Submitted by Laxton. *Laxton. GB. 1862.*

GUSTAVE DORÉ. Double. Red/White. Tube. Red. Sepals. Red. Corolla. White. Named after a French Painter !833-83). GC. Vol 22 1884 P310 6/9/1884 Exhibited at Bath by J Lye. 1st (Light). HC. Cat. 1882, 1885, 1890, 1891, 1896, 1898. BSW Cat. 1888. GO. "Select" 1887-1889. Dobbies Cat. 1893/4. *Lemoine, Nancy. France. 1880.*

GUSTAVE FLAUBERT. Double. Red/Purple. Tube. Bright Carmine. (Carmine Pink) Sepals. Bright carmine. (Rose carmine). Corolla. Lilac Mauve. Unuusual colour. Vigourous and very floriferous. Named after a French novelist (1821-80). B. Cat. 1892. JF. Cat. 1892. L. Cat. 1892. *Lemoine, Nancy. France. 1891.*

GUSTAVE HEITZ. Double. Red/Purple. Tube. Red. Sepals. Red. Corolla. Purple. "Not in the first selection" P126 4th Edition by Porcher 1874. RH. P295 1887. Being grown as a standard at Twickel. Nr. Arnhem. *Cornelissen. Belgium. 1866.*

GUSTAVE NADAUD. Double. Red/Purple. Tube. Red. Sepals. Red. Completely reflexed. Corolla. Violet Plum. Long. L. Cat. 1892. B. Cat. 1892. *Lemoine. Nancy. France. 1892.*

GUY DAUPHINE. Double. Red/Purple. Tube. Clear Crimson. Sepals. Clear crimson. Corolla. Exterior carmine, interior plum. Very full. Good habit. L. Cat. 1913. *Rozain. Lyons. France. 1913.*

GUY DE MAUPASSANT. Double. Red/White. Tube. Dark wine red. Sepals. Dark wine red. (Dark cherry). Corolla. Creamy White. Very full. Good habit. Named after a French Novelist (1850-93). L. Cat. 1892. B. Cat. 1892. *Lemoine. Nancy. France. 1890.*

GYPSY GIRL. ND. White/ND.Tube. White. Sepals. White. Corolla. ND. CG. P454 1865. NK. NK. *GB. 1864?*

GYPSY. Single. Red/Purple. Tube. Dark red. Sepals. Dark red. Corolla. Dark maroon. GC. P143 4/3/1848 Listed by R. Cooper, Croydon. GC. P298 8/3/1847 Intro by Barkways. *Barkway. GB. 1847.*

H. DUTERAIL. Double. Red/Purple. Tube. Carmine. Sepals. Carmine. Long. Corolla. Plum to rose marked carmine. Long. L. Cat. 1906. *Rozain. Lyons. France. 1905.*

H. LECOQ. Single. Red/Red. Tube. Carmine red at base. Rose at summit. 1 1/2 to 2" long. Sepals. Straw coloured. Recurved. Corolla. Rosy orange. Dwarf branching habit. Similar to "Ed. Andre" but distinct. B. Cat. 1878-1881. HC. Cat. P78 1882. Vol.19 P6. 1881. Dominiana X Serratifolia. *Lemoine. Nancy. France. 1878.*

HAFIZ. Single. Red/White. Tube. Rosy carmine. Sepals. Rosy carmine. Well reflexed. Corolla. Pure white. Dickson's Chester Cat.1907-1908. *Dickson, Chester. GB. 1907.*

HAIDEE. Single. Red/White. Tube. Carmine. Sepals. Carmine. Very broad. Recurved. Corolla. White suffused pink, veined carmine. Bell shaped. B. Cat. 1901. *Bull, W. Chelsea. GB. 1901.*

HAILSTORM. Single. ND/ND. Tube. ND. Sepals. ND. Corolla. ND. GC. P153 4/3/1848 Listed by R. Cooper, Croydon. P224 14/4/1849 by R. Whibley, Kennington. GC. P199 27/3/1847 Intro. by J. Fowles. *Fowles, J. London. GB. 1847.*

HALLALI. Single. Red/Purple. Tube. Red. Sepals. Red. Paised up. Corolla. Purple red. Large. L. Cat. 1913. *Rozain, Lyons. France. 1913.*

HALLOWEEN. Single. Red/Purple. Tube. Crimson. Overshort. Sepals. Crimson. Immense. Broad. Long. Recurved. Corolla. Slatey blue, veined crimson at base. Good variety for pillars. B. Cat. 1901. *Bull, W. Chelsea. GB. 1901.*

HAMLET (a). Single. Red/Purple. Tube. Bright crimson. Sepals. Bright crimson. Corolla. Purple. Several flowers at each leaf joint. Base of footstalk to pistil is 6". GC. P162 14/3/1846 & P184 13/3/1847 Listed by W. Miller, Ramsgate. GC. P206 29/3/1845 Intro. by G. Smith, Tollington Nursery. *Smith, G. Islington. GB. 1845.*

HAMLET (b). Double. Red/Purple. Tube. Brilliant Scarlet. Sepals. Brilliant Scarlet. Corolla. Violet. L. Cat. 1898. JF. Cat. 1898. NK. NK. *France. 1898.*

HANDEL. Single. Red/Purple. Tube. Crimson. Sepals. Crimson. Broad. Hood corolla. Corolla. Bluish tinted rose at base. Large. L. Cat. 1906. B. Cat. 1905. *Bull, W. Chelsea. GB. 1905.*

HARDY HYBRID No. 1. Single. Red/Purple. Tube. Red. Sepals. Red. Corolla. Purple. A perfect "Globosa" in shape, and at bud burst. Excels the old variety for graceful habit. Growth 4' to 8' high. HC. Cat. 1882 P79. Intro. by Cannell. *Bland, E. Fordham. GB. 1873.*

HARDY HYBRID No. 2. Single. Red/Purple. Tube. Red. Sepals. Red. Corolla. Purple. Profuse bloomer. Medium size. Bright Coloured flowers. Evidently a cross with "Gracilis". HC. Cat. 1882. Intro. by H. Cannell. *Bland, E. Fordham GB. 1873.*

HARDY HYBRID No. 3. Single. Red/Purple. Tube. Red. Sepals. Red. Corolla. Purple. Somewhat similiar to "Hardy Hybrid No. 2". Valuable outdoor variety for a mild climate. HC. Cat. P79 1882. Intro. by H. Cannell. *Bland, E. Fordham. GB. 1873.*

HARDY HYBRID No. 4. Single. Red/Purple. Tube. Red. Sepals. Red. Corolla. Purple. Has the largest blooms and evidently a cross between "Globosa" and "Try me O". Strong flower. Profuse. HC. Cat. P79 1882. Intro. by H. Cannell. *Bland, E. Fordham GB. 1873.*

HARLEQUIN. Single. Red/Purple. Tube. Rich carmine. Sepals. Rich carmine. Broad. Reflexed. Corolla. Bluish Purple striped rose pink. Immense. B. Cat. 1888-1892. L. Cat. 1891. Intro. by W. Bull, Chelsea. *Eckford. GB. 1888.*

HARMONY. Single. Red/Purple. Tube. Rich crimson. Sepals. Rich crimson. Very long. Broad. Horizontal. Corolla. Violet blue. A pretty colour. B. Cat. 1872-1873. *Bull, W. Chelsea. GB. 1872.*

HARMONY (c). Single. Red/Purple. Tube. Carmine. Sepals. Carmine. Corolla. Purple. RB. Cat 1937. NK. NK. NK. NK.

HARMONIE (Harmoine). Single. Pink/Purple. Tube. Whitish rose. Sepals. Whitish rose. Reflexed. Corolla. Soft lilac. Good habit. B. Cat. 1888-1894. *Lemoine. Nancy. France. 1884.*

HARRIET LYE. Single. White/Pink. Tube. Cream. (creamy white). Sepals. Creamy white (cream). Corolla. Lilac pink edged carmine. Free Bloomer. B. Cat. 1883. GC. Vol 22 P310 6/9/1884 Exhibited at Bath by J.Lye GC. Vol 28 1887 1st 9 pot class. GC. Vol 23 Fig. 39 Illustrated. HC. Cat 1885-1890. *Lye, J. Market Lavington. GB. 1883.*

HARRISONII. Single. Red/Purple. Tube. Bright scarlet. Sepals. Bright scarlet. Reflex back. Corolla. Dark purple. Spreading. GC. P374 26/4/1862. Intro. by J.H. Harrison. *Harrison, J.H. Dereham. GB. 1862.*

HARRY ALIS. Double. Red/Red. Tube. Carmine. Sepals. Carmine. Well recurved. Corolla. Clear rose edge white. Very double and compact. Globular form. B. Cat. 1894-1895. *Lemoine, Nancy. France. 1894.*

HARRY BROOKE. See Henry Brooke.

HARRY FELTON. Double. Red/Purple. Tube. Bright crimson. Sepals. Bright crimson. Reflexed. regularly curled. Corolla. Bright mauve. Long. Full. Well expanded. GC. P320 20/3/1869 Intro. by Felton & Son, Birmingham. *Felton, Birmingham. GB. 1869.*

HARRY GEORGE HENDERSON. Single. Red/Purple. Tube. Bright coral. Sepals. Bright coral. Recurved. Corolla. Plum blue merging into violet red. Margins slightly revolute. Almost flat outline. Very large round parachute formed corolla. B. Cat.1870-1873. BSW. Cat. 1878. F&P P56 March 1866. GC. P382 28/4/1866 Intro. by E.G. Henderson. *Banks, E. Deal. GB. 1866.*

HARRY WILLIAMS. Double. Red/Purple. Tube. Scarlet. (Shining crimson). Short. Sepals. Scarlet. (Shining crimson). Horizontal. Points down. Corolla. Purple tinged carmine at base. (Violet Blue washed red). (Intense violet). Globular buds. Robust. Compact. P68 Vol 4 J of RHS, Chiswick trials 1873. BSW. Cat. 1878. GC. P510 20/4/1871. Intro. by B&S Williams. *Bland, E. Fordham GB. 1871.*

HARVEST HOME. Double. Red/Purple. Tube. Pink. Long. Sepals. Scarlet. Broad. Recurved. Corolla. Violet with pale flakes of rose. Large. Open. GC. P1554 2/12/1871 Review by H. Cannell. GC. P375 19/3/1870 Intro. by E.G. Henderson, St. Johns Wood. *Henderson E.G. St. Johns Wood. GB. 1870.*

HARVIN. Double. Red/Purple. Tube. Red. Sepals. Red. Corolla. Purple. 4th Ed. by Porcher 1874. "Not in the first selection". *Lemoine, Nancy. France. 1868.*

HATTERAS. Single. Pink/Purple. Tube. Clear Flesh. Sepals. Clear Flesh. Corolla. Violet Blue P77 Witte 1882. *Lemoine, Nancy. France. 1876.*

HAYDEE See Haidee

HEATHER BELL. Single. Pink/Red. Tube. Greenish white. Long 15 mms. Thick. Sepals. Pink. Reflexed round. Corolla. Vermillion tinged carmine. Tinged white at base. Spiralled petals. Similar to "Elegans". Pedicel 60 mms. P118 4th. Ed. by Porcher 1874. Intro. by E.G. Henderson, St. Johns Wood. *Henderson, E.G. St. John's Wood. GB. 1869.*

HEBE (a). Single. ND/ND. Tube. ND. Sepals. ND. Corolla. ND. GC. P98 17/2/1844 Listed by Youell, Gt. Yarmouth. GC. P112 17/2/1844 & P66 1/2/1845 listed by W. Miller, Ramsgate. *Standish, Bagshot. GB. 1843.*

HEBE (b). Single. White/Red. Tube. Pure glossy white. Sepals. Pure glossy white. Corolla. Deep Crimson. Globular shape. Purchased last season. GC. P505 31/7/1847 Listed by G. Smith, Islington. GC. P297 8/5/1847 Intro. by J. Bell, Warwick. *Bell, J. Warwick. GB. 1847.*

HEBE. (c) Single. White/Red. Tube. Waxy white. Sepals. Waxy White. Corolla. Ruby. Blooms 5" to 6" long. GC. P505 31/7/1847 Listed by G. Smith, Islington. GC. P338 22/5/1847 Intro. by Turville, Chelmsford. *Turville, Chelmsford GB. 1847.*

HEBE (d). Single. White/Red. Tube. White. Sepals. White. Reflex gracefully. Corolla. Scarlet. GC. P183 "Select". GC. P207 27/3/1852 Listed by H. Walton, Burnley. GC. P151 5/3/1853 1st rate for exhibition. GC. P279 30/4/1853 "Light green stemmed" GC. P497 10/8/1850 Intro. By Mayle, Birmingham. *Mayle, Birmingham GB. 1850*

HECLA. Double. Red/White. Tube. Bright rosy red. Short. Sepals. Bright rosy red. Well reflexed. Corolla. White suffused at base with magenta rose. Large. B. Cat. 1901. Intro. by W. Bull, Chelsea. *Bull, W. Chelsea. GB. 1901.*

HECTOR. (a). Single. Red/Red. Tube. Carmine red. Sepals. Carmine red. Corolla. Carmine red. GC. P66 1/2/1845 Listed by W. Miller, Ramsgate. GC. P146 8/3/1845 Listed by Youell, Gt. Yarmouth. GC. P234 11/4/1846 Listed by by A.J. Stewart, Windsor. RH. P24 1846. GC. P193 30/3/1844 Intro. by J. Smith, Dalston. *Smith, J., Dalston GB. 1844.*

HECTOR (b). Single. Red/Purple. Tube. Ruby red. Sepals. Ruby red. Completely reflexed. Corolla. Rich purple. Well formed. Largely expanded. B. Cat. 1870. *Bull, W. Chelsea. GB. 1868?*

HECTOR (c) Single. Red/Purple. Tube. Dark crimson. Sepals. Dark crimson. Broad. Well reflexed. Corolla. Crimson Purple, light crimson at base. L. Cat. 1901. B. Cat. 1898-1901. Intro. by W. Bull. *Bull, W. Chelsea. GB. 1898.*

HEINRICH FELDTMANN. ND ND/ND. Tube. ND. Sepals. ND. Corolla. ND. Essig. Goliath X. *Curio. Germany. 1884.*

HEINZEL MÄNNCHEN. ND. ND/ND. Tube. ND. Sepals. ND. Corolla. ND. Essig. Cupido x James Lye. *Brembach Germany 1911.*

HELLFARBIG. Single. ND/ND. Tube. ND. Sepals. ND. Corolla. ND. Essig. Globosa x F. Fulgens *Meillez. Lille. France 1845.*

HELENA. Single. ND/Red. Tube. ND. Sepals. ND. Corolla. Red. GC. P162 14/3/1846 & P184 13/3/1847 Listed by W. Miller, Ramsgate. GC. P216 27/3/1847 Listed by R. Cooper, Croydon. GC. P254 19/4/1845. Intro. by J. Smith. *Smith, J. Dalston. GB. 1845.*

HÉLÈNE. Single. Red/White. Tube. Light red. Sepals. Light red. Corolla. White veined rose. P81 Witte 1882. RH. P311 1889 "Select" by E. A. Carrière. *Twrdy, Brno. Austria. 1876.*

HELIGOLAND. Single. Red/Purple. Tube. Carmine Scarlet. (Brilliant red). Thick. 15mm long. Sepals. Carmine Scarlet. Recurved. (Reflexed round). Corolla. Rich violet blue. washed rose. Bell shaped. 4th Ed. by Porcher 1874 Pedicel 50mm. Remarkable for its form and colouration. BSW. Cat. 1878 GC. P430 29/3/1873 Intro. by E. G. Henderson. *Henderson, E.G. St. Johns Wood.GB. 1873.*

HENDERSONII. Double. Red/Purple. Tube. Deep crimson. Sepals. Deep crimson. Beautifully reflexed. Corolla. Blue purple. Globular mass of petals. Medium size. (Semi-double varities now in cultivation bear no comparison). Raiser could be a North of England amateur or as below. Vol P3 J of RHS 1863. GC. P130 21/2/1852 Intro. by E. G. Henderson. *Smith S, Liverpool. GB. 1852*

HENGIST. Single. Red/Purple. Tube. Red. Sepals. Red. Corolla. Purple. Vigourous. Branching little. Remarkable for the coral coloured buds. GC. P122 Review of new Fuchsias of 1853. GC. P211 26/3/1853 Listed by W. Rumley, Richmond. *Salter. GB. 1853.*

HENRI ETIENNE. Double. Red/Purple. Tube. Carmine reddish purple, Short.Sepals. Carmine reddish purple. Large. Corolla. Amarinth watered blue. Spherical. L. Cat. 1888-9. *Rozain, Lyons. France. 1887.*

HENRI D'ORLÉANS. Double. Red/Red. Tube. Red. Sepals. Red. Corolla. Wine red. Petals veined scarlet. Named after a French aristocrat and traveller (1867-1901). RB. Cat. 1898. L. Cat. 1898.JF. Cat. 1899. *Rozain, Lyons. France. 1898.*

HENRI DE BORNIER Double. Red/Purple. Tube. Red. Short. Sepals. Red. Corolla. Violet Purple. BSW. Cat. 1878-1888. *Lemoine, Nancy. France. 1877.*

HENRI DE LA POMMERAYE. Double. Red/White. Tube. Coral pink. (Coral red). Sepals. Coral Pink (Coral red). Corolla. Pinkish white. (Rosy white). Very full. Floriferous. Pyramidical growth. B. Cat. 1892-1895. L. Cat. 1892. *Lemoine, Nancy. France. 1890.*

HENRI DUNANT. Double. Red/Purple. Tube. Red. Sepals. Red. Corolla. Bluish violet. Exterior petals blotched pink, striped white. Very large. Named after a Swiss philanthropist, (1828-1901). Founder of the Red Cross. 1st winner of Nobel Peace Prize 1901. L. Cat 1902. *Lemoine, Nancy. France. 1902.*

HENRI JACOTET. Double. Red/Purple. Tube. Red. Sepals. Red. Corolla. Purple. P126 4th. Ed. by Porcher 1874. *Lemoine. Nancy. France. 1868.*

HENRI MEILHAC. Double. Red/Red. Tube. Blood red. Sepals. Blood red. Corolla. Red and Rose. Inner petals Rose veined carmine. Named after a French playright and lyricist. (1831-1897). L. Cat. 1898. *Lemoine. Nancy. France. 1898.*

HENRI POINCARÉ. Single. Red/Purple. Tube. Blood red. Sepals. Blood red. Reflexed. Long. Broad. Corolla. Plum Violet. Bell shaped. Long. Broad. Named after a French mathematician, born in Nancy, (1854-1912). L. Cat. 1906. *Lemoine. Nancy. France. 1905.*

HENRY ABTS. ND. Red/White. Tube. Red. Sepals. Red. Corolla. White. CG P454 1865. J of H. Vol 8. P454. NK. NK. NK. NK.

HENRY BROOKE. Single. Red/Purple. Tube. Bright red. Sepals. Bright red. Corolla. Plum. GO. "Select" 1890-1891. GC. Vol 20 P280. G.Vol 26 P375 6/9/1884. Exhibited by J. Lye. JF. Cat. 1885. Dobies. Cat. 1892-4. Vol. 26 GC. 1886 RHS Trials at Chiswick. *Lye,J. Market Lavington. GB. 1885.*

HENRY MONTEITH. Single. Red/Purple. Tube. Rich crimson. Sepals. Rich crimson. Corolla. Deep purple. GC. P401 24/6/1854 Listed by H. Walton, Burnley. GC.P466 22/7/1854 Listed by Bass & Brown, Sudbury. GC. P194 1/4/1854. Intro. by Kimberley, Coventry. *Kimberley, Coventry. GB. 1854.*

HENRY OF NAVARRE. Single. ND/ND. Tube. ND. Sepals. ND. Corolla. ND. GC. P226 13/4/1850 Listed by Poole Nurseries. NK. NK. NK. NK.

HERA. S/Double. Red/Purple. Tube. Crimson. Sepals. Crimson. Corolla. Soft purplish rose. Displays a tuft of petaloid segments at the base, same colour as corolla. Bruant Cat. 1911. Dicksons, Chester Cat. 1907. *Dickson, Chester. GB. 1907.*

HERALD (a). Single. Red/Purple. Tube. Bright rose. Small. Sepals. Bright rose. (Pale red). Horizontally reflexed. Corolla. Bright blue fading violet pink. (Light reddish violet veined at the base) Dwarf and Free. Pcxvi Vol III RHS 1872. Report of fuchsias grown for trial at Chiswick 1872. B. Cat.

1870-1873. GC. P414 17/4/1869 Intro. by W. Bull. *Bull W. Chelsea. GB. 1869.*

HERALD (b). Single. Red/Purple. Tube. Red. Sepals. Red. Long. Well reflexed. Corolla. Plum purple. HC. Cat. 1890. H.J. Jones, Lower Sydenham Cat. 1901. *Sankey. GB. 1887.*

HERBERT. ND. ND/ND. Tube. ND. Sepals. ND. Corolla. ND. GC. P756 20/7/1867 Exhibited at the RHS Show, Bury St. Edmunds by D.T. Fish, Gr. to Lady Callum, Hardwicke House, Bury St. Edmunds. An old free blooming kind. NK. NK. NK. NK.

HERCULE. Double. Red/Purple. Tube. Red. Sepals. Red. Corolla. Violet. P135 4th Ed. by Porcher 1874. *Twrdy, Brno. Austria. 1874.*

HERCULES (a). Single. ND/Red. Tube. ND. Sepals. ND. Corolla. Red. GC. P66 1/2/1845 & P184 13/3/1847 Listed by W. Miller, Ramsgate. *Stedman. GB. 1844.*

HERCULES (b). Single. ND/ND. Tube. ND. Sepals. ND. Corolla. ND. GC. P224 14/4/1849 Listed by Bass & Brown, Sudbury. *Salter, Versailles. France. 1848.*

HERCULES (c). Double. Red/Purple. Tube. Red. Slender. Sepals. Red. Broad. Spreading. Corolla. Deep violet. SG. P459 1866 "Recommended". Pcxv Vol J of RHS 1872. Fuchsia trials at Chiswick. Good habit. In the way of "Sir Colin Campbell" but different. GC. P122 7/2/1863 GC. P344 11/4/1863 Intro. by G. Smith, Islington. *Smith, G. Islington. GB. 1863.*

HERCULES (d). Single. Red/Purple. Tube. Coral red. Sepals. Coral red. Beautifully relexed. Corolla. Intense Bright Blue. (Purple). Barrel shaped. HC. Cat. 1882, Dwarf grower. Largest flower yet sent out. P115 4th. Edition by Porcher 1874 Not in 1st selection. B. Cat. 1876-1878. *Banks, E. Deal. GB. 1872.*

HÉRISSÉ. Single.Red/White. Tube. Coral. Sepals. Coral. Corolla. White. L. Cat. 1888-9. Gartenflora 1888. *Rozain, Lyons. France. 1887.*

HER MAJESTY. Single. White/ND. Tube. White. Sepals. White. Corolla. ND. After the size of the "Duchess of Lancaster" but eclipses this variety. Its ponderous flowers are twice the size. P120 4th. Ed. by Porcher 1874. Not in the 1st Selection. GC. P960 26/10/1861 Purchased and intro. by W. Bull, Chelsea. *Bull, W. Chelsea. GB. 1862.*

HERMINE. Double. Red/White. Tube. Light rose. Sepals. Light rose. Corolla. Pinkish white. P83 Witte 1882. *Twrdy, Brno. Austria 1879.*

HERMIONE. ND. Red/Purple. Tube. Red. Sepals. Red. Spreading and reflexed. Corolla. Purple. Vol. P3 J of RHS 1863. Fuchsias grown for trial at Chiswick 1862. Small and compactly arranged. Branching habit. Neat foliage. Smooth. Bright colours. Awarded ***. *Henderson, E.G. St. Johns Wood. GB. 1861?*

HERO (a). Single. ND/ND. Tube. ND. Sepals. ND. Corolla. ND. GC. P705 14/10/1843 Listed by John Whitley, Sulcoates Nursery, Wakefield. *Whitley, J. Wakefield. GB. 1843.*

HERO (b), Single. Red/Purple. Tube. Rich vermilion. Sepals. Rich vermilion. Much reflexed. Corolla. Rosy Purple. GC. P162 14/3/1846 Listed by W. Miller, Ramsgate. GC. P146 8/3/1845 Intro. by Youells, Gt. Yarmouth. *Youell, Gt. Yarmouth. GB. 1845.*

HERO (c). Single. Red/Red. Tube. Crimson. Sepals. Rich crimson. Corolla. Deep rose. GC. P184 13/3/1847 Listed by W. Miller, Ramsgate. GC. P270 26/4/1845 Intro. by G. Sclater, Exeter. *Mayne. GB. 1845.*

HERO (d). Single. White/Red. Tube. White. Sepals. White. Corolla. Scarlet. GC. P259 28/4/1849 & P241 20/4/1850 Listed by W. Rendle, Plymouth. GC. P338 22/5/1847 Intro. by Turville, Chelmsford. *Turville, Chelmsford GB. 1847.*

HERO (e). Single. Red/Red. Tube. Light red. Sepals. Light red. Reflexed. Wide and long. Corolla. Lake. Immense. To be sent out 13/10/1862. GC. P952 11/10/1862. Intro. by W. Bull, Chelsea. *Bull, W. Chelsea. GB. 1862.*

HERO OF SUFFOLK. Single. Red/Purple. Tube. Crimson vermilion. Short. Sepals. Crimson vermilion. Reflex well back. Corolla. Purple. Like "Magniflora" only better. GC. P98 17/2/1844 Listed by Youells, Gt. Yarmouth. GC. P66 1/2/1845 & P112 17/2/1846 Listed by W. Miller, Ramsgate. GC. P177 23/3/1844 Intro. by Girling, Stowmarket. *Girling, Stowmarket. GB. 1844.*

HERO OF WILTS. Double. Red/Purple. Tube. Scarlet. Sepals. Scarlet. Rose pink on inside. Corolla. Light violet. Vol. P1 J of RHS 1859 P79 Report by Floral C'tee. Inferior flowers. Corolla Irregular and confused. GC. P560 30/6/1860. Listed by F. Godwin, Sheffield. GC. P359 21/4/1860 Intro. by G. Wheeler. *Wheeler, G. Warminster. GB. 1860.*

HEROINE (a). Single. ND/ND. Tube. ND. Sepals. ND. Corolla. ND. GC. P199 27/3/1847 Listed by H. Walton, Burnley. GC. P216 27/3/1847 Listed by R. Cooper, Croydon. GC. P254 19/4/1845 Intro. by J. Smith, Dalston. *Smith, J. Dalston. GB. 1845.*

HEROINE (b), Single. ND/ND. Tube. ND. Sepals. ND. Corolla. ND. GC. P224 14/4/1849 Listed by Bass & Brown, Sudbury. GC. P256 21/4/1849 Listed by R. Cooper, Croydon. *Knight. GB. 1848.*

HEROINE (c). Single. White/Red. Tube. White lined pink. Sepals. White. Corolla. Bright carmine. Excellent habit. JF. Cat. 1889-1890. B Cat. 1889-1893. *Lye, J. Market Lavington. GB. 1889.*

HERON. Single. Red/Purple. Tube. Rosy carmine. Short. Sepals. Rosy carmine. Broad. Corolla. Rich Bluish Purple. B. Cat. 1888-1893. *Bull, W. Chelsea. GB. 1886.*

HIDALGO. Double. Red/Purple. Tube. Coral red. Short. Sepals. Coral red. Completely reflexed. Corolla. Rich rosy purple, splashed and suffused at base with rosy purple. Dicksons, Chester Cat. 1907. *Dickson, Chester. GB. 1907.*

HIGHLAND CHIEF (a). Single. Red/Purple. Tube. Coral. Sepals. Coral. Corolla. Rosy purple. GC.P140 27/2/1847 Good dark variety. GC. P162 14/3/1846 & P184 13/3/1847 Listed by W. Miller, Ramsgate. GC. P162 8/3/1845 Intro. by J.Hally. *Hally, J. Blackheath GB. 1845.*

HIGHLAND CHIEF (b). Single. Red/Purple. Tube. Bright crimson. Sepals. Bright crimson. Elegantly reflexed. Corolla. Deep purple. Large. Bell shaped. Expands as flower ages. Retains its deep colour to the last. B. Cat. 1875-1882. GC. P427 3/4/1875 Intro. by W. Bull. *Bull, W. Chelsea. GB. 1875.*

HILDA. Double. Red/Purple. Tube. Deep rosy red. Thin. Short. Sepals. Deep rosy red. Horizontal. Corolla. Purplish plum, marked rose at base. (Two shades of violet, washed with red). The Gardener P435 1875 Resembles Harry Williams". 4th. Ed. by Porcher 1874. B. Cat. 1872-1876. *Bull, W. Chelsea. GB. 1872.*

HOCHE. Double. Red/Purple. Tube. Rose. Sepals. Rose. Completely reflexed. Corolla. Rosy lilac. Good shape. New Colour. Full. B. Cat 1888-1889. *Lemoine. Nancy. France. 1886.*

HOGARTH. Double. Red/Purple. Tube. Bright carmine. Slender. Sepals. Bright carmine. Reflexed.

1" long. Corolla. Blue. Blotched and striped bright rose. (Reddish purple). Medium size. Pcxv Vol 3 J of RHS 1872. Fuchsia trial at Chiswick. Ill shaped and inferior flower. B. Cat. 1870-1873. GC. P414 17/4/1869 Intro. by W. Bull. *Bull, W. Chelsea. GB. 1870.*

HOLLOWAY RIVAL. Single. Red/Purple. Tube. Bright red. Short. Sepals. Bright red. Well reflexed. Reflex round. Corolla. Rich deep violet. (Violet blue washed red). Petals spiral. P109 4th. Ed. by Porcher 1874. Pedicel 50mm. GC. P486 9/4/1870 Intro. by B&S Williams. *Bland, E. Fordham GB. 1870.*

HOLSTEIN. Single. Red/Pink. Tube. Carmine red. Sepals. Carmine red. Reflexing. Corolla. Orchid pink. Good market variety. Very floriferous. Vigorous. L. Cat. 1912. *Schadendorff. Germany. 1912.*

HON. MRS. HAY. Single. Red/Purple. Tube. Red. Sepals. Red. Corolla. Purple. GC. P183 "Recommended". Exhibited at Trowbridge 1877 2nd, 1884 1st, 1883 1st Bath 1st, 1887 Bath 1st. Illustration GC. Vol 23 1885 P209. Plate 39. *Lye. J. Market Lavington. GB. 1878.*

HONEYBELL. Single. White/Purple. Tube. White. Sepals. White. Reflex well. Corolla. Lilac. Good stout flower. GC. P580 9/7/1859 & P607 16/7/1859 Exhibited by H. Cannell gr. to E. Groves, Tulse Hill at RBS Show. GC. P449 17/7/1852 Listed by H. Walton, Burnley. GC. P223 10/4/1852 Intro. by C. Turner, Slough. *Banks, E. Deal. GB. 1852.*

HOPE. Single. ND/ND. Tube. ND. Sepals. ND. Corolla. ND. GC. P820 12/1844 "Recommended". P410 20/6/1846 Exhibited by Robinson Gr. to J. Simpson. GC. P265 24/4/1847 Listed by W. Rendle, Plymouth. NK. NK. *GB. 1843?*

HOPVERRII. Single. ND/ND. Tube. ND. Sepals. ND. Corolla. ND. GC. P393 June 1842. Listed by Youell, Great Yarmouth. GC. P112 17/2/1844 by W. Miller, Ramsgate. GC. 28/3/1846 by Shilling, Odiham. NK. NK. *GB. 1841.*

H.RAWSON. Single. Red/Purple. Tube. Rose. Sepals. Rose. Corolla. Light Purple. Dicksons, Chester Cat. 1907. NK. NK. *GB. NK.*

HUGH MILLER. Single. Pink/Purple. Tube. Pink. Slender. Sepals. Pink. Tipped green. Spreading. Corolla. Purple. P217 Vol 4 J of RHS Report on Fuchsia trials at Chiswick. Spreading. Free vigorous, bushy but drooping habit. Distinct large flower. Same as "Hugh Mollen".?

HUGH MOLLEN. Single. Pink/Purple. Tube. Pale pink. Sepals. Pale pink. Corolla. Reddish Purple. GC. P749 17/8/1861 RHS Floral C'tee "Commended". GC. P426 10/5/1862. Intro. by Veitch & Co. Confused with Hugh Miller?. *Mollen, H. GB. 1862.*

HUMBOLDT. ND. ND/ND. Tube. ND. Sepals. ND. Corolla. ND. F&A Smith possess entire stock. GC. P376 26/4/1862 Intro by F&A Smith. Hackney. *Smith F & A. Hackney GB. 1862.*

HUMBOLTII. Single. ND/ND. Tube. ND. Sepals. ND. Corolla. ND. GC. P250 19/4/1842 for sale by auction by T. Ansell, Camden Town. NK. NK. NK. *1841.*

HUME. Single. Red/Purple. Tube. Deep rose. Short. Sepals. Deep rose. Corolla. Rich Dark blue. B. Cat. 1881-1883. *Bull, W. Chelsea. GB. 1881.*

HUMILIS. Single. ND/ND. Tube. ND. Sepals. ND. Corolla. ND. Exhibited at Bot. and Hort. Scty of Exeter show on 9/6/1843 by Sclater & Sons, Summerlands, Exeter. NK. NK. *GB. NK.*

HUTCHINSONII. Single. ND/ND. Tube. ND. Sepals. ND. Corolla. ND. Exhibited by Catleugh, H.S. Show, London 18/5/1844. GC. P337 25/5/1844 & P375 4/6/1844. NK. NK. *GB. 1844.*

HYBRIDA COCCINEA. Single. ND/ND. Tube. ND. Sepals. ND. Corolla. ND. GC. P393 June 1842 Listed by Youell, Great Yarmouth. NK. NK. *GB. NK.*

HYBRIDA RUBRA. Single. Red/Red. Tube. Crimson. Sepals. Crimson. Corolla. Scarlet. Blooms 3" in length. Plant 3' high. Said to have been in bloom since October last. Exhibited at RHS Show London 22/3/1881 by Wells Gr to Mr Ravenhill of Windsor. Dominiana x Serratifolia. *Wells, Windsor. GB 1880.*

HYLAS. Single. Pink/Red. Tube. Light pink. Sepals. Light pink. Corolla. Cherry. GC. P338 22/5/1847 Intro. by Turville. *Turville. Chelmsford GB. 1847.*

IANTHE. Single. Red/Purple. Tube. Bright crimson. Short. Sepals. Bright crimson. Wide. Well reflexed. Corolla. Rich bright plum. B. Cat. 1872-1875. *Bull, W. Chelsea. GB. 1872.*

IBRAHIM PASHA. Single. ND/ND. Tube. ND. Sepals. ND. Corolla. ND. GC. P224 14/4/1849 Listed by Bass & Brown Sudbury. *Knight, St Leonards. GB. NK.*

ICARUS. Single. Red/White. Tube. Carmine. Sepals. Carmine. Completely recurved. Corolla. Blush white, veined rosy carmine. Suffused carmine at base. L. Cat. 1901. B. Cat. 1899-1901. Intro. by W. Bull. *Bull, W. Chelsea. GB. 1899.*

ICHTYANA. Single. Red/Red. Tube. Clear red. Short. Sepals. Clear red. Well open. Corolla. Orange violet. Very large 4 cms. App. to RH. 1851 by Porcher. NK. NK. NK.

IDA. Single Red/White. Tube. Bright red. Short. Sepals. Bright red. Well reflexed. Double. White veined carmine. Widely expanded. Dicksons, Chester Cat. 1907. *Dickson, Chester. GB. 1907.*

IDRA. Single. Red/Purple. Tube. Salmon red. Sepals. Salmon red. Well extended. Corolla. Lilac Purple. B. Cat. 1901. Intro. by W. Bull. *Bull, W. Chelsea. GB. 1899.*

IGNEA. Single. Red/Purple. Tube. Dark red. (Bright crimson). Long. Sepals. Dark red. (Bright crimson). Broad. Large. Corolla. Deep purple. (Deep violet purple). Good in shape. GC. P487 2/8/1851 Visit to Frasers Nurseries, Lea Bridge - 3 times the size of "Formosa Elegans". GC. P649 11/10/1851 Exhibited at RHS of Cornwall Show 9/9/1851 by W. Friend. GC. P387 15/6/1850 Listed by H. Walton, Burnley. GC. P465 27/7/1850 Listed by G. Smith, Islington. GC. P632 6/10/1849 & P236 13/4/1850. Intro. by Veitch, Exeter. *Story, W.H. Newton Abbot GB. 1849.*

IGNESCENS. Single. ND/ND. Tube. ND. Sepals. ND. Corolla. ND. GC. P473 16/7/1842.Exhibited at Hort. Scty Show. *Beck, Isleworth. GB. 1842.*

IL TROVATORE. Single. White/Red. Tube. White. Sepals. White. Corolla. Scarlet Pink. Large. Corolla is apt to become deficient. GC. P55 19/1/1867. Review by H. Cannell. NK. NK. NK. NK.

ILIAD. Single. Red/Purple. Tube. Crimson. Short. Broad. Sepals. Crimson. Long. Corolla. Violet Purple veined crimson. L. Cat. 1906. *Bull, W. Chelsea. GB. 1905.*

ILLICIFOLIA. Single. ND/ND. Tube. ND. Sepals. ND. Corolla. ND. GC. P393 6/1842 Listed by Youells, Gt. Yarmouth. GC. P481 5/7/1843 Exhibited at H.S. Show, London 12/7/1843 by Gaines, Battersea. GC. P345 28/5/1842 Intro. by J. Smith, Dalston. *Smith, J. Dalston. GB. 1842.*

ILLUSTRATION. ND. ND/ND. Tube. ND. Sepals. ND. Corolla. ND. Essig. *Lemoine, Nancy. France. 1875.*

IMPERATRICE (a). ND. ND/ND. Tube. ND. Sepals. ND. Corolla. ND. RH. P311 1889 Select by E. André. NK. NK. NK.

IMPERATRICE EUGENIE. ND. ND/ND. Tube. ND. Sepals. ND. Corolla. ND. GC. P146 7/3/1857 Listed by W. Rumley, Richmond. GC. P251 11/4/1857 Listed by W. Masters, Canterbury. NK. NK. NK. *1856.*

IMPERATRICE ELIZABETH. Double. Red/White. Tube. Rose. Sepals. Rose. Recurved. Corolla. Pure white, tipped carmine. P131 4th Ed. by Porcher 1874. Not in the first selection. B. Cat. 1870. Introduced by Wm. Bull. *Cornelissen, Arras. Belgium. 1866.*

IMPERIAL WHITE. Single. White/Purple. Tube. Pure white. Thick. Sepals. White, tinged pink. Recurved. Horizontal. Corolla. Rich violet rose. (Violet margined bright red. Shading to white at base). Multiflowered. Similar to "Signora" and "Schiller". P118 4th. Ed. by Porcher 1874. GC. P375 19/3/1870 Intro. by E.G. Henderson. *Carter. GB. 1870.*

IMPERIAL. Single. Red/Purple. Tube. Rosy carmine. Sepals. Rosy carmine. Elegantly recurved. Corolla. Glossy Plum, striped and flaked pink. Huge. Well formed. B. Cat. 1882. Intro. by Wm. Bull. *Eckford. GB. 1882.*

IMPERIALIS FLORE PLENO. ND. ND/ND. Tube. ND. Sepals. ND. Corolla. ND. RH. P295 1887 Growing as a standard at Twickel, (Nr. Arnhem). RH. P170 1857. *Demureaux France. 1857.*

IMPERIALIS. Single. Red/Purple. Tube. Crimson. Sepals. Crimson. Glossy. Corolla. Dark violet. GC. P162 14/3/1846 & P147 13/3/1847 Listed by W. Miller, Ramsgate. GC. P270 26/4/1845 Intro. by G. Sclater. *Sclater, G. Exeter GB. 1845.*

IMPROVEMENT (a). Single. Red/Purple. Tube. Brilliant crimson. Thick. (Glossy carmine). Sepals. Brilliant Crimson. (Vermilion) Reflexed round. Corolla. Indigo blue, splashed red at base. (Deep Violet Blue, tinged carmine). P137 Elite variety. P109 4th Ed. by Porcher 1874. Dwarf bush. Vigorous. Pedicel 35mm. Pcxvi Vol 3 P of RHS 1872. Chiswick Fuchsia Trial 1872. Coarse. Inferior. GC. P211 17/2/1877 West Country variety. Intro. by E.G. Henderson. *Henderson, E.G. St. John's Wood. GB. 1871.*

IMPROVEMENT (b). Single. White/Red. Tube. Pure white. Sepals. Pure white. Well reflexed.

Corolla. Carmine shading to rose. HC. Cat. 1882-1885. BSW. Cat. 1878. GC. P521 28/4/1877 Intro. by B.S. Williams. Duchess of Lancaster X. *Bland, E. Fordham GB. 1877.*

INACCESSIBLE. Single. Red/Purple. Tube. Glossy crimson. Short. Sepals. Glossy crimson. Very Broad. Corolla. Deep violet purple. Twice the size of "Williamsii". GC. p535 23/8/1851 Exhibited at Vauxhall Garden Show. 1GC. P387 15/6/1850 & P706 9/11/1850 Listed by H.Walton, Burnley. GC. P465 27/7/1850 & P144 8/3/1851 by W. Rumley, Richmond. GC. P177 23/3/1850 Intro.by Kimberley. Williamsii X. *Kimberley, Coventry. GB. 1850.*

INCARNATA. Single. Pink/Red. Tube. Flesh. Sepals. Flesh. Corolla. Orange red. GC. P66 1/2/1845 & P184 13/3/1847 Listed by W. Miller, Ramsgate, GC. P146 8/3/1845 Listed by Youell, Gt. Yarmouth. GC. P193 30/3/1844 Intro. by J. Smith, Dalston. *Smith, J. Dalston. GB. 1844.*

INCOMPARIBLE (a). Single. ND/ND. Tube. ND. Sepals. ND. Corolla. ND. GC. P97 18/2/1843 Listed by Youell, Gt. Yarmouth. NK. *GB.* NK.

INCOMPARIBLE (b). Single. White/ND. Tube. ND. Sepals. ND. Corolla. ND. GC. P146 8/3/1845 Listed by Youells, Gt. Yarmouth. GC. P184 13/3/1847 Listed by W. Miller, Ramsgate. GC. P216 27/3/1847 Listed by R. Cooper, Croydon. GC. P145 9/3/1850 Listed by W. Rumley, Richmond. GC. P309 10/5/1845 Intro. by Wm. May, Bedale. *Foxton. GB. 1845.*

INCOMPARIBLE (c). Single. Red/Purple. Tube. Red. Sepals. Red. Recurved. Corolla. Purple. Coloured Plate The Florist March 1853. GC.P151 5/3/1853 First Rate. GC. P337 28/5/1853 Listed by Bass & Brown, Sudbury. GC.. P385 18/6/1853 Listed by W. Rumley, Richmond. GC. P465 23/7/1853 Listed by Harrison, Darlington. GC. P627 1/10/1853 Listed by S. Fenney, Gateshead. GC. P147 11/3/1854 Listed by H. Walton, Burnley. GC. P213 8/4/1854 Listed by C. H. Gardiner, Maidstone. GC. P248 15/4/1854 Listed by Mitchell & Co, Brighton. Purity X. *Mayle, Birmingham. GB. 1853.*

INCOMPARIBLE (d). Single. Red/Purple. Tube. Bright crimson. Sepals. Bright crimson. Long. Broad. Finely reflexed. Corolla. Rich purple. Unusual length. Short jointed. Free bloomer. GC. P864 28/9/1861. Intro. by W. Bull, Chelsea. GC. P19/10/1861 Sent out. *Bull, W. Chelsea. GB. 1861.*

INDIAN CHIEF. Single. Red/Purple. Tube. Carmine pink. Sepals. Carmine pink. Finely

recurved. Corolla. Violet blue, shaded with red from the base. Large. Open. B. Cat. 1877-1881. HC. Cat. 1882. *Bull, W. Chelsea. GB. 1876.*

INDO CHINE. S/Double. Red/Red. Tube. Red. Sepals. Red. Large. Corolla. Clear rosy lilac. New colour. Bushy growth. GC. Vol 23 P213 14/2/1885 New from Lemoine. BSW. Cat. 1888. *Lemoine. Nancy. France. 1885.*

INFLATA ARBOREA. Single. Red/Purple. Tube. Deep crimson. Sepals. Deep crimson, tipped green. Corolla. Purplish. Quite a tree fuchsia. Foliage large and distinct. GC. P112 17/2/1844 Listed by W. Miller, Ramsgate. P82 Intro. by W. Dean, Jedburgh. *Dean, W. Jedburgh GB. 1843.*

INFLATA FULGIDA. Single. Pink/Pink. Tube. Bright Pink. Sepals. Bright pink. Expanded. Points tipped white/green. Corolla. Bright Pink. Glacous dark green foliage. GC. P393 6/1842 Listed by Youells, Gt. Yarmouth. GC. P112 17/2/1844 Listed by W. Miller, Ramsgate. GC. P337 26/5/1842. Intro. by J. May, Tottenham. *May, W. Bedale. GB. 1842.*

INFLATA. Single. Red/Purple. Tube. Red. Sepals. Red. Corolla. Purple. GC. P630 25/9/1841 One of the best of the Chilean varieties. GC. P668 11/10/1841 Exhibited at the RHS of Cornwall Show. GC. P241 15/4/1843 Listed by F&A Smith, Hackney. *Ivery, Peckham. GB.* NK

INGEGNOLI DESIDERATA. Double. Red/Purple. Tube. Bright red. Sepals. Bright red. Wide. Reflexed. Corolla. Slate Violet. Enormous. Very Full and extended. L. Cat. 1901. *Lemoine. Nancy. France. 1899.*

INIMITABLE (a). Single. ND/ND. Tube. ND. Sepals. ND. Corolla. ND. GC. P386 15/6/1850. New Fuchsia exhibited by G. Smith. R.B.S. Garden Show. *Smith, G. Islington. GB. 1850.*

INIMITABLE (b). S/Double. Red/Purple. Tube. Scarlet crimson. Short. Sepals. Scarlet Crimson. Reflexed. Corolla. Bluish violet. Washed red. P109 4th. Ed. by Porcher. 1874. Dwarf. Free. Medium size. Trials at Chiswick 1875 FCC. Pcxvi Vol 3 J of RHS 1872 . P311 RH 1889 by E. A. Carrieré "Select". Intro. by E.G. Henderson. *Henderson, E.G. St. John's Wood. GB. 1870.*

INNOCENCE. Single. White/Red. Tube. Pure white. Sepals. Pure white. Symmetrically reflexed. Recurved. Corolla. Violet rose margined lake. (Compact deep red paler at the base). Very much like "Lustre". Pcxiii Vol 3 J of RHS Fuchsia Trial at Chiswick. B. Cat. 1870. *Bull, W. Chelsea.? GB. 1868?*

INSPECTOR (a). Double. Red/Purple. Tube. Crimson. Sepals. Crimson. Reflexed. Corolla. Purple. Very large and full. P126 4th Ed. by Porcher 1874 Not in the first selection. B. Cat. 1870-1873. *Bland E., Fordham GB. 1868.*

INSPECTOR (b). Single. White/Red. Tube. White. Sepals. White. Prettily reflexed. Corolla. Bright rosy pink. Cup shaped. P136 4th Ed. by Porcher 1874. Intro. by E.G. Henderson. *Henderson, E.G. St. John's Wood. GB. 1874.*

INSTANCE. Double. Red/White. Tube. Bright carmine. Sepals. Bright carmine. Well reflexed. Corolla. White beautifully marked violet rose at base. B. Cat. 1870-1873. *Bull, W. Chelsea. GB. 1869.*

INSTIGATOR. Single. Red/Purple. Tube. Crimson red. Thick. Short. Sepals. Crimson red. Reflexed. (Dark crimson). Corolla. Lilac Violet. (Bluish Purple). Similar to "Beauty of Sholden" and "Rhoderick Dhu". P109 4th. Ed. by Porcher 1874. B. Cat. 1870-1873. *Bull, W. Chelsea. GB. 1869.*

INTENSITY. Single. Red/Purple. Tube. Carmine. Sepals. Carmine. Beautifully reflexed. Corolla. Dark purple. B. Cat. 1877-1879. *Bull, W. Chelsea. GB. 1877.*

INTERNATIONAL. Double. Red/Purple. Tube. Light red. Slender. Sepals. Light red. Corolla. Purple. Striped and blotched red at base. GC. P406 2/5/1863 Listed by Hussey, Norwich. Vol P3 J of RHS P90 Fuchsia Trials at Chiswick 1862. Dwarf, Free blooming. GC. P960 26/10/1861 & GC. P108 1/2/1862 Intro. by W. Bull. *Bull, W. Chelsea. GB. 1862.*

INVINCIBLE. Single. Red/Red. Tube. Red. Sepals. Bright carmine tipped green. Short. Corolla. Violet red. Large leaves. Free bloomer. GC. P668 11/10/1841 Exhibited at RHS of Ireland show. GC. P393 6/1842. Listed by Youells, Gt. Yarmouth. P13 FC Vol IX 1841. GC. P241 15/4/1843 Listed by F&A Smith, Hackney. Fulgens X. *Smith, J. Dalston. GB. 1841.*

IONA. Single. Red/Purple. Tube. Carmine rose. Sepals. Carmine rose. Short. Broad. Corolla. Pinkish purple, veined rose at base. L. Cat. 1906. *Bull, W. Chelsea. GB. 1905.*

IPHIGÉNIE. ND. ND/ND. Tube. ND. Sepals. ND. Corolla. ND. Essig. *Lemoine, Nancy. France. 1854.*

IRENE (a). Single. Red/Purple. Tube. Delicate rosy transparent pink. Sepals. Delicate rosy transparent pink. Tipped green. Corolla. Richest Purple. Great bloomer. GC. P146 8/3/1845 Intro. by Youells, Gt. Yarmouth. *Youell, Gt. Yarmouth GB. 1845.*

IRENE (b). Double. Red/Purple. Tube. Rosy crimson. Sepals. Rosy crimson. Broad. Good substance. Corolla. Bluish purple striped rose. Very full. (Bluish violet streaked with bright rose. The marking is not constant throughout the season). P134 4th Ed. by Porcher 1874. B. Cat. 1872-1875. Intro. by W. Bull. *Bull, W. Chelsea. GB. 1872.*

IRENE (c). Single. Red/Purple. Tube. Red. Sepals. Red. Reflexed. Corolla. Reddish Violet. Crimson at base. Extended. B. Cat. 1898-1901. Intro. by W. Bull. *Bull, W. Chelsea. GB. 1896.*

IRIS (a). Single. Red/Purple. Tube. Bright red. Sepals. Bright red. Corolla. Purple. GC. P338 22/5/1847 Intro. by Turville, Chelmsford. *Turville, Chelmsford GB. 1847.*

IRIS (b) Double. Red/White. Tube. Carmine. Sepals. Carmine. Corolla. White shaded rose, flaked rose pink. GC. P579 May 1896. B. Cat. 1898-1899. Intro. by W. Bull. *Bull, W. Chelsea. GB. 1896.*

IRMA. Single. Red/Purple. Tube. Bright rosy carmine. Sepals. Rosy carmine. Horizontal. Extra long. Curled. Corolla. Rosy purple. Long. B. Cat. 1888-1893. Intro. by W. Bull. *Bull, W. Chelsea. GB. 1887.*

ISA CRAIG. Single. Red/Purple. Tube. Red. Sepals. Red. Reflexed. Corolla. Purple. Large. Expanded. Long drop like buds. Loose habit. Yellowish leaves. Vol 3 J of RHS 1863 Fuchsia Trials at Chiswick. GC. P426 12/5/1860 Listed by F. Godwin, Sheffield. GC. P165 26/2/1859 Intro. by E.G. Henderson. *Banks, E. Deal. GB. 1859.*

ISABEL. Single. White/Purple. Tube. White. Sepals. White. Corolla. Orange purple. Similar to "Ichtyana". Mediocre. App to RH. 1851 by Porcher. GC. P210 6/4/1850 Listed by H. Walton, Burnley. GC. P225 14/4/1849 Intro. by T. Sorrell. *Sorrell, T. Chelmsford. GB. 1849.*

ISABELLA. Single. ND/ND. Tube. ND. Sepals. ND. Corolla. ND. GC. P122 17/2/1844 & P66 1/2/1845 Listed by W. Miller, Ramsgate. NK. *GB. 1843.*

ISABELLE. Double. Red/White. Tube. Carmine pink. Sepals. Carmine Pink. Reflexed. Corolla.

White veined carmine. Very large. L Cat. *Rozain. Lyons. France. 1913.*

ISADORE DUNCAN. Single. White/White. Tube. Pale pink. Sepals. Pale pink to white at tips. Horizontal. Long. Corolla. Creamy white. Named after a celebrated American dancer (1878-1927). L. Cat. 1914. *Lemoine. Nancy. France. 1914.*

ISIGNIS. Single. Red/Purple. Tube. Crimson Very long. Sepals. Carmine. Recurved. Corolla. Rosy violet. Profuse. Foliage resembes F. corymbiflora. P13 Vol IX 1841. GC. P668 11/10/1841 Exhibited at RHS of Ireland show. GC. P393 June 1842 Listed by Youell, Gt. Yarmouth. GC. P241 15/4/1843 Listed by F&A Smith. *Smith, J. Dalston. GB. 1841.*

ISMAILIA. ND. ND/ND. Tube. ND. Sepals. ND. Corolla. ND. Essig. *Lemoine, Nancy. France. 1870.*

IVERYANA. Single. Red/Purple. Tube. Red. Sepals. Red. Corolla. Purple. GC. P98 17/2/1844 & P146 8/3/1845 Listed by Youell, Gt. Yarmouth. GC. P112 17/2/1844 & P66 1/2/1845 Listed by W. Miller, Ramsgate. GC. P201 1/4/1843 Exhibited by Ivery at HS Show 1842. *Ivery. Peckham. GB. 1843.*

IVOIRE. Double. ND/White. Tube. ND. Sepals. ND. Corolla. Whitish Ivory. RB. Cat. 1934. *Rozain. Lyons. France. 1934.*

IXION. Single. White/Red. Tube. White. Sepals. White. Corolla. Orange red. Good strong habit. Named after a mythological Thessalian King who was punished in the internal regions by being bound to a perpetually revolving fiery wheel. HC. Cat. 1890. NK. NK. NK. NK.

JACKY FRENCH. ND. ND/ND. Tube. ND. Sepals. ND. Corolla. ND. JF. Cat. 1920. NK. NK. NK.

JACQUES ROZE. Double. Red/Blue. Tube. Crimson. Sepals. Crimson. Corolla. Marine Blue, flamed pink. Enormous. Very full. L. Cat. 1909. *Rozain. Lyons. 1909.*

J. ALDRUFEU. Double. Red/Purple. Tube. Carmine. Sepals. Carmine. Corolla. Bluish Violet, webbed carmine. Very Long. L. Cat. 1892. JF. Cat. 1892. *Rozain. Lyons. France. 1891.*

JAMES DEUCHARS. Double. Pink/White. Tube. Clear pink. Sepals. Clear Pink. Corolla. White veined crimson. Free flowering. JF. Cat. 1912. NK. NK. *1912.*

JAMES HOOD. Single. Red/Purple. Tube. Red. Sepals. Red. Corolla. Rosy mauve. Large. HC. Cat. 1896. JF. Cat. 1898. *Banks, E. Deal. GB. 1896.*

JAMES HUNTLEY. Single. Red/Purple. Tube. Bright vermillion. Short. Thick .Sepals. Bright vermillion crimson. Thick. Horizontal. Corolla. Purple crimson.(Rich plum). James Huntley was the Show Secretary of the Trowbridge H.S. for over 20 years. GC. P280 1/9/1883. B. Cat. 1878, 1879. BSW Cat 1878. GC. P722 9/6/1877 New Seedling. T277 Floral magazine 1877 *Lye, J. Market Lavington. GB. 1877.*

JAMES LYE. Single. Red/Purple. Tube. Dark red. Sepals. Dark red. Corolla. Dark Violet Purple. "An improved Perfection" P120 4th Ed. by Porcher 1874. Not in the 1st selection. B. Cat. 1878, 1879, 1880. BSW. Cat 1878. GC. P722 9/6/1877. GO. "Select" 1880-1891. JF Cat. 1885. HC. Cat. 1882. *Lye, J. Market Lavington. GB. 1873.*

JAMES WELCH. Single. Red/Purple. Tube. Bright rosy red. Sepals. Bright rosy red. Reflexed. Corolla. Pale maroon shaded bright purple. GC. Vol 24 1885, P277. New for 1886. GC. P183 1888 Recommended. JF. Cat.1886. Dobbies Cat. 1888 B. Cat 1889, 1892, 1893. BSW. Cat. 1888. Vol 36. G P277 21/9/1889 Exhibited at Bath 3rd. *Lye, J. Market Lavington. GB. 1886.*

JAMES WILSON. Double. Red/Purple. Tube. Scarlet. Sepals. Scarlet. Corolla. Light Purple. Large. JF. Cat. 1912. NK. *GB. 1912.*

JANUS. Double. Red/White. Tube. Carmine. Sepals. Carmine. Corolla. White, veined rose at base. B. Cat. 1899. L. Cat. 1901.*Bull, W. Chelsea GB. 1899.*

JARRY-DESLOGES. Double. Red/White. Tube. Clear red. Sepals. Clear Red. Corolla. White, rosy carmine at base. Enormous. L. Cat. 1901, 1903. *Rozain. Lyons. France. 1895.*

JASON. Single. Red/Purple. Tube. Bright deep crimson. Sepals. Bright deep crimson. Very large. Long. Reflexed. Corolla. Intense black purple. 1½" long. B. Cat. 1878 - 1893. *Bland, E. Fordham. GB. 1878.*

JAYII. ND. ND/ND. Tube. ND. Sepals. ND. Corolla. ND. GC. P257 22/4/1843 Listed by Youells, Gt. Yarmouth. NK. NK. NK

J.B. VARRONNE. Double. Red/Blue. Tube. Red. Sepals. Red. Corolla. Light blue veined red. RB. Cat

1897. Fuchsiaphiles Vol 2/3 1990. *Rozain, Lyons. France. 1885.*

J. DE LA PERRIÈRE Double. Red/Pink. Tube. Bright Coral Red. Sepals. Bright Coral Red. Reflexed. Corolla. Flesh Pink edged flesh. Large. L. Cat. 1908. *Rozain, Lyons. France. 1908.*

J. DESIDERATA. Double.. Red/Purple. Tube. Bright scarlet. Sepals. Bright Scarlet. Well reflexed. Corolla. Violet. Large. Full. JF. Cat. 1900. NK. NK. *1900.*

JEANNE BENOITON. Single. Red/Purple. Tube. Red. Sepals. Red. Corolla. Purple. P115 4th. Ed. by Porcher. Not in the 1st selection. *Lemoine, Nancy. France. 1866.*

JEAN CORNELISSEN. Single. Red/White. Tube. Bright crimson. Sepals. Bright crimson. Corolla. Pure white, veined crimson. Immense. B. Cat. 1870. *Cornelissen. Belgium 1868?*

JEANNE CHAUVIN Double. Red/White. Tube. Carmine. Sepals. Carmine. Reflexed. Corolla. White. JF. Cat 1899. L. Cat. 1901. NK. *France. 1898.*

JEANNE D'ARC (a). S/Double. Red/Purple. Tube. Crimson. Sepals. Crimson. Perpendicular reflexed. Corolla. Dark Violet, carmine at base. P126 4th Ed. by Porcher 1874. Not in the 1st selection. B. Cat. 1870. *Cornelissen. Belgium. 1868.*

JEANNE D'ARC (b). Single. Red/White. Tube. Carmine. Well proportioned. Sepals. Carmine. Large. Very elongate and well turned back. Corolla. Pure white. Very large petals. Round. Very much expanded. The character of this plant is not displayed in all the other red/white varieties. B. Cat. 1875-1879. HC. Cat. 1882. BSW. Cat. 1888. GO. "Select" 1880. *Lemoine. Nancy. France. 1875.*

JEANNE D'ARC (c). Double. White/Purple. Tube. Pinkish white. Sepals. Pinkish white. Reflexed. Corolla. Light violet fading to violet mauve. Base of petals are pinkish white. It is the old Venus Victrix with double flowers. The plant is covered with flowers in the Springtime. Nice branching habit without pinching. L. Cat. 1910. JF. Cat 1912. *Lemoine. Nancy. France. 1910.*

JEANNE SAMARY. Double. Red/White. Tube. Red. Sepals. Red. Completely reflexed flat against the tube. Corolla. Whitish salmon. Centre petals tubular. Full. Regular. B. Cat. 1892, 1893. L. Cat. 1892. *Lemoine. Nancy. France. 1891.*

JEAN SISLEY. Single. Red/Red. Tube. Crimson Scarlet. 1½" long. ½" in diam.at the mouth. Sepals. Crimson at base Green at tips 1" long. 1?" Spread. Corolla. Orange Scarlet. Leaves 4" x 2" Olive Green above, purple underneath. HC.Cat. 1882. Col Pl. in RH 1878 P410. Cross between F. Denticulata (Spectablis) and Dominiana. F. dent. x Dominiana. *Lemoine. Nancy. France.1880?*

JEHU. Single. Red/Purple. Tube. Red. Sepals. Red. Corolla. Purple. New seedling. Large globe, like Candidate, but much finer with larger corolla. GC. P66 1/2/1845, P184 13/3/1847. Listed by W. Miller, Ramsgate. GC.P232 1/4/1848, P256 21/4/1849 by R. Cooper Croydon, etc. *Miller, W. Ramsgate GB. 1845.*

JENNY LIND (a). Single. White/Red. Tube. Pearly white.Good size. (Flesh pink) (strong). Sepals. Pearly white. Well reflexed. 3½" across. Large. Corolla. Rich carmine. (vermillion purple) Very short. App. to RH. 1851 by Porcher. GC P537. 12/8/1848 by G. Smith, Islington. P161 17/3/1849 by W. Rumley, Richmond. etc. GC. P234 8/4/1848 Tiley, E., Bath. Named after Swedish singer 1820-1887. *Tiley, E. Bath. GB. 1848.*

JENNY LIND (b). Single. ND/ND. Tube. ND. Sepals. ND. Corolla. ND. P8 App to RH. 1851 by Porcher. "Mediocre". *Reid. GB. 1848?*

JESSICA. Double. Red/Purple. Tube. Bright rosy crimson. Sepals. Bright rosy crimson. Well reflexed. Corolla. Rich purple, striped and blotched bright rose. Very full. B. Cat. 1872, 1873, 1875. *Bull, W. Chelsea. GB. 1871.*

JESSY DOUGLAS. Single. Red/Purple. Tube. Crimson. Sepals. Crimson.(Coral) Corolla. Violet crimson. (Purple) Vol. P1 J of RHS. P241 1860 Floral C'tee. No award. GC. P450 19/5/1860. Adv. by J & C. Lee. *Lee J & C. Hammersmith. GB. 1860.*

J.F. McELROY. Single. Red/Purple. Tube. Carmine Red. (Red). Sepals. Carmine Red. Finely reflexed. Curved back to tube. Corolla. Blue, occasionally striped red.(Very fine blue) Improvement on Lord Derby (Intense violet with red Veining). Barrel Shaped. Coloured Plate F&P March 1870. GC. P1554 2/12/1871 Review by Cannell. BSW. Cat. 1878. *Banks, E. Deal. GB. 1870.*

J.J. ROUSSEAU. Double. Red/Purple. Tube. Red. (Bright crimson). Sepals. Red. (Bright crimson). Corolla. Violet. (Bluish violet). Very double. Named after a 18th. century Swiss political philospher and writer, who made his home in France.(1712-78). He coined the phrase Liberty, Equality, Fraternity. L. Cat. 1885. HC. Cat. 1885, 1890. *Lemoine. Nancy. France. 1883.*

J. LEJEUNE. Double. Red/Purple. Tube. Scarlet. Sepals. Scarlet. Reflexed. Corolla. Bright plum, veined rose on the exterior of petals. Very Large.. L. Cat. 1903. JF. Cat. 1904. *Rozain. Lyons. France. 1903.*

JOAN OF ARC. Single. White/Red. Tube. Waxy white. Stout. Sepals. Waxy White. Corolla. Rosy Scarlet. Well formed. Originally exhibited in 1851 by G. Smith as Beauty of Deal. However C. Turner had introduced another cultivar by Banks earlier, so was renamed. GC. P241 17/4/1852 Intro. by G.Smith. GC. P279 30/4/1853 Light green stem *Banks, E. Deal. GB. 1852.*

JOCELYN. Double. Red/Purple. Tube. Bright crimson. Thick. Sepals. Bright crimson. Horizontal. Corolla. Violet washed brown and red. Spiralled. Good colouring. P124 4th. Ed. by Porcher. 1874. *Lemoine. Nancy. France. 1869.*

JOHN BRIGHT. Single. ND.Attributed to J. Lye. Not to be confused with The Rt.Hon John Bright. No further reference..

JOHN DICKSON. Double. Red/Pink. Tube. Bright red. Sepals. Bright red. Corolla. Rose veined crimson. Large. Extra Fine. JF. Cat. 1912. *Forbes, J. Hawick. GB. 1912.*

JOHN FRASER. Single. Red/Purple. Tube. Very bright scarlet. Sepals. Bright scarlet. Horizontal. Corolla. Very dark violet shaded with black. Compact. Very free. Large. Well formed. P69 Vol 4 JofRHS 1877 Report on Fuchsia Trial at Chiswick 1873. No award. *Fraser. GB. 1873.*

JOHN FORBES. Double. Red/Purple. Tube. Crimson. Sepals. Crimson Corolla. Purplish Violet. JF. Cat. 1921. *Forbes, J. Hawick GB. 1921.*

JOHN GIBBONS. Single. Red/Purple. Tube. Dark Crimson. Sepals. Dark crimson. Corolla. Deep Blue. Very long. Synonomous with JOHN GIBSON (b). Dobies Cat. 1892, 1893, 1894. NK. *GB.* NK.

JOHN GIBSON (a). Single. Red/Purple. Tube. Bright Scarlet. Sepals. Bright scarlet. Well reflexed. Corolla. Lavender purple. Beautiful shape. B. Cat. 1877, 1878, 1879, 1880, 1881, 1882. JF.Cat. 1885. GC. P491 17/4/1875 Intro. by B & S Williams. *Bland E., Fordham. GB. 1875.*

JOHN GIBSON.(b) Single. Red/Purple. Tube. Deep carmine. Sepals. Deep carmine. Corolla. Intense indigo Blue, almost black. Free. Dwarf. Synonomous with John Gibbons. HC. Cat. 1882. NK. *GB.* NK.

JOHN JENNINGS. Single. ND/ND. Tube. ND. Sepals. ND. Corolla. ND. GC. P216 27/3/1847. Listed by R. Cooper, Croydon. NK. *GB. 1847.*

JOLLY. Single. White/Red. Tube. White. Thick 15 mm long. Sepals. White. Rose on underside. Large. Reflexed. Round. Corolla. Bright red, stained white at base. HC. Cat. 1882 an improvement on Fair Oriana. 4th Ed. by Porcher 1874. GC. P597 6/7/1868. Intro. by Felton & Holliday in 1867. *Felton. Birmingham. GB. 1867.*

JOSEFA. Single. Red/Purple. Tube. Dark crimson. Sepals. Dark crimson. Elegantly reflexed. Great substance. Corolla. Rich dark purple. GC. P74 24/1/1863. Intro. by W. Bull, Chelsea. *Bull, W. Chelsea. GB. 1863.*

JOSÉPHINE. Single. White/Red. Tube. White tinted rose. (Blush) Long. Thick. 20mm (?"). Sepals. White tinted rose. Horizontal.Tips turned up. Short Corolla. Rose carmine shaded white.(carmine red). P118 4TH. Ed. 1874 by Porcher. P215 Vol 4 J of RHS 1877 FCC. Dwarf. Stocky Pcxii Vol. 3 J of RHS 1872 Chiswick trial *. Sepals Green tipped . Corolla. Long. Spreading. *Henderson. St. Johns Wood. GB. 1871.*

JOSEF NAGY. ND. ND. Tube. ND. Sepals. ND. Corolla. ND. Fuchsiaphiles Vol 1 2/3 1990 *Boucharlet. Lyons France. 1880.*

JOSEPH ROZAIN. Double. Red/Purple. Tube. Red. Sepals. Red. Corolla. Pale violet. Striped. Laings Cat circa 1890 Fuchsiaphile Vol 1 2/3 1990. *Rozain. Lyons. France. 1881.*

JOSEPH SADA. Double. Red/Purple. Tube. Crimson red. Sepals. Crimson red. Large. Reflexed. Corolla. Bluish violet splashed red. Very full. Large. P123 4th Ed. by Porcher 1874. *Crousse France. 1867.*

JOSEPHUS. Single. ND/ND. Tube. ND. Sepals. ND. Corolla. ND. GC. P234 11/4/1846. Listed by A.J. Stewart, Salthill Nursery, Windsor. NK. NK. NK.

J. MOINS. Double. Red/Purple. Tube. Currant red (Rose). Sepals. Currant red. (Rose). Corolla. Slate mauve. (Rosy mauve). Long. Enormous. L. Cat. 1902. JF. Cat. 1904. Fuchsiaphile Vol 1 2/3 1990. *Rozain, Lyons. France. 1902.*

J. PERINI. Double. Red/Purple. Tube. Carmine rose. Sepals. Bright Carmine rose. Corolla. Pinkish purple. Centre bright lavender. Fuchsiaphile Vol 1 2/3 1990. L. Cat. 1906. *Rozain, Lyons. France. 1904.*

J. T. BRIGHT. Single. ND/ND. Tube. ND. Sepals. ND. Corolla. ND. GC. Sept 85. New fuchsia. *Lye, J. Market Lavington. GB. 1886.*

JUBILEE. Single. White/Red. Tube. Waxy White. Massive. Sepals. Waxy white. Broad. Corolla. Rosy red. GC. Vol 22 P295 1897. Vol 24 J of RHS 1900. P342 *Lye, J. Market Lavington. GB. 1897.*

JUBILEE QUEEN. Single. White/Red. Tube. White. Waxlike. Sepals. White. Waxlike. Corolla. Deep red. Very large. Striking. JF. Cat 1901. *Lye. J. Market Lavington. GB. 1901.*

JUBILÉ Single. nd/nd. Tube. ND. Sepals. ND. Corolla. ND. L. Cat. 1892. Fuchsiaphiles Vol 1 2/3 1991 *Rozain, Lyons France. 1888.*

JULES CALOT. Single. Red/Red. Tube. Orange red. Sepals. Orange red. Long. Large. Reflexed. Corolla. Orange crimson. Irregularly formed. B. Cat. 1870. P115 4th Ed. by Porcher 1874. Not in the first selection. *Lemoine. Nancy. France. 1867.*

JULES CHRÉTIEN. Double. Red/Purple. Tube. Red. Sepals. Red. Large. Corolla. Dark blue stained carmine at the outside. Enormous. L. Cat. 1892. *Rozain, Lyons. France. 1891.*

JULES FERRY. Single. Red/Purple. Tube. Scarlet. Sepals. Scarlet. Corolla. Violet mottled white. Perfect form. HC. Cat. 1882, 1885. BSW. Cat.1888. *Lemoine. Nancy. France. 1881.*

JULES MONGES. ND. ND/ND Tube. ND. Sepals. ND. Corolla. ND. P295 RH. 1887 Grown as a standard at Twickel. Nr. Arnhem. Fuchsiaphiles Vol. 1 2/3 1989. *Boucharlet, Lyons. France. 1881.*

JULES NORIAC. Single. Red/Purple. Tube. Light rosy red. Sepals. Light rosy red. Corolla. Soft mauve. Flowers rather small. Very pretty and free. HC. Cat. 1882. *Lemoine. Nancy. France. 1880.*

JULIA DE GUEST. Single. Red/Purple. Tube. Light scarlet. Sepals. Light scarlet. Recurved. Corolla. Lavender blue. Cup shaped. Vol 2 J of RHS. 1870 Fuchsia trials at Chiswick "Passed over". GC. P382 28/4/1866 Intro. by E. G. Henderson. *Banks, E. Deal. GB. 1866.*

JULIA GRISI. Single. White/Red. Tube. Blush. Tipped green (Pale flesh). Sepals. Blush tipped green. (Pale flesh) Corolla. Rosy scarlet. (Light cerise red). Bell shaped. Listed by G. Smith. GC. P497 11/8/1849 GC. P145 9/3/1850 by W. Rumley, Richmond. App. to RH 1851 by Porcher. GC. P427 7/7/1849 Intro. by Youells, Gt. Yarmouth. *Meillez, Lille. France. 1849.*

JULIET (a). Single. White/ND. Tube. ND. Sepals. Light. ND. Corolla. ND. P170 Floricultural Cabinet Vol XIII Exhibited at Hort. Scty. Show May 1845 by Kendall. GC. P153 4/3/1848 Listed by R. Cooper Croydon as Julia. *Kendall. London GB. 1845.*

JULIET (b). Double. Red/White. Tube. Bright crimson. Sepals. Bright crimson. Corolla. White shaded rose. Large. JF. Cat. 1913. NK. NK. NK.

JULIETTE. Double. ND/ND. Tube. ND. Sepals. ND. Corolla. ND. Garden 15.12.1883 P503. See colour plate L'Illustration Horticulture Vol 30 P174. *Mahon, J. Brussels. Belgium 1883.*

JULIETTE ADAM. Double. Red/White. Tube. Carmine Vermillion. Sepals. Carmine Vermillion. Reflexed. Corolla. Pinkish white. Upright habit. Full. Good for market. Average sized flowers. L. Cat. 1909. *Lemoine. Nancy. France. 1909.*

JUMNA. Double. Red/Purple. Tube. Crimson. Short. Sepals. Bright crimson. Very broad. Corolla. Rich purple, marked rosy crimson at base. Enormous. B. Cat. 1888, 1889, 1892, 1893, 1894, 1895. JF. Cat. 1886. *Bull, W. Chelsea. GB. 1885.*

JUNIUS.(a). Single. White/Red. Tube. Light blush. Sepals. Light blush. Tipped Green. Expanding. Corolla. Orange Scarlet. GC. P66 1/2/1845. P162 14/3/1846, P184 13/3/1847 Listed by Millers, Ramsgate. GC P206 29/3/1845 Intro. by G. Smith. *Smith, G. Islington. GB. 1845.*

JUNIUS.(b). Single. Pink/Purple. Tube. Light pink. Very large. Sepals. Light pink. Large but short. Corolla. Violet Pink. Suffers from a defect of the flowers not opening. App. to RH. 1851 by Porcher. *Morot. GB. 1849.*

JUNO. Single. Red/Purple. Tube. Crimson. Short. Sepals. Crimson. Broad . Well reflexed. Corolla. Deep purple marked rosy pink at base. B. Cat. 1888, 1889, 1892. *Bull, W. Chelsea. GB. 1888.*

JUNON. Single. Red/White. Tube. Coral. Sepals. Coral. Corolla. White, veined rose at base.. L. Cat 1906. *Bull, W. Chelsea. GB. 1905.*

JUPITER. Double. ND/ND. Tube. ND. Sepals. ND. Corolla. ND. L. Cat.1892. Fuchsiaphile Vol 1 2/3 1900. *Rozain, Lyons. France. 1889.*

JUSSIEUX. ND. ND/ND. Tube. ND. Sepals. ND. Corolla. ND. Fuchsiaphiles Vol. 1 2/3.1990. *Rozain, Lyons. France. 1898.*

KAISERII. Single. Red/Purple. Tube. Red. Sepals. Red. Corolla. Purple. GC. P406 1846 Listed as a good fuchsia. Choice kind. Dark. *Kendall, Stoke Newington. GB. 1844?*

KENTISH BRIDE. Single. Red/Purple. Tube. Bright rosy scarlet. Sepals. Bright rosy scarlet. Corolla. Bright violet purple. Very Large. Like "Formosa Elegans". GC. P820 1844 "Recommended". GC P112 17/2/1844 & P66 1/2/1845 Listed by Millers, Ramsgate etc. GC. P821 25/11/1843 & P97 17/2/1844 Intro by W.J. Epps, Ramsgate. *Busby, H. Hemstead. GB. 1843.*

KENTISH HERO. Single. Red/Purple. Tube. Vermillion red. Sepals. Vermillion red. Well expanded. Corolla. Puce purple. Resembles "Curtisii", only more prolific bloomer. 6 flowers from 1 joint. GC. P596 Oct. 1844. GC. P117 17/2/1844 Listed by Millers, Ramsgate. GC. P97 17/2/1844 Intro. by W.J. Epps, Maidstone. *Epps, W.J. Maidstone GB. 1844.*

KETELEERI. Single. Pink/Red. Tube. Salmon tinted. Sepals. Salmon Tinted. Spreading. Green tipped. Corolla. Crimson. Vol 3 J of RHS. P91 Report on fuchsias grown for trial at Chiswick 1862. No merit. *Henderson, E. G. St.Johns Wood. GB. 1862.*

KHÉDIVE. Double. ND/ND.. Double. Red/Purple. Tube. Turkey red. Sepals. Turkey red. Curled Back. Corolla. Purple red, splashed blue. Enormous. L. Cat. 1912. *Rozain. Lyons. France. 1912.*

KILLIECRANKIE. Single. Red/Purple. Tube. Carmine Red. (Crimson red). Short. Sepals. Carmine Red. (Crimson red). Reflexed. Broad. Short. Corolla. Rich violet black. (Violet shaded red and brown). Petals spiral. Perfect shape. Early Blooming. Habit compact. Very large corolla. GC. P567/8 23/4/1870 4th. Ed. by Porcher 1874. HC. Cat. 1882. GO. "Select" 1880-1889. Jof RHS Vol 4 P69 1877. Intro by E.G. Henderson. *Banks, E. Deal. GB. 1867.*

KING. ND. ND/ND. Tube. ND. Sepals. ND. Corolla. ND. Very large. GC. P97 18/2/1843 & P98 17/2/1844 Listed by Youells, Gt. Yarmouth. P112

17/2/1844, P66 1/2/1845 by Millers, Ramsgate NK. NK. NK. *1843?*

KING ALFONSO. Double. Red/Purple. Tube. Crimson. Sepals. Crimson. Broad. Corolla. Deep violet. Named after the King Alfonso XII of Spain (1857-85). B. Cat. 1877, 1878, 1879, 1880, 1881, 1882. BSW. Cat. 1875 and GC. P491 17/4/1875. Intro. by B & S Williams. *Bland, E. Fordham. GB. 1875.*

KING CHARMING. Single. White/Purple. Tube. White. Thick. Sepals. White. Horizontal. Corolla. Purple flushed crimson. Colour plate The Florist March 1853. GC. P151 5/3/1853. GC. P337 28/5/1853 Listed by Bass & Brown, Sudbury. GC. P385 18/6/1853 Listed by W. Rumley, Richmond. P483 30/7/1853 by H. Walton, Burnley. Champion of England x Roseola. *Mayle, Birmingham. GB. 1853.*

KING JOHN. Single. Pink/Red. Tube. Salmon. Sepals. Salmon. Corolla. Scarlet. Like "Chandlerii" but twice as big. GC. P559 17/8/1844 with the habit of Chandlerii". GC. P369 8/6/1844 Listed by T. Cripps. GC. P66 1/2/1845 Listed by Millers Ramsgate. RH. P24 1846. GC. P162 16/3/1844. *Hally, J. Blackheath GB. 1844.*

KING OF BEAUTIES. Single. White/ND.. Tube. White . Sepals. White. Corolla. ND. GC. P184 13/3/1847 P250 27/4/1847 Listed by Millers, Ramsgate. GC. P455 8/7/1847 Exhibited by Mr. Bray RBS Show London. *Fairbeard. London. GB. 1846.*

KING OF DENMARK.ND ND. ND/ND. Tube. ND. Sepals. ND. Corolla. ND. GC. P338 15/4/1865 Listed by W. Rumley, Richmond. NK. NK. NK. *1864.*

KING OF DOUBLES. Double. ND/ND. Tube. ND. Sepals. ND.Corolla. ND. GC. P778 23/10/1858 Listed by H. Walton, Burnley. NK. NK. NK. *1858.*

KING OF THE DOUBLES. Double. Red/Purple. Tube. Dark Scarlet Sepals. Dark Scarlet. Broad. Reflexed. Corolla. Rich purple, distinctly striped with red. Large. Long. GC. P55 19/1/1867 F&P P57 March 1866. HC.Cat.1882. GO "Select" 1886 - 1891. *Bland, E. Fordham GB. 1866.*

KING OF THE FUCHSIAS. Single. Red/Purple. Tube. Carmine. (Rose). Stoutish. ⅜" long. Sepals. Carmine. (Rose) Broad. Spreading. 1" long. Corolla. Rich violet purple. ¾". A bad grower and not very free". Vol, 4 Jof RHS 1877 P69. *** Vol 3 P of RHS

1872 Neat and dwarf in habit. Free. Pcxvi Vol 3 P of RHS 1872. B. Cat. 1870, 1872, 1873. HC. Cat. 1882. 1885. *Banks, E. Deal. GB. 1868.*

KING OF THE STRIPES. Single. Red/Purple. Tube. Red. (Crimson). Sepals. Red. (Crimson). Reflexed. Corolla. Violet Blue. Each petal is striped with red. GC. P488 9/4/1870 HC Advert. FW & GG 4/1/1870 Habit of the "Souvenir of Chiswick" P143 4th Ed. by Porcher Bushy but not vigourous. GO. "Select" 1880-1891. HC. Cat. 1885, 1890, 1891, 1896, 1898. *Banks, E. Deal. GB. 1870.*

KING OF PURPLES. ND. Red/Purple. Tube. Red. Sepals. Red.. Corolla. Purple. GC. P595 29/6/1861 Listed by Godwin & Padman, Sheffield. GC. P771 24/8/1861 Listed by H. Walton Burnley. GC. P358 20/4/1861 Intro. by G. Smith. *Smith, G. Islington GB. 1861.*

KINGSBURYANA. Double. Red/White. Tube. Bright red. Sepals. Bright red. Reflexed. Corolla. White. Open and spreading. Illustrated HC. Cat. 1882 P71, 1885, 1890, 1891. GO. "Select" 1880-1891. B.Cat. 1877-1892. NK. NK. *GB. 1876.*

KITTY TYRRELL. Single. Red/Purple. Tube. Scarlet. Sepals. Scarlet. Corolla. Violet. GC. P539 10/7/1858 Listed by F. Godwin, Sheffield. GC. P571 24/7/1858 Listed by H. Walton, Burnley GC. P238 19/3/1859 Listed by W. Rumley, Richmond. RH. P95 1859. Intro. by E. G. Henderson. *Banks, E. Deal. GB. 1858.*

KLÉBER Double. White/Purple. Tube. Rosy White. Sepals. Rosy white. Tipped green. Horizontal. Corolla. Violet blue. B. Cat. 1888-1893. Named after a French Commander. Assinated Cairo 1800. *Lemoine. Nancy. France. 1886.*

KNIGHT OF THE GARTER. Double. Red/Purple. Tube. Red. Sepals. Red. Corolla. Bluish Violet. Very big. P136 Appendix of 4th Ed. by Porcher 1874. *Williams, B&S, London. GB. 1874.*

KNIGHTS MASTER ND. ND/ND. Tube. ND. Sepals. ND. Corolla. ND. GC. P250 17/4/1847 Listed by J. Hally, Blackheath. *Knight. St. Leonards GB. 1846.*

KOH I NOOR. Single. Red/Purple. Tube. Crimson. Sepals. Crimson. Corolla. Purple. GC. P545 30/8/1851 Listed by G. Smith, Isleworth. GC. P177 20/3/1852 Listed by W. Rumley, Richmond. GC. P207 27/3/1852 Listed by H. Walton, Burnley GC. P304 10/5/1851 Intro. by E. Tiley, Bath. *Tiley, E. Bath GB. 1851.*

KOSSUTH. Single. Red/Purple. Tube. Bright crimson.Sepals. Bright crimson. Reflexed. Corolla. Violet Purple. Bell shaped blooms. Habit and growth of "Corollina". GC. P410 6/7/1850 Listed by H. Walton, Burnley. etc. Named after a Hungarian patriot,who settled in England. GC. P226 13/4/1850 Intro. by G. Smith. *Smith, G. Islington. GB. 1850.*

KRÜGER. Double. Red/Purple. Tube. Carmine. Sepals. Carmine. Large. Corolla. Blue. Large. Full. Named after a Boer leader (1825-1904). L. Cat. P149 1901. *Rozain, Lyons. France. 1901.*

LA BELLE ELISE. ND. ND/ND. Tube. ND. Sepals. ND. Corolla. ND. "Good market variety". GC. P181 7/2/1880. NK.NK. NK. NK.

LA CHINOIS Single. ND/ND. Tube. ND. Sepals. ND. Corolla. ND. GC. P241 20/4/1850 Listed by W. Rendle, Plymouth. *Salter, Versailles. France. 1848.* (SEE LE CHINOIS)

LACÉDÉMONE. Double. Red/Cream. Tube. Coral. Sepals. Coral. Corolla. Cream. Plant very vigourous. Full. L. Cat. 1911. *Lemoine. Nancy. France. 1911.*

LACONII. Single. Red/Purple. Tube. Rich vermillion. Sepals. Rich vermillion. Expand well. Corolla. Deep rosy purple. Immense size. Prolific bloomer. GC. Dec 1844. GC. P808 Nov 1846 Recommended "dark". GC. P146 8/3/1845 Intro. by Youells, Gt. Yarmouth. *Youell. Gt.Yarmouth. GB. 1845.*

LA CORÉE. Double. White/Red. Tube. Waxy white. Sepals. Waxy White. Reflexed. Corolla. Rosy pink. L. Cat. No. 149 1901. *Lemoine. Nancy. France. 1901.*

LACORDAIRE. Double. ND/ND. Tube. ND. Sepals. ND. Corolla. ND. Fuchsiaphile Vol. 1. 2/3.1990. L. Cat. *1901 Rozain. Lyons. France. 1898.*

LA CRINOLINE. Single. Red/Purple. Tube. Crimson. Sepals. Crimson. Corolla. Blue. Large. Opens out flat. Vol. P3 JofRHS 1863 Fuchsia Trial at Chiswick - Free Flowering. Bushy. Short corolla, broadly expanded. Resembles "Prince Imperial". GC. P665 26/2/1859 Intro. by E.G. Henderson, St. Johns Wood. *Banks, E. Deal. GB. 1859.*

LADY ALICE PEEL. Single. Red/Purple. Tube. Rosy red. Sepals. Rosy red, tipped green. Corolla. Crimson Purple. GC. P146 8/3/1845 Listed by Youells, Gt. Yarmouth. GC. P153 4/3/1848 Listed by R. Cooper, Croydon. GC. P1 6/1/1844 Intro. by

Youells, Gt. Yarmouth. *Youell, Gt. Yarmouth GB. 1844.*

LADY BLANCHE. ND. Red/White. Tube. Red. Sepals. Red. Corolla. White. GC. P376 26/4/1862. *F&A Smith, Dulwich. GB. 1862.*

LADY BRIDPORT. Single. Red/Purple. Tube. Coral Scarlet. Large. Sepals. Coral Scarlet. Corolla. Deep Violet, finely flaked scarlet through the centre of the petals. Open parachute shape. BSW. Cat. 1878. HC. Cat. 1882. B. Cat. 1877, 1878. NK. *GB. 1876.*

LADY BRODIE. Single. White/Pink. Tube. Blush white. Medium sized. Sepals. Blush white. Well recurved. Corolla. Rich rose with carmine belt. Free bloomer. HC. Cat. 1882. B. Cat. 1877, 1878, 1879. *Todman. GB. 1875.*

LADY BUXTON (a). Single. Red/Red. Tube. Brilliant rosy crimson. Sepals. Brilliant rosy crimson. Corolla. Rosy crimson. GC. P224 14/4/1849 Listed by Bass & Brown, Sudbury and R. Whibley, Kennington. GC. P256 21/4/1849 Listed by R. Cooper, Croydon. GC. P313 13/5/1848 Intro. by Barkways. *Barkway. GB. 1848.*

LADY BUXTON (b). Single. ND/ND. Tube. ND. Sepals. ND. Corolla. ND. GC. P161 17/3/1849 Listed by W. Rumley, Richmond. *Tiley, Bath GB. 1848.*

LADY CHARLOTTE DENISON. Double. Red/Purple. Tube. Red. Nearly ½" long. Sepals. Red. Slender ⅞" long. Corolla. Purple. ¾" Pcxv Vol. 3 JofRHS 1872 Fuchsia Trial at Chiswick. Habit weak. Medium size. Inferior. NK. *GB.* NK.

LADY COTTON SHEPHERD. Single. White/Purple. Tube. White. Long. Sepals. White. Nearly free of green tips. Corolla. Purple. GC. P201 27/3/1847 Listed by Hart & Nickling, Guildford. GC. P265 24/4/1847 Listed by W. Rendle. Plymouth. GC. P234 11/4/1846 Intro. by G. Rogers, Uttoxeter. *Rogers, G. Uttoxeter GB. 1846.*

LADY DARTMOUTH. Single. White/ND. Tube. White. Sepals. White. Corolla. ND. GC. P151 5/3/1853. Light variety. Good for exhibition. GC. P199 19/3/1853 Recommended. GC. P706 9/11/1850 Listed by H. Walton, Burnley. GC. P289 11/5/1850 Intro. by Mayle, Birmingham.(1 of 7 new introductions). *Mayle, Birmingham GB. 1850.*

LADY DE VERE. Single. Red/Purple. Tube. Red. Sepals. Red. Corolla. Purple. GC. P146 8/3/1846 Listed by Youells, Gt. Yarmouth. NK. *GB. 1845.*

LADY DOREEN LONG. Single. White/Pink. Tube. Creamy White. Sepals. Creamy White. Smooth and Stout in texture. Corolla. Deep Pink, shaded pale violet. Robust. Very free. GO. 1889. HC. Cat. 1890. JF. Cat. 1888. Laings Cat. Circa 1890. B. Cat. 1888. BSW. Cat. 1888. GC. P374 4/9/1887. Exhibited at Market Lavington by J. Lye. *Lye, J. Market Lavington. GB. 1888.*

LADY DOROTHY NEVILLE. Single. Red/Purple. Tube. Bright Carmine. Short. Thick. Sepals. Bright Carmine. Reflexed. Broad. Corolla. Mauve Pink. (Rosy Mauve). (Lavender). Bell Mouthed. Large. Smooth. Expanded like "La Crinoline". P109 4th Ed. by Porcher 1874 Pedicel 50 mms. BSW. Cat. 1878. GC. P396 22/3/1873 Intro. by B.S. Williams. *Bland, E. Fordham GB. 1873.*

LADY DOUGLAS. Single. Red/Purple. Tube. Dark Scarlet. Sepals. Dark Scarlet. Recurved. Corolla. Dark crimson purple. Expanded. Small flowers. Vol P3 J of RHS 1863 Fuchsia trial at Chiswick 1862. Dwarf Habit. GC. P450 17/5/1862 Intro. by B.W. Knight, Battle. *Knight. B.W., Battle. GB. 1862.*

LADY DOVER. Single. ND/ND. Tube. ND. Sepals. ND. Corolla. ND. GC. P184 13/3/1847 Listed by Millers, Ramsgate. *MacFarling. GB. 1847.*

LADY DUMBELLO. Single. Red/Purple. Tube. Carmine. (Crimson) Sepals. Carmine (Crimson). Corolla. Lavender blue and Purple. Cup Shaped. CG. P506 1866. (Mauve) Large. B. Cat. 1870. GC. P382 28/4/1866 Intro. by E.G. Henderson, St. Johns Wood. *Banks, E. Deal. GB. 1866.*

LADY EMILY CAVENDISH. Single. Pink/Purple. Tube. Pink. Sepals. Pink. Corolla. Rich Purple. P79 Floricultural Cabinet 1855. GC. P279 30/4/1853 Light green stemmed. GC. P385 18/6/1853 Listed by W. Rumley, Richmond. P465 27/7/1853 Listed by Harrison, Darlington. P483 30/7/1853 Listed by H. Walton, Burnley etc. NK. NK. *GB. 1853.*

LADY FRANKLIN. Single. White/Purple. Tube. White. Sepals. White. Corolla. Purple. GC. P385 18/6/1853 Listed by W. Rumley, Richmond. GC. P465 23/7/1853 Listed by Harrison, Darlington. GC. P627 1/10/1853 Listed by S. Fenney, Gateshead. GC. P162 18/3/1854 Listed by H. Walton Burnley. GC. P98 12/2/1853 Intro. by G. Smith, Islington. Venus Victrix X. *Smith, G. Islington. GB. 1853.*

LADY HEYTESBURY. Single. White/Purple. Tube. White. Slender. Tapered downwards (Cone shaped) Sepals. White. Somewhat reflexed 1" long. Corolla. Rosy Purple.(Deep Lake with white feather at base). ⅛". Vol 2 1870 J of RHS Fuchsia Trials at Chiswick. Vol. 3 1872 Awarded ***.GC. P824 27/6/1885 Fuchsia trials "Best in class" GC. P55 19/1/1867 Review by Cannell. BSW. Cat. 1878. HC. Cat. 1882. etc. *Wheeler, Warminster. GB. 1866*

LADY HEYTESBURY IMPROVED. Single. White/Purple. Tube. ND. Sepals. ND. Corolla. ND. B. Cat. 1888 An improvement on Lady Heytesbury, both in habit and flower. HC. Cat. 1885 New Seedling from Lady Heytesbury. More attractive colour. NK. NK. *GB. 1885.*

LADY JULIA. Single. White/Red. Tube. Waxy white. Sepals. Waxy White. Green tips. Corolla. Vivid crimson. GC. P140 27/2/1847 Good. GC. P250 17/4/1847 Listed by Epps. GC. P216 27/3/1847 Listed by R. Cooper Crmydon. GC. P265 24/4/1847 Listed by W. Rendle, Plymouth. GC. P113 14/2/1846 Intro. by Epps. Maidstone. *Epps, W.J. Maidstone. GB. 1846.*

LADY MONTAGUE. Single. Pink/Purple. Tube. Pink. Sepals. Pink. Corolla. Purple. Vol 2. F.F.& GM. Vol 2. P204 1/7/1853. Label of Commendation. GC. P483 30/7/1853 Listed by H. Walton, Burnley. GC. P529 20/8/1853 Listed by Youells, Gt. Yarmouth. GC.P535 20/8/1853 seen at C. Turners, Slough. *Turner, C. Slough. GB. 1853.*

LADY OF THE LAKE (a). Single. ND/ND. Tube. ND. Sepals. ND. Corolla. ND. GC. P234 11/4/1846 Listed by A. J. Stewart, Windsor. GC. P265 24/4/1847 and P241 20/4/1850 Listed by W. Rendle Plymouth. NK. NK. *GB.* NK.

LADY OF THE LAKE (b). Single. ND/ND. Tube. ND. Sepals. ND. Corolla. ND. GC. P207 27/3/1852 & P275 1/5/1852 Listed by H. Walton Burnley. NK. NK. *GB.* NK.

LADY OF THE LAKE (c). Single. Red/White. Tube. Crimson. Sepals. Crimson. Corolla. Blush white. GC. P467 14/7/1855 Listed by Bass & Brown, Sudbury and H. Walton, Burnley. GC. P529 11/8/1855 Listed by W.J.Epps, Maidstone. GC.P530 11/8/1855 Listed by Bainbridge & Hewison, York. GC. P18 13/1/1855 Intro. by E.G. Henderson. St. Johns Wood. *Banks, E. Deal. GB. 1855.*

LADY OF THE SEA. ND. ND. Tube. ND.

Sepals. ND. Corolla. ND. GC. P382 29/4/1865 Intro. by E.G. Henderson, St. Johns Wood. *Banks, E. Deal. GB. 1865.*

LADY PEEL. See Lady Alice Peel.

LADY RAE REID. Single. ND/ND. Tube. ND. Sepals. ND. Corolla. ND. Dark variety. GC. P98 17/3/1844, P146 8/3/1845 Listed by Youells, Gt. Yarmouth. *Youell, Gt. Yarmouth GB. 1843.*

LADY SALE (a). Single. Red/Purple. Tube. Red. Sepals. Red. Corolla. Purple. GC. P66 1/2/1845 Listed by Millers, Ramsgate. GC. P146 8/3/1845 Listed by Youells, Gt. Yarmouth *Youell, Gt. Yarmouth GB. 1844.*

LADY SALE (b). Single. Pink/Red. Tube. Flushed pink. Sepals. Flushed pink. Green tips. Corolla. Vermillion GC. P184 13/3/1847 Listed by Millers, Ramsgate. Vol IV P204 1846 Floricultural Cabinet. Exhibited at RBS Show 20/4/1846 by Kendalls, Stoke Newington. GC. P238 12/4/1845 Intro. by Rogers, Uttoxeter. *Rogers, Uttoxeter. GB. 1845.*

LADY SALE (c). Double. White/Purple. Tube. Pearl White. (Blush white) Sepals. Pearl White. (Blush white). Nicely reflexed. Corolla. Brilliant purple, flamed and striped bright carmine. (Dark carmine shaded purple) GC. P567/8 23/9/1870. HC. Cat. 1882. RH. P311 1889 "Select" by E. A. Carriere. GC. P597 6/7/1868 Intro. by Felton and Holiday, Birmingham. *Felton, G. Birmingham GB. 1868.*

LADY SONDES. Single. Red/Purple. Tube. Red. Sepals. Red. Corolla. Purple. GC. P98 17/2/1844 & P146 8/3/1845 Listed by Youells, Gt. Yarmouth. *Youell, Gt. Yarmouth GB. 1843.*

LADY STANLEY. Single. White/Purple. Tube. White. Sepals. White. Corolla. Purple. Sent out Feb 1850. GC. P610 29/9/1849 Intro. by W.Skirving, Walton, Liverpool. *Skirving, W. Liverpool. GB. 1850.*

LADY WALSINGHAM. Single. Red/Purple. Tube. Rosy vermillion. Sepals. Rosy Vermillion. Upswept. Corolla. Purple Crimson. GC. P820 Dec 1844 "Recommended" GC. P808 Nov 1846 "Recommended dark variety" GC. P140 27/2/1847 Good dark variety. GC. P146 3/3/1846 Listed by Youells. GC. P1 6/1/1844 Intro. by Youells, Gt. Yarmouth. *Youell, Gt. Yarmouth GB. 1844*

LADY WATERLOW. Single. White/Purple. Tube. White. Sepals. White. Much reflexed. Corolla. Rich magenta, beautifully striped and flaked scarlet. Profuse. B. Cat. 1877, 1878, 1879. HC. Cat. 1882. GC. P491 17/4/1875 Intro. by B.S. Williams. *Bland, E. Fordham GB. 1875.*

LADY WILLIAM POWLETT. Single. Pink/Red. Tube. Pink. Sepals. Pink. Corolla. Scarlet. GC. P153 4/3/1848 & P232 1/4/1848 Listed by R. Cooper, Croydon. GC. P298 8/5/1847 Intro. by Tiley, Bath. *Tiley, Bath. GB. 1847.*

LAFAYETTE. S/Double. Red/Purple. Tube. Crimson. (Dark red). Sepals. Crimson. (Dark red) Long. Broad. Corolla. Rich plum. Enormous. Named after a French reformer who helped the Americans in the Civil War. He was also prominent after the French revolution. (1757-1834). JF. Cat. 1898. B. Cat. 1898 Intro. by W. Bull, Chelsea. *Lemoine. Nancy. France. 1896.*

LA FRANCE. Double. Red/Purple. Tube. Bright red. Sepals. Bright red. Recurved. Large. Corolla. Cobalt Blue. (Chinese and Cobalt Blue).(Dark blue). Large. Perfect form. Very vigorous. GC. P518 28/4/1888 Listed by Daniels, Norwich. J. Laings Cat. circa 1890. Dobbies Cat. 1893/4. B. Cat. 1888, 1889, 1892, 1893. BSW. Cat. 1888. *Lemoine. Nancy. France. 1885.*

LAINGS HYBRID. Single. GC. Vol 2 P73 7/7/1885 Exhibited by J. Laing, Forest Hill, Surrey. Hybrid between F. fulgens and a large flowered dark. Stems stoutish red. Leaves ovate. Red petioles. Flowers in clusters. Rich orange. Tube 1¼" long. Pointed sepals. Bright crimson scarlet corolla. See Earl of Beaconsfield. and also Lord Beaconsfield.

LAMARTINE (a). Single. Red/Purple. Tube. Carmine red. Thick. Short. Sepals. Carmine red. Large. Reflexed. Round. Corolla. Violet Blue, tinted red. Expanded. P109 4th Ed. by Porcher 1874. Named after a French poet, historian and statesman. 1790-1869. NK NK. NK. *1869*

LAMARTINE (b). Double. Red/Purple. Tube. Red. Sepals. Clear Red. Short. Horizontally reflexed. Corolla. Lilac shade of sky blue. (Velvety bluish violet). Perfect form. Plant of dwarf habit and very floriferous. B. Cat. 1893, 1894, 1895, 1898, 1899. *Rozain, Lyons. France. 1897.*

LAMENNAIS Double. Red/White. Tube. Rosy Carmine. Sepals. Rosy Carmine. Corolla. Pure White. Dwarf and free. Flowers globular, having about thirty petals. Named after a French writer and politician (1782-1854). Dobbies Cat. 1893, 1894. BSW. Cat. 1888. HC. Cat. 1885, 1890. *Lemoine. Nancy. France. 1883.*

LAMEUNAIS. Double. Red / White. See LAMENNAIS.

LAMORICIÈRE. Single. Red/Purple. Tube. Light crimson. Sepals. Light crimson. Recurved and Reflexed. Corolla. Violet marked bright rose. Large. Named after a French General (1806-65) B. Cat. 1870. NK. NK. *France. 1866?*

LAMUS. Single. Red/Purple. Tube. Rich scarlet. Short. Sepals. Rich scarlet. Recurved. Corolla. Dark satiny purple. Intro. by W. Bull Chelsea. B. Cat. 1881, 1882, 1883, 1888, 1889, 1892, 1893. *Bull, W. Chelsea. GB. 1881*

LA NATION. Double. Red/Purple. Tube. Clear red. Sepals. Clear red. Broad. Recurved. Corolla. Brilliant Violet mauve. Large. Full. HC. Cat. 1882, 1885, 1890. RH. P311 1889 "Select" by E.A. Carrière. B. Cat. 1878, 1879, *Lemoine. Nancy. France. 1877.*

LANCASHIRE WITCH. Single. Pink/Pink. Tube. Flesh. Sepals. Flesh. Extended. Corolla. Bright pink. 2nd Ed. by Porcher 1848. GC. P259 28/4/1849 & P241 30/4/1850 Listed by W. Rendle, Plymouth. NK. NK. *GB. NK.*

LAND OF PLENTY. Single. Red/Purple. Tube. Scarlet red. Glossy. Sepals. Scarlet red. Gracefully recurved. Corolla. Rich violet black. Barrel shape. Lobes well cupped. Held back for a year for intense hybridisation. A perfect flower. GC. P55 19/1/1867 Review by H. Cannell. GC. P382 28/4/1866. Intro. by E.G. Henderson, St. John's Wood. *Banks, E. Deal. GB. 1866.*

LA NEIGE. Double. Red/White. Tube. Crimson Red. Thick. Sepals. Crimson Red. Horizontal. Green tips. Large. Corolla. Pure White, Paint striped. Petals folded. Corolla Expanded. A little short. P128 4th Ed. by Porcher. 1874. GC. P206 17/2/1877. GO. "Select" 1881-1885. HC. Cat. P74 1882. RH. P311 1889 "Select" *Lemoine. Nancy. France. 1873.*

LANEII. Single. Red/Purple. Tube. Red. Long. Sepals. Red. Drooping. Corolla. Carmine rose. GC. P97 18/2/1843 Listed by Youells, Gt. Yarmouth. GC. P321 24/6/1842 Exhibited at H.S. Show by Lanes. GC. P833 17/12/1841 Immense flowers of Globosa type, similar to "Standishi", but more expansive petals. *Lane. Berkhampstead. GB. 1841.*

LANSEZEUR. Single. Red/Purple. Tube. Carmine. Sepals. Carmine. Corolla. Chocolate Lake. RH. P24 1846. *Salter, J. Versailles. France 1846.*

LA POLKA. Single. Red/Purple. Tube. Carmine. Sepals. Carmine. Corolla. Crimson Purple. GC. P162 14/3/1846 and P184 13/3/1847 Listed by W.

Miller, Ramsgate. GC. P164 8/3/1845 Intro. by E. Tiley, Bath. *Tiley, E. Bath. GB. 1845.*

LA PROPHÈTE. Single. Red/Purple. Tube. Brilliant Carmine. Thick. Short. Sepals. Brilliant Carmine. Large. Reflexed. Corolla. Violet Blue, washed red at base. Full. Bell shaped. Large leaves. P109 4th. Ed. by Porcher 1874. Vol. P3 JofRHS 1863. Grown for trial at Chiswick. GC. P165 24/2/1859 Intro. by E.G. Henderson. St. Johns Wood. Similar to "Wonderful" *Banks, E. Deal. GB. 1859.*

LA QUINTINYE. Double. Red/Purple. Tube. Red. Sepals.Red. Corolla. Dark Amaranth. Petals are horizontal. JF. Cat. 1901. L. Cat. 1901. *Lemoine. Nancy. France. 1900.*

LA SYLPHIDE. Single. ND/ND. Tube. ND. Sepals. ND. Corolla. ND. GC. P250 17/4/1847 Listed by J. Hally, Blackheath. NK. NK. *GB. 1846.*

LATONA. Double. Red/White. Tube. Coral Crimson. Sepals. Coral Crimson. Recurved. Corolla. White, shaded deep rose at base. GC. Vol. 21 1/5/1897. Intro. by W. Bull, Chelsea. B. Cat. 1898. *Bull, W. Chelsea. GB. 1897.*

LAURA. Single. Pink/Purple. Tube. Delicate Bright pink. Sepals. Delicate Bright pink. Slightly tipped green. Corolla. Light rosy purple. GC. 7/2/1846 Intro. by Youell's, Gt. Yarmouth. *Youell, Gt. Yarmouth GB. 1846.*

LA TRAVIATA. Single. Red/Purple. Tube. Carmine Scarlet. Short. Sepals. Carmine Scarlet. Broad. Well recurved. Corolla. Lavender Blue. Cup shaped. (Habit of "Rifleman"). GC. P55 19/1/1867 Review by H. Cannell. One of the best for small pots. P109 4th Ed. by Porcher 1874. GC. P983 15/10/1864, P1 7/1/1865 Intro. by E.G. Henderson. St Johns Wood, *Banks, E. Deal. GB. 1865.*

LAURENT PALMAERT. Single. Red/White. Tube. Clear red. Thin. Sepals. Clear red. Large. Reflexed. Corolla. Pure white, striped rose at base. Vigorous. Not free flowering. 4th Ed. by Porcher 1874. *Cornelissen, Arras. Belgium. 1864.*

L'AVENIR. Single. Red/Purple. Tube. Rosy Crimson. Short. Sepals. Rosy crimson. Tipped green. Recurved. Double. Blue, Rose and White. Fine expanded tricoloured corolla. Very free bloomer. Intro. by Wm. Bull, Cat. 1882, 1883, 1888, 1889, 1892. *Rozain, Lyons. France. 1882.*

LAVINA. Double. Red/Purple. Tube. Rosy Crimson. Short. Sepals. Rosy crimson. Well reflexed. Corolla.

Purple Plum. Full. Good flower. B. Cat. 1872, 1873, 1875. *Bull, W. Chelsea. GB. 1871.*

LÉA. Single. Pink/Purple. Tube. Pinkish lilac. Very large. Sepals. Pinkish lilac. Large. Spreading. Arched. Corolla. Violet shaded pink. App. to RH. 1851 by Porcher. *Corbell. France. 1850.*

LEADER. Single. Red/Purple. Tube. Crimson. Sepals. Crimson. Corolla. Violet. Free-grower and bloomer. GC. P449 17/7/1852 & P209 26/3/1853 Listed by H. Walton, Burnley. GC. P211 26/3/1853 Listed by W. Rumley, Richmond etc. GC. P241 17/4/1852 Intro. by G. Smith, Islington. *Banks, E. Deal. GB. 1852.*

LEAH. Single. White/Purple. Tube. White. Stout. (Very thick. Long. 20 mms.). Sepals. White. Well reflexed. Corolla. Rich purple crimson, margined bright crimson.(Rose carmine bordered fire red, stained white) P118 4th Ed. 1874 by Porcher. GC. P1554 2/12/1871 by Cannell. GC.P476 15/4/1871 Intro. by W. Bull. B. Cat. 1872, 1873, 1875. *Weston. GB. 1871.*

LE CHINOIS (a). Single. Red/Purple. Tube. Carmine red. (Purple crimson) Sepals. Carmine red. (Purple crimson) Reflexed. Corolla. Lake. (Violet red). Stout. GC. P479 20/7/1844 Exhibited by Hendersons, Pineapple Place. GC. P66 1/2/1845 & P147 15/3/1847 Listed by Millers Ramsgate. RH. P24 1846. GC. P694 7/10/1843 Exhibited by Salter in Paris 19/8/1843. *Salter, J. Versailles. France. 1843.* (SEE LA CHINOIS)

LE CHINOIS (b). Single. White/Purple. Tube. White. Very thick. 15mms long. Sepals. White, washed rose. Reflexed. Round. Corolla. Violet lilac, bordered bright rose. Spiralled petals. Pedicel 50mms. Foilage is clear green. 4th Ed. by Porcher 1874. *Rendatler. NK. France. 1870.*

LE COMMANDEUR. Single. Red/Purple. Tube. Bright rose Pink. Very large. Sepals. Bright rose pink. Large. Horizontal. Corolla. Violet shaded pink. Very floriferous. Similar to "Perfection" by Meillez. App. to RH. 1851 by Porcher. *Racine. NK. France. 1850.*

LECOQ DE BOISBAUDRAN. Double. Red/Purple. Tube. Brick Coral. Sepals. Brick Coral. Broad. Long. Twisted. Corolla. Bluish Violet marked scarlet. Very full. Well formed. L. Cat. 1906. *Lemoine.Nancy. France. 1905.*

LE CYGNE. Double. Red/White. Tube. Deep Pink. (Red). Sepals. Deep pink. (Red). Corolla. White.

Long. GO. "Select" 1885 - 1891. Laings Cat. circa 1890. HC. Cat. 1885, 1890, 1891. Dobbies Cat. 1893, 1894. *Rozain. Lyons. France. 1880*

LÉDA. Single. Red/Purple. Tube. Crimson. Short. Sepals. Crimson. Reflexed. Corolla. Blush violet veined crimson. Much expanded. Irregular. L. Cat. 1902. B. Cat. 1898, 1899, 1901. GC. Vol 19, P579 May 1896. Intro. by W. Bull. *Bull, W. Chelsea. GB. 1896.*

LEELERE DU SABLON. Double. Red/White. Tube. Clear red. Sepals. Clear red. Completely reflexed. Corolla. Off white tinted mauve. Average size. L. Cat.1906. *Lemoine. Nancy. France. 1904.*

LEE'S DARK. Single. Red/Purple. Tube. ND. Sepals. ND. Corolla. ND. GC. P476 16/6/1842. Exhibited at Nottingham Floral Show by Mr. Pearson. NK. NK. *GB.* NK.

LE GAULOIS. Single. Red/Purple. Tube. Brilliant Carmine red. Sepals. Brilliant Carmine red. Long. Wide. Reflexed. Corolla. Dark Blue veined rosy carmine at base. Cylindrical shape. Large. B. Cat. 1875, 1876, 1877, 1878. NK. NK. NK. *1875.*

LE GLOBE. Double. Red/White. Tube. Clear crimson. Very short. Sepals. Clear crimson. Large. Reflexed. (Slightly recurved) Corolla. Pure white shaded rose and carmine at base. Petals short and numerous. Very open. Dwarf. Globular variety. Free Bloomer. P128 4th Ed. by Porcher 1874. B. Cat. 1870. *Crousse. France. 1866.*

L'ELEGANTE. Single. White/Red. Tube. White. Sepals. White. Reflexed. Corolla. Vermillion. Good Habit. CG. Vol. 6 P272 1853. Exhibited by Turner. Pale, reflexes like "Elizabeth". GC. P211 26/3/1853. Listed by W. Rumley, Richmond. GC. P248 15/4/1854 Listed by Mitchell, Brighton. GC. P223 10/4/1852 Intro. by Turner, Slough. *Turner, C. Slough GB. 1852.*

L'ELISIR D'AMORE. Single. Red/Purple. Tube. Red. Sepals. Red. Reflexed. Corolla. Purple marked with red stripes. Large. Moderately expanded. Moderately free habit. Vol 2 JofRHS 1870 Report on Fuchsia trials at Chiswick 1868. First Class. Sent by E.G. Henderson. St. Johns Wood. NK. NK. *GB.* NK.

LEMICHEZ. Single. Pink/Purple. Tube. Pink. Sepals. Pink. Green tips. Horizontal. Large. Corolla. Lilac Pink. P70 2nd Ed. by Porcher. GC. P250 17/4/1847 Listed by J. Hally, Blackheath. *Salter. Versailles. France. 1846.*

L'EMPEREUR. Single. Red/White. Tube. Bright Scarlet. Slender ⅜" long. Sepals. Bright Scarlet. Broad. Spreading. 1" long. Corolla. White with rosy veins. Pcxiii Vol. 3 JofRHS 1872 and Vol 4 Jof RHS. Report on Fuchsia trials at Chiswick 1873 and 1874. 2nd Class Cert. Sent by H. Cannell. NK. NK. NK. NK.

LENA. Double. ND/ND Tube. ND. Sepals. ND. Corolla. ND. JF. Cat. 1920.NK. NK. NK. NK.

LENÒTRE (a). Single. Red/Purple. Tube. Red. Sepals. Red. Corolla. Purple. Not in the first rank. P115 4th. Ed. by Porcher 1874. *Lemoine. Nancy. France. 1867.*

LENÒTRE. (b). Single. Red/Purple. Tube. Coral Pink. Sepals. Coral Pink. Curl back to form a circle. Corolla. Violet Purple. Large. Very long. JF. Cat. 1901. L. Cat. P149 1901. *Lemoine. Nancy. France. 1900.*

LÉO DELIBES. Single. Pink/Purple. Tube. Clear Pink. Short. Thick Sepals. Clear Pink. Long and large, curl back to tube. Corolla. Reddish Violet. Long. B. Cat. 1892, 1893. JF. Cat. 1892. Named after a French composer who wrote the music for the Ballet Coppelia. (1836-1891) L. Cat. 1892. *Lemoine. Nancy. France. 1891.*

LEOLINE. Single. Red/Purple. Tube. Crimson. Sepals. Crimson. Broad. Spreading. Corolla. Violet Blue. (Purple) GC. P260 24/3/1860 Listed by Wm. Hussey, Norwich. GC. P426 12/5/1860 Listed by F. Godwin, Sheffield. Vol. P3 JofRHS 1863 Report on Fuchsia Trial at Chiswick 1862. GC. P165 26/2/1859 Intro. by E.G. Henderson. St. Johns Wood. *Banks, E. Deal. GB. 1859.*

LEONARD. Double. Red/Purple. Tube. Bright crimson. Sepals. Bright crimson. Well recurved. Corolla. Rich Purple striped with rose at base. Short thick flower. B. Cat. 1872, 1873, 1875. GC. P476 15/4/1871 Intro. by W. Bull. *Bull, W. Chelsea. GB. 1871.*

LEONARD DE VINCI. Double. Red/Purple. Tube. Pale Red. Sepals. Pale Red. Corolla. Rich shade of Purple. Named after an Italian Painter, Sculptor, Architect (1452-1510). L. Cat. 1914. *Rozain, Lyons France. 1914.*

LEONCAVALLO. Double. ND/ND. Tube. ND. Sepals. ND. Corolla. ND. Named after an Italian composer. L. Cat. 1901. *Lemoine. Nancy. France. 1898.*

LEO XIII. Double. Red/Purple. Tube. Carmine red. Sepals. Carmine Red. Corolla. Blue. Laings. Cat. circa 1890. Fuchsiaphile Vol.1 2/3.1990. *Rozain, Lyons. 1885.*

LÉONIDAS. Single. ND/ND. Tube. ND. Sepals. ND. Corolla. ND. L. Cat. 1892. *Lemoine. Nancy. France. 1890.*

LEON DES COMBATS. Single. Red/Purple. Tube. Red. Sepals. Red. Spreading. Corolla. Purple. Small close corolla. Vol. P3 J of RHS 1863 Report of fuchsias grown for trial at Chiswick 1862. GC. P571 24/7//1856 Listed by H. Walton, Burnley. NK. NK. NK. NK.

LE PACHA. Single. Red/Pink. Tube. Red. Sepals. Red. Horizontal. Corolla. Pinkish White, webbed carmine. Compact. L. Cat. 1892. *Hoste. 1890.*

LE PASCAL. Double. Red/Purple. Tube. Red. Sepals. Red. Corolla. Dark blue shaded violet. Large. L. Cat. 1906. *Rozain, Lyons. France. 1905.*

LE PÉRE HYACINTHE. ND. Red/Purple. Tube. Red. Sepals. Red. Corolla. Purple. Not in the first selection. P115 4th Ed. by Porcher 1874. *Lemoine. Nancy. France. 1868.*

LE PHARE (a). Single. Red/Purple. Tube. Brilliant red. Short. Thick. Sepals. Brilliant red. Well reflexed. Corolla. Rich Violet veined bright red. Globular. B. Cat. 1876, 1877, 1878, 1879, 1880, 1885. BSW. Cat. 1878 NK. NK. NK. NK.

LE PHARE (b). Single. ND/ND. Tube. ND. Sepals. ND. Corolla. ND. L. Cat. 1890. *Comte. France 1890.*

LE ROBUSTE. Double. Red/Purple. Tube. Rose. Sepals. Rose. Twisted. (Bright pink). Corolla. Violet striped rose and white. (Violet blue striped rose and flesh pink). Large. Lengthening. JF. Cat. 1904. L. Cat. 1903. *Rozain, Lyons. France. 1903.*

L'ESPÉRANCE. Single. White/Purple. Tube. White (Flesh pink). Sepals. White. (Flesh Pink). Corolla. Deep blue. (Dark Blue). GC. P283 25/4/1857 Listed by Wm. Cutbush, Highgate. GC. P286 25/4/1857 Listed by H. Low. RH. P169 1857. Intro. by H. Low. *Demoureaux. France. 1856.*

LES REINE. ND. ND/ND. Tube. ND. Sepals. ND. Corolla. ND. GC. P201 27/3/1847 Listed by Hart & Nicklin, Guildford. NK. NK. NK. NK.

LE TRAVATORE ND. ND/ND. P459 SG. 1866 Recommended light variety. Nothing further found, possibly confused with Il Trovatore.

LETTY LYE. Single. White/Purple. Tube. Delicate blush. (Flesh Pink) (Blush white). Sepals. Delicate Blush. (Flesh Pink). (Blush white). Corolla. Deep Carmine tinted purple. BSW. Cat. 1878. GC. P722 9/6/1877. GC. P503 20/10/1887 T.277 Floral Magazine. P342 Vol 24 Jof RHS. 1900 A good bedder. HC. Cat 1882 P79. A good kind but the flower does not reflex well. Arabella Imp. x James Lye. *Lye, J. Market Lavington. GB. 1877.*

LEUCANTHA. Single. White/Red. Tube. Greenish white tinted pink. Thick. Sepals. Greenish white tinted pink. Green points. Corolla. Cerise red. Small. Short pedicels. 2nd Ed. by Porcher 1848. GC. P153 8/5/1847 & P232 1/4/1848 & P256 21/4/1849 Listed by R.Cooper, Croydon. GC. P201 25/3/1848 Listed by W. Rumley Richmond etc. GC. P297 8/5/1847 Intro. by H. Low. *Wright. GB. 1846.*

LEVERRIER (a). Single. Red/Purple. Tube. Reddish violet. Thick. Sepals. Reddish violet. Large. Reflexed. Corolla. Violet. P70 2nd Ed. by Porcher 1848. App. to RH 1851 by Porcher. First class variety. Named after a French astronomer 1811-77. *Salter, Versailles. France. 1846.*

LEVERRIER (b). Single. Red/Purple. Tube. Dark red. Sepals. Dark red. Large. Reflexed. Corolla. Plum. Bright centre. Remarkable for planting in the open. B. Cat. 1892, 1893. Named after a French astronomer (1811-77). GO. P141 1891 "New Continental variety". L. Cat. 1892. *Lemoine. Nancy. France. 1890.*

LEVIATHAN. Single. Red/Purple. Tube. Rich crimson. Sepals. Rich crimson. Broad. Completely reflexed and incurved. Corolla. Deep Purple. Well expanded. Very large bold flower. Vol P3 JofRHS 1863 Report on fuchsias grown for trial at Chiswick. GC. P560 30/6/1860 Listed by F. Godwin, Sheffield. GC. P18 14/1/1860 Intro. by W. Rollinson, Tooting. *Rollinson, W. Tooting GB. 1860.*

LEWALD. Single. Red/Purple. Tube. Bright crimson. Thick. Short. Sepals. Bright crimson. Reflexed round. Large. Corolla. Blue violet (Rich violet purple). Well expanded. Bell shaped. P110 4th Ed. by Porcher 1874. Vigourous. Similar to "Marvellous". GC. P502 13/4/1872 Intro. by W. Bull. B. Cat. 1872, 1873, 1875, 1876. *Bull, W. Chelsea. GB. 1872.*

LIEUTENANT MARITZ. Double. Red/White. Tube. Scarlet. Sepals. Scarlet. Reflexed. Corolla. Blush White. Enormous. Well formed. JF. Cat. 1895. Intro. by W. Bull. Cat. 1894, 1895. NK. NK. NK. *1894.*

LIEUTENANT MIZON. Double. Red/Purple. Tube. Brilliant Carmine. Sepals. Brilliant Carmine. Corolla. Clear Violet. Large Petals. B. Cat. 1894. 1895. Intro. by W. Bull, Chelsea. NK. NK. NK. *1894.*

LIGHT HEART. Single. Red/Purple. Tube. Red. Very short. Thick. Sepals. Red. Very large. Reflexed. Corolla. Blackish Purple fading to violet plum when fully expanded. (Violet Blue washed red). Fully Expanded. Vol. 2 JofRHS 1870. GC. P55 19/1/1867 Review by H. Cannell. P110 4th Ed. by Porcher 1874. GC. P382 29/4/1865 Intro by E.G. Henderson, St. Johns Wood. *Banks, E. Deal. GB. 1865.*

LILLAH. Single. Red/Purple. Tube. Crimson Red. Short. Thick. Sepals. Crimson. (Carmine Red). Very Broad. Horizontal. Corolla. Bluish Violet, with red overtones. (Rich satiny purple). 4th. Ed. by Porcher 1874. GC. P502 13/4/1872 Intro. by W. Bull, Chelsea. B. Cat. 1872, 1873, 1875, 1876. *Bull, W. Chelsea. GB. 1872.*

LILY BOULANGER. Double. White/White. Tube. White. Sepals. White. Corolla. Creamy white or pale flesh. Compact. L. Cat. 1914 Page 2. *Lemoine. Nancy. France. 1914.*

LILY OF KILLARNEY. ND. ND/ND. Tube. ND. Sepals. ND. Corolla. ND. GC. P406 2/5/1863 Listed by Wm Hussey Norwich. NK. NK. NK. *1862.*

LIMA. Double. Red/Purple. Tube. Crimson. Sepals. Crimson. Corolla. Purple Red bordered plum. L. Cat. 1910. *Rozain, Lyons. France 1910.*

LINA. Single. Red/Purple. Tube. Bright Crimson. Sepals. Bright crimson. Long and most elegantly reflexed. Corolla. Dark Purple. Distinct. B. Cat. 1872, 1873, 1875. Intro. by W. Bull. *Bull, W. Chelsea. GB. 1872.*

LINA VON MAINZ. Single. White/Red. Tube. White. Thin. Long. 15mms. Sepals. White. Long. Narrow. Horizontal. Green tips. Corolla. Rosy red. Vol P3 JofRHS 1863 P92 Fuchsia trials at Chiswick. Poor. 3rd Ed. by Porcher 1858, sometimes referred to as Lina De Mayence. GC.P366 25/3/1857. Intro. by E.G. Henderson, St. Johns Wood. Souvenir de la Reine X. *Koch. Germany. 1857.*

LINDA. Single. Red/Purple. Tube. Coral Red. Short. Sepals. Coral red. Broad. Corolla. Lavender Blue veined crimson at base. JF. Cat. 1990. L. Cat. 1901. B. Cat. 1899, 1901. Intro. by W.Bull, Chelsea. *Bull, W. Chelsea. GB. 1899.*

LINDLEYANA. Single. Red/Red. Tube. Vermillion. Long. Sepals. Vermillion. Expanded. (Crimson vermillion). Corolla. Crimson vermillion. (Dark Vermillion). GC. P146 8/3/1845. GC. P446 1/7/1843. RH. P24 1846. Somewhat inflated Tube. GC. P1 6/1/1844 Intro. by Youells, Gt. Yarmouth, purchased entire stock. *Youell, Gt. Yarmouth. GB. 1844.*

LITTLE ALICE. Double. Red/White. Tube. Scarlet. Sepals. Scarlet. Corolla. White. GC. P1554 2/12/1871 Neat Minature growth. Very free. Small foliage. GC. Vol. 26 1886 RHS Trials at Chiswick "Neat" HC. Cat. P74 1882, 1885. *Bland, E. Fordham GB. 1870.*

LITTLE BOBBY. Double. Red/Purple. Tube. Red. Sepals. Red. Corolla. Rich mauve. P79 HC. Cat. 1882. First double fuchsia possessing that highly rich mauve colour of Mr. Banks varieties. Very Dwarf. Free Bloomer. *Bland, E. Fordham. GB. 1874.*

LITTLE BO PEEP. Single. Red/Purple. Tube. Scarlet. Rather small. ⅜" long. Sepals. Scarlet. Spreading ⅞" long. Corolla. Violet Purple, red at base. Pcxvi Vol III PofRHS 1872. Fuchsia Trial at Chiswick. Dwarf habit. Rather small-⅝". Moderately expanded. GC. P515 25/7/1857 Listed by H. Walton, Burnley. GC. P210 28/3/1857 Intro. by E.G. Henderson. St. Johns Wood. *Banks, E. Deal. GB. 1857.*

LITTLE DORRIT. Single. Red/Purple. Tube. Red. Sepals. Red. (Violet crimson). Reflexed. Corolla. Blue (Purple). Broadly Expanded. Dwarf. Dense habit. Free. Abundant bloomer. Vol P3 JofRHS 1863 Fuchsia Trials at Chiswick awarded **. GC. P426 12/5/1860 Listed by F. Godwin, Sheffield. GC. P165 26/2/1859 Intro. by E.G. Henderson, St. Johns Wood. *Banks, E. Deal. GB. 1859.*

LITTLE GEM. Single. Red/Purple. Tube. Glossy Pink. Sepals. Glossy Pink. (Red). Corolla. Cobalt Blue. (Purple). P115 4th. Ed. by Porcher 1874. "Not in the first rank". GC. P452 6/4/1872 Intro. by E.G. Henderson. *Henderson, E.G. St. Johns Wood. GB. 1872.*

LITTLE HARRY (a). Single. Red/Purple. Tube. Scarlet. Sepals. Scarlet. Corolla. Mauve Lavender. HC. Cat. 1882. *Bland, E. Fordham. GB. 1870.*

LITTLE HARRY (b). Double. Red/White. Tube. Scarlet. Sepals. Scarlet. Corolla. White. Very dwarf growth. Free and profuse bloomer. Requires no stakes. Unsurpassable for bedding. JF. Cat. 1885. NK. NK. *GB.* NK.

LITTLE TREASURE. Single. Red/Purple. Tube. Red. Sepals. Red. Reflexed. Corolla. Purple. Expanded. Small flowers. Vol. P3 J of RHS 1863 Fuchsia Trials at Chiswick. *Fraser. Edinburgh. GB. 1863.*

LITTRÉ Single. Red/Purple. Tube. Soft rose. Short. Sepals. Soft rose. Large and elegantly recurved. Corolla. Dark Violet, whitish at base. Beautifully formed flower. Named after a French lexicographer and Philospher (1801-81). B. Cat. 1879, 1880, 1881, 1882, 1883, 1888, 1889, 1892, 1893. *Lemoine. Nancy. France. 1879.*

LIZZIE HEXHAM. Single. Red/Purple. Tube. Crimson. Sepals. Crimson. Recurved. Corolla. Plum almost Black. Cup or Bell shaped. Fades to Maroon crimson. CG. P506 19/12/1865. GC. P55 19/1/1867 Review by H. Cannell. P115 4th Ed. by Porcher 1874. GC. P382 28/4/1866 Like "Guiding Star". B. Cat. 1870. GC. P382 18/4/1866 Intro. by E.G. Henderson, St. Johns Wood. *Banks, E. Deal. GB. 1866.*

LOAD ME WELL. Single. Red/Purple. Tube. Red. Sepals. Red. Corolla. Purple. G. 6/9/1884 Exhibited by G. Tucker at Trowbridge Hort. Scty Show. 2nd. GC. Vol 24 P277 28/8/1885 Exhibited by G. Tucker Trowbridge Hort. Scty Show 2nd 4 pot class. NK. NK. *GB.* NK.

LOCH KATRINE. ND. ND/ND. Tube. ND. Sepals. ND. Corolla. ND. GC. P778 23/10/1858 Listed by H. Walton, Burnley. NK. NK. *GB. 1858.*

LOGANII. Single. ND. Tube. ND. Sepals. ND. Corolla. ND. P25 1849 Annals of Horticulture "Best Varieties". NK. NK. *GB.* NK.

LOHENGRIN. Double. Red/White. Tube. Carmine Red. Long 15mms. Sepals. Carmine red. Large. Reflexed. Corolla. Greyish White, splashed rose. Very full. Pedicel 50 mms. P128 4th. Ed. by Porcher 1874. *Twrdy. Brno. Austria. 1873.*

LOIE FULLER. Double. Red/Purple. Tube. Carmine. Sepals. Carmine. Reflexed. Corolla. Mauve splashed carmine pink. Corolla spreads out like a crinoline. Large. Full. L. Cat. 1909. *Lemoine. Nancy. France. 1909.*

LONDON RIVAL. Single. Red/Purple. Tube. Dark purplish vermillion. Sepals. Dark purplish vermillion. Reflexed. Corolla. Bright crimson purple. Long. GC. P487 15/7/1843 H.S. Show 12/7/1843. Pretty good after the manner of "Standishii". GC. P66 1/2/1845 Listed by Millers, Ramsgate. GC. P177 17/2/1844 Intro. by G. Smith. *Smith, G. Islington. GB. 1844.*

LONGIFLORA ELEGANS. Single. Red/Purple. Tube. Cerise Red. 3.5cms long. Thin. Sepals. Cerise red. Divergent. Corolla. Reddish Violet. GC. P668 11/10/1841 Exhibited at RHS of Cornwall Show. GC. 8/5/1841 Listed by James May of Edmonton. *May. W. Bedale. GB. 1841.*

LONGIFLORA HYBRIDA. Single. Red/Red. Tube. Red. Thin. 5 cms. Sepals. Dull Red. Spreading. Raised up. Corolla. Dull red. Leaves 5cms x 3 cms green tinted violet with a whitish overlay. GC. P98 17/2/1844 Listed by Youells, Gt. Yarmouth. GC. P112 17/2/1844 & P66 1/2/1845 Listed by Millers, *Ramsgate. Standish, Bagshot. GB. 1843.*

LONGIFLORA SPLENDENS. Single. Red/Purple. Tube. Red. Long. Sepals. Red. (Coral Scarlet). Horizontal turned at tips. Corolla. Bluish Purple. GC. P630 25/9/1841 One of the best of the Chilean varieties. P192 Vol 3 Floral Cabinet Seed parent of "St. Clare". HC. Cat. 1882 etc. GC. P289 29/4/1841 Listed by H. Low. *Doubleday, H. Epping. GB. 1840?*

LONGFELLOW. Single. Red/Purple. Tube. Rich deep scarlet. Sepals. Rich deep scarlet. Well recurved. Corolla. Intense violet. Slightly expanded. Vol. P3 JofRHS 1863 Fuchsia Trial at Chiswick "A brightly coloured sort". GC. P594 30/6/1860 Listed by F. Godwin, Sheffield. GC. P215 10/3/1860 Intro. by E.G. Henderson, St. Johns Wood. *Banks, E. Deal. GB. 1860.*

LONGIPES. Single. Red/Purple. Tube. Flesh. Sepals. Rose tipped green. Corolla. Lilac. The flower is regular, but is less than 10mms long. The petals are on filaments and longer than the sepals. GC. P545 30/8/1851 Listed by G. Smith, Islington. App. to RH. 1851 by Porcher. *Meillez, Lille. France. 1851.*

L'OPULENT. Single. Red/Red. Tube. Red. Sepals. Red. Reflexed. Corolla. Carmine red. Very vigourous and floriferous. L. Cat. 1892. JF. Cat. 1892. *Hoste. France 1891.*

LORD ARDILAUN. Single. Red/Red. Tube. Rich crimson scarlet. 2" long. Sepals. Rich crimson scarlet. Corolla. ND. Flowers are in clusters. GC.

108

P659 23/5/1885 Intro. by B&S Williams. *Williams B. GB. 1885.*

LORD ASHLEY. Single. Red/Purple. Tube. Reddish Purple. Very thick. Sepals. Reddish purple. Green tips. Large. Corolla. Violet red. 2nd. Ed. by Porcher 1848. GC. P162 14/3/1864 & P184 13/3/1847 Listed by Millers, Ramsgate. GC. P234 11/4/1846 Listed By A. J. Stewart, Windsor. GC. P254 19/4/1845 Intro. by J. Smith, Dalston. *Smith, J, Dalston. GB. 1845.*

LORD BEACONSFIELD. GC. P73 17/7/1875. See Earl of Beaconsfield.

LORD BYRON. Single. Red/Purple. Tube. Bright crimson. Sepals. Bright crimson. Well recurved. Corolla. Black. (Dark Purple). Large. Open. Bell Shaped. Fine habit. B. Cat. 1877, 1878, 1879. BSW. Cat. 1878. Laings Cat. 1890. HC. Cat. 1882, 1885. NK. NK. *GB. 1876.*

LORD CALTHORPE. Double. Red/Purple. Tube. Red. Sepals. Red. Corolla. Purple. Floral World and Garden Guide P4 Jan. 1870. NK. NK. *GB. NK.*

LORD CLYDE. Double. Red/Pink. Tube. Glossy Scarlet. Sepals. Glossy Scarlet. Perfectly reflexed. Corolla. Rosy Pink flaked with Broad stripes of Violet Purple. P295 RH. 1887 Grown as a standard at Twickel. Illustrated in Flore des Serres Vol 8, 1858. etc. GC. P259 26/3/1859 Intro. by Youells, Gt. Yarmouth. *Youell, Gt. Yarmouth GB. 1859.*

LORD DERBY. Single. Red/Purple. Tube. Brilliant red. (Bright crimson). Sepals. Brilliant red.(Bright crimson). Very big. Recurved. Corolla. Violet with red overtones. (Bright blue occasionally striped light pink). Good shape. Bell shaped. Large. See "Guardsman" P110 4th. Ed by Porcher 1874. B. Cat. 1870. *Banks, E. Deal. GB. 1868.*

LORD ELCHO. Single. Red/Purple. Tube. Bright crimson. Short. Sepals. Bright Crimson. Very long. Large. Reflex round. Corolla. Blue Violet veined red. Not Expanding. Larger and less expanding than "Prince Leopold". GC. P689 28/7/1860 Awarded FCC by Hort. Scty. GC. P110 4th Ed. by Porcher 1874. Vol. 1 JofRHS 1860 P262 Vol 2 1870 J of RHS etc. etc. *Banks, E. Deal. GB. 1861.*

LORD FALMOUTH. Single. Red/Purple. Tube. Carmine Scarlet. Sepals. Carmine Scarlet. Corolla. Rich Violet Blue. Perfect shape and great substance. Free bloomer. HC. Cat. 1882, 1885. GO. "Select" 1880 - 1886. B. Cat. 1876, 1877, 1878. *Banks, E. Deal. GB. 1876.*

LORD HERSHELL. Single. Red/Red. Tube. Rose. Sepals. Rose. Corolla. Bronzy Scarlet. Grand habit. JF. Cat. 1893. NK. NK. *GB. 1893.*

LORD HILL. Single. Red/Purple. Tube. Dark red. Sepals. Dark red. Corolla. Lilac crimson. 2nd. Ed. by Porcher 1848. GC. P185 20/3/1847 2nd in seedling prize RBS 1846. GC. P184 Listed by Millers, Ramsgate. GC. P185 20/3/1847 Intro. by Gaines, Battersea. GC. P445 8/7/1847 Exhibited at RBS 1847. *Gaines, Battersea. GB. 1846.*

LORD HOLMESDALE. Single. Red/Purple. Tube. Carmine. Sepals. Carmine. Recurved. Corolla. Rich plum purple. GC. P478 12/5/1866 Intro. by G. Fry. *Fry, G. Lee GB. 1866.*

LORD JOHN RUSSELL. Single. Red/Purple. Tube. Red. Sepals. Red. Corolla. Violet. Expanded. Similar to "Prince Arthur".Vol P1 JofRHS 1860 P262/3 Floral C'tee - no award. *Banks, E. Deal. GB. 1860.*

LORD LEWISHAM. Single. ND/ND. Tube. ND. Sepals. ND. Corolla. ND. GC. P250 17/4/1847 Listed by J. Hally, Blackheath. GC. P234 16/4/1846. Listed by A.J. Stewart, Salthill Nurseries, Windsor. *Meade. GB. NK.*

LORD LYONS. Double. Red/Purple. Tube. Red. (Coral red). Sepals. Red (Coral red). Reflexing. Corolla. Deep Violet. (Plum Coloured). (Violet). Very large. Laings Cat. 1890 B. Cat 1889, 1892, 1893. BSW. Cat. 1897. NK. NK. NK. NK.

LORD MACAULEY. Single. Red/Purple. Tube. Red. Sepals. Red. Recurved. (Reflexed). Corolla. Deep violet. (Purple). Spreading. GC. P594 30/6/1860 Listed by F. Godwin, Sheffield. Vol 3(P3) JofRHS 1863 Fuchsia Trial at Chiswick 1862. etc. GC. P215 10/3/1860 Intro. by E.G. Henderson, St. Johns Wood. *Banks, E. Deal. GB. 1860.*

LORD NELSON (a). Single. White/ND. Tube. White. Sepals. White. Corolla. ND. GC. P184 13/3/1847 & P250 20/4/1847 Listed by W. Miller, Ramsgate. *Fairbeard. GB. 1846.*

LORD NELSON (b) Single. Red/Red. Tube. Carmine rose shaded orange. Large. Sepals. Pink Vermillion. Very large and spread out. Corolla. Bright amarinth crimson. Style rose. Stigma Brownish. App. to RH. 1851 by Porcher. RH. P168 1857. GC. P145 9/3/1850 Listed by W. Rumley, Richmond. etc. etc. GC. P49 27/1/1849 & P497 11/8/1849 Intro. by G. Smith. *Smith, G. Islington. GB. 1849.*

LORD OF THE ISLES.(a) Single. ND/ND. Tube. ND. Tube. ND. Corolla. ND. GC. P207 27/3/1852 & P275 1/5/1852 Listed by H. Walton, Burnley. GC. P290 10/5/1851 Intro. by E.G. Henderson, St. Johns Wood. *Henderson E.G. St.Johns Wood. GB. 1851.*

LORD OF THE ISLES.(b). Double. Red/Purple. Tube. Scarlet. Sepals. Scarlet. Spreading. Corolla. Dark Purple. P1 JofRHS P78 Floral C'tee. Inferior flower. Irregular and confused. Vol P3 JofRHS P90 1863.Fuchsia Trial at Chiswick. Habit branching and bushy. GC. P359 21/4/1860 Intro. by G. Wheeler, Warminster. *Wheeler, G. Warminster GB. 1860.*

LORD OF THE MANOR. Double. ND/ND. Tube. ND. Sepals. ND. Completely reflexed. Corolla. ND. 3 or 4 flowers at each joint. Immense size. GC. P338 15/4/1865 Listed by W. Rumley, Richmond. GC. P312 2/4/1864 Intro. by G. Fry, Manor Nurseries, Lee. *Fry, G. Lee. GB. 1864.*

LORD PALMERSTON. ND. ND/ND. Tube. ND. Sepals. ND. Corolla. ND. GC. P553 28/7/1857 Listed by H. Walton, Burnley. NK. NK. *GB. 1857.*

LORD RAGLAN. ND. ND/ND. Tube. ND. Sepals. ND. Corolla. ND. GC. P82 9/2/1856 Intro. by G. Smith, Islington. *Banks, E. Deal. GB. 1856.*

LORD ROBERTS. Double. Red/Purple. Tube. Carmine Red. Sepals. Carmine red. Very Broad. Horizontal. Corolla. Indigo. Enormous. L. Cat. 1909. *Lemoine. Nancy. France. 1909.*

LORD SANDON. Single Red/Purple. Tube. Bright crimson. Sepals. Bright crimson. Horizontal. Corolla. Purple. GC. P162 14/3/1846 & P184 13/3/1847 Listed by W. Miller, Ramsgate. GC. P238 12/4/1845. Intro. by Rogers, Uttoxeter.*Rogers, Uttoxeter GB. 1845.*

LORD STANLEY. Single. Red/Purple. Tube. Bright red. Sepals. Bright red. Recurved. Corolla. Mauve. GC. P488 9/4/1870 by H. Cannell. Floral World and Gardeners Guide Page 4 1870. *Banks, E. Deal. GB. 1870.*

LORD WARDEN. Single. Red/Purple. Tube. Bright Crimson. Short. Thick. Sepals. Bright crimson. Large. Recurved. Corolla. Violet blue, splashed red. Very much expanded. Similar to "Lord Elcho" in formation and colour of flower. P110 4th. Ed by Porcher 1874. GC. P55 19/1/1867 Review by H. Cannell. Vol. P3 JofRHS 1863 Report on Fuchsia Trials. Awarded ***. etc. *Banks, E. Deal. GB. 1862.*

LORD WOLSELEY. Single. Red/Purple. Tube. Vinous red. Sepals. Vinous red. Broad. Well reflexed. Corolla. Soft rosy crimson, veined red, margined bluish purple. Well expanded. GC. P824 27/6/1885 Fuchsia Trials at Chiswick "Best in its class". HC. Cat. 1885, 1890, 1891, 1896. GC. P495 21/4/1883. Sent out after death of G. Smith. *Smith, G. Islington. GB. 1883.*

LOTHAIR (a). Double Red/Purple. Tube. Red. Sepals. Red. Corolla Purple. Fine Large flowered. HC. Cat 1885, 1890. NK. NK. NK. NK.

LOTHAIR. Double. Red/Purple. Tube. Carmine red. Short. Sepals. Carmine red. Completely recurved. Corolla. Lavender purple, shaded rose at base. Large. B. Cat. 1901. *Bull, W. Chelsea. GB. 1900.*

LOTTIE. Single. White/Red. Tube. Creamy delicate blush pink. Sepals. Pink. Corolla. Bright carmine. Very pleasing flower of fine shape. Excellent grower. JF. Cat. 1890. Laings Cat. 1890. L. Cat. 1892. B. Cat. 1889 Intro. by W. Bull. *Lye, J. Market Lavington. GB. 1889.*

LOUDONII. Single. Red/Red. Tube. Dark cerise. Thin. Sepals. Dark cerise. Divergent. Corolla. Cerise. GC. P383 June 1842 Listed by Youells, Gt. Yarmouth. GC. P112 17/2/1844 Listed by Millers, Ramsgate. 2nd. Ed. by Porcher 1848. NK. NK. *GB. NK.*

LOUISA. Single. Red/Purple. Tube. Dull cerise. Sepals. Dull cerise. Half up. Corolla. Violet reddish vermillion. 2nd. Ed. by Porcher 1848. GC. P146 8/3/1845 Listed by Youells, Gt. Yarmouth. NK. NK. *GB. 1844.*

LOUISA BALFOUR. Single. White/NK. Tube. White. Sepals. White. Corolla. ND. "A light seedling of my own". Used as a seed parent. P342 Vol 24 J. of RHS. *Lye, J. Market Lavington. GB. NK.*

LOUISA LELANDAIS. Single. ND/ND. Tube. ND. Sepals. ND. Corolla. ND. GC. P211 26/3/1853 Listed by W. Rumley, Richmond. NK. NK NK. *1852.*

LOUIS BERGER. See M. Louis Berger.

LOUIS DE SMET. Single. Red/Purple. Tube. Red. Sepals. Red. Corolla. Purple. Not in the first selection. P115 4th. Ed. by Porcher 1874. *Cornelissen, Arras. Belgium. 1867.*

LOUISE Single. Red/White. Tube. Bright crimson. Sepals. Bright crimson. Large. Completely reflexed. Corolla. White, veined deep rose. B. Cat. 1901. Intro. by W. Bull, Chelsea. *Bull, W. Chelsea. GB. 1900.*

LOUIS FAUÇON. Double. Red/Purple. Tube. Pinky red. Sepals. Pinky red. Corolla. Wine red with violet. (Rich plum shaded violet). Enormous. Full. (Large like "Phenomenal") B. Cat. 1892. L. Cat. 1892. *Rozain, Lyons. France. 1892.*

LOUIS FIGUIER. Double. Red/Purple. Tube. Scarlet. Sepals. Scarlet. Corolla. Lilac Mauve. Large. Globular. Named after a French writer (1819-94). JF. Cat. 1898. NK. NK. *France. 1897.*

LOUISE MEILLEZ Single. Pink/Red. Tube. Pale rose. Sepals. Pale Rose. Green tips. Corolla. Carmine. Good flower, opens perfectly. App. to RH. 1851 by Porcher. GC. P548 30/8/1851 Listed by G. Smith, Islington. GC. P177 20/3/1852 Listed by W. Rumley, Richmond. *Meillez. Lille. France. 1851.*

LOUIS NAPOLEON Single. Red/Purple. Tube. Crimson. Sepals. Crimson. Well reflexed. Corolla. Violet. Selected from 3,000 seedlings. To be sent out 1/4/1856, by Stewart & Neilsen, Liscard, Ches. GC. P611 15/9/1855. *Stewart & Neilsen. GB. 1856.*

LOUIS-PHILLIPE. Single. ND/ND. Tube. ND. Sepals. ND. Corolla. ND. GC. P66 1/2/1845 and P184 13/3/1847 Listed by W. Miller, Ramsgate. NK. NK. NK. NK.

LOUIS TRICON. Single. Red/Purple. Tube. Dark red. Sepals. Dark Red. Corolla. Reddish plum veined fire red. L. Cat. 1906. *Rozain. Lyons. France. 1905.*

LOUIS VAN HOUTTE. Double. Red/White. Tube. Brilliant Crimson. Long. Thin. Sepals. Brilliant crimson. Large. Reflexed round. Corolla. Pure white, striped red at base. P129 4th. Ed. by Porcher 1874. *L'Huillier. France. 1864.*

LOVELINESS (a). Single. White/ND. Tube. White. Sepals. White. Corolla. ND. GC. P545 30/8/1851 Listed by G. Smith, Islington. GC. P207 27/3/1852 Listed by H. Walton, Burnley. GC. P209 5/4/1851 Intro. by C. Turner, Slough. *Banks, E. Deal. GB. 1851.*

LOVELINESS (b) Single. White/Purple. Tube. Creamy White. Sepals. Pale blush. Long. Stout. Corolla. Pale Violet Pink, margined carmine. GO. 1889. HC. Cat. 1890. JF. Cat. 1888. Laings. Cat. 1890. B. Cat. 1888. BSW. Cat. 1888. *Lye, J. Market Lavington. GB. 1888.*

LOVELY. Single. White/Red. Tube. Pure white. Sepals. Pure white. Corolla. Brilliant carmine, slightly shaded magenta. JF. Cat. 1888. Laings Cat. 1890. B. Cat. 1888. *Lye, J. Market Lavington. GB. 1887.*

LOWEII. Single. Red/Purple. Tube. Red. Sepals. Red. Corolla. Purple. Raised by H. Lowe from seed sent from Port Famine. See F. Discolour. GC. P560 3/11/1883. *Lowe. H. GB. 1830.*

LOWERYII. Single. Red/Purple. Tube. Crimson. (Bright scarlet). Sepals. Crimson. (Bright scarlet). (Coral). Corolla. Blue. (Deep purple). Dwarf. Long. Distinct. Small leaves, slender growing. GC. P359 17/8/1844 Noted at Standish's Nursery. GC. P559 17/8/1843 Improvement on "Formosa Elegans". GC. P554 12/8/1843 Intro. by J. Hancock, Durham. *Lowery. GB. 1843?*

LUCILLE LEMOINIER. ND. ND/ND. Tube. ND. Sepals. ND. Corolla. ND. RH. P311 1889. Select by E.A. Carrière. *Boucharlet, Lyons. France. 1880.*

LUCIEN DANIEL. Double. Red/Purple. Tube. Bright red. Sepals. Bright red. Short. Corolla. Mauve. Full. L. Cat. 1906. *Lemoine. Nancy. France. 1904.*

LUCIENNE BREVAL. Double. Red/White. Tube. Crimson red. Sepals. Crimson. Rolled back. Corolla. Milk White. Good habit. Very floriferous. Large. L. Cat. 1912. *Lemoine. Nancy. France. 1912.*

LUCIEN DESMOULINS. Double. Red/White. Tube. Red. Sepals. Red. Well reflexed. Twisted. Corolla. Pure white, shaded pink. Rosette type flowers. Compact. Well open. Long. JF. Cat. 1907. L. Cat. 1906. *Lemoine. Nancy. France. 1906.*

LUCIUS. Single. Red/White. Tube. Crimson. Sepals. Crimson. Reflexed. Corolla. White veined rose. Large. B. Cat. 1898, 1899, 1901. GC. Vol. 21 1/5/1897 Intro. by W. Bull. *Bull, W. Chelsea. GB. 1897.*

LUC-OLIVER MERSON. Double. Red/White. Tube. Carmine red. Sepals. Carmine red. Spread out. Reflexed. Corolla. White marked pink. Enormous. Full. L. Cat. 1910. *Lemoine. Nancy. France. 1910.*

LUCREZIA BORGIA. Single. Red/Purple. Tube. Bright red. Short. Thick. Sepals. Bright red. Reflex right back to tube. Corolla. Blue violet. Streaked red and violet. (Purple nicely striped). Vol. 1 JofRHS 1861 FCC. 6/7/1864. HC. Cat. 1882, 1885. GC. P653 9/7/1864 RBS Show awarded Certificate. P110

4th Ed. by Porcher 1874. Intro. by E.G. Henderson, St. Johns Wood. *Banks, E. Deal. GB. 1864.*

LUCY MILLS. Single. White/Pink. Tube. White. Long. Thick. 155 mms. Sepals. White. Reflexed. Corolla. Light pink edged bright rose. (after the style of "Marginata"). P118 4th. Ed by Porcher 1874 Bright rose margined fire red. Vol. 2 1870 Vol 4. 1877 J of RHS Fuchsia Trails at Chiswick 1870 1873. No Award. GC. P382 29/4/1865 Intro. by E.G.Henderson, St. Johns Wood. *Banks, E. Deal. GB. 1865.*

LUDOVICI. Single. Red/White. Tube. Greenish white, tinted pink. Sepals. Greenish white, tinted pink. Pink tips. Large. Corolla. Scarlet red. Illustrated in "L'Instructeur Jardinier". Annals of Horticulture P25 1849. App. to RH. 1851 by Porcher. *Verschaffelt. NK. 1849.*

LUIGI CATTANEO. Double. Red/Purple. Tube. Red. Sepals. Red. Corolla. Purple. P126 4th Ed. by Porcher 1874. Not in the first selection. *Crousse France.1869.*

LURLINE. Single. Red/White. Tube. Rose. Sepals. Rose. Corolla. Pure white, margined violet. Dentated corolla. P131 4th Ed. By Porcher 1874. Not in the first selection. B. Cat. 1870, 1872, 1873. *Bull, W. Chelsea. GB. 1869*

LUSTRE. Single. White/Red. Tube. White. ⅛" long. Sepals. White (Blush) Recurved. ¾" long. Corolla. Crimson vermillion. (Vivid crimson edged pale orange). (Deep red paler at base). Compact. ⅝". P120 4th Ed. by Porcher 1874. Vol. 3 1872 Vol. 4 J of RHS. Fuchsia trials. Not free.. Inferior. B. Cat. 1870, 1872, 1873. GC. P473 Dec 1867. Intro. by W. Bull, Chelsea. GO "Select" 1880 - 1891. *Bull, W. Chelsea. GB. 1868.*

LUSTROUS (IMPROVED). Single. White/Red. Tube. White. Sepals. White. Corolla. Orange Scarlet. Larger. Bolder. More Intense. Seedling of Lustrous (?Lustre). Dobbies Cat. 1892, 1893, 1894. HC. Cat. 1885.(New) NK. NK. *GB. 1883?*

LYDIA. Single. White/Red. Tube. Pure white. Sepals. Pure white. Reflexed. Corolla. Rich carmine scarlet. GC. P74 24/1/1863 Intro. by W. Bull. Chelsea. *Bull, W. Chelsea. GB. 1863.*

LYE'S ADVANCE. Single. Red/ND. Tube. Red. Sepals. Red. Corolla. ND. GC. P653 20/9/1897. *Lye, J. Market Lavington. GB. 1897.*

LYE'S ECLIPSE. Single. White/Red.Tube. White. Sepals. White. Corolla. Cerise red. More massive than "W.H. Mould". GM. P59 2/2/1895. GC. Vol 22 1897. *Lye, J. Market Lavington. GB. 1894.*

LYE'S EXCELSIOR. Single. White/Red. Tube. Cream tinted emerald. (Creamy white). Sepals. Cream tinted emerald. (Creamy white). Corolla. Rich deep rosy magenta flushed carmine. JF. Cat. 1886 FCC Bath 2/9/1885. Laings Cat. 1890. BSW. Cat. 1888. GC. Vol. 24 1885 P277. Lye's seedlings for 1886. *Lye, J. Market Lavington. GB. 1886.*

LYE'S FAVOURITE. Single. White/Purple. Tube. White. Sepals. White. Corolla. Rich magenta. Blooms born in elegant clusters. B. Cat. 1880 1881, 1882. GC. P450 10/4/1880 Adv. by J. Lye. GC. P716 5/6/1880 Coloured Plate T396 in Floral Magazine 1880. GC. Vol 18 P215 Exhibited by J Lye. at Devizes Hort. Scty. Arabella Imp. x James Lye. *Lye, J. Market Lavington. GB. 1880.*

LYE'S OWN. Single. White/Red. Tube. White. Sepals. White. Corolla. Scarlet tinted. (Pink). GC. P389 Vol 21 1897 Noted as a bedder. JF. Cat. 1891. HC. Cat. 1890. "New" *Lye, J. Market Lavington. GB. 1890.*

LYE'S PERFECTION. Single White/Red. Tube. Cream suffused pink. Sepals. Cream suffused pink. Reflexed. Corolla. Bright carmine. GC. Vol. 24 1885 P277. JF. Cat. 1886. B. Cat. 1888. Laings Cat. 1890. FCC Bath. 2/9/1885. *Lye, J. Market Lavington. GB. 1886.*

LYE'S RIVAL. Single. Red/Purple. Tube. Red. Sepals. Red. Corolla. Violet purple. Flowers in clusters at end of shoots. B. Cat. 1883. GC. Vol 20. P307 15/9//1887 Exhibited Bath Floral Fete by J. Lye 1st 9 pot class. Laings Cat. 1890. JF. Cat. 1885. *Lye, J. Market Lavington. GB. 1883.*

LYRA. Single. Red/Purple. Tube. Crimson Short. Sepals. Crimson. Large. Broad. Elegantly reflexed. Corolla. Purple rose. (Purple mauve) Large. L. Cat. P149 1901. B. Cat. 1901. *Bull, W. Chelsea. GB. 1901.*

LYSIAS. Double. Red/Purple. Tube. Bright red. Sepals. Bright red. Broad. Shell shaped. Extended. Corolla. Rosy purple. Well expanded. B. Cat. 1901. *Bull, W. Chelsea. GB. 1900.*

MABEL. Single. White/ND. Tube. White. Sepals. White. Corolla. ND. G. 6/9/1884 Exhibited at Trowbridge Hort.Scty. Show 20/8/1884 by Pocock 2nd. GC. Vol. 20 P280 1/9/1883 Exhibited at

Trowbridge Hort.Scty. Show by Pocock-3rd in 6" pot class. NK. NK. *GB*. NK.

MACBETH. Single. Red/Purple. Tube. Bright purple red. Long. 15mms. Sepals. Bright purple red. Large. Totally reflexed. Corolla. Violet blue, veined purple. Large petals. 3rd Ed. by Porcher 1858. GC. P401 24/6/1854 Listed by H. Walton, Burnley. GC. P407 16/6/1855 Exhibited at RBS Show. GC. P375 31/5/1856 Exhibited as a 7' high pyramid at Crystal Palace by Boussie. *Banks, E. Deal. GB. 1854.*

MACMAHON. Double. Red/Purple. Tube. Bright crimson. Short. Thick. Sepals. Bright crimson. Large. Horizontal. Points arched. Corolla. Bluish Violet washed red. Spread out though a little short. Pedicel 40mm. Very full. First class variety. P123 4th Ed. by Porcher 1874. Named after French Marshall & President of France 1873-9. *Lemoine. Nancy. France. 1872.*

MACNABIANA. Single. ND/ND. Tube. ND. Sepals. ND. Corolla. ND. GC. P393 June 1842 Listed by Youells, Gt. Yarmouth. GC. P66 1/2/1845 Listed by Millers, Ramsgate. NK. NK *GB. 1841?*

MACROSTEMMA. Single. Red/Purple. Tube. Red. Sepals. Red. Corolla. Purple. Loddiges Botanical Cabinet Vol XI P1062 1825. Flowered in 1824. Coloured illustration in Maunds Botanic Garden Vol 10 Plate 935 1830. From Lima. "Flora Peruviana". GC. P537 21/7/1841 Will survive in open ground.

MACROSTEMMA VARIEGATA. Single. Red/Purple. Tube. ND. Sepals. ND. Corolla. ND. G. Vol 33. P178 25/8/1888 The above is like Gracilis Variegata. Both being grown in No. 4 House at Kew. NK. NK. *GB*. NK.

MACROSTEMMA Var.RECURVATA. Single. Red/Purple. Tube. ND. Sepals. ND. Corolla. ND. Raised by Mr.Niven. Glasnevin Botanic Garden, Dublin. Coloured illustration Marnocks Florists Magazine P137 11/1836. *Niven, Dublin. Ireland. 1834?*

MACULATA SUPERBA. Single. ND/ND. Tube. ND. Sepals. ND. Corolla. ND. GC. P531 11/8/1855 Listed by Joseph Courcha. Beautiful variegated foliage. NK. NK. *GB. 1855.*

MADAME AMBROISE VERSCHAFFELT. Double. Red/Pink. Tube. Bright crimson. (Purplish red). Thin. Sepals. Bright crimson. (Purplish red). Large. Reflexed. Corolla. Clear rose veined carmine.

Each petal scalloped at base. (Pure white striped bright rose). 4th Ed. by Porcher 1874. B. Cat. 1870. *Cornelissen. Arras. Belgium. 1868.*

MADAME A. ROZAIN. Double. Red/Pink. Tube. Red. Sepals. Red. Corolla. Flesh pink veined bright crimson. Roz. Cat. 1897, 1898. L. Cat. 1901. Fuchsiaphile Vol 1.2/3. *Rozain. Lyons. France. 1895.*

MADAME AUBERGE. ND. ND/ND. Tube. ND. Sepals. ND. Corolla. ND. GC. P146 10/3/1855 Listed by W. Rumley, Richmond. "Best fuchsias of 1854". NK. NK. NK. 1854.

MADAME AUBIN. Single. Pink/Red. Tube. Soft pink. Sepals. Soft pink. Thick. Bulbous. Corolla. Magenta rose, stained orange at base. RH. P311 1889 "Select" by E.A. Carrière. HC. Cat. P89 1885 Large fine Orange yellow flowers. *Aubin, R. Bagnolet. France. 1883?*

MADAME BOUCHARLET. Double. Red/Purple. Tube. Red. Sepals. Red. Corolla. Purple. P126 4th. Ed. by Porcher 1874. Not in the first selection. *Lemoine. Nancy. France. 1864.*

MADAME BRAVY. Single. Red/Red. Tube. Bright Pink. Thick. Sepals. Bright pink. Reflexed. Corolla. Cerise red. 2nd Ed. by Porcher 1848. GC. P184 13/3/1847 Listed by Miller, Ramsgate. GC. P505 31/7/1847 Listed by G. Smith, Islington. GC. P232 1/4/1848 & P256 21/4/1849 Listed by R. Cooper, Croydon. GC. P256 16/4/1848 Listed by G. Rogers, Uttoxeter. GC. P274 5/5/1849 Listed by H. Walton, Burnley. GC. P226 13/4/1850 Listed by Poole Nurseries. *Salter, J. Versailles. France. 1846.*

MADAME BRUANT (a). Double. Red/Purple. Tube. Bright red. Sepals. Bright red. Corolla. Lilac mauve, maculated and veined rose. L. Cat. 1901. B. Cat. 1893-1895. *Bruant. Poitiers. France. 1893.*

MADAME BRUANT (b). Single. 6Red/Purple. Tube. Crimson. Very short. Sepals. Crimson. Reflexed round. Corolla. Violet Blue, shaded red.(Violet mauve). Very expanded. Dwarf bush. Branching. P110 4th Ed. by Porcher. 1874. B. Cat. 1870. *Lemoine. Nancy. France. 1867.*

MADAME CAMBIER. Double. Red/White. Tube. Red. Sepals. Red. Corolla. White. P131 4th Ed. by Porcher 1874 Not in the first selection. *Cornelissen, Arras. Belgium 1866.*

MADAME CARNOT. Double. Red/White. Tube. Crimson. Short. Sepals. Crimson. (Reddish carmine). Corolla. White, veined and suffused pink. (Pale flesh veined carmine). GC. Vol.21 P471 1/5/1897 Listed by H.J. Jones, Lower Sydenham. G.C. P198 11/9/1897 Seen at Bull's nursery. L. Cat. 1901. B. Cat. 1895. *Lemoine. Nancy. France. 1895.*

MADAME CORNELISSEN. Double. Red/White. Tube. Red. Sepals. Red. Reflexed. Corolla. White. Vol. P3 J of RHS P91 1863 Fuchsias Grown for trial at Chiswick. A free habited variety, with very handsome flowers, the sepals are red and reflexed, the corolla double, white and when the plants are young and when well grown full. Compact and effective, but all the double flowered varieties with white corollas are liable to become single or to have the petaloid parts confused when they are old or ill grown. In its best state, this is a very handsome fuchsia. Awarded ***. P131 4th Ed. by Porcher 1874 Not in the first selection. Vigorous bush but flowers are semi double. Excellent in the open ground. GC. P309 6/4/1861 & P771 24/8/1861 Listed by H. Walton, Burnley. GC. P594 29/6/1861 Listed by Godwin & Padman, Sheffield. SG. P459 1866 "Recommended". RH. P295 1887. Grown as a standard at Twickel. GC. Vol. 20 P289 1/9/1883 Exhibited at Trowbridge Hort. Scty Show by Pocock. 3rd. GC. P1103 15/12/1860 Intro. by E.G. Henderson, St. Johns Wood. *Cornelissen, Arras. Belgium 1860.*

MADAME DEPROOST. Single. Red/White. Tube. Crimson. Sepals. Crimson. Corolla. Blush white. Large. Beautifully formed. P131 4th Ed. by Porcher 1874. Not in the first selection. B. Cat. 1870. *Cornelissen, Arras. Belgium. 1867.*

MADAME DIEULAFOY. Single. White/Pink. Tube. White. Long. Sepals. White. Large. Recurved. Corolla. Rose, brightening at the margin. Good Habit. Floriferous. L. Cat. 1892. B. Cat. 1889. *Lemoine. Nancy. France. 1889.*

MADAME EMILE CHATÉ. Single. White/Red. Tube. Greenish White. Sepals. Greenish White. Large. Reflexed back. Corolla. Carmine rose, margined fire red. Bell shaped. Pedicel 50/60 mms. Vigorous dwarf bush. Floriferous. P119 4th Ed. by Porcher 1874. *Chaté. NK. France. 1873.*

MADAME GALLI-MARIÉ. Double. Red/White. Tube. Rosy red. Sepals. Rosy red. Large. Long. Recurved. Corolla. Alabaster White. Large. Full double. Vol 6 J of RHS 1880 FCC. GO. P109 1881 Good size. Free flowering. B. Cat. 1879-1893. *Lemoine. Nancy. France. 1879.*

MADAME GUIGNARD. Single. Red/White. Tube. Bright Carmine. Sepals. Bright Carmine. Corolla. White veined scarlet. Fine. JF. Cat. 1892. *Rozain. Lyons. France. 1891.*

MADAME HAQUIN. Single. Pink/Red. Tube. Flesh. Sepals. Rose. Green tips. Corolla. Lilac carmine with a touch of orange. Very Large flowers. App. to RH. 1851 by Porcher. *Meillez. Lille. France. 1851.*

MADAME IRELAND. Single. ND/ND. Tube. ND. Sepals. ND. Corolla. ND. GC. P241 20/4/1850 Listed by W. Rendle, Plymouth. NK. NK. *GB. 1850.*

MADAME JULES CHRÉTIEN. Double. Red/White. Tube. Reddish crimson. Short. Sepals. Reddish crimson. Well reflexed. Corolla. Snowy white, veined and flaked carmine. GO. Select 1885-1891. RH. P311 "Select" by E.A. Carrière. GC. Vol 25 P389 27/3/1886 Listed by Daniel Bros, Norwich. B. Cat. 1882-1893. HC. Cat. 1885-1898. *Boucharlet, Lyons. France. 1891.*

MADAME JULES MÉNOREAU. Single. Red/Purple. Tube. Red. Sepals. Red. Corolla. Purple. P115 4th Ed. by Porcher 1874. Not in the first selection. *Lemoine. Nancy. France. 1867.*

MADAME KARL SCHICKLER. Single. Red/White. Tube. Carmine red. Sepals. Carmine red. Large. Reflexed. Corolla. White, washed lilac rose. Very full. Floriferous. 1st class because it is an intermediate between a pure white corolla and that with a clear violet. Pedicel 50mms. Dark Green foliage. P129 4th Ed. by Porcher 1874. *Twrdy, Brno. Austria 1872.*

MADAME LEBOIS. Single. Red/Red. Tube. Carmine rose. Sepals. Carmine rose. Green tips. Extended. Corolla. Carmine. Enormous. GC. P545 30/8/1851 Listed by G. Smith, Islington. GC. P258 17/4/1852 Listed by W. Rumley, Richmond. App. to RH. 1851 by Porcher. *Meillez, Lille. France. 1851.*

MADAME LEGRELLE D'HONIS. ND. ND/ND. Tube. ND. Sepals. ND. Corolla. ND. GC. P1015 23/10/1864 Out in 1864. Seen on visit to nursery of B&S Williams. NK. NK. NK. *1864.*

MADAME LELANDAIS. Single. Red/Pink. Tube. Red. Sepals. Red, striped white. Large. Spreading. Corolla. Bright rose. App. to RH. 1851 by Porcher. *Corbell. France. 1850.*

MADAME LEMOINE. Double. Red/White. Tube. Carmine rose. Sepals. Carmine rose. Reflexed right up. Corolla. Pure white with some stripes of rose at the base. Long. Very Double. P129 4th Ed. by Porcher 1874 Pedicel 40mms. Distinguished by its vigour, and the formation and size of flower. RH. P311 1889 "Select" by E.A. Carrière. *Twrdy, Brno. Austria. 1872.*

MADAME MEILLEZ. Single. White/Purple. Tube. Yellowish. Sepals. White and pale rose. Well reflexed. Corolla. Lilac blue shaded maroon. RH. P95 1859. *Dubus, Lille. France. 1859.*

MADAME MELDERT. ND. ND/ND. Tube. ND. Sepals. ND. Corolla. ND. GC. P406 2/5/1863 Listed by Wm. Hussey, Norwich. NK. NK. NK. *1862.*

MADAME MILLET ROBINET. Single. White/Pink. Tube. White. Great length. Sepals. Greenish white. Corolla. Clear rose pink. Large. Long. L. Cat. 1892. B. Cat. 1891. *Lemoine. Nancy. France. 1889.*

MADAME PANIS. Double. Red/White. Tube. Red. Sepals. Red. Corolla. White. P131 4th Ed. by Porcher 1874. Not in the first selection. *Cornelissen, Arras. Belgium 1866.*

MADAME PATTI. Single. Red/Purple. Tube. Carmine Red. Short. Sepals. Carmine red. Large. Reflexed, round. Corolla. Violet blue shaded red. Expanded. Good variety. Named after an Italian Opera singer who appeared in London in 1861. P109 4th Ed. by Porcher 1874. *Banks, E. Deal. GB. 1863.*

MADAME PELE. Single. Pink/Red. Tube. Salmon pink. Medium. Sepals. Salmon Pink. Green tips. Large. Divergent. Corolla. Violet red. 2nd Ed. by Porcher 1848. GC. P505 31/7/1847 Listed by G. Smith, Islington. GC. P153 4/3/1848 Listed by R. Cooper, Croydon. GC. P256 16/4/1848 Listed by G. Rogers, Uttoxeter. *Salter, Versailles. France. 1846.*

MADAME PICHEREAU. Single. Red/Red. Tube. Rosy red. Large. Short. Sepals. Rosy red. Horizontal. Corolla. Vermillion red. Like a poppy. Petals thrown back poppylike. App. to RH. 1851 by Porcher. *Pichereau. France. 1850.*

MADAME ROSTAING. Double. Red/White. Tube. Scarlet. Sepals. Scarlet. Corolla. Blush white veined carmine. Large. JF. Cat. 1895. *Rozain, Lyons. France. 1894.*

MADAME ROZAIN. ND. ND/ND. Tube. ND. Sepals. ND. Corolla. ND. GC. P518 28/4/1888 Listed by Daniels of Norwich. Gartenflora P149 1888. *Rozain, Lyons. France. 1886.*

MADAME SONTAG (a). Single. White/Red. Tube. White. Short. Sepals. Waxy white. Thrown back to expose coralla. Corolla. Rich crimson. Partially exposed base of corolla clear white. GC. P545 30/8/1851 Listed by G. Smith, Islington. GC. P290 10/5/1851 Intro. by E.G. Henderson. *Henderson, E.G. St. Johns Wood. GB. 1851.*

MADAME SONTAG (b). Single. White/Red. Tube. White. Sepals. White. Corolla. Vermillion. GC. P545 30/8/1851 Listed by G. Smith, Islington. GC. P177 20/3/1852 by W. Rumley, Richmond. GC. P207 27/3/1852 Listed by H. Walton, Burnley. GC. P209 5/4/1851 Intro. by C. Turner, Slough. *Banks, E. Deal. GB. 1851.*

MADAME THIBAUT (a). Single. Red/Red. Tube. Scarlet pink. Long. Thin. Sepals. Scarlet pink. Green tips. Sepals only open a little. Corolla. Vermillion red. GC. P201 25/3/1848 Listed by W. Rumley, Richmond. 2nd.Ed. by Porcher 1848. *Salter, J. Versailles. France. 1847.*

MADAME THIBAUT (b). Double. Red/White. Tube. Carmine. Sepals. Carmine. Recurved. Corolla. Carmine bordered white. (White margined rose). (Rose margined white) B. Cat. 1888-1893. GC. Vol.26 1886 Fuchsias at Chiswick 31/7/1886. (Single by Lemoine) Large trusses at end of shoots. GC. Vol 25 P386 27/3/1886 Listed by Daniel Bros, Norwich. Laings Cat. 1890 Single. BSW. Cat. 1897. *Lemoine. Nancy. France. 1885.*

MADAME TREBELLI.(See MDLLE TREBELLI)

MADAME VERGEOT. ND. Red/Red. Tube. Rose. Sepals. Rose. Corolla. Scarlet. JF. Cat. 1898. *Berger, L.M. Bagnolet. France. 1895.*

MADAME WALNER. Single. ND/ND. Tube. ND. Sepals. ND. Corolla. ND. GC. P216 27/3/1847 Listed by R. Cooper, Croydon. NK. NK NK. NK.

M. ADRIEN CORRET. Double. ND/ND. Tube. ND. Sepals. ND. Corolla. ND. L. Cat. 1892. *Hoste. France. 1888.*

MADONNA. Single. White/Red. Tube. Flesh. (White). Green tips. Sepals. Flesh. (White). Horizontal. Corolla. Scarlet. (Pinky red). P225 Floricultural Cabinet Vol XI 1843. RH. P24 1846. GC. P98 17/2/1844 & P146 8/3/1845 Listed by Youells as their raising. GC. P66 1/2/1845 Listed by Millers, Ramsgate. *Harrison, Dereham. GB. 1843.*

MAGICIAN. Single. ND/ND. Tube. ND. Rather large. Sepals. ND. Corolla. ND. More highly coloured than "Magnificent". See "Rudolphus". All are similar. GC. P112 17/2/1844 & GC. P66 1/2/1845 Listed by Millers, Ramsgate. *Bell, W. Thirsk. GB. 1841?*

MAGIC FLUTE. Single. Red/Purple. Tube. Crimson. Sepals. Crimson. Corolla. Purple. GC. P260 24/3/1860 Listed by Wm. Hussey, Norwich. GC. P426 12/5/1860 Listed by F. Godwin, Sheffield. P89 Vol P3 1863 J of RHS Report of fuchsia trials at Chiswick. GC. P165 26/2/1859 Intro. by E.G. Henderson, St. Johns Wood. *Banks, E. Deal. GB. 1859.*

MAGGIE. ND. White/ND. Tube. White. Sepals. White. Corolla. ND. G. 6/9/1884 Exhibited at Trowbridge Hort. Scty. Show by Pocock 3rd. GC. Vol 20 1/9/1883 P280 Exhibited at Trowbridge Hort. Scty. Show by Pocock. 2nd. NK. NK. NK. NK.

MAGNA MULTIFLORA. ND. Pink/Purple. Tube. Pale Pink. Short. Sepals. Pale Pink. Corolla. Deep reddish purple. Vol P1 P230 1859 J of RHS Floral Committee report. *Keynes, Salisbury. GB. 1859.*

MAGNATE. Single. Red/Purple. Tube. Red. Sepals. Red. Long. Broad. Corolla. Rich purple marked with rosy crimson at base. B. Cat. 1901. *Bull, W. Chelsea. GB. 1900.*

MAGNET (a). Single. Red/Purple. Tube. Bright vermillion. Sepals. Bright vermillion. Corolla. Bluish purple. GC. P820 Dec 1844 "Recommended". GC. P162 14/3/1846 & P184 13/3/1847 Listed by Millers, Ramsgate. GC. P216 27/3/1847 Listed by R. Cooper, Croydon. GC.P254 19/4/1845. Intro. by J. Smith. *Smith, J. Dalston. GB. 1845.*

MAGNET (b). Single. Red/Purple. Tube. Red. Sepals. Red. Corolla. Purple. GC. P66 1/2/1845 Listed by Millers, Ramsgate. GC. P146 8/3/1845 Listed by Youells, Gt. Yarmouth. GC. P161 16/3/1844 W. Pawley, White Hart Hotel, Bromley purchased entire stock. *Pawley, W. Bromley GB. 1844.*

MAGNET (c). Single. Red/Purple. Tube. Scarlet. Sepals. Scarlet. Corolla. Purple. JF. Cat. 1903. NK. NK. NK. NK.

MAGNIFICA (a). Single. Red/Red. Tube. Carmine. Sepals. Crimson. Reflexed. Petals exposed to view. Corolla. Rosy crimson. GC. P393 6/8/1842 & P257 22/4/1843 & P98 17/2/1844 Listed by Youells, Gt.

Yarmouth. GC. P112 17/2/1844 & P66 1/2/1845 Listed by Millers, Ramsgate. Floral Cabinet P13 1841. Fulgens X. *Smith, J. Dalston. GB. 1841.*

MAGNIFICA (b). Single. Red/Red. Tube. Light rose. Sepals. Light rose. Corolla. Rosy Purple. GC. P481 15/7/1843 H.S. Show 12/7/1843 Exhibited by Lanes, Berkhampstead. Compact and dwarf plant of F. fulgens. GC. P393 6/1842 & P257 22/4/1843. GC. P241 15/4/1843 Listed by F&A Smith, Hackney. *May. J. Bedale. GB. 1841.*

MAGNIFICA (c). Single. Red/Purple. Tube. Crimson. Sepals. Crimson. Corolla. Purple. GC. P401 24/6/1854 & P258 21/4/1855 Listed by H. Walton, Burnley. GC. P466 22/7/1854 Listed by Bass & Brown, Sudbury. GC. P530 11/8/1855 Listed by Bainbridge & Hewison, York. GC. P194 1/4/1854 Intro. by C. Turner, Slough. *Banks, E. Deal. GB. 1854 .*

MAGNIFICENT (a). Single. ND/ND. Tube. ND. Sepals. ND. Corolla. ND. GC. 28/8/1843 Tube longer and more highly coloured than "Rudolphus". See also" Magician". GC. P112 17/2/1844 & P66 1/2/1845 Listed by Millers, Ramsgate. *Bell, W. Thirsk GB. 1841?*

MAGNIFICENT (b). Single. ND/ND. Tube. ND. Sepals. ND. Corolla. ND. GC. P97 18/2/1843 & P98 17/2/1844 Listed by Youells, Gt. Yarmouth. NK. NK. *GB.* NK.

MAGNIFICENT (c). Single. Red/Red. Tube. Vermillion. Sepals. Vermillion. Corolla. Dark crimson. Extraordinary large flower. Smooth in texture. GC. 7/2/1846 Intro. by Youells, Gt. Yarmouth. *Youell, Gt. Yarmouth GB. 1846.*

MAGNIFICENT (d). Single. Red/Purple. Tube. Rosy salmon. Thin. Sepals. Rosy salmon. Large. Spreading. Corolla. Reddish purple. App. to RH. 1851 by Porcher. *Dodd. GB. 1849.*

MAGNIFICENT (e). Single. ND/ND. Tube. ND. Sepals. ND. Corolla. ND. GC. P423 7/1851 & P535 23/8/1851. Exhibited by H. Low, Clapton at Vauxhall Garden Show. GC. P211 26/3/1853 Listed by W. Rumley, Richmond. NK. NK. NK. NK.

MAGNIFLORA (a). Single. ND/ND. Tube. ND. Sepals. ND. Corolla. ND. GC. P139 26/2/1842 Included in sale at Ansells of Camden Town. NK. NK. *GB.* NK.

MAGNIFLORA (b). Single. Red/Purple. Tube. Red. Sepals. Red. Corolla. Purple. GC. P375

*Plate 9 - Eclat &
Sir Colin Campbell*

*Plate 10 - Queen Victoria,
Prince Albert & Mrs Story*

*Plate 11 - Smiths Gigantia
& Superba*

*Plate 12 - Attractor, President
& Colossus*

Plate 13 - Fuchsia Macrostemma

Plate 14 - Madonna & Goldfinch

Plate 15 - Multiflora

Plate 16 - Village Maid

4/6/1844 Exhibited by J. Smith at H.S. Show. GC. P820 Dec 1844 "Recommended". GC. P162 14/3/1846 & P184 13/3/1847 Listed by Millers, Ramsgate. GC. P254 19/4/1845 Raised and introduced by J. Smith. *Smith, J. Dalston. GB. 1845.*

MAGNIFLORA (c). Single. Red/Purple. Tube. Crimson Scarlet. Sepals. Crimson scarlet. Corolla. Deep violet. GC. P659 23/5/1885 New fuchsia from B.S. Williams. BSW. Cat. 1888. *Williams, B.S.,Holloway. GB. 1885.*

MAGNUN BONUM (a). Single. Red/Purple. Tube. Crimson. Sepals. Crimson. Corolla. Dark crimson purple. Small foliage. Bold dark flower larger than "Duke of York". GC. P183 13/3/1847 Intro. by Millers. Ramsgate. *Miller, W. Ramsgate. GB. 1847.*

MAGNUM BONUM (b). Single. Red/Red. Tube. Scarlet. Large. Very long. Sepals. Scarlet. Well reflexed. Broad. Corolla. Rich crimson. Long. Finely shaped. Blooms 7" long. GC. P594 30/6/1860 Listed by F. Godwin, Sheffield. GC. P359 21/4/1860 Intro. by G. Wheeler, Warminster. *Wheeler, G. Warminster. GB. 1860.*

MAGNUM BONUM (c). Double. Red/Purple. Tube. Red. Sepals. Red. Reflexed. Corolla. Purple. Moderately full. Vol P3 J of RHS 1863 P90 Report on Fuchsia trials at Chiswick. Submitted by E.G. Henderson. NK. NK. NK. NK.

MAGNUM BONUM (d). Single. Red/Purple. Tube. Brilliant red. Sepals. Brilliant red. Broad. Stout. Large. Corolla. Richest violet purple. GO. "Select" 1883-1889. Vol 6 J of RHS 1880. HC. Cat. 1882. Laings Cat. 1890. B. Cat. 1881-1888. GC. P424 2/4/1881 Intro. by G. Smith, Islington. *Smith, G. Islington GB. 1881.*

MAID OF HONOUR (a). Single. Red/White. Tube. Bright rose. Very long. Slender. Sepals. Bright rose. Reflexed. Recurved. 1" long. Corolla. Pure white, striped violet rose at base. Vol 2 J of RHS 1872 Pcxiv Fuchsia trials at Chiswick 1872. White streaked and flushed at base with rosy red. The rosy red predominates. B. Cat. 1870-1873. *Bull, W. Chelsea. GB. 1870.*

MAID OF HONOUR (b). Single. White/Purple. Tube. Ivory white. Sepals. Ivory white. Gracefully recurved. Corolla. Rich magenta rose. Upright habit. B. Cat. 1877-1879. BSW. Cat. 1878. HC. Cat. 1882-1885. *Todman. GB. 1876.*

MAID OF KENT. Single. White/Purple. Tube. Waxy White. Sepals. Waxy White. Corolla. Rich

plum puce. Great clusters of blooms GC. P368 26/5/1855 Listed by E. G. Henderson. GC. P467 14/7/1855 Listed by Bass & Brown, Sudbury, and H. Walton, Burnley. GC. P34 20/1/1855 Intro. by Epps. *Banks, E. Deal. GB. 1855.*

MAID OF SURREY. ND. ND/ND. Tube. White. Sepals. White. Well reflexed. Corolla. ND. Laings Cat. 1890 NK. NK. NK. NK.

MAJESTIC (a). Single. Red/Purple. Tube. Scarlet. Sepals. Scarlet. Reflex to tube. Corolla. Bluish Violet. Base of petals feathered crimson. Vol 2 J of RHS 1870 Fuchsia trials "Passed over". GC. P287 1/4/1865 Intro. by Williams. *Williams, B. Holloway. GB. 1865.*

MAJESTIC (b). Double. Red/Purple. Tube. Scarlet. Stout. Waxy. Sepals. Scarlet. Well reflexed. Corolla. Purple flamed carmine. Large. Full. Expanded. B. Cat. 1870-1873. GC. P451 2/4/1870 Intro. by Felton & Son, B'ham. *Felton. Birmingham GB. 1870.*

MAJESTICA (a). Single. ND/ND. Tube. ND. Sepals. ND. Corolla. ND. GC. P688 11/10/1841 Exhibited at RHS of Cornwall Show. GC. P630 25/9/1841. GC. 8/5/1841 Listed by J. May of Edmonton. *May, W. Bedale. GB. 1841.*

MAJESTICA (b). Single. Red/Purple. Tube. Red. Sepals. Red. Corolla. Purple. GC. P98 17/2/1844 Listed by Youells, Gt. Yarmouth, and Girlings, Stowmarket. GC. P112 17/2/1844 & P66 1/2/1845 Listed by Millers, Ramsgate. GC. P375 4/6/1844 Exhibited by Cole at Hort. Scty Show. *Smith, J. Dalston. GB. 1843.*

MAJESTICA (c). Single. Pink/Purple. Tube. Light Pink. Sepals. Light Pink. Corolla. Violet. GC. P338 22/5/1847 Intro. by Turville, Chelmsford. *Turville, Chelmsford GB. 1847.*

MAJESTICA MULTIFLORA. Single. ND/ND. Tube. ND. Sepals. ND. Corolla. ND. GC. P98 17/2/1844 Listed by Girlings, Stowmarket. GC. P112 17/2/1844 Listed by Millers, Ramsgate. GC. P241 15/4/1843 Intro. by B.W. Knight, St. Leonards. *Knight, B.W. St. Leonards. GB. 1843.*

MAJESTICA SUPERBA. Single. Red/Purple. Tube. Red. Sepals. Red. Expanded. Corolla. Purple Crimson. GC. P184 13/3/1847 Listed by W. Miller, Ramsgate. GC. P113 17/2/1845 Intro. by Barnes, Warwick. *Barnes. Warwick. GB. 1845.*

MALAKOFF. Double. Red/Purple. Tube. Crimson. Sepals. Crimson. Well open. Corolla. Purple. Very full. Perfect form. RH. P170 1857. GC. P338 17/5/1856 Raised and Introduced by Veitch, Exeter. *Veitch, Exeter. GB. 1856.*

M. ALPHAND. Double. Red/Purple. Tube. Scarlet. Sepals. Scarlet. Horizontal. Corolla. Amaranth Violet. Very good in the open ground. B. Cat. 1892-1893. JF. Cat. 1893. L. Cat. 1892. *Lemoine. Nancy. France. 1892.*

MALVINA. Double. Red/Pink. Tube. Blood red. Sepals. Blood red. Reflexed. Corolla. Flesh Pink. Irregular. L. Cat. P149 1901. *Lemoine. Nancy. France. 1901.*

MAMMOTH (a). Single. ND/ND. Tube. ND. Sepals. ND. Corolla. ND. GC. P199 27/3/1847 Listed by H. Walton, Burnley. NK. NK. NK. NK.

MAMMOTH (b). Double. Red/Purple. Tube. Red. Sepals. Red. Horizontal Divergent. Corolla. Purple. Full and bold. Wanting in refinement. Dwarfish and compact. Vol P3 J of RHS 1863. FCC. Vol. 1 J of RHS 1861. GC. P116 9/2/1861 Life size drawing. GC. P358 20/4/1861 Intro. by G. Smith. *Smith, G. Islington. GB. 1861.*

MANDARIN. Double. Red/Purple. Tube. Deep crimson. Short. Sepals. Deep crimson. Reflexed. Peculiarly curled. Corolla. Light Bluish Purple shaded violet. Peculiarly formed. GC. P502 13/4/1872. Intro. by W. Bull. B. Cat. 1872-1876. Not in the first selection. P126 4th Ed. by Porcher 1874. *Bull, W. Chelsea. GB. 1872.*

MANGLESSII. Single. ND. Tube. ND. Sepals. ND. Corolla. ND. GC. P112 17/2/1844 Listed by W. Miller, Ramsgate. *Standish, Bagshot. GB. 1842.*

MANTLE (a). Single. Red/Purple. Tube. Crimson. Short. Sepals. Crimson. Well reflexed. Corolla. Dark violet blue. (Rich plum). Large. P110 4th Ed. by Porcher 1874 Sepals recurved to tube. Petals spiralled. Pedicel 40mms. B. Cat. 1872-1873. *Bull, W. Chelsea. GB. 1871.*

MANTLE (b). Double. Red/Purple. Tube. Crimson. Sepals. Crimson. Short. Corolla. Rich purple. Full. Large. Corolla segments somewhat fimbriated. GC. P647 22/5/1880 Intro. by W. Bull. *Bland,E. Fordham GB. 1880.*

MAORI CHIEF. Single. Red/Purple. Tube. Scarlet. (Bright crimson). Thin. Sepals. Scarlet. (Bright crimson). Large. Reflexed. Corolla. Rich dark plum. (Indigo blue washed reddish brown). P111 4th Ed. by Porcher 1874 Vigorous. Upright. Floriferous.

Dark green foliage. B. Cat. 1873-1879. Intro. by W. Bull, Chelsea. Killiecrankie X. *Bull, W. Chelsea. GB. 1873.*

MARATHON. Single. Red/Purple. Tube. Rich crimson. Short. Sepals. Rich crimson. Elegantly reflexed. Corolla. Rich Purplish plum shaded rose at base. B. Cat. 1873-1876. Intro. by W. Bull, Chelsea. *Bull, W. Chelsea. GB. 1873.*

MARCEAU. ND. ND/ND. Tube. ND. Sepals. ND. Corolla. ND. Gartenflora P149 1888 New fuchsia. *Lemoine. Nancy. France. 1886.*

MARCEL LINBERTHELOT. Double. Red/Purple. Tube. Carmine rose. Sepals. Carmine rose. Broad. Corolla. Bluish violet. Very full. L. Cat. 1906. *Lemoine. Nancy. France. 1905.*

MARCEL MONNIER. Double. Red/Pink. Tube. Coral. Sepals. Coral. Recurved. Corolla. Salmon white. (Scarlet blush). Enormous. Very floriferous. Named after a French writer (1829-85). B. Cat. 1894, 1895. JF. Cat. 1895. L. Cat. 1901. *Lemoine. Nancy. France. 1894.*

MARCEL PRÉVOST. Double. Red/White. Tube. Bright red. Sepals. Bright red. Reflexed. Corolla. Blush white, profusely flamed scarlet. Named after a French writer (1862-1941). B. Cat. 1894-1895. NK. NK. *France. 1894.*

MARCHIONESS. ND. White/ND. Tube. White. Sepals. White. Corolla. ND. GC. P515 25/7/1857 Listed by H. Walton, Burnley. GC. P357 7/4/1858 Listed by C.E. Allen, Stoke Newington. SG P459 1866. Compact habit. Prolific flowers. NK. NK. *GB. 1857.*

MARCHIONESS CORNWALLIS. Single. White/ND. Tube. White. Sepals. White. Corolla. ND. GC. P184 13/3/1847 Listed by W. Miller, Ramsgate. *Epps, W.J. Maidstone GB. 1846.*

MARCHIONESS OF ANGLESEY. Double. Red/White. Tube. Red. Sepals. Red. Corolla. White. Dwarf, Stiff habit and growth. HC. Cat. P74 1882. Intro. by H. Cannell. *Bland, E. Fordham. GB. 1873.*

MARCHIONESS OF BATH. ND. ND/ND. Tube. ND. Sepals. ND. Corolla. ND. GC. P311 8/9/1877 Exhibited at Trowbridge Hort. Scty. Show. by Matthews. 1st. P3 J of RHS 1863 Floral Committee Exhibited by G. Wheeler, Warminster. *Wheeler, G. Warminster. GB. 1863.*

MARCHIONESS OF CAMDEN. Single. Pink/Red. Tube. Pink. Sepals. Pink. Well expanded. Corolla. Rich crimson. Resembles "Queen Victoria" by Smith. GC. 6/2/1847 & P216 27/3/1847 & P232 1/4/1848 Listed by R. Cooper, Croydon. GC. 13/3/1847 Listed by W. Miller, Ramsgate. GC. P175 14/3/1846 Intro. by Hally, Blackheath. *Hally, Blackheath. GB. 1846.*

MARCHIONESS OF HASTINGS. Single. ND/ND. Tube. ND. Sepals. ND. Corolla. ND. GC. P120 23/2/1850 Select dark variety. CG. Vol III P272 1850 "Fuchsias for exhibition - new ones". NK. NK. *GB. 1849.*

MARCHIONESS OF NORMANBY. Single. Red/Purple. Tube. Scarlet. Sepals. Scarlet. Corolla. Purple. GC. P1 6/1/1844 and GC. P146 8/3/1845 Intro. by Youell, Gt. Yarmouth. *Youell, Gt. Yarmouth. GB. 1844.*

MARCHIONESS OF ORMONDE. Single. Red/Purple. Tube. Red. Sepals. Red. Corolla. Purple. GC. P98 17/2/1844 & P146 8/3/1845 Listed by Youells, Gt. Yarmouth. *Youell, Gt. Yarmouth. GB. 1843.*

MARDUIS. Single. ND/ND. Tube. ND. Sepals. ND. Corolla. ND. GC. P610 2/9/1843 Practical Floral & Hort. Scty of Ireland Show 25/8/1843 exhibited by T. Farrell. NK. NK. NK.

MARÉCHAL McMAHON. Single. Red/Purple. Tube. Red. Longish. Sepals. Red. Partially spreading. Corolla. Reddish purple. Small. A coarse looking variety, flowering in bunches at the end of the shoots. Submitted by C. Turner, Slough. Vol P3 P89 1863 J of RHS. Fuchsia trials at Chiswick 1862. Named after a Marshall of France (1808-93).NK. NK. *France.* NK.

MARGARET. Single. Red/Purple. Tube. Red. Short. Sepals. Red. Completely reflexed. Corolla. Blue. Large. Long. Expanded. Novel in shape. GC. P74 24/1/1863 Intro. by W. Bull, Chelsea. *Bull, W. Chelsea. GB. 1863.*

MARGINATA (a). Single. Red/Red. Tube. Scarlet. Sepals. Scarlet. Corolla. Crimson, scarlet margin around petal. GC. P369 8/6/1844 Listed by T. Cripps. GC. P66 1/2/1845 & P184 13/3/1847 Listed by W. Miller, Ramsgate. GC. P146 8/3/1845 Listed by Youells. GC. P162 16/3/1844 Intro. by Hally, Blackheath. *Hally, Blackheath. GB. 1844.*

MARGINATA (b). Single. White/Pink. Tube. White. (Blush). Short. Sepals. White. (Blush).

Reflexed. Corolla. Pink margined scarlet. (Rose margined crimson). GO. "Select" 1880-1891. Vol P3 J of RHS 1863 Fuchsia trial at Chiswick 1862. GC. Fuchsia trials at Chiswick 1874 Free. Bushy habit. Free bloomer. FCC. P120 4th Ed. by Porcher 1874. Not in the first selection. HC. Cat. 1882-1885. GC. P311 8/9/1877 Exhibited at Trowbridge H.S. Show 1st. prize Matthews, 2nd. prize J. Lye. *Banks, E. Deal. GB. 1862*

MARGUERITA. Single. White/Purple. Tube. Blush white. Sepals. Blush white. Broad. Well reflexed. Corolla. Bright mauve, edged with rosy lake. Rather small. Free flowering. First rate in habit. No Award. Submitted by E.G. Henderson. Vol 4 J of RHS P69 1877 Report on Fuchsias grown for trial at Chiswick 1873. NK. NK. *GB.1872.*

MARGUERITE. Single. Red/Purple. Tube. Red. Sepals. Red. Corolla. Purple. P115 4th Ed. by Porcher 1874. Not in the first selection. *Bull, W. Chelsea. GB. 1865.*

MARIA (a) Single. Red/Purple. Tube. Rose. Sepals. Rose. Corolla. Bluish purple. Large. GC. P369 8/6/1844 Listed by T. Cripps, Maidstone. GC. P112 17/2/1844 & P66 1/2/1845 Listed by Miller, Ramsgate. (Sent for appraisal, to Editor of GC by J.W. Tenterden Kent in 1843). GC. P97 17/2/1844 Intro. by W.J.Epps. *Epps, W.J. Maidstone GB. 1844.*

MARIA (b). ND. ND/ND. Tube. ND. Sepals. ND. Corolla. ND. GC. P418 22/5/1858 Listed by H. Walton, Burnley. NK. NK. *GB. 1857.*

MARIA LOUISA. Single. White/ND. Tube. White. Sepals. White. Corolla. ND. GC. P184 13/3/1847 & P250 18/4/1847 Listed by Millers, Ramsgate. NK. NK. *GB. 1846.*

MARIE AUBIN. HC. Cat. 1885 A pretty and distinct new variety, very free. Red and Purple. Most likely confused with Madam Aubin.

MARIE COMTE. Single. ND/ND. Tube. ND. Sepals. ND. Corolla. ND. L. Cat. 1892. *Comte. France. 1890.*

MARIE CORNELISSEN. S/Double. Red/White. Tube. Light red. Very short. Sepals. Light red. Long. Spreading. Partially reflexed. Corolla. White. Rather irregular form. Long droplike buds. Awarded ** Vol P3 J of RHS 1863 Fuchsia Trials at Chiswick. CG. P454 1865. SG. P459 1866 Recommended. P131 4th Ed. by Porcher. 1874. Not in the first selection Good in the open ground. RH. P311 1889 "Select" by E.A. Carriére. *Cornelissen, Arras. Belgium. 1861.*

119

MARIE McMINTOSH. Double. Red/Purple. Tube. Red. Sepals. Red. Corolla. Purple. Vol P3 J of RHS 1863 P90 Fuchsia trials at Chiswick. A poor irregular sort. Submitted by Scott. NK. NK. *GB*. NK.

MARIE PARENT. Single. Red/Purple. Tube. Red. Sepals. Red. Recurved. Corolla. Purple. Scarcely expanded. Vol P3 J of RHS 1863 Fuchsia trials at Chiswick 1862. *Low. GB. 1861.*

MARIE WEINRICH. ND. ND/ND Tube. ND. Sepals. ND. Corolla. ND. P120 4th Ed. by Porcher 1874 Not in the first selection. *Weinrich. Germany. 1867.*

MARINER. Single. Red/Purple. Tube. Bright crimson. Sepals. Bright crimson. Broad. Reflexed. Corolla. Purple blotched and flaked bright crimson. B. Cat. 1870-1873. NK. NK. NK. *1869.*

MARION. Single. Red/Purple. Tube. Carmine scarlet. Sepals. Carmine scarlet. Broad. Recurved. Corolla. Rosy Purple. Well expanded. GC. P450 17/5/1862. Intro. by B.W. Knight, Battle. *Knight, B.W. Battle. GB. 1862.*

MARKSMAN (a). Double. Red/Purple. Tube. Bright carmine. Long. Slender. Sepals. Bright carmine Broad. Spreading. Corolla. Violet purple. reddish towards the base. A most useful market sort, which never seeds. Habit dwarf. Free. Vol 3 Pcxiv J of RHS 1872 Fuchsia trial at Chiswick awarded ***. P217 Vol 4 J of RHS. Fuchsia Trials at Chiswick 1877 "Certificate confirmed". GC. P269 26/8/1876 Mr. Kinghorn notes this is a good hardy bedder. Bushy. Compact. B. Cat. 1870-1873. NK. NK. *GB. 1868.*

MARKSMAN (b). Double. Red/White. Tube. Bright carmine. Sepals. Bright carmine. Corolla. Pure white. JF. Cat. 1885. NK. NK. *GB*. NK.

MARMION. Single. Red/White. Tube. Crimson. Sepals. Crimson. Scarcely 1". Broad. Well reflexed. Corolla. White. Rosy scarlet veins. Medium size. Similar to "Pursuit" but not equalling it. Pcxiv Vol 3 J of RHS 1872 Fuchsia trial at Chiswick 1872. P131 4th Ed. by Porcher 1874. Not in the first selection. B. Cat. 1872, 1873. Intro. by W. Bull. *Bull, W. Chelsea. GB. 1871.*

MARTIUS. S/Double. Red/Purple. Tube. Crimson red. Sepals. Crimson red. Corolla. Purple Rose. Irregular. L. Cat. 1906. *Bull, W. Chelsea. GB. 1905.*

MARVEL. Single. Red/Purple. Tube. Bright carmine. Sepals. Bright carmine. Broad. Well reflexed. Corolla. Lavender Blue. Irregularly shaped. Free bloomer. Good habit. B. Cat. 1870-1873. *Bull, W. Chelsea. GB. 1870.*

MARVELLOUS. (a). Double. Red/Purple. Tube. Rich crimson. Sepals. Rich crimson. Broad. Slightly Spreading. Corolla. Almost Black. Very full. Much richer and darker than "Sir Colin Campbell". Vol P3 J of RHS 1863 Fuchsia trials at Chiswick 1862 GC. P595 30/6/1860 Listed by F. Godwin, Sheffield. GC. P18 14/1/1860 Intro. by Wm. Rollinson. *Rollinson, W. Tooting GB. 1860.*

MARVELLOUS (b). Single. Red/Purple. Tube. Carmine. Thin. Short. Sepals. Carmine. Long. Wide. Horizontally curved. Corolla. Violet tinted plum. Very expanded 2" in diameter. Did not flower well. P111 4th. Ed. by Porcher 1874. GC. P988 15/10/1864 & P1 7/1/1865 Intro. by E.G. Henderson, St. Johns Wood. *Banks, E. Deal. GB. 1864.*

MARVELLOUS (c). Double. Red/Purple. Tube. Deep rose. Sepals. Deep rose. Oval in shape. Reflexed. Corolla. Bright blue. Full. Rosette form. JF. Cat. 1885. HC. Cat. 1885. B. Cat 1882-1893. Intro. by W. Bull. *Eckford. GB. 1882.*

MARY. Single. Red/Red. Tube. Brilliant Crimson Scarlet. Sepals. Brilliant Crimson Scarlet. Corolla. Scarlet. Flowers In clusters. One of the first hybrids of F. triphylla. L. Cat. 1901. JF. Cat. 1903. *Bonstedt, Gottingen. Germany 1897.*

MARY ANDERSON. Single. White/Red. Tube. White. Sepals. White. Corolla. Red. JF. Cat. 1892. HC. Cat. 1890. *Lye, J. Market Lavington. GB. 1890.*

MARY ANN. Single. White/Red. Tube. Nearly white. Short. Sepals. White. Expanded. Large. Corolla. Bright red. April delivery. GC. P184 13/3/1847 & P250 27/4/1847 Listed by W. Miller, Ramsgate. GC. P201 27 /3/1847 Listed by Hart & Nickling, Guildford. GC. P161 14/3/1846 Intro. by J. Barkway, East Dereham. *Barkway, J. Dereham GB. 1846.*

MARY REID. Single. White/Pink. Tube. Ivory White. Sepals. Ivory White. Corolla. Delicate Pink. Well formed. GM. P59 2/2/1895 Dobbies Cat. 1893. *Lye, J. Market Lavington. GB. 1892.*

MASANIELLO. Single. Red/Purple. Tube. Brilliant Crimson. Sepals. Brilliant Crimson. Reflexed. Corolla. Violet veined rose. RH. P95 1859. GC. P539 10/7/1858 Listed by F. Godwin, Sheffield. GC. P571 24/7/1858 Listed by H. Walton,

Burnley. GC. P238 19/3/1859 Listed by W. Rumley, Richmond. Intro. by E.G. Henderson. *Banks, E. Deal. GB. 1858.*

MASTER LONGFIELD. Single. White/Red. Tube. Flesh. (White). Enlarged at base. Sepals. Flesh. (White). 1" long. Well reflexed. Green at tips. Corolla. Bright carmine rose, with crimson margins. Lake, paler at base). Loose. Vol 3 Pcxii J of RHS 1872 Fuchsia Trials at Chiswick. P120 4th Ed. by Porcher 1874 Not in the first selection. GC. P314 20/3/1868 Intro. by E.G. Henderson an improvement on Todmans "Beauty of Clapton". *Todman. GB. 1868.*

MASTERPIECE (a). Single. Red/Purple. Tube. Scarlet Crimson. Sepals. Scarlet Crimson. Well reflexed. Corolla. Rich Maroon. Thick. GC. P595 29/6/1861 Listed by Godwin & Padman, Sheffield. GC. P771 24/8/1861 Listed by H. Walton, Burnley. GC. P140 16/2/1861 Intro. by F&A Smith. *Smith F&A, Dulwich GB. 1861.*

MASTERPIECE (b). Single. Red/Purple. Tube. Red. Sepals. Red. Corolla. Purple. P324 Vol 3 J of RHS 1900 "A valuable free blooming variety of vigorous growth and lasting a long time in bloom". IF. Cat. 1901. GC. P198 31/8/1911. *Lye,J. Market Lavington. GB. 1901.*

MASTODONTE. Double. Red/Purple. Tube. Red. Sepals. Red. Corolla. Purple. P126 4th Ed. by Porcher 1874. Not in the first selection. RH. P295 1887 Grown as a standard at Twickel. Mastodonte is the French word for mammoth. *Lemoine. Nancy. France. 1862.*

MATCHLESS (a). Single. ND/ND. Tube. ND. Sepals. ND. Corolla. ND. GC. P224 14/4/1849 Listed by *R. Whibley, Kennington Cross. GB.* NK.

MATCHLESS (b). Double. Red/Purple. Tube. Dark scarlet. Sepals. Dark scarlet. Well reflexed. Corolla. Rich Purple. Immensely large. GC. P74 24/1/1863 Intro. by W. Bull, Chelsea. *Bull,W. Chelsea. GB. 1863.*

MATCHLESS (c). Single. Red/Purple. Tube. Deep crimson. Sepals. Deep crimson. Broad. Elegantly reflexed. Corolla. Rich purple striped and flaked rose. B. Cat. 1882-1883. JF. Cat. 1885. Intro. by W. Bull, Chelsea. *Bland, E. Fordham. GB. 1882*

MATHIAS DUVAL. Double. Red/Purple. Tube. Scarlet. Small. Sepals. Scarlet. Large. Corolla. Bright Blue. (Dark violet). Serrated petals. GO. P141 1891 "Continental Fuchsias of 1890". B. Cat.

1892, 1893. L. Cat. 1892. *Lemoine. Nancy. France. 1890.*

MATHILDE. ND. ND/ND. Tube. ND. Sepals. ND. Corolla. ND. Striped. G. 15/12/1883 P503. See Col Pl. in L'Illustration Horticole P174. *Mahon, J. Belgium. 1883.*

MATILDA. Single. White/Red. Tube. White tinted rose. Sepals. White tinted rose. Large. Well open. Corolla. Cerise red. Small. 1st Class variety. App.to RH. 1851 by Porcher. GC. P455 8/7/1847 Exhibited at RBS Show London by Gaines. *Gaines. Battersea. GB. 1848.*

MAUD. Single. White/Pink. Tube. White. Sepals. White. Corolla. Pink shaded violet. Laings Cat. 1890. BSW. Cat.1897. NK. NK. *GB.* NK.

MAUVE PETTICOAT. ND. ND/ND. Tube. ND. Sepals. ND. Corolla. ND. GC. P338 15/4/1865 Listed by W. Rumley, Richmond. NK. NK.*GB. 1864.*

MAUVE QUEEN. Single. Red/Purple. Tube. Scarlet. Sepals. Scarlet. Corolla. Bright Mauve. FW. & GG. 1872 Review by H. Cannell.HC. Cat. 1882. *Banks, E. Deal. GB. 1872.*

MAXIMA SPLENDENS. Single. ND/ND. Tube. ND. Sepals. ND. Corolla. ND. GC.P112 17/2/1844 Listed by W. Miller, Ramsgate. NK. NK. *GB.* NK.

MAY FELTON. Double. Red/Purple. Tube. Light red. (Bright crimson red). Almost non existant. Sepals. Light red. (Bright crimson red). Reflexed. Corolla. Mauve edged light mauve.(Dark violet blue veined red). Compact. Regular. P124 4th. Ed. by Porcher 1874. B. Cat. 1870-1873. GC. P451 2/4/1870 Intro. by Felton & Sons, Birmingham. *Felton, Birmingham. GB. 1870.*

MAYFLOWER. Single. Red/Purple. Tube. Carmine red. Average size. Sepals. Carmine red. Reflexed round to tube. Corolla. Violet washed red and white. Pedicel 45mms. P111 4th Ed. by Porcher 1874. *Smith F&A. Dulwich. GB. 1866.*

MAY QUEEN. Single. White/Pink. Tube. Pure white (white washed rose). Thick. Long. 20mms. Sepals. Pure white. Recurved. (Horizontal) Green tips. Corolla. Violet rose. Long. Symetrical form (Bright rose pink shaded violet and white bordered red). Similar to "Taglioni" and "Arabella Improved" P119 4th Ed. by Porcher 1874. Pcxii Vol 3 J of RHS 1872 Habit stiff erect. Flowers large. Tube 1". Sepals scarcely spreading. Green tipped. Corolla 1".

121

Conical. Pcxii Vol 3 J of RHS 1872. Sent for trial at Chiswick 1877 by F&A Smith. No Award. "The exact counterpart of "Starlight" in every respect except that the corolla is a very bright pure lake. P69 Vol 4 J of RHS 1877. GC. P414 17/4/1869 Intro by W. Bull. B. Cat. 1870-1873. *Bull, W. Chelsea. GB. 1869.*

MAZEPPA. Single. Red/Red. Tube. Orange rose. Sepals. Orange rose. Very open. Corolla. Flaming red. (A darker shade of orange). Vigorous. RH. P169 1857. App to RH. 1851 by Porcher. RH. P311 1889 "Select" by E. A. Carrière. GC. P177 20/3/1852 Listed by W. Rumley, Richmond. GC. P545 30/8/1851 Intro. by G. Smith Islington into this country. *Meillez, Lille. France. 1851.*

M. BISCHOFFSHEIM. Single. Red/Red. Tube. Fiery Salmon. Long. Sepals. Fiery Salmon. Corolla. Rosy red, marked orange at base. L. Cat. 1892. B. Cat. 1888-1889. *Lemoine. Nancy. France. 1888.*

M. BÉRAUD-MASSARD. Double. ND/ND. Tube. ND. Sepals. ND. Corolla. ND. L. Cat 1892. *Hoste. France. 1888.*

M. LE BORGNE. Single. Red/Purple. Tube. Carmine Scarlet. Sepals. Carmine Scarlet. Long. Corolla. Dark amaranth. Long. Enormous. JF. Cat. 1900. L. Cat. 1901. *Rozain, Lyons. France. 1899.*

M. BONFIGLIOLI. Double. Red/Purple. Tube. Light red. Sepals. Light red. Roll back to tube. Corolla. Bluish Purple veined scarlet. Large. Full. JF. Cat. 1900. L. Cat. 1901. *Rozain, Lyons France. 1899.*

M. BROWN-SÉQUARD. Double. Red/White. Tube. Scarlet. Sepals. Scarlet. Well recurved. Perfectly shaped. Corolla. Creamy White. GO. P141 1891 "New Continental Fuchsias of 1890". L. Cat. 1892. B. Cat. 1892-1893. Named after a French Physiologist (1817-94). *Lemoine. Nancy. France. 1890.*

M. BRUANT. Single. Red/White. Tube. Red. Sepals. Red. Corolla. White GC. P406 2/5/1863 Listed by Wm Hussey, Norwich. Vol 2 J of RHS 1870 Fuchsia trials at Chiswick. RH. P295 1887. Fuchsias grown as standards at Twickel. *Cornelissen, Arras. Belgium. 1862.*

M. CH. GAILLY. Single. Red/Purple. Tube. Crimson. Sepals. Crimson. Horizontal. Corolla. Dark Violet shaded. B. Cat. 1870. NK. NK. *France.* NK.

M. CH. POTIGNY. Double. Red/Purple. Tube Crimson. Sepals. Crimson . Short. Corolla. Blu fading to Violet. Globular. L. Cat. 1892. *Host France 1892.*

M. CL. COQUET. Double. ND/ND. Tube. NI Sepals. ND. Corolla. ND. L. Cat. 1892. *Hos France. 1888.*

MDLLE. TIETJENS Single. White/Red. Tub White. Sepals. White. Corolla. Pink/Scarlet. Name after a Hungarian Operatic soprano (1831-77). GC P55 19/1/1867 Review by H. Cannell. NK. NK. *GI* NK.

MDLLE TREBELLI. Single. Red/Purple. Tub Crimson red. Thick. Short. Sepals. Crimson re Large reflexed and round. Corolla. Clear Lila Violet. Spiralled. Very expanded. Bushy habit. P11 4th. Ed. by Porcher 1874. GC. P806 30/8/1862 Intr by E.G. Henderson, St. Johns Wood. *Banks, E. Dea GB. 1862.*

M. DUFAURE. Single. White/Red. Tube. White (Yellowish salmon) Sepals. White. (Yellowis salmon with green tips) Corolla. Rosy Lake. (Ros salmon). JF. Cat. 1888. Dobbies Cat. 1893/4. B. Ca 1888-1892. Named after a French Statesmar Premier of France 1877-9 (1798-1881). *Lemoine Nancy. France. 1879.*

M. DYBOWSKI. Double. Red/Pink. Tube. Cora red. Sepals. Coral red. Reflexed. Corolla. Lilac pink A new colour. (Lilac rose). Full. Medium size. B Cat. 1892, 1893. L. Cat. 1892. *Lemoine. Nancy France. 1892.*

MEDINA. Double. Red/Purple. Tube. Crimson Sepals. Crimson. Corolla. Violet blue splashe reddish brown. Adheres to sepals. Large buds in th form of bells. Pedicel 25mms. This variety is note for its foliage, which takes on a copper tint. P12 4th. Ed. by Porcher 1874. B. Cat. 1872, 1873. *Bul W. Chelsea. GB. 1871.*

MEDORA (a) Single. ND/ND. Tube. ND. Sepals ND. Corolla. ND. GC. P66 1/2/1845 Listed b Millers, Ramsgate. *Harrison,Dereham.GB.* NK.

MEDORA. (b) Single. Pink/Purple. Tube. Very ligh pink. Sepals. Very light pink. Corolla. Purple. Long New seedling. GC. P146 8/3/1845. Intro. by Youells *Youell, Gt. Yarmouth. GB.1845.*

MEDORA (c). Single. Red/Purple. Tube. Crimso red. Thick. Long. 15mms. Sepals. Crimson red Reflexed. Corolla. Blue Violet. Very expanded. Th flower is long lasting. P111 4th. Ed. by Porcher 1874. *Banks, E. Deal. GB. 1863.*

MEDORA (d). Double. Red/White. Tube. Bright carmine. Sepals. Bright Carmine. Completely reflexed. Corolla. White veined carmine. Large. L. Cat. 1901. B. Cat. 1901. Intro. by W. Bull. *Bull, W. Chelsea. GB. 1901.*

MEILLEZI. Single. Violet Rose. Tube. Violet rose. Almost nil. Sepals. Violet rose. Small. Corolla. Small Violet rose. This variety is an enclandra hybrid. GC. P368 26/5/1855. Intro by G. Smith, Islington. GC. P282 25/9/1857 Listed by Youells, Gt. Yarmouth. 3rd. Ed. by Porcher 1858. *Smith,G. Islington. GB.1854.*

MEMNON. Double. Red/Purple. Tube. Bright rose. Sepals. Bright rose. Horizontal. Corolla. Bright violet blue blotched rose at base. B. Cat. 1870-1875. *Bull, W. Chelsea. GB. 1870.*

MEMPHIS (a). Single. Red/Purple. Tube. Rich crimson. Sepals. Rich crimson. Gracefully reflexed. Corolla. Rich purple. Large. Well expanded. B. Cat. 1878-1893. Intro. by W. Bull. *Bland, E. Fordham. GB. 1878.*

MEMPHIS (b). ND. Red/White. Tube. Rich crimson. Sepals. Rich crimson. Corolla. Pure white. JF. Cat. 1885. NK. NK. *GB.* NK.

MENÉLIK. Double. Red/Purple. Tube. Red. Sepals. Red. Corolla. Dark plum purple. Large petals. L. Cat. 1901. *Rozain, Lyons. France. 1899.*

MENTO. Double. Red/Purple. Tube. Reddish crimson. Sepals. Reddish crimson. Broad. Recurved. Corolla. Bluish purple. Immense. L. Cat. 1901. B. Cat. 1899-1901. Intro. by W. Bull. *Bull, W. Chelsea. GB 1899.*

MENTOR (a). Double. Red/Purple. Tube. Rich deep crimson. Sepals. Rich deep crimson. Horizontal. Corolla. Deep rich purple. Short but thick. B. Cat. 1873-1876. *Bull, W. Chelsea. GB. 1873.*

MENTOR (b). Single. Red/Purple. Tube. Bright red. Sepals. Bright red. Uplifted. Corolla. Purple Violet. L. Cat. 1901. NK. NK. NK.

MÉROPE. Single. ND/ND. Tube. ND. Sepals. ND. Corolla. ND. L. Cat. 1892. *Rozain, Lyons. France. 1889.*

MERRY MAID. Single. White/Red. Tube. White. Sepals. White. Corolla. Scarlet or Pink. HC. Cat.

1882 Splendid little Fuchsia. Fine for small pots. GC. P55 19/1/1867 Review by H. Cannell. *Banks, E. Deal. GB. 1866.*

MERRY MONARCH. Single. ND/ND. Tube. ND. Sepals. ND. Corolla. ND. GC. P184 13/3/1847 & P250 27/4/1847 Listed by W. Miller, Ramsgate. *Fairbeard. GB. 1846.*

MESSÈNE. Double. Red/Purple. Tube. Crimson. Sepals. Crimson. Spread out. Corolla. Dark violet purple. Full. L. Cat. 1911. *Lemoine. Nancy. GB. 1911.*

M. E. VAUCHER. Double. Red/Purple. Tube. Dark red. Sepals. Dark Red. Reflexed. Corolla. Violet blue shaded blue and marked carmine (Violet Purple shaded blue, carmine at base) B. Cat. 1892. L. Cat. 1892. *Rozain, Lyons. France. 1892.*

METEOR (a). Single. Red/Red. Tube. Dark crimson. Thin. Sepals. Dark crimson. Expanded. Open. Corolla. Violet crimson. Floriferous. Brilliant colouration. Stems and leaf veins violet. 4cms. 2nd Ed. by Porcher 1848. GC. P241 15/4/1843 Listed by F&A Smith, Hackney. GC. P112 17/2/1844 & P66 1/2/1845 Listed by W. Miller, Ramsgate. *Harrison, Dereham GB. 1842.*

METEOR (b). S/Double. Red/Purple. Tube. Red. Sepals. Red. Corolla. Reddish purple. Plant illustrated in Floral Magazine July 1862. GC. P493 31/5/1862 Listed by F&A Smith, Dulwich. JofH & CG. Vol 3 P294 1863 Cert. of Merit by the RBS. Foliage plant with leaves rich golden yellow variegated with bronze. Received from the Continent and distributed by Messrs Carter. GC. P462 Extract from the American Gardeners Monthly. Bedding Fuchsias- A few of the newer ones bear the hottest sun, and bloom wonderfully. None surpasses "Meteor" who with golden and crimson hues are born of tropical heat. The more sun the better". Vol. 4 Jof RHS P69 1877 Report on plants grown for trial at Chiswick. No Award. Habit very robust, the foliage at the ends of all branches is a very bright red, rendering the plant very distinct and effective. P77 HC. Cat. 1882 Lower leaves buff yellow, upper ones rich crimson. 1st class for a climber or small pots. RH. P311 1889 "Select" by E.A. Carrière. Vol 33 The Garden 1888 Young leaves suffused with crimson until the leaf is mature, when it changes to yellow. Now called "Autumnale". GC. P282 29/3/1862 Intro. by J. Carter, Crystal Palace sent out on 1/5/1862. GC. P374 26/4/1862. NK. NK. NK. *1861.*

METIS. Double. Red/White. Tube. Rose. Sepals. Rose. Well reflexed. Corolla. White marked deep rose at base. Expanded. GC. Vol 19 P579 May 1896. Intro. by W. Bull. B. Cat. 1898-1899. *Bull, W. Chelsea. GB. 1896.*

METZ. Double. Red/White. Tube. Yellowish white. Thin. Short. Sepals. Crimson red. Reflexed. Rounded to tube. Corolla. White. This variety is not vigorous or floriferous but does not belong to the second selection. P129 4th. Ed. by Porcher 1874. HC. Cat. 1882. *Lemoine,Nancy. France. 1874.*

MEYERBEER. Double. Red/White. Tube. Carmine. Sepals. Carmine. Horizontal. Corolla. White marbled carmine. Very floriferous. Named after a German composer (1791-1864). L. Cat. 1892. *Lemoine. Nancy. France. 1892.*

M. GINDRE. Double. ND/ND. Tube. ND. Sepals. ND. Corolla. ND. L. Cat. 1892. *Rozain. Lyons. France. 1899.*

M. GLADSTONE. Double. Red/Purple. Tube. Clear red. Sepals. Clear red. Corolla. Violet plum. Immense. Very double. Named after an English statesman and Prime Minister. B. Cat 1894. *Lemoine. Nancy. France. 1894.*

M. HERMITE. Double. Red/Purple. Tube. Reddish crimson. Short. Sepals. Reddish crimson. Corolla. Violet. Large. Irregular. Very double. Named after a French mathematician (1822-1901). B. Cat. 1893-1895. NK. NK. *France. 1893.*

MIARKA. Double. Red/White. Tube. Coral. Sepals. Coral. Short. Relaxed. Corolla. White. Large. *Lemoine. Nancy. France. 1906.*

MICHEL ANGE. Double. Red/Purple. Tube. Clear crimson. Sepals. Clear crimson. Corolla. Dark plum violet, Veined red. Enormous. Good habit. L. Cat. 1914. *Rozain, Lyons France. 1914.*

MICROPHYLLA MAJOR. Single. Purple/Purple. GC. P630 25/9/1841. It is a fine variety with much larger flowers than microphylla. NK. NK. *GB. 1841.*

MICROPHYLLA ALBA ROSA. HC. Cat. P79 1892.NK. NK. NK. NK.

MIDDLETONIA. Single. Red/Purple. Tube. Purplish red. Thick. Short. Sepals. Purplish red. Turned up to tube. Corolla. Violet. Resembles "Paragon". Large foliage 6cms x 3cms. P46 2nd. Ed. by Porcher 1848. GC. P393 6/1842 Listed by Youells, Gt. Yarmouth. GC. P241 15/4/1843 Listed by F&A Smith, Hackney. *Middleton? GB. 1842.*

MIDNIGHT. Single. Red/Purple. Tube. Deep glossy crimson. Sepals. Deep glossy crimson. Corolla. Dark Purple. Large. B. Cat. 1877-1878. Intro. by Wm. Bull. *Bull, W. Chelsea. GB. 1877.*

MIKADO. Single. Red/Pink. Tube. Bright red. Sepals. Bright red. Lift back. Corolla. Bright flesh pink. Very big. L. Cat. 1912. *Rozain, Lyons. France. 1912.*

MILDRED. Single. Red/Purple. Tube. Dark crimson. Sepals. Dark crimson. Reflexed. Round to tube. Sometimes horizontal. Corolla. Purple. (Indigo blue washed rose). P124 4th Ed. by Porcher 1874. Spiralled. Double Average size. Pedicel 30 mms. GC. P74 24/1/1863 Intro. by Wm. Bull. *Bull, W. Chelsea. GB. 1863.*

MILNE EDWARDS. Double. Red/Purple. Tube. Coral red. Sepals. Coral red. Corolla. Blue shaded violet. Named after a French naturalist (1800-85). Laings Cat. 1890. *Lemoine. Nancy. France. 1882.*

MINATURE. Single. Red/Purple. Tube. Red. Sepals. Red. Corolla. Purple. Hybrid of "Myrtifolia". Dwarf. L. Cat. 1901. *Lemoine. Nancy. France. 1894.*

MINERVA SUPERBA. Single. ND/ND. Tube. ND. Sepals. ND. Corolla. ND. GC. P663 18/10/1851 Exhibited at York Hort. Scty. Show 24/9/1851 by J. Roper. App. to RH. 1851 by Porcher. *Gaines. Battersea.GB. 1850.*

MINERVA (a). Double. Red/White. Tube. Carmine. Sepals. Carmine. Corolla. White. B. Cat. 1878-1888. JF. Cat. 1885. GC. P146 1895. Intro. by W. Bull. *Bland, E. Fordham GB. 1878*

MINERVA (b). ND. ND/ND. Tube. ND. Sepals. ND. Corolla. ND. RH. 1887, P295 Fuchsias grown as standards at Twickel. GC. P824 27/6/1885 Fuchsia trials at Chiswick "Best in Class". Single. Dark. *Boucharlet, Lyons. France. 1881.*

MINIATA. Single. Red/Red. Tube. Orange scarlet. Sepals. Orange scarlet. Corolla. Orange scarlet. A very distinct beautiful species of good habit forming a moderately sized branching and compact shrub like "F. Serratifolia". The flowers are produced in terminal bunches of a brilliant orange scarlet. Direct importation of M. Linden. GC. P226 9/4/1853 Intro. by L. Van Houtte, Ghent. GC. P337 28/5/1853 & P369 11/6/1853 Listed by Bass & Brown, Sudbury

10/6d each. GC. P369 11/6/1853 Offered by E.G. Henderson. A new species flowering in bunches of scarlet crimson tubed flowers. Habit of Serratifola. GC. P248 10/4/1854 Listed by Mitchell, Bristol Nurseries, Kemptown, Brighton. Gartenflora Vol 2. 1852 P185. Colour plate Flore Des Serres et Des Jardins, Vol VIII, p.754 1852-3.

MINISTRE BOUCHER. Double. Red/Purple. Tube. Dark scarlet. Sepals. Dark scarlet. Corolla. Purple. Very large. Long. JF. Cat. 1899. L. Cat. 1901. *Lemoine. Nancy. France. 1898.*

MINNIE. Single. Red/Purple. Tube. Red. Sepals. Red. Corolla. Purple. GC. P406 2/5/1863 Listed by Wm. Hussey, Norwich. P115 4th Ed. by Porcher 1874 Not in the first selection. *Bull, W. Chelsea. GB. 1862.*

MINNIE BANKS. Single. White/Purple. Tube. White. Thick. Stout. Sepals. White. Stout. Short. Reflexed. Recurved. Broad. Corolla. Lilac rose, stained white at base. (Scarlet or pink). (Clear pale purple). GC. P689 28/7/1860 FCC Hort. Scty. Show, London. GC. P653 9/7/1864 RBS Show 22/7/1864 Noted. CG P257 1865 "Best of 1864 varieties". SG. P459 1866 "Recommended". GC. P55 19/1/1867 Review by H. Cannell One of the best out. Splendid corolla. Cup shaped. P119 4th Ed. by Porcher 1874 Multiflowered. Vol. 1 J of RHS 1861 FCC 26/7/1860. HC. Cat. 1882-1885. P69 Vol 4 J of RHS 1877 Fuchsia trial at Chiswick 1873 Habit good. Free flowering, distinct, white tinted rose. Sepals Short, stout and reflexed. Corolla, Clear pale purple. Good. *Banks, E. Deal. GB. 1862.*

MINOS (a). S/Double. Red/Purple. Tube. Red. Sepals. Red. Corolla. Rosy Magenta. Dwarf. F. Myrtifolia X. *Lemoine. Nancy. France. 1896.*

MINOS (b). Double. Red/Purple. Tube. Crimson. Sepals. Crimson. Reverse rose. (Clear red). Broad. Corolla. Purple veined rose at base. JF. Cat. 1904. L. Cat. 1902. *Rozain. Lyons. France. 1902.*

MINOTAUR. Double. Red/Purple. Tube. Glossy carmine. Sepals. Glossy carmine. Corolla. Lavender Blue. Three corollas in one. "From a well known raiser in the North of England". GC. P191 27/2/1864 Intro. by B&S. Williams. NK. NK. *GB. 1864.*

MINSTREL (a). Single. Pink/Purple. Tube. Pink. Sepals. Pink. Horizontal. Corolla. Rose Lavender. B. Cat. 1870. NK. NK. NK. NK.

MINSTREL (b). Double. Red/White. Tube. Rosy crimson. Short. Sepals. Rosy crimson. Broad.

Recurved. Corolla. Ivory white striped rose at base. Fully double. Intro. by W. Bull. B. Cat. 1882-1888. HC. Cat. 1885-1891. *Eckford. GB. 1882.*

MINSTREL (c). ND. Red/ND. Tube. Red. Sepals. Red. Corolla. Striped. Laings Cat. 1890. NK. NK. *GB. NK.*

MIRABLIS (a). Single. Red/Purple. Tube. Crimson. Sepals. Crimson. Inside rosy crimson. Tipped green. Recurved. Corolla. Violet red. Large and exposed to view. Vigorous and free. GC. P393 6/1842 Listed by Youells, Gt. Yarmouth. GC. P241 15/4/1843 Listed by F&A Smith, Hackney. GC. P705 14/10/1843 Listed by J. Whitley, Wakefield. FC. Vol IX P214 1841. X Fulgens. *Smith, J. Dalston. GB. 1841.*

MIRABLIS (b). Single. Red/Purple. Tube. Scarlet. Sepals. Scarlet. Corolla. Lively scarlet. Bell shaped. Early bloomer. GC. P357 15/6/1850 Listed by H. Walton, Burnley. GC. P465 27/7/1850 Listed by G. Smith, Islington. GC. P226 13/4/1850 Intro. by Veitch, Exeter. *Story, W.H., Newton Abbott. GB. 1850.*

MIRACLE. ND. ND/ND. Tube. ND. Sepals. ND. Corolla. ND. RH. P295 1887 Fuchsias grown as standards at Twickel. *Demoureaux. Lille. France. NK.*

MIRANA. Single. Red/Purple. Tube. Deep rose. Sepals. Deep rose. Well reflexed. Corolla. Bluish purple, marked rose at base. A very pretty flower. B. Cat. 1872-1875. *Bull, W. Chelsea. GB. 1872.*

MIRANDA (a). Single. Pink/Red. Tube. Flesh. Sepals. Flesh. Corolla. Rosy Pink. GC. P216 27/3/1847 & P153 4/3/1848 & P232 1/4/1848 Listed by R. Cooper, Croydon. GC. P338 22/5/1847 Intro. by Knight, St. Leonards. *Knight, St. Leonards. GB. 1847.*

MIRANDA (b). Single. ND/ND. Tube. ND. Sepals. ND. Corolla.ND. GC. P279 30/4/1853 "Dark wooded stem". *Turner, C. Slough. GB. NK.*

MISAI. Double. Red/Purple. Tube. Red. Sepals. Red. Corolla. Violet ribboned with red. P133 4th Ed. by Porcher 1874. Not in the first selection. *Coene. Ghent. Belgium.1870.*

MISS BAILEY. ND. ND/ND. Double. ND. Sepals. ND. Corolla. ND. GC. P515 25/7/1857 & P418 22/5/1858 Listed by H. Walton, Burnley. NK. NK. *GB. 1857.*

MISS BERRAGE. Single. White/Red. Tube. White, faintly tinted pale rose. Sepals. White, faintly tinted pale rose. Corolla. Rosy carmine passing to scarlet at the margin with whitish veins. Laings. Cat. 1890. NK. NK. *GB*. NK.

MISS BURDETT COUTTS. Single. Red/White. Tube. Red. Sepals. Red. Corolla. White. Dwarf habit. Free bloomer. Continously in flower. HC. Cat. 1882. NK.NK. *GB*. NK.

MISS C. JONES. Single. White/Red. Tube. White. Sepals. White. Well reflexed. Corolla. Scarlet. Long. Large. GC. P95 4/2/1860 Intro. by Stewart and Nielsen, Liscard. *Stewart & Nielsen, Liscard. GB. 1860.*

MISS DORCAS WEBBER. ND. ND/ND. Tube. ND. Sepals. ND. Corolla. ND. GC. P338 15/4/1865 Listed by W. Rumley, Richmond. NK. NK. *GB. 1864.*

MISS E. MEARA. Single. Red/Purple. Tube. Carmine Scarlet. Sepals. Carmine Scarlet. Beautifully reflexed. Corolla. Rich dark marine blue. GO. "Select" HC. Cat. 1882. B. Cat. 1876. *Bull, W. Chelsea. GB. 1876.*

MISS. GRANT. Single. White/Red. Tube. Blush. Sepals. Blush. Corolla. Orange carmine. Very effective. JF. Cat. 1885. NK. NK. *GB*. NK.

MISS HAWTREY. Single. White/Red. Tube. White. 20mms long. Sepals. White. Uplifted. Corolla. Vermillion red. GC. P146 10/3/1855 "Best fuchsias of 1854". Listed by W. Rumley, Richmond. GC. P407 16/6/1855 RBS Show, Regents Park held on 13/6/1855- Finest light variety. Intro. by C. Turner, Slough. *Turner, C. Slough. GB. 1854.*

MISS LIZZIE VIDLER. Double Red/Purple. Tube. Rosy red. (Carmine red). Sepals. Rosy red. (Carmine red). Corolla. Mauve. (Rich mauve). GO. "Select" 1881-1886. HC. Cat. 1882. Laings Cat. 1890. Dobbies Cat. 1893/4. GC. P457 9/4/1881 Intro. By Jones & North, Hope Nurseries, Lewisham. To be sent out 12/4/1881. *Fry, G. Lea. GB. 1881.*

MISS LUCY FINNIS Double. Red/White. Tube. Coral red. Sepals. Coral red. Corolla. White. Immense size. GO. "Select" 1880-1891. HC. Cat. 1882-1898. Habit dwarf. Very Double. GC. Vol 26 P379 Exhibited at Bath Floral Fete by G Tucker 2nd 9 pot class. JF. Cat. 1885. Laings Cat. 1890. BSW. Cat 1897. Dobbies Cat. 1893/4. *Simmonds. GB. 1878*

MISS LYE. Single. White/Red. Tube. Blush. Suffused a delicate rosy pink. (White). Sepals. Blush. (White) Well recurved. Corolla. Rose,slightly shaded violet. (Carmine red flushed violet). GC. P206 17/2/1877 Like "Arabella" but darker petals. GC. P722 9/6/1877. B. Cat. 1878-1882. BSW. Cat. 1878. HC. Cat. 1882. JF. Cat. 1885. Laings Cat. 1890. *Lye, J. Market Lavington. GB. 1877.*

MISS MAY CAMERON. Single. Red/Purple. Tube. Red. Sepals. Red. Corolla. Lilac rose. HC. Cat. 1896. *Banks, E. Deal. GB. 1896.*

MISS PRETTYMAN. Single. White/Purple. Tube. White. Sepals. White. Corolla. Blood Purple. GC. P184 13/3/1847 & P250 27/4/1847. Listed by W. Miller, Ramsgate. GC. P216 27/3/1847. Listed by R. Cooper, Croydon. GC. P49 24/1/1846 Intro. by W. Miller, Ramsgate. *Miller, W. Ramsgate. GB. 1846.*

MISS ROBERTS. ND. ND/ND. Tube. ND. Sepals. ND. Corolla. ND. GC. P455 8/7/1847 Shown at RBS Show, London by Mr. Bray, Gardener to Mr. Goldsmith. NK. NK. NK. NK.

MISS STANLEY. Single. White/ND. Tube. White. Sepals. White. Corolla. ND. Midland Florist P133 1856 "Ten White Fuchsias". NK. NK. *GB*. NK.

MISS TALFOURD. Single. Red/Red. Tube. Carmine red. Sepals. Carmine red. Large. Pendant. Corolla. Lake. Long flowers. A nice shade of red. GC. P66 1/2/1845 Listed by Millers, Ramsgate. RH. P24 1846. RH. P167 1857. Exhibited at RBS Show July 1845 by Gaines. *Salter, Versailles. France. 1844.*

MISS VYSE. Single. Red/Purple. Tube. Rosy scarlet. Short. Sepals. Rosy scarlet. Broad. Recurved. Corolla. Rich blue. Very large. Very firm. GC. P450 Intro. by B.W. Knight, Battle. *Knight, B W. Battle. GB. 1862.*

MISS WELSH. Single. Pink/Red. Tube. Blush. Sepals. Blush. Corolla. Orange carmine. Very effective. JF. Cat. 1885. NK. NK. *GB. 1885.*

MISTRAL. Single. Red/Purple. Tube. Scarlet. Short. Sepals. Scarlet. Well reflexed. Corolla. Reddish violet. Robust. Very floriferous. B. Cat. 1891. L. Cat. 1892.Named after wind of the South of France. *Lemoine. Nancy. France. 1889.*

MISTRESS PUNCH. Single. ND/ND. Tube. ND. Sepals. ND. Corolla. ND. App. to RH. 1851 by Porcher. In a catalogue but flowers not seen or description obtained. *Kendall. GB.* NK.

MIZPAH. Single. White/Purple. Tube. White. Sepals. White. Corolla. Rich violet crimson. BSW. Cat. 1878. HC. Cat. 1882-1885. *Henderson, E.G. St. Johns Wood. GB. 1877.*

M. JOULE. Single. Red/Purple. Tube. Red. Sepals. Red. Corolla. Pretty sky blue colour marked white at base. (Lilac shaded blue). P141 GO. 1891. B. Cat. 1892-1893. Named after an French physicist (1818-89). L. Cat. 1892. *Lemoine. Nancy. France. 1890.*

M. LEQUET. Double. Red/White. Tube. Bright rose. Sepals. Bright rose. Well reflexed. Corolla. White veined rose. JF. Cat. 1904. *Rozain, Lyons. France. 1902.*

MLLE. DELNA. Double. Red/White. Tube. Red. Sepals. Red. Large. Twisted. Circular. Corolla. White veined pink. Good habit. JF. Cat. 1901. L. Cat. 1901. *Lemoine. Nancy. France. 1900.*

M. KETELEER. Single. White/Red. Tube. White. Sepals. White. Corolla. Clear scarlet. JF. Cat. 1898. NK. NK. *France. NK.*

M. KOCH. Double. Red/Pink. Tube. Bright carmine. Sepals. Bright carmine. Raised back to tube. Corolla. Soft Rose. L. Cat. 1912. *Lemoine. Nancy. France. 1912.*

M. LOMBARD. Double. Red/Purple. Tube. Coral red. (Red). Sepals. Coral red. (Red). Reflexed. Corolla. Clear lilac margined white. (Light lilac margined and striped white. Comes almost pure white on occasions). HC. Cat. 1882-1885. B. Cat. 1880-1883. *Boucharlet, Lyons. France. 1880.*

M. LOMBROSO. Double. Red/Purple. Tube. Rich crimson. Sepals. Rich crimson. Corolla. Bluish Violet. GO. P141 1891 "Continental Fuchsias of 1890". B. Cat. 1892, 1893. L. Cat. 1892. Named after the Italian founder of the science of criminology (1836-1909). *Lemoine. Nancy. France. 1890.*

M. LUQUET. Double. Red/Purple. Tube. Coral. Sepals. Coral. Corolla. Reddish purple, veined rose at base. L. Cat. 1902. *Rozain, Lyons. France. 1902.*

MME. CHAMBEYRON Double. Red/Pink. Tube. Dull red. Sepals. Dull red. Corolla. Pinkish white, veined purple. Broad. Full. L. Cat.1906. *Rozain, Lyons. France. 1905.*

MME. DANJOUX. Single. Red/Pink. Tube. Carmine pink. Sepals. Carmine pink. Corolla. Flesh pink. Centre petals pink veined carmine. Large. *Rozain. Lyons. France. 1902.*

MME. DE THÈBES. S/Double. Pink/White. Tube. Clear pink. Sepals. Clear pink. Large. Well reflexed. Corolla. Nice white. Vigourous. L. Cat. 1906. *Lemoine. Nancy. France. 1905*

MME. DU GAST. Double. White/Purple. Tube. White. Sepals. White with pink tinge. Green tips. Reflexed. Corolla. Violet fading purple violet. Full. L. Cat. 1913. *Lemoine. Nancy. France. 1913.*

MME. JACQUES FEUILLET. Double. Red/White. Tube. Crimson carmine. Sepals. Crimson Carmine. Reflexed. Corolla. White marked rose. Enormous. L. Cat. 1913. *Lemoine. Nancy. France. 1913.*

MME. LANTELME. Double. Red/White. Tube. Crimson. Sepals. Crimson. Reflexed. Corolla. Soft whitish pink. Full. L. Cat. 1912. *Lemoine. Nancy. France. 1912.*

MME. VIGÉE-LEBRUN. Double. Red/White. Tube. Bright red. Sepals. Bright red. Corolla. White overlaid pink. L. Cat. 1910. *Lemoine. Nancy. France. 1910.*

MODEL (a). Single. White/Red. Tube. Blush white. (Pure white flesh coloured at base). Very long. Sepals. Blush White. (Pure white). Corolla. Orange and Scarlet. (Rosy pink shaded orange). GC. P145 9/3/1850. GC. P210 6/4/1850 Listed by H. Walton, Burnley. GC. P241 20/4/1850 Listed by W. Rendle, Plymouth. GC. P307 14/5/1853 Listed by B.R. Cant, Colchester. GC. P423 7/7/1849 Intro. by Youells, Gt. Yarmouth. *Youell. Gt.Yarmouth. GB. 1849.*

MODEL (b). Single. Red/Purple. Tube. Bright Reddish Purple. Short. Sepals. Bright Reddish purple. Large. Reflexed. Corolla. Violet Blue. Small. GC. P391 12/6/1852. "Has many sterling qualities". GC. P307 14/5/1853 Listed by B.R. Cant, Colchester. GC. P385 18/6/1853 Listed by H. Walton, Burnley. GC. P627 1/10/1853 Listed by S. Fenney, Gateshead. P185 3rd Ed. by Porcher 1858. Intro. by C. Turner, Slough. *Banks, E. Deal. GB. 1853.*

MODEL (c). Single. Red/Purple. Tube. Shining crimson. Thick. Short. Sepals. Shining crimson. Large. Reflexed. Corolla. Indigo blue. almost black. washed red and brown. Bell shaped. Large. Well formed. HC. Cat. 1882. B. Cat. 1870-1873. P111 4th Ed. by Porcher 1874. Meritorius for its form, habit and colour. Pedicel 35mms. *Banks, E. Deal. GB. 1868.*

MODEL (d). Double. Red/Purple. Tube. Bright red. Sepals. Bright red. Corolla. Dark purple flamed carmine. Full. Regular. GC. P406 29/9/1877 Noted on a Visit to H. Cannell,Swanley. B. Cat. 1870, 1872. BSW. Cat. 1878. GC. P451 2/4/1870 Intro. by Felton & Son, Birmingham. *Felton, Birmingham. GB. 1870.*

MODEL (e) Double. Red/White. Tube. Cherry red. Sepals. Cherry Red. Corolla. White. Laings Cat. circa 1890. NK. NK. NK. NK.

MODESTA. Single. Pink/Red. Tube. Flesh. Sepals. Flesh. Corolla. Vermillion. GC. P375 4/6/1844 Exhibited by J. Smith, H.S. Show, London. GC. P66 1/2/1845 Listed by W.Miller, Ramsgate. GC. P146 8/3/1845 Listed by Youell, Gt. Yarmouth. RH. P24 1846. GC. P193 30/3/1844 Intro. by J. Smith *Smith, J. Dalston. GB. 1844.*

MODIOLA. Single. Red/White. Tube. Bright rosy crimson. Sepals. Bright rosy crimson. Well reflexed. Corolla. Waxy white, striped crimson rose at base of sepals. B. Cat. 1875, 1876. NK. NK.NK.NK.

MOLESWORTH. Double. Red/White. Tube. Red.(Carmine).Sepals. Red. (Carmine). Well reflexed. Corolla. Pure white. (Pure Ivory white). HC. Cat. 1890. L. Cat. 1892. Laings Cat. 1890. Dobbies Cat. 1893/4. B. Cat. 1889-1893. BSW. Cat. 1888-1897. JF. Cat. 1895. GC. Vol. 7 24/5/1890. Intro. by Hender & Son, Plymouth. *Rundle, G. Molesworth. GB. 1888.*

MOLIÈRE (a). Single. Red/Purple. Tube. Bright red. Sepals. Bright red. Long. Spreading. Corolla. Violet blue. App. to RH. 1851 by Porcher. 2nd. Class, but superior to "Victor Hugo". Named after French playwright. Corallina X. *Baudinat. France. 1849.*

MOLIÈRE (b). Single. Red/Purple. Tube. Wine red. Sepals. Wine red. Large. Recurved. Corolla. Plum. Large. B. Cat. 1898, 1899. NK. NK. NK. *1898.*

MONA. Double. Red/Purple. Tube. Rich crimson. Sepals. Rich crimson. Elegantly reflexed. Corolla. Deep purple. B. Cat. 1872-1875. Intro. by W. Bull, Chelsea. *Bull, W. Chelsea. GB. 1872.*

MONARCH (a). Single. Red/Purple. Tube. Purplish vermillion. Stout. Sepals. Purplish vermillion. Corolla. Crimson purple. GC. P574 19/8/1843 Exhibited at H.S. Show by Epps on 15/8/1843. GC. P375 4/6/1844 Exhibited by Catleugh at H.S. Show. Floricultural Cabinet P219 Vol Xi 1843 "Bears the greatest resemblance in form and habit to "Globosa Major"". GC. P146 8/3/1845 Listed by Youell, Gt. Yarmouth. GC. P561 12/8/1843 Intro. by W.J. Epps.

Epps, W.J. Maidstone GB. 1844.

MONARCH (b). Single. Red/Purple. Tube. Scarlet. Sepals. Scarlet. Great width. Corolla. Light blue violet. Fine. Expanded. GC. P401 24/6/1854 Listed by H. Walton, Burnley. GC, P466 28/7/1854. Listed by Bass & Brown, Sudbury. GC. P530 11/8/1855 Listed by Bainbridge & Hewison, York. GC. P178 25/3/1853. *Henderson, E.G. St. GB. 1854.*

MONARCH (c). Double. Red/Purple. Tube. Crimson. Sepals. Crimson. Reflexed. Corolla. Purple. Large. GC. P952 11/10/1862 Intro. by W. Bull, Chelsea. To be sent out 13/10/1862. *Bull, W. Chelsea. GB. 1862.*

MONARCH (d). Single. Red/Red. Tube. Light Lake red. Rather slender. Tapered. Sepals. Light lake red. Spreading. 1½" long. Reflexed. Corolla. Light lake red. Conical shape 1¼". Similar colour to sepals. Very large. Well expanded. Pcxvii Vol 3 P of RHS 1872 Fuchsia trials at Chiswick 1872. HC. Cat. 1882-1898. GC. Vol 26 1886 Fuchsia trial at Chiswick. B. Cat 1872-1876. GC. P299 4/3/1876 List of Selfs. GC. P476 15/4/1871 Intro. by W. Bull, Chelsea. *Bull, W. Chelsea. GB. 1871.*

MONEYPENNI. Single. Red/Purple. Tube. Cerise red. Thick. Sepals. Bright cerise red. Open. Corolla. Violet. The flowers are more than half as big as "Standishii", blooms in racemes of a highly beautiful Rosy Carmine, and of a strong and magnificent habit. 1st Banksian Medal at the Hort. Scty. Show. Named after Capt. Monypenny, Todd's employer. GC. P393 6/1842 & P98 17/2/1844 & P146 8/3/1845 Listed by Youells, Gt.Yarmouth. GC. P112 17/2/1844 Listed by W. Miller, Ramsgate. GC. P216 27/3/1847 Listed by R. Cooper, Croydon. GC. P625 Intro. by M. Todd, Rolvenden. *Todd, M., Rolvenden GB. 1841.*

MONSIEUR ACKERMAN. Double. Red/Purple. Tube. Carmine. (Shining crimson) Almost nil. Sepals. Shining crimson. (Carmine). Corolla. Bright carmine shaded dark blue. (Violet blue streaked red). Inside of the petals area different shade. P131 4th Ed. by Porcher 1874. B. Cat. 1870-1873. *Cornelissen, Arras. Belgium. 1868.*

MONSIEUR ALDEBERT. Double. Red/White. Tube. Clear red. Thin. Sepals. Clear red. Reflexed. Corolla. Pure white, pin striped with red. Full. Large. P129 4th Ed. by Porcher 1874. *L'Huillier France. 1868.*

MONSIEUR CHARLES GAILLY. Double. Red/Purple. Tube. Red. Sepals. Red. Corolla. Purple. P126 4th Ed. by Porcher 1874. Not in the first selection. *Cornelissen, Arras. Belgium. 1868.*

MONSIEUR FILLION. Double. Red/Purple. Tube. Crimson red. Almost nil. Sepals. Crimson red. Large. Reflexed right up. Corolla. Violet, splashed and streaked with red. Petals folded and spreading. Pedicel 35/40 mms. Foliage.Dark Green. Oval shaped and elongated. Very dentate. P132 4th. Ed. by Porcher 1874. JF. Cat. 1885. *Crousse. France.1868.*

MONSIEUR KLEIN. Single. White/Red. Tube. White. Thick. Swollen at top. 18mm long. Sepals. White. Reflexed. Corolla. Carmine red, margined fire red. Spiralled. Expanded. *L'Huiller France. 1869.*

MONSIEUR LAURENTIUS. ND. ND/ND. Tube. ND. Sepals. ND. Corolla. ND. RH. P295 1887. Grown as a standard at Twickel. *Cornelissen. Arras. Belgium. NK.*

MONSIEUR LAUTH. Single. Red/Purple. Tube. Carmine red. Sepals. Carmine red. Well reflexed. Corolla. Violet striped rose (Plum often striped with rose). Well expanded. Large. Compact flowers. P111 4th. Ed. by Porcher 1874. HC. Cat. 1882-1885. *Lemoine. Nancy. France. 1874.*

MONSIEUR LOUIS BERGER. Single. Red/Red. Tube. Bright scarlet. Sepals. Bright scarlet. Corolla. Carmine. Grand form and habit. JF. Cat. 1898. L. Cat. 1901. *Berger, L. Bagnolet. France. 1897.*

MONSIEUR MAIL. Double. Red/White. Tube. Crimson. Sepals. Crimson. Reflexed. Rounded to tube. Corolla. White. striped bright rose. P129 4th Ed. by Porcher 1874. *Cornelissen. Arras. Belgium. 1865.*

MONSIEUR PORCHER. Double. Red/Purple. Tube. Bright crimson red. Thick. 15mm long. Sepals. Bright crimson red. Very big. Reflexed. Corolla. Bluish violet washed red. Floriferous. Strong pyramidical growth. Pedicel 45 mms. P124 4th Ed. by Porcher 1874. *L'Huillier. France. 1868.*

MONSIEUR TAGLIARUE. Double. Red/Purple. Tube. Red. Sepals. Red. Corolla. Purple. P126 4th Ed. by Porcher 1874. Not in the first selection. *Cornelissen. Arras. Belgium. 1863.*

MONSIEUR. THIBAUT. ND. ND/ND. Tube. ND. Sepals. ND. Corolla. ND. RH. P311 1889 "Select" by E.A. Carrière. NK. NK. NK. NK.

MONSTER. Double. Red/Purple. Tube. Scarlet. Sepals. Scarlet. Corolla. Purple. Measures 2" to 2½" across, or as large as a small rose. GC. P55 19/1/1867 Review by H. Cannell. P56 F&P 1866. Intro. by H. Cannell. *Bland,E. Fordham. GB. 1866.*

MONSTROSA (a). Single. Red/Purple. Tube. Red. Sepals. Red. Corolla. Purple. GC. P162 14/3/1846 & P184 13/3/1847 Listed by W. Miller, Ramsgate. GC. P201 28/3/1846 Like "Standishii", but twice as large. GC. P186 20/3/1847 Three times the size of "Standishi". Sepals expand. GC. 6/2/1847 & P216 27/3/1847 & P232 1/4/1848 & P256 21/4/1849 Listed by R. Cooper, Croydon. GC.P201 28/3/1846 Intro. by Standish. *Standish, Bagshot. GB. 1846.*

MONSTROSA (b). Double. Red/White. Tube. Crimson red. Sepals. Crimson red. Large. Raised up. Corolla. Pure white, striped with crimson red at base. Vigourous bush. Good foliage and flower. P129 4th Ed. by Porcher 1874. NK. NK. *GB. 1868.*

MONSTROSA (c). Double. Red/Purple. Tube. Carmine scarlet.Sepals. Carmine scarlet. Well reflexed. Corolla. Deep purple, striped fiery crimson. Petals are 1" broad and arranged to show two separate corollas. GC. P371 11/4/1868 Intro. by B. S. Williams, Holloway. NK. NK. *GB. 1868.*

MONSTROSITY. Double. Red/Purple. Tube. Red. Short. Stout. Sepals. Red. Divergent. Corolla. Purple shaded violet. BSW. Cat. 1878. GC. P521 28/41877. Intro. by B&S Williams. *Bland, E. Fordham. GB. 1877.*

MONSTRUOSA PLENA. Double. Red/Red. Tube. Dark coral red. Short. Sepals. Dark coral red. Well recurved. Corolla. Bright reddish crimson. Extended. Good habit. Vigourous. Enormous flowers. B. Cat. 1879-1883. *Bull, W. Chelsea. GB. 1879.*

MONTGOMERY. Single. Red/Purple. Tube. Crimson. Short. Sepals. Crimson. Horizontal. Corolla. Rich purplish crimson, flaked mottled rose. B. Cat. 1881-1883.Intro. by W Bull, Chelsea. *Bland, E. Fordham. GB. 1881.*

MONTROSE. Double. Red/White. Tube. Bright rose. Sepals. Bright rose. Broad. Well reflexed. Green tips. Corolla. White. Flower neat and compact. GC. P414 17/4/1869. B. Cat. 1870-1873.Intro. by W. Bull, Chelsea. *Bland, E. Fordham. GB. 1869.*

MONUMENT. Double. Red/Purple. Tube. Rosy crimson. Sepals. Rosy crimson. Horizontal. Corolla.

Deep purple striped rosy carmine. JF. Cat. 1885. B. Cat. 1882-1893. Intro. by W. Bull. *Eckford. GB. 1882.*

MORAVIA. Double. Red/White. Tube. Red. Sepals. Red. Corolla. White, streaked carmine rose. Full. Large. P135 4th Ed. by Porcher 1874. *Twrdy, Brno. Austria. 1873.*

MOUNT BLANC. Single. White/Purple. Tube. Pure white. Sepals. Pure white. Corolla. Amarinth rose. App. to RH. 1851 by Porcher. GC. P537 12/8/1848 Listed by G. Smith, Islington. GC. P161 17/3/1849 Listed by W. Rumley, Richmond. GC. P224 14/4/1849 Listed by R. Whibley, Kennington Cross. GC. P256 21/4/1849 Listed by R. Cooper, Croydon. GC. P274 5/5/1849 Listed by H. Walton, Burnley. GC P153 4/3/1848 Intro. by Kendall. *Kendall, Stoke Newington. GB. 1848.*

MR. A. HUGGETT. SingleRed/Purple. Tube. Carmine. Sepals. Carmine. Corolla. Rosy mauve. Most profuse. Laings. Cat. circa 1890. Countess of Aberdeen X. NK. NK. *GB. 1890?*

MR. CHARLES PALMER. Single. White/Red. Tube. White. Sepals. White. Broad. Inverted. Corolla. Scarlet. GC. P213 8/4/1854 Listed by H. Low. GC. P401 24/6/1854 Listed by H. Walton, Burnley. GC. P466 26/7/1854 Listed by Bass & Brown, Sudbury. GC. P238 14/4/1855 Listed by J. Hoade, Addlestone. GC. P83 11/2/1854 Intro. by T. Batten, Clapton. *Batten, T. Clapton. GB. 1854.*

MR. DISRAELI. Single. Red/Purple. Tube. Bright crimson red. (Bright Scarlet). Sepals. Bright crimson red.(Bright scarlet). Perfectly reflexed. Corolla. Violet washed red. (Intense Mauve).Good colour. Floriferous. Short pedicals hold flowers erect, and gradually incline to horizontal. Very large. Elegantly shaped. Very large. Same style and colour as "Count Cavour". P111 4th Ed. by Porcher 1874. B. Cat. 1870-1873. NK. NK. *GB. 1870.*

MR. D.T. FISH. ND. Red/Purple. Tube. Dark scarlet. Sepals. Dark scarlet. Corolla. Plum. BSW. Cat. 1878. GO. P109 1881. "Select" NK. NK. *GB. 1878?.*

MR. E. BENNETT. NK. NK. NK. GC. 1894. Vol I. P146. Intro. by H. Cannell. *Bland, E. Fordham. GB. 1873.*

MR. EWART. ND. ND/ND. Tube. ND. Sepals. ND. Corolla. ND. GC. P314 10/5/1856 Listed by H. Walton, Burnley. NK. NK. *GB. 1855.*

MR. F. BRIGHT. Single. Red/Purple. Tube. Deep rosy red. (Pink). Sepals. Deep rosy red. (Pink) Corolla. Rose margined with rich blue purple. (Rose purple). GC. Vol 24 P277 1885. JF. Cat. 1886. Laings. Cat. 1890. BSW. Cat. 1888. *Lye,J. Market Lavington. GB. 1886.*

MR. F. GLASS. Single. Red/Purple. Tube. Deep crimson. Sepals. Deep crimson. Corolla. Purple maroon. GC. Vol. 24 P277 1885. JF. Cat. 1886. Laings. Cat. circa 1890. B. Cat. 1888-1892. BSW. Cat. 1888. *Lye J. Market Lavington. GB. 1886.*

MR. GLADSTONE. Double. Red/Purple. Tube. Scarlet. Sepals. Scarlet. Corolla. Violet. Enormously Large. JF. Cat. 1898. See M. GLADSTONE.

MR. HOOPER TAYLOR. Single. Red/Purple. Tube. Red. Sepals. Red. Corolla. Light magenta purple. Coloured illustration Plate 426 Floral Magazine Nov 1880. *Lye,J. Market Lavington. GB. 1880.*

MR. JAMES HUNTLEY. SEE JAMES HUNTLEY.

MR. J. LAWRENCE. Single. ND/ND. Tube. ND. Sepals. ND. Corolla. ND. GC. P314 10/5/1856 Listed by W. Rumley, Richmond. NK. NK. *GB. 1855.*

MR. LYNDOE. Double. Red/Purple. Tube. Scarlet. Sepals. Scarlet. (Pale red). Greatly reflexed. Corolla. Purple. Bold but irregular. Free growing. Very long flowers. Vol. 4 J of RHS. P217 1877 FCC. Fuchsia trials at Chiswick. NK. NK. *GB.* NK.

MR POWELL. Single. Red/Purple. Tube. Deep carmine. Sepals. Deep carmine. Corolla. Purple. Compact habit. GO. P97 1882. GC. Vol 17 20/5/1882 Intro. by B&S Williams. *Bland, E. Fordham GB. 1882.*

MR. RICHARD PEXTON. Single. Red/Purple. Tube. Crimson red. Sepals. Crimson red. Large. Reflexed. Corolla. Dark Purple. Perfect form. Very large. Very dark. P111 4th. Ed. by Porcher 1874. P73 HC. Cat. 1882-1885. *Banks, E. Deal. GB. 1872.*

M. RIBOULON. Double. Red/White. Tube. Carmine. Sepals. Carmine. Corolla. White veined carmine. Petals mixed with carmine. JF. Cat. 1901. L. Cat. No. 149, 1901. *Rozain. Lyons. France. 1900.*

M. RIVOLI. Double. Red/Purple. Tube. Scarlet. Sepals. Scarlet. Corolla. Violet. Very Large. JF. Cat. 1907, 1910. NK. NK. NK. *1907.*

MR. RUNDELL. Single. White/Red. Tube. White. Sepals. White. Corolla. Red. Similar to Earl of Beaconsfield, (whose flowers are common and misshapen). Beautiful shaped flower. HC. Cat. 1885. Intro. by H. Cannell. Earl of Beaconsfield X. NK. NK. *GB. 1881.*

MRS. A. HUGGETT. Double. White/ND. Tube. White. Sepals. White. Recurved. Corolla. ND. Laings Cat. circa 1890. NK. NK. *GB.* NK.

MRS. BALLANTINE. Double. Red/White. Tube. Scarlet. Sepals. Scarlet. Corolla. White. Fully expanded. Floral World and Garden Guide P4 Jan 1870. GC. P567/8 23/4/1870. JF. Cat. 1885. GC. P146 1895. Intro. by H. Cannell. *Bland, E. Fordham. GB. 1871.*

MRS. BARRY. ND. White/ND. Tube. Creamy yellow. Sepals. Creamy yellow. Green tips. Corolla. ND. Stamens are creamy yellow. GC. P659 23/5/1885. Intro. by B&S Williams. BSW. Cat. 1888. *Williams, B & S. GB. 1885.*

MRS. BAYLEY. ND. ND/ND. Tube. ND. Sepals. ND. Corolla. ND. GC. P162 14/3/1846 & P184 13/3/1847 Listed by W. Miller, Ramsgate. Light variety. NK. NK. *GB.* NK.

MRS. BERRAGE. ND. Pink/Red. Tube. Pale rose. Sepals. Pale rose. Corolla. Scarlet. BSW. Cat. 1897. NK. NK. *GB.* NK.

MRS. BLAND. Single. Red/White. Tube. Scarlet. Sepals. Scarlet. Rather narrow. Well reflexed. Corolla. White. Barrel shaped. It is generally assumed that a plant with this colour of flowers has a long slender of habit of growth , but this has a dwarf vigorous habit. Foliage broad and bold. GC. P1554 2/12/1871 Review by H.Cannell. P131 4th Ed. by Porcher 1874. *Bland, E. Fordham. GB. 1871.*

MRS. BOUCH. ND. ND/ND. Tube. ND. Sepals. ND. Corolla. ND. GC P314 10/5/1856 Listed by W. Rumley. Richmond. NK. NK. *GB. 1855.*

MRS BRIGHT. Single. White/Red. Tube. Waxy white. Sepals. Waxy white. Corolla. Orange scarlet. Free bloomer. FCC at Bath 1881. GC. P824 27/6/1885 RHS Fuchsia trials at Chiswick "Best in its class" G. 6/9/1884 Exhibited at Trowbridge Hort. Scty. Show 20/8/1884 by J. Lye. GC. Vol 20 1883 P243 & P280 Exhibited at Trowbridge Hort. Scty. show 22/8/1883 by J. Lye 1st 9 pot class. *Lye, J. Market Lavington. GB. 1883.*

MRS. BURROUGHS. Single. White/Red. Tube. Pure white. Long. Stout. Sepals. Pure white. Much reflexed. Corolla. Crimson Lake. Barrel shaped. BSW. Cat. 1878.GC. P521 28/4/1877 Intro. by B&S Williams. *Bland, E. Fordham. GB. 1877.*

MRS. CHARLES DANIELS. Double. Red/White. Tube. Crimson red. Sepals. Crimson red. Reflexed. Corolla. White veined carmine. Enormous. L. Cat. 1892. JF. Cat. 1892. *Rozain. Lyons. France. 1891.*

MRS. E. BENNETT. Single. Red/White. Tube. Crimson red. Short. Sepals. Crimson red. Large. Long. Uplifted. Corolla. Pure white. Spiralled. Floriferous. Large. Upright. Dark green foliage. Oval. Elongated. Very dentate. Pedicel 50mms. P129 4th Ed. by Porcher 1874. Free blooming. Erect habit. P216 Vol. 4 J of RHS Fuchsia trials at Chiswick FCC. GO 1881-1888 "Select". HC. Cat.1882-1885 One of the best for exhibition. RH. P311 1889 "Select" by E.A. Carrière. Intro. by H. Cannell. *Bland, E. Fordham. GB. 1872.*

MRS. E.G. HILL. Double. Red/White. Tube. Scarlet. (Dark red). Sepals. Scarlet. (Dark red). Well reflexed. Corolla. Pure white. (Creamy White). Very large. L. Cat. 1892. Laings Cat. 1890. Dobbies Cat. 1893/4. B. Cat. 1888. Gartenflora 1888. *Lemoine. Nancy. France. 1887.*

MRS. EUSTACE SMITH. Double. White/Purple. Tube. White. Sepals. White. Corolla. Violet. Large. JF. Cat. 1912. NK. NK. *GB. 1912.*

MRS. FREDERICK MILLBANK. Single. White/Purple. Tube. White tinted rose. Sepals. White tinted rose. Large. Extended. Open. Green tips. Corolla. Violet cerise. Previously called "Nonpareil". GC. P216 27/3/1847 Listed by R. Cooper. GC. P184 13/3/1847 Listed by W. Miller, Ramsgate. GC. P201 25/3/1848 Listed by W. Rumley, Richmond. GC. P129 28/2/1846 Intro. by W. Jackson. *Jackson, W. Bedale GB. 1846.*

MRS. F. GLASS. Single. White/Red. Tube. Creamy white. Stout, Sepals. Creamy white. Corolla.Bright carmine. (Pink). An improvement on "Beauty of Trowbridge". GC. Vol. 24 P277 1885. G. Vol 36 P277 21/9/1889 exhibited at Bath Floral Fete by J. Lye - 3rd 9 pot class. JF. Cat. 1886-1888. B. Cat. 1888. Laings Cat. 1890. *Lye, J. Market Lavington. GB. 1886.*

MRS. FRY. Single. Red/Purple. Tube. Rosy vermillion. Medium. Sepals. Rosy vermillion. Divergent. Green tips. Corolla. Violet red. Small. GC. P162 14/3/1847 & P184 13/3/1847 Listed by W.

Miller, Ramsgate. GC. P201 27/3/1847 Listed by Hart & Nickling, Guildford. GC. P216 27/3/1847 Listed by R. Cooper, Croydon. GC. P254 19/4/1845 Intro. by J. Smith, Dalston. *Smith, J. Dalston. GB. 1845.*

MRS. GADDICK DITTON. Single. White/Red. Tube. White. Sepals. White. Recurved. Lanceolate. Corolla. Bright carmine. Produced in large terminal clusters. B. Cat. 1877-1879. BSW. Cat. 1878. HC. Cat. 1882. GO. "Select" 1883-1887. *Todman GB. 1876.*

MRS. GIDEON BROWN. Double. Red/Purple. Tube. Scarlet.Sepals. Scarlet. Corolla. Violet Purple. Large. Full. Free. JF. Cat. 1912. NK. NK. *GB.1912.*

MRS. GLADSTONE. Single. Red/White. Tube. Scarlet. Sepals. Scarlet. Broad. Reflexed. Corolla. White, with a beautiful scarlet feather. Perfect shape. Bell shaped. Equal to "Guiding Star". GC. P55 19/1/1867 Review by H. Cannell. F&P P57 3/1866. Intro.by H. Cannell. *Bland,E. Fordham.GB.1874..*

MRS. GRANT. Single. White/Red. Tube. Blush. Sepals. Blush. Corolla. Orange red. B. Cat. 1879-1883. NK. NK. *GB.* NK.

MRS. GEORGE GROTE. Single. White/Pink. Tube. White. Sepals. White. Corolla. Pink. HC. Cat. 1885, 1890. A very fine variety, useful for baskets. Laings Cat. circa 1890. NK. NK. *GB.* NK.

MRS. H. CANNELL. Double. Red/White. Tube. Bright Carmine. Sepals. Bright Carmine. Corolla. White. Large. Full. Illustration in H. Cannell Cat. Page 71 1882. HC. Cat. 1882-1890 Very late. B. Cat. 1875-1879. BSW. Cat. 1878. GC. P363 20/3/1875 Intro. by H. Cannell, of Woolwich. *Swaffield. GB. 1875.*

MRS. HOBHOUSE. Single. White/Red. Tube. White. Sepals. White. Corolla. Rosy red. GM. P653 1896 Noted. GC. Vol 22 P249 1897. *Lye, J. Market Lavington. GB. 1897.*

MRS. HOOPER TAYLOR. Single. White/Red. Tube. White. Sepals. White. Well reflexed. Corolla. Cerise Pink. (Dark rose) Coloured illustration Plate 426 Floral Magazine Nov. 1880. JF. Cat. 1885. *Lye, J. Market Lavington. GB. 1880.*

MRS. HUNTLEY. Sepals. White/Red. Tube. White. Sepals. Delicate flesh. Corolla. Brilliant Carmine. GC. P722 9/6/1877. GC. P503 20/10/1877 refers to coloured illustration Plate T277 in Floral Magazine. GO. "Select" 1880-1891. HC. Cat. 1882.

Dobbies Cat. 1893-4. *Lye, J. Market Lavington. GB. 1877.*

MRS. J. DOEL. Single. White/Red. Tube. White. Sepals. White. Corolla. Carmine red. GC. P881 1873 Exhibited at the RHS Show at Bath, by J. Lye. Light like "Arabella". NK. NK. *GB. 1873.*

MRS. J. LYE. Single. White/Purple. Tube. Creamy white. Short. Sepals. Creamy white. Long. Well reflexed. Corolla. Dark red shaded purple. HC. Cat. 1882 One of the best for pyramids. GC. P211 17/2/1877 Fuchsias grown at Trowbridge. GO. "Select" 1880-1891. B.Cat 1875/76. BSW. Cat. 1878. GC Vol 20 P243 1883 & Vol 26 P403 1886. *Lye, J. Market Lavington. GB. 1875.*

MRS. J. NAYLOR. Single. Red/Red. Tube. Crimson. Sepals. Crimson. Corolla. Fine Puce. GC. P611 15/9/1855 Selected from 3000 seedlings. To be sent out 1/4/1856. Intro. by Stewart & Nielsen, Liscard. *Stewart & Nielsen, Liscard. GB. 1856.*

MRS. JOYNSON. Single. White/Purple. Tube. Waxy white. Sepals. Waxy white. Well reflexed. Corolla. Lilac edged crimson. Large. GC. P95 4/2/1860 Intro. by Stewart & Nielsen. *Stewart & Nielsen, Liscard. GB. 1860.*

MRS. KING. Single. White/Red. Tube. White. Sepals. White. Corolla. Rich carmine. Expands with age. GC. Vol 20 P243 25/8/1883. JF. Cat. 1885. Laings Cat. 1890. B. Cat. 1883. *Lye, J. Market Lavington. GB. 1883.*

MRS. LANE. Single. ND/ND. Tube. ND. Sepals. ND. Corolla. ND. GC. P436 21/6/1845 Exhibited at H.S. Show by Lane. GC. P797 28/11/1845 To be sent out in 1846. GC. P410 20/6/1846 Winner of challenge originated by W. Miller, Ramsgate. GC. P216 27/3/1847 & P232 1/4/1848 Listed by R. Cooper,Croydon. GC. P265 24/4/1847 & P259 29/4/1849 Listed by W. Rendle, Plymouth. *Lane, Berkhamstead. GB. 1846.*

MRS. MARSHALL. Single. White/Red. Tube. Pure white. Sepals. Pure white. Well reflexed. Corolla. Dark rose. (Red). GC. P1331 1871 Grown as a bedder in Hyde Park. Vol 2 J of RHS 1870 Fuchsia trial at Chiswick. A free bloomer, flowers with a lengthened tube, spreading. small red corolla. Pcxii Vol 3 J of RHS 1872. Fuchsia Trial at Chiswick, considered to be identical with "Arabella". Laings. Cat. circa 1890. GC. P424 11/5/1861 Intro. by Stewart & Nielsen,Liscard. *Stewart & Nielsen, Liscard. GB. 1861.*

MRS. MEIN. Single. Red/White. Tube. Bright carmine. (Scarlet). Sepals. Bright carmine. (Scarlet). Well reflexed. Corolla. Pure white. Beautifully formed flower. Perfect shape. GC. Vol. 26 1886 Fuchsia trial at Chiswick 11/7/1886. B. Cat. 1877-1879. HC. Cat. 1882-1891. JF. Cat. 1885. GC. P491 17/4/1875 Intro. by B&S Williams. *Bland, E. Fordham. GB. 1875.*

MRS MOULD. Single. ND/ND. Tube. ND. Sepals. ND. Corolla. ND. GC. P84 18/7/1874 Exhibited at H.S. Show 15/7/1874 by F.G. Mould. *Mould, F.G. GB. 1874.*

MRS. PATTERSON. Single. White/Purple. Tube. White. Sepals. White. Single. Light violet purple. GC. P385 18/6/1853 & P147 11/3/1854 Listed by W. Rumley, Richmond. GC. P465 23/7/1853 by J. Harrison, Darlington. GC. P483 30/7/1853 & P162 18/3/1854 Listed by H. Walton, Burnley. GC. P627 1/10/1883 Listed by S. Fenney, Gateshead. GC. P213 8/4/1854 Listed by C.H. Gardiner, Maidstone. GC. P248 15/4/1854 Listed by Mitchell & Co, Brighton. GC. P358 26/5/1855 Listed by Hart & Nicklen, Guildford. GC. P98 12/2/1853 Intro. by G. Smith, Islington. *Patterson. GB. 1853.*

MRS. RUNDELL. Single. White/Red. Tube. Tinted warm salmon. Sepals. Warm salmon tint. Corolla. Vermillion red. JF. Cat. 1885 An improvement on "Earl of Beaconsfield". Laings. Cat. circa 1890, An orange improvement on the "Aurora Superba" type (Spelt Rundle). Dobbies Cat. 1893/4 (Spelt Rundle). GO. "Select" 1884-1891. BSW. Cat. 1888-1897. HC. Cat. P86 1885 Seedling from "Earl of Beaconsfield". Earl of Beaconsfield X. GO. P97 1882. Intro. by H. Cannell. NK.NK. *GB. 1881.*

MRS. SCOTT. ND. ND/ND. Tube. ND. Sepals. ND. Corolla. ND. GC. P338 15/4/1865 Listed by W. Rumley, Richmond. NK. NK. *GB. 1864.*

MRS. SHIRLEY HIBBERD. Single. White/Pink. Tube. Pure white. Sepals. Pure white. Perfectly reflexed. No green on tips. Corolla. Bright pink, suffused with purple. Large. Expanded. P69 Vol 4 J of RHS 1877. Fuchsia trials at Chiswick 1873. No Award. Compact and branching. Tube and sepals white, tinged with rose. Corolla. Bright lake margined crimson. Not a desirable variety. GC. P488 9/8/1870 Intro. by H. Cannell. *Banks, E. Deal. GB. 1870.*

MRS. SHORT. Double. Red/White. Tube. Bright rose. Sepals. Bright rose. Corolla. White. (like Miss Lucy Finnis) G. Vol 36 P384 1889. Laings. Cat. circa 1890 The raiser describes this as the finest double

white yet sent out. B. Cat. 1888-1892. Intro by W. Bull. NK. NK. *GB. 1888.*

MRS. SIMPSON. Single. Red/Purple. Tube. Bright glossy crimson. Sepals. Bright glossy crimson. Reflexed perfectly. Corolla. Velvet Purple. Long. GC. P280 11/8/1857 Raised and intro. by J&C Lee. *Lee J&C, Hammersmith GB. 1857.*

MRS. STORY. Single. Red/White. Tube. Scarlet. Sepals. Scarlet. Corolla. Clear white. Named by W.H. Story, as it was, in his opinion, his finest. Coloured illustration in L' Illustration Horticole. Vol. 2. Plate 42 1855. GC. P368 26/5/1855 Listed by E.G. Henderson. GC. P467 14/7/1855 Listed by Bass & Brown, Sudbury & H. Walton, Burnley. GC. P529 11/8/1855 Listed by W.J. Epps, Maidstone. GC. P530 11/8/1855 & P208 22/3/1856 Listed by Bainbridge & Hewison, York. GC. P531 11/8/1855 Listed by J. Courcha. GC. P314 10/5/1856 Listed by W. Rumley, Richmond & Listed by Youell, Gt. Yarmouth. GC. P451 Listed by J. Clarke, Cheltenham. *Story, W.H. Newton Abbott. GB. 1855.*

MRS. TODMAN. Single. White/Red. Tube. White mixed with rose. Sepals. White mixed with rose. (Rose). Corolla. Rosy scarlet. Very floriferous. Coloured Plate in The Garden Vol 55 P530/1. Laings Cat. circa. 1890. BSW. Cat. 1897. *Todman. GB. NK.*

MRS. WADDILOVE. Single. Red/Purple. Tube. Bright scarlet. Sepals. Bright scarlet. Well reflexed. Corolla. Rich mauve. Free bloomer. B. Cat. 1876 Intro. by W. Bull. *Bull, W. Chelsea. GB. 1876.*

MRS. WILLS. Single. White/Red. Tube. White. Sepals. White. Corolla. Scarlet. JF. Cat. 1885. NK. NK. *GB. NK.*

MRS. WM. CRAIK. Double. Red/White. Tube. Scarlet. Sepals. Scarlet. Corolla. White, veined crimson. JF. Cat. 1912. NK. NK. *GB. 1912.*

MRS. W TAYLOR. Single. ND/ND. Tube. ND. Sepals. ND. Corolla. ND. GC. P417 6/7/1850 & P706 8/11/1850 Listed by H. Walton, Burnley. GC. P465 27/7/1850 Listed by W. Rumley. Richmond & G. Smith, Islington. *Glasscock. GB. 1850.*

M. SALLIER. ND. Red/ND. Tube. Bright red. Sepals. Bright red. Corolla. ND. Good habit and growth. JF. Cat. 1898. L. Cat. 1897. *Berger,L. Bagnolet. France. 1897.*

MULTIPLEX. Double. Red/Purple. Tube. Red. Long. Sepals. Red. Well reflexed. Corolla. Intense purple. Distinct from "Duplex". Free bloomer. Like a large double violet. GC. P632 6/10/1849 Originally called "Multifida". GC. P226 13/4/1850. GC. P387 15/6/1850 Listed by H. Walton, Burnley. GC. P465 27/7/1850 Listed by W. Rumley, Richmond & G. Smith, Islington. GC. P568 8/9/1849 Intro. by Veitch, Exeter. *Story, W.H, Newton Abbott. GB. 1850.*

MULTIFLORA. Single. Red/Purple. Tube. Red. Sepals. Red. Corolla. Purple. First raised in 1820 by the Horticultural Society. Loddiges Botanical Cabinet Vol 15 1828 Plate 1415. NK. NK. *GB. 1820.*

MULTIFLORA COCCINEA. Single. ND/ND. Tube. ND. Sepals. ND. Sepals. ND. Corolla. ND. GC. P98 17/2/1844 Listed by Girling, Stowmarket. GC. P112 17/2/1844 & P66 1/2/1845 Listed by W Miller, Ramsgate. GC. P241 15/4/1843 Intro. by B.W. Knight, St Leonards on Sea. *Knight, B.W. St Leonards. GB. 1843.*

MULTIFLORA ERECTA. Single. Red/Red. Tube. Deep fulgens red. Sepals. Deep fulgens red. Corolla. Deep fulgens red. Flowers produced in terminal racemes 5" long and 20 flowers on each. GC. 23/1/1841 Best new Plant. GC. P393 6/1842 Listed by Youells. GC. 8/5/1841 Intro. by J. May. *May, W. Bedale. GB. 1840.*

MULTIFLORA PENDULA PLEINA. ND. ND/ND. Tube. ND. Sepals. ND. Corolla. ND. GC. P338 15/4/1865 Listed by W. Rumley, Richmond. NK. NK. NK. *1864.*

MULTIFLORE. ND. ND/ND. Tube. ND. Sepals. ND. Corolla. ND. RH. P311 1889 "Select" by E.A. Carrière". NK. NK. NK. NK.

MURAT. ND. ND/ND. Tube. ND. Sepals. ND. Corolla. ND. GC. P824 8/9/1860 Listed by F. Godwin, Sheffield. *Cornelissen, Arras. Belgium. 1859.*

MUTABLIS. Single. Red/Purple. Tube. Red. Sepals. Red. Divergent. Corolla. Purple. GC. P833 18/12/1841 "Recommended 6 next best". Floral Cabinet Vol. 3 P192 1835 Coloured plate P168. NK. NK. *GB. 1834.*

NABOB. Single. Red/Purple. Tube. Brilliant red. ½" long. Sepals. Reflexed round. Large. Spreading. 1½" long. Corolla. Violet blue, washed red. (Dark dull lake red). Spriral shaped. Dwarf. Floriferous. Good habit. P111 4th Ed. by Porcher 1874. Pcxviii Vol 3 P of RHS 1872 Fuchsia Trials. GC. P1554 2/12/1871 Review by H. Cannell. *E.G. Henderson, St. Johns Wood. GB. 1871.*

NADAR. ND. ND/ND. Tube. ND. Tube. ND. Corolla. ND. P311 RH. 1889 "Select by E.A. Carrière". NK. NK. NK. NK.

NAEGELI. Double. Red/White. Tube. Wine red. Sepals. Wine red. Relaxed. Corolla. Flesh white. Large petals. Full. Vigourous. Numerous flowers. Named after a Swiss botanist and physicist (1817-1891). L. Cat. 1906. *Lemoine. Nancy. France. 1905.*

NANCY. Double. Red/Purple. Tube. Corol red. Sepals. Coral red. Corolla. Violet blue (Violet purple with blue reflections). Very large. B. Cat. 1888-1896. Laings. Cat. circa 1890. L. Cat. 1892. Intro. in 1888. *Lemoine. Nancy. France. 1888.*

NAPOLEON. Single. White/ND. Tube. White. Sepals. White. Corolla. ND. GC. P279 30/4/1853. "Light green stemmed". App. to RH. 1851 by Porcher "First class variety". GC. P140 27/2/1847 "Good light tariety". GC. P184 13/3/1847 & P250 17/4/1847 Listed by W. Miller, Ramsgate. GC. P211 27/3/1847 Listed by Hart & Nickling, Guildford. GC. P216 27/3/1847 & P231 1/4/1848 & P256 21/4/1849 Listed by R. Cooper, Croydon.GC. P259 28/4/1849 & P241 20/4/1850 Listed by W. Rendle, Plymouth. GC. P226 13/4/1850 Listed by Poole Nurseries. GC. P274 5/5/1849 Listed by H. Walton, Burnley. *Meillez. Lille. France. 1846.*

NAPOLEON III. ND. ND/ND. Tube. ND. Sepals. ND. Corolla. ND. GC. P529 11/8/1855 Listed by W.J. Epps, Maidstone. GC. P531 11/8/1855 Listed by J. Courcha. GC. P208 22/3/1856 Listed by Bainbridge & Hewison, York. GC. P451 5/7/1856 Listed by J. Clarke, Cheltenham. NK. NK. NK. NK.

NARDY FRÈRES. Double. Red/White. Tube. Red. 1?" Long. Slender. Sepals. Red. Spreading. 1". Corolla. White. Petals folded. Large. Inferior. Pcxii Vol 3 J of RHS 1872 Fuchsia trials. P131 4th Ed. by Porcher 1874 Not in the first selection. *L'Huillier. France. 1865.*

NEGRO. Single. Red/Purple. Tube. Bright red. Sepals. Bright red. Corolla. Deep reddish purple. GC. P689 28/7/1860 "Commended" by Hort.Scty See also Vol 1 J of RHS 1860. *Smith,G. Islington. GB. 1860.*

NELLIE. Single. White/Pink. Tube. Creamy white. Sepals. Creamy White. Corolla. Pink suffused pinkish mauve, deepening to clear mauve. GC. Vol 24 1885. JF. Cat. 1886. Laings. Cat. Circa. 1890. B. Cat. 1888-1889. *Lye, J. Market Lavington. GB. 1886.*

NELLIE MORTON. Double. Red/White. Tube. Red. Sepals. Red. Corolla. White. Has fewer and broader petals than "Miss Lucy Finnis". GC. Vol26 1886 RHS Trials at Chiswick 31/7/1886 Immense size. JF. Cat. 1885. HC. Cat. 1882-1898. Intro. by H. Cannell. Miss Lucy Finnis X. *Dr. Morton. GB. 1882.*

NELLY. Single. White/Pink. Tube. Pure white. Sepals. Pure white. Reflexed. Corolla. Bright rosine. Pure white at base. GA. P74 24/1/1863 Intro. by W. Bull, Chelsea. *Bull, W. Chelsea. GB. 1863.*

NE PLUS ULTRA. Single. Red/Purple. Tube. Bright red. Narrow. Sepals. Bright red. Broad. Expanded enough to show corolla. Corolla. Violet. (Rich dark purple). AH. P25 1849 Best. CG. P272 Vol 3 1850 "For Exhibition". App. to RH. 1851 by Porcher, Foliage thick and very dentate. Gracious, Elegant, but delicate. CG. Vol 2 1849 P455 wrongly attributed to Knight. GC. P537 12/8/1848 Listed by G. Smith, Islington. GC. P161 17/3/1849 Listed by W. Rumley, Richmond. GC. P224 14/4/1849 Listed by Bass & Brown, Sudbury, and R. Whibley, Kennington Cross. GC. P256 21/4/1849 Listed by R. Cooper, Croydon. GC. P2274 4/5/1850 Listed by Bass & Brown, Sudbury. *Willmore, J. Birmingham GB. 1848.*

NEPTUNE (a). Single. Red/Purple. Tube. Carmine. Very long. Sepals. Carmine. Corolla. Maroon. GC. P146 8/3/1845 Listed by Youells, Gt. Yarmouth. GC. P216 27/3/1847 Listed by R. Cooper, Croydon. RH. P24 1846. GC. P193 30/3/1844 Intro. by J. Smith, Dalston. *Smith, J. Dalston. GB. 1844*

NEPTUNE (b). Double. Red/Purple. Tube. Bright crimson. Sepals. Bright crimson. Corolla. Bluish violet. From a well known grower in the North of England. SG. P459 1866 Recommended. GC. P338 15/4/1865 Listed by W. Rumley, Richmond. GC. P191 27/2/1864 Intro. by B&S. Williams, Slough. NK. NK. *GB. 1864.*

NEPTUNE (c). Single. Red/Purple. Tube. Bright crimson. ½" long. Sepals. Bright crimson. 1"long. Spreading. Corolla. Purple blotched rose at base. (Violet Purple reddish at base). Pcxvi Vol 3 P of RHS 1872. Fuchsia trial at Chiswick Habit dwarf and free. Inferior. Corolla Expanded. B. Cat. 1870. *Bull, W. Chelsea. GB. 1869*

NESTOR (a). Double. Red/Purple. Tube. Carmine. Sepals. Carmine. Reflexed. Corolla. Purple/Crimson. Very large. Much expanded. B. Cat. 1878-1883. Intro. by W. Bull, Chelsea. *Bland, E. Fordham. GB. 1878.*

NESTOR (b). ND. ND. Tube. ND. Sepals. ND. Corolla. ND. L. Cat. 1892. Riccartonii X. *Lemoine. Nancy. France. 1887.*

NEWTON. ND. Red/Purple. Tube. Red. Short. Sepals. Red. Corolla. Deep Violet striped rose carmine. Free. HC. Cat. 1882 P76. *Lemoine. Nancy. France. 1880.*

NEWTONIENSIS. Single. Red/Purple. Tube. Crimson Scarlet. Sepals. Crimson Scarlet. Corolla. Purple. GC. P226 14/4/1849 & P241 21/4/1849. GC. P568 11/8/1849 Listed by G. Smith, Islington. GC. P145 9/3/1850 Listed by W. Rumley, Richmond. GC. P210 6/4/1850 Listed by H. Walton, Burnley. GC. P241 20/4/1850 Listed by W. Rendle, Plymouth. GC. P274 4/5/1850 Listed by Bass & Brown, Sudbury. App. to RH. 1851 by Porcher. Offspring of "Corallina". GC. P120 23/2/1850 "Select". GC. P650 30/9/1848 Intro. by Veitch, Exeter for delivery May 1849. *Story, W.H. Newton Abbott. GB. 1849.*

NICHOLSII. Single. Red/Purple. Tube. Bright Carmine. Sepals. Bright Carmine. Corolla. Purple Maroon. GC. P184 13/3/1847 & P250 17/4/1847 Listed by Miller, Ramsgate. GC. P201 25/3/1848 Listed by W. Rumley, Richmond. GC P49 24/1/1846 Intro. by G. Nicholls, Leeds. *Nicholls, G.,Leeds GB 1846.*

NIL DESPERANDUM. Single. Red/Purple. Tube. Waxy bright scarlet. Sepals. Waxy bright scarlet. Well reflexed. Corolla. Deep violet. GC. P727 11/1851 Awarded Certificate by National Floral Committee. Florist P276 Dec 1851. GC.P449 17/7/1852 & P209 26/3/1853 Listed by H. Walton, Burnley. GC. P307 14/5/1853 & P369 11/6/1853 Listed by B.R. Cant, Colchester. GC. P213 8/4/1854 Listed by C.H. Gardiner, Maidstone. GC. P284 22/4/1854 Listed by Hart & Nicklin, Guildford. GC. P238 14/4/1855 Listed by J. Hoade, Addlestone. GC. P279 30/4/1853 Dark wooded stem. MF. P133 1856 "Ten Dark" GC. P241 17/4/1852 Intro. by G. Smith, Islington. *Smith, G. Islington GB. 1852.*

NIMROD (a). Single. ND/ND. Tube. ND. Sepals. ND. Corolla. ND. GC. P375 4/6/1844 Exhibited by J. Smith, Dalston at Hort. Scty Show. *Smith, J. Dalston. GB. 1844.*

NIMROD (b). Single. White/Purple. Tube. White. Sepals. White. Corolla. Light Purple. Good form. Free Bloomer. GC. P531 11/8/1855 Listed by Joseph Courcha. GC. P314 10/5/1856 Listed by W. Rumley, Richmond. GC. P218 7/4/1855 Intro. by G. Smith. Islington. *Smith, G. Islington. GB. 1855.*

NIMROD (c). Double. Red/Purple. Tube. Crimson. Sepals. Crimson. Corolla. Purplish Plum. Full Double. B. Cat. 1872-1873. *Bull, W. Chelsea. GB. 1871.*

NINON DE LENCLOS. Single. Pink/Red. Tube. Light rose. Swollen. Sepals. Light rose. Open well. Globular Buds. Corolla. Rosy Salmon. App. to RH. 1851 by Porcher. *Racine. France. 1850.*

NOBILIS. Single. Red/Purple. Tube. Dark crimson. Sepals. Dark crimson. Corolla. Light purple. GC. P112 17/2/1844 & P66 1/2/1845 & P184 13/3/1847 Listed by W. Miller, Ramsgate. GC. P82 11/2/1843 Intro. by W. Dean, Jedburgh. *Dean, W. Jedburgh. GB. 1843.*

NOBLESSE (a). Single. Red/Purple. Tube. Dark crimson. Sepals. Dark crimson. Completely reflexed. Corolla. Black. GC. P1054 7/11/1863. Intro. by W. Bull, Chelsea. *Bull, W. Chelsea. GB. 1863.*

NOBLESSE (b). Single. Red/Purple. Tube. Crimson Scarlet. Slender. Sepals. Crimson Scarlet. (Bright crimson). Spreading. Corolla. Deep maroon. Darkest in collection.(Blue Violet) (Rich maroon, flushed and veined towards the base with red. Good habit. Free. FCC.Pcxv Vol 3 J of RHS 1872 Fuchsia trials at Chiswick 1872. Habit good and free, Flowers medium. Tube ½". Slender sepals. Spreading. P67 Vol 4 J of RHS 1873 Report of Fuchsia trials at Chiswick. FCC. P216 J of RHS 1877 Fuchsia trials at Chiswick. Certificate previously awarded is confirmed. P112 4th Ed. by Porcher 1874 Elite. vigourous. BSW. Cat. 1878. HC. Cat. 1882. *Henderson, E.G. St.Johns Wood. GB. 1871.*

NOBLISSIMA. Single. ND/ND. Tube. ND. Sepals. ND. Corolla. ND. GC. P98 17/2/1844 & P142 14/3/1845 Listed by Youell, Gt. Yarmouth (Dark Variety). GC. P112 17/2/1844 & P66 1/2/1845 Listed by W. Miller, Ramsgate. *Smith, J. Dalston. GB. 1844.*

NONPAREIL (a). Single. ND/ND. Tube. ND. Sepals. ND. Corolla. ND. GC. P265 22/4/1848 Intro. by J. Smith, Dalston. *Smith, J. Dalston. GB. 1848.*

NONPAREIL (b). Single. Red/Purple. Tube. Crimson red. Short. Thin. Sepals. Crimson red. Narrow. Very long. Corolla. Dark reddish violet. Large. App. to RH. 1851 by Porcher. GC. P535 23/8/1851 Dark variety. Exhibited at Vauxhall Garden Show. GC. P465 27/7/1850 Listed by G. Smith, Islington. GC. P144 8/3/1851 Listed by W. Rumley, Richmond. *Dubus, France. 1850.*

NONPAREIL (c). Double. Red/White. Tube. Crimson red. (Cherry). Sepals. Crimson red. Horizontal. Points raised up or down. Corolla. White. Pin striped or veined with crimson red. Large. Spiralled This is a nice variety despite sometimes the flowers open badly, and the sepals do not open well. P129 4th Ed. by Porcher 1874. B. Cat. 1870. Vol 1 J of RHS 1861 FCC on 5.9.1860. NK. NK. GB. 1860.

NONSUCH. Single. Red/Purple. Tube. Crimson. Sepals. Crimson. Corolla. Dark Purple. Good shape. Small free bloomer. GC. P727 Nov 1851 Awarded Certificate by National Floriculture Committee. GC. P279 30/4/1853 Light green stemmed. GC. P449 17/7/1852 & P209 26/3/1853 Listed by H. Walton, Burnley. GC. P211 26/3/1853 Listed by W. Rumley, Richmond. GC. P248 15/4/1854 Listed by Mitchell & Co, Brighton. GC. P199 19/3/1853 "Recommended". GC. P223 10/4/1852 Intro. by C. Turner, Slough. *Banks, E. Deal. GB. 1852.*

NORA. Double. Red/Purple. Tube. Crimson. (Clear red). Very short. Sepals. Crimson. (Clear red). Long. Reflexed. Corolla. Purple flaked bright crimson. (Indigo Blue). Petals folded and spiralled. Large. P124 4th Ed. by Porcher 1874. GC. P171 21/2/1863 Intro. by Wm. Bull, Chelsea. *Bull, W. Chelsea. GB. 1863.*

NORFOLK GIANT. See Norfolk Hero. GC. P55 19/1/1865 Review by H. Cannell

NORFOLK HERO (a). Single. Pink/Pink. Tube. Delicate Pink. Sepals. Delicate Pink. Corolla. Rose with a tinge of purple.GC. P820 Dec 1844 & P820 1/2/1845 "Recommended". GC. P66 1/2/1845 & P184 13/3/1847 Listed by W. Miller, Ramsgate. GC. P201 27/3/1847 Listed by Hart & Nickling, Guildford. GC. P216 27/3/1847 Listed by R. Cooper, Croydon. GC. P618 14/9/1844 Intro by J. Barkway. *Barkway, J. East Dereham. GB. 1844.*

NORFOLK HERO (b). Double. Red/Purple. Tube. Carmine. Sepals. Carmine. (Scarlet). Corolla. Rich Violet blue. (Purple) Colossal size. GC. P55 19/1/1867 Review by H. Cannell Good habit. Small Leaves. Superior to "Universal". P126 4th Ed. by Porcher 1874. Not in the first selection. GC. P1134 1/12/1866 Intro. by E.G.Henderson. *Henderson E. G. St. Johns Wood. GB. 1866.*

NORMA. (a). ND. ND/ND. Tube. ND. Sepals. ND. Corolla. ND. RH. P311 1889 Select by E.A. Carrie˅'re. NK. NK. NK. NK.

NORMA (b). ND. ND/ND. Tube. ND. Sepals. ND. Corolla. ND. L. Cat. 1901. Myrtifolia X. *Lemoine. Nancy. France. 1896.*

NORTHERN BEAUTY. Single. White/Red. Tube. White tinged rose. Sepals. White tinged rose. Corolla. Deep rosy carmine. GC. P177 20/3/1852 Listed by W. Rumley. GC. P321 24/5/1851 Intro. by W. Rumley, Richmond. *Rumley, W. Richmond. GB. 1851.*

NORTHERN LIGHT. Single. Red/Purple. Tube. Bright carmine. (Scarlet carmine). Sepals. Bright carmine. (Scarlet Carmine). Corolla. Bluish purple. (Light violet washed bright rose). Similar to "Souvenir de Chiswick" P112 4th Ed. by Porcher 1874 Bell shaped. Colouration like "Beauty of Sholden". GC. P55 19/1/1867 Review by H. Cannell. GC. P863 12/9/1863 Intro. by E.G. Henderson, St. Johns Wood. *Banks, E. Deal. GB. 1863.*

NOVEAU MASTODONTE. Double. Red/Purple. Tube. Red Sepals. Red. Reflex to cover tube. Corolla. Dark violet veined red. Floriferous. Globular formation. H.C. Cat. 1882-1891 Extra Large. Beautifully striped. B. Cat. 1880-1893. *Lemoine. Nancy. France. 1880.*

NOVELTY (a). Double. Red/Purple. Tube. Lively red. Waxy. Sepals. Lively red. Waxy. Much reflexed. Corolla. Dense violet. Very double. GC. P449 17/7/1852 & P209 26/3/1853 Listed by H. Walton, Burnley. GC. P307 14/5/1853 & P369 11/6/1853 Listed by Benj. R. Cant, Colchester. GC. P32 10/1/1852 Intro. by W. J. Epps. *Epps.W.J. Maidstone. GB. 1852.*

NOVELTY. (b). Single. White/Purple. Tube. Pale Green. Sepals. Paler Green. Large. Corolla. Crimson Purple. GC. P184 13/3/1847 & P250 27/4/1847 Listed by W. Miller, Ramsgate. GC. P49 24/1/1846 Intro. by Nicholls, Leeds. *Nicholls. Leeds. GB. 1846.*

NOVELTY (c). ND. ND/ND. Tube. ND. Sepals. ND. Corolla. ND. GC. P465 17/8/1850 Listed by G. Smith, Islington. *Kendall, Stoke Newington. GB. 1850.*

NUBIAN. Double. Red/Purple. Tube. Crimson. Short. Sepals. Deep rose. Broad. Corolla. Rich purplish crimson, marked rose at base. Globular shaped corolla. Large. B. Cat. 1875-1876. NK. NK. *GB. 1873.*

NYMPH. Single. White/Purple. Tube. Pure white. Sepals. White lightly veined pink. Expanded. Green tips. Corolla. Bright velvet plum. Large. GC. P455 8/7/1847 Exhibited by Mr. Robinson at RBS Show. GC. P66 1/2/1845 & P162 14/3/1846 & P1184 13/3/1847 Listed by W. Miller, Ramsgate. GC. P216 27/3/1847 Listed by R. Cooper, Croydon. GC. P265 24/4/1847 & P259 28/4/1849 Listed by W. Rendle, Plymouth. GC. P33 18/1/1845 Intro. by W.J. Epps. *Epps, W.J. Maidstone. GB. 1845.*

NYSA. Single. Red/Purple. Tube. Scarlet. Sepals. Scarlet. Beautifully recurving. Corolla. Purplish crimson. Very fine. B. Cat. 1875. GC. P427 3/4/1875 Intro. by W. Bull, Chelsea. *Bull, W. Chelsea. GB. 1875.*

OBÉRON. Single. Red/Purple. Tube. Crimson red. Sepals. Crimson red. Horizontal. Corolla. Violet crimson. App. to RH. 1851 by Porcher 2nd class variety. *Low, H. GB. 1849.*

OBERON (a). Single. Red/Purple. Tube. Bright crimson. Thick. Short. Sepals. Bright crimson. Reflexed round. Corolla. Violet blue washed red. Very expanded like a Petunia. P112 4th. Ed. 1874 by Porcher. *Banks, E. Deal. GB. 1864.*

OBERON (b). Single. White/Red. Tube. White Sepals. White. Semi reflexed. Corolla. Rose carmine shaded magenta. B. Cat. 1898-1899. L. Cat. 1901. GC. Vol 21 1/5/1897 Intro. by W. Bull. *Bull, W. Chelsea. GB. 1897.*

O BOTTERI. Double. Red/Purple. Tube. Carmine pink. Sepals. Carmine Pink. Uplifted. Corolla. Intense blue. Large. JF. Cat. 1892. L. Cat. 1892. *Rozain, Lyons. France. 1891.*

OCTAVIE. S/Double Red/Purple. Tube. Bright rose. Sepals. Bright rose. Corolla. Light blue. B. Cat. 1872-1875. *Bull, W. Chelsea. GB. 1871.*

OCTAVE FEUILLET. S/Double Red/Purple. Tube. Bright red. Sepals. Bright red. Corolla. Mauve Pink. Irregular. Floriferous. Suitable for culture in vases. Named after a French novelist (1821-90). B. Cat. 1892-1893. L. Cat. 1892. *Lemoine. Nancy. France. 1891.*

OLDFORDENSIS. ND. ND/ND. Tube. ND. Corolla. ND. Corolla. ND. GC. P274 5/5/1849 Listed by H. Walton, Burnley.NK. NK. *GB. 1848.*

OLYMPIA. Single. Red/Red. Tube. Salmon Pink. Sepals. Salmon Pink. Corolla. Carmine Scarlet. Laings. Cat. 1890. NK. NK. NK. NK.

OLYNTHUS. Single. Red/Purple. Tube. Bright rich crimson. Very short. Sepals. Rich crimson. Broad. Symetrically reflexed. Corolla. Deep rich violet. B. Cat. 1875-1879. *Bull, W. Chelsea. GB. 1874.*

OMEGA (a). Single. ND/ND. Tube. ND. Sepals. ND. Corolla. ND. GC. P483 15/7/1843 Exhibited at H.S. Show 12/7/1843 by Catleugh. NK. NK. *GB. 1843.*

OMEGA (b). Single. Red/Purple. Tube. Crimson. Sepals. Crimson. Corolla. Bright lilac. Very dissimilar to all other varieties. GC. P401 24/6/1854 Listed by B.R. Cant, Colchester & H. Walton, Burnley. GC. P238 14/4/1855 Listed by J. Hoade, Addlestone. GC. P258 21/4/1855 Listed by H. Walton, Burnley. GC. P353 26/5/1855 Listed by Hart & Nicklin, Guildford. GC. P530 11/8/1855 Listed by Bainbridge & Hewison, York. GC. P194 1/4/1854 Intro. by C. Turner, Slough. *Banks, E. Deal. GB. 1854.*

OMER PACHA (a). Single. Red/Purple. Tube. Dark crimson. Sepals. Dark crimson. Corolla. Velvet Purple. GC. P467 14/7/1855 Listed by Bass & Brown, Sudbury & H. Walton, Burnley. GC. P529 11/8/1855 Listed by W. J. Epps, Maidstone. GC. P530 11/8/1855 & P208 22/3/56 Listed by Bainbridge & Hewison, York. GC. P531 11/8/1855 Listed by J. Courcha. GC. P314 10/5/1856 Listed by W. Rumley, Richmond & Youell, Gt. Yarmouth. GC. P34 20/1/1855 Intro. by W.J. Epps, Maidstone. *Banks, E. Deal. GB. 1855.*

OMER PASHA (b). Single. Red/Purple. Tube. Bright waxy crimson scarlet. Short. Stout. Sepals. Bright waxy crimson scarlet. Well reflexed. Corolla. Deep violet. Good shape. Fine habit. Profuse bloomer. GC. P467 14/4/1855 Listed by Bass & Brown, Sudbury & H. Walton, Burnley. GC. P531 11/8/1855 Listed by J. Courcha. GC. P314 10/5/1856 Listed by W. Rumley, Richmond. GC. P218 7/4/1855 Intro. by G. Smith, Islington. *Smith, G. Islington. GB. 1855.*

ONE OF THE RING. Single. White/Red. Tube. White. Sepals. White. Horizontal. Corolla. Scarlet. (Cerise Purple). App. to RH. 1851 by Porcher. Makes an allusion to a stone in a ring. 1st Class variety. GC. P120 23/2/1850 "Select". GC. P535 23/8/1851 Exhibited at Vauxhall Garden Show. GC. P232 1/4/1848 & P256 21/4/1849 Listed by R. Cooper, Croydon. GC. P201 25/3/1848 Listed by W. Rumley, Richmond. GC. P224 14/4/1849 Listed by R. Whibley, Kennington. GC. P259 28/4/1849 & P241 20/4/1850 Listed by W. Rendle, Plymouth. GC. P338 22/5/1847 Intro. by Turville, Chelmsford. *Turville, Chelmsford. GB. 1847.*

OPHELIA (a). Single. White/Purple. Tube. White. Sepals. White. Corolla. Violet crimson. GC. P537 12/8/1848 Listed by G. Smith, Islington. GC. P537 12/8/1848 Listed by R. Cooper, Croydon. GC. P274 5/5/1849 Listed by H. Walton, Burnley. GC. P153 4/3/1848 Intro. by W. H. Holmes, Sudbury, Derbys. *Holmes, W. Sudbury. GB. 1848.*

OPHELIA (b). Single. Red/Purple. Tube. Bright red. Sepals. Bright red. Large. Long. Corolla. Purple. GC. P1054 7/11/1863 Intro. by W. Bull, Chelsea. *Bull, W. Chelsea. GB. 1863.*

ORACLE. Double. Red/Purple. Tube. Bright crimson. (Carmine red).Thin. Long. Sepals. Bright crimson. Horizontal. Elongated. Raised up. Corolla. Rich violet purple, bright pink at base. (Bluish violet striped red). P124 4th Ed. by Porcher 1874. Vigorous bush. Branches flexible. Long jointed. Pedicel 40 mm. Long petals. Spiralled. GC. P476 15/4/1871 Intro. by W. Bull, Chelsea. *Bull, W. Chelsea. GB. 1871.*

ORANGE BOVEN. Single. ND/ND. Tube. ND. Sepals. ND. Corolla. ND. Smallest variety, forming a neat dwarf compact plant. Its golden leaf ground being prettily tinted with bronze in the young growth. P134 4th Ed. by Porcher 1874 Not in the first selection. GC. P375 19/3/1870 Intro. by E.G.Henderson. *Henderson, E.G. St. Johns Wood. GB. 1870.*

ORESTES. Single. Red/Purple. Tube. Red. Sepals. Red. Corolla. Purple. GC. P535 23/8/1851 Dark variety, exhibited at Vauxhall Garden Show. *Salter, T. Vauxhall GB. 1851.*

ORION (a). Single. White/Purple. Tube. Greenish white, Sepals. Greenish white, tinted rose. Well spread. Corolla. Crimson purple. Similar to "Purity". App. to RH. 1851 by Porcher. GC. P265 22/4/1848 Intro. by J. Smith, Dalston. *Smith, J. Dalston. GB. 1848.*

ORION (b). Single. Red/Purple. Tube. Dark crimson. Sepals. Dark crimson. Corolla. Rosy purple. Large. Free bloomer. GC. P535 23/8/1851 Exhibited at Vauxhall Garden Show. GC. P647 11/10/1851 Exhibited at RHS of Cornwall show 9/9/1851 by F. H. Earle of Falmouth. GC. P454 16/7/1853 Exhibited at H.S. Show 9/7/1853 by M. Wiggins. App. to RH. 1851 by Porcher. Confused with Orion (a) above. *Smith, G. Islington. GB. 1850.*

ORLANDO (a). Single. Red/Purple. Tube. Dark crimson. Sepals. Dark crimson. Reflexed. Corolla. Intense Purple. GC. P531 11/8/1855 Listed by J.

Courcha. GC. P314 10/5/1856 Listed by W. Rumley, Richmond. GC. P218 7/4/1855 Intro. by G. Smith, Islington. *Smith, G. Islington. GB. 1855.*

ORLANDO (b). Double. Red/Purple. Tube. Carmine. Sepals. Carmine. Corolla. Light violet purple. Large. GO. "Select" 1881-1888. BSW. Cat. 1888. B. Cat. 1880-1881. Intro. by W. Bull, Chelsea. *Smith, G. Islington. GB. 1880.*

ORPHEUS. Double. Red/Pink. Tube. Coral red. Sepals. Coral red. Corolla. Clear pink. Large. L. Cat. 1906. *Veitch. GB. 1904.*

OTHELLO (a). Single. ND/ND. Tube. ND. Sepals. ND. Corolla. ND. GC. P66 1/2/1845 & P162 14/3/1846 & P184 13/3/1847 Listed by W. Miller, Ramsgate. GC. P216 Listed by R. Cooper, Croydon. GC. P265 24/4/1847 Listed by W. Rendle, Plymouth. GC. P113 22/2/1845 Intro. by A. Kendall. *Kendall,A. Stoke Newington. GB. 1845.*

OTHELLO (b). ND. ND/ND. Tube. ND. Sepals. ND. Corolla. ND. GC. P375 31/5/1856 Exhibited at Crystal Palace by Mr. Bousie as a 7' high pyramid. GC. P401 24/6/1854 Listed by H. Walton, Burnley. GC. P238 14/4/1855 Listed by J. Hoade, Addlestone. NK. NK. NK. *1854.*

OTHELLO (c) Single. Red/Red. Tube. Bright crimson. Very short. Sepals. Bright crimson. Reflexed round. Corolla. Crimson washed brown. Bell shaped. Good colouration. P112 4th Ed. 1874 by Porcher. *Lemoine. Nancy. France. 1869.*

OTTO NORDENSKJOELD. Double. Red/Pink. Tube. Brilliant red. Sepals. Brilliant red. Long. Corolla. Clear pinkish violet. Very full. Large. Long. Named after a Swedish explorer (1869-1928) who led an expedition to Antartica 1901-3. L. Cat. 1906. *Lemoine. Nancy. France. 1905.*

OUR FUTURE QUEEN. Single. White/Red. Tube. White. Long 20mms. Swollen at the end. Sepals. White, washed rose.. Large. Reflexed round. Corolla. Carmine red margined fire red. P119 4th Ed by Porcher 1874. Bell shaped. Beautiful variety. Floriferous but delicate. B. Cat. 1876-1878. HC. Cat. 1882. *Banks, E. Deal. GB. 1872.*

OXONIAN. Single. ND/ND. Tube. ND. Sepals. ND. Corolla. ND. GC. P66 1/2/1845 Listed by W. Miller, Ramsgate. *Day. GB. 1844.*

OVID (a). Single. ND/ND. Tube. ND. Sepals. ND. Corolla. ND. GC. P66 1/2/1845 Listed by W. Miller, Ramsgate. NK.NK. NK. NK.

OVID (b). Double. Red/White. Tube. Coral red. Sepals. Coral red. Well reflexed. Corolla. White shaded magenta. Immense. B. Cat. 1898-1899. GC. Vol 21 1897 Intro. by W. Bull, Chelsea. *Bull, W. Chelsea. GB. 1897.*

PAGODA. Single. Red/Purple. Tube. Red. Sepals. Red. Corolla. Purple. GC. P545 30/8/1851 Listed By G. Smith, Islington. GC. P177 20/3/1852 Listed by W. Rumley, Richmond. GC. P337 24/5/1851 Intro. by Batten, Clapham. *Batten. Clapham. GB. 1851.*

PAGODIENSIS. Single. ND/ND. Tube. ND. Sepals. ND. Corolla. ND. GC. P250 17/4/1847 Listed by J. Hally, Blackheath. NK. NK. *GB. 1846.*

PAINTER. ND. ND/ND. Tube. ND. Sepals. ND. Corolla. ND. GC. P314 10/5/1856 Listed by W. Rumley, Richmond. NK. NK. *GB. 1855.*

PALATINE. S/Double. Red/Purple. Tube. Red. Sepals. Red. Long. Broad. Completely recurved. Corolla. Rich ruby purple. Very large. Fine shape. B. Cat. 1901. *Bull, W. Chelsea. GB. 1900.*

PANMURE GORDON. Single. Red/Purple. Tube. Red. Sepals. Red. Corolla. Dark Violet Purple. JF. Cat. 1898. HC. Cat. 1896. *Banks, E. Deal. GB. 1896.*

PAPIN. Double. Red/Purple. Tube. Red. Sepals. Red. Corolla. Deep Violet. Full. P115 4th Ed. by Porcher 1874 Not in the first selection. RH. P295 1887 Grown as a standard at Twickel. HC. Cat. 1882, 1885. *Lemoine. Nancy. France. 1867.*

PARACHUTE. Single. Red/Purple. Tube. Reddish Scarlet. Sepals. Reddish Scarlet. Short. Broad. Recurved. Corolla. Violet Lake, marked red. Large. Well Expanded. Intro. by W. Bull, Chelsea. B. Cat. 1883-1888. *Bull, W. Chelsea. GB. 1883.*

PARAGON. Single. Red/Purple. Tube. Red. Sepals. Red. Corolla. Purple. GC. P610 2/9/1843 Exhibited at Practical Floral & Hort Scty. of Ireland by T. Farrell. GC. P820 Dec 1844. P140 27/2/1847 & P808 Nov 1846 Recommended. GC. P441 1/7/1843 Listed by Marnock and Manby. GC.P98 17/2/1844 & P146 8/3/1845 Listed by Youell, Gt. Yarmouth. GC. P98 17/2/1844 Listed by Girling, Danecroft Nurseries, Stowmarket. GC. P216 27/3/1847 Listed by R. Cooper, Croydon. GC. P657 1843 Listed by James Piper. GC. P112 17/2/1844 & P66 8/3/1845 Listed by W. Miller, Ramsgate. *Smith, J. Dalston. GB. 1843.*

PARIS MURCIE. Double. Red/White. Tube. Bright rose. Sepals. Bright rose. Corolla. White. RH.

P295 1887 Grown as a standard at Twickel. BSW. Cat. 1888. *Lemoine. Nancy. France. 1880.*

PARTHENOPE. Single. Red/Pink. Tube. Violet. Sepals. Violet. Well reflexed. Corolla. Rosy blush. Very attractive. JF. Cat. 1898. NK. NK. NK. *1898.*

PASCAL. ND. Red/Purple. Tube. Scarlet. Sepals. Scarlet. Well reflexed. Corolla. Deep violet carmine. Named after a French mathematician (1623-62). JF. Cat. 1882. *Lemoine. Nancy. France. 1880.*

PASHA. Double. Red/Purple. Tube. Deep rose. Sepals. Deep rose. Corolla. Rich purplish plum. B. Cat. 1872-1876. *Bull, W. Chelsea. GB. 1871.*

PASTEUR. Double. Red/White. Tube. Red. Sepals. Red. Large. Well recurved. Corolla. Pure white. Long. Named after a French Chemist (1822-1895). L. Cat. 1893. B. Cat. 1893-1895. *Lemoine. Nancy. France. 1893.*

PARTRICIAN. Single. Red/Purple. Tube. Rich crimson. Sepals. Rich crimson. Broad. Well reflexed. Corolla. Deep purple. B. Cat. 1872-1873. NK. NK. NK. *1871.*

PATRIE. Double. ND. Tube. ND. Sepals. ND. Corolla. ND. L. Cat. 1888. Gartenflora 1888. *Rozain. Lyons. France. 1887.*

PATRIOT. Single. Red/Purple. Tube. Scarlet Carmine. Sepals. Scarlet Carmine. Reflexed. Well shaped. Corolla. Pale rose margined lilac. GC. Vol.17 20/5/1882 New fuchsia from B.S. Williams. GO. P97 1882. *Bland, E. Fordham GB. 1882.*

PATRIOTE. Single. Red/Purple. Tube. Rich carmine. Large. Sepals. Rich carmine. Long. Reflexed. Corolla. Violet purple, veined scarlet at base.. Involute form. Immense. B. Cat. 1875-1882. NK. NK. NK. *1875.*

PATTERN Double. Red/Purple. Tube. Rosy crimson. Short. Sepals. Rosy crimson. Broad. Corolla. Light bluish purple shaded and flaked with rose. Intro. by W. Bull. B. Cat. 1888-1895. L. Cat. 1886. JF. Cat. 1886. *Bull, W. Chelsea. GB. 1885.*

PAUL CAMBON. Double. Red/Purple. Tube. Carmine red. Sepals. Carmine red. Large. Reflexed. Corolla. Indigo. Vigorous. Floriferous. Named after the French Ambassador to London between 1898-1921 (1843-1924). L. Cat. 1909. *Lemoine. Nancy. France. 1909.*

PAUL DE DÉROULÈDE Double. Red/Purple. Tube. Scarlet. Sepals. Scarlet. Large. Horizontal. Corolla. Violet fading to red. Large petals. Vigorous. New colour in the doubles. Named after a French poet and politician (1846-1914). L. Cat. 1887. *Lemoine. Nancy. France. 1887.*

PAUL ET VIRGINIE. Single. ND/ND. Tube. ND. Sepals. ND. Corolla. ND. Flowers not obtained, but listed in catalogue. App. to RH. 1851 by Porcher. *Dubus. France. 1851.*

PAUL GAILLARD. Double. Red/Purple. Tube. Bright red. Sepals. Bright red. Corolla. Plum violet. Exterior petals carmine mingled with orange. JF. Cat. 1901. L. Cat. No. 149. 1901. *Rozain. Lyons France. 1900.*

PAULINE. Single. Red/Purple. Tube. Vermillion. Sepals. Vermillion. Reflex back to tube. Corolla. Rich purple. Thick. Well formed. GC. P881 1873 Exhibited at Bath RHS Show by J.H. Wilcox (1st) and J. Lye (2nd). GC. P211 17/2/1877 Growers of the West Country. GC. P311 8/9/1877 Exhibited at Trowbridge by Matthews (1st). *Bull, W. Chelsea. GB. 1863.*

PAUL MEYER. Double. Red/Purple. Tube. Carmine Red. Sepals. Carmine red. Broad. Twisted. Corolla. Clear Violet carmine with rose in centre. L. Cat. 1907. *Lemoine. Nancy. France. 1907.*

PAVILLON BLANC. Single. Red/White. Tube. Red. Sepals. Red. Corolla. White. 4th Ed. by Porcher 1874. Not in the first selection. *Crousse. France. 1867.*

P. BRONDEL. Double. Red/Purple. Tube. Coral Pink. Sepals. Coral pink. Long. Reflexed. Corolla. Sea Blue veined and margined rose. L. Cat. 1901. *Rozain. Lyons. France. 1899.*

PEARL. Single. White/Red. Tube. Flesh. Sepals. Flesh. Corolla. Scarlet. GC. P686 12/10/1844 Exhibited at RHS of Cornwall Show. GC 2/7/1845 Exhibited by Gaines at RBS Show. GC. P265 24/4/1847 Listed by W. Rendle, Plymouth. RH. P24 1846. *Harrison. Dereham GB. 1843.*

PEARL OF ENGLAND. Single. White/Red. Tube. Pearly white. (Light rose). Swollen. Sepals. Pearly white. (Light rose). Very open. Corolla. Scarlet. (Red). Bell shaped. GC. P423 6/1851 Exhibited at RBS Show by H. Low, Clapton. GC. P535 23/8/1851 Exhibited at Vauxhall Garden Show. GC. P663 18/10/1851 Exhibited at York Horticultural Scty. Show by Mrs. Staplyton. GC. P454 16/7/1853

Exhibited at HS. Show 9/7/1853 by Mr. Wiggins. GC. P438 6/7/1854 Exhibited at RBS Show by Mr. Bray as a 7 foot pyramid. App. to RH. 1851 by Porcher, First Class variety. GC. P465 27/7/1850 & P144 8/3/1851 Listed by W. Rumley, Richmond. GC. P242 20/4/1850 Intro. by E.G. Henderson, St. Johns Wood. *Henderson, E.G. St Johns Wood. GB. 1850.*

PEASANT GIRL (a). Double. Red/Purple. Tube. Scarlet. Sepals. Scarlet. Corolla. Dark porcelain blue. BSW. Cat. 1878. NK. NK. *GB.* NK.

PEASANT GIRL (b). Single. White/Red. Tube. White. Sepals. White. Tinted with the most delicate blush. Corolla. Pink and Carmine slightly shaded violet. B. Cat. 1889. JF. Cat. 1890. L. Cat. 1892. *Lye, J. Market Lavington. GB. 1889.*

PECULIARITY. Double. Red/Purple. Tube. Red. Short. Sepals. Red. Corolla. Purple, striped deep rose. GC. P593 20/9/1851 Entire stock purchased by J. Dobson, Woodlands Nurseries, Isleworth of the 1850 Seedling. GC. P449 17/7/1852 & P209 26/3/1853 Listed by H. Walton, Burnley. GC. P248 15/4/1854 Listed by C. Mitchell, Brighton. GC. P143 6/3/1852 Intro. by J. Dobson. *Story, W. Newton Abbot. GB. 1852.*

PEERLESS. Single. White/Red. Tube. White. Sepals. White. Horizontal. Corolla. Vermillion. B. Cat. 1870. NK. NK. *GB.* NK.

PEGASUS. S/Double. Red/Purple. Tube. Bright crimson. Sepals. Red. Bright crimson. Broad. Well reflexed. Corolla. Bluish veined crimson. Short. B. Cat 1870 10/6d. *Bull, W. Chelsea. GB. 1870.*

PENDANT. S/Double. Red/Purple. Tube. Carmine pink. Short. Sepals. Carmine pink. Extended. Corolla. Rich plum shaded deep rose. Drooping. B. Cat. 1897-1901. *Bull, W. Chelsea. GB. 1897.*

PENDULA (a). Single. ND. Tube. ND. Sepals. ND. Corolla. ND. GC. P97 18/2/1843 & P98 17/2/1844 Listed by Youell, Great Yarmouth. *Young. GB.* NK.

PENDULA (b). Single. Red/Purple. Tube. Rich crimson. Sepals. Rich crimson. Corolla. Purple violet. Pyramidical with pendulous branches. Middle sized flower. Raised by J. Smith, manager of T. Whalleys Nursery, Liverpool or a celebrated amateur from the North of England. GC. P449 17/7/1852 & P209 20/3/1853 Listed by H. Walton, Burnley. GC. P211 26/3/1853 Listed by W. Rumley, Richmond. GC. P209 20/3/1853 & P303 14/5/1853 Listed by B. R. Cant, Colchester. GC. P130

21/2/1852 Intro. By E. G. Henderson, St Johns Wood. *Smith, J. Liverpool. GB. 1852.*

PENDULA ELEGANS. Single. Red/Purple. Tube. Red. Sepals. Red Corolla. Shaded purple. GC. P162 16/3/1844. Intro. by Rogers, Uttoxeter. *Rogers, Uttoxeter. GB. 1844.*

PENDULAEFLORA. Single. Red/Red. Tube. Rich crimson shaded maroon. Trumpet shaped 3-5" Long. Sepals. Rich crimson. Corolla. Rich crimson. Flowers in clusters from the axils of the leaves. Leaves 3" to 4" long. Acuminate. Glabrous. Violet midrib. Illustrated in Cannells Catalogue of 1882. Vol 6 J of RHS 1880 Awarded FCC. GC. P521 28/4/1877. Coloured plate in Floral Magazine 411 July 1880 Character of Corymbiflora in minature. GC. Vol 26 1886 RHS Trials at Chiswick 21/7/1886. G. P383 Vol 19 1881. Winter flowering at Swanley. A kind similar to, if not identical, with the pendulous F. Boliviana. Clusters of rosy crimson flowers 2" in length. JF. Cat. 1885. BSW Cat. 1888. Intro. by B. S. Williams. BSW. Cat. 1877. *Williams B.S. Holloway. GB. 1877.*

PENDULA SPLENDENS. Single. ND. Tube. ND. Sepals. ND. Corolla. ND. GC. P668 11/10/1841 Exhibited at RHS of Cornwall show. GC. 8/5/1841 Listed by J. May, Edmonton. *May, W. Bedale. GB. 1840.*

PENDULA TERMINALIS. Single. Red/Purple. Tube. Deep red. Sepals. Deep red. Corolla. Purple, tinged carmine. P13 Floral Cabinet Vol IX 1841. GC. 23/1/1841 Best new plant. GC. 11/10/1841 Exhibited at RHS of Cornwall show. GC. P287 29/5/1841 Listed by H. Low, Clapton. GC. P393 6/1842 Listed by Youell, Gt. Yarmouth. GC. 8/5/1841 Listed by J. May, Edmonton. *May, W. Bedale GB. 1840.*

PENDULINA. Single. Red/Pink. Tube. Carmine Sepals. Carmine. Corolla. Deep pink. Very glossy. GC. P338 17/5/1856 A very distinct and beautiful hybrid raised between Serratifolia and a pendulous Peruvian species with flowers produced on even a small plant. Fine corymbs carrying flowers 3" in length. Awarded C of M by N.F.S. 4/10/1856. P169 RH. 1857. Intro. by Veitch, Exeter. F. serratifolia X. *Veitch. Exeter. GB. 1856.*

PENDULOUS Single. Red/ND. Tube. Rosy red. Sepals. Greenish. Corolla. ND. GC. P192 Vol 21 1897. F. splendens X Ordinary greenhouse variety. Pendulous. F. splendens X NK. NK. NK. *1897.*

PENELOPE (a). Single. White/Purple. Tube. Waxy white. Sepals. Waxy white. Corolla. Violet purple. GC. P259 28/4/1849 & P241 20/4/1850 Listed by W. Rendle, Plymouth. GC. P338 22/5/1847 Intro. by Turville, Chelmsford. *Turville, Chelmsford GB. 1847.*

PENELOPE (b). Single. Red/White. Tube. Bright red. Sepals. Bright red. Corolla. White. Long. Large. Good shape. B. Cat. 1888. *Bull, W. Chelsea. GB. 1884?*

PENTHEUS. Single. Red/Purple. Tube. Deep crimson. Short. Sepals. Deep crimson. Horizontal. Very Broad. Corolla. Dark Purple Plum. Open saucer shaped. B. Cat. 1874-1883. *Bull, W. Chelsea. GB. 1874?*

PERA. Single. Red/Purple. Tube. Bright coral red. Short. Sepals. Bright coral red. Horizontal. Corolla. Bluish purple. Long. B. Cat. 1888-1892. *Bull, W. Chelsea. GB. 1887.*

PERCY. Double. Red/Purple. Tube. Dark crimson. Sepals. Dark crimson. Reflexed. Corolla. Purple. Large. Full. GC. P1054 7/11/1863 Intro. by W. Bull. *Bull, W. Chelsea. GB. 1863.*

PERFECTION (a). Single. Red/Red. Tube. Crimson. (Bright rose). Short. Sepals. Crimson.(Bright rose). Shorter than tube. Horizontal. Corolla. Red and lilac. (Violet rose). (Violet). RH. P168 1857. App. to RH. 1851 by Porcher. Globular form. 1st class variety. GC. P497 11/8/1849 Listed by G. Smith. Islington. GC. P145 9/3/1850 Listed By W. Rumley. GC. P210 6/4/1850 Listed by H. Walton, Burnley. GC. P423 7/7/1849 Intro. by Youell. *Youell. Gt. Yarmouth. GB. 1849.*

PERFECTION (b). Single. Red/Purple. Tube. Coral Red. Sepals. Coral Red. Reflexed sufficiently. Remarkable for their breadth. Corolla. Deep purple. GC. P535 20/8/1853 Seen at C. Turner, Slough. GC. P438 6/7/1854 Exhibited at RBS Show, Regents Park by Mr. Bray 7' pyramid. GC. P391 6/1852 Show report on Seedlings. GC. P369 11/6/1853 Listed by Bass & Brown. GC. P385 18/6/1853 & P147 11/3/1854 Listed by W. Rumley, Richmond. GC. P483 30/7/1853 & P162 18/3/1854 Listed by H. Walton, Burnley. GC. P627 1/10/1853 Listed by S. Fenney, Gateshead. GC. P213 8/4/1854 Listed by C. H. Gardiner, Maidstone. GC. P337 28/5/1853 Intro. by Bass & Brown, Sudbury. *Banks, E. Deal. GB. 1853.*

PERFECTION (c). Single. ND/ND. Tube. ND. Sepals. ND. Corolla. ND. GC. P401 24/6/1854

Listed by B. Cant, Colchester & H. Walton, Burnley. GC. P466 22/7/1854 Listed by Bass & Brown, Sudbury. GC. P238 14/4/1855 Listed by J. Hoad, Addlestone. *Standish, Bagshot. GB. 1854.*

PERFECTION (d). Single. Red/Purple. Tube. Rich coral red. Sepals. Rich coral red. Beautifully recurved. Corolla. Rich purple. Goblet shaped. GC. P885 2/7/1870 Review by H. Cannell. Small flowers. Very free bloomer. Difficult to grow. GC. P881 1873 Exhibited at RHS Show, Bath by J. Lye. GC. P885 2/7/1870 Not being sent out until July. GC. P83 14/7/1879 Greenhouse Favourites. B. Cat. 1870. GC. P488 9/4/1870 Intro. by H. Cannell. *Banks, E. Deal. GB. 1870.*

PERICLES. Single. Red/Purple. Tube. Crimson scarlet. (Light Red). Sepals. Crimson scarlet. Smooth. Reflexed. Corolla. Violet Purple. GC. P260 24/3/1860 Abundant blooms. Average Size. Vol. P3 1863 J of RHS Fuchsia trial at Chiswick 1862. A free and showy sort. GC. P426 12/5/1860 Listed by W. Hussey, Norwich & F. Godwin, Sheffield. GC. P90 5/2/1859. Intro. by G. Smith. *Smith, G. Islington. GB. 1859.*

PERLE. Single. Pink/Red. Tube. Pearl pink.long. Sepals. Pearl pink. White points. Corolla. Red. Large panicles. L. Cat. 1907-1908. *Bonstedt, Gottingen. Germany. 1905.*

PERSEVERANCE. ND. ND/ND. Tube. ND. Sepals. ND. Corolla. ND. GC. P594 29/6/1861 Listed by Godwin & Padman, Sheffield. GC. P771 24/8/1861 Listed by H. Walton, Burnley. NK. NK. *GB. 1861.*

PERSUASIVE. Single. Red/Purple. Tube. Deep crimson. Sepals. Deep crimson. Well reflexed. Corolla. Violet purple. B. Cat. 1872-1873. NK. NK. *GB. 1871.*

PERUGINO. Single. Red/Purple. Tube. Scarlet. Sepals. Scarlet. Well reflexed. Corolla. Rose and purple stripes. Free flowering. GC. P276 28/4/1855 Not to be sent out because the nursery is unable to supply plants of sufficient strength. GC. P18 13/1/1855 Intro. by E.G. Henderson. *Story, W. Newton Abbot. GB. 1855.*

PET. Double. Red/Purple. Tube. Dark crimson. Sepals. Dark crimson. Reflexed. Corolla. Violet Purple. Bedding variety. Fine. Dwarf bushy type of growth 18" to 20" high. Profusely loaded with fine reflexed flowers. GC. P449 17/7/1852 & P209 26/3/1853 Listed By H. Walton, Burnley. GC. P211 26/3/1853 Listed by W. Rumley, Richmond. GC.

P130 21/2/1852 Intro. by E.G.Henderson, St. Johns Wood. *Whalley, T. Liverpool. GB. 1852*

PETRARCH. S/Double. Red/Purple. Tube. Bright crimson. Sepals. Bright crimson. Corolla. Rich purplish crimson marked rose at base. B. Cat. 1872-1876. *Bull, W. Chelsea. GB. 1872.*

PHARAON. Double. Red/White. Tube. Bright red. Long. Sepals. Bright red. Corolla. White veined carmine. L. Cat. 1912. *Rozain. Lyons. France. 1912.*

PHASIS. Single, Red/Purple. Tube. Rosy crimson. Sepals. Rosy crimson. Completely reflexed. Corolla. Crimson purple. Well expanded. B. Cat. 1883. *Bull, W. Chelsea. GB. 1883.*

PHENOMENAL (a). Double. Red/Purple. Tube. Rose with white. Thick. Long. Very large. Sepals. Rose with white. Held out. Corolla. Red shaded violet. P112 4th Ed. by Porcher 1874. This variety is an example of dimorphism within the genus. Thus the filaments of the stamens are united with pedicels of the petals and at their extremity the rudiments of a petal, within the centre, one finds a portion of the anthers. Pedicel 70mms. *Lemoine. Nancy. France. 1869.*

PHENOMENAL (b). Double. Red/Purple. Tube. Reddish carmine. Short. Sepals. Reddish carmine. Reflexed. Corolla. Azure violet flaked red. (Dark purple). GO. Select 1884-1891. RH. P311 1889 Select by E. A. Carrière. B. Cat. 1882-1894. JF. Cat. 1885. BSW. Cat. 1897. *Lemoine. Nancy. France. 1882.*

PHIDIAS Double. Red/White. Tube. Crimson red. 12mms long. Sepals. Crimson red. Reflexed. Round. Large. Corolla. Greyish white. Full. Short. Pedicel 10mms. Dark green foliage. Distinguished from the others by its shade of tube and sepals, nice and dark. P130 4th Ed. by Porcher 1874. *Demay H. Arras. Belgium. 1873.*

PHILÉMON. Double. Red/Purple. Tube. Dark blood red. Sepals. Dark blood red. Horizontal. Corolla. Bright purple. Flared. L. Cat. 1901. NK. NK. NK. *1901.*

PHILLIS COUSINS. ND. ND/ND. Tube. ND. Sepals. ND. Corolla. ND. GC. P184 13/3/1847 Listed by W. Miller, Ramsgate. NK. *GB. 1846.*

PHOENIX. Single. ND/ND. Tube. ND. Sepals. ND. Corolla. ND. GC. P112 17/2/1844 Listed by W. Miller, Ramsgate. NK. *GB. 1843.*

PHYNEANA. Single. ND/ND. Tube. ND. Sepals. ND. Corolla. ND. GC. P241 15/4/1843 Listed by F & A Smith, Hackney. NK. *GB. 1843.*

PHYRNE. Single. Red/White. Tube. Carmine. Sepals. Carmine. Corolla. White veined carmine. JF. Cat. 1921. NK. *GB. 1921.*

PICCO. Double. Red/Purple. Tube. Crimson. Sepals. Crimson. Broad. Well recurved. Corolla. Purplish plum. Large. B. Cat. 1872-1876. GC. P502 13/4/1872 Intro. by W. Bull, Chelsea. *Bull, W. Chelsea. GB. 1872.*

PICTA. Single. Pink/Red. Tube. Delicate bright pink. Sepals. Delicate bright pink, Green tips. Corolla. Rosy crimson tinged lilac. GC. P162 14/3/1846 & P184 13/3/1847 Listed by W. Miller, Ramsgate. GC. P153 4/3/1847 & P 232 1/4/1848 Listed by R. Cooper, Croydon. GC. P265 Listed by W. Rendle, Plymouth. GC. P650 28/9/1844 Intro. by Piper, Parkstone Nursery, Poole. *Piper, Poole. GB. 1844.*

PICTURATA. Single. Red/White. Tube. Red. Sepals. Red. Corolla. White. Floral World & Garden Guide 4 Jan 1870. NK. NK. NK.

PICKWICK. Single. Pink/Red. Tube. Light flesh. Sepals. Light flesh. Corolla. Rich carmine. Large. Globose. GC.P541 10/8/1844 Exhibited at HS. Meeting by Cormack, Deptford. GC. P162 14/3/1845 Listed by J. Miller, Ramsgate. FC. P224 Vol XII 1844. GC. P341 24/5/1845 Intro. by Cormack, Deptford. *Cormack, Deptford. GB. 1845.*

PIERRE BONNIER. Double. Red/White. Tube. Brilliant carmine. Sepals. Brilliant Carmine. Short. Relaxed. Corolla. Rich violet marbled with pink. Full. Very Large. Petals well open. L. Cat. 1906. *Lemoine. Nancy. France. 1905.*

PIERRE JOIGNEAUX (a). Double. Pink/Purple. Tube. Light yellowish rose. Sepals. Light yellowish rose. Green tips. Reflexed. Corolla. Rosy purple shaded violet. Irregularly formed. B. Cat 1879-1880. HC. Cat. 1882 Light red tipped green shaded white. Peculiar formation of deep reddish carmine. *Lemoine. Nancy. France. 1879.*

PIERRE JOIGNEAUX (b). Double. Red/Purple. Tube. Bright rose. Sepals. Bright rose. Short. Corolla. Dark mauve. B. Cat 1893. L. Cat. 1893. *Lemoine. Nancy. France. 1893.*

PIERRE LOTI. Double. Red/Purple. Tube. Bright red. Sepals. Bright red. Large. Corolla. Bluish violet.

Enormous. B. Cat. 1889-1893. L. Cat 1892. Named after the pen name of a French author Louis Viaud (1850-1923). *Lemoine. Nancy. France. 1889.*

PIERRE MOUILLEFÉRT. Double. Red/Pink. Tube. Bright coral. Sepals. Bright coral. Extremely broad. Corolla. Carmine pink splashed coral red. Petals adhere to sepals. L. Cat. 1906. *Lemoine. Nancy. France. 1904.*

PIETRO. Double. Red/White. Tube. Clear carmine red, lined white. Thick. Long. 35mms. Sepals. Carmine red. Horizontal. Large. Corolla. Pure white striped carmine. Full. Good size. Pedicel 40 mms. P130 4th Ed. by Porcher 1874. RH. P311 1889 Select by E. Carrière. *Twrdy, Brno. Austria. 1872.*

PILLAR OF BEAUTY. Single. Red/Purple. Tube. Red. Sepals. Red. Corolla. Purple. GC. P66 1/2/1845 & P162 14/3/1846 & P184 13/3/1847 by W. Miller, Ramsgate. GC. P216 27/3/1847 Listed by R. Cooper, Croydon. GC. P265 24/4/1847 Listed by W. Rendle, Plymouth. GC. P113 22/2/1845 Intro. by Kendall. *Kendall, Stoke Newington. GB. 1845.*

PILLAR OF GOLD. Single. Red/Purple. Tube. Red. Sepals. Red. Corolla. Violet Purple. Vol 1 J of RHS 1861 Commended. Exhibited by F & A Smith. GC. P1015 26/10/1864 Nursery visit. Rich gold variegation on olive green ground. GO. "Select" 1880-1883. SG. P459 1866 "Recommended". P69 Vol 4 J of RHS 1877 Fuchsia trials at Chiswick, No Award. A small grower of tolerable habit, the leaves pale green edged and streaked yellow. B. Cat. 1872-1878. GC. P287 26/2/1864 Listed by E.G. Henderson. GC. P410 30/4/1864 Listed by F & A Smith. HC. Cat. 1882. NK. *GB. 1864.*

PILOT. Double. Red/Purple. Tube. Scarlet. Long. Sepals. Scarlet. Well reflexed. Corolla. Dark Purple. Large. GC. P51 26/1/1856 To be sent out in May by W. Fuller, Florist, Newton Bushel formerly gardener to W.H. Story of Whitehill. *Story W. H. Newton Abbot. GB. 1856.*

PINK GLOBE. Single. ND/ND. Tube. ND. Sepals. ND. Corolla. ND. GC. P208 25/3/1848. Listed by Hart & Nicklin, Guildford. NK. *GB. 1847.*

PINK PERFECTION. Single. White/Pink. Tube. Creamy white. Sepals. Creamy white. Corolla. Rich pink and violet, dashed violet. GC. Vol 18 P215 1882. Exhibited at Devizes Hort Scty Show by J. Lye. (1st Prize). GC. Vol 22 P310 6/9/1884 Exhibited at Bath Show 3/4 Sept 1884 by J. Lye (1st 9 pot class) GC. Vol 26 P375 18/9/1886 Exhibited at Bath Floral Fete by J. Lye (1st 9 pot class). GC. Vol

23 1885 P209 Figure 39 Illustrated. Vol 36 G. 1889 21/9/1889 Exhibited at Bath Floral Fete by J. Lye (3rd 9 pot class) JF. Cat. 1885. B. Cat. 1879-1883. *Lye, J. Market Lavington. GB. 1879.*

PIONEER. Single. Red/Purple. Tube. Crimson. Sepals. Crimson. Corolla. Light purple. Large. J of H & CG. P406 20/8/1861. GC. P594 29/6/1861 Listed by Godwin & Padman, Sheffield. GC. P771 24/8/1861 Listed by H. Walton, Burnley. GC. P358 20/4/1861 Intro. by G. Smith, Tollington Nurseries. *Smith, G. Islington. GB. 1861.*

PIROLLE. Single. Red/Red. Tube. Rose. Sepals. Rose. Corolla. Lake. RH. P24 1846. F.C. Vol XIV P31 1846. Report on H.S. Show July 1845, exhibited by Gaines (2nd). NK. *France. 1845.*

PISTILLUM ALBUM. Single. ND/ND. Tube. ND. Sepals. ND. Corolla. ND. GC. P97 18/2/1843 Listed by Youells, Gt. Yarmouth. NK. *GB. NK.*

PITTO. Single. Pink/Purple. Tube. Pale Pink. Sepals. Orange. Corolla. Pale Lilac. GC. P338 22/5/1847 Intro. by Turville, Chelmsford. *Turville, Chelmsford GB. 1847.*

PIUS IX. Single. ND/ND. Tube. ND. Sepals. ND. Corolla. ND. App. to RH. 1851 by Porcher. 1st class variety. GC. P537 12/8/1848 Listed by G. Smith, Islington. GC. P224 14/4/1849 Listed by Bass & Brown, Sudbury. GC. P256 21/4/1849 Listed by R. Cooper, Croydon. GC. P279 5/5/1849 Listed by H. Walton, Burnley. *Salter, Versailles. France. 1848.*

PLATO. Double. Red/Purple. Tube. Deep rosy red. Short. Sepals. Deep rosy red. Wide. Horizontally reflexed. Corolla. Purple plum. Large. Full. B. Cat. 1872-1876. P127 4th Ed. by Porcher 1874 Not in the first selection. GC. P502 13/4/1872 Intro. by W. Bull, Chelsea. *Bull, W. Chelsea. GB. 1872.*

PLUTO. Single. ND/ND. Tube. ND. Sepals. ND. Corolla. ND. GC. P162 14/3/1846 & P184 13/3/1847 & P250 17/4/1847 Listed by W. Miller, Ramsgate. NK. NK. *GB. 1845.*

POLYHYMNIA. Single. Red/Red. Tube. Orange scarlet. Sepals. Orange scarlet. Corolla. Golden orange. Petals incurved. Dwarf graceful drooping habit. BSW. Cat. 1878. HC. Cat. 1882. NK. NK. NK.

POMONA. Single. ND/ND. Tube. ND. Sepals. ND. Corolla. ND. GC. P202 28/3/1846 Listed by W.C. Brown. GC. P250 17/4/1847 Listed by J. Hally, Blackheath. App. to RH. 1851 by Porcher 1st class variety. *Meade. GB. 1845.*

POMPIEN. Double. Red/Purple. Tube. Red. Sepals. Red. Corolla. purple violet. L. Cat. 1907. *Rozain. Lyons. France. 1907.*

PONDII. Single. Red/Red. Tube. Bright crimson. Sepals. Bright crimson. Corolla. Dark crimson. GC. P66 1/2/1845 Listed by W. Miller, Ramsgate. GC. P177 23/3/1846 Intro. by J. Kitley, Lyncombe Vale Nursery. *Pond. GB. 1844.*

PONTEY'S TRICOLOUR. Single. Pink/Purple. Tube. Delicate pale pink. Sepals. Delicate pale pink. Tipped green. Corolla. A fine purple. GI. P342 15/5/1841 Nursery visit. Among the plants in flower a seedling fuchsia called Tricolour. After the way of "Standishii" but the colours are quite distinct. GC. P433 11/6/1841 Report on Devon & Exeter HS show. Mr. Pontey had also a new variety called Tricolour. Delicate pink with green tips. Free grower and good bloomer. GC. P793 4/12/1841 Intro. by A. Pontey, Exeter. *Pontey, A. Exeter. GB. 1841.*

POOT. Single. Pink/Red. Tube. Flesh Pink. Sepals. Flesh pink. Large. Corolla. Brick red. Similar to "Crimson King". Long pedicels. App. to RH. 1851 by Porcher. *De Jonghe. France. 1850.*

PORT ARTHUR. Single. Red/Purple. Tube. Scarlet. Sepals. Scarlet. Very large. Well reflexed. Corolla. Violet. JF. Cat. 1898. *Rozain. Lyons. France. 1895.*

PORTENA. Double. Red/Purple. Tube. Crimson. Short. Sepals. Crimson. Completely reflexed. Corolla. Purplish crimson. Loose Open Double. B. Cat. 1876-1878. *Bull, W. Chelsea. GB. 1876.*

PORT SAY. Double. Red/Purple. Tube. Bright pink. Sepals. Bright pink. Large. Corolla. Bluish plum. L. Cat. 1908. *Rozain. Lyons. France. 1908.*

P. RADAELLI. Double. Red/Purple. Tube. Bright red. Sepals. Bright red. Recurved. Corolla. Bluish violet striated carmine rose. Enormous. B. Cat. 1893-1895. *Rozain. Lyons. France. 1893.*

PREDOMINANT. Single. Red/Red. Tube. Red. Sepals. Red. Corolla. Red. GC. P410 20/6/1846 Exhibited by J. Robinson Gr to J. Simpson at HS Show. FC. Vol XIV P206 1846. Certificate given to Fairbairn. NK. *GB. 1845.*

PREMIER (a). Single. Red/Purple. Tube. Red. Sepals. Red. Corolla. Rich crimson plum. GC. P483 30/7/1853 & P162 18/3/1854 Listed by H. Walton, Burnley. GC. P627 1/10/1853 Listed by S. Fenney, Gateshead. GC. P147 11/3/1854 Listed By W.

Rumley, Richmond. GC. P213 8/4/1854 Listed by C.H. Gardiner, Maidstone. GC. P248 15/4/1854 Listed by Mitchell & Co, Brighton. GC P353 26/5/1855 Listed by Hart & Nicklin, Guildford. GC. P226 9/4/1853 Raised and Intro. by E.G. Henderson, Wellington Nurseries. *Henderson, E.G. St. Johns Wood. GB. 1853.*

PREMIER (b). Double. Red/Purple. Tube. Bright crimson. Sepals. Bright crimson. Very wide up to the point. Corolla. Rich purple, sometimes flaked rose. Dwarf. Free bloomer. GC. P824 8/9/1860 Listed by F. Godwin, Sheffield. GC. P378 30/4/1859 Intro. by C. Kimberley, Stoke Nurseries, Coventry. *Kimberley, C. Coventry. GB. 1859*

PRESIDENT (a). Single. Red/Purple. Tube. Red. Sepals. Red. Corolla. Purple. GC. P574 19/8/1843 HS Show 15/8/1843 Exhibited by Standish. Parentage "Formosa Elegans x Corymbiflora then selfed". FJ. Page 78 4/1845 (Formosa X Corymbiflora) resultant seedlings pretty and free growing but not much different from hybrids with F. Fulgens, Progeny selfed and found in 1843 that three plants had a longer and more bolder flower more in the way of "Standishii" but with a much better corolla. See also "Colossus, Attractor and Antagonist" Illustrated in Paxton's magazine of Botany March 1844. GC. P401 22/6/1844 Being sent out. GC. P146 8/3/1845 Listed by Youell, Gt. Yarmouth. *Standish. Bagshot. GB. 1843.*

PRESIDENT (b). ND. ND/ND. Tube. ND. Sepals. ND. Corolla. ND. GC. P145 9/3/1850 Listed by W. Rumley, Richmond. GC. P210 6/4/1850 Listed by H. Walton, Burnley. GC. P241 20/4/1850 Listed by W. Rendle, Plymouth. NK. *GB. NK.*

PRESIDENT (c). ND ND/ND. Tube. ND. Sepals. ND. Corolla. ND. GC. P594 29/6/1861 Listed by Godwin & Padman, Sheffield. GC. P771 24/8/1861 Listed by H. Walton, Burnley. NK. *GB. 1861.*

PRESIDENT (d). Single. Red/Purple. Tube. Carmine. Sepals. Carmine. Large. Broad. Horizontally reflexed. Corolla. Rich purple. B. Cat. 1870-1873. *Bull, W. Chelsea. GB. 1869.*

PRESIDENT (e). Single. Red/Purple. Tube. Bright vermillion. Sepals. Bright vermillion. Well recurved. Corolla. Rich violet. Beautiful formed corolla. GC. P824 27/6/1885 Fuchsia trials at Chiswick 1885. Best in class. GO. "Select" 1886-1891. HC. Cat. 1882-1885. B. Cat. 1881-1889. GC. P424 9/4/1881 Intro. by G. Smith, Tollington Nursery. *Smith, G. Islington. GB. 1881.*

PRESIDENT (f). Single. Red/Purple. Tube. Deep red. Sepals. Deep red. Corolla.Rich Black blue. Good habit. Dobbies Cat. 1893-4. NK. NK. NK.

PRESIDENT CARNOT. Double. Red/Purple. Tube. Rosy crimson. Sepals. Rosy crimson. Reflexed. Corolla. Violet blue. Named after a President of France M.F.Carnot (1837-94) chosen Premier in 1887, assassinated 1894. B. Cat. 1888-1893. L. Cat. 1892. *Lemoine. Nancy. France. 1888.*

PRESIDENT DAVIS. ND. ND. ND/ND. Tube. ND. Sepals. ND. Corolla. ND. Named after the President of the Confederate States of America during the civil war. GC. P338 15/4/1865 Listed by W. Rumley, Richmond. NK. NK. NK.

PRESIDENT F. GUNTHIER. Double. Red/Purple. Tube. Red. Sepals. Red. Corolla. Rich violet. Dobbies Cat. 1893-4. NK. NK. NK.

PRESIDENT GRÉVY. Double. Red/Pink. Tube. Rosy lake. Sepals. Rosy lake. Well reflexed. Corolla. Peculiar shade of rose. Dwarf. Free. Very large. Fine form. Named after a President of France between 1879-87. Vol 13 J of RHS Pcxxxviii Highly commended.B. Cat. 1888-1893. Gartenflora P149 1888 new from Lemoine. *Lemoine. Nancy. France. 1886.*

PRESIDENT HARN. Single. White/Red. Tube. White. Sepals. White. Corolla. Red. P120 4th Ed. by Porcher 1874 Not meritorious enough to be included in the first selection. *Weinrich. Germany. 1866.*

PRESIDENT HUMANN. Double. Red/Purple. Tube. Clear carmine red. Sepals. Clear carmine red. Large. Reflexed. Rounded. Corolla. Rose violet, splashed red at base. P124 4th Ed. by Porcher 1874 Good foliage. Nice shade. *Lemoine. Nancy. France. 1868.*

PRESIDENT MULLER. NK. NK/NK. Tube. NK. Sepals. NK. Corolla. NK. RH. P295 1887 Grown as a standard at Twickel. GC. P406 Listed by Wm. Hussey, Norwich. *Cornelissen, Arras. Belgium. 1866.*

PRESIDENT PORCHER (a). Single. Red/Purple. Tube. Bright red. Sepals. Bright red. Paler than the tube. Corolla. Reddish purple. Style rose. Stigma brown. Perfection of "Zenobie" and "Comte de Beaulieu" 1st class variety. App. to RH. 1851 by Porcher. GC. P465 27/7/1850 Listed by G. Smith, Islington. *Meillez, Lille. France. 1850.*

PRESIDENT PORCHER (b). Double. Red/Purple. Tube. Bright crimson. Long. 15mms. Sepals. Bright crimson. Large. Elongated. Reflexed. Corolla. Violet blue, stained red at base. P124 4th Ed. by Porcher 1874 Although this variety is 12 years old and dedicated to me, it is still better than some more recent introductions. *Lemoine. Nancy. France. 1862.*

PRÉSIDENT VAN DAN HECKE. Double. Red/Purple. Tube. Red. Sepals. Red. Corolla. Purple. P127 4th Ed by Porcher 1874 Not in the first selection. *Coene, Ghent. Belgium 1865.*

P. RESTELLI. Double. Red/Purple. Tube. Bright red. Sepals. Bright red. Corolla. Deep blue. Very large. Long. JF. Cat. 1898. *Rozain, Lyons. France. 1897.*

PRESTIGE. Single. Red/Purple. Tube. Carmine. Sepals. Carmine. Broad. Short. Completely reflexed. Corolla. Purple marked rose. B. Cat. 1870-1873. *Bull, W. Chelsea. GB. 1869.*

PRIAM (a). Single. White/ND. Tube. White. Sepals. White. Corolla. ND. Floricultural Cabinet Vol XIII P170 1845 Exhibited at H.S. show June by Gaines. *Gaines.* NK. NK. *1845?*

PRIAM (b). Double. Red/Purple. Tube. Crimson. Short. Sepals. Crimson. Broad. Reflexed. Corolla. Violet Purple blotched carmine. Very thick. B. Cat. 1872-1876. *Bull, W. Chelsea. GB. 1871.*

PRIDE OF PECKHAM. Single. Pink/Red. Tube. Flesh. Sepals. Flesh. Tipped green. Corolla. Scarlet. GC. P66 1/2/1845 & P184 12/3/1847 Listed by W. Miller, Ramsgate. GC. P225 13/4/1844 Intro. by Ivery, Peckham. *Ivery, Peckham GB. 1844.*

PRIDE OF WOOLWICH. Single. Red/Purple. Tube. Scarlet. (Coral red). (Light coral). Sepals. Scarlet. (Coral Red). (Light coral). Recurved. Corolla. Rich purplish blue. (Dark blue) (Bright blue plum). GC. P1554 2/12/1871 Review by H. Cannell. Perfect shape. B. Cat. 1870-1876. HC. Cat. 1882. GC. P488 9/4/1870 Intro. by H. Cannell, Woolwich. *Banks, E. Deal. GB. 1870.*

PRIMA DONNA (a). Single. Pink/Red. Tube. Pale pink. (Rose salmon) (Lilac rose). Sepals. Pale Pink. (Rose salmon) (Lilac rose). Green tips. Corolla. Orange bordered crimson. Coloured plate. F.C. P145 1/7/1843. GC. P820 12/1844 "Recommended". RH. P24 1846. RH. P167 1857. GC. P66 1/2/1845 & P184 13/3/1847 Listed by W. Miller, Ramsgate. GC. P216 27/3/1847 & P232 1/4/1848 Listed by R. Cooper, Croydon. F. splendens X F. fulgens. *Harrison, Dereham GB. 1843.*

PRIMA DONNA (b). Single. White/Red. Tube. White. Stout. Sepals. White. Well reflexed. Corolla. Bright rose, edged scarlet. Very large. An improvement of "Duchess of Lancaster". GC. P475 13/6/1855 "Best three of the season". GC. P571 24/7/1858 Listed by H. Walton Burnley. GC. P85 6/2/1858 Intro. by G. Smith, Islington. *Smith, G. Islington. GB. 1858.*

PRIME MINISTER. Single. Red/Purple. Tube. Crimson. Sepals. Crimson. Corolla. Purple. GC. P545 30/8/1851 Listed by G. Smith, Islington. GC. P290 10/5/1851 Intro. by E.G. Henderson, St. Johns Wood. *Henderson, E.G. St.Johns Wood. GB. 1851.*

PRINCE ALBERT (a). Single. Pink/Red. Tube. Pale pink. Sepals. Pale pink. Corolla. Crimson. GC. P473 16/7/1842 Exhibited at HS Show by Brown, Bedford Nurseries. It is not of much value. GC. P112 17/2/1844 & P66 1/2/1845 Listed by W.Miller, Ramsgate. GC. P553 12/8/1843 Intro. by Brown, Bedford Nursery, Hampstead Rd. London. *Brown, London. GB. 1843.*

PRINCE ALBERT (b). Single. Red/Purple. Tube. Red. Sepals. Red. Corolla. Purple. GC. P98 17/2/1844 & P143 8/3/1845 Listed by Youells, Gt. Yarmouth. *Youell, Gt. Yarmouth. GB. 1844.*

PRINCE ALBERT (c). Single. ND/ND. Tube. ND. Sepals. ND. Corolla. ND. GC. P66 1/2/1845 Listed by W. Miller, Ramsgate. *Bell, Thirsk. GB. 1844.*

PRINCE ALBERT (d). Single. Red/Purple. Tube. Pale waxy rose. Sepals. Pale waxy rose. Reflexed. Corolla. Crimson Purple. Very large. All exposed. 20-30 flowers from each joint. Superb habit. 1st prize Bath R.H. show 18/7/1844. GC. P234 11/4/1846 Listed by A.J. Stewart, Salthill Nursery, Windsor. GC. P164 8/3/1845 Intro. by E. Tiley, Bath. *Tiley E. Bath GB. 1845.*

PRINCE ALBERT (e). Single. Red/Purple. Tube. Dark red. Sepals. Crimson. A little open. Corolla. Violet red. Small flowers. App. to RH. 1851 by Porcher 2nd class. GC. P216 27/3/1847 & P232 1/4/1848 Listed by R. Cooper, Croydon. GC. P274 5/5/1849 Listed by H. Walton, Burnley. *Jennings. GB. 1847.*

PRINCE ALBERT (f). Single. Red/Purple. Tube. Scarlet crimson. Sepals. Scarlet crimson. Reflexed. Corolla. Rich violet. Coloured plate in Florist Feb 1855. Colour Plate 42 Vol 2 L'Illustration Horticole 1855. GC. P435 30/6/1855 Listed by H. Groom. GC. P467 19/7/1855 Listed by Bass & Brown, Sudbury & H. Walton, Burnley. GC. P529 11/8/1855 & P208

22/3/1856 Listed by Bainbridge & Hewison, York. GC. P531 11/8/1855 Listed by Joseph Courcha. GC. P314 12/5/1856 & P146 7/3/1857 Listed by W. Rumley, Richmond. GC. P314 10/5/1856 Listed by Youell, Gt. Yarmouth. GC. P456 5/7/1856 Listed by T. Clarke, Cheltenham. GC. P18 13/1/1855 Intro. by E.G. Henderson, St. Johns Wood. *Banks, E. Deal. GB. 1855.*

PRINCE ALFRED (a). Single. ND/ND. Tube. ND. Sepals. ND. Corolla. ND. GC. P216 27/3/1847 Listed by R. Cooper, Croydon. NK. NK. NK.

PRINCE ALFRED (b). Single. White/Purple. Tube. Blush Pink. Striped. Sepals. Blush Pink. Inner side white. Wide. Finely recurved. Corolla. Deep plum or mulberry. Base of petals pure white extending to half the length. Dense flower clusters. GC. P824 27/6/1885 Fuchsia Trials at Chiswick "Best in its class", single light. HC. Cat. 1882-1885 Must be well stopped when young. Vol 3 J of RHS P92 Fuchsia trials at Chiswick 1863. A small sort with whitish reflexed sepals and a purplish corolla. GC. P55 19/1/1867 Review by H. Cannell. Profuse bloomer. GC. P560 30/6/1860 Listed by F. Godwin, Sheffield. GC. P215 10/3/1860 Intro. by E.G. Henderson, St. Johns Wood. *Banks, E. Deal. GB. 1860.*

PRINCE ARTHUR (a). Single. White/Red. Tube. Pure white. Sepals. Pure white. Reflex upwards 3½" to 4" across. Corolla. Deep rosy crimson. GC. P177 20/3/1852 Listed by W. Rumley, Richmond. GC. P207 27/3/1852 Listed by H. Walton, Burnley. GC. P481 3/8/1850 Intro. by Nicholls, Leeds. *Nicholls, Leeds. GB. 1850.*

PRINCE ARTHUR (b). Double. Red/Purple. Tube. Red. Sepals. Red. Corolla. Purple. GC. P545 30/8/1851 Listed by G. Smith, Islington. P351 Gartenflora Vol 2. GC. P274 3/5/1851 Intro. by Veitch, Exeter. *Story, W.H. Newton Abbot. GB. 1851.*

PRINCE ARTHUR (c). Single. Red/Purple. Tube. Red. Sepals. Red. Corolla. Violet. Expanded. Similar to "Lord John Russell". Vol P1 J of RHS P262/3 1860. *Banks, E. Deal. GB. 1860.*

PRINCE DE LAMBELLES. Single. ND/ND. Tube. ND. Sepals. ND. Corolla. ND. GC. P224 14/4/1849 Listed by Bass & Brown, Sudbury. *Meillez, Lille. France. 1848.*

PRINCE D'ESSLING. Double. Red/Purple. Tube. Cardinel red. Sepals. Cardinal red. Reflexed. Corolla. Red Purple splashed scarlet. L. Cat. 1911. *Rozain, Lyons France. 1911.*

PRINCE DE WERNIGERODE. SEE. FURST OTTO VAN WERNIGERODE.

PRINCE FREDERICK WILLIAM OF PRUSSIA. Single. Red/Purple. Tube. Carmine. Sepals. Carmine. Corolla. Blue fading purple. RH. P95 1859. GC. P539 10/7/1858 Listed by F. Godwin, Sheffield. GC. P571 Listed by H. Walton, Burnley. GC. P238 19/3/1859 Listed by W. Rumley, Richmond. GC. P308 9/4/1859 Listed by Epps Nurseries, Maidstone. *Banks, E. Deal. GB. 1858.*

PRINCE FREDERICK WILLIAM. Double. Red/Purple. Tube. Red. Sepals. Red. About 1" long. Broad. Corolla. Reddish Purple. Uneven. Pcxv Vol 3 J of RHS Fuchsia trials at Chiswick 1872. NK. *GB.* NK.

PRINCE GEORGES (a). Double. Red/Purple. Tube. Dark blood red. Sepals. Dark Blood Red. Extended. Corolla. Reddish plum violet. Large. Full. Expanded. L. Cat. 1901. *Lemoine. Nancy. GB. 1899.*

PRINCE GEORGES (b) Double. Red/Purple Tube. Crimson. Sepals Crimson. Corolla. Purple. Large. Full. JF. Cat 1921. *Rozain, Lyons. France. 1915.*

PRINCE GHIKA. Single. Red/Purple. Tube. Red. Tube.Red. Corolla. Purple. Striped. Small. Vol. P3 J of RHS P90 1863 Fuchsia trials at Chiswick. GC. P824 8/9/1860 Listed by F. Godwin, Sheffield. *Cornelissen, Arras. Belgium 1859.*

PRINCE IMPERIAL. Single. Red/Purple. Tube. Scarlet. Short Sepals. Scarlet. Broad. Recurved. Corolla. Violet. Vol P3 J of RHS 1863 Fuchsia Trials at Chiswick Awarded **. Free variety, erect habit. Near "La Crinoline". Expanded. GC. P594 30/6/1860 Listed by F. Godwin, Sheffield. GC. P215 10/3/1860 Intro. by E.G. Henderson. *Banks, E. Deal. GB. 1860.*

PRINCE LEOPOLD (a). Single. Red/Purple. Tube. Red. Stout. ½" long. Sepals. Red. Slender. Tapered. Spreading. 1¼" long. Corolla. Violet purple, reddish towards the base. Petals overlap. 1½" across. Conically expanded. Vol 1 J of RHS 1861 Floral Committee, awarded FCC. Vol III pcxvi J of RHS 1872 Fuchsia trials at Chiswick. Vol V J of H & CG P406 20/8/1861 Well cupped. P115 4th Ed. by Porcher 1874 Not in the first selection. GC. P595 29/6/1861 Listed by Godwin & Padman, Sheffield. GC. P771 24/8/1861 Listed by H. Walton, Burnley. GC. P653 9/7/1864. Exhibited at RBS show. *Banks, E. Deal. GB. 1861.*

PRINCE LEOPOLD (b). Double. Red/Purple. Tube. Deep crimson. Short. Sepals. Deep crimson. Broad. Well reflexed. Corolla. Deep violet, upper parts shaded carmine. (Violet Blue stained red at base). Spiralled. Regular. GC. P146 1895. P124 4th Ed. by Porcher 1874. Vigorous. Good foliage, having a pronounced yellowish tint. Pedicel 30mms. P217 Vol 4 J of RHS 1877 Fuchsia trials at Chiswick FCC. Bushy. Drooping habit. Free. Compact corolla. HC. Cat. 1882 P79 Profuse bloomer. Good habit. RH. P311 1889 Select by E.A. Carrière. GC. P419 30/3/1872 Intro. by B.S. Williams, Holloway. *Bland E. Fordham GB. 1872.*

PRINCE OF ORANGE (a). Single. Red/Red. Tube. Orange. (Clear vermillion). Long. Thin. Sepals. Orange. (Bright green to orange). Corolla. Crimson. App to RH. 1851 by Porcher. An ordinary variety, it is not distinguished by its colour. GC. P465 27/7/1850 Listed by W. Rumley, Richmond. GC. P242 24/4/1850 Intro. by E. G. Henderson. *Henderson, E.G. St. Johns Wood. GB. 1850.*

PRINCE OF ORANGE (b). Single. Red/Purple. Tube. Bright crimson red. Sepals. Crimson red. Large. Short. Bent. Corolla. Violet red, paler than the tube. Small. App. to RH. 1850 by Porcher. *Racine. France. 1850.*

PRINCE OF ORANGE (c). Single. Red/Purple. Tube. Scarlet. Sepals. Scarlet. Well recurved. Wide. Reflexed. Corolla. Purple. Expanded. GC. P1331 1871 Grown in Hyde Park as a bedder. RH. P311 1889 "Select" by E.A. Carrière. Vol 3 P3 J of RHS 1863 Fuchsia trials at Chiswick A free bloomer. HC. Cat 1882 A fine old exhibition variety. More of this grown for Covent Garden than any other. GC. P215 10/3/1860 Intro. by E.G. Henderson. *Banks, E. Deal. GB. 1860.*

PRINCE OF ORANGE (d). Single. Pink/Orange. Tube. Orange pink. Short. Sepals. Orange pink. Green tips. Corolla. Orange vermillion. L. Cat. No. 149 1901. B. Cat. 1901 Intro. by W. Bull, Chelsea. *Bull, W. Chelsea. GB. 1901.*

PRINCE OF WALES (a). Single. Red/Purple. Tube. Red. Sepals. Red. Corolla. Purple. GC. P112 17/2/1844 Listed by W. Miller, Ramsgate. GC. P146 8/3/1845 Listed by Youell, Gt. Yarmouth. GC. P97 17/2/1841 Intro. by W.J. Epps, Maidstone. *Busby. Hemstead. GB. 1841.*

PRINCE OF WALES (b). Single. Red/Red. Tube. Carmine red. Very long. Sepals. Carmine red. Corolla. Carmine red with a tinge of purple. GC. P417 17/6/1843 Assessed. GC. P112 17/2/1844 &

148

P66 1/2/1845 Listed by W. Miller, Ramsgate. RH. P24 1846. GC. P553 28/8/1843 Intro. by W. Bell, Thirsk. *Bell, W. Thirsk. GB. 1843.*

PRINCE OF WALES (c). Single. Red/Purple. Tube. Rosy vermillion. Sepals. Rosy vermillion. Green tips. Corolla. Maroon Purple. GC. P146 8/3/1845 Listed by Youell, Gt. Yarmouth. GC. P1 6/1/1844 Intro. by Youell, Gt. Yarmouth. *Youell, Gt. Yarmouth. GB. 1844.*

PRINCE OF WALES (d). Single. Red/Purple. Tube. Bright crimson. Sepals. Bright crimson. Corolla. Violet. Large. GC. P369 8/6/1844 Listed by T. Cripps. GC. P66 1/2/1845 Listed by W. Miller, Ramsgate. GC. P146 8/3/1845 Listed by Youell, Gt. Yarmouth. GC. P161 16/3/1844 Entire stock purchased and intro. by W. Pawley, White Hart Hotel, Bromley. *Pawley, W. Bromley. GB. 1844.*

PRINCE OF WALES (e). Single. ND/ND. Tube. ND. Sepals. ND. Corolla. ND. GC. P369 8/6/1844 Listed by T. Cripps. *Lengelier. GB. 1844.*

PRINCE OF WALES (f). Single. Red/Purple. Tube. Red. Sepals. Red. Corolla. Purple. GC. P706 9/11/1850 Listed by H. Walton, Burnley. GC. P151 5/3/1853 Dark variety, good for exhibition. GC. P289 11/5/1850 Intro. by Mayle, Birmingham. *Mayle, Birmingham. GB. 1850.*

PRINCE OF WALES (g). Single. Red/Purple. Tube. Rosy crimson. Sepals. Rosy Crimson. Corolla. Dark Violet. Dwarf. Selected from 3,000 seedlings. Out on 1/4/1856. GC. P451 5/7/1856 & P642 27/9/1856 Listed by H. Walton, Burnley. GC. P690 18/10/1856 & P146 7/3/1857 Listed by W. Rumley, Richmond. GC. P 251 11/4/1857 Listed by W. Masters, Canterbury. GC.P611 15/9/1855 Intro by Stewart & Nielsen, Liscard. *Stewart & Nielsen, Liscard. GB. 1856.*

PRINCE OF WALES (h). Single. Red/Purple. Tube. Crimson red. Very short. Sepals. Crimson red. Large sepals. Reflexed. Corolla. Violet washed red. Very expanded. Pedicel 30 mms. P112 4th. Ed. by Porcher 1874. GC. P338 15/4/1865 Listed by W. Rumley, Richmond. *F&A Smith. Hackney.GB. 1863.*

PRINCE OF WATERLOO. Single. ND/ND. Tube. ND. Sepals. ND. Corolla. ND. GC. P409 22/6/1844 Exhibited by R. Oswald, Gardener to Orphan Hospital at the Royal Caledonian Show. *Oswald. Edinburgh? GB. 1844.*

PRINCEPS (a). Single. ND/ND. Tube. ND. Sepals. ND. Corolla. ND. GC. P393 June 1842 Listed by

Youell, Gt. Yarmouth. GC. P241 15/4/1843 Listed by F & A Smith, Hackney (as Princess). GC. P98 17/2/1844 Listed by Youell, Gt.Yarmouth. GC. P112 17/2/1844 Listed by W. Miller, Ramsgate. GC. P345 28/5/1842 Intro by J. Smith, Dalston. *Smith, J. Dalston. GB. 1842.*

PRINCEPS (b). Single. Red/Purple. Tube. Scarlet Lake. (Deep rose). Sepals. Scarlet Lake. (Deep rose). Corolla. Deep blue. (Purple). Tube and Sepals 3" long. GC. P614 4/10/1851 Seen on Nursery visit noted as "Princess". Corrected on P629 11/10/1851. GC. P661 18/10/1851 I have a plant of the sort 14 feet high. Never been covered. J. Gould Arnbeck. GC. P353 5/6/1852 Out on 5/7/1852 Sepals reflex to a greater degree than any other. GC. P660 Nov 1851. New fuchsia in the way of "Corallina" loaded with 3 to 7 of the gorgeous flowers. Branches forced downwards with their weight. GC. P199 3/1853 "Recommended". GC. P162 18/3/1854 Listed by H. Walton, Burnley. *Pince, Exeter. GB. 1852.*

PRINCE ROUGE. Double. Red/ Red. Tube. Crimson. Sepals. Crimson. Corolla. Fiery red. Sport of "Black Prince". L. Cat. 1892. *Stingue. France. 1890.*

PRINCESS. Single. White/Red. Tube. White. Sepals. White. Corolla. Red. GC. P545 30/8/1851 Listed by G. Smith, Islington. GC. P177 20/3/1852 Listed by W. Rumley, Richmond GC. P245 15/4/1854 Listed by Mitchell & Co, Brighton. GC. P368 26/5/1855 Listed by Hart & Nicklin, Guildford. GC. P209 5/4/1851 Intro. by C. Turner, Slough. *Banks, E. Deal. GB. 1851.*

PRINCESS ALEXANDER (a). Single. White/ND. Tube. White. Sepals. White. Corolla. ND. P120 4th. Ed by Porcher 1874. Not in the first selection. *Smith, F&A. GB. 1863.*

PRINCESS ALEXANDER (b). Double. Red/White. Tube. Rose pink. (Carmine). Sepals. Rose pink. (Carmine). Well reflexed. Corolla. White. Very double. P130 4th. Ed by Porcher 1874 Sepals elevated. Large. Delicate. GO. 1880 "Select". BSW Cat. 1878. GC. P430 29/3/1873 Intro. by E.G. Henderson. *Henderson, E.G. St. Johns Wood. GB. 1873.*

PRINCESS ALICE (a). Single. White/Red. Tube. White. Sepals. White. Corolla. Red. Selected from a large number of seedlings, raised by W. Knight Gr. to the Duke of Kent. GC. P539 10/1/1858 Listed by F. Godwin, Sheffield. GC. P238 Listed by W. Rumley, Richmond. GC. P126 20/2/1858 Intro. by W. Rollisson, Upper Tooting. *Knight, W. GB. 1858.*

149

PRINCESS ALICE (b). Single. White/Purple. Tube. White. Sepals. White. Well reflexed. Corolla. Rosy purple tinted maroon. Continual bloomer. Style of "Maid of Kent". SG. P459 1866 "Recommended". Vol P3 J of RHS 1863 P91 Fuchsia trials at Chiswick. Awarded ** A very elegant free blooming decorative variety. GC. P215 10/3/1860 Intro. by E. G. Henderson, St. Johns Wood. *Banks, E. Deal. GB. 1860.*

PRINCESS ALICE (c). Single. Red/White. Tube. Coral red. Sepals. Coral red. Corolla. White streaked red. Vol P1 J of RHS 1860 P293 Floral C'tee. Inferior to "Princess of Prussia" and "Fascination". *Veitch, Exeter. GB. 1861.*

PRINCESS ALICE (d). Single. Red/Purple. Tube. Red. Sepals. Red. Corolla. Purple. P115 4th Ed. by Porcher 1874. Not in the first selection. *Smith, G. Islington. GB. 1863.*

PRINCESS ALICE MAUD (a).. Single. ND/ND. Tube. ND. Sepals. ND. Corolla. ND. GC. P184 13/3/1841 & P250 27/4/1841 Listed by W. Miller, Ramsgate. *Fairbeard. GB. 1841.*

PRINCESS ALICE MAUD (b). Single. Pink/ND. Tube. Flesh. Sepals. Pink. Corolla. ND. GC. P375 4/6/1844 Exhibited at H.S. Show by Mr Wright Gr. to Hon Mrs. Rushout. GC. P66 1/2/1845 Listed by W. Miller, Ramsgate. GC. P250 17/4/1847 Listed by J. Hally, Blackheath. GC.P265 24/4/1847 & P259 20/4/1849 Listed by W. Rendle, Plymouth. *Wright. GB. 1844.*

PRINCESS BEATRICE. Single. White/Pink. Tube. Waxy white. short. Stout. (Blush white). Sepals. Waxy white. (Blush white). Beautifully reflexed. Corolla. Bright Pink. (Light lake margined with rose vermillion). Vol 4 J of RHS 1877 P69. Fuchsia trials at Chiswick. No award. Habit very compact and robust and a free flowerer. GC. P1233 27/11/1869 A correspondent writes "Cuttings struck in February. Started flowering first week in August. Now 8 foot high and 4 foot 6 inches in diameter. B. Cat. 1870. HC. Cat. 1882-1885. *Banks, E. Deal. GB. 1867.*

PRINCESS DESTRICHEN. Double. Red/Purple. Tube. Red, Sepals. Red. Corolla. Purple. P127 4th Ed. by Porcher 1874. Not in the first selection. *Twrdy, Brno. Austria. 1866.*

PRINCESS HELEN. Single. ND/ND. Tube. ND. Sepals. ND. Corolla. ND. GC. P224 14/4/1849 Listed by R. Whibley, Kennington Cross. NK. *GB.* NK.

PRINCESS LOUISE (a). Single. Pink/Red. Tube. Salmon. Sepals. Salmon. Green tips. Corolla. Deep Carmine, tinged rosy purple. Free bloomer. GC. P146 8/4/1845 Intro. by Youell, Gt. Yarmouth. *Youell, Gt.Yarmouth. GB. 1845.*

PRINCESS LOUISE (b). Single. Red/White. Tube. Carmine. Sepals. Carmine. Well reflexed. Corolla. Pure white. Dwarf. GC. P146 1895. GC. P510 28/4/1871 Intro. by B.S. Williams, Holloway. *Bland, E. Fordham. GB. 1871.*

PRINCESS MARY. Single. ND/ND. Tube. ND. Sepals. ND. Corolla. ND, Floricultural Cabinet. Vol XIV P206 1846 Exhibited at RBS Show 20/5/1846 by Gaines, Battersea. NK. *GB. 1846.*

PRINCESS MATHILDE. ND. ND/ND. Tube. ND. Sepals. ND. Corolla. ND. RH. P311 1889. "Select" by E.A. Carrière. NK. NK. NK.

PRINCESS MAY. Single. White/Red. Tube. White slightly tinted blush. Sepals. White slightly tinted blush. Corolla. Clear scarlet. (Orange scarlet). (Rosy coral deepening at edge of petals). Very free. Graceful. Dwarf. A of M Temple show. GO. P151 1895. GC. Vol 27 P 411 1/5/1897 Listed by H.J. Jones, Lower Sydenham. JF. Cat. 1895. B. Cat. 1894 -1895. HC. Cat. 1894-1896. Intro. by H. Cannell. *Banks, E. Deal. GB. 1894.*

PRINCESS OF PRUSSIA (a). ND. ND/ND. Tube. ND. Sepals. ND. Corolla. ND. GC. P368 26/5/1855 Listed by E.G. Henderson, St. Johns Wood. GC. P531 11/8/1855 Listed by J. Courcha. GC. P314 10/4/1856 Listed by W. Rumley, Richmond, & Youell, Gt. Yarmouth. GC. P146 7/3/1857 Listed by W. Rumley, Richmond.NK. NK. *1855.*

PRINCESS OF PRUSSIA (b). Single. Red/White. Tube. Red. Sepals. Red. Long. Narrowish. Reflexed. Corolla. White. Well folded. Large. (Pure white). Moderate size, petals veined red at base. Elegant habit. Equal to "Nil Desperandum". Six flowers at each joint. Exceed 5" in length. RH. P95 1859. Vol P3 J of RHS 1863 P91. Fuchsia Trials at Chiswick 1862 Awarded **. An elegant free blooming variety. GC. P475 13/6/1858 Listed by C.E. Allen. GC. P571 24/7/1858 Listed by H. Walton, Burnley. GC. P238 19/8/1859 Listed by W. Rumley, Richmond. GC. P308 9/4/1859 Listed by Epps Nursery, Maidstone. GC. P260 24/3/1860 Listed by Wm Hussey, Norwich. GC. P85 6/2/1858 Intro. by G. Smith, Islington. *Smith, G. Islington. GB. 1858.*

PRINCESS ROYAL (a). Single. Pink/Red. Tube. Long. Light rose. Sepals. Light rose. Tipped green.

Corolla. Scarlet Lake. Resembles "Chandlerii" with a longer tube. GC. P417 17/6/1843 Assessed by Editor (as from Mowbray). GC. P112 17/2/1844 & P66 1/3/1845 Listed by W. Miller, Ramsgate. GC. 28/8/1843 Intro. by W. Bell, Thirsk. *Mowbray. GB. 1843.*

PRINCESS ROYAL (b). Single. Red/ND. Tube. Red. Sepals. Red. Corolla. ND. Large. 4" from the pod to the pistil. GC. P146 8/3/1845 Listed by Youell. GC. P1 6/1/1844 Intro. by Youell, Gt. Yarmouth. *Youell, Gt. Yarmouth. GB. 1844.*

PRINCESS ROYAL (c). Single. White/Red. Tube. White. Sepals. White. Sepals not reflexed. Corolla. Dark rose. Selected from 3,000 seedlings. To be sent out 1/4/1856. Raised and intro by Stewart & Nielsen, Liscard, Ches. *Stewart & Nielsen, Liscard. GB. 1856.*

PRINCESS ROYAL (d). Single. Red/White. Tube. Scarlet. Sepals. Scarlet. Corolla. White. Free blooming and undoubtably the best habit of all the white corolla varieties. GC. P471 14/7/1855 Exhibited at HS Show 11/7/1855 (? by E.G. Henderson). GC. 23/5/1857 Now being sent out by E.G. Henderson. GC. P515 25/7/1857 Listed by H. Walton, Burnley. GC. P171 14/3/1857 Intro. by Veitch, Exeter. *Veitch, Exeter. GB. 1857.*

PRINCESS OF WALES (a). Single. Red/Purple. Tube. Red. Sepals. Red. Corolla. Purple. GC. P338 15/4/1865 Listed by W. Rumley, Richmond. P115 4th Ed. by Porcher 1874 Not in the first selection. *Banks, E. Deal. GB. 1863.*

PRINCESS OF WALES (b). Double. Red/White. Tube. Scarlet. (Glossy coral scarlet). Sepals. Scarlet. (Glossy coral scarlet). Reflexed. Corolla. White. (Pure white). GC. P1554 2/12/1870 Review by H. Cannell. GC. P257 27/8/1887 Exhibited at Trowbridge by Pocock (2nd). GC. P330 13/3/1875 Listed by T. Fletcher, Chesterfield. B. Cat. 1872-1873. BSW. Cat. 1878. GC. P488 9/4/1870 Intro. by H. Cannell, Swanley. *Bland, E. Fordham. GB. 1870.*

PRINCESS SOPHIA. Single. Red/Purple. Tube. Glossy vermillion. Sepalq. Vermillion. Corolla. Dark purplish rose. GC. P66 1/2/1845 Listed by W. Miller, Ramsgate. GC. P146 8/3/1845 Listed by Youell, Gt. Yarmouth. GC. P218 27/3/1847 Listed by R. Cooper, Croydon. GC. P161 16/3/1844 Purchased and intro. by Marnock & Manby, Hackney. *Marnock & Manby, Hackney. GB. 1844.*

PRINCESS SUPERB. ND. ND/ND. Tube. ND. Sepals. ND. Corolla. ND. GC. P571 24/7/1858 Listed by H. Walton, Burnley. NK. NK. *1858.*

PRINTAIR. ND. ND/ND. Tube. ND. Sepals. ND. Corolla. ND. CG. P257 1865. "Best of 1864 varieties". NK. NK. *1864.*

PRISTINE. Single. Red/Red. Tube. Carmine. Sepals. Carmine. Well reflexed. Corolla. Lake. GC. P1054 7/11/1863 Intro. by W. Bull, Chelsea. *Bull, W. Chelsea. GB. 1863.*

PRIVATEER. Double. Red/Purple. Tube. Rose. Sepals. Rose. Corolla. Lavender blue. Globular flowers. B. Cat. 1870-1873. NK. *GB. NK.*

PRIX NOBEL. Double. Red/Pink. Tube. Carmine. Sepals. Carmine. Broad. Corolla. Whitish salmon pink. Large. Well formed. Full. L. Cat. 1902. *Lemoine. Nancy. France. 1902.*

PROFESSEUR LIPPMAN. Double. Red/Purple. Tube. Carmine lake. Sepals. Carmine Lake. Lay on corolla. Corolla. Indigo fading to plum violet. Full. Named after a French physicist (1845-1920) who was a Nobel prizewinner in 1908. L. Cat. 1909. *Lemoine. Nancy. France. 1909.*

PROFESSEUR ROENTGEN. Double. Red/Purple. Tube. Scarlet. Sepals. Scarlet. Corolla. Violet, alternated with red bands. Compact. Very full and voluminious. JF. Cat. 1904. L. Cat. 1902. *Lemoine. Nancy. France. 1902.*

PROFUSA. Single. Red/Purple. Tube. Red. Sepals. Red. Spreading. ½". Corolla. Purple, reddish at base. Prominent. (? should be Profusion). P of RHS 1872 Vol III Pcxvi Fuchsia Trials at Chiswick 1872. Habit neat. Dwarf. Free. Small flowers. NK. NK. NK.

PROFUSION (a). ND ND/ND. Tube. ND. Sepals. ND. Corolla. ND. Vol. 2 J of RHS 1870 Fuchsia trials at Chiswick. "Passed over". GC. P338 15/4/1865 Listed by W. Rumley, Richmond. NK. NK. *1863.*

PROFUSION (b). Single. Red/Purple. Tube. Red. Sepals. Red. Corolla. Violet. Laing Cat. 1890 an extremely floriferous variety. Habit very compact. Most beautiful. Gartenflora P149 1887. L. Cat. 1892. X Riccartonii. *Lemoine. Nancy. France. 1887.*

PROFUSION (c). Double. Red/Purple. Tube. Red. Sepals. Red. Corolla. Clear blue veined carmine. Floriferous. L. Cat. P149 1901. *Rozain. Lyons. France. 1901.*

PROGRÈSS. Single. Red/Purple. Tube. Bright red. Sepals. Bright red. Very long. Corolla. Rich violet. B. Cat. 1888-1889. RH. P311 1889 "Select" by E.A. Carrière. NK. NK. *1887.*

PROSTRATA. Single. Red/Purple. Tube. Bright pink. Sepals. Bright pink. Corolla. Deep violet. P13 Floral Cabinet Vol IX 1841 This variety is perfectly prostrate, hanging all around the pot. Free bloomer. *Schofield. GB. 1841.*

PROVOST MARSHAL. Double. Red/White. Tube. Brilliant scarlet. Sepals. Brilliant scarlet. Double. White. Large flowers. Good form. Very free. JF. Cat. 1895. NK. NK. *1895.*

PSYCHE (a). Single. White/Red. Tube. Pure white. Sepals. Pure white. Reflexed. Corolla. Scarlet. Long. Similar to "Dr. Jephson". GC. P545 30/8/1851 Listed by G. Smith. GC. P177 20/3/1852 Listed by W. Rumley, Richmond. GC. P207 27/3/1852 Listed by H. Walton, Burnley. GC. P83 8/2/1851 Intro. by G. Smith. Islington. *Smith, G. Islington. GB. 1851.*

PHYSCHÉ (b). Single. White/Red. Tube. Yellow suffused green. Sepals. Yellowish white. Green tips. Corolla. Crimson red. App. to RH 1851 by Porcher. Unique colouring. *Meillez, Lille. France. 1851.*

PSYCHE (c). Single. Red/White. Tube. Red. Sepals. Red. Reflexed. Corolla. Whitish pink. Elongated. P135 4th Ed. by Porcher 1874. *Twrdy, Brno. Austria. 1873.*

PULCHELLA. Single. ND/ND. Tube. ND. Sepals. ND. Corolla. ND. A hybrid between "Stylosa Conspicua (Fulgens X)" X "Fulgens". Large and Bright Foliage, much serrated. GC.P393 6/1842 & P98 13/2/1844 Listed by Youell, Gt. Yarmouth. GC. P112 17/2/1844 Listed by W. Miller, Ramsgate. GC. P337 26/5/1842 Listed by James May (Tottenham), Edmonton. X Fulgens. *W. May, Bedale. GB. 1842.*

PULCHELLA CARNEA. Single. Pink/Purple. Tube. Pale Flesh. Stout. Short. Sepals. Pale flesh. Reflex. Corolla. Purple crimson. GC. P162 14/3/1846 & P184 13/3/1847 Listed by W. Miller, Ramsgate. GC. P216 27/3/1847 Listed by R. Cooper, Croydon. GC. P2 4/1/1845 Intro. by Girling, Stowmarket. *Girling, Stowmarket. GB. 1845.*

PULCHERRIMA (a). Single. Red/Purple. Tube. Crimson.Sepals. Crimson. Corolla. Purple. What a fine variety, bedecked with blooms. GC. P473 16/7/1842. *Story, W.H. Isleworth. GB. 1842.*

PULCHERRIMA (b). Single. Pink/Red. Tube. Pink. (Pale pink). Sepals. Pink. Green tips. Corolla. Rosy red. (Rose Pink) Barrel shaped corolla. Coloured Plate Floricultural Cabinet April 1843. GC. P97 18/2/1843 & P98 17/2/1844 Listed by Youell, Gt. Yarmouth. GC. P243 15/4/1843 Listed

by A.J. Stewart, Windsor. GC. P112 17/2/1846 & P66 1/2/1845 & P184 13/3/1847 Listed by W. Miller, Ramsgate. P74 Floricultural Cabinet 1843 To be introduced by Harrison, Dereham. *Harrison, Dereham. GB.1842*

PUMILA. Single. Red/Purple. Tube. Red. (Crimson). Sepals. Red. (Crimson). Corolla. Blue Violet. (Purple). P267 Floricultural Cabinet Vol XVII 1849. This pretty plant grows about a foot high. Foliage very small, Profuse bloomer. B. Cat. 1872-1873 Dense compact habit. For edgings and small beds. NK. *GB. 1848.*

PURITANI. Single. Red/White. Tube. Scarlet. Bulged. Sepals. Scarlet. Spreading. Corolla. White, with rosy scarlet feathery veins. GC. P55 19/1/1867 Review by H. Cannell "one of the best for small pots". GC. P567/8 Extremely free blooming. F&P P57 March 1866 Best habit. P131 4th Ed. by Porcher 1874 Not in the first selection. Good for the open garden. GC. P84 18/7/1874 RHS Show held on 15/7/1874 Exhibited by Mr King Gr to R.V. Leach, Devizes. GC. P206 17/2/1877 Growers of the West Country- varieties. GC. P311 8/9/1877 Exhibited at Trowbridge H.S. by J. Lye (2nd) GO. 1880-1890 "Select". P1 J of RHS 1872 Pcxiii Fuchsia trials at Chiswick 1872. Habit dwarf. Drooping. Elegant. Flowers medium size. Awarded ***. J of RHS Vol 4 1872 P216 Fuchsia trials at Chiswick. Certificate confirmed. *Banks, E. Deal. GB. 1864.*

PURITY (a). Single. ND/ND. Tube. ND. Sepals. ND. Corolla. ND. GC. P153 4/3/1848 & P232 1/4/1848 Listed by R. Cooper, Croydon. GC. P202 27/3/1847 Intro. by Wm. May Bedale. *May, W. Bedale. GB. 1847.*

PURITY (b). Single. White/Purple. Tube. White. Sepals. White. Corolla. Purple. Small. GC. P120 23/2/1850 "Select". GC. P535 22/8/1851 Exhibited at Vauxhall Garden Show. GC. P663 24/9/1851 Exhibted at York H.S. Show by Mr. Roper CG. Vol III P272 1850 "Fuchsias for exhibition". GC. P256 16/4/1848 Listed by G. Rogers, Uttoxeter. GC. P256 21/4/1849 Listed by R. Cooper, Croydon. GC. P259 28/4/1849 & P241 20/4/1851 Listed by W. Rendle, Plymouth. GC. P274 5/5/1849 Listed by H. Walton, Burnley. GC. P226 13/4/1850 Listed by Poole Nurseries. GC. P298 8/5/1847 Intro. by Barkway. *Barkway. GB. 1847*

PURITY (c). Single. White/ND. Tube. White. Sepals. White. Corolla. ND. GC. P151 5/3/1853 Good for exhibition. GC. P274 4/5/1850 Listed by Bass & Brown, Sudbury. GC. P248 15/4/1854 Listed by G. Mitchell, Brighton. *Mayle, Birmingham GB. 1849.*

152

PURITY (d). Single. White/Purple. Tube. White. Sepals. White. Corolla. Purplish rose. Vol. P1 J of RHS 1860 P262/3 Floral Committee report. *Banks, E. Deal.? GB. 1860.*

PURITY (e). Single. Red/White. Tube. Bright crimson. Sepals. Bright crimson. Perfectly reflexed. Corolla. Pure white. Regular. P131 4th Ed. by Porcher 1874. Not in the first selection. P79 HC. Cat. 1882. GC. P146 1895 Blands Chronicle. GC. P419 30/3/1872 Intro. by B.S. Williams. *Bland, E. Fordham. GB. 1872.*

PURPEREA ELEGANS. ND. ND/ND. Tube. ND. Sepals. ND. Corolla. ND. GC. P305 13/5/1850 Listed by Hart & Nicklin, Guildford. NK. NK. NK.

PURPLE FINNIS. Double. Red/Purple. Tube. Red. Sepals. Red. Corolla. Purple. Sport of "Miss Lucy Finnis". L. Cat. 1892. JF. Cat. 1892. Intro. by H. Cannell, Swanley. Pxiv. Cat. 1890. NK. *GB. 1890.*

PURPLE PERFECTION. Single. Red/Purple. Tube. Red. Sepals. Red. Corolla. Purple. Style of "Ne Plus Ultra" but twice the size. Raised in Liverpool. GC. P483 30/7/1853 & P162 18/3/1854 Listed by H. Walton, Burnley. GC. P627 Listed by S. Fenney, Gateshead. GC. P248 15/4/1854 Listed by Mitchell & Co., Brighton. GC. P226 9/4/1853 Intro. by E.G. Henderson. NK *Liverpool. GB. 1853.*

PURPLE PRINCE. Double. Red/Purple. Tube. Waxy carmine scarlet. ½" long. Bulged. Sepals. Waxy carmine Scarlet. Deflexed as in "Globosa". Corolla. Rich Violet. (Reddish Violet). ½" long. 1½" Broad. Shallow but much expanded. Regular. A large showy rough flower. GC. P1554 2/12/1871 Review by H. Cannell. Vol 3 J of RHS 1872 Fuchsia trials at Chiswick. Awarded ***. GO. "Select" 1880-1886. B. Cat. 1870-1873. GC. P294 26/2/1870 Intro. by G. Smith. *Smith, G. Islington. GB. 1870.*

PURSUIT. Single. Red/White. Tube. Scarlet Crimson. Sepals. Scarlet crimson. Horizontal. Scacely spreading 1". Corolla. Pure White. Conspicious rosy scarlet veins. Somewhat expanded. Vol 3 J of RHS 1872 Pcxiii Habit free and elegant. Medium size. Awarded ***. Vol 4 J of RHS 1877 P216 Chiswick trials. Certificate confirmed. B. Cat. 1870. NK. *GB. 1869.*

PYRAMIDALIS. Single. ND/ND. Tube. ND. Sepals. ND. Corolla. ND. GC. P545 5/8/1843 Flowers sent to Editor for appraisal. "Bright rich colours". GC. P112 17/2/1844. Listed by W. Miller, Ramsgate. *Wheeler, Tenterden. GB. 1844.*

PYRENE. Double. Red/Purple. Tube. Crimson red. (Deep crimson). Long. Thin. Sepals. Crimson red. (Deep crimson). Reflexed. Rounded. Corolla. Bluish Violet stained red. (Dark violet purple). P125 4th Ed. by Porcher 1874. Nice variety but tube is not in proportion. B. Cat. 1872-1876. GC. P502 13/4/1872. Intro. by W. Bull, Chelsea. *Bull, W. Chelsea. GB. 1872.*

PYRRHUS. Double. Red/Purple. Tube. Bright rose. Sepals. Bright rose. Horizontal. Reflexed and Incurved. Corolla. Blue. Intro. by W. Bull, Chelsea. B. Cat. 1882-1883. *Bull, W. Chelsea. GB. 1882.*

PYTHAGORE. Double. Red/Purple. Tube. Dull coral. (Coral red). Short. Sepals. Dull coral. (Coral red). Corolla. Dark plum. Large. JF. Cat. 1904. L Cat. 1902. *Rozain. Lyons. France. 1902.*

QUEEN (a). Single. Pink/Pink. Tube. Delicate pale pink. Sepals. Delicate pale pink. Green tips. Corolla. Deep rose. GC. P545 1843 Flowers sent to Editor for appraisal by J Winser, Tenterden. Large flower. Good. Colour. Corolla too crumpled. GC. P146 8/3/1845 Listed by Youell, Gt. Yarmouth. GC. P369 8/6/1846 Listed by T. Cripps, Maidstone. GC. P184 13/3/1847 Listed by W. Miller, Ramsgate. GC. P161 16/3/1844 Entire stock purchased by Wm. Pawley, White Hart Hotel, Bromley. *Winser, J. Tenterden GB. 1844.*

QUEEN (b). Single. ND/ND. Tube. ND. Sepals. ND. Corolla. ND. GC. P177 20/3/1852 Listed by Wm. Rumley, Richmond. NK. NK. *GB. 1851.*

QUEEN (c). ND. ND/ND. Tube. ND. Sepals. ND. Corolla. ND. GC. P483 30/7/1853 Listed by H. Walton, Burnley. GC. P147 11/3/1854 Listed by Wm. Rumley, Richmond. NK. NK. *GB. 1853.*

QUEEN ADELAIDE (a). Single. Red/Purple. Tube. Bright carmine. Sepals. Bright carmine. Tipped Green. Corolla. Crimson purple. Large Foliage. GC. P721 14/10/1843 Appraised by Editor of GC. P551 17/8/1844 Listed by T. Cripps, Maidstone. GC. P66 1/2/1845 Listed by Youell, Gt. Yarmouth. GC. 28/3/1846 Listed by S. Schilling, Odiham. *Holmes. GB. 1844.*

QUEEN ADELAIDE (b). GC. P676 1/2/1845 Listed by W. Miller, Ramsgate. See "QUEEN (a)"

QUEEN ELIZABETH. ND. ND/ND. Tube. ND. Sepals. ND. Corolla. ND. GC. P535 23/8/1851 Light variety exhibited at Vauxhall Garden Show. NK. NK. *GB. 1851.*

QUEEN OF DENMARK. Single. White/Pink. Tube. White. Sepals. White. Corolla. Pink. ND. Laings Cat. 1890. NK. NK. *GB. 1890?*

QUEEN OF ENGLAND. ND. ND/ND. Tube. ND. Sepals. ND. Corolla. ND. GC. P177 20/3/1852 Listed by W. Rumley, Richmond. GC. P283 22/4/1854 Listed by Hart & Nicklin, Guildford. NK. NK. *GB. 1851.*

QUEEN OF HANOVER. Single. White/Red. Tube. White. Sepals. White. Stout. Reflex handsomely Corolla. Carmine. GC. P375 31/5/1856 Exhibited at Crystal Palace by Mr. Bousie as a 7 foot high pyramid. SG. P459 1866 Dwarf compact habit. Prolific flowerer. GC. P580 9/7/1859 & P607 16/7/1959 Exhibited at RBS Show 6/7/1859 by H.Cannell & E. Groves, Tulse Hill. GC. P401 24/6/1854 Listed by B.R. Cant, Colchester & H. Marsden, Burnley. GC. P466 22/7/1854 Listed by Bass & Brown, Sudbury. GC. P238 14/4/1855 Listed by J. Hoade Addlestone. GC. P258 21/4/1855 Listed by H. Walton, Burnley. GC. P383 21/4/1855 Listed by Hart & Nicklin, Guildford. GC. P530 11/8/1855 Listed by Bainbridge & Hewison, York. GC. P194 1/4/1854 Intrto. by C. Turner, Slough. *Banks, E. Deal. GB. 1854.*

QUEEN OF MAY. Single. White/Purple. Sepals. White. Sepals. White. Green tips. Corolla. Rosy lilac. Midland Florist P133 1856 In list of ten white fuchsias. GC. P226 13/4/1850 Intro. by G. Smith. Islington. *Smith, G. Islington. GB. 1850.*

QUEEN OF ROSES. ND. ND/ND. Tube. ND. Sepals. ND. Corolla. ND GC. P314 10/5/1856 & P146 7/3/1857 Listed by W. Rumley, Richmond. NK. NK. *GB. 1855.*

QUEEN OF SHEBA. ND. ND/ND. Tube. ND. Sepals. ND. Corolla. ND. GC. P234 11/4/1846 Listed by A.J. Stewart, Salthill Nurseries, Nr. Windsor. NK. NK. *GB. 1845.*

QUEEN OF SUMMER. Single. White/Red. Tube. White. Bulged. Sepals. White. 1" long. Recurved. Stout. Corolla. Lake, paler at the base. Pcxii Vol 3 J of RHS 1872 Fuchsia trials at Chiswick - Habit neat. Flowers medium size. Spreading. P70 Vol 4 J of RHS 1877 Fuchsia Trial at Chiswick 1873. No Award. The same in every respect as "Fairest of the Fair". GC. P376 20/4/1862 F&A Smith possess entire stock. *Smith F&A. Dulwich GB. 1862.*

QUEEN OF THE BEAUTIES (a). Single. White/Purple. Tube. Pale ochorous white. (Waxy light buff). Sepals. Pale ochorous white. (Waxy light buff). Green tips Corolla. Purple crimson (Dark crimson blood coloured tinged purple) Large blooms. GC. P820 Dec 1844. "Recommended" Florists Journal P96 1845 "Recommended". GC P66 1/2/1845 & P162 14/3/1846 & P184 13/3/1847 Listed by W. Miller, Ramsgate. GC. P216 27/3/1847 & P232 1/4/1848 Listed by R. Cooper, Croydon GC. P265 24/4/1847 Listed by W. Rendle Plymouth. GC. P33 18/1/1845 Intro. by W.J. Epps Maidstone. *Epps, W.J. Maidstone. GB. 1845.*

QUEEN OF THE BEAUTIES (b). Single White/Red. Tube. Pure white. Sepals. Pure white Broad. Well recurved. Corolla. Rose shade crimson. GC. P191 27/2/1864 Raised by a well known raiser in the north of England and intro. by B.S. Williams, Holloway. GC. P338 15/4/1865 Listed by W. Rumley Richmond. *Williams B.S. Holloway. GB. 1864.*

QUEEN OF THE BOURBONS. Single. ND/ND Tube. ND. Sepals. ND. Corolla. ND. Floricultural Cabinet P204 Vol XIV 1846. Exhibited at RBS Show by Gaines. NK. NK. *GB. 1846.*

QUEEN OF THE FAIRIES (a). Single. ND/ND Tube. ND. Sepals. ND. Corolla. ND. GC. P250 17/4/1847 Listed by W.J. Epps, Maidstone. NK. NK *GB. 1847.*

QUEEN OF THE FAIRIES (b). Single. White/Red. Tube. Pure white. Sepals. Pure white. Corolla. Bright carmine. Compact Grower. FCC London Hort. Scty Show Sept 1849. App. to RH. 1851 by Porcher. GC. P210 6/4/1850 Intro. by J. Vickers, Brixton. *Vickers, J. Brixton. GB. 1850.*

QUEEN OF THE SEA. Single. Red/Purple. Tube. Red. Sepals. Red. Recurved. Corolla. Purple. Vol P3 J of RHS 1863 Fuchsia trials at Chiswick 1862. Expanded. Stiff. Erect. Dark coloured bark. RH. P95 1859. GC. P539 10/7/1858 Listed by F. Godwin, Sheffield. Gc. P571 24/7/1858 Listed by H. Walton, Burnley. GC. P238 19/3/1859 Listed by W. Rumley, Richmond. Intro. by E.G. Henderson, St. Johns Wood. *Banks, E. Deal. GB. 1858.*

QUEEN OF THE WEST. Single. White/Red. Tube. White, blushed pink. Sepals. White, blushed pink. Corolla. Bright crimson. GC. P234 11/4/1846 Listed by W.J. Epps, Maidstone. GC. P270 26/4/1845 Intro. by G. Sclater, Exeter. *Sclater, G. Exeter. GB. 1845.*

QUEEN OF THE WHITES. Double. Red/White. Tube. Coral red. Sepals. Coral red. Broad. Well reflexed. Corolla. Pure white. GC. P55 19/1/1867 Review by H. Cannell. Dwarf. Free blooming. Best for small pots. P131 4th Ed. by Porcher 1874. Not in the first selection. GO. "Select" 1880-1890. GC. P122 10/2/1866 Intro. by G. Smith. *Smith, G. Islington. GB. 1866.*

QUEEN POMARE. Single. ND/ND. Tube. ND. Sepals. ND. Corolla. ND. GC. P455 8/7/1847 Exhibited by Gaines, RBS Show. NK. NK. *GB. 1847.*

QUEEN SUPERB. Single. White/Red. Tube. White. Sepals. White. Corolla. Scarlet. GC. P146 8/3/1845 Listed by Youell, Gt. Yarmouth. RH. P24 1846. *Bell. Thirsk. GB. 1844.*

QUEEN VICTORIA (a). Single. Pink/Purple. Tube. Pale Pink. Sepals. Pale pink. Corolla. Purplish. (Dark crimson). (Crimson). RH. P117 1845 Flowers 6cms in length. GC. P820 Dec 1844 & GC. P808 Nov 1846 "Recommended". GC. P98 17/2/1844 & P146 8/3/1845 Listed by Youell, Gt. Yarmouth. GC.P112 17/2/1844 & P66 1/2/1845 Listed by W. Miller, Ramsgate. GC.P216 27/3/1847 & P232 1/4/1848 Listed by R. Cooper, Croydon. GC. P446 1/7/1843 Intro. by J. Smith, Dalston. *Smith, J. Dalston. GB. 1843.*

QUEEN VICTORIA (b). Single. Red/Purple. Tube. Bright vermilion. Sepals. Bright vermilion. Corolla. Purple rose. GC. P146 8/3/1845 Listed by Youells, Gt. Yarmouth. GC. P1 6/1/1844 Intro by Youells. *Youell, Gt. Yarmouth GB. 1844.*

QUEEN VICTORIA (c). Single. Pink/Purple. Tube. Light flesh. Sepals. Light flesh. Corolla. Crimson purple. Very large. Good habit like "Eppsii". GC. P162 14/3/1846 & P184 13/3/1847 Listed by W. Miller, Ramsgate. GC. P66 1/2/1845 Intro. by W. Miller. *Miller, W. Ramsgate. GB. 1846.*

QUEEN VICTORIA (d). Single. White/Red. Tube. White. Long. Sepals. White. Green tips. Corolla. Red. Floral Cabinet Vol XIII Plate 145 1/2/1845 Coloured plate. GC. P184 13/3/1847 Listed by W. Miller, Ramsgate. GC. P216 27/3/1847 Listed by R. Cooper, Croydon. *Harrison, Dereham GB. 1845.*

QUEEN VICTORIA (e). Single. Red/White. Tube. Scarlet. Sepals. Scarlet. Corolla. White. Small flowers. Midland Florist P133 1856. Coloured Plate No.97 1855. Colour plate in L'Illustration Horticole Vol 2 Plate 42 1855. GC. P368 26/5/1855 Listed by E.G. Henderson. GC. P435 30/6/1855 Listed by H. Groom. GC. P467 14/7/1855 Listed by Bass & Brown, Sudbury. GC. P467 14/7/1855 Listed by H. Walton, Burnley. GC. P529 11/8/1855 Listed by W.J. Epps, Maidstone. GC. P530 11/8/1855 & P208

22/3/1856 Listed by Bainbridge & Hewison, York. GC. P531 11/8/1855 Listed by J. Courcha. GC. P314 10/5/1856 Listed by W. Rumley, Richmond. GC.P314 10/5/1856 Listed by Youell, Gt. Yarmouth. GC. P456 5/7/1856 Listed by J. Clarke, Cheltenham. GC. P18 13/1/1855 Intro. by E.G. Henderson. *Story, W.H. Newton Abbott. GB. 1855.*

QUEEN VICTORIA (f). Single. Red/Red. Tube. Rose. Sepals. Rose. Well raised. Green points. Corolla. Dark crimson. Long. Large flowers. RH. P167 1857 Recommended for its good habit and brightness of its flowers. NK. NK. NK. NK.

QUEEN VICTORIA (g). Single. White/Red. Tube. White. Sepals. White. Corolla. Dark red. GC. P206 17/2/1877. GC. P311 8/9/1879 Exhibited at Trowbridge by J. Lye (2nd) GC. Vol 20 1/9/1883 Exhibited by Tucker (2nd 6 pot class). *Doel. GB. 1877.*

RACEMIFLORA. Single. Pink/Pink. Tube. Pink. 2" long. Sepals. Pink. Corolla. Pink. Flowers 4" long from leaf stalk. Large foliage 3" x 2". Awarded seedling prize Oxford Hort.Scty. 6/8/1840. GC. 19/6/1841 Listed by H. Low, Clapton. GC. P657 9/10/1841 Listed by Rogers, Uttoxeter. GC. P289 29/3/1841 Listed by H. Low, Clapton. GC. P393 6/1842 & P97 2/1843 & P98 17/2/1844 & P146 8/3/1845 Listed by Youell, Gt. Yarmouth. GC. P241 15/4/1843 Listed by F&A Smith, Hackney. GC. P112 17/2/1844 Listed by W. Miller, Ramsgate. GC. P274 1841 Intro. by W. Day, Victoria Nursery. Raised by Mr. Dick, Gardener to the late A. Annesley, Bletchington Park. F.Fulgens X Grandiflora. *Dick, Oxford. GB. 1841.*

RACEMIFLORA ELEGANS (a). Single. Red/Red. Tube. Deep red. Sepals. Deep red. Long. Corolla. Deep red. Flowers 2" long. Droop around the main stem of the plant. GC. P97 2/1843 & P98 17/2/1844 Listed by Youell, Gt. Yarmouth. GC. P112 17/2/1844 Listed by W. Miller, Ramsgate. GC. P489 23/7/1842 Intro. by Maule. *Maule, Bristol. GB. 1842.*

RACEMIFLORA ELEGANS (b). Single. Red/Purple. Tube. Cerise red. Sepals. Cerise red. Corolla. Rosy carmine. Size and colour similar to "Moneypenni" but greatly superior in habit. GC. P112 17/2/1844 Listed by W. Miller, Ramsgate. GC. P146 8/3/1845 Listed by Youell, Gt. Yarmouth. GC. P82 11/2/1843 Intro by W.Dean, Jedburgh. *Dean,W Jedburgh. GB. 1843.*

RACEMOSA. Single. ND/ND. Tube. ND. Sepals. ND. Corolla. ND. GC. P97 10/2/1843 & P98

17/2/1844 Listed by Youell, Gt. Yarmouth. GC. P112 17/2/1844 & P66 1/2/1845 Listed by W. Miller, Ramsgate. GC. P345 28/5/1842 Intro. by J. Smith, Dalston. *Smith, J. Dalston. GB. 1842.*

RACHEL. Single. Red/Pink. Tube. Salmon red, splashed white. Sepals. Salmon red, splashed white. Extended. Corolla. Bright rose. App. to RH. 1851 by Porcher. *Baudinet. France. 1850.*

RACHILDE. Double. Red/White. Tube. Carmine coral. Sepals. Carmine coral. Corolla. White. Very vigorous. Floriferous. Good habit. L. Cat. 1912. *Lemoine, Nancy. France. 1912.*

RACINE. Double. Red/Purple. Tube. Rose. Sepals. Rose. Interior soft rose. Well recurved. Corolla. Clear lilac. JF. Cat. 1898. B. Cat. 1898. *Lemoine. Nancy. France. 1897.*

RAFFAELLE. Single. Red/Purple. Tube. Crimson. Sepals. Crimson. Well reflexed. Corolla. Rich chocolate flaked rose. GC. P368 26/5/1855 Listed by E.G. Henderson. GC. P529 11/8/1855 Listed by W.J.Epps, Maidstone. GC. P530 11/8/1855 & P209 22/3/1856 Listed by Bainbridge & Hewison, York. GC. P531 11/8/1855 Listed by J. Courcha. GC. P314 10/5/1856 Listed by W. Rumley, Richmond & Youell, Gt. Yarmouth. GC. P18 13/1/1855 Intro. by E.G. Henderson, St. Johns Wood, 10/6d. *Story, W.H., Newton Abbot. GB. 1855.*

RAINBOW. Double. Red/White. Tube. Bright carmine. Sepals. Bright carmine. Nicely reflexed. Corolla. White. An extremely pretty variety with attractive variegated leaves, the colours of which are rose, white, and crimson, on a light green background. B. Cat. 1878-1881. G. Vol 35 1889. Similar to "Sunray" but with more pointed leaves. Delicate. *Bull, W. Chelsea. GB. 1877.*

RAJAH. Single. Red/Purple. Tube. Bright red. Sepals. Bright red. Fully reflexed. Corolla. Purple. GC. P256 21/4/1849 Listed by R. Cooper, Croydon. GC. P209 7/4/1849 Purchased from J. Willmore and intro. by H. Low, Clapton. *Willmore, J. Birmingham. GB. 1849.*

RANGER. Double. Red/Purple. Tube. Rosy crimson. Short. Sepals. Rosy crimson. Completely recurved. Corolla. Light bluish purple, shaded rose at base. B. Cat. 1888-1893. JF. Cat. 1886. NK. NK. *GB. 1885.*

RANUNCULAEFLORA. Double. Red/White. Tube. Scarlet. Sepals. Scarlet. Corolla. White. GC. P18 13/1/1855 This was considered the best of the only two double whites flowered by Mr. Story. The other double we do not appear to have received. GC. P141 10/3/1855 Price now 21/-. GC. P276 28/4/1855 Not to be sent out because EGH are unable to supply plants of sufficient strength. GC. P82 23/2/1856 To be sent out with others. GC. P642 27/9/1856 Listed by H. Walton, Burnley. GC. P283 25/4/1857 Listed by Wm. Cutbush, Highgate. RH. P170 1857. Very double. Corolla striped rose. (See also GALANTHAFLORA PLENA). *Story, W.H. Newton Abbot. GB. 1855.*

RAOUL PUGNO. S/Double. Red/Purple. Tube. Coral red. Sepals. Coral red. Corolla. Clear plum. The nice form and ampleness of the calyx is the merit of this variety. *Lemoine. Nancy. France. 1910.*

RAOUL TOCHÉ. Double. Red/White. Tube. Red. Sepals. Red. Arched. Large. Long. Corolla. Pure white. Very large. Very full. B. Cat. 1892-1893. L. Cat. 1892. *Lemoine. Nancy. France. 1892.*

RAPHAEL (a). Single. Red/Purple. Tube. Light rose pink. Sepals. Light rose pink. Well reflexed. Corolla. Violet purple. GC. P594 29/6/1861 Listed by Godwin & Padnam, Sheffield. GC. P771 24/8/1861 Listed by H Walton, Burnley. GC. P140 16/2/1861 Intro. by F&A Smith. *Smith F&A., Dulwich. GB. 1861.*

RAPHAEL (b). Single. Red/Purple. Tube. Scarlet. Sepals. Scarlet. Well reflexed. Corolla. Violet. JF. Cat. 1898. NK. NK. NK. *1898.*

RAPHAELLO. Single. Red/White. Sepals. Cerise red. Sepals. Cerise red. Reflexed. Corolla. Pure white. Flowers until December. RH. P170 1857. NK. NK. NK. *1857.*

RAPPER. Single. Red/Purple. Tube. Scarlet. Sepals. Scarlet. Corolla. Purple scarlet. Shading commences one third down on petals. Long. GC. P120 8/2/1868 Intro. by G. Smith. Tollington Nurseries. *Smith, G. Islington. GB. 1868.*

RAOUL D'ALLARD. Single. Red/Purple. Tube. Intense red. (Crimson). Sepals. Intense red. (Crimson). Uplifted. Corolla. Reddish plum. Exterior of petals carmine. (Rosy plum). JF. Cat. 1904. L. Cat. 1902. *Rozain. Lyons. France. 1902.*

REAPER. Double. Red/Purple. Tube. Rosy carmine. Short. Sepals. Rosy carmine. Extremely wide. Corolla. Rich purplish crimson. B. Cat. 1880-1893. *Bull, W. Chelsea. GB. 1880.*

156

RECURVA (a). Single. Red/Purple. Tube. Dark crimson. Sepals. Dark crimson. Corolla. Light purple. GC. P112 17/2/1844 & P66 1/2/1845 Listed by W. Miller, Ramsgate. GC. P82 11/2/1843 Raised and intro. by W. Deans, The Nursery, Jedburgh. *Dean, W. Jedburgh. GB. 1843.*

RECURVA (b). Single. ND/ND. Tube. ND. Sepals. ND. Corolla. ND. GC. P216 27/3/1847 Listed by R. Cooper, Croydon. GC. P254 19/4/1845 Intro. by J. Smith. *Smith, J. Dalston. GB. 1845.*

RECURVA (c). Single. ND/ND. Tube. ND. Sepals. ND. Corolla. ND. GC. P234 11/4/1846 Listed by A.J. Stewart, Windsor. *Harrison, Dereham. GB. 1845.*

RECURVATA. Single. Red/Purple. Tube. Red. Sepals. Red. Corolla. Purple. Marnocks Florists Magazine P137 11/1836 Colour plate. Raised by Mr. Niven of Glassnevin Botanic Garden, Dublin. (See Botanical Register). *Niven, Dublin. Ireland. 1836.*

RED MARSHALL. Single. Red/ND. Tube. Red. Sepals. Red. Corolla. ND. GC.P181 7/2/1880 Good market variety. Vol. 26 GC P403 1/5/1886. Good kind. NK. NK. *GB. NK.*

RED ROVER. ND. ND/ND. Tube. ND. Sepals. ND. Corolla. ND. GC. P883 1873 RHS. Show at Bath. Exhibited by J. Lye, 2nd 6 pot class. NK. NK. *GB. NK.*

REDWING. Double. Red/Purple. Tube. Bright red. Short. Sepals. Bright red. Short. Broad. Corolla. Rosy purple flaked carmine. JF. Cat. 1886. B. Cat. 1888-1892. NK. NK. *GB. 1885.*

REFLEXA (a). Single. Red/Red. Tube. Red. Sepals. Red. Corolla. Red. GC. P144 4/3/1843 Recommended for the open border. Vol 3 P192 Floral Cabinet. 1835 Hybrid of Encliandra type. Vol 19 G. P318 A small flowered type from Glassnevin. Used to produce "Wormaldii". X Microphylla. *Niven, Dublin. Ireland. 1835.*

REFLEXA (b). Single. Red/Purple. Tube. Carmine. Sepals. Carmine. Corolla. Purple. (Rosy purple). P200 Vol XI Floricultural Cabinet 1843 Exhibited at RBS as a seedling and selected for a prize. Large flowers. Sepals turning up exposing the whole of the corolla. *Smith, J. Dalston. GB. 1844.*

REFLEXA (c). ND. ND/ND. Tube. ND. Sepals. ND. Corolla. ND. GC.P66 1/2/1845 & P184 13/3/1847 Listed by W. Miller, Ramsgate. GC. P216 27/3/1847 Listed by R. Cooper, Croydon. *Bell, Thirsk. GB. 1844.*

REFLEXA (d). S/Double. Red/Purple. Tube. Red. Sepals. Red. Long. Spreading. Corolla. Purple. Vol P3 J of RHS 1863 P90. Fuchsia trials at Chiswick 1862. Submitted by Turner. NK.NK. *GB.* NK.

REFRACTION. Single. ND/ND. Tube. ND. Sepals. ND. Corolla. ND. GC. P410 20/6/1846 Exhibited at H.S. Show by Mr. Robinson Gr. to J. Simpson. NK. NK. *GB. 1846.*

REFULGENS. Single. ND/ND. Tube. ND. Sepals. ND. Corolla. ND. GC. Exhibited at H.S. Show on 17th July 1841 by Mr. Kyle, Gr.tm R. Barclay, Leyton. GC. P241 15/4/1843 Listed by F&A Smith, Hackney. NK. NK. *GB.* NK.

REGALIA (a). Single. Red/Purple. Tube. Rich crimson. Sepals. Rich crimson. Corolla. Deep purple. GC. P488 9/4/1870 Ornamental foliage. Beautiful golden leaves shaded bronze, veined crimson. B. Cat. 1872-1875. Vol 4 P70 J of RHS 1877 Fuchsia trials at Chiswick. No Award. Sent by RHS. Leaves of a bright golden hue with red veins. Very distinct but a weak grower. F&P. P282 Dec 1868. From the gardens of the RHS at Chiswick, one of a batch of seedlings which had been raised there. The upper surface of its leaves was golden yellow and the underside claret red, with veins of a similar hue. It was awarded an FCC as a desirable and effective bedding plant. FCC RHS 20/10/1868. HC. Cat. 1882 P77. Habit beautiful forming itself into a perfect medium sized pyramidical plant. Its intense bright golden bronzy foliage is veined ruby red. *Bousie, Chiswick. GB. 1868.*

REGALIA (b). Double. Red/Purple. Tube. Bright crimson. Sepals. Bright crimson. Nicely reflexed. Corolla. Violet purple, blotched red at base. P134 4th Ed by Porcher 1874 Not in the first selection. NK. NK. *GB. 1868.*

REGENT. S/Double. Red/Purple. Tube. Bright red. Sepals. Bright red. Shell shaped. Partially reflexing. Corolla. Lavender purple, shaded rose. Irregular. B. Cat. 1901. *Bull, W. Chelsea. GB. 1900.*

REGULUS. Single. Red/Purple. Tube. Red. Sepals. Red. Corolla. Purple. P115 4th Ed. by Porcher 1874. Not in the first selection. *Rollinson, Tooting. GB. 1862.*

REINE BLANCHE. Single. White/Red. Tube. Pure white. Long. Sepals. Blush white. Recurva-reflexed. Corolla. Scarlet. Vol P3 J of RHS 1863 P91 Fuchsia Trials at Chiswick 1862. A lively looking variety. Awarded **. Submitted by E.G. Henderson. NK. NK. NK. *1862.*

REINE CLAUDE. Single. White/Pink. Tube. White. Sepals. White Corolla. Pink. Free. Vol. 2 J of RHS. 1870 Fuchsia trials at Chiswick. NK. NK. NK. NK.

REINE DE FRANCAIS. Single. Pink/Red. Tube. Pale pink. 9/10cms long. Sepals. Pale pink. Corolla. Vermilion red. RH. P205 1847. Result of crosses between Fulgens, Corymbiflora (Boliviana) and Macrostema GC. P250 17/4/1847 Listed by Hart & Nicklin, Guildford. *Salter, J. Versailles. France. 1844.*

RELIANCE. Double. Red/Purple. Tube. Light red.Sepals. Light red. Reflexed. Corolla. Light blue. 10/6d. GC. P1054 7/11/1863 Intro. by W. Bull. Chelsea. *Bull,W. Chelsea. GB. 1863.*

REMBRANDT. Single. Red/Purple. Tube. Red. Sepals. Red. Corolla. Purple. GC. P184 13/3/1847 Listed by W. Miller, Ramsgate. GC. P270 26/4/1845 Intro. by Gaines, Battersea. *Gaines, Battersea. GB. 1845.*

REMOR. Double. Red/Purple. Tube. Red. Sepals. Red. Corolla. Purple. P127 4th Ed. by Porcher 1874 Not in the first selection. *Coene. Ghent. Belgium. 1870.*

RENAULT-MORLIÈRE. Double. Red/Purple. Tube. Clear crimson. Sepals. Clear crimson. Corolla. Plum violet. Round. Good habit. L. Cat. 1906. *Rozain. Lyons. France. 1904.*

RENOWN (a). Single. ND/ND. Tube. ND. Sepals. ND. Corolla. ND. GC. P216 27/3/1847 & P153 4/3/1847 & P232 1/4/1848 Listed by R. Cooper, Croydon. *Jennings. GB. 1846.*

RENOWN (b). Single. Red/Purple. Tube. Pale red. Sepals. Pale red. Corolla. Purple shaded maroon. Vigorous. JF. Cat. 1890. L. Cat. 1892. B. Cat. 1889. *Lye, J. Market Lavington. GB. 1889.*

RENOWN (c). Single. Red/Purple. Tube. Carmine red. Sepals. Carmine red. Well reflexed. Corolla. Rosy purple. GC. P344 4/4/1868 Intro by B.W. Knioght, Battle. *Knight, B.W., Battle GB. 1868*

RESOLUTION. Single. Red/Purple. Tube. Red. (Bright red). Very short. Sepals. Red. (Bright red). Upraised. (Reflexed). Corolla. Plum coloured blotched and striped carmine. (Violet shaded red). Expanded. B. Cat. 1870-1873. P112 4th Ed. by Porcher 1874. *Bull,W. Chelsea. GB. 1867.*

RESPLENDENT (a). Single. Red/Purple. Tube. Crimson. Sepals. Crimson. Double. Purple. GC.

P545 30/8/1852 Listed by G. Smith, Tollington Nurseries. GC. P177 20/3/1852 Listed by W. Rumley, Richmond. GC. P207 27/3/1852 Listed by H. Walton, Burnley. GC. P307 15/5/1853 & P369 11/6/1853 Listed by B.R. Cant, Colchester. GC. P248 15/4/1854 Listed by Mitchell & Co, Kemptown. Brighton. GC. P290 10/5/1851 Intro. by E.G. Henderson. St. Johns˜üWood. *Henderson, E.G. St. Johns Wood. GB. 1851.*

RESPLENDENT (b). Single. Red/Purple. Tube. Bright crimson red. Average size. Sepals. Bright crimson red. Large. Reflexed. Round. Corolla. Dark blue violet. Spiralled. P112 4th. Ed. by Porcher Dark green foliage. Central vein violet red. Oval. Very denticulate. Pedicel 40mm. One of the family of "Lord Derby, Model, Noblesse". HC. Cat. 1882-1885. In the way of "Lord Elcho". GC. P146 1895 Bland's Chronicle. *Bland, E. Fordham. GB. 1873.*

RETORTA. Single. Red/Purple. Tube. Red. Sepals. Red. Corolla. Purple. GC. P299 1841 Probably a garden variety appeared from Mr. Jackson of Kingston. Allied to "Gracilis" with reflexed sepals. *Jackson, Kingston. GB. 1841.*

RÊVE D'AMOUR. Single. Pink/Purple. Tube. Soft Pink. Good thickness. Sepals. Soft pink. Longer than the tube. Horizontal. Corolla. Lilac violet. P80 2nd Ed. by Porcher 1848. GC. P201 27/3/1847 Listed by Hart & Nicklin, Guildford. GC. P250 17/4/1847 Listed by J. Hally, Blackheath. *Salter, J. Versailles. France. 1846.*

REV. J. TOBIN. Single. Red/Purple. Tube. Light crimson. Sepals. Light crimson. Well reflexed. Corolla. Puce. Funnel shaped. Good habit. Free bloomer. GC. P95 4/2/1860 Intro. by Stewart & Nielsen, Liscard. *Stewart & Nielsen. GB. 1860.*

REVOLOTA. Single. ND/ND. Tube. ND. Sepals. ND. Corolla. ND. GC. P251 11/4/1857 "New fuchsias of 1856" listed by W. Masters, Exotic Nurseries and Fant Nurseries, Canterbury and Maidstone. NK. NK. *GB. 1856.*

REV. T. WILTSHIRE. Single. Red/Purple. Tube. Fine crimson. Sepals. Fine crimson. Corolla. Bright blue. Large. In the "Lord Elcho" or bright blue corolla class. B. Cat. 1876-1877. BSW. Cat. 1878. HC. Cat. 1882-1885. GO. "Select" 1880-1891. *Banks, E. Deal. GB. 1875.*

REV. W.F.FREEMAN. Single. White/Red. Tube. White. Strong. Sepals. White. (Pale rose, interior bright rose). Spreading. Corolla. Crimson Scarlet. (Vermilion shaded carmine˜rose). App. to RH. 1851

158

by Porcher 1st class variety. GC.P226 14/4/1849 Intro. by T. Barnes successor to S. Girling (Deceased). *Girling, S. Stowmarket. GB. 1849.*

RHODERICK DHU (a). Single. Red/Red. Tube. Carmine rose. Long. Sepals. Carmine rose. Corolla. Lake. GC. P162 14/3/1846 & P184 12/3/1847 Listed by W. Miller, Ramsgate. GC. P216 27/3/1847 Listed by R. Cooper, Croydon. RH. P24 1846. *Salter, J. Versailles. France. 1845.*

RHODERICK DHU (b). Single. Red/Purple. Tube. Scarlet. (Crimson red). (Bright salmon tinted scarlet). Short. Thick. Sepals. Scarlet. (Bright crimson). (Bright salmon tinted scarlet). Large. Reflexed. (Recurved). Corolla. Violet Purple. (Violet washed red). (Dark lavender blue). Very expanded. (Umbrella shaped). B. Cat. 1870. Vol 2 J of RHS 1870 Fuchsia trials at Chiswick. Dwarf branching habit, with short broad red closely reflexed sepals and a very much expanded corolla. Free. 2nd class in 1868. P67 J of RHS 1873 Fuchsia trials at Chiswick 1873. Awarded FCC. Habit good, tube and sepals bright scarlet. Sepals well reflexed. Corolla. Expanded Lavender blue. GC. P652 Exhibited at RHS Show. HC. Cat. 1882-1885. B. Cat. 1893. GO. "Select" 1880. GC. P55 19/1/1867 Review by Cannell. Very large, opening out like "La Crinoline". GC. P83 1867 RHS Show 24/6/1866 awarded FCC. F&P P56 March 1866 Free bloomer. Sepals well recurved. Corolla lavender blue. Very large, Opens out. Fine colour. P112 4th Ed. by Porcher 1874 Pedicel 50 mms GC. P382 29/4/1865 Intro by E.G. Henderson. *Banks, E. Deal. GB. 1865.*

RICCARTONII. Single. Red/Purple. Tube. Red. Sepals. Red. Corolla. Purple. GC. P833 18/12/1841 & P273 23/4/1842 "Recommended". GC. P393 6/1842 & P97 10/3/1843 & P98 17/2/1844 & P146 18/3/1845 Listed by Youell Gt. Yarmouth. B. Cat. 1879-1881. HC. Cat. 1882-1885. F.globosa X F.discolour. *Young. Edinburgh. GB. 1835.*

RICCARTONII VARIEGATED. Single. Red/Purple. Tube. Red. Sepals. Red. Corolla. Purple. RH. P539 1911 Recently introduced from England. Low growing bush with small leaves, about 15-20 cms high. Its flowering like other variegated ones is not profuse. Presented to National Committee of Horticulture by Vilmorin Andrieux and awarded certificate of merit. NK. NK. *GB.* NK.

RICKARDII GRANDIFLORA. Single. ND/ND. Tube. ND. Sepals. ND. Corolla. ND. GC. P523 29/7/1843 Exhibited at RHS of Cornwall show, by Veitch. *Rickard,Truro. GB. 1840.*

RICKARDIANA, Single. Red/Purple. Tube. Bright crimson. Sepals. Bright crimson. Beautifully reflexed. Corolla. Purple. GC. P387 19/6/1852 Novel globular flower. Intro. by J. Rickard, Truro. *Rickard,J. Truro. GB. 1852.*

RIFLARD. Single. ND/ND. Tube. ND. Sepals. ND. Corolla. ND. L. Cat. 1892. *Rozain, Lyons, France. 1888.*

RIFLEMAN (a). ND. ND/ND. Tube. ND. Sepals. ND. Corolla. ND. GC. P594 29/6/1861 Listed by Godwin & Padnam, Sheffield. GC. P771 24/8/1861 Listed by H. Walton, Burnley. NK. NK. *GB. 1861.*

RIFLEMAN (b). Double. Red/Purple. Tube. Scarlet. Sepals. Scarlet. Corolla. Dark purple. F&P March 1863. GC. P55 19/1/1867 Review by H. Cannell Similar to "Sir Colin Campbell" but far superior. GC. P376 20/4/1862 Entire stock purchased and Intro. by F&A Smith, Dulwich. *Smith F&A, Dulwich. GB. 1862.*

RIFLEMAN (c). Single. Red/Purple. Tube. Scarlet. Sepals. Scarlet. Corolla. Lavender purple. Beautiful pot plant. Small leaves. Densely branched. GC. P55 19/1/1867 Review by H. Cannell A little gem. Dwarf. Good habit. Most profuse bloomer. Young plants will bloom all winter. GC. P338 15/4/1865 Listed by W. Rumley, Richmond. GC. P863 12/9/1863 Intro. by E. G. Henderson. *Banks, E. Deal. GB. 1863.*

RIGOLBOCKE. Single. Red/Purple. Tube. Rosy red. Sepals. Rosy red. Long, Slender. Corolla. Rosy Purple. Narrow petals. Vol P3 J of RHS 1863 Fuchsia trial at Chiswick. A weedy looking sort. *Bull,W. Chelsea. GB. 1863.*

RIVAL. Single. Red/Purple. Tube. Red. Sepals. Red. Corolla. Purple. GC. P571 24/7/1858 & P778 23/10/1858 Listed by H. Walton, Burnley. Vol P3 J of RHS 1863 Fuchsia trial at Chiswick 1862 A poor coarse red and purple. JF. Cat. 1885. NK. NK. *GB. 1858.*

ROBERT BLATRY. Single. White/Pink. Tube. Creamy white.(Pinky white). Long. Sepals. Creamy white. (Pinky white). Large. Corolla. Bright pink tinted flesh. (Salmon carmine). In Corymbiflora class like "Heinrich Heinkel/Souvenir de H Henkel". L. Cat. 1906. RH. P455 1905 Intro. by A. Nonin. *Nonin,A. France. 1904.*

ROBIN HOOD. Double. ND/ND. Tube. ND. Sepals. ND. Corolla. ND GC. P59 29/6/1861 Listed by Godwin & Padnam, Sheffield. GC. P771

159

24/8/1861 Listed by H. Walton, Burnley. FF & GM 1860 Florist P89 1860. P1 J of RHS 1859 P79 Floral Committee Inferior flowers. Corolla irregular and confused. *Wheeler, Warminster GB. 1860.*

ROBINSONII (a). Single. Red/Purple. Tube. Red. Sepals. Red. Corolla. Purple. Plate T4 Page 61 1836 Coloured plate in Marnocks Floricultural Magazine. *Backhouse, York. GB. 1835.*

ROBINSONII (b). Single. ND/ND. Tube. ND. Sepals. ND. Corolla. ND. Floricultural Cabinet Vol XIV 1846 P12 & P29 & P51. Exhibited at RBS Show June 1845 and at the HS Show 1845 by Robinson, Gr. to J. Simpson. *Robinson. GB. 1845.*

ROBUSTA. Single. Red/Purple. Tube. Scarlet. Sepals. Scarlet. Corolla. Purple. GC. P481 15/7/1843 Exhibited by Catbush RBS Show - Dwarf. Compact. GC. P610 2/9/1843 Exhibited by T. Farrell at Practical Floral and Hort Scty of Ireland show. GC. P820 Dec 1844 "Recommended". GC. P98 17/2/1844 & P146 8/3/1845 Listed by Youell, Gt. Yarmouth. GC. P657 1843 Listed by J. Piper. GC. P705 1843 Listed by J. Whiteley, Wakefield. *Smith, J. Dalston. GB. 1843.*

ROCHAMBEAU. Double. Red/Pink. Tube. Carmine. Sepals. Carmine. Reflexed. Corolla. Pink Mauve. Large petals. Full. L. Cat. 1903. *Lemoine, Nancy. France. 1903.*

RODIN. Double. Red/Purple. Tube. Brilliant scarlet. Sepals. Brilliant scarlet. Corolla. Bluish violet. Enormous. JF. Cat. 1893. NK. NK. NK. *1892.*

ROGERSIANA. Single. Red/Red. Tube. Carmine. Sepals. Carmine. Corolla. Violet vermilion. Leaves 9cm x 6cm. Upright. Vigourous. P51 2nd. Ed. by Porcher 1848. GC. P169 18/3/1843 Floricultural Cabinet March 1843. GC. P98 17/2/1844 & P146 8/3/1845 Listed by Youell, Gt.Yarmouth. GC. P112 17/2/1844 & P66 1/2/1845 Listed by W. Miller, Ramsgate. *Rogers, W. Uttoxeter. GB. 1843.*

ROI DES BLANCS. ND. ND/ND. Tube. ND. Sepals. ND. Corolla. ND. RH. P170 1857. NK. NK. *France. 1857.*

ROI DE REINE. ND. ND/ND. Tube. ND. Sepals. ND. Corolla. ND. GC. P418 22/5/1858 Listed by H. Walton, Burnley. NK. NK. NK. *1857.*

ROI DE ROME. Single. White/Red. Tube. White. (Does not pink). Short. Sepals. White. Corolla. Brilliant scarlet. P96 Vol II Midland Florist 1848 Very beautiful and superior to "Napoleon". GC.

P224 14/4/1849 Listed by Bass & Brown, Sudbury. GC. P274 5/5/1849 Listed by H. Walton, Burnley. P81 2nd. Ed. by Porcher 1848. Napoleon X. *Meillez, Lille. France. 1847.*

ROI DES FUCHSIAS. ND. ND/ND. Tube. ND. Sepals. ND. Corolla. ND. GC. P162 18/3/1854 Listed by H. Walton, Burnley. GC. P211 26/3/1853 Listed by W. Rumley, Richmond. NK. NK. NK. *1853.*

ROLAND (a). Single. Red/Purple. Tube. Coral Red. Sepals. Coral red. Reflexed. Corolla. Light blue. Large. Long. Very distinct 7/6d. GC. P74 24/1/1863. Intro. by W. Bull, Chelsea. *Bull,W. Chelsea. GB. 1863.*

ROLAND (b). Double. Red/Purple. Tube. Red. Sepals. Red Corolla. Dark violet. Vigorous. Full. L. Cat. 1913. NK. NK. NK. *1912.*

ROLLA. Double. Pink/White. Tube. Soft Pink. Sepals. Soft pink. Reflexed. Corolla. Pure white. Average size. Good vegetation. L. Cat. 1913. *Lemoine, Nancy. France. 1913.*

ROLLINSONII. Single. Red/Purple. Tube. Red. Sepals. Red. Reflexed. Corolla. Purple. Small. Vol P3 J of RHS 1862 Fuchsias grown for trial 1862. *Turner,C. Slough. GB. 1861.*

ROMEO. Single. Red/Purple. Tube. Crimson. Sepals. Crimson. Elegantly recurved. Very symmetrical. Corolla. Rich purple plum, marked rose at base. *Bull,W. Chelsea. GB. 1901.*

ROMOLA. Single. Red/White. Tube. Rosy red. Sepals. Rosy red. Corolla. White, striped rose at base. B. Cat. 1872-1876. *Bull,W. Chelsea. GB. 1872.*

RONSARD. Single. Red/Purple. Tube. Red. Sepals. Red. Corolla. Violet. Hardy. L. Cat. 1901. F.coccinea X. *Lemoine, Nancy. France. 1897*

ROSABELL. Single. Red/Red. Tube. Bright purple rose. Sepals. Bright purple rose. ((Rosy lilac). Corolla. Bright purple rose. (Lake). Quite distinct from anything yet send out. RH. P24 1846. GC. P163 14/3/1846 & P184 13/3/1847 Listed by W. Miller, Ramsgate. GC. P216 27/3/1847 Listed by R. Cooper, Croydon. GC. P265 24/4/1847 & P259 28/4/1848 Listed by W. Rendle Plymouth. *Hally, J. Blackheath GB. 1845.*

ROSA BONHEUR. Single. White/Pink. Tube. Blush white. Sepals. Blush white. Well recurved. Corolla. Rich rose shaded carmine. Flowers

160

produced in terminal drooping clusters. Free. Erect Habit. HC. Cat. 1882-1885. B. Cat. 1877-1879. *Todman. GB. 1876.*

ROSALBA. ND. ND/ND. Tube. ND. Sepals. ND. Corolla. ND. Gartenflora Vol 6 1857 P283 (P1156 Flore des Serres). NK. NK. NK. NK.

ROSALIA. Single. Red/Purple. Tube. Crimson red. Sepals. Crimson red. Corolla. Purple. App. to RH. 1851 by Porcher. Corolla a little paler than the calyx. GC. P256 16/4/1848 Listed by G. Rogers, Uttoxeter. GC. P224 14/4/1848 Listed by R. Whibley, Kennington Cross. GC. P259 28/4/1849 & P241 20/4/1850 Listed by W. Rendle, Plymouth. GC. P144 8/3/1851 Listed by W. Rendle, Plymouth. GC. P249 27/4/1847 Intro. by W. Rendle, Plymouth. *Passingham, Truro. GB. 1847.*

ROSALIE (a). Single. Pink/Pink. Tube. Deep blush. Sepals. Deep blush. Corolla. Rose pink edged scarlet.Vol P3 J of RHS 1863 Report on fuchsias grown for trial 1862 Small. Dwarf habited sort. Sent by E.G. Henderson. *Henderson, E.G. St. John's Wood. GB. 1861.*

ROSALIE (b). Double. Red/White. Tube. Crimson. Sepals. Crimson. Horizontal. Corolla. White veined cerise pink. B. Cat. 1898-1901. GC. P579 May 1896 Intro. by W. Bull, Chelsea. *Bull,W. Chelsea. GB. 1896.*

ROSALIE FRANCK. Double. Red/White. Tube. Bright crimson. Short. Sepals. Bright crimson. Very long. Reflexed. Corolla. Pure white, pin striped with crimson red. P130 4th Ed. by Porcher 1874. *Crousse. France. 1866.*

ROSALIND. Single. White/Pink. Tube. White. Large. Waxy. (Tinted blush). Sepals. Waxy white. (Tinted blush). Corolla. Pale rosy pink (Pale rosy pink margined with carmine). Very stout. B. Cat. 1888-1889. BSW. Cat 1888. GO. 1889. HC. Cat. 1890. JF. Cat 1888. *Lye, J. Market Lavington. GB. 1888.*

ROSAMUNDE. Exhibited at HS Show 11/7/1849 (in the way of "Beaute Supreme" but larger) See "FAIR ROSAMOND". GC. P275 1/5/1852 Listed by H. Walton, Burnley.

ROSA LEUCANTHA. ND. ND/ND. Tube. ND. Sepals. ND. Corolla. ND GC. P241 20/4/1850 Listed by W. Rendle, Plymouth. NK. NK. *GB. 1850.*

ROSA MUNDI. Single. Pink/Red. Tube. Bright pink. Sepals. Bright pink. Green tips. Corolla. Bright

scarlet. GC. P2 4/1/1845 Intro. by Girling, Stowmarket. *Girling, Stowmarket. GB. 1845.*

ROSA QUINTAL. Single. White/Red. Tube. White, tinted vermilion. Sepals. White tinted vermilion. Green tips. Horizontal. Corolla. Vermilion. Small. GC. P454 16/7/1853 Exhibited by Mr. Wiggins, at H.S. Show 9/7/1853. Awarded 2nd Prize as a standard. GC. P537 12/8/1848 Listed by G. Smith, Islington. GC. P256 21/4/1849 Listed by R. Cooper, Croydon. GC. P241 20/4/1850 Listed by W. Rendle Plymouth. *Salter,J. Versailles. France. 1848.*

ROSCHEN Single. Red/Purple. Tube. Bright crimson. Sepals. Bright crimson. Horizontal. Corolla. Rich bluish purple. Good Size. B. Cat. 1872-1876. *Bull, W. Chelsea. GB. 1872.*

ROSEA ALBA. Single. Pink/Pink. Tube. White ageing to pink. Sepals. White ageing to pink. Corolla. Pink. GC. P393 6/1842 Rosy white fuchsia. This is a neat and pretty variety and flowers very freely. Raised by Mr.J. Bell of Bracondale Nr. Norwich. Originated in Norfolk in 1841. The plant is a free grower and vigorous. P51 2nd Ed. by Porcher 1848 Nice plant. Bushy. Delicate. Small oval lanceolate leaves, with violet veins. Short tube, with extended sepals. Corolla is bright pink. This variety does not have pure white flowers. Also named as "Albiflora" or "Bellidifolia". *Bell,J. Norwich. GB. 1841.*

ROSEA ELEGANS. ND. ND/ND. Tube. ND. Sepals. ND. Corolla. ND. GC. 10/2/1843 Listed by Youell, Gt. Yarmouth. NK. NK. *GB. 1843.*

ROSEA SUPERBA. ND. ND/ND. Tube. ND. Sepals. ND. Corolla. ND. GC. P234 11/4/1846 Listed by A. J. Stewert, Windsor. GC. P184 13/3/1847 Listed by W. Miller, Ramsgate. *Stewart, Windsor. GB. 1847.*

ROSE D'AMOUR. Single. RH. P205 1847. SEE REVE D'AMOUR.

ROSE D'AMOUR. Single. Red/Purple. Tube. Rose. Sepals. Rose. Corolla. Purple. GC. P216 27/3/1847 & P153 4/3/1848 & P232 1/4/1848 Listed by R. Cooper, Croydon. GC. P226 13/4/1850 Listed by Poole Nurseries. GC. P338 22/5/1847 Intro. by Knight, St. Leonards. *Knight. St Leonards. GB. 1847.*

ROSE OF CASTILLE. Single. White/Purple. Tube. White. (Blush White). (White tinged flesh). Short. Sepals. White. (Blush white). (Edged rose). Horizontal. Corolla. Violet Rose, striped white at base. (Lilac Blue). (Rosy purple). GC. P580 9/7/1859 & P607 16/7/1859 Exhibited at RBS Show Regents Park, by H. Cannell Gr. to R.E. Grove, Tulse Hill. RH. P95 1859. GC. P57 18/7/1856 "Recommended". SG P459 1866 "Recommended" P119 4th Ed. by Porcher 1874 Short pedicel. Spiralled. GC. P211 17/2/1877 Growers of the West Country-varieties. Vol P3 J of RHS 1863 P92 Fuchsia trials at Chiswick 1862. A free blooming and useful decorative sort with stiff erect shrubby habit. Flowers blush white, sepals spreading, Corolla moderately expanded. Pcxi Vol 3 J of RHS 1872 Fuchsia trials at Chiswick Awarded ** Habit stiff, compact, profuse flowering. Tube ½" bulged. Sepals spreading. Green at tip. Corolla. Clear rosy purple with white feather at base. GC. Vol IV J of RHS P218 Fuchsia trials. Previous certificate confirmed. GC. P311 8/9/1877 Exhibited at Trowbridge show. Matthews 1st, J. Lye 2nd. G. 6/9/1884 Exhibited at Trowbridge by Pocock 2nd. GC. Vol. 20 P280 1/9/1883 Exhibited at Trowbridge H.S. Show by J. Lye 1st 4" pot class. Vol 18 1882 P215 Exhibited at Devizes H.S. Show 7/8/1882 by J. Lye (1st) and T. Chandler (2nd). RH. P295 1886. Fuchsias grown as standards at Twickel. GC P1331 1871 Grown as a bedder in Hyde Park. GC. 539 10/7/1858 Listed by F. Godwin, Sheffield. GC. P571 24/7/1858 Listed by H. Walton, Burnley. GC. P238 19/3/1859 Listed by W. Rumley, Richmond. GC. P260 24/3/1860 Listed by W. Hussey, Norwich. Dobbies Cat. 1893-4. Dwarf. Free. Hardy. *Banks E. Deal. GB. 1858.*

ROSE OF CASTILLE IMPROVED. Single. White/Purple. Tube. Blush. Sepals. Blush. Corolla. Purple. JF. Cat. 1888 Fine habit. Laings Cat. 1890. Dobbies Cat. 1893/4. Has all the good qualities of its parent with larger finer flowers. B. Cat. 1888-1889. A great improvment on the old favourite. Free. Good growth. BSW. Cat. 1897. A plant of this cultivar being grown at Wallington Gardens in Northumberland is reputed to be the oldest growing fuchsia in this country, and planted in 1905. *Rowson. GB. 1887.*

ROSE OF DENMARK. Single. White/Pink. Tube. White. (Glossy white). (White tinged yellow). Sepals. White. (Glossy white). (White tinged yellow). Horizontal. Corolla. Light pink margined rose. (Lilac rose margined pink). (Bright pink belted rose). GC. P652 15/7/1865 "Recommended". GC. P55 19/1/1867 Review by H. Cannell Strong habit. Blooms very freely at the points. Distinct. F&P P57 3/1866 Corolla cup shaped. P119 4th Ed. by Porcher 1874 Sepals rose pink on underside, reflexed and rounded. Spiralled. B. Cat. 1870. HC. Cat. 1882-1885. Vol 2 J of RHS 1870 Fuchia trials at Chiswick

1870 - passed over. Vol 3 J of RHS 1872 Fuchsia trials at Chiswick Tube long, tapered upward. Sepals. Recurved tinged with pink. Corolla full. Rather spreading. Lively rose pink. A pretty variety. GC. Vol 26 1886 RHS Trials at Chiswick. GC. P382 29/4/1865 Intro. by E. G. Henderson. *Banks, E. Deal. GB. 1865.*

ROSEOLA. Single. Red/Purple. Tube. Red. Sepals. Red. Corolla. Purple. GC. P207 27/3/1852 Listed by H. Walton, Burnley. GC. P151 5/3/1853 Dark variety. Good for exhibtion. *Mayle, Birmingham. GB. 1851.*

ROSE PHENOMENAL. Double. Red/Purple. Tube. Red. Sepals. Red. Corolla. Bluish mauve. Sport from "Phenomenal". HC. Cat. 1896. JF. Cat 1899. B. Cat. 1894-1895 Similar to "Phenomenal" the corolla a new shade of rose. *Westley. GB. 1894.*

ROSSINI. Single. Red/Purple. Tube. Violet red. Long. Thick. Sepals. Violet red. Reflexed. Rounded. Corolla. Violet washed red. Bell shaped. The whole assembly constitutes a good and effective flower. P112 4th Ed. by Porcher 1874. Named after a composer of operas 1792-1868. *Lemoine. Nancy. France. 1869.*

ROUGE ET BLANC. Single. Red/White. Tube. Deep scarlet. Sepals. Deep scarlet. Well reflexed. Corolla. White. Very elegant. P79 Floricultural Cabinet 1855. GC. P368 26/5/1855 Listed by E.G. Henderson. NK. NK. NK. *1854.*

ROUGET DE L'ISLE. Double. Pink/Purple. Tube. Clear pink. Sepals. Clear pink. Roll up to tube. Remarkable new shade. Corolla. Dark plum. Named after a French Army Officer who composed the Marseillaise (1760-1836). L. Cat. 1903. *Lemoine. Nancy. France. 1903.*

ROWENA. ND. ND/ND. Tube. ND. Sepals. ND. Corolla. ND. Vol P3 J of RHS 1863 Report on fuchsias grown for trial at Chiswick 1862. A free blooming sort with globular buds and having reflexed sepals and a small expanded corolla of good colour. *Laxton. GB. 1861.*

ROYALIST. ND. ND/ND. Tube. ND. Sepals. ND. Corolla. ND. GC. P145 9/8/1850 Listed by W. Rumley, Richmond. NK. NK. *GB. 1850.*

ROYAL OSBORNE. Single. White/Red. Tube. White. Sepals. White. Corolla. Deep rose. JF. Cat. 1920. HC. Cat. 1885. NK. NK. *GB. 1883.*

ROYAL PRINCE. Double. Red/Purple. Tube. Bright red. Sepals. Bright red. Recurved. Corolla. Purple carmine. (Bright purple veined carmine). P127 4th Ed. by Porcher 1874. Not in the first selection. B. Cat. 1870-1873. GC. P451 2/4/1870 Intro. by Felton & Son. *Felton. Birmingham. GB. 1870.*

ROYAL PURPLE ND. ND/ND. Tube. ND. Sepals. ND. Corolla. ND. GC. Vol 21 P411 1/5/1897 Listed by H.J. Jones. NK. NK. *GB. 1896?*

ROYAL STANDARD. Single. Red/Purple. Tube. Bright red. Sepals. Bright red. Corolla. Plum purple. BSW. Cat. 1878. GC. P503 20/10/1877 See Floral Magazine Plate T277 1877. GO. "Select" 1880-1881. HC. Cat. 1882 Fine strong growing plant. One of the best for large plants. Laings Cat. 1890. *Lye, J. Market Lavington. GB. 1877.*

ROYAL VICTORIA. Single. White/Red. Tube. White. Sepals. White. Reflexed. Corolla. Light red. Vol. P3 J of RHS 1863 P92 Fuchsia trial at Chiswick 1862. GC. P515 25/7/1857 & P418 22/5/1858 Listed by H. Walton, Burnley. GC. P231 4/4/1857 Intro. by J. Keynes, Salisbury. *Pond. GB. 1857.*

R.P. OLIVER. Double. Red/White. Tube. Bright carmine. Sepals. Bright carmine. Corolla. Pure white. JF. Cat. 1899. L. Cat. 1901. *Rozain, Lyons. France. 1898,*

RUBENS (a). Single. Pink/Red. Tube. Flesh. Sepals. Flesh. Green tips. Corolla. Red. Large. GC. P183 13/3/1847 Raised by Mr. Evans Gr. to J.B. Freeland and Intro. by W. Miller, Ramsgate. *Evans. GB. 1847.*

RUBENS (b). Double. Red/Purple. Tube. Red. Sepals. Red. Corolla. Dark violet. Variegated yellow, bordered golden yellow. B. Cat. 1883. Vol. 33 The Garden 1887 Another yellow leaved variety. Very double. Dark flowered blossoms. *Bull,W. Chelsea. GB. 1883.*

RUBENS (c). Double. Red/Purple. Tube. Crimson. Sepals. Crimson. Corolla. Blue. (Dark blue outside. Petals amarinth). Fine habit. L. Cat. 1901. JF. Cat. 1900. *Rozain, Lyons. France. 1899.*

RUBLUM. Single. Red/Red. Tube. Deep crimson. Sepals. Deep crimson. Corolla. Orange red. FCC. RHS. HC. Cat. 1882 5/-. Illustration in catalogue. Dominiana x F.serratifolia. *Cannell, H. Swanley. GB. 1882.*

RUDOLPHUS. Single. Red/Red. Tube. Deep rose vermillion. Sepals. Deep rose vermillion. Corolla. Reddish purple. GC. P112 17/2/1844 & P66 1/2/1845 Listed by W. Miller, Ramsgate. GC. P553 12/8/1843 Intro. by W. Bell, Thirsk. GC. P417 17/6/1843 Sent by Mawbray to Editor GC. for assessment. *Maybray. GB. 1843.*

RUFUS. Double. Red/Purple. Tube. Scarlet. Sepals. Scarlet. Corolla. Purple, flamed and striped bright carmine. GC. P570 30/5/1868 Intro. by Felton & Holiday, Birmingham. *Felton, Birmingham. GB. 1868*

RUPERT. Single. Red/Purple. Tube. Carmine red. Short. Sepals. Carmine red. Broad. Recurved. Corolla. Bright purple. Long. Spreading. B. Cat. 1899-1901. JF. Cat. 1899. L. Cat. 1901. B. Cat. 1898 intro. by W. Bull, Chelsea. 5/-. *Bull,W. Chelsea. GB. 1898.*

RUSTIC. Double. Red/Purple. Tube. Dark crimson. Short. Sepals. Dark crimson. Immense breadth. Well reflexed. Corolla. Rich dark purple, marked rose at base. B. Cat. 1872-1875. P125 4th Ed. by Porcher 1874. Makes a nice bush without too much pinching. Flowers abundantly. Pedicel 40 mm. Tube thin. Short. Sepals elongated. Horizontal. Turned up points. Corolla Violet blue, marked red at base. Double without being too full. Spiralled. *Bull,W. Chelsea. GB. 1871.*

RUY BLAS (a). Double. ND/ND. Tube. ND. Sepals. ND. Corolla. ND. P113 4th Ed. by Porcher 1874. *Rollinson, Tooting. GB. 1862.*

RUY BLAS (b). Single. Red/Purple. Tube. Crimson. Short. Sepals. Crimson. Large. Reflexed. Corolla. Bluish violet washed red. Spreading. Medium size. P113 4th Ed. by Porcher 1874. *Lemoine, Nancy. France. 1868.*

RUY BLAS (c). Single. Red/Red. Tube. Carmine rose. Sepals. Carmine rose. Corolla. Carmine rose. L. Cat. 1888. *Aubin R., Bagnolet. France. 1888.*

SALOMON. Single. White/Red. Tube. Clear Pink. Short. Thick. Sepals. White flushed flesh pink. Reflexed. Corolla. Carmine Pink. L. Cat. 1888. *Aubin,R. Bagnolet. France. 1888.*

SABINE. Single. White/Red. Tube. White. Sepals. White. Long. Broad. Well extended. Corolla. Magenta Carmine. JF. Cat. 1903. B. Cat. 1901. *Bull,W. Chelsea. GB. 1900.*

SAINTINE. Single. Red/Purple. Tube. Bright red. Sepals. Bright red. Corolla. Mauve. Globular. BSW. Cat. 1878. NK. NK. NK. *1877.*

SALAMANDER. Single. ND/ND. Tube. ND. Sepals. ND. Corolla. ND. GC. P177 20/3/1852 Listed by W. Rumley, Richmond. NK. NK. NK. *1850.*

SALMONIA. Single. Pink/Red. Tube. Clear pink. Sepals. Clear Pink. Green tips. Reflexed to the tube. Corolla. Vermilion. Flowers 35 mm long. P51 2nd Ed. by Porcher 1848. Foliage Bright Green. Acuminate. Charming variety. GC. P97 Feb 1843 & P98 17/2/1844 & P146 8/3/1845 Listed by Youell, Gt. Yarmouth. GC. P112 17/2/1844 & P66 1/2/1845 Listed by W. Miller, Ramsgate. *Smith, J. Dalston. GB. 1842.*

SALMO. Single. Red/Purple. Tube. Deep rose. Sepals. Deep rose. Very broad. Horizontal. Corolla. Deep bluish purple. B. Cat. 1881-1883. *Bull,W. Chelsea. GB. 1881.*

SALOPIA. Single. Red/Purple. Tube. Crimson. Sepals. Crimson. Corolla. Light purple. Handsomely expanded. 3½" across. HC.Cat. 1890 Illustration No.4. L. Cat. 1892. *Sankey. GB. 1888.*

SALTERII. Single. Red/Red. Tube. Clear crimson. Thin. Sepals. Crimson. Less bright than tube. Green tips. Open. Corolla. Violet vermilion red. P51 2nd Ed. by Porcher 1848 Upright. Leaves 9cm by 7cm. Flowers 55 mms long. GC. P66 1/2/1845 & P184 13/3/1847 Listed by W. Miller, Ramsgate. *Salter, J. Versailles. France. 1844.*

SANGUINEA. Single. ND/ND. Tube. ND. Sepals. ND. Corolla. ND. GC. P289 29/5/1841 Listed by H. Low, Upper Clapton. GC. P97 2/1843 & P98 17/2/1844 & P146 8/3/1845 Listed by Youell, Gt. Yarmouth. P79 HC. Cat. 1882. *Smith, J. Dalston. GB. 1840.*

SANGUINEA SUPERBA. Single. Red/Purple. Tube. Crimson purple. 45 mm long. Sepals. Crimson purple. Large. Short. Open. Corolla. Violet vermilion. Leaves 5cm by 4 cm. *Salter, J. Versailles. France. 1842.*

SANGUINOLENTA Single. Red/ND. Tube. Dark crimson. 4cms long. Sepals. Dark crimson. Large. Stout. Pendant. Corolla. ND. P51 2nd. Ed. by Porcher 1848 Leaves oval-oblong 8cm by 4cm, often tinged with red. Mediocre. NK. NK. NK. NK.

SANGUINIVEA. Single. White/Red. Tube. White. Sepals. White. Corolla. Crimson. (Vermilion). GC. P559 17/8/1844 Habit of "Chandlerii". GC. P820 12/1844 "Recommended". GC. P369 3/6/1844 Listed by T. Cripps, Maidstone. RH. P24 1846. GC.P146 8/3/1845 Listed by Youell, Gt. Yarmouth. GC. P66 1/2/1845 & P147 13/3/1847 Listed by W. Miller, Ramsgate. GC. P162 16/3/1844 Intro. by *Hally. Blackheath GB. 1844.*

SANSPAREIL (a). Single. White/Purple. Tube. White. Medium. Sepals. White. Reflexed. Strongly shaded green. Corolla. Cerise red. Flower 3" in length. 3 times the size of "Venus Victrix". P81 2nd Ed. by Porcher 1848. Resembles "Lady Julia" and "Diana". GC. P808 11/1846 & P140 27/2/1847 "Recommended". GC. 7/2/1846 Intro. by Youells. Gt. Yarmouth. Venus Victrix X. *Youell. Gt. Yarmouth GB. 1846.*

SANSPAREIL (b). Single. Red/White. Tube. Scarlet. Sepals. Scarlet. Underside lighter. Finely recurved. Corolla. Pure white. Long. GC. P643 12/7/1862 Awarded FCC at RBS Exhibition held on 9/7/1862. GC. P344 11/4/1863 see Floral Magazine Feb 1863. GC. P122 1/2/1863 Intro. by G. Smith Islington. *Smith, G. Islington. GB. 1863.*

SAPHIR. Double. Red/Purple. Tube. Red. Sepals. Red. Corolla. Slate blue violet, veined red. L. Cat. 1911. *Rozain. Lyons. France. 1911.*

SAPPHO. Single. Red/Purple. Tube. Bright scarlet. Long. Similar to "Cormackii". Sepals. Scarlet. Corolla. Scarlet with a rich purple tinge. GC. P184 13/3/1847 & P250 27/4/1847 Listed by W. Miller, Ramsgate. GC. P82 6/2/1845 Intro. by Bass & Brown, Sudbury. *Bass & Brown. Sudbury GB. 1845.*

SAPHO. ND. ND/ND. Tube. ND. Sepals. ND. Corolla. ND. P120 4th Ed. by Porcher 1874. Not in the first selection. *Demay, H. Arras. Belgium. 1868.*

SAPPHIRE (a). Single. ND/ND. Tube. ND. Sepals. ND. Corolla. ND. GC. P146 8/3/1845 Listed by Youell. Gt. Yarmouth. NK. NK. NK. *1844.*

SAPPHIRE (b). Single. Red/Purple. Tube. Coral. Sepals. Coral. Reflex to tube. Corolla. Dark blue. CG. Vol 3 P272 1850 "Fuchsias for exhibition". GC. P210 6/4/1850 Listed by H. Walton, Burnley. GC. P339 2/6/1849 Purchased from Mr. Denham, Birmingham, and intro. by Luccome & Pince, Exeter. *Denham. Birmingham. GB. 1849.*

SARAH BERNHARDT. Double. Pink/White. Tube. Brilliant pink. Sepals. Brilliant pink. Turned back. Corolla. Whitish pink. Very full. Named after a French actress 1844-1923. L. Cat. 1901. *Lemoine, Nancy. France. 1899.*

SATRAPE. Double. Red/Purple. Tube. Carmine. Sepals. Carmine. Horizontal. Corolla. Lilac bordered red. L. Cat. 1913. *Lemoine, Nancy. France. 1912.*

S. BOREL. Double. Red/Pink. Tube. Clear crimson. Sepals. Clear crimson. Corolla. Carmine pink veined china rose. L.Cat. 1906. *Rozain, Lyons. France. 1904.*

SCARAMOUCHE. Single. Red/Purple. Tube. Lilac pink. Thick. Sepals. Lilac pink. Open. Green points. Corolla. Lilac. P81 2nd Ed. by Porcher 1848 Similar to "Sylphe" and "Esmeralda" (which is superior). GC. P216 27/3/1847 & P232 1/4/1848 Listed by R. Cooper, Croydon. *Meillez. Lille. France. 1846.*

SCARCITY. Single. Red/Purple. Tube. Scarlet. Sepals. Scarlet. Corolla. Purple. Laings Cat. circa 1890. BSW Cat. 1897. NK. NK. *GB. 1890?*

SCARLETINA REFLEXA. Single. Red/Purple. Tube. Scarlet. Sepals. Scarlet. Corolla. Purple. GC. P151 5/3/1853 "Good for exhibition" GC. P279 30/4/1853 Dark wooded stem. GC. P454 16/7/1853 Exhibited at HS Show by Salter. CG. Vol III 1850 . P272 New Fuchsias for exhibition. App. to RH. 1851 by Porcher Hybrid from Corallina. Similar in colour. Defect is the shoots elongate haphazardly. Early pinching is necessary. GC. P537 12/8/1848 Listed by G. Smith, Islington. GC. P224 14/4/1849 Listed by Bass & Brown, Sudbury. GC. P224 14/4/1849 Listed by R. Whibley, Kennington Cross. GC. P256 21/4/1849 Listed by R. Cooper, Croydon. GC. P274 5/5/1849 Listed by H. Walton, Burnley. GC. P241 20/4/1850 Listed by W. Rendle, Plymouth. GC. P226 13/4/1850 Listed by Poole Nurseries. GC. P537 14/8/1847 Intro. by J. Sherriff, Handsworth. *Sherriff,J. Handsworth. GB. 1847.*

SCARLET KING. Single. ND/ND. Tube. ND. Sepals. ND. Corolla. ND. GC. P311 8/9/1877 Exhibited at Trowbridge Show, by J. Lye. NK. NK. NK. NK.

SCHILLER. Single. White/Purple. Tube. White. (Flesh pink to white). Long. 15mm. Sepals. White. (Flesh pink to white). Large. Corolla. Rich deep purple, Pure white blotch at base of each petal. (Violet blue washed and streaked white at base). Bell shaped. P119 4th. Ed. by Porcher 1874. CG. & JH. P361 "Select 12" CG. & JH. P406 20/8/1861 A long

drooping elegant flower. Vol P3 J of RHS 1863 P92 Fuchsia trials at Chiswick. A blush variety with loose spreading reflexed sepals and a purple corolla. Vol 2 J of RHS 1870 Fuchsia trials at Chiswick "Passed over". Pcxi Vol 3 J of RHS 1872 Fuchsia trials at Chiswick 1872. Habit loose. Flowers large. Tube ½". Sepals 1" long. Broad. Spreading. Green at tips. Clear rosy purple with white feather at base. Vol 4 J of RHS 1873 Fuchsia trials at Chiswick. Awarded FCC. Free. Bushy. Drooping habit. Tube and sepals blush. Sepals spreading. Corolla is purple. Flowers are larger and better than "Rose of Castille" which they resemble in colour. Vol 4 P67 J of RHS 1877 Fuchsia trials at Chiswick. Awarded FCC. Habit somewhat loose. Flowers large. Tube and broad spreading sepals are white, green at tip. Corolla is a clear rosy purple with a white feather at base. GC. P594 30/6/1860 Listed by F. Godwin, Sheffield. *Banks, E. Deal. GB. 1860.*

SCHLIEMANN. Double. Red/Pink. Tube. Brilliant coral. Sepals. Brilliant coral. Horizontal. Large. Corolla. Greyish pink. (Rosy red). Serrated corolla. Very double. Compact. JF. Cat. 1892. B. Cat. 1892. L. Cat. 1892. *Lemoine. Nancy. France. 1891.*

SCHNEEPYRAMIDE. Double. Red/White. Tube. Clear crimson. Very short. Almost non existant. Sepals crimson. Large. Reflexed to tube. Corolla. Pure white with faint stripes of rose. Full. P130 4th Ed. by Porcher 1874 Good. Strong upright. *Twrdy. Brno. Austria. 1870.*

SCHWAN. Single. Red/White. Tube. Red. Sepals. Red. Corolla. White. P131 4th Ed. by Porcher 1874 Not in the first selection. *Twrdy. Brno. Austria. 1866.*

SCIPIO. Single. Red/Purple. Tube. Coral red. Short. (Moderate length). Sepals. Coral red. Broad. Corolla. Violet purple. An improvement on Globosa varieties. GC. P90 5/2/1859 awarded FCC by N.F.C. Vol P3 J of RHS 1863 Fuchsia trial at Chiswick. Awarded **. Good habit. Free bloomer. Corolla half expanded. *Smith, G. Islington. GB. 1859.*

SCIPION. Double. Red/Purple. Tube. Carmine pink. Sepals. Carmine Pink. Uplifted. Corolla. Mauve. L. Cat. 1902. *Rozain. Lyons. France. 1902.*

SCRIBE. Single. Red/Purple. Tube. Red. Sepals. Red. Long. Spreading. Corolla. Purple. Petals isolate themselves from one another, and then combine to form a turban. App. to RH 1851. Hybrid from Corallina. Corallina X. *Baudinet. France. 1849.*

SCULPTOR BARTHOLOMÉ. Single. Red/ Purple. Tube. Bright red. (Scarlet). Sepals. Bright red. (Scarlet). Large. Reflexed. Corolla. Clear violet. Enormous. Regular. Funnel shaped. Named after a French sculptor 1848-1928. JF. Cat. 1901. L. Cat. No 149. 1901. *Lemoine, Nancy. France. 1900.*

SECRETAIRE MATTIN. ND. ND/ND. Tube. ND. Sepals. ND. Corolla. ND. GC. P406 1/5/1863 Listed by Wm. Hussey. Norwich. NK. NK. NK. *1862.*

SEDAN. Single. Red/Red. Tube. Crimson. (Bright scarlet). (Deep red). (Bright rose). Sepals. Crimson. (Bright scarlet). (Deep red). (Bright rose). Corolla. Crimson. (Scarlet lake). Nearly a self. GC. P1554 2/12/1871 Review by H. Cannell. Similar to "Duke of Wellington". GC. P299 4/3/1872 Listed as a self. P74 Vol 4 J of RHS Fuchsia trials at Chiswick. No award. Habit excellent and exceedingly floriferous. Corolla Large and of fine form. A very showy and first rate variety. GC. Vol 26 31/7/1886 Fuchsia trials at Chiswick. HC. Cat. 1882-1898 A favourite, especially for market. Laings Cat. circa 1890. Dobbies Cat. 1893/4. Introduced by *Hock. Weinrich. Germany. 1871.*

SEMPERFLORENS. ND. ND/ND. Tube. ND. Sepals. ND. Corolla. ND. L. Cat. 1892. *Rozain, Lyons. France. 1888.*

SENATEUR BERLET. Double. Red/Purple. Tube. Brilliant carmine. Sepals. Brilliant carmine. Long. Broad. Well reflexed. Corolla. Violet. Perfect globular shape. B. Cat. 1888-1893. GO. 1887 "Select". *Lemoine, Nancy. France. 1884.*

SENATOR. Single. Red/Purple. Tube. Bright waxy crimson. Sepals. Bright waxy crimson. Well reflexed. Corolla. Rich violet. GC. P93 4/2/1860. FCC. R.B.S. CG & JH. P361 1861 "Select 12". Vol P3 J of RHS 1863 Fuchsia trials at Chiswick 1862 Long reflexed sepals. GC. P594 30/3/1860 Listed by F. Godwin, Sheffield. GC. P93 4/2/1860 Intro. by G. Smith, Islington. Awarded FCC by R.B.S. *Smith, G. Islington. GB. 1860.*

SENSATION. Single. Red/Purple. Tube. Bright crimson. Sepals. Bright crimson. Beautifully reflexed. Corolla. Rich purple. Expands almost horizontally. New shape. GC. P960 26/10/1861. P115 4th Ed. by Porcher 1874 Not in the first selection. Vol P3 J of RHS 1863 Fuchsia trials at Chiswick. Flower small. Tube slender. Sepals 1" spreading. Corolla prominent reddish purple, darker at the edges. Poor and undesirable. Vol. P3 J of RHS 1863 P89. GC. P108 1/2/1862 Intro. by W. Bull. *Bull, W. Chelsea. GB. 1862.*

SERENA. Double. Red/Pink. Tube. Rose red. Short. Sepals. Rose red. Completely reflexed. Corolla. Blush rose. Spreading. B. Cat. 1898-1899. GC. Vol 19 P579 5/1896 Intro. by W. Bull, Chelsea. *Bull, W. Chelsea. GB. 1896.*

SERRATIFOLIA ALBA. Single. White/Red. Tube. White. Sepals. ND. Corolla. ND. App to RH 1851 by Porcher. Raised from seeds of F.serratifolia crossed with "Napoleon". Placed in commerce by M. Van Houtte. The reddish tube is replaced by white. More floriferous than F. serratifolia. The branches instead of resting and then elongating, cover the base with abundant flowers. F. serratifolia X Napoleon. *Delbaere. France. 1849.*

SERRATIFOLIA MULTIFLORA. Single. Red/Red. Tube. Rose cerise shading to rose pink. Sepals. Tipped green. Short. Spreading. Corolla. Red. Small. App. to RH. 1851 by Porcher. The plant is a dwarf and more floriferous than the type from which it was raised. Foliage is a darker shade of green and less oblong. GC. P275 5/5/1849 Listed by E.G. Henderson. GC. P241 20/4/1850 Listed by W. Rendle, Plymouth. NK. NK. *France. 1849.*

SERRATIFOLIA GRANDIFLORA. Single. Red/Red. Tube. Bright carmine rose at top. Very pale in the length. Sepals. Green tips. Spread out. Star shaped. Reflexed. Corolla. Clear vermilion. Cultivate in shade. Under glass in Autumn will continue to flower in abundance. P113 4th Ed. by Porcher 1874. Dwarf well branched bush. Foliage elongated and nice shade of green. *L'Huillier. France. 1873.*

SERRATIPETALA. Single. Red/Purple. Tube. Scarlet. Sepals. Scarlet. Reflex to tube, showing feathered base of petals. Corolla. Rich mulberry. Each petal evenly serrated. Barrel shaped. GC. P287 1/4/1865 Intro. by B.S. Williams, Holloway. *Williams, B.S. Holloway. GB. 1865.*

SÉVERINE. Double. Red/White. Tube. Carmine red. Sepals. Carmine red. Broad. Turned up. Corolla. White. Full. Most probably named after the Italian tenor, Severini 1883-1966. L cat?. *Lemoine, Nancy. France. 1911.*

SHAKESPEARE (a). Single. ND/ND. Tube. ND. Sepals. ND. Corolla. ND. GC. P162 14/3/1846 & P184 13/3/1847 Listed by W. Miller, Ramsgate. NK. NK. *GB. 1845.*

SHAKESPEARE (b). ND. Red/Purple. Tube. Red. Sepals. Red. Corolla. Purple. CG. P454 1865. NK. NK. *GB. NK.*

SHAKESPEARE (c). Double. Red/Purple. Tube. Red. Sepals. Red. Corolla. Purple. GC. P994 23/7/1870 Exhibited at RHS Show at Oxford. Best fuchsias were from Mr. Mapplebeck of Birmingham. A seedling, exhibited as a 4½' conical. *Mapplebeck, Birmingham. GB. 1868?*

SHIRLEY HIBBERD. Double. Red/Purple. Tube. Crimson scarlet. Sepals. Crimson scarlet. Nicely recurved. Broad. Corolla. Purple. Named after a horticultural journalist (1825-90) and Editor of the Gardeners Magazine 1861-90. Laings Cat. (circa 1890). NK. NK. *GB. 1891?*

SHYLOCK. Single. Pink/Red. Tube. Light pink. Sepals. Light pink. Corolla. Rosy crimson striped rose. A decided improvement on "Beauty of Leeds". GC. P423 6/1851 Exhibited at RBS Show by H. Low. App. to RH. 1851 by Porcher. Mediocre. GC. P497 11/8/1849 Listed by G. Smith, Tollington Nurseries. GC. P274 4/5/1850 Listed by Bass & Brown, Sudbury. GC. P226 14/4/1849 Intro. by Turville, Chelmsford. *Turville, Chelmsford GB. 1849.*

SIDMOUTHII. Single. ND/ND. Tube. ND. Sepals. ND. Corolla. ND. Strong grower. Prolific bloomer. GC. P112 17/2/1844 & P66 1/2/1845 & P184 13/3/1847 Listed by W. Miller, Ramsgate. GC. P216 27/3/1847 Listed by R. Cooper, Croydon. GC. P265 24/4/1847 & P259 28/4/1849 Listed by W. Rendle, Plymouth. GC. P81 10/2/1844 Raised last year. *Bartlett, Sidmouth. GB. 1844.*

SIDONIA. Single. White/Purple. Tube. Blush white. Sepals. Blush white. Green tips. Well reflexed. Corolla. Violet purple. 3 times the size of "Venus Victrix" GC. P183 20/3/1852 "Select". GC. P199 19/3/1853 "Recommended". GC. P545 30/8/1851 Listed by G. Smith. GC. P69 12/6/1854 Listed by J. Moore, Birmingham. GC. P83 8/2/1851 Intro. by G. Smith, Tollington Nurseries. *Smith, G. Islington. GB. 1851.*

SIGNORA. Single. White/Purple. Tube. Whitish pink. Sepals. Whitish pink. Corolla. Violet washed rose and marked white. P119 4th Ed. by Porcher 1874 Similar to "Schiller" but flowers more larger. Vol P3 J of RHS P91 1863 Fuchsia trials at Chiswick 1862. Awarded **. A variety of fresh erect branching habit, blooming abundantly. It is in the way of "Rose of Castille" but purer in colour. *Banks, E. Deal. GB. 1862.*

SILISTRIA. Single. Red/Purple. Tube. Dark crimson. (Crimson red). Thick. Short. Sepals. Dark crimson. (Crimson red). Broadly reflexed. Corolla.

Dark purple marked light crimson at base. (Bluish violet veined red). Free bloomer. P113 4th Ed by Porcher 1874 Pedicel 50mm. Bell shaped. Well open. Expanded, 1st class. Multiflowered. B. Cat. 1872-1876. *Bull,W. Chelsea. GB. 1872.*

SILVER GLOBE. Single. White/Purple. Tube. White. Sepals. White. Expand well. Corolla. Lilac. Globe shaped flower. Compact. Tube and sepals more silvery and corolla more lilac than "Nymph". GC. 6/2/1847 & P183 13/3/1847 & P216 27/3/1847 & P232 1/4/1848 Listed by R. Cooper, Croydon. GC. P184 13/3/1847 Listed by W. Miller, Ramsgate. GC. P201 27/3/1847 Listed by Hart & Nicklin, Guildford. GC. P175 14/3/1846 Intro. by Hally, Blackheath. *Hally, Blackheath. GB. 1846.*

SILVERY BEAM. Double. Red/White. Tube. Carmine. Sepals. Carmine. Very broad. Beautifully reflexed. Corolla. White. B. Cat. 1877-1879. JF. Cat. 1885. *Bull,W. Chelsea. GB. 1877.*

SIMS REEVES. Single. Red/Purple. Tube. Rosy red. Large. Long. Sepals. Rosy red. Large. Same length as tube. Corolla. Violet red. Small. App. to RH. 1851 by Porcher. Named after the first English tenor 1818-1900. *Henderson,E.G.St. John's Wood. GB. 1850.*

SIR BARTLE FRERE. Single. Red/Purple. Tube. Carmine. (Bright Crimson red). (Purplish violet). Very large. P113 4th Ed. by Porcher. Pedicel 30mm. Bell shaped. 1st class. Named after a Governor of Bombay and the Cape (1815-1884). BSW Cat. 1878. GO. Select 1882-3. HC. Cat. 1882-1885. GC. P396 22/3/1873 Intro. by B.S. Williams, Holloway. GC. P146 1895 Blands Chronicle. *Bland, E. Fordham. GB. 1873.*

SIR BEVOIS. Double. Red/Purple. Tube. Dark scarlet. Sepals. Dark scarlet. Beautifully reflexed. Corolla. Intense dark violet. Expanded. GC. P287 31/3/1860 Intro. by W. Windebank, Bevois Valley Nursery, Southampton. For release on 1/5/1860 at 10/6d each. *Windebank, W. Southampton. GB. 1860.*

SIR CHARLES NAPIER. Single. Red/Purple. Tube. Red. Sepals. Red. Corolla. Purple. Much superior to "Colossus". Named after a British Admiral (1786-1860) who distinguished himself in the Napoleonic wars. GC. P497 11/8/1849 Listed by G. Smith, Islington. GC. P145 9/3/1850 Listed by W. Rumley, Richmond. GC. P210 6/4/1850 Listed by H. Walton, Burnley. GC. P274 4/5/1850 Listed by Bass & Brown, Sudbury. GC. P289 12/5/1849 Intro. by E. Tiley, Bath. *Tiley, E. Bath. GB. 1849.*

SIR COLIN CAMPBELL. Double. Red/Purple. Tube. Dark scarlet. Sepals. Dark scarlet. Corolla. Purple. Large. SG P459 1866 "Recommended". GC. P1331 1871 Grown as a bedder in Hyde Park. GC. P665 4/9/1858 Awarded an FCC by the National Floricultural Committee. Named after a distinguished English soldier, who is buried in Westminster Abbey. GC. P260 24/3/1860 Listed by Wm. Hussey, Norwich. GC. P426 12/5/1860 Listed by F. Godwin, Sheffield. P33 Florist 1858 Coloured Plate No 148. P3 J of RHS 1863 Fuchsia trials at Chiswick 1862 Awarded *** Best. A showy variety of fine free blooming habit. The flowers are of elegant form, with a longish slender tube, moderately reflexed red sepals and a dense compact corolla. One of the most ornamental kinds yet raised. GC. P234 19/3/1859 Intro. by G. Wheeler, Warminster. *Wheeler, G. Warminster. GB. 1859.*

SIR COUTTS T. LINDSAY. Double. Red/Purple. Tube. Carmine. Sepals. Carmine. Well reflexed. Corolla. Deep bluish purple. GC. P240 17/3/1866 Intro. by Downey, Laird & Lang, Stanstead Park, Forest Hill. SE. *Downie, Forest Hill. GB. 1866.*

SIR GARNET WOLSESLEY. Double. Red/ Purple. Tube. Bright flame. Sepals. Bright flame. Reflexed. Corolla. Deep purplish Violet. Base flaked bright scarlet. Named after a distinguished British soldier 1833-1913. P136 4th Ed. by Porcher 1874. P311 RH 1889 "Select" by E.A. Carrière. GO. "Select" 1880-1890. HC. Cat. 1882. Laing. Cat. circa 1890. BSW. Cat. 1878. GC. P363 21/3/1874 Intro. by B.S. Williams, Holloway. *Bland, E. Fordham. GB. 1874.*

SIR GEORGE MACKENZIE. Single. Red/Red. Tube. Bright vermilion. (Purple red). Very large. Sepals. Bright vermilion. (Purple red). Reflexed. Large. Corolla. Pink, of the finest form. (Crimson). P82 2nd Ed. by Porcher 1848. Recommended for its brilliant colours. GC. 7/2/1846 Intro. by Youell, Gt. Yarmouth. *Youell, Gt. Yarmouth GB. 1846.*

SIR HARRY SMITH. Single. White/ND. Tube. White. Sepals. White. Corolla. ND. Named after an English soldier 1788-1860. GC. P328 13/5/1848 Intro. by E. Mitchell, Bristol Nursery, Brighton. *Mitchell, E. Brighton. GB. 1848.*

SIR H. POTTINGER. Single. Pink/Purple. Tube. Light flesh. Slightly veined pink. Sepals. Light flesh. Well expanded.(Only open a little). Corolla. Dark crimson purple. P82 2nd Ed. by Porcher 1848 45mm. Nice variety. GC. P455 8/7/1847 Exhibited at LHS show by W. Bray, Gr. to Mr. Goldsmid. P145 J of RHS 1892 Sent out by Ivery, raised by Mr. P

Cole. GC. P162 14/3/1846 & P184 13/3/1847 Listed by W. Miller, Ramsgate. GC. P201 27/3/1847 Listed by Hart & Nicklin, Guildford. GC. P216 27/3/1847 & P232 1/4/1848 Listed by R. Cooper, Croydon. GC. P224 14/4/1849 Listed by R. Whibley, Kennington Cross. GC. P226 13/4/1850 Listed by Poole Nurseries. GC. P113 22/2/1845 Intro. by Ivery, Peckham. *Cole, P. GB. 1845.*

SIR JOHN FALSTAFF. Single. Red/Purple. Tube. Red. Sepals. Red. Corolla. Purple. GC. P535 23/8/1851 Exhibited at Vauxhall Garden show. GC. P647 11/10/1851 Exhibited at RHS of Cornwall Show 9/9/1851 by F.H. Earle. GC. P387 15/6/1850 Listed by H. Walton, Burnley. GC. P465 27/8/1850 Listed by G. Smith, Islington. GC. P817 29/12/1849 Intro by C. Turner, Slough. *Hocken. GB. 1850.*

SIR J. PAXTON. ND. ND/ND. Tube. ND. Sepals. ND. Corolla. ND. Named after the English gardener and Architect, designer of the Crystal Palace. 1801-1863. GC. P147 11/3/1854 Listed by W. Rumley, Richmond "Best new varieties of 1853". NK. *NK. GB. 1853.*

SIR ROBERT PEEL (a). Single. Red/Purple. Tube. Red. Sepals. Red. Corolla. Purple. GC. P535 23/8/1851 Exhibited at Vauxhall Garden Show. App. to RH. 1851 by Porcher - mediocre. GC. P423 18/6/1851 Exhibited at RBS show by H. Low, Clapton Nurseries. Exhibited at LHS Show 11/7/1849 by Robinson. *Reid. GB. 1849*

SIR ROBERT PEEL (b). Single. Red/Purple. Tube. Bright red. Sepals. Bright red. Reflexed. Thick. Smooth. Corolla. Deep purple. Well expanded. Vol P3 J of RHS 1863 Fuchsia trials at Chiswick 1862. Awarded ***. Dwarfish growing sort. Firm branching habit. Small neat foliage. Named after an English statesman who reorganised the London Police. Hence Bobbies or Peelers, names given to the Police. GC. P653 9/7/1864 RBS Show 2/7/1864 Noted. *Banks, E. Deal. GB. 1860.*

SIR. R. SALE. Single. ND/ND. Tube. ND. Sepals. ND. Corolla. ND. Named after an English soldier 1782-1845. GC. P234 11/4/1846 Listed by A.J. Stewart, Windsor. GC. P66 1/2/1845 Listed by W. Miller, Ramsgate. *Bell, Thirsk. GB. 1845.*

SIR W. MAGNAY. Single. Red/Red. Tube. Reddish purple. Short. Sepals. Reddish Purple. Reflexed. Corolla. Dull vermilion. P82 2nd Ed. by Porcher 1848. GC. P113 22/2/1845 Far superior to "Stanwelliana". GC. P162 14/3/1846 & P184 13/3/1847 Listed by W. Miller, Ramsgate. GC.P217 27/3/1847 Listed by R. Cooper, Croydon. GC. P265

24/4/1847 & P259 28/4/1849 & P241 20/4/1850 Listed by W. Rendle, Plymouth. GC. P113 22/2/1845 Intro. by *W. Ivery. Cole. GB. 1845*

SIR W.G. ARMSTRONG. Single. Red/Purple. Tube. Deep red. Sepals. Deep red. Reflexed. Corolla. Bright dark blue marked light crimson at base. Very free blooming. GO. 1881 "Select" Named after an English inventor and engineer of Newcastle. Famous for his ordnance and heavy engineering. B. Cat. 1876. *Banks, E.Deal. GB. 1876.*

SKYLARK (a).Single. ND/ND. Tube. ND. Sepals. ND. Corolla. ND. GC. P145 9/3/1850 Listed by W. Rumley, Richmond. NK. NK. *GB. 1849.*

SKYLARK (b). Single. White/Purple. Tube. White. Sepals. White. Elegantly reflexed. Corolla. Bright plum purple. GC. P597 6/7/1868 Intro. by Felton & Holiday, Birmingham. *Felton. Birmingham. GB. 1868*

SMILAY. Single. Red/Red. Sepals. Red. Sepals. Red. Expanded. Corolla. Red. GC. P338 22/5/1847 Intro. by Turville, Chelmsford. *Turville. Chelmsford GB. 1847.*

SMITHII. Single. ND/ND. Tube. ND. Sepals. ND. Corolla. ND. GC. P393 June 1842 & P97 Feb 1843 & P98 17/2/1844 Listed by Youell, Gt. Yarmouth. GC. P473 1844 Listed by Wm. Wood, Uckfield. NK. NK. *GB. 1842.*

SNOWBALL. Single. White/Red. Tube. White, striped rose. Sepals. Pure white. Very long. Globular. Much larger than any yet sent out. Corolla. Crimson. GC. P162 14/3/1846 & P184 13/3/1847 Listed by W. Miller, Ramsgate. GC. P162 8/3/1845 Intro. by J. Hally, Blackheath. *Hally, J. Blackheath GB. 1845.*

SNOWCLOUD. Single. Red/White. Tube. Red. Sepals. Red. Corolla. White. GC. P599 5/11/1882 Advert by W. Hender of Plymouth states "Edelwiess" is far superior. NK. NK. *GB. NK.*

SNOWDROP (a). Single. White/Red, Tube. Creamy white. Sepals. Creamy white. Green tips. Corolla. Scarlet. Midland Florist P195 1847. GC. P281 1/5/1847 Purchased from the raiser, Mr. Brown Gr. to A Lowe, Highfield House, Nottingham. by W. Miller, Ramsgate and introduced by him. *Brown. Nottingham. GB. 1847.*

SNOWDROP (b). Single. ND/ND. Tube. ND. Sepals. ND. Corolla. ND. GC. P161 17/3/1849 & P145 9/3/1850 Listed by W. Rumley, Richmond. *Keynes. GB. 1848.*

SNOWDROP (c). Double. Red/White. Tube. Red. Sepals. Red. Corolla. White. GC. P18 13/1/1855 & P34 20/1/1855 Puchased from W. Story, but Luccombe and Pince of Exeter introduced "Galanthiflora plena" which is very similar to the above, which had been purchased from a jobbing gardener who had worked at W.H. Story's. GC. P114 24/2/1855 If the full set of nine are taken "Snowdrop" will be included. This was received from Mr. Story as having a double white corolla and described by himself and others who saw it in flower as a very beautiful variety. It was the first double white raised by him, but the plant did not flower in the Wellington Road nursery, after it was received by Hendersons, and though three stout branches had been broken off, it did not quite correspond with the description, given by Mr. Story and others a few months after, to Mr. A. Henderson, when at Newton making enquries respecting the plant. Consequently no charge will be made for it, but will be presented when every set is ordered. GC. P467 14/7/1855 Listed by Bass & Brown, Sudbury. GC. P467 14/7/1855 Listed by H. Walton, Burnley. GC. P529 11/8/1855 Listed by W.J. Epps, Maidstone. GC. P530 11/8/1855 & P208 22/3/1856 Listed by Bainbridge & Hewison, York. GC. P531 11/8/1851 Listed by Joseph Courcha. *Story,W.H. Newton Abbot GB. 1855.*

SNOWDROP (d). Single. White/Purple. Tube. White. Short. Swollen, Sepals. White. Corolla. Rosy lilac. Vol P1 J of RHS 1860 Floral Committee report. *Banks, E. Deal. GB. 1860.*

SNOWDROP (e). ND. Red/White. Tube. Red. Sepals. Red. Corolla. White. P133 4th Ed. by Porcher 1874 Not in the first selection. *Henderson, E.G. St. Johns Wood. GB. 1868.*

SNOWDROP (f). S/Double. Red/White. Tube. Red. Sepals. Red. Corolla. White. Petticoat shape. Long globular buds. Vol 22 GC. P295 1897 New from J. Lye. GC. P342 Vol 24 J of RHS 1900. *Lye, J. Market Lavington. GB. 1897.*

SNOWDROP (g). Single. Red/White. Tube. Scarlet. Sepals. Scarlet. Corolla. Pure white. Long. GC. P344 4/4/1868 Intro. by B.W, Knight, Battle. *Knight, B.W. Battle. GB. 1868.*

SOCIAL. Single. Red/White. Tube. Crimson. Sepals. Crimson. Reflexed. Corolla. Pure white. B. Cat. 1870-1873. *Bull, W. Chelsea. GB. 1869.*

SOCRATE. Single. Red/White. Tube. Red. Sepals. Red. Corolla. White. Expanded. Large. P136 Appendix to 4th Ed. by Porcher 1874. New for 1875. *Lemoine. Nancy. France. 1875.*

169

SOCRATES. Single. Red/Purple. Tube. Rose carmine. Sepals. Rose carmine. Corolla. Violet plum. BSW. Cat. 1878. NK. NK. *GB.* NK.

SOLFERINO (a). Single. Red/Purple. Tube. Bright red. Short. Sepals. Bright red. (Crimson red). Perpendicular reflexed. Corolla. Rich purple, veined crimson. Florist 1860 P89 Colour plate. Dwarf. Free flowering. Long. Vol P1 J of RHS 1859 Commended 25/7/1859. In the habit of "Souvenir de Chiswick" Vol 1 J of RHS 1861. GC. P594 30/6/1860 Listed by F. Godwin, Sheffield. GC. P93 4/2/1860 Intro. by G. Smith, Tollington Nurseries. *Smith, G. Islington. GB. 1860.*

SOLFERINO (b). Double. Red/Purple. Tube. Red. Sepals. Red. Lay on Corolla. Corolla. Purple. Illustrated in Flore des Serres. Gold Medal Societe Imperial D'Horticulture. Vol 7 P251 L'Illustration Horticole Coloured Plate. P127 4th Ed. by Porcher 1874 Not in the first selection. Vol P3 J of RHS 1863 Fuchsia trials at Chiswick. A slender free habited sort with recurved red sepals and a small purple corolla. GC. P771 24/8/1861 Listed by H. Marsden, Burnley. *Lemoine. Nancy. France. 1860.*

SOLON. Single. Red/Purple. Tube. Bright crimson red. Sepals. Bright crimson red. Perpendicular reflexed. Corolla. Purple with crimson veining at base, becomes reddish with age. Florist P89 1860 Coloured plate. P1 J of RHS 1859 Floral Committee. Large flowers. Dwarf . Free flowering. FF & GM 1860. *Smith, G. Islington. GB. 1860.*

SOUTH DEVON. Single. Red/Purple. Tube. Bright red. Rather thin. Sepals. Bright red. Pointed and twice the height of the tube. Corolla. Dark violet. Large. Showy. Beautifully proportioned. GC. P226 18/4/1850 Light blue. Compact. GC. P387 15/6/1850 Listed by H. Marsden, Burnley. GC. P632 6/10/1849 Intro. by Veitch, Exeter. *Story, W.H. Newton Abbot. GB. 1860.*

SOUVENIR DE CHISWICK. Single. Red/Purple. Tube. Red. Sepals. Red. 1?". Reflexed. Corolla. Reddish purple,prominent. GC. P580 9/7/1858 & P607 16/7/1858 Exhibited at RBS Show by H. Cannell Gr to E. Grove, Tulse Hill. SG P459 1886 "Recommended". Vol P3 J of RHS 1863 Fuchsia trials at Chiswick Awarded ***. Flowers are rather long tubed. Broad reflexed sepals. Moderately expanded corolla. GC. P515 25/7/1857 & P418 22/5/1858. Listed by H. Walton, Burnley. GC. P357 7/4/1858 Listed by C.E. Allen, Stoke Newington. GC. P260 24/3/1860 Listed by Wm. Hussey, Norwich. GC. P210 28/3/1857 Intro. by E. G. Henderson, St. Johns Wood. *Banks, E. Deal. GB. 1857.*

SOUVENIR DE CORNELISSEN. Double. Red/Purple. Tube. Red. Sepals. Red. Corolla. Purple. P127 4th Ed. by Porcher 1874 Not in the first selection. RH. P295 1887 Fuchsias grown as standards at Twickel. *Cornelissen. Arras. Belgium. 1864.*

SOUVENIR DE GENDBRUGGE. Double. Red/Purple. Tube. Red. Short. Sepals. Red. Reflexed or introverted. Corolla. Violet blue streaked red. P132 4th Ed. by Porcher 1874. Vigorous bush. Medium dark green foliage. Pedicel 30mms. Flower buds in the shape of small bells. A feature is the expansion of the flower but does not open well and is not floriferous. *Coene. Ghent. Belgium. 1869.*

SOUVENIR DE H. HENKEL. Single. Red/Red. Tube. Crimson red. Long. Sepals. Crimson red. Corolla. Crimson red. Hybrid of triphylla by another species. Col pl. Revue Horticole 1909. p.180. L. Cat. 1902. Triphylla X. *Henkel. Germany. 1902.*

SOUVENIR DE LA REINE. Single. Red/Red. Tube. Bright rosy Crimson. 1" long. Sepals. Rosy crimson. White tips. Corolla. Rosy carmine. Blossoms have a strong likeness to F. Cordata. P234 Vol 5 Gartenflora ? Serratifolia X. FC.P98 1854 Exhibited at Florale de Societe d'Horticulture at Gand 1853. GC. P368 26/5/1855 Intro. by E.G. Henderson, St Johns Wood. *Coene. Ghent. Belgium. 1853*

SOUVENIR DE MRS TODMAN. Single. Red/Purple. Tube. Rosy carmine. Sepals. Rosy carmine. Corolla. Bright purple. (indigo). Laings Cat. circa 1890. BSW. Cat. 1897. NK. *GB.* NK.

SPANISH INFANTA. Single. Pink/Red. Tube. Light flesh. Large Sepals. Light flesh. Large. Bent inwards. Corolla. Vermillion red to purple. App. to RH 1851 by Porcher 1st class variety. GC. P120 23/2/1850 "Select". GC. P256 21/4/1849 Listed by R.Cooper, Croydon. GC. P274 5/5/1849 Listed by H. Walton, Burnley. GC. P153 4/3/1848 Intro. by Kendall, Stoke Newington. *Kendall. Stoke Newington. GB. 1848.*

SPARTAN. Double. Red/Purple. Tube. Dark crimson. Sepals. Dark crimson. Horizontal. Corolla. Purplish plum. B. Cat. 1875-1876. *Bull,W. Chelsea. GB. 1873.*

SPECIAL. Single. Red/Purple. Tube. Bright red. Sepals. Bright red. Reflex to tube. Corolla. Bright blue marked red at base. Large. GC. P952 11/10/1862 Intro. by W. Bull, Chelsea. *Bull,W. Chelsea. GB. 1862.*

170

SPECIOSA. Single. ND/ND. Tube. ND. Sepals. ND. Corolla. ND. GC. P610 2/9/1843 Exhibited at Devon & Exeter Bot. Scty. Show on 28/7/1843 by Veitch, Exeter. GC. P438 6/7/1854 Exhibited at RBS Show, Regents Park by Mr. Bray as a 7 ft. pyramid. GC. P66 1/2/1845 Listed by W. Miller, Ramsgate. HC. Cat. P89 1885 Orange yellow flowers. A very free flowering and showy variety. *Veitch. Exeter. GB. 1843.*

SPECTABLIS. Single. Red/ND. Tube. Cerise red. Short. Sepals. Cerise red. Twice as long as the tube. Pendant. Corolla. ND. P52 2nd Ed. by Porcher Small 3cms. Erect habit. Oval leaves. Dull green. Mediocre. GC. P242 11/4/1843 Listed by A.J. Stewart, Windsor. GC. P112 17/2/1844 Listed by W. Miller, Ramsgate. *Harrison. Dereham. GB. 1842.*

SPITFIRE. Single. Red/Purple. Tube. Bright scarlet red. Sepals. Bright scarlet red. Corolla. Pale purple. (Deep magenta). GC. P824 27/2/1885 Fuchsia trials at Chiswick "Best in class". JF. Cat. 1885 Large bold flower. HC. Cat. 1885. Very showy and distinct. NK. NK. *GB.* NK.

SPLENDENS (a). Single. Red/Purple. Tube. Red. Sepals. Red. Upturn slightly. Corolla. Purple. Vol 3 Floral Cabinet P192 1835. NK. NK. *GB. 1835.*

SPLENDENS (b). Single. ND/ND. Tube. ND. Sepals. ND. Corolla. ND. GC. P431 24/6/1843 HS. Show London Exhibited by Catleugh. A large flower but deficient in colour. GC. P481 15/7/1843 HS. Show 12/7/1843 exhibited by Catleugh. Does not seem to open too well. *Salter, J. Versailles. France. 1842.*

SPLENDIDA (a). Single. Red/Red. Tube. Red. Sepals. Red. Corolla. Red. JofH. P25 1849 "Best". GC. P393 6/1842, P97 2/1843. P98 17/2/1844, P146 8/3/1845 Listed by Youell, Gt. Yarmouth. GC. P184 13/3/1847 Listed by W. Miller, Ramsgate. GC. P705 1843 Listed by J. Whiteley, Wakefield. NK. NK. *GB. 1842.*

SPLENDIDA (b). Single. Red/Purple. Tube. Bright red. Thin. Short. Sepals. Bright red. Fully reflexed along the length of the tube. Corolla. Purple. GC. P199 19/3/1853 Recommended. GC. P535 23/8/1851 Exhibited at Vauxhall Garden Show. App to RH. 1851 by Porcher. Small flowers. From "Criterion", but the flowers are a little too small. CG. Vol III P272 1850 For exhibition. GC. P256 21/4/1849 Listed by R. Cooper, Croydon. GC. P145 9/3/1850 Listed by W. Rumley, Richmond. GC. P210 6/4/1850 Listed by H. Walton, Burnley. GC. P274 4/5/1850 Listed by Bass & Brown, Sudbury.

GC. P209 7/4/1849 Purchased from J. Wilmore and introduced by H. Low, Clapton. *Wilmore, J. Birmingham. GB. 1849.*

SPLENDIDISSIMA. Single. Red/Purple. Tube. Crimson. Sepals. Crimson. Well reflexed. Corolla. Purple Violet. Large. GC. P279 30/4/1853 "Dark wooded stem". GC. P130 21/2/1852 Raised by either J. Smith, manager of Whalley's Nursery, or a celebrated amateur from the North of England. GC. P449 17/7/1852 & P209 26/3/1853 Listed by H. Walton, Burnley. GC. P307 14/5/1853 & P369 11/6/1853 Listed by Ben. R. Cant, Colchester. GC. P248 18/4/1854 Listed by Mitchell & Co. Kemptown, Brighton. GC. P130 21/2/1852 Intro. by E.G. Henderson. NK. NK. *GB. 1852.*

SPLENDISSIMA. Single. Red/Purple. Tube. Crimson. Very long. Sepals. Crimson. Corolla. Crimson purple. Very large. GC. P66 1/2/1845. Listed by W. Miller, Ramsgate. *Miller, W. Ramsgate GB. 1845.*

SPLENDOUR. Single. Red/Purple. Tube. Scarlet. Sepals. Scarlet. Reflex to a perfect crown. Corolla. Dark purple. Long. Spreading. Immense. GC. P488 9/4/1870. FW & GG Jan 1870. GC. P1554 2/12/1872 Review by H. Cannell. B. Cat. 1870. F&P. Mar 1870 Colour Plate. Diameter of expanded corolla is 3". Intro. by H. Cannell. *Banks, E. Deal. GB. 1870.*

STANDARD (a). Single. ND/ND. Tube. ND. Sepals. ND. Corolla. ND. GC. P449 17/7/1852 & P209 26/3/1853 Listed by H. Walton, Burnley. GC. P211 26/3/1853 Listed by W. Rumley, Richmond. *Turner, C. Slough. GB. 1852.*

STANDARD (b). Single. Red/Purple. Tube. Rosy Pink. Great length. Sepals. Cherry pink tipped white. Very broad. 2" long. Corolla. Rich violet purple, flamed deep rose. Large. B. Cat. 1872-1878. GC. P476 15/4/1871 Intro. by W. Bull, Chelsea. *Bull, W. Chelsea. GB. 1871.*

STANDARD OF PERFECTION (a). Single. Red/Purple. Tube. Scarlet. Sepals. Scarlet. Corolla. Purple. GC. P151 5/3/1853 Good for exhibition. GC. P199 19/3/1853 "Recommended". GC. P706 9/11/1850 Listed by H. Walton, Burnley. GC. P289 11/5/1850. Intro. by Mayle, Birmingham. *Mayle. Birmingham. GB. 1850.*

STANDARD OF PERFECTION (b). Single. Red/Purple. Tube. Bright waxy coral red. Sepals. Waxy coral red. Reflexed. Corolla. Dense violet blue slightly veined purple. Very stout. Blooms as large as

171

"Don Giovanni". GC. P449 17/7/1852 & P209 26/3/1853 Listed by H. Walton, Burnley. GC. P211 26/3/1853 Listed by W. Rumley, Richmond. GC. P307 14/5/1853 & P369 11/6/1853 Listed by Benj. R. Cant, Colchester. GC. P32 10/1/1852 Intro by W.J. Epps, Maidstone. *Epps W.J., Maidstone. GB. 1852.*

STANDISHII. Single. Red/Purple. Tube. Red. Sepals. Red. Corolla. Purple. GC 23/1/1841 "Best new plant". GC. 8/5/1841 Listed by J. May Edmonton. GC. 13/2/1841 Listed by W. Masters, Canterbury. GC P289 29/5/1841 Listed by H. Low, Upper Clapton. GC. P630 25/9/1841. GC. P668 11/10/1841 Exhibited by Messrs. Keefe at RHS of Ireland show. GC. P668 11/10/1841 Exhibited at RHS of Cornwall show. GC. P393 6/1842 & P97 2/1843 & P98 17/2/1844 Listed by Youell, Gt. Yarmouth. F. fulgens X. *Standish, Bagshot. GB. 1840.*

STANLEY. Double. Red/Purple. Tube. Bright rose. Sepals. Bright rose. Broad. Reflexing. Corolla. Dark blue. GC. P1054 7/11/1863. Intro. by W. Bull. Chelsea, 10/6d. *Bull,W. Chelsea. GB. 1863.*

STANWELLIANA. Single. Pink/Red. Tube. Red. Sepals. Red. Reflexed. Corolla. Lake. (Blush). RH. P168 1857 Globular. Leaves very dentate. RH. P24 1846. GC. P513 29/7/1843 Listed by H. Low, Clapton. GC. P98 17/2/1844 & P146 18/3/1845 Listed by Youells. GC. P112 17/2/1844 & P184 13/3/1847 & P66 1/2/1845 Listed by W. Miller, Ramsgate. GC. 28/3/1846 Listed by J&S Schilling, Odiham. GC.P497 22/7/1843 Intro. by T. Cripps. Tunbridge Wells. *Cripps, T. Tunbridge Wells. GB. 1843.*

STAR. Double. Red/Purple. Tube. Red. Short. Sepals. Red. Well reflexed. Corolla. Purple. GC. P690 18/10/1856 & P146 7/3/1857 Listed by W. Rumley, Richmond. GC. P51 26/1/1856 To be sent out in May by W. Fuller, Newton Bushell, formerly gardener to W.H. Story of Whitehill. GC. P690 18/10/1856 & P146 7/3/1857 Listed by W. Rumley, Richmond. *Story, W.H. Newton Abbot. GB. 1856.*

STARLIGHT. Single. White/Red. Tube. White. Sepals. White. Spreading. Green tips. Blushed. Corolla. Clear lake. Pcvi J of RHS Vol III 1872. RHS Trials at Chiswick. Good habit. Free blooming. Awarded ***. P67 J of RHS 1877 Fuchsia trial at Chiswick 1873 Awarded FCC. A fine variety, not sufficiently known. It has the same habit as "Lady Heytesbury", but the corolla is a bright carmine lake. It is a first class fuchsia. P215 Vol 4 J of RHS. Chiswick trials. Awarded FCC. Free growing, free

blooming, excellent habit. Large flowers. G. P473 12/1867 New. B. Cat. 1870-1873. GO "Select" 1880-1891. HC. Cat. 1882. *Bull,W. Chelsea. GB. 1868.*

STAR OF THE NIGHT. Single. Red/Purple. Tube. Carmine. Sepals. Carmine. Recurved. (Reflexed round). Corolla. Violet purple. (Bluish violet veined red). Expanded. 1½" across. Finely cupped. JH&CG. P406 1864 Dark. Well cupped. P113 4th Ed. by Porcher 1874 This variety along with "Lord Elcho" are the two best varieties known and are again superior to certain novelties. Similar to "Prophète". Pedicel 60 mms. Vol P3 J of RHS 1863 Fuchsia trials at Chiswick 1862. A variety of erect bushy habit with dark coloured shoots. Flowers are of a bright red purple having small recurved sepals and a large expanded corolla. RH. P295 1887 Grown as a standard at Twickel, Nr. Arnhem. GC. P515 25/7/1857 & P418 22/5/1858 & P771 24/8/1861 Listed by H. Walton, Burnley. See also GC. P283 25/4/1857. GC. P357 7/4/1858 Listed by C.E. Allen, Stoke Newington. GC. P594 29/6/1861 Listed by Godwin & Padman, Sheffield. GC. P210 28/3/1857 To be sent out in May. Intro. by E.G. Henderson, St. Johns Wood. *Banks, E. Deal. GB. 1857.*

STAR OF THE WEST. Single. White/Purple. Tube. White. Sepals. White. Corolla. Deep purple. P195 Midland Florist 1847 An improvement on Smith's "Queen Victoria". Deep rose tinted at base. GC. P286 16/4/1848 Listed by C. Rogers, Uttoxeter. GC. P224 14/4/1849 Listed by R. Whibley, Kennington Cross. GC. P259 28/4/1849 & P259 20/4/1850 Listed by W. Rendle, Plymouth. GC. P249 27/4/1847 Intro. by W. Rendle, Plymouth. *Passingham, Truro. GB. 1847.*

STAR OF WILTS. Single. White/Purple. Tube. Cream. Sepals. Cream. Corolla. Violet with a distinct margin of orange. G. 6/9/1884 Exhibited at Trowbridge Hort. Scty. Show 20/8/1884 by J. Lye, 1st 4 pot class. GC. P310 6/9/1884 Exhibited at Bath Floral Fete by J. Lye. 1st 9 pot class. HC. Cat. 1882 A pretty and effective variety. GC. Vol 23 1885 P209 Fig. 39 Illustration. L. Cat. 1890. B. Cat 1879-1880. *Lye, J. Market Lavington. GB. 1879.*

STARTLER. Double. Red/Purple. Tube. Rose crimson. Sepals. Rose crimson. Reflexed. Corolla. Rich purple striped and flaked rosy carmine. B. Cat. 1882-1883 Intro. by W. Bull. Chelsea. JF. Cat. 1885. *Eckford. GB. 1882.*

STATUAIRE DALON. Double. Red/Purple. Tube. Coral red. Sepals. Bright coral red. Twisted. Corolla. Violet with a rosy base. Enormous. Globular. L. Cat. 1901. JF. Cat 1901. *Lemoine, Nancy. France. 1900.*

172

ST. CLARE. Single. Red/Purple. Tube. Bright carmine. 3" long. Sepals. Bright carmine. Corolla. Rosy purple. GC. P633 24/9/1842 Raised by Mr. Meehan (actually Mr. Meehan's son), Gardener to Col. Harcourt of St Clare, IOW. GC. P83, 1900. Conference on hybridisation. Several dozen plants were raised, all being from one berry, but no two of the seedlings were alike. Some nearly approached the female, others the male parent. None could fairly be said to be intermediate. GC. P97 18/2/1843 & P98 17/2/1844 & P146 8/3/1845 Listed by Youell, Gt. Yarmouth. GC. P112 17/2/1844 Listed by W. Miller, Ramsgate. F.fulgens X Longiflora. *Meehan, St. Clare. GB. 1842.*

STEPHEN PINCHON. Double. Red/Purple. Tube. Coral red. Sepals. Coral red. Large. Corolla. Plum Violet. Extended. Enormous. Full. L. Cat. 1901. *Lemoine, Nancy. France. 1901.*

STEWARTII. Single. ND/ND. Tube. ND. Sepals. ND. Corolla. ND. GC. P202 26/3/1842 Sale by Auction, the property of Mr. Henbury, a well known florist. GC. P97 2/1843 & P98 17/2/1844. Listed by Youell, Gt. Yarmouth. NK. NK. *GB. 1841.*

STORMONTII. Single. ND/ND. Tube. ND. Sepals. ND. Corolla. ND. P52 2nd Ed. by Porcher 1848. Upright habit. Leaves similar to "Globosa", oval, acuminate and dentate. GC. P369 3/6/1844 Listed by T. Cripps. Tunbridge Wells. GC P375 4/6/1844 Exhibited by Catleugh at the HS Show. NK. NK. *GB. 1843.*

STRADELLA. Single. Red/Purple. Tube. Scarlet. Sepals. Scarlet. Corolla. Violet tinted black. Occasionally striped. Vol P3 J of RHS 1863 Fuchsia trials at Chiswick 1862. A red and purple with reflexed sepals and a small corolla. GC. P426 12/5/1860 Listed by F. Godwin, Sheffield. GC. P165 26/3/1859 Intro. by E.G. Henderson, St. Johns Wood. *Banks, E. Deal. GB. 1859.*

STRIATA (a). Single. Red/Red. Tube. Red. Sepals. Red. Corolla. Crimson, striped with purple like a flake Carnation. Florist 3/1850 Illustrated. GC. P632 6/10/1849. App. to RH. 1851 by Porcher. This is considered a very beautiful variety with streaked flowers are partly red and violet. GC. P201 1875 In the opinion of Mr. Porcher nothing after the one from Story until "Carl Halt" 1869 and "Striata Perfecta". GC. P387 15/6/1850 Listed by H. Walton, Burnley. GC. P465 27/7/1850 & P144 8/3/1851 Listed by W. Rumley, Richmond. GC. P465 27/7/1850 Listed by G. Smith, Islington. GC. P568 8/9/1849 & GC. P226 13/4/1850 Intro. and listed by Veitch & Co. Exeter. *Story, W.H. Newton Abbot. GB. 1849.*

STRIATA (b). Single. Red/Purple. Tube. Bright vermilion. Sepals. Bright vermilion. Finely reflexed. Corolla. Dark violet plum striped and shaded rose scarlet. GC. P594 29/6/1861 Listed by Godwin & Padman, Sheffield. GC. P771 24/8/1861 Listed by H. Walton, Burnley. GC. P140 16/2/1861 Intro. by F&A Smith, Dulwich. *Smith F. Dulwich GB. 1861.*

STRIATA FLORA PLENO. ND. ND/ND. Tube. ND. Sepals. ND. Corolla. ND. GC. P338 15/4/1865 Listed by W. Rumley, Richmond. NK. NK. NK. *1864.*

STRIATA FORMOSISSIMA. Single. Red/Purple. Tube. Coral red. Sepals. Coral red. Corolla. Amarinth strongly striped with white and pink. RH. P170 1857. *Coene. Ghent. Belgium. 1856.*

STRIATA INCOMPARIBLE. Single. ND/ND. Tube. ND. Sepals. ND. Corolla. ND. P133 4th Ed. by Porcher 1874 Not in the first selection. Inconsistancy in the petals. *Twrdy, Brno. Austria 1868.*

STRIATA PERFECTA (a). Single. Red/Purple. Tube. Crimson. Very short. Sepals. Crimson. Large. Horizontal. Points raised. Corolla. Pale Violet washed white, banded and striped pink. P132 4th Ed. by Porcher Sometimes the petals are only of the principal shade. Although not perfect it is a nice variety. P70 Vol 4 J of RHS 1877 Fuchsia trials at Chiswick. Very free flowering, but the corolla is ragged. No award. B. Cat. 1870-1873 Bloomed for 3 years to prove its constancy. Beautifully marked from top to bottom of corolla. Scarlet and Light mauve striped scarlet. BSW. Cat. 1878. *Banks, E. Deal. GB. 1868.*

STRIATA PERFECTA (b). Single. White/Red. Tube. Waxy white Sepals. Waxy white. Corolla. Bright carmine striped with broad lines of pure white. GC. P1554 2/12/1871 Review by H. Cannell. This is a continental variety. First light tube with a striped corolla. P132 4th Ed by Porcher 1874 Under this name Williams has sent out a variety identical with "Carl Halt" It is a turn up of the German variety and is not new. Tube and sepals yellowish white long tube 20mms. Sepals tinged with rose. Large. Reflexed. Corolla vermilion, spotted with white. It is bizarre. According to Bland this was raised by him and introduced by Williams in 1870. GC. P276 29/8/1874 Exhibited at Belfast. Pcxiii Vol 3 J of RHS 1872. Fuchsia trials at Chiswick 1872. Flowers large. Tube greenish. Sepals 1". Spreading, strongly tipped with green. Corolla 1" bright red with medium flame of white, crumpled and folded inside, pinkish edged with red. An inferior sort. GC. P486

9/4/1870 Intro. by B. S. Williams. *Bland, E. Fordham. GB. 1870.*

STRIATA SPLENDIDA. Single. Red/Purple. Tube. Dark scarlet. Sepals. Dark scarlet. Corolla. Plum striped red. BSW. Cat. 1878. HC. Cat. 1882-1890 Most regularly striped yet sent out. Sepals completely reflexed. GO. "Select" 1883-1891. P133 4th Ed. by Porcher 1874 Tube and sepals crimson red. Well reflexed. Large petals. *Banks, E. Deal. GB. 1872.*

STRIPED QUEEN. Single. Red/Purple. Tube. Red. Long. Narrow. Sepals. Red. Slightly spreading. Corolla. Purple. Small. Slightly striped. Vol P3 J of RHS 1863 Fuchsia trials at Chiswick 1862, submitted by Scott. GC. P571 24/7/1858 Listed by H. Walton, Burnley. NK. NK. *GB. 1858.*

STRIPED UNIQUE. Double. Red/Purple. Tube. Bright crimson. Thick. 20mm long. Sepals. Bright crimson. Large. Reflexed round. Corolla. Dark violet blue, striped and variegated with red. P133 4th Ed. by Porcher 1874. P76 HC. Cat. 1882 A most conspicuous flower with bright scarlet stripes running 3 parts of the way down the corolla. GO. "Select" 1883-1884. *Smith, G. Islington. GB. 1868.*

STUPENDOUS. Double. Red/Purple. Tube. Bright scarlet. Sepals. Bright scarlet. Corolla. Dark purple plum. Immense. Very Large. B. Cat. 1875-1876. P135 4th Ed. by Porcher. RH. P2951887 Grown as a standard at Twickel, Nr. Arnhem. *Bland, E. Fordham. GB. 1873.*

STYLOSA CONSPICUA. Single. ND/ND. Tube. ND. Sepals. ND. Corolla. ND. GC. 8/5/1841 Listed by James May, Edmonton. GC. 23/1/1841 Best new plant. GC. P630 25/9/1841 GC. P393 6/1842 Illustrated Florists Magazine 1840/41 p.16. col pl L1. Listed by Youell, Gt.Yarmouth. F. fulgens X. *May, W. Bedale. GB. 1840.*

STYLOSA ELEGANS. Single. ND/ND. Tube. ND. Sepals. ND. Corolla. ND. GC. P393 6/1842 & P97 2/1843 & P98 17/2/1844 Listed by Youell, Gt. Yarmouth. GC. P112 17/2/1844 Listed by W. Miller, Ramsgate. NK. NK. *GB. 1840.*

STYLOSA MAXIMA. Single. Red/Red. Tube. Bright vermilion Sepals. Bright vermilion. Corolla. Bright red. GC. P337 26/5/1842 Intro. by James May, Tottenham. Seedling from "Stylosa conspicua" The flowers are longer and more globular. GC. P393 6/1842 & P97 2/1843 & P98 2/1844 & P146 8/3/1845 Listed by Youell, Gt.Yarmouth. Stylosa Conspica X Fulgens. *May, W. Bedale. GB. 1842.*

STYLOSA SUPERBA. Single. ND/ND Tube. ND. Sepals. ND. Corolla. ND. GC. P833 18/12/1841 "Recommended Best 6" NK. NK. *GB. 1840.*

SULLY-PRUDHOMME. Double. Red/Purple. Tube. Blood red. Sepals. Blood red. Broad. Reflexed. Corolla. Rich purple. Full. Enormous. Named after a French poet 1839-1907. L. Cat. 1902. *Lemoine. Nancy. France. 1902.*

SULTAN (a). Single. ND/ND. Tube. ND. Sepals. ND. Corolla. ND. GC. P162 14/3/1846 & P184 13/3/1847 Listed by W. Miller, Ramsgate. *Miller, W. Ramsgate. GB. 1846.*

SULTAN (b). Single. Red/Purple. Tube. Scarlet. (Crimson red). Waxy. Short. Stout. Sepals. Scarlet. (Crimson red). Well reflexed. (Reflexed round). Corolla. Deep violet, splashed and striped red at base. (Bluish violet). (Light purple changing early to reddish purple). Bell shaped. Well expanded. Good colour. P113 4th Ed by Porcher 1874. Pedicel 60 mm. Vol 4 J of RHS P70 1877 Fuchsia trials at Chiswick 1873. No award. Habit robust but not desirable and not a very free bloomer. B. Cat. 1870-1873. GC. P294 26/2/1870 Intro. by G. Smith. Islington. *Smith, G. Islington. GB. 1870.*

SULTAN (c). Double. Red/Purple. Tube. Red. Sepals. Red. Corolla. Plum violet marked red. Full. L. Cat. 1913. *Rozain. Lyons. France. 1912.*

SULTANA. Single. ND/ND. Tube. ND. Sepals. ND. Corolla. ND. GC. P265 22/4/1848 Intro. by J. Smith, Dalston. *Smith, J. Dalston. GB. 1848.*

SUNRAY. Single. Red/Purple. Tube. Scarlet. Short and thick. Sepals. Scarlet. Horizontal. Corolla. Light purple. P134 4th Ed. by Porcher 1874. Red white and green foliage. Corolla Amarinth red. Spiralled. Mediocre. GC. P151 1/2/1873. Listed by J. Leigh, Sandy Lane, Lowton, Lancs. GC. P432 6/4/1872 Being sent out by H. Milner, Bradford. FCC RHS 10/7/1871. GC. P264 26/8/1875 Raised by G. Rudd of Undercliffe, Bradford, who made the cross "Cloth of Gold" x with a cultivar with a white tube and sepals and a red corolla. Several seedlings came from the cross, but Mr. Rudd observed a spot of white on the leaf of one of them. He cut the plant back to that particular leaf in the Autumn. The next Spring the plant broke into the lovely variegated plant now called Sunray. GO.1881 "Select". Vol 4 J of RHS P70 1877 Fuchsia trials at Chiswick 1873. No award. Habit compact and branching. Small flowers not reflexed. A good grower and distinct in foliage. P218 Vol 4 J of RHS Chiswick trials 1877. Finest yet sent out FCC for variegation. HC.

Cat.1882. (See also Rainbow 1877). (Sunray often reverts to a green leaf cultivar with identical flowers Ed). Dobbies Cat. 1893-1894. BSW. Cat. 1897. JF. Cat. 1888. B. Cat. 1872-1881. *Rudd, Bradford. GB. 1873.*

SUNSET. Single. Pink/Red. Tube. Pale rose. Sepals. Pale rose. Horizontal. Corolla. Vermilion red, shaded purple. App. to RH. 1851 by Porcher. The principal merit is the colour of the corolla. *Low, H., Clapton. GB. 1849.*

SUNSHINE (a). Single. Red/Purple. Tube. Pure carmine rose. (Scarlet). (Crimson red). Almost non existant. Sepals. Pure carmine rose. (Scarlet). (Crimson red). Reflex. Corolla. Rosy lavender or mauve. (Clear violet washed rose and white). Expanded. GC. P1015 22/10/1864 Seen at B.S. Williams nursery. CG. P257 1865 Best of the 1864 varieties. SG. P459 1866 Dwarf compact habit. Prolific flowering. GC. P55 19/1/1867 Review by H. Cannell. P113 4th. Ed. by Porcher. Pedicel 30-35 mm. Vol 2 J of RHS 1870 Fuchsia trials at Chiswick. Passed over. *Banks, E. Deal. GB. 1864.*

SUNSHINE (b). Single. White/Red. Tube. Creamy white. Sepals. Delicate blush. Corolla. Bright carmine. GO. 1889 New for 1889 from B.S. Williams. HC. Cat. 1890. JF. Cat 1888. Laings Cat. 1890. B. Cat 1888. BSW Cat. 1888. *Lye,J. Market Lavington. GB. 1888*

SUPERB (a). Single. Red/Purple. Tube. Crimson. Sepals. Crimson. Corolla. Blue. Florists Journal 1843 T13.52 Coloured plate. An improvement on Globosa. Raised by C. Matlock Gr at Herne House Derbyshire. GC. P112 17/2/1844 Listed by W. Miller, Ramsgate. *Matlock, Derbys. GB. 1843.*

SUPERB (b). ND. ND/ND. Tube. ND. Sepals. ND. Corolla. ND. GC. P778 23/10/1858 Listed by H. Walton, Burnley. NK. *GB. 1858.*

SURPASS. ND. ND/ND. Tube. ND. Sepals. ND. Corolla. ND. GC. P162 14/3/1846 Listed by W. Miller, Ramsgate. NK. NK. *GB. 1845.*

SUPASSE VANQUEUR DE PUEBLA. Double. Red/White. Tube. Crimson Red. 75 mm long. Sepals. Crimson red. Reflex round. Corolla. Pure white, striped at the base with bright pink. P130 4th Ed. by Porcher 1874. A good variety with an astonishing floriferousness, and florists are impressed with its ability to replace "Madame and Marie Cornelissen". *Boucharlet,L. Lyons France 1867.*

SUPREME. Single. Red/White. Tube. Scarlet crimson. Sepals. Scarlet crimson. Reflexed. Corolla. Pure white. Free bloomer. B. Cat. 1870. NK. NK. *GB. 1870.*

SURPRISE (a). Single. ND/ND. Tube. ND. Sepals. ND. Corolla. ND. GC. P146 8/3/1845 Listed by Youell, Gt. Yarmouth. NK. NK. *GB. 1844.*

SURPRISE (b). Single. Single. Tube. Red. Sepals. Red. Entirely reflexed. Corolla. Rose pink striped blue. Very large. Perfectly shaped flower. P169 RH. 1856. Vol P3 J of RHS 1863 P89 Fuchsia trials at Chiswick, A large coarse light red with spreading sepals and a reddish variegated corolla. GC. P283 25/4/1856 Listed by Wm. Cutbush, Highgate. GC. 286 25/4/1856 Intro. by H. Low, Clapton. *Dubus. France. 1855.*

SURPRISE (c). Single. White/Red. Tube. Rich crimson. Sepals. Rich crimson. Corolla. Pure white. Neat habit. Free blooming. Good market plant. B. Cat. 1877-1879. HC. Cat. 1882. GC. P491 17/4/1875 Intro. by B.S. Williams

SURPRISE (d). Single. White/Purple. Tube. White. Sepals. White. Corolla. Magenta. (Carmine). Very stout. JF. Cat. 1888. B. Cat. 1888-1889. Laings Cat. 1890. L. Cat. 1892. *Lye, J. Market Lavington. GB. 1887.*

SWALESII. Single. ND/ND. Tube. ND. Sepals. ND. Corolla. ND. GC. P98 17/2/1844 Listed by Girlings, Danecroft Nursery, Stowmarket. NK. NK. *GB. 1844.*

SWANLEY GEM. Single. Red/Pink. Tube. Coral scarlet. Sepals. Coral scarlet. Prettily reflexed. Corolla. Rose. Frilled shape of flower, free on blooming and splendid habit. HC. Cat. 1882 Illustrated on P72. HC. Cat. 1885. GC. P211 17/2/1877 Rose. Finely frilled. GO. "Select" 1885-1888. Dobbies Cat. 1893-1894. (The cultivar now grown under this name is "First of the Day" Ed.) *Banks, E. Deal. GB. 1878.*

SYBIL. Double. Red/White. Tube. Carmine. Sepals. Carmine. Corolla. Pure white. P131 4th Ed. by Porcher 1874. Not in the first selection. B. Cat. 1870. *Bull,W. Chelsea. GB. 1869.*

SYLPH (a). Single. ND/ND. Tube. ND. Sepals. ND. Corolla. ND. GC. P98 17/2/1844 & P146 8/3/1845 Listed by Youell, Gt. Yarmouth. NK. NK. *GB. 1844.*

SYLPH (b). Single. Pink/Purple. Tube. Pale blush. Sepals. Pale blush. Expanded. Corolla. Purple

carmine. GC. P162 14/3/1846 & P184 13/3/1847
Listed by W. Miller, Ramsgate. GC. P234 11/4/1846
Listed by Epps, Maidstone. GC. P216 27/3/1847
Listed by R. Cooper, Croydon. GC. P270 26/4/1845
Intro. by Sclater, Exeter. *Sclater, Exeter. GB. 1845.*

SYLVANUS. Double. Red/Purple. Tube. Rosy
carmine. Short. Sepals. Rosy carmine. Long.
Corolla. Bluish purple. B. Cat. 1888-1895. *Bull, W.*
Chelsea. GB. 1888.

SYLVIA. Double. Red/White. Tube. Scarlet. Sepals.
Scarlet Corolla. White. Large. JF. Cat. 1905. L. Cat.
1906. Illustrated Revue Horticole 1909. p.180.
Veitch. GB. 1904.

SYMBOL. Double. Red/White. Tube. Crimson.
(Bright scarlet). Sepals. Crimson. (Bright scarlet).
Corolla. Creamy white. P70 Vol 4 J of RHS 1877.
Fuchsia trials at Chiswick 1873. No award. Habit
lanky. A splendid flower but not of a desirable habit.
B. Cat. 1870-1873. *Bull, W. Chelsea. GB. 1870.*

SYMMETRY. Single. Red/Purple. Tube. Reddish
crimson. Sepals. Reddish crimson. Reflexed.
Corolla. Rich violet plum. P134 4th Ed. by Porcher
1874. BSW. Cat. 1878. HC. Cat. 1882-1885. GC.
P146 1895 Blands Chronicle. GC. P363 21/3/1874
Intro. by B.S. Williams. *Bland, E. Fordham. GB.*
1874.

SYROS. Single. Red/Purple. Tube. Deep rose.
Sepals. Deep rose. Broad. Horizontally reflexed.
Corolla. Deep bluish purple. B. Cat. 1880-1883. GC.
P647 22/5/1880 Intro. by W. Bull. *Bull, W. Chelsea.*
GB. 1880.

TAGLIONI. Single. White/Purple. Tube. White.
Thick. 15mm long. Sepals. White. Reflexed round.
Corolla. Violet rose stained white at base. P119 4th
Ed. by Porcher 1874 resembles "May Queen". P70
Vol 4 J of RHS 1877 Fuchsia trials at Chiswick 1873.
No award. Habit good, but not by any means a
desirable variety. Stout tube and sepals which are not
reflexed are white stained with rose. Corolla lake
margined with crimson. Named after famous French
ballerina. *Lemoine, Nancy. France. 1868.*

TAGLIONII. Single. ND/ND. Tube. ND. Sepals.
ND. Corolla. ND. GC. P98 17/2/1844 & P146
8/3/1845 Listed by Youell, Gt. Yarmouth. NK. NK.
NK. *1844.*

TAKOU. Single. Red/Purple. Tube. Red. Sepals.
Red. Corolla. Bluish violet shaded white. Bell
shaped. Long. L. Cat. 1901. *Lemoine, Nancy.*
France. 1901.

TALMA. Double. Red/Purple. Tube. Red. Sepals.
Red. Corolla. Purple. P127 4th Ed. by Porcher 1874
not in the first selection. Laings Cat. 1890. *Lemoine,*
Nancy. France. 1869.

TAMPICO. Single. Red/Purple. Tube. Bright
crimson. Sepals. Bright crimson. Elegantly
recurved. Corolla. Purplish crimson. B. Cat. 1883.
Bull, W. Chelsea. GB. 1883.

TANCRÈDE. Double. Red/Purple. Tube. Bright
crimson red. Sepals. Bright crimson red. Large.
Reflexing. Corolla. Indigo blue. P125 4th Ed. by
Porcher 1874 Easily opens out fully. Petioles, veins
and young wood are violet red. Foliage is dark green,
oval and elongated. *Demay, H. Arras. Belgium.*
1872.

TARTAR. Single. Red/White. Tube. Dark crimson.
Sepals. Dark crimson. Reflexed. Double. Pinkish
white veined crimson pink at base. *Large L. Cat.*
1906. Bull, W. Chelsea. GB.1905.

TAURUS. Single. ND/ND. Tube. ND. Sepals. ND.
Corolla. ND. GC. P216 27/3/1847 & P232 1/4/1848
& P256 21/4/1849 Listed by R. Cooper, Croydon.
NK. NK. NK. NK.

TEKAPO. Single. Red/Purple. Tube. Rosy crimson.
Short. Sepals. Rosy crimson. Well reflexed. Double.
Deep purplish crimson. Large. Expanded. B. Cat.
1881. *Bull, W. Chelsea. GB. 1881.*

TELEGRAPH (a). Single. Red/Purple. Tube.
Bright coral red. Sepals. Bright coral red. Thick.
Broad. Well reflexed. Corolla. Deep violet. Good
size. Circular. Equal to and distinct from "Glory"
and "Nil desperandum". GC. P401 24/6/1854 &
P258 21/4/1855 Listed by H. Walton, Burnley. GC.
P466 22/7/1854 Listed by Bass & Brown, Sudbury.
GC. P353 26/5/1855 Listed by Hart & Nicklin,
Guildford. GC. P530 11/8/1855 Listed by
Bainbridge & Hewison, York. GC. P163 18/3/1854
Intro. by G. Smith, Tollington Nurseries. *Smith, G.*
Islington. GB. 1854.

TELEGRAPH (b). ND. ND/ND. Tube. ND. Sepals.
ND. Corolla. ND. P149 Gartenflora 1888 "New
from Lemoine". *Lemoine. Nancy. France. 1887.*

TERANO. Single. Red/Purple. Tube. Rosy crimson.
Sepals. Rosy crimson. Completely reflexed. Corolla.
Bluish purple marked rose at base. B. Cat. 1883.
Bull, W. Chelsea. GB. 1883.

TERPSICHORE. Single. Red/Purple. Tube.
Crimson. 15mm long. Sepals. Crimson. Large.

Reflexed. Corolla. Pale violet washed red. Bell shaped. P114 4th Ed. by Porcher 1874. This variety is recommended for its form and colouring of its flower. Named after God of Dance.*Lemoine, Nancy. GB. 1860.*

THAIS. Single. Pink/White. Tube. Whitish pink. Sepals. Whitish pink. Corolla. Pure white.L Cat. *Lemoine, Nancy. France. 1913.*

THALABA. Single. White/Red. Tube. White. Sepals. White. Corolla. Red. GC. P146 8/3/1845 Listed by Youell, Gt. Yarmouth. Foxton. NK. *GB. 1845.*

THALIA (a). Single. White/Red. Tube. White. Sepals. White. Corolla. Deep rose. GC. P330 19/5/1855 Listed by Bass & Brown, Sudbury. GC. P314 10/5/1856 Listed by W. Rumley, Richmond & Youell, Gt. Yarmouth. See "Propagation and improvement of cultivated Plants 1878". Venus Victrix X. *Turner, C. Slough GB. 1855.*

THALIA (b). S/Double. Red/White. Tube. Coral crimson. Sepals. Coral crimson. Reflexed. Corolla. White veined deep pink suffused rose. Veined crimson at base. JF. Cat. 1898. B. Cat. 1898-1899. GC. P579 Vol 19 5/1896 Intro. by W. Bull, Chelsea. *Bull, W. Chelsea. GB. 1896.*

THALIA (c). Single. Red/Red. Tube. Coral red. Sepals. Coral red. Corolla. Coral red. Purple foliage. L. Cat. 1908. *Bonstedt. Gottingen. Germany. 1905.*

THE ADMIRAL. Single. Red/Purple. Tube. Crimson. Long. Sepals. Dark Crimson. Long. Expanding well. Corolla. Deep purple. Flowers nearly 5" in length. GC. P162 14/3/1846 & P184 13/3/1847 Listed by W. Miller, Ramsgate. GC. P162 8/3/1845 Intro. by J. Hally, Blackheath. *Hally, J. Blackheath GB. 1845.*

THE AMERICAN BANNER. Single. Red/Purple. Tube. Crimson red. Sepals. Crimson red. Corolla. Bluish violet splashed underneath with red. P133 4th Ed. by Porcher 1874. Dark green foliage. Pedicel 6/7 cms. The petals are half coloured violet blue, the other with crimson red. A first class variety if the petals retain the constant colouring. *Banks, E. Deal. GB. 1871.*

THE BEST. Single. Red/White. Tube. Bright scarlet. Sepals. Bright scarlet. Elegantly reflexed. Corolla. White. Long. Shapely. Vol P3 J of RHS 1863 P91 Fuchsia trials at Chiswick 1862. A large flowered sort with long decurved red sepals, spreading at the points. A close white corolla veined

red. GC. P406 2/5/1863 Listed by Wm. Hussey, Norwich. GC. P960 26/10/1861 & P108 1/2/1862 Intro. by W. Bull, Chelsea. *Bull, W. Chelsea. GB. 1862.*

THE BIG UMBRELLA. Single. ND/ND. Tube. ND. Sepals. ND. Corolla. ND. GC. P338 15/4/1865 Listed by W. Rumley, Richmond. NK. NK. *GB. 1864.*

THE BRIDE. Single. White/Purple. Tube. White. Short. Thick. Sepals. Purplish. Reflexing. Corolla. Light rose. Vol. P3 J of RHS 1863 Fuchsia trials at Chiswick 1862. Submitted by Turner. A free and showy variety. GC. P338 15/4/1865 Listed by W. Rumley, Richmond. *Turner, C. Slough. GB. 1862.*

THE FAIR ORIANA. Single. White/Red. Tube. White. Sepals. White. Corolla. Pure scarlet. GC. P515 25/7/1857 Listed by H. Walton, Burnley. GC. P357 2/4/1858 Listed by C.E. Allen, Stoke Newington. GC. P210 28/3/1857 & P283 25/4/1857 Intro. by E.G. Henderson, St. Johns Wood. *Banks, E. Deal. GB. 1857.*

THE FAIRY. Single. Pink/Red. Tube. Pale flesh. Waxy. Sepals. Pale flesh. Tipped green. Corolla. Bright pink edged carmine. GC. P241 17/4/1852 Intro. by J & C Lee of Hammersmith. *Lee J&C. Hammersmith. GB. 1852.*

THE LITTLE TREASURE. Single. Red/Purple. Tube. Scarlet. Sepals. Scarlet. Corolla. Purple. GC. P515 25/7/1857 & P418 22/5/1858 Listed by H. Walton, Burnley. GC. P357 7/4/1858 Listed by C.E. Allen, Stoke Newington. GC. P210 28/3/1857 & P283 25/4/1857 Intro. by E. G. Henderson, St. Johns Wood. *Banks, E. Deal. GB. 1857.*

THE MAGNIFICENT. ND. ND/ND. Tube. ND. Sepals. ND. Corolla. ND. GC. P338 15/4/1865 Listed by W. Rumley, Richmond. NK. NK. *GB. 1864.*

THEOPHRASTUS. Single. Red/Purple. Tube. Light crimson. Short. Sepals. Light crimson. Long. Reflex to tube. Tipped green. Corolla. Purple. Named after a Greek philosopher (372-286 BC). GC. P162 14/3/1846 & P184 13/3/1847 Listed by W. Miller, Ramsgate. GC. P216 27/3/1847 Listed by R. Cooper, Croydon. GC. P238 12/4/1845 Intro. by Rogers, Uttoxeter. *Rogers. Uttoxeter GB. 1845.*

THE OSPREY. ND. ND/ND. Tube. ND. Sepals. ND. Corolla. ND. GC. P338 15/4/1865 Listed by W. Rumley, Richmond. NK. NK. *GB. 1864*

THE PARACHUTE. ND. ND/ND. Tube. ND. Sepals. ND. Corolla. ND. GC. P338 15/4/1865 Listed by W. Rumley, Richmond. NK. NK. *GB. 1864.*

THE PERFECT CURE. Double. Red/Purple. Tube. Red. Sepals. Red. Corolla. Purple. P127 4th Ed. by Porcher 1874 Put into commerce in 1872 by Jennings. The flower, like "Barillet Deschamps" offers a singularity of having two corollas superimposed on one another. Vol 2 J of RHS 1870 Fuchsia trials at Chiswick. Good habit, Petals unequal in length so as to form an irregular corolla. HC. Cat. 1882 P77 Corolla is formed on the tip of each stamen . Measures 3" to 4" from top to tip. *Rendatler NK. 1869.*

THE PERFECT GLOBE. ND. ND/ND. Tube. ND. Sepals. ND. Corolla. ND. GC. P353 26/5/1855 Listed by Hart & Nicklin, Guildford. NK.NK. *GB. 1855.*

THE PRESIDENT. Single. Pink/Pink. Tube. Pink. Sepals. Pink. Reflex. Corolla. Deep rose. (Reddish violet). App. to RH 1851 by Porcher. This cultivar has the habit of throwing five or six sepals and petals. GC. P369 16/6/1849 Intro. by Youell, Gt Yarmouth. *Youell, Gt. Yarmouth GB. 1849.*

THERA. Single. Red/Purple. Tube. Light carmine rose. Short. Waxlike. Sepals. Light carmine rose. Broad. Horizontal. Wax like. Corolla. Deep purplish plum. B. Cat. 1880-1882. GC. P647 22/5/1880 Intro.by W. Bull

THE RAJAH. Single. Red/Purple. Tube. Bright red. Very small. Sepals. Bright red. Reflex as a Turkcap lily. Corolla. Violet. (Violet blue). App. to RH. 1851 by Porcher. Small flowers. Sepals totally reflex round to tube. GC. P145 9/3/1850 Listed by W. Rumley, Richmond. GC. P241 21/4/1849 Purchased by H. Low, Clapton from Wilmore. *Wilmore, Birmingham. GB. 1849.*

THERESA. Single. White/Red. Tube. White. Sepals. White. Reflexed. Corolla. Rich crimson lake. B. Cat. 1872-1873. *Bull,W. Chelsea. GB. 1870.*

THE RIGHT HON JOHN BRIGHT. Single. Red/Purple. Tube. Coral scarlet. Sepals. Coral scarlet. Completely reflexed. Corolla. Light lavender or mauve. Cup shaped. GC. P1554 2/12/1871 Review by H. Cannell. GO "Select" 1880-1881. F&P March 1870 Colour Plate. B. Cat. 1873-1875. HC. Cat. 1885. GC. P313 Feb 11/3/1871 Intro. by H. Cannell. An improvement on "Beauty of Sholden" and "Disraeli". *Banks, E. Deal. GB. 1870.*

THEROIGNE DE MÉRICOURT. Double. Red/White. Tube. Bright red. Sepals. Bright red. Corolla. Creamy white. Globular corolla. Very full. Enormous. JF. Cat. 1904. L. Cat. 1903. *Lemoine. Nancy. France. 1903.*

THE SHAH. Single. Red/Purple. Tube. Crimson Sepals. Crimson. (Scarlet). Corolla. Regularly striped purple and rose. (Violet blue). B. Cat. 1877-1878. BSW Cat. 1897. NK. NK. *GB. 1875.*

THE SILVER SWAN. Single. White/Purple. Tube. White. Sepals. White. Corolla. Rosy lilac. SG. P45 1866. Compact habit. Prolific flowerering. P120 4th Ed. by Porcher 1874. Not in the first selection. GC. P515 25/7/1857 Listed by H. Walton, Burnley. GC. P210 28/3/1857 & P283 25/4/1857 Intro. by E.G. Henderson, St. Johns Wood. *Banks, E. Deal. GB. 1857.*

THE TRIUMPH OF 1864. ND. ND/ND. Tube. ND. Sepals. ND. Corolla. ND. GC. P338 15/4/1865 Listed by W. Rumley, Richmond. NK. NK. *GB. 1864.*

THE VILLAGE PET. Single. Red/Purple. Tube. Crimson red. Thick. Short. Sepals. Crimson red. Reflex. Corolla. Pale violet shading to white at centre and striped red at base. P114 4th Ed. by Porcher 1874 bell shaped. Expanded. Dwarf bush. GC. P382 29/4/1865 Intro. by E.G. Henderson, St. Johns Wood. *Banks, E. Deal. GB. 1865.*

THE WONDER. ND. ND/ND. Tube. ND. Sepals. ND. Corolla. ND. GC. P338 15/4/1865 Listed by W. Rumley, Richmond. NK. NK. *GB. 1864*

THOMAS KING. Single. Red/Purple. Tube. Crimson scarlet. Sepals. Soft coral red. (Scarlet). Corolla. Deep purple, sometimes striped pale red. Very free. P109 GO. 1885 "New Fuchsias of 1884". GC. Vol 20 1883 P243 New from J. Lye. GC. Vol 26 1886 RHS Trials at Chiswick 31/7/1886. GO. "Select" 1890-1891. GC. Vol 26 P379 Exhibited at Bath Floral Fete by J. Lye 1st - 9 pot class. JF. Cat. 1885. B. Cat. 1883-1893. *Lye, J. Market Lavington. GB. 1883.*

THOMPSONII. Single. Red/Purple. Tube. Red. Sepals. Red. Corolla. Purple. GC. P630 25/9/1841 One of the best Chilean varieties. Raised by Thompson, Gr. to Lady Gambier Iver House. *Thompson. GB. 1839.*

THOMPSONIANA (SUPERBA). Single. Red/Purple. Tube. Red. Sepals. Red. Corolla. Purple. GM. P555 1837 Exhibited at Whitehaven

Horticultural Show 17/8/1837 by Mr. Randelson. GC. P89 11/2/1843 "Recommended for the open ground without protection". GC. P393 6/1842 & P97 17/2/1844 Listed by Youell, Gt. Yarmouth. *Thompson. GB. NK.*

THORNTONII. ND. ND/ND. Tube. ND. Sepals. ND. Corolla. ND. GC. P146 10/3/1855 "Best new fuchsias of 1854" Listed by W. Rumley, Richmond. NK. *GB. 1854.*

TIMOUR. Single. Red/White. Tube. Rosy crimson. Sepals. Rosy crimson. Corolla. White. Long. B. Cat. 1875-1877. NK. NK. NK. *1874.*

TIBBY. Single. Red/Purple. Tube. Bright carmine. Sepals. Bright carmine. Completely reflexed. Corolla. Light blue. Large. Expanded. P115 4th Ed. by Porcher 1874 Not in the first selection. GC. P74 24/1/1863 Intro. by W. Bull, Chelsea. *Bull, W. Chelsea. GB. 1863.*

TIENTSIN. Double. Red/Purple. Tube. Wine red. Sepals. Wine red. Short. Corolla. Clear violet, variegated light pink on the exterior of the petals. *Lemoine. Nancy. France. 1901.*

TIMANDRA. Single. Red/Purple. Tube. Red. Sepals. Red. Corolla. Purple. GC. P146 8/3/1845 Listed by Youell, Gt. Yarmouth. NK. NK. *GB. 1845.*

TILLERYANA. Single. ND/ND. Tube. ND. Sepals. ND. Corolla. ND. GC. P289 29/5/1841 Listed by H. Low, Clapton. GC. P241 15/4/1843 Listed by F&A Smith, Hackney. NK. NK. *GB. 1841.*

TINTED VENUS. Single. Red/White. Tube. Scarlet. Sepals. Scarlet. Fine shape. Well reflexed. Corolla. White tinted violet blue. (White, tinted and feathered violet rose). Good form. Profuse. Corolla somewhat imperfect. Bell shaped. B. Cat. 1870-1873. GC. P567/8 23/4/1870 Intro. by W. Bull, Chelsea. *Bland, E. Fordham. GB. 1869.*

TITIAN. Single. Red/Purple. Tube. Rosy crimson. Sepals. Rosy crimson. Corolla. Reddish with a purple base. JF. Cat. 1904. NK. NK. *GB. 1904.*

TITUS. Single. Red/Purple. Tube. Rosy red. Sepals. Rosy red. Corolla. Rosy purple. Like "Globosa Major" but larger. GC. P338 22/5/1847. Intro. by Turville, Chelmsford. *Turville, Chelmsford GB. 1847.*

TODDIANA. Single. Red/Pink. Tube. Bright red. 4" in length. Sepals. Bright red. Corolla. Pale puce. GC. P97 1843 Purchased by T. Cripps, Tunbridge Wells, from Mr. Todd, Gr. to the late Capt. Moneypenny. GC. P97 2/1843 & P98 17/2/1844 & P146 8/3/1845 Listed by Youell Gt. Yarmouth. GC. P112 17/2/1844 & P66 1/2/1845 Listed by W. Miller, Ramsgate. *Todd. GB. 1843.*

TOLLORIS (OR CURIOSA). Single. ND/ND. Tube. ND. Sepals. ND. Corolla. ND. GC. P66 1/2/1845 Listed by W. Miller, Ramsgate. NK. NK. *GB. 1845.*

TOM POUCE. Single. Red/Purple. Tube. Cerise red. Fat. Short. Sepals. Large Equal in length to the tube. Corolla. Violet pink. Small. App. to RH 1851 by Porcher, Flower is almost globular. Floriferous but placed in the second rank because the corolla is of little extent. *Baudinet. France. 1850.*

TOM THUMB. Single. Red/Purple. Tube. Red. Sepals. Red. Corolla. Purple. P78 HC. Cat. 1882 Very neat, small growing plant with an abundance of small flowers. Synonomous with "Pumila". NK. NK. *GB. NK.*

TORPILLEUR. Double. Red/Pink. Tube. Intense red. Sepals. Intense red. Corolla. Flesh pink mixed with pink. (Carmine). Large. Well open. JF. Cat. 1904. L. Cat. 1903. *Rozain. Lyons. France. 1903.*

TOURVILLE. Double. Red/Purple. Tube. Red. Sepals. Red. Corolla. Purple. P127 4th Ed. by Porcher 1874 Not in the first selection. *Demay, H. Arras. Belgium. 1872.*

TOWARDII. Single. Red/Red. Tube. Dark carmine. Sepals. Dark carmine. Corolla. Dark carmine. Fl. Cab. P185 1841. Hort. Scty Show 17/7/1841 from Standish of Bagshot. A common hybrid, the sepals and petals coloured throughout a brilliant hue between crimson and carmine. GC. P393 June 1841 & P97 2/1843 & P98 17/2/1844 & P146 8/3/1846 Listed by Youell, Gt. Yarmouth. GC. P112 17/2/1844 Listed by W. Miller, Ramsgate. *Standish, Bagshot. GB. 1841.*

TOWER OF LONDON. Double. Red/Purple. Tube. Crimson red. 16mm long. Slender. Sepals. Crimson red. Large. Reflexed. 25 mm. Concave. Deflexed. Corolla. Bluish violet washed red. 19mm. Irregular. P125 4th Ed. by Porcher 1874 Largest known flower. Pcxv Vol 3 J of RHS 1872 Fuchsia trials at Chiswick. An inferior sort with crumpled flowers. GC. P330 13/3/1875 Listed by T. Fletcher, Chesterfield. HC. Cat. 1882 Resembles "Sir Colin Campbell" in foliage and habit. RH. P311 1889 "Select" by E.A. Carrière. Intro. by E.G. Henderson. *Bundy. GB. 1870.*

179

TRAFALGAR. Single. Red/Purple. Tube. Red. Sepals. Red. Tipped green. Reflexing. Corolla. Dark purple. GC. 6/2/1847 & P216 27/3/1847 & P232 1/4/1848 Listed by R. Cooper, Croydon. GC. P250 17/4/1847 Listed by W. Miller, Ramsgate & Epps, Maidstone. GC. P265 24/4/1847 & P259 29/4/1849 & P241 30/4/1850 Listed by W. Rendle, Plymouth. GC. P250 18/4/1846 Intro. by Ivery, Peckham. *Ivery, Peckham. GB. 1846.*

TRAILING QUEEN. Single. Red/Red. Tube. Carmine rose. Sepals. Carmine rose. Corolla. Deeper shade of carmine rose. Distinct drooping habit, Useful for hanging baskets. JF. Cat. 1901. NK. NK. *GB. 1900.*

TRANSPARENS (a). Single. Pink/Red. Tube. Delicate, transparent pink. Sepals. Pink. Green tips. Corolla. Rosy carmine. Erect habit. Profuse bloomer. GC. P98 17/2/1844 & P146 8/3/1845 Listed by Youells, Gt. Yarmouth. GC. P112 17/2/1844 & P66 1/2/1845 Listed by W. Miller, Ramsgate. GC. P97 18/2/1843 Intro. by Youell, Gt. Yarmouth. *Youell. Gt. Yarmouth. GB. 1843.*

TRANSPARENS (b). Single. ND/ND. Tube. ND. Sepals. ND. Corolla. ND. GC. P354 1/6/1844 Listed by T. Cripps, Maidstone. *Hardy. GB. 1844.*

TRANSPARENS (c). Single. ND/ND. Tube. ND. Sepals. ND. Corolla. ND. GC. P551 17/8/1844 Listed by T. Cripps, Maidstone. *Ouding. GB. 1844.*

TRAUDCHEN BONSTEDT. Single. Red/Red. Tube. Orange red. Long. Sepals. Orange red. Green points. Corolla. Clear orange. Panicles. L. Cat. 1908. *Bonstedt. Gottingen. Germany. 1905.*

TREASURE. Double, Red/Purple. Tube. Rich crimson. Short. Thick. Sepals. Rich crimson. Well reflexed. Corolla. Violet plum. Full. B. Cat. 1872-5. GC. P476 15/4/1871 Intro. by Wm. Bull, Chelsea. *Bull, W. Chelsea. GB. 1871.*

TRENTHAM. Single. Red/Purple. Tube. Brilliant scarlet. Sepals. Brilliant scarlet. Broad. Gracefully reflexed. Corolla. Purplish mozarine blue. Smooth. Velvety. Foliage is large, fleshy and handsome. GC. P771 3/12/1853 Out in Spring 1854. GC. P401 24/6/1854 Listed by Benj. R. Cant, Colchester and H. Walton, Burnley. GC. P466 22/7/1854 Listed by Bass & Brown, Sudbury. GC. P258 21/4/1855 Listed by H. Walton, Burnley. GC. P162 18/3/1854 Intro. by Cole & Sharp, Birmingham. NK. NK. *GB. 1854.*

TRIBUNE. Single. Red/Purple. Tube. Deep scarlet. (Crimson). Sepals. Deep scarlet. (Crimson). Broad. Long. Reflexed. Corolla. Bright plum. (Rich plum shaded violet). Very large. Immense length. Good brancher. Very free flowering. B. Cat. 1870-1875. GC. P567/8 23/4/1870 Intro. by W. Bull. *Bull, W. Chelsea. GB. 1869.*

TRIBUTE. Single. Red/Purple. Tube. Reddish crimson. Sepals. Bright crimson. Completely reflexed. Corolla. Violet purple, red at base. G. P198 11/9/1897 Seen at Bull's nursery. L. Cat. 1901. B. Cat. 1898-1901. GC. Vol 21 1897 1/5/1897 Intro. by W. Bull, Chelsea. *Bull, W. Chelsea. GB. 1897.*

TRICOLOR (a). Single. ND/ND. Tube. ND. Sepals. ND. Corolla. ND. GC. P669 11/10/1841 Exhibited at RHS of Cornwall show by Mr. Rickard. GC. P393 6/1842 & P97 2/1843 & P98 17/2/1844 Listed by Youell, Gt.Yarmouth. GC. P112 17/2/1844, & P184 13/3/1847 & P66 1/2/1845 Listed by W. Miller. Ramsgate. NK. NK. *GB. NK.*

TRICOLOR (b). Single. Pink/Red. Tube. Pale blush. Sepals. Pale blush. Bright green tips. Corolla. Deep crimson. GC. P431 24/6/1843 Exhibited at HS Show by Lane. *Lane, Berkhamstead GB. 1843.*

TRICOLOR (c). Double. Red/Purple. Tube. Red. Sepals. Red. Corolla. Purple. Vol P3 J of RHS 1863 Fuchsia trials at Chiswick 1862, submitted by Scott. A slender, free, small flowered variety. NK. NK. *GB. 1863.*

TRICOLOR (d). Single. Red/White. Tube. Scarlet. Sepals. Scarlet. Green tips. Well reflexed. Corolla. Blue rose. RH. P95 1859. GC. P308 9/4/1859 Listed by Epps, Maidstone. RH. P295 1887 Grown as a standard at Twickel. *Dubus. France. 1859.*

TRICOLOURED BEAUTY. Single. Red/Purple. Tube. Bright carmine. (Bright rose). Sepals. Bright carmine. Recurved. Raised right up. Corolla. Pure slate blue on dark lavender, fading to violet. P133 4th Ed. by Porcher 1874. Good foliage. Clear green. Pedicel 30mm. Bell shaped. Large. GC. P430 29/3/1873 A distinct and effective variety for the first row in a competitive group. Intro. by E.G. Henderson. HC. Cat. 1882. *Henderson, E.G. St. Johns Wood. GB.1873.*

TRICOLOUR SUPERBA. ND. ND/ND. Tube. ND. Sepals. ND. Corolla. ND. GC. P145 9/3/1850 Listed by W. Rumley, Richmond. NK. NK. NK. *1849.*

TRIOMPHE DE BRUXELLES. ND. ND/ND. Tube. ND. Sepals. ND. Corolla. ND. Gartenflora P122 1858. *Cornelissen. Belgium. 1857.*

TRIOMPHE DE BRUNN. Single. Red/Purple. Tube. Red. Sepals. Red Corolla. Rosy violet. P135 Appendix to 4th Ed. by Porcher 1874 New variety. Flower very large. *Twrdy, Brno. Austria. 1873.*

TRIOMPHE DE CORNELISSEN. Double. Red/Purple. Tube. Red. Sepals. Red. Long. Reflexed. Corolla. Purple. Vol P3 J of RHS 1863 Fuchsia trial at Chiswick 1862 Awarded **. A vigorous growing variety with much the character of "Sir Colin Campbell", but not thought equal to it in merit, though flowers are larger. Corolla frequently confused. *Cornelissen. Arras. Belgium 1861.*

TRIPHYLLA HYBRIDA. Single. Red/Red. Tube. Red. Sepals. Red. Corolla. Crimson red. L. Cat. 1901. Triphylla x Boliviana. *Lemoine. Nancy. France. 1895.*

TRIPHYLLA SUPERBA. Single. Red/Red. Tube. Scarlet. Sepals. Scarlet. Corolla. Red. GO. 1898 New Fuchsia of 1897 by R. Veitch. A pretty fuchsia with panicles of scarlet flowers. AM. RHS 21/8/1897. *Veitch,J. Exeter. GB. 1897.*

TRISTRAM SHANDY. Single. Red/Purple. Tube. Scarlet. Sepals. Scarlet. Corolla. Pale Blue lilac. GC. P515 25/7/1857 & P418 22/5/1858 Listed by H. Walton, Burnley. GC. P357 7/4/1858 Listed by C.E. Allen, Stoke Newington. GC. P283 25/4/1857 Intro. by E.G. Henderson. *Banks, E. Deal. GB. 1857.*

TRITON (a). Single. Red/Purple. Tube. Bright crimson. Short. Sepals. Bright crimson. Completely reflexed. Corolla. Rich purplish crimson. (Violet blue). Large. Fully expanded. P114 4th Ed by Porcher Good variety. Good form. B. Cat. 1873-1876. *Bull, W. Chelsea. GB. 1873.*

TRITON (b). Double. Red/Purple. Tube. Crimson. Short. Sepals. Crimson. Long. Well reflexed. Corolla. Bright lavender flaked with bright rosy pink. B. Cat. 1888-1889. *Bull, W. Chelsea. GB. 1887.*

TRIUMPH (a). Single. Red/Purple. Tube. Dark red. Sepals. Dark red. Corolla. Purple. Extra large. GC. P281 29/4/1848 Intro. by J.G. Hine, successor to W. Miller (Deceased). *Miller, W. Ramsgate. GB. 1848.*

TRIUMPH (b). ND. ND/ND. Tube. ND. Sepals. ND. Corolla. ND. GC. P224 14/4/1849 Listed by Bass & Brown, Sudbury. *Meillez, Lille. France. 1848.*

TRIUMPHANS (a). Single. Red/Red. Tube. Red. Sepals. Red. Corolla. Red. Floricultural Cabinet P185 Vol IX A curious variety of which it would be difficult to give a better notion than is conveyed in the declaration that it was like fulgens in an unusually high state of culture and was shown by W. H. Story. The stems, leaves and flowers were amazingly large but otherwise resembling those of F. Fulgens. GC. P97 2/1843 & P98 17/2/1844 Listed by Youell, Gt.Yarmouth. GC. P241 15/4/1843 Listed by F&A Smith, Hackney. GC. P112 17/2/1844 Listed by W. Miller, Ramsgate. GC. P609 1841 Shown by Mr. Kyle Gardener to R. Barclay of Leyton at the Hort. Scty Show on 17th July 1841. Very long and large with carmine sepals (like F. Fulgens). *Kyle, Leyton. GB. 1841.*

TRIUMPHANS (b). Double. Red/Purple. Tube. Rich crimson. Sepals. Rich crimson. Corolla. Intense violet, suffused crimson at base. Large and very regular petals. Laings Cat. circa 1890. BSW. Cat. 1897. GC. P146 1895 Blands Chronicle. GC. P486 9/4/1870. Intro. by B.S. Williams, Holloway. *Bland, E. Fordham. GB. 1870.*

TRIUMPHANT (a). Single. ND/ND. Tube. ND. Sepals. ND. Corolla. ND. GC. P66 1/2/1845 Listed by W. Miller, Ramsgate. *Smith, J. Dalston. GB. 1844.*

TRIUMPHANT (b). Double. Red/Purple. Tube. Crimson. (Pale red). Slender. Sepals. Crimson. (Pale red). Broad. Short. Turned up. Corolla. Purple flushed crimson at base. Vol 4 P70 J of RHS 1877 Chiswick trials 1873. Habit good. Free flowering. No award. P217 Chiswick trials 1877 Awarded FCC. Firm and well formed flower. GC. P952 11/10/1862 Intro. by W. Bull. *Bull, W. Chelsea. GB. 1862.*

TROPHÉE. Double. Red/Purple. Tube. Bright red. Sepals. Bright red. Corolla. Violet blue. GO. P141 1891 "New Continental fuchsias of 1890". L. Cat. 1892. *Rozain. Lyons. France. 1890.*

TROPHY (a). Single. Red/Purple. Tube. Bright scarlet. Sepals. Bright scarlet. Great length. Well reflexed. Corolla. Deep violet purple. Very stout. Spreading. GC. P374 26/4/1862. Intro. by J.H. Harrison, Dedham. *Harrison, J.H. Dereham. GB. 1862.*

TROPHY (b). Single. White/Purple. Tube. Pure white. Sepals. Pure white. Corolla. Carmine shaded violet. B. Cat. 1870. NK. NK. *GB. 1869.*

TROUBADOR (a). Single. Red/Purple. Tube. Red. Sepals. Red. Broad. Elegantly recurved. Corolla. Olive black that does not fade. Cup Shaped. GC. P1 7/1/1865. GC. P983 15/10/1864 Intro. by E.G.

Henderson, St. Johns Wood. *Banks, E. Deal. GB. 1864.*

TROUBADOR (b). Double. Red/Purple. Tube. Crimson. Thin. 13mm long. Sepals. Crimson. Extremely wide. Elegantly recurved. 22mm long. Corolla. Purple marked crimson at base. 22mm long. Vigorous. Compact. Extremely floriferous. P125 4th Ed. by Porcher 1874 Nice coloured flower. Large. Spriralled. Pedicel 5/6 cm. Vol III Pcxv P. of RHS. 1872 Fuchsia trials at Chiswick 1872. Flowers elongated. A coarse and inferior variety. B. Cat. 1870-1873 Intro. by Wm. Bull, Chelsea. *Bland,E. Fordham GB. 1869.*

TRUE BLUE. Double. Red/Purple. Tube. Red. Sepals. Red. Corolla. Dense slaty blue. Vol P3 J of RHS 1863 Fuchsia trials 1862. A distinct looking variety having large globose buds. Sepals converge closely over the full corolla. GC. P342 12/4/1862 Listed by E.G. Henderson. GC. P922 19/10/1861 Intro. by W. Bull. *W. Bull, W.,Chelsea. GB. 1861.*

TRUMPETER. Single. Red/Red. Tube. Salmon red. Sepals. Salmon red. Large. Narrowish. Corolla. Magenta rose. Vol 15 G. P420 1881. Petals are rolled outwards at the edges to give a trumpet shaped outline. HC. Cat. 1882. JF. Cat. 1885. Laings Cat. circa 1890. GC. P359 4/1881 & P457 9/4/1881 Intro. by Jones & North, Lewisham. *Fry, G. Lee. GB. 1881.*

TRUTH. Single. Red/Purple. Tube. Bright scarlet. Sepals. Bright scarlet. Corolla. Rosy mauve. Very large. Excellent shape. HC. Cat. 1882. BSW. Cat. 1878. B. Cat. 1876-1877. *Banks, E. Deal. GB. 1875.*

TRY ME O. Single. Red/Purple. Tube. Scarlet. (Crimson). Short. Sepals. Scarlet. (Crimson). Reflexed round. Corolla. Purple. (Blue washed red). (Dark violet blue). Bell shaped. Medium size. Small flowers. Very free. P4 Floral World & GG Jan 1870. P114 4th Ed by Porcher1874. Vol 4 P70 J of RHS 1877 Fuchsia trial at Chiswick No Award. Habit compact and dwarf, exceedingly free flowering and a great favourite for market growers. B. Cat. 1870. HC. Cat. 1882-1885. Dobbies Cat. 1893-1894. RH. P295 1887 Grown as a standard at Twickel. *Banks, E. Deal. GB. 1868.*

TSAR. Double. Red/Purple. Tube. Dark scarlet. Sepals. Dark scarlet. Corolla. Purple marked red on exterior. Enormous. L. Cat. 1912. *Rozain. Lyons. France.1912.*

T.T. LAWDEN. Single. Red/Purple. Tube. Scarlet. Sepals. Scarlet. Corolla. Dark blue. GO. "Select"

1880-1891. HC. Cat. 1882. BSW. Cat. 1878. NK. NK. *GB. 1878.*

TUCKER'S FAVOURITE. ND. ND/ND. Tube. ND. Sepals. ND. Corolla. ND. GC. P283 1899 Exhibited at Bath by G. Tucker. *Tucker, G. Trowbridge. GB. 1897.*

TULIP. Single. Red/Purple. Tube. Crimson. Sepals. Crimson. Completely reflexed. Corolla. Rich purple. Large. Expanded. Tulip shaped. B. Cat. 1882-1893. HC. Cat. 1885. Intro by W. Bull. *Eckford. GB. 1882.*

TURBAN (a). ND. ND/ND. Tube. ND. Sepals. ND. Corolla. ND. GC. P234 11/4/1846 Listed by A.J. Stewart, Salthill Nurseries, Windsor. NK. NK. *GB. 1845.*

TURBAN (b). Single. Red/Purple. Tube. Crimson Sepals. Crimson. Broad. Corolla. Smooth reddish purple. Beautifully formed. GC. P960 26/10/1861 & P108 1/2/1862 Intro. by W. Bull, Chelsea. GC. P406 2/5/1863 Listed by Wm. Hussey, Norwich. *Bull,W. Chelsea. GB. 1862.*

TURENNE. Double. Red/White. Tube. Bright crimson. Thin. Sepals. Bright crimson. Large. Horizontal. Tips upturned. Corolla. Pure white, striped rose at base. Full. Large foliage. Nice shade of green. Pedicel 50mm. P130 4th Ed. by Porcher 1874. *Demay, H., Arras. Belgium. 1869.*

TWRDY J.N. Single. Red/Purple. Tube. Bright crimson. Short. Thick. Brightly coloured. Sepals. Bright crimson. Reflexed round. Corolla. Violet washed red. Very expanded. Good variety. Pedicel 50mm. P114 4th Ed. by Porcher 1874. *Lemoine. Nancy. France. 1868.*

ULYSSE. ND. Red/White. Tube. Bright carmine. Sepals. Bright carmine. Corolla. White. HC. Cat. 1885. NK. NK. NK. NK.

ULYSSE BONDON. Single. Red/White. Tube. Bright red. Sepals. Bright red. Corolla. White. L. Cat. 1908. *Rozain. Lyons. France. 1908.*

ULYSSE TRÉLAT. Double. Red/White. Tube. Bright red. Sepals. Bright red. Corolla. White suffused rose. (White shaded deep red). GO. P141 1891 "New Continental varieties of 1890". L. Cat. 1892. B. Cat. 1892-1893. *Lemoine. Nancy. France. 1890.*

UMPIRE. Single. Red/Purple. Tube. Rich crimson. Short. Corolla. Rich crimson. Reflexed. Wide. Corolla. Very blue purple, blotched rosy carmine. P133 4th Ed. by Porcher 1874. B. Cat. 1872-1875.

GC. P476 15/4/1871 Intro. by W. Bull. *Bull, W. Chelsea. GB. 1871.*

UNA (a). Single. Red/Red. Tube. Bright red. Sepals. Bright red, tipped white. Corolla. Crimson. GC. P473 16/7/1842 H.S. Show. Exhibited by Catleugh. GC. P481 15/7/1842 H.S. Show Exhibited by Catleugh. *Catleugh, Chelsea. GB. 1842.*

UNA (b). Single. White/Red. Tube. White. Sepals. White. Expanded. Corolla. Rosy vermilion. GC. P161 17/3/1849 Listed by W. Rumley, Richmond. GC. P224 14/4/1849 Listed by R. Whibley, Kennington Cross. GC. P259 28/4/1849 & P241 20/4/1850 & GC. P330 20/5/1848 Intro. and listed by W.E. Rendle. Plymouth. *Hocking. GB. 1848.*

UNA (c). ND. ND/ND. Tube. ND. Sepals. ND. Corolla. ND. GC. P515 25/7/1857 & GC. P418 22/5/1858 Listed by H. Walton, Burnley. GC. P357 7/4/1850 Listed by C.E. Allen, Stoke Newington. NK. NK. *GB. 1857.*

UNICOLOUR. Single. Red/Red. Tube. Dull rosy pink. Sepals. Dull rosy pink. Corolla. Rosy pink purple. Vol P3 J of RHS 1863 Fuchsia trial at Chiswick 1862. Submitted by Scott. Poor. GC. P571 24/7/1858 Listed by H. Walton, Burnley. NK. NK. *GB. 1858.*

UNIQUE (a). Single. Red/Purple. Tube. Red. Sepals. Red. Expand well. Corolla. Rosy purple. GC. P81 10/2/1844 Raised and Intro. by G. Croft, Reading. GC. P112 17/2/1844 & P66 1/2/1845 Listed by W. Miller, Ramsgate. *Croft, G. Reading. GB. 1844.*

UNIQUE (b). Single. Red/Purple. Tube. Glossy crimson. Sepals. Glossy crimson. Corolla. Dark purple. Equal to "Formosa elegans". GC. P66 1/2/1845 & P162 14/3/1846 & P184 13/3/1847 Intro. by W. Miller, Ramsgate. *Miller, W. Ramsgate. GB. 1845.*

UNIQUE (c). Single. White/Purple. Tube. Nearly white. Sepals. Nearly white. Corolla. Violet crimson. GC. P184 13/3/1847 Listed by W. Miller, Ramsgate. GC. P162 8/3/1845 Intro. by Hally, Blackheath. *Hally, Blackheath. GB. 1845.*

UNIQUE (d). Single. Red/Purple. Tube. Bright glossy scarlet. (Amarinth red). Very short. Sepals. Bright glossy scarlet. (Amarinth red). Large. Corolla. Deep purple. (Violet Blue). Well formed. 2 blooms at each leaf axil 10/6d. App. to RH. 1851 by Porcher. Petals entwined like a turban. Florist March 1850 illustrated. GC. P387 15/6/1850 Listed by H.

Walton, Burnley. GC. P465 27/7/1850 Listed by G. Smith, Islington. GC. P226 13/4/1850 Intro. by Veitch, Exeter. *Story, W.H. Newton Abbot. GB. 1850.*

UNIVERSAL. Double. Red/Purple. Tube. Bright crimson. Sepals. Bright crimson. Corolla. Deep violet. GC. P55 19/1/1867 Review by H. Cannell. Vol 1 J of RHS 1861 Fuchsia trials at Chiswick Commended 24/9/1961. Vol 2 J of RHS 1870 Fuchsia trials at Chiswick. Passed over. Vol P3 J of RHS 1863 P90 Fuchsia trials at Chiswick Awarded ***. A showy variety of moderately dwarf, free flowering habit and producing very large globose cherry like buds. Corolla is compact in the early stages but becomes loose and irregular when old. Altogether one of the best double flowered sorts. GC. P864 28/9/1861 RHS Floral Committee Commended. GC. P65 25/1/1862 Intro. by G. Smith, Tollington Nurseries. *Smith, G. Islington. GB. 1862.*

URANIA. Double. Red/Pink. Tube. Coral red. Sepals. Coral red. Corolla. Dark pink veined carmine rose. L. Cat. 1906. *Bull, W. Chelsea. GB. 1905.*

USHERII. Single. Pink/Pink. Tube. Pink. Sepals. Pink. Green tips. Corolla. Pink. Neat. Compact. Foliage bright shining brown. GC. P393 6/1842 & P97 2/1843 Listed by Youell, Gt. Yarmouth. GC. P112 17/2/1844 Listed by W. Miller, Ramsgate. GC. P337 26/5/1842 Intro. by James May of Tottenham. Fulgens X Atkinsii. *May, W. Bedale. GB. 1842.*

UTERPE (a). ND. ND/ND. Tube. ND. Sepals. ND. Corolla. ND. GC. P314 12/5/1855 Listed by Youell, Gt. Yarmouth. NK. NK. *GB. 1855.*

UTERPE (b). Single. Red/Purple. Tube. Coral red. Short. Sepals. Coral red. Recurved. Corolla. Dark plum, shaded rosy crimson at base. B. Cat. 1888-1892. *Bull, W. Chelsea. GB. 1887.*

UTTOXETER BEAUTY. Single. Red/Purple. Tube. Bright rosy red. Sepals. Bright rosy red. Corolla. Purple vermilion. Very long pistil. GC. P146 8/3/1845 Listed by Youell, Gt. Yarmouth. GC. P184 13/3/1847 & P66 1/2/1845 Listed by W. Miller, Ramsgate. GC. P259 28/4/1849 Listed by W. Rendle, Plymouth. GC. P162 16/3/1844. Intr. by Rogers, Uttoxeter. *Rogers, Uttoxeter. GB. 1844.*

UTTOXETER RIVAL. Single. Red/Purple. Tube. Rosy carmine. Sepals. Rosy carmine. Green tips. Freely expanded. Corolla. Rosy purple. GC. P146 8/3/1845 Listed by Youell, Gt. Yarmouth. GC. P184 13/3/1847 & P66 1/2/1845 Listed by W. Miller, Ramsgate. GC. P162 16/3/1844 Intro. by Rogers, Uttoxeter. *Rogers, Uttoxeter. GB. 1844.*

VAINQUEUR DE PUEBLA. Double. Red/White. Tube. Bright red. (bright crimson). Thin. 18mm long. Sepals. Bright red. (Bright crimson). Reflex round. Broad. 22mm long. Corolla. Pure white, striped bright rose at base. P130 4th Ed. by Porcher This variety has been neglected by the appearance of the variety called "Surpasse" with which it is similar. Vol 2 J of RHS 1870 Fuchsia trials at Chiswick. Sent by A Henderson. Fine habit. Beautiful variety for vases and decorative purposes. Vol 4 P70 J of RHS 1877 Fuchsia trials at Chiswick 1873. This variety retains its high character as a free blooming and exceedingly useful decorative plant. Pcxviii Vol 3 J of RHS 1872 Awarded **. A model as to habit. GC. P55 19/1/1867 Review by H. Cannell. Best double out. F&P. P57 3/1866 Far superior to Madame Cornelissen. RH. P311 1889 "Select" by E.A. Carrière. GC. P303 13/3/1875 Listed by T. Fletcher, Chesterfield. BSW. Cat. 1878. *L'Huillier. France. 1864.*

VALIANT. Single. Red/Red. Tube. Coral red. Sepals. Coral red. Well reflexed. Corolla. Bright crimson red. (Brilliant crimson). JF. Cat. 1900. L. Cat. 1901. B. Cat. 1899 Intro. by W. Bull. *Bull,W. Chelsea. GB. 1899.*

VANDA. ND. ND/ND. Tube. ND. Sepals. ND. Corolla. ND. RH. P311 1889 "Select" by E.A. Carrière. NK, NK. *GB.* NK.

VAN DYKE (a). ND. ND/ND. Tube. ND. Sepals. ND. Corolla. ND. GC. P234 15/4/1854 Listed by W. Rumley, Richmond. NK. NK. *GB. 1853.*

VAN DYKE (b). Double. Red/Purple. Tube. Crimson. Sepals. Crimson. Corolla. Clear purple. L. Cat. 1914. *Rozain. Lyons. France. 1914.*

VANGUARD (a). Single. Red/Purple. Tube. Crimson. Sepals. Crimson. Corolla. Dark Purple. MF. P133 1856 "Ten good Dark varieties". GC. P401 24/6/1854 Listed by Benj. R. Cant, Colchester & H. Walton, Burnley. GC. P466 22/7/1854 Listed by Bass & Brown, Sudbury. GC. P239 14/4/1855 Listed by John Hoade, Addlestone. GC. P259 21/4/1855 Listed by H. Walton, Burnley. GC. P353 26/5/1855 Listed by Hart & Nicklen, Guildford. GC. P530 11/8/1855 Listed by Bainbridge & Hewison, York. GC. P194 1/4/1854 Intro. by C. Turner, Slough. *Banks, E. Deal. GB. 1854.*

VANGUARD (b). Single. Red/Red. Tube. Light rose. Sepals. Light rose. Corolla. Lake. RH. P24 1846. NK. NK. NK. *1845.*

VAN T'HOFF. Double. Red/Purple. Tube. Red. Sepals. Red. Corolla. Clear lilac mauve. Very full

with long petals of a new colour. Named after a Dutch chemist who was the first winner of the Nobel Peace prize for Chemistry in 1901. L Cat. *Lemoine, Nancy. France. 1902.*

VARONNE. ND. Red/Purple. Tube. Carmine. Sepals. Carmine. Corolla. Violet. Laings Cat. circa 1890. NK. NK. NK. NK.

VAUBAN. ND. ND/ND. Tube. ND. Sepals. ND. Corolla. ND. GC. P147 11/3/1853 Best Varieties of 1852. Listed by W. Rumley, Richmond. NK. NK. NK. *1852.*

VECTIS. Single. Red/Purple. Tube. Deep rose. Sepals. Deep rose. Horizontal. Corolla. Purple crimson. B. Cat. 1883. *Bull,W. Chelsea. GB. 1883.*

VÉLASQUEZ. Double. Red/White. Tube. Dark carmine red. Sepals. Dark carmine red. Corolla. White veined carmine. Enormous. L. Cat. 1914. *Rozain. Lyons. France. 1914.*

VELUTINA. ND. ND/ND. Tube. ND. Sepals. ND. Corolla. ND. G. Vol 19 P603 24/12/1881 A very elegant fuchsia from Sir George Macleary's garden. It is a distinct species with flowers 2" long, but remarkable for the velvety look of its leaves, which are a soft dark olive green, large and good in form. The foliage is very beautiful. NK. NK. *GB. 1881.*

VENETIA. ND. ND/ND. Tube. ND. Sepals. ND. Corolla. ND. GC. P594 29/6/1861 Listed by Godwin & Padman, Sheffield. GC. P771 24/8/1861 Listed by H. Walton Burnley, NK. NK. *GB. 1861.*

VENUS DE MEDICI. Single. White/Purple. Tube. White. Sepals. Blush pink on white, shaded and striped pink. Corolla. Deep violet blue. Flower large and elegantly formed. GC. P483 19/7/1856 This fuchsia is much improved when grown in a shady part of the greenhouse and not exposed to the power of the sun. Florist Vol VI March 1856 Coloured Plate 3. P120 4th Ed. by Porcher 1874 This fuchsia was a grest success and I find it being revived in 1874. Vol 3 P93 L'Illustration Horticole coloured plate. SG. P459 1866 "Recommended light variety". GC. P580 9/7/1859 Exhibited at RBS Show Regents Park 6/7/1959 by H. Cannell, Gr. to E. Groves, Tulse Hill. GC. P419 21/6/1856 Listed by Bainbridge & Hewison, York 3/6d. GC. P497 26/7/1856 Listed by Fowle & Son, Holland St., Brixton 1/6d. GC. P690 18/10/1856 & P146 7/3/1857 Listed by W. Rumley, Richmond. GC. P251 11/4/1857 Listed by W. Masters, Canterbury. GC. P283 25/4/1857 Listed by W. Cutbush, Highgate. GC. P260 24/3/1860 Listed by Wm. Hussey, Norwich. HC. Cat. P79 1882. JF.

Cat. 1886. GC. P114 23/2/1856 Intro. by E.G. Henderson, St. Johns Wood

VENUSTA (a). Single. White/Purple. Tube. Pure white. Sepals. Pure white. Corolla. Purple. GC. P264 24/4/1847 Listed by W. Rendle, Plymouth, flowers more globose and large than "Venus Victrix. GC. P808 11/1846 "Recommended". GC. P140 27/2/1847 "Good". GC. P254 19/4/1845 & P557 16/8/1845 Intro. by J. Smith, Dalston. *Smith, J. Dalston. GB. 1845.*

VENUSTA (b). Single. ND/ND. Tube. ND. Sepals. ND. Corolla. ND. GC. P820 12/1844 "Recommended light variety". GC. P241 15/4/1843 Listed by F&A Smith, Hackney. GC. P112 17/2/1844 Listed by W. Miller, Ramsgate. *Harrison, Dereham. GB. 1842.*

VENUS VICTRIX. Single. White/Purple. Tube. White. Sepals. White. Corolla. Purple. GC. P153 5/3/1842 T. Cripps has purchased entire stock from Mr. Gulliver of Tunbridge Wells, gardener to Rev. S. Marriott of Horsmonden. The same size as "Gracilis" of which it is belived to be an accidental variety. GC. P375 4/6/1844 Exhibited at HS Show by Cole. GC. P421 26/3/1870 Corresdpondent Edward Bennett,- found in Ireland and re-introduced by H. Cannell in 1870. GC. P475 12/10/1877 VV was a chance seedling from F. gracilis. RH. P24 1846. GC. P393 6/1844 & P97 2/1843 & P146 8/3/1845 & P184 13/3/1847. Illustrated in Floricultural Cabinet August 1842 P169. Listed by Youell, Gt. Yarmouth. GC. P216 27/3/1847 & P232 1/4/1848 & P256 21/4/1849 Listed by R. Cooper, Croydon. HC. Cat. 1882. JF. Cat. 1888. *Gulliver, Tunbridge Wells. GB. 1842.*

VENUS VICTRIX IMPROVED. Single. White/Purple. Tube. White. Sepals. White. Corolla. Dark purple. B. Cat. 1888-1893. JF. Cat. 1888. L. Cat. 1892. *Rowson. GB. 1888.*

VERDI. Single. Red/Red. Tube. Carmine red. Sepals. Carmine red. Large. Horizontal. Corolla. Wine red. Very expanded. Bell shaped. Enormous. L. Cat. 1892. JF. Cat. 1893.Named after an Italian composer of operas (1813-1901). *Lemoine, Nancy. France. 1892.*

VERNALIS. ND. ND/ND. Tube. ND. Sepals. ND. Corolla. ND. GC. P393 6/1842 & P97 2/1843 Listed by Youell, Gt. Yarmouth. GC. P112 14/2/1844 & P184 13/3/1847 Listed by W. Miller (Light). GC. P345 28/5/1842 Intro. by J. Smith, Dalston. *Smith, J. Dalston. GB. 1842.*

VERONA. Single. Red/White. Tube. Intense bright crimson. Sepals. Bright crimson. Long. Well reflexed. Corolla. Pure white, striped crimson at base. B. Cat. 1872-1875. *Bull,W. Chelsea. GB. 1871.*

VERA SERGINE. S/Double. White/White. Tube. White. Sepals. White slightly tinged pink. Well expanded. Corolla. Pure white. L. Cat. P2 1914. *Lemoine, Nancy. France. 1914.*

VERRIO. Single. Red/Purple. Tube. Dark crimson. Sepals. Dark crimson. Reflexed. Corolla. Dark purple. Fine flower. GC. P279 30/9/1853 Dark wooded stem. GC. P454 16/7/1853 Exhibited at HS Show 9/7/1853 by Mr. Bousie Gr. to Rt. Hon Laboutiere as a Pyramid. GC. P449 17/7/1852 & P209 26/3/1853 Listed by H. Walton, Burnley. GC. P211 26/3/1853 Listed by W. Rumley, Richmond. GC. P223 10/4/1852 Intro. by C. Turner, Slough. *Turner, C. Slough. GB. 1852.*

VESTA (a). Single. Pink/Red. Tube. Flesh. Sepals. Flesh Corolla. Deep crimson. GC. P502 22/7/1843 Exhibited at RBS show. GC. P375 4/6/1844 Exhibited by J. Smith at HS Show London. GC. P820 12/1844 "Recommended". GC. P146 8/3/1845 Listed by Youell, Gt. Yarmouth. GC. P216 27/3/1847 & P232 1/4/1848 Listed by R. Cooper, Croydon. GC. P66 1/2/1845 Listed by W. Miller, Ramsgate. GC. P226 23/4/1850 Listed by Poole Nurseries. RH. P24 1846. GC. P193 30/3/1844 Intro. by J. Smith, Dalston. *Smith, J. Dalston. GB. 1844.*

VESTA (b). ND. ND/ND. Tube. ND. Sepals. ND. Corolla. ND. GC. P184 13/3/1847 Listed by W. Miller (Dark). NK. NK. *GB. 1846.*

VESTA (c). Single. White/Red. Tube. White. Sepals. White. Corolla. Rosy pink. GC. P385 18/6/1853 & P147 11/3/1854 Listed by W. Rumley, Richmond. GC. P465 23/7/1853 Listed by J. Harrison, Darlington. GC. P483 30/7/1853 & P162 18/3/54 Listed by H. Walton, Burnley. GC. P98 12/2/1853 Intro. by G. Smith, Islington. *Patterson. GB. 1853.*

VESTA (d). Single. Red/Purple. Tube. Red. Sepals. Red. Corolla. Purple. FW&GG Jan 1870 P4. In the way of "Try me O", but better. GC. P1554 2/12/1871 Review by H. Cannell. An advance on older kinds, but scarcely wanted. GC. P488 9/4/1870 Intro. by H. Cannell. JF. Cat. 1888. *Banks, E. Deal. GB. 1870.*

VESTA (e). Double. Red/White. Tube. Carmine. 13mm long. Sepals. Carmine. 25mm long. Scarcely spreading. Corolla. White, rosy scarlet veins. Vol 3 J of RHS Pcxiv 1872 Fuchsia trial at Chiswick 1872

Has small petals in the interior. The tube and sepals too pale in colour to be effective. B. Cat. 1870-1873. *Bull,W. Chelsea. GB. 1869.*

VESTA (f). Double. ND/ND. Tube. ND. Sepals. ND. Corolla. ND. L. Cat. 1901 *Rozain. Lyons. France. 1896*

VESTAL. Single. White/Red. Tube. White. Long. Sepals. White. Recurved. Corolla. Bright rosy carmine. B. Cat. 1901. *Bull,W. Chelsea. GB. 1900.*

VIALA. Single. Pink/Purple. Tube. Pale pink. Sepals. Pale pink. Large. Horizontal. Corolla. Lilac rose. App. to RH. 1851 by Porcher. 1st class variety. This flower is distinguishable by its expansion and the freshness of its colouring. *Lefevre. France. 1849.*

VICE ADMIRAL TEGETTHOFF. ND. Red/White. Tube. Red. Sepals. Red. Corolla. White. P131 4th Ed. by Porcher 1874. Not in the first selection. Named after an Austrian Admiral (1827-71). *Twrdy, Brno. Austria. 1867.*

VICTOR. Double. Red/Purple. Tube. Crimson. Sepals. Crimson. (Brilliant red). Large. Reflexed. Corolla. Rich blue. Petals are peculiarly arranged and being expanded have the appearance of a fine single corolla with a surrounding frill. P125 4th Ed. by Porcher 1874 Small foliage. P67 Vol 4 J of RHS 1877 Fuchsia trials at Chiswick 1873. 2nd Class Certificate. Habit strong and compact. Very bright Scarlet tube and sepals, the latter not much reflexed. Corolla is of an immense size, but coarse and irregular, pale purple changing to reddish purple. Not a very desirable fuchsia. GC. Intro. by W. Bull. B. Cat. 1870-1876. *Bull,W. Chelsea. GB. 1870.*

VICTOR DE LAPRADE. Double. Red/White. Tube. Crimson. Sepals. Crimson. Corolla. White, with pink veins.at base. GO "Select" 1891. L. Cat. 1890. *Hoste. NK. 1889.*

VICTOR EMMANUEL (a). ND. ND/ND. Tube. ND. Sepals. ND. Corolla. ND. GC. P771 24/8/1861 Listed by H. Walton, Burnley. NK. NK. NK. *1861.*

VICTOR EMMANUEL (b). Single. Red/Purple. Tube. Crimson red. Almost non existant. Sepals. Crimson red. Reflexed round. Corolla. Lilac violet washed pink. Bell shaped. Yellowish green foliage. Similar to "Comte De Cavour" and "Terpischore". GC. P55 19/1/1867 Review by H. Cannell. HC. Cat.1882. Intro. by E.G. Henderson. *Banks, E. Deal. GB. 1862.*

VICTOR HUGO (a). Single. Red/Purple. Tube. Reddish purple. Sepals. Reddish purple. Corolla. Violet purple. App to RH. 1851 by Porcher. Much brighter than "Corallina". Corallina X. *Baudinet. France. 1849.*

VICTOR HUGO.(b). Tube. Red/Purple. Tube. Light rosy red. Sepals. Light rosy red. Corolla. Soft mauve. HC. Cat. 1885. Laings Cat. circa 1890. BSW. Cat 1888. NK. NK. NK. *1884?*

VICTOR HUGO (c). Double. Red/Purple. Tube. Blood red (Clear rose). Sepals. Blood red. (Clear rose). Corolla. Purple violet marbled with rose. (Rosy lilac). B. Cat 1898-1899. JF. Cat. 1898. L. Cat. 1897. Named after a French author and politician (1802-1885). *Lemoine, Nancy. France. 1897.*

VICTORIA. ND. ND/ND. Tube. ND. Sepals. ND. Corolla. ND. GC. P481 15/7/1843 Exhibited at Bot. & Hort. Scty, Exeter show by Sclater, Summerlands. GC. P97 2/1843 & P98 17/2/1844 Listed by Youell, Gt. Yarmouth. GC. P241 15/4/1843 Listed by F&A Smith, Hackney. *Salter, J. Versailles. France. 1842.*

VICTORIEN SARDOU (a). Double. Red/Purple. Tube. Red. Sepals. Red. Corolla. Purple. P127 4th Ed. by Porcher 1874. Not in the first selection. *Lemoine, Nancy. France. 1866.*

VICTORIEN SARDOU (b). Double. Red/Purple. Tube. Coral red. Sepals. Coral red. Large. Reflexed. Corolla. Clear plum purple. Large. Full. L. Cat. 1907. *Lemoine, Nancy. France. 1907.*

VICTORINE. Single. ND/ND. Tube. ND. Sepals. ND. Corolla. ND. GC. P537 25/5/1844 Exhibited at HS Show 18/5/1844 by Mr. Cole and Catleugh. NK. NK. NK. NK.

VICTOR MASSÉ. S/Double. Red/Purple. Tube. Bright red. Sepals. Bright red. Long. Broad. Corolla. Mauve Violet. L. Cat. 1903. *Lemoine, Nancy. France. 1903.*

VICTORY. Single. ND/ND. Tube. ND. Sepals. ND. Corolla. ND. GC.P481 15/7/1843 Exhibited at HS Show 12/7/1843 by Catleugh. GC. P610 2/9/1843 Exhibited at Practical Floral and Hort. Scty of Ireland by T. Farrell. GC. P98 17/2/1844 & P146 8/3/1845 Listed by Youell, Gt. Yarmouth. *Smith, J. Dalston., GB. 1843.*

VILLAGE MAID. Single. White/Purple. Tube. White. Sepals. White. Green tips. Corolla. Bluish violet. Neat habit. Makes bush 2 1/2 feet high with stiff branches. Illustrated in Floral Cabinet, P53 Nov. 1844. *Harrison, Dereham. GB. 1844.*

VILLAGE PRIDE. ND. ND/ND. Tube. ND. Sepals. ND. Corolla. ND. GC. P426 12/5/1860 & P824 8/9/1860 Listed by F. Godwin, Sheffield. NK. NK. *GB. 1859.*

VILLE DE LYON. Double. Red/White. Tube. Crimson red. Thick. Sepals. Crimsdon red. Horizontal. Corolla. White, veined carmine. Enormous. L. Cat. 1890. *Rozain, Lyons. France. 1890.*

VILLE DE NANCY. Double. Red/Purple. Tube. Pale carmine red. Sepals. Pale carmine red. Very wide. Recurved. Corolla. Dark violet. Large. RH. P311 "Select" by E.A. Carrière. BSW. Cat. 1885. B. Cat. 1875-1883. *Lemoine, Nancy. France. 1875.*

VINCENT D'INDY. Double. Red/Purple. Tube. Scarlet. Sepals. Scarlet. Broad. Reflexed. Corolla. Pansy violet. Broad. Spreading. Named after a French composer (1851-1931). *Lemoine, Nancy. France. 1910.*

VIOLAEFLORA PLENA. Double. Red/Purple. Tube. Red. Sepals. Red. Reflexed. Double. Purple. (Dark fiery red). Very full. RH. P170 1857. GC. P467 14/7/1855 Listed by A. Walton, Burnley. GC. P531 11/8/1855 Listed by J. Courca. GC. P314 10/5/1856 Listed by W. Rumley & Youell, Gt. Yarmouth. GC. P273 28/4/1855 Intro. by *Luccombe & Pince. Exeter. GB. 1855.*

VIOLLET-LE-DUC. Double. Red/Purple. Tube. Crimson. Sepals. Crimson. Corolla. Metallic Violet. Short. Expanded. Floriferous. Beautifully marked. Named after a French architect and church restorer (1814-79). B. Cat. 1879-1893. HC. Cat. 1882. *Lemoine, Nancy. France. 1879.*

VIOLET QUEEN. ND. ND/ND. Tube. ND. Sepals. ND. Corolla. ND. JF. Cat. 1920. NK. NK. NK. *1920.*

VIRGINAL (a). Double. Red/White. Tube. Pink. Sepals. Pink. Raised up. Corolla. White. L. Cat. 1892. *Rozain. Lyons. France. 1891.*

VIRGINAL (b). ND. ND/ND. Tube. ND. Sepals. ND. Corolla. ND. GC. P265 24/4/1847 & P259 28/4/1849 Listed by W. Rendle, Plymouth. NK. NK. *GB. 1846.*

VIRGINIA. Single. White/Purple. Tube. White suffused flesh. Waxy. Sepals. White, Waxy. Corolla. Pale carmine flecked violet. GO.1889 "New fuchsias of 1888". HC. Cat. 1890. GC. "Select"

1891. JF. Cat. 1888. B. Cat. 1888-1889. Laings. Cat. circa 1890. BSW Cat. 1888. *Lye, J. Market Lavington. GB. 1888.*

VIRGIN QUEEN. Single. White/Purple. Tube. Waxy white. Sepals. Waxy white. Corolla. Deep purple crimson. GC. P426 10/1/1862 Intro. by Veitch & Co. *Mollen, H. GB. 1862.*

VIRGO (a). ND. ND/ND. Tube. ND. Sepals. ND. Corolla. ND. GC. P418 22/5/1858 Listed by H. Walton, Burnley. NK. NK. *GB. 1857.*

VIRGO (b). Single. White/Purple. Tube. Pure white. Sepals. Pure white. Gracefully reflexed to form a perfect crown. Corolla. Magenta. Novel shade. P120 4th Ed. by Porcher 1874 Not in the first selection. B. Cat. 1873-1883. *Bull,W. Chelsea. GB. 1873.*

VIRGO MARIA. Single. White/Red. Tube. White. Sepals. White. Corolla. Vermilion. P116 4th Ed. by Porcher 1874. Similar to "Baroness Burdett Coutts", & P120 Good old variety. Pedicel 15mms. Spiralled. A little short. RH. P170 1857. RH. P295 1887 Grown as a standard at Twickel. *Demouveaux. France. 1857.*

VISCOUNTESS. ND. ND/ND. Tube. ND. Sepals. ND. Corolla. ND. GC. P177 20/3/1852 Listed by W. Rumley, Richmond. *Maynard. GB. 1852.*

VIZIER. Single. Red/Purple. Tube. Carmine red. Sepals. Carmine red. Long. Recurved. Corolla. Lilac pink. Expanded L. Cat. 1906. *Bull,W. Chelsea. GB. 1905.*

VOILE BLUE. Double. Red/Purple. Tube. Carmine pink. Sepals. Carmine pink. Rolled back. Corolla. Azure violet. L. Cat. 1908. *Lemoine. Nancy. France. 1908.*

VOIX DU PEUPLE. Double. Red/White. Tube. Rosy carmine. Sepals. Rosy carmine. Corolla. Milky white. Expanded to give a large flower. B. Cat. 1875-1889. BSW. Cat. 1878-1888. *Lemoine. Nancy. France. 1874.*

VOLCANO DI AQUA. Single. Red/Purple. Tube. Rich glossy scarlet. Sepals. Rich glossy scarlet. Well reflexed. Corolla. Violet. Extra large. GC. P451 5/7/1856 & P642 27/9/1856 Listed by H. Walton, Burnley. GC. P497 26/7/1856 Listed by Fowle & Son, Brixton. GC. P690 18/10/1856 Listed by W Rumley, Richmond. GC. P283 25/4/1857 Listed by W. Cutbush, Highgate. GC. P134 23/2/1856 Intro. by E.G. Henderson, St. Johns Wood. *Banks, E. Deal. GB. 1856.*

VOLTAIRE (a). Single. Red/Red. Tube. Red. Long. Sepals. Bright red. Double. Crimson red. App. to RH. 1851 by Porcher 2nd class. *Racine. France. 1850.*

VOLTAIRE (b). Double. Red/Purple. Tube. Red. Sepals. Red. Short. Broad. Reflexed. Corolla. Plum. Petals veined rose. B. Cat. 1898-1899. NK. NK. NK. *1898.*

VOLTIGEUR (a). Single. White/Red. Tube. White. Sepals. White. Corolla. Deep rose. GC. P321 24/5/1851 & P177 20/3/1851 Intro. by W. Rumley, Richmond. *Rumley, W. Richmond GB. 1851.*

VOLTIGEUR (b). Single. Red/Purple. Tube. Crimson. Sepals. Crimson. Corolla. Dark purple. Named after a Hungarian patriot who was active in England at the time. GC. P545 30/8/1851 Listed by G. Smith, Tollington Nurseries. GC. P177 20/3/1852 Listed by W. Rumley, Richmond. GC. P207 27/3/1852 Listed by H. Walton, Burnley, P351 Gartenflora 1852. GC. P209 5/4/1851 Intro. by C. Turner, Slough. *Banks, E. Deal. GB. 1851.*

VOLUNTAIRE. Single. Red/Purple. Tube. Red. Sepals. Red Corolla. Purple. P149 Gartenflora 1888 New from Lemoine. Riccartonii X. *Lemoine, Nancy. France. 1887.*

VULCAIN. Single. Red/Red. Tube. Red. Sepals. Red. Corolla. Dark carmine. P24 RH.1846. *Salter, J. Versailles. France. 1846.*

VUURBERG. Single. Pink/Red. Tube. Pale pink. Sepals. Rose pink. Deflexed. Corolla. Red. GC. P221 5/4/1845 Intro. by J. Fowle, Brixton. GC. P265 24/9/1847 Listed by W. Rendle, Plymouth. Coloured Plate in Florists Journal P93 Plate 71. *Fowle, J. Brixton. GB.1845.*

WAGNERIAN. Single. Red/Purple. Tube. Crimson. Sepals. Crimson. Beautifully reflexed. Corolla. Deep crimson purple. Very Large. Glossy. Good habit. Very free. B. Cat. 1877-1882. *Bull, W. Chelsea. GB. 1877.*

WALTER LONG. Single. Red/Purple. Tube. Bright coral red. Sepals. Bright coral red. Corolla. Clear violet deepening in colour towards the edges. GC. P374 24/8/1887 Exhibited at Market Lavington by J. Lye. JF. Cat. 1888. BSW. Cat. 1888. B. Cat. 1889-93. HC. Cat. 1892. GO. 1889 "New fuchsias of 1888" *Lye, J. Market Lavington. GB. 1888.*

WAR EAGLE. Single. Red/Purple. Tube. Scarlet. Short. Thick. Sepals. Scarlet. Reflexed round. Small.

Much reflexed. Corolla. Violet purple washed and striped red. Much expanded. Rather thin. Vol 36 G. Being grown in Regents Park. 20/7/1889. P114 4th Ed. by Porcher 1874. Bell shaped. Good foliage. Pedicel 45mm. GC. P652 15/7/1865 Exhibited at RHS Show. GC. P55 19/1/1867 Review by H. Cannell. P70 Vol 4 J of RHS 1877 Fuchsia trials at Chiswick 1873. No award. Compact habit. Branching. HC. Cat. 1875-1882. GC. P382 29/4/1865 Intro. by E.G. Henderson, St. Johns Wood. *Banks, E. Deal. GB. 1865.*

WARRIOR (a). ND. ND/ND. Tube. ND. Sepals. ND. Corolla. ND. GC. P87 1/2/1862 Eiven free with purchases of "Cedo Nulli, Conquest, & Blondin " by R. Rea. Similar to these three. *Rea, R. Ipswich. GB. 1862.*

WARRIOR (b). Double. Red/Purple. Tube. Red. Sepals. Red. Broad. Well reflexed. Corolla. Deep violet purple. Large. Very double. GC. P450 17/5/1862 Intro. by B.W. Knight, Battle. *Knight, B.W. Battle. GB. 1862.*

WARRIOR (c). Double. Red/Purple. Tube. Vermilion. Sepals. Vermilion. Reflexed. Corolla. Purple plum. Very large. P126 4th Ed. by Porcher 1874 Not in the first selection. B. Cat. 1870. *Bull,W. Chelsea. GB. 1866.*

WARRIOR (d). Single. Red/Purple. Tube. Crimson red. Short. Sepals. Crimson red. Large. Reflexed. Corolla. Violet blue washed bright red. P114 4th Ed. by Porcher 1874. *Smith, G. Islington. GB. 1868.*

WARRIOR QUEEN. Single. Red/Purple. Tube. Scarlet. Sepals. Scarlet. (Brilliant carmine). Corolla. Bluish violet. (Violet washed red). P115th Ed. by Porcher 1874 Good variety. Pedicel 40 mm. GC. P20 4/7/1874 Exhibited at Saffron Walden show. RH. P311 "Select" by E.A. Carrière. Laings. Cat. circa 1890. GC. P375 19/3/1870 Intro. by E.G. Henderson, St. Johns Wood. *Henderson, E.G., St. Johns Wood. GB. 1870.*

WASHINGTON (a). Single. ND/ND. Tube. ND. Sepals. ND. Corolla. ND. GC. P146 8/3/1845 Listed by Youell, Gt. Yarmouth. NK. NK. *GB. 1844.*

WASHINGTON (b). Double. Red/Pink. Tube. Red. Sepals. Red. Large. Corolla. Rose. Large. B. Cat. 1893-1895. *Bull,W. Chelsea. GB. 1893.*

WATER NYMPH (a). Single. Red/White. Tube. Scarlet crimson. Sepals. Scarlet crimson. Corolla. Clear white. Crimson Globe. GC. P467 19/7/1855 Listed by Bass & Brown, Sudbury & H. Walton,

Burnley. GC. P529 11/8/1855 Listed by W. J. Epps, Maidstone. GC. P530 11/8/1855 & P208 22/3/1856 Listed by Bainbridge & Hewison York. GC. P531 11/8/1855 Listed by J. Courcha. GC. P314 10/5/1856 Listed by W. Rumley, Richmond & Youell, Gt. Yarmouth. GC. P451 5/7/1856 Listed by J. Clarke, Cheltenham. GC. P18 13/1/1855 & P368 26/5/1855 Intro. by E. G. Henderson. *Story, W.H. Newton Abbot. GB. 1855.*

WATER NYMPH (b). Single. White/Purple. Tube. White washed pink. Thick. Long. 15mms. Sepals. White washed pink. Large. Uplifted. Corolla. Violet margined rose. Stained white at base. P120 4th. Ed. by Porcher 1874. The fault in the branches are not strong enough to bear the weight of the flowers. P70 Vol 4 J of RHS Fuchsia trials 1873 No award. Compact. P215 Vol 4 J of RHS 1877 Fuchsia trials at Chiswick. Awarded F.C.C. Dwarf. Free flowering. Bushy habit. Sepals straight. Corolla crimson. *E.G. Henderson, St. Johns Wood. GB. 1871.*

WAT TYLER. Single. Red/Red. Tube. Light rose. Very large. Sepals. Light rose. Corolla. Scarlet. GC. P146 8/3/1845 Listed by Youell, Gt. Yarmouth. GC. P162 16/3/1844 Intro. by J. Hally, Blackheath. *Hally, J. Blackheath GB. 1844.*

WAVE OF LIFE. Single. Red/Purple. Tube. Scarlet. (Coral red). Short. Sepals. Scarlet. (Coral red). Broad. Reflexed. Corolla. Violet blue. Gold tinted foliage. P67 J of RHS Fuchsia trials at Chiswick 1873 F.C.C. Habit compact and good. Leaves pale yellow at points. A distinct and really good fuchsia. P216 Vol 4 J of RHS 1877 Chiswick trials 1877 Awarded FCC. Weak, drooping, dense habit. Vol 3 P of RHS 1872 Pcxvii Tube 13mm tapered. Sepals 25 mm reflexed. Corolla 20 mm Reddish purple stained red at base. HC. Cat. 1885. BSW. Cat. 1897. Dobbies Cat. 1893-1894. Laings Cat. circa 1890. GO. "Select" 1880-1883. NK. NK. *GB. 1870?*

W.B. LEAF. Single. Red/Purple. Tube. Red. Sepals. Red. Corolla. Deep mauve shaded rose. Very wide. HC. Cat. 1896. JF. Cat. 1898. *Banks, E. Deal. GB. 1896.*

WEBBII. ND. ND/ND. Tube. ND. Sepals. ND. Corolla. ND. GC. P250 27/4/1847 Listed by W.J. Epps, Maidstone. NK. NK. *GB. 1847.*

WEEPING BEAUTY (a). Single. Red/Purple. Tube. Crimson scarlet. Rather bulged. Sepals. Bright crimson scarlet. Broadish. Corolla. Rich deep purple. Moderately expanded. P67 Vol 4 J of RHS 1877 Fuchsia trials 1873. A very fine fuchsia. Pcxvi Vol 3 P of RHS 1872 Fuchsia trials at Chiswick 1872

Awarded ***. Habit dwarf. Free. Good. Tube. Medium sized tube 19mm Sepals 25mm. Corolla 16 mm. Moderately expanded. NK. *GB. 1871?*

WEEPING BEAUTY (b). Single. Red/Purple. Tube. Scarlet. Sepals. Scarlet. Corolla. Blue. Large. Expanded. BSW. Cat. 1878. NK. NK. *GB.* NK.

WESTERN BEAUTY. Single. White/Red. Tube. White. Sepals. White. Corolla. Deep pink. (Various tints of scarlet). HC. Cat. 1890. JF. Cat. 1892. *Lye, J. Market Lavington. GB. 1890.*

WHIDENIA. ND. ND/ND. Tube. ND. Sepals. ND. Corolla. ND. GC. P690 18/10/1856 & P146 7/3/1857 Listed by W. Rumley, Richmond. NK. NK. *GB. 1856.*

WHITE EAGLE. Single. Red/White. Tube. Scarlet. Sepals. Scarlet. Corolla. White. 3 flowers at each axil. P131 4th Ed. by Porcher 1874 Not in the first selection. Upright. Not free flowered. P70 Vol 4 J of RHS 1877 Fuchsia trials at Chiswick 1873 No Award. Habit good, but by no means a desirable variety. Flowers are very badly shaped.GC. P375 19/3/1870 Intro. by. E.G. Henderson. *Henderson E.G., St Johns Wood. GB. 1870.*

WHITE GIANT. Double. Red/White. Tube. Red. Sepals. Red. Corolla. White. Produces long racemes of flowers of immense size. One of the largest white doubles. GO. "Select" 1880-1891. B. Cat. 1878-1893. NK. NK. *GB. 1877.*

WHITE LADY. Single. Red/White. Tube. Red. Sepals. Red. Corolla. White. SG. P459 1866 "Recommended". Vol 2 J of RHS 1870 mentioned similar to "Floribunda" by Bland. Vol P3 J of RHS 1863 Fuchsia trials at Chiswick 1862. A free blooming sort, with long, narrow, decurved sepals.Vol 2 J of RHS 1870 "Passed over". *Henderson, E.G.,St Johns Wood. GB. 1862.*

WHITE PERFECTION (a). Single. Red/White. Tube. White. Sepals. White. Corolla. Crimson. App. to RH. 1851 by Porcher. Inferior to "Duchess of Bordeaux" 1st class variety. GC. P184 27/3/1847 Listed by W. Miller, Ramsgate. GC. P216 27/3/1847 & P153 4/3/1848 & P202 1/4/1848 & P256 21/4/1849. Listed by R. Cooper, Croydon. GC. P337 22/5/1847 Listed by J. Hancock, Durham. GC. P259 28/4/1849 & P241 20/4/1850 Listed by W. Rendle, Plymouth. GC. P274 5/5/1849 Listed by H. Walton, Burnley. GC. P226 13/4/1850 Listed by Poole Nursery. GC. P737 7/11/1846 Intro. by F. Jennings, Gravesend. *Jennings, F. Gravesend. GB. 1847.*

WHITE PERFECTION (b). Single. White/Red. Tube. White. Sepals. Blush white. Long. Narrow. Corolla. Lake crimson and rose. P67 J of RHS 1877 Fuchsia trials at Chiswick 1873. Awarded *** Habit Good. Floriferous. Drooping. Submitted by Henderson. *Henderson E.G., St. Johns Wood. GB. 1872.*

WHITE PERFECTION (c). Single. Red/White. Tube. Rosy carmine. Sepals. Rosy carmine. Reflex to tube. Corolla. Pure white. Dwarf. Compact. Short jointed. 10/6d. GC. P344 4/4/1868 Intro. by B.W. Knight, Battle. *Knight, B.W. Battle. GB. 1868.*

WHITE PHENOMENAL. Double. Red/White. Tube. Scarlet. Sepals. Scarlet. Corolla. White. Sport from "Phenomenal". B. Cat. 1894-1895. BSW. Cat. 1897. HC. Cat. 1896 Illustrated. JF. Cat. 1899. *Wesley. GB. 1894*

WHITE QUEEN. Single. White/Red. Tube. White. Sepals. White. Corolla. Vermilion. JF. Cat. 1901. *Lye, J. Market Lavington. GB. 1901.*

WHITE SOUVENIR DE CHISWICK. Single. White/Red. Tube. Pure white. Long. Sepals. Pure white. Long. Reflexed. Corolla. Bright rose pink. Cup shaped. GO. "Select" 1881-1890. GC. P206 17/2/1877. HC. Cat. 1882 Resembles the dark variety "Souvenir de Chiswick". BSW. Cat. 1878. B. Cat. 1876. *Lye, J. Market Lavington. GB. 1875.*

WHITE UNIQUE. Double. Red/White. Tube. Bright carmine. Sepals. Bright carmine. Reflexed. Corolla. Pure white. Solid. Compact. P136 4th Ed. by Porcher 1874 Perfection of "Avalanche". BSW. Cat. 1878-1888. GC. P622 16/1/1874 Intro. by G. Smith, Tollington Nurseries. *Smith,G. Islington. GB. 1874.*

W.H. MOULD. Single. White/Red. Tube. White. Sepals. White. Corolla. Cerise red. GC. Vol 22 P295. *Lye, J. Market Lavington. GB. 1897.*

W.H. ROWE. Single. Red/Purple. Tube. Red. Sepals. Red. Corolla. Rosy mauve. Large. Good shape. Fine form. HC. Cat. 1896. JF. Cat. 1898. *Banks, E. Deal. GB. 1896.*

WILHELM PFITZER. S/Double. Red/Purple. Tube. Dull red. Sepals. Dull red. Long. Narrow. Pointed. Spreading. Corolla. Slaty red. RH. P311 1889 "Select" by E.A. Carrière. P89 Vol P3 J of RHS 1863 Fuchsia trials at Chiswick. A large coarse flowered sort. Submitted by H. Low. Vol 8 P339 Gartenflora. NK.NK. NK. NK.

WILHELM PABIT. Double. Red/Purple. Tube. Red. Sepals. Red. Corolla. Purple. P127 4th Ed. by Porcher 1874 Not in the first selection. *Weinrich. Germany 1866.*

WILLIAM IGGULDEN. Single. Red/Purple. Tube. Red. Sepals. Red. Corolla. Purple. GM. P59 2/2//1895 Article on James Lye. *Lye, J. Market Lavington. GB. 1894.*

WILLIAMSII. Single. Red/Purple. Tube. Reddish purple. Very short. A little swollen. Sepals. Reddish purple. Large. Totally reflexed. Corolla. Violet blue. App. to RH 1851 by Porcher. Resembles "Criterion". Flowers are a little too small. GC. P305 18/5/1850 Listed by Hart & Nicklin, Guildford. See also "Inaccessible". Corallina X. *Pope. GB. 1849.*

WILLMORII. Single. ND/ND. Tube. ND. Sepals. ND. Corolla. ND. GC. 22/7/1847 Exhibited at H.S. Show by Mr. Wiltshire, Gardener to J.H Reynolds. NK. NK. *1846*

WILL SELL. Single. Red/Purple. Tube. Coral scarlet. Sepals. Coral scarlet. Perfectly reflexed to form a perfect crown. Corolla. Satiny magenta. GC. P1554 2/12/1871 Review by H. Cannell. Free bloomer. Small neat foliage. Like "Killiecrankie". *Banks, E. Deal. GB. 1869.*

WILTSHIRE GIANT. S/Double. Red/Purple. Tube. Pale orange carmine. Stout. Sepals. Orange carmine. Broad. Corolla. Deep magenta. P342 Vol 24 J of RHS 1900 "I never used double corollas, but had two or three semi double. This one I thought good enough". Dobbies Cat. 1893-1894. *Lye, J. Market Lavington. GB. 1892.*

WILTSHIRE LASS. Single. White/Red. Tube. Waxy white. Sepals. Waxy white. Reflexed. Corolla. Rich dark puce. (Purplish rose). GC. P653 9/7/1864 Noted at RBS Show. SG. P459 1866 Dwarf. Compact habit. Prolific flowering. GC. P277 29/8/1885 Exhibited at Trowbridge H.S. Show by Matthews - 1st 4 pot class. Vol P3 J of RHS 1863. Fuchsia trials at Chiswick 1862. A very free and ornamental variety. Still one of the most desirous of the light coloured group. Awarded ***. Laings Cat. circa 1890. GC. P234 19/3/1859 Intro. by G. Wheeler, Warminster. *Wheeler, G. Warminster. GB. 1859.*

WINIFRED GLASS. Single. White/Red. Tube. Blush. Sepals. Blush. Corolla. Rich carmine. (Rich carmine shaded magenta). B. Cat. 1888-1892. Laings Cat. circa 1890. *Lye, J. Market Lavington. GB. 1886.*

WINSERII. Single. Red/Red. Tube. Rosy crimson. Long. Smooth. Sepals. Rosy crimson. Green tips. Open wide. Corolla. Rosy vermilion. Short. GC. P545 5/8/1843 Sent to editor of GC for appraisal by J.W. (Winser?), Tenterden. GC. P112 17/2/1844 Listed by W. Miller, Ramsgate. GC. P146 8/3/1845 Listed by Youell, Gt. Yarmouth. GC. P97 17/2/1844 Intro. by W.J. Epps, Maidstone. *Winser, J. Tenterden. GB. 1844.*

WM. PERRY. Double. Red/Purple. Tube. Crimson. Sepals. Crimson. Corolla. Dark purple. Very large. Free. JF. Cat. 1912. NK. NK. *GB. 1912.*

WOODSII. ND. ND/ND. Tube. ND. Sepals. ND. Corolla. ND. GC. P97 2/1843 & P257 4/1843 Listed by Youell, Gt. Yarmouth. GC. P112 2/1844 & P66 1/2/1845 Listed by W. Miller, Ramsgate. *May, Bedale. GB. 1842.*

WONDER. ND. ND/ND. Tube. ND. Sepals. ND. Corolla. ND. GC. P177 20/3/1852 Listed by W. Rumley, Richmond. NK. NK. NK. *1851.*

WONDERFUL (a). Single. Red/Purple. Tube. Scarlet. Sepals. Scarlet. Waxy. Reflexed. Corolla. Dark violet. Immense. Expanded. 37 mm in diameter. P3 J of RHS 1863 P89 Fuchsia trials at Chiswick 1862 A coarse red and purple. GC. P419 21/6/1856 Listed by Bainbridge & Hewison, York. GC. P451 5/7/1856 & P646 17/9/1856 Listed by H. Walton, Burnley. GC. P690 18/10/1856 Listed by W. Rumley, Richmond. GC. P251 11/4/1857 Listed by W.Masters, Canterbury. P115 23/2/1856 Intro. by W.J. Epps, Maidstone. *Epps, W.J. Maidstone GB. 1856.*

WONDERFUL (b). ND. ND/ND. Tube. ND. Sepals. ND. Corolla. ND. GC. P571 24/7/1858 Listed by H. Walton, Burnley. GC. P308 9/4/1859 Listed by W. Epps, Maidstone. GC. P580 9/7/1859 & P607 16/7/1859 Exhibited by H. Cannell, Gr to E. Grove, Tulse Hill, at RBS Show 6/7/1859. *Cornelissen. Arras. Belgium. 1858.*

WORDSWORTH. Single. Red/Purple. Tube. Carmine scarlet. Short. Sepals. Carmine scarlet. Recurved. Broad. Purplish plum. B. Cat. 1881-1883. *Bull,W. Chelsea. GB. 1881.*

WORMALDII. Single. ND/ND. Tube. ND. Sepals. ND. Corolla. ND. Colour plate in Floral Cabinet Vol VII Plate 239, 1839. GC. P833 18/12/1841 Spelling corrected (originally shown as Normaldii). GC. P685 16/10/1841 Raised by H. Wormald of Sawley Hall, Nr. Ripon. P668 11/10/1841 Exhibited at RHS of Cornwall show by Mr. J. Rickard, on 21/9/1841.

GC. P273 23/4/1842 Habit of Microphylla. Arborescens X Reflexa. *Wormald, H. Ripon. GB. 1838.*

W.S.GOVER. Sepals. ND/Pink. Tube. ND. Short. Sepals. ND. Long. Reflexed. Corolla. Silvery rose. Laings Cat. circa 1890. NK. NK. *GB.* NK.

WYVERN. S/Double. Red/Purple. Tube. Rosy crimson. Short. Sepals. Rosy crimson. Well reflexed. Long. Corolla. Purple. B. Cat. 1889-1893. *Bull,W. Chelsea. GB. 1888.*

XENOPHON. ND. ND/ND. Tube. ND. Sepals. ND. Corolla. ND. GC. P250 17/4/1847 Listed by W. Miller, Ramsgate. NK. NK. NK. *1846.*

YORKSHIRE ECLIPSE. Single. White/Purple. Tube. Pale blush. Sepals. Pale blush. Green tips. Corolla. Bright orange purple. GC. P658 20/10/1849 To be released in May 1850. GC. P387 15/6/1850 Listed by H. Walton, Burnley. GC. P465 27/7/1850 Listed by G. Smith, Islington. GC. P 465 27/7/1850 & P144 8/3/1851 Intro. by Wm. Rumley. *Rumley, W. Richmond. GB. 1850.*

YOUNG MAY MORN. Single. Pink/Red. Tube. Light salmon. Sepals. Light salmon. Corolla. Crimson. P170 Floricultural Cabinet Vol XIII 1845 H.S. Show Exhibited by Kendall, & P220 Exhibited at RBS Show by Kendall. *Kendall, Stoke Newington. GB. 1845.*

YVES DELAGE. Double. Red/Purple. Tube. Wine red. Sepals. Wine red. Broad. Corolla. Plum. Expanded. Full. Special formation of flowers. L. Cat. 1906. *Lemoine. Nancy. France. 1904.*

YVONNE DE BRAY. Single. White/White. Tube. White. Sepals. White hardly suffused pink. Large. Broad. Reflexed. Corolla. White. Very good habit. L. Cat. 1914. *Lemoine. Nancy. GB. 1914.*

ZAMPA. Double. Red/Purple. Tube. Reddish crimson. Sepals. Reddish crimson. Corolla. Purple. Enormous. BSW. Cat. 1888. *Lemoine. Nancy. France. 1882.*

ZEBRINA. Single. Red/Purple. Tube. Red. Sepals. Red. Corolla. Purple. GC. P184 13/3/1847 & P66 1/2/1845 Listed by W. Miller, Ramsgate. *Miller, W. Ramsgate. NK. 1844.*

ZELINDA. Double. Red/White. Tube. Rose. Sepals. Rose. Tipped green. Well reflexed. Corolla. White. B. Cat. 1870-1873. *Bull, W. Chelsea. GB. 1870.*

ZENOBIA. Single. Red/Red. Tube. Carmine rose. Sepals. Carmine rose. Corolla. Lake. RH. P24 1846. Floricultural Cabinet Vol XIV.P29 1846 Exhibited at RBS Show 2/7/1845 by Gaines. *Harrison, Dereham. GB. 1844.*

ZINGARA. Single. White/Purple. Tube. Pure white. Sepals. Pure white. Reflexed. Corolla. Lilac. Raised by W. Knight Gr. to the Duke of Kent. GC. P539 10/7/1858 Listed by F. Godwin, Sheffield. GC. P126 20/2/1858 Intro. by W. Rollinson. *Knight, W. GB. 1858.*

ZOMME DE BRAY. JF. Cat. 1920. Most likely "Yvonne de Bray".

EDWARD R R G BANKS (1820-1910)

Living at Sholden Hall, Deal, Kent, Edward Banks developed a thriving floricultural business propagating fuchsias. He supplied such famous firms as Henry Cannell Nurseries, Swanley and E G Henderson, St Johns Wood, London. He became one of the largest growers of Fuchsias of his times, employing up to ten gardeners, and producing many new cultivars each year. Fuchsias which are attributed to him in contemporary literature are listed below. His Forget Me Not Fuchsia is the Emblem of the British Fuchsia Society.

ALBERT SMITH	1857
ALBERT VICTOR	1878
ALEXANDRINA	1866
ANNA BULLEYN	1864
ARABELLA	1866
ARIEL	1852
AUTOCRAT	1854
BACCHUS	1863
BARCELONA	1873
BARONESS BURDETT COUTTS	1872
BEAUTY	1865
BEAUTY OF DEAL	1852
BEAUTY OF KENT	1870
BEAUTY OF SHOLDEN	1868
BEAUTY OF THE BOWER	1855
BEAUTY'S BLOOM	1866
BEN E GLOE	1866
BIANCA MARGINATA	1862
BLACK PRINCE	1861
BLANCHETTE	1866
BLUE BEAUTY	1864
BRIDAL BOQUET	1862?
BRILLIANT	1851
BRILLIANT	1867
BRITISH SAILOR	1858
CATHERINE HAYES	1857
CATHERINE PARR	1866
CHARLEMANGE	1856
CHARMER	1854
CLIMAX	1855
CLIO	1854
COEUR DE LION	1857
COLLEGIAN	1853
COLONEL HARCOURT	1876
COMET	1862
CONQUEST	1866
CONSOLATION	1865
CONSPICUA	1851
CONSTANCE	1860
CORTONA	1852
COUNT CAVOUR	1860
CROWN JEWEL	1859
DAY DREAM	1865?
DIADEM	1852

DON GIOVANNI	1864
DONNA JOAQUINA	1856
DR KITTO GIDDINGS	1878?
DR LINDLEY	1853
DR LIVINGSTONE	1860
DUKE OF CONNAUGHT	1894
DUKE OF EDINBURGH	1872
DUKE OF EDINBURGH	1894
DUKE OF FIFE	1894
DUKE OF YORK	1894
EDITH	1862
ELECT	1851
ELEGANS	1854
ELEGANTISSIMA	1862
EMBLEMATIC	1863
EMPEROR NAPOLEON	1856
ENOCH ARDEN	1865
ÉTOILE DU NORD	1857
EUTERPE	1854
EVENING STAR	1868
EXPANSION	1851
FAIR ORIANA	1857
FAIREST OF THE FAIR	1857
FAIRY QUEEN	1855
FATHER IGNATUS	1865
FAVOURITE	1855
FINSBURY VOLUNTEER	1861?
FIRST OF THE DAY	1870
FLOWER OF FRANCE	1859
FORGET ME NOT	1861
FRANK VINE	1860?
GAIETY	1852
GARIBALDI	1860
GEORGE BRUNNING	1872
GLORY	1853
GUIDING STAR	1856
HARRY GEORGE HENDERSON	1866
HERCULES	1872
HONEYBELL	1852
ISA CRAIG	1859
JAMES HOOD	1896
JF McELROY	1870
JOAN OF ARC	1852
JULIA DE GUEST	1866
KILLIECRANKIE	1867
KING OF THE FUCHSIAS	1868
KING OF THE STRIPES	1870
KITTY TYRRELL	1858
LA CRINOLINE	1859
LADY DUMBELLO	1866
LADY OF THE LAKE	1855
LADY OF THE SEA	1865
LAND OF PLENTY	1866
LA PROPHETE	1859
LA TRAVIATA	1865
LEADER	1852
LEOLINE	1859

		PURITANI	1864
LIGHT HEART	1865	PURITY	1860
LITTLE DORRIT	1859	QUEEN OF HANOVER	1854
LIZZIE HEXHAM	1866	QUEEN OF THE SEA	1858
LONG FELLOW	1860	REV T WILTSHIRE	1875
LORD DERBY	1868	RHODERICK DHU	1865
LORD ELCHO	1861	RIFLEMAN	1863
LORD FALMOUTH	1867	ROSE OF CASTILLE	1858
LORD JOHN RUSSELL	1860	ROSE OF DENMARK	1865
LORD MACAULEY	1860	SCHILLER	1860
LORD STANLEY	1870	SIGNORA	1862
LORD WARDEN	1862	SIR ROBERT PEEL	1860
LOVELINESS	1851	SIR W G ARMSTONG	1876
LUCREZIA BORGIA	1864	SNOW DROP	1860
LUCY MILLS	1865	SOUVENIR DE CHISWICK	1857
MACBETH	1854	SPLENDOUR	1870
MADAME PATTI	1863	STAR OF THE NIGHT	1857
MADAME SONTAG	1851	STRADELLA	1859
MAGIC FLUTE	1859	STRIATA PERFECTA	1868
MAGNIFICA	1854	STRIATA SPLENDIDA	1872
MAID OF KENT	1855	SUNSHINE	1864
MARGINATA	1862	SWANLEY GEM	1878
MARVELLOUS	1864	THE AMERICAN BANNER	1871
MASANIELLO	1858	THE FAIR ORIANA	1857
MAUVE QUEEN	1872	THE LITTLE TREASURE	1857
MDLLE TREBELLI	1862	THE RIGHT HON JOHN BRIGHT	1870
MEDORA	1863	THE SILVER SWAN	1857
MERRY MAID	1866	THE VILLAGE PET	1865
MINNIE BANKS	1862	TRISTRAM SHANDY	1857
MISS MAY CAMERON	1896	TROUBADOR	1864
MODEL	1853	TRUTH	1875
MODEL	1868	TRY ME O	1868
MR RICHARD PEXTON	1872	VANGUARD	1854
MRS SHIRLEY HIBBERD	1870	VENUS DE MEDICI	1856
NONSUCH	1852	VESTA	1870
NORTHERN LIGHT	1863	VICTOR EMMANUEL	1862
OBERON	1864	VOLCANO DI AQUA	1856
OMEGA	1854	VOLTIGEUR	1851
OMER PACHA	1855	WAR EAGLE	1865
OUR FUTURE QUEEN	1872	W.B. LEAF	1896
PANMURE GORDON	1896	W.H. ROWE	1896
PERFECTION	1853	WILL SELL	1869
PERFECTION	1870		
PRIDE OF WOOLWICH	1870		
PRINCE ALBERT	1855		
PRINCE ALFRED	1860		
PRINCE ARTHUR	1860		
PRINCE FREDERICK WILLIAM OF			
PRUSSIA	1858		
PRINCE IMPERIAL	1860		
PRINCE LEOPOLD	1861		
PRINCE OF ORANGE	1860		
PRINCESS	1851		
PRINCESS ALICE	1860		
PRINCESS BEATRICE	1867		
PRINCESS MAY	1894		
PRINCESS OF WALES	1863		

J EDMUND BLAND

Gardener on several estates in Richmond, Surrey area. Gardener to S K Mainwaring at Oteley Park, Shropshire, 1881. His own account of his life and a portrait is given in the Gardeners Chronicle 1894 Vol I page 146. He raised many fuchsia varieties, as listed below:

ADDISON	1881
ADINE	1878
ALBERT MEMORIAL	1871
ATTRACTION	1881
BEATRICE	1877
BIRD OF PARADISE	1870

BLANDS NEW STRIPED	1873
BLANDS FLORIBUNDA	1867
CANNELS GEM	1873
CARMINATA	1877
CHAMPION OF THE WORLD	1870
CHASTITY	1882
CLARINDA	1880
CLIPPER	1877
COLOSSUS	1883
COQUETTE	1873
CREUSA	1880
CRITERION	1882
DESIDERATUM	1874
DR. HESSLE	1873
EMPEROR OF BRAZIL	1872
EMPRESS OF GERMANY	1871
ENCHANTRESS	1870
FAVOURITE	1868
FLORIBUNDA	1867
FORMOSA	1870
FORMOSA	1882
GALATEA	1878
GASPAR	1880
GENERAL GARFIELD	1882
GERALD	1882
GRAND DUCHESS MARIE	1874
GRANDIDENS	1874
HARDY HYBRID No 1	1873
HARDY HYBRID No 2	1873
HARDY HYBRID No 3	1873
HARDY HYBRID No 4	1873
HARRY WILLIAMS	1871
HOLLOWAY RIVAL	1870
IMPROVEMENT	1877
INSPECTOR	1868
JASON	1878
JOHN GIBSON	1875
KING ALFONSO	1875
KING OF THE DOUBLES	1866
LADY DOROTHY NEVILLE	1873
LADY WATERLOW	1875
LITTLE ALICE	1870
LITTLE BOBBY	1874
LITTLE HARRY	1870
MANTLE	1880
MARCHIONESS OF ANGLESEY	1873
MATCHLESS	1882
MEMPHIS	1878
MINERVA	1878
MONSTER	1866
MONSTROSITY	1877
MONTGOMERY	1881
MONTROSE	1869
MR E BENNETT	1873
MR POWELL	1882
MRS BALLANTINE	1871
MRS BLAND	1871

MRS BURROUGHS	1877
MRS E BENNETT	1872
MRS GLADSTONE	1874
MRS MEIN	1875
NESTOR	1878
PATRIOT	1882
PRINCE LEOPOLD	1872
PRINCESS LOUISE	1871
PRINCESS OF WALES	1870
PURITY	1872
RESPLENDENT	1873
SIR BARTLE FRERE	1873
SIR GARNET WOLSESLEY	1874
STRIATA PERFECTA	1870
STUPENDOUS	1873
SURPRISE	1875
SYMMETRY	1874
TINTED VENUS	1869
TRIUMPHANS	1870
TROUBADOR	1869

LAURENT BOUCHARLAT (1807-1903)

In 1830 he founded a nursery at "Montée des Chartreux", Lyons, where he collected and hybridized a whole variety of plants, including petunias, pelargoniums, dahlias, chrysanthemums and, of course, fuchsias. He had an extremely distinguished career in horticulture, and was awarded many medals of merit in recognition of his work. His niece, Francoise Marie Boucharlat married Joseph Rozain (*q.v.*) who continued the nursery in Lyons. Their son Benoit Rozain-Boucharlat also continued the business. Further details of their lives are found in Fuchsiaphiles 1989-90, researched by B. Fournier. Laurent Boucharlat, hybridized the following Fuchsias:

ABONDANCE	?
AMELIE BOTTERI	1881
ANNA	1856
BEAUTÉ	1880
CIEL D'AZUR	1883
CLÉOPÂTRE	1884
COMPACTA FLORIBUNDA	1880?
COMPACTA SUPERBA	1880?
CREPUSCULE	1883
DOCTEUR COMPIN	1883
ESMERALDA	1884
FRÈRE MICHEL	1881
GEANT DES BATAILLES	1881?
JOSEF NAGY	1880
JULES MONGES	1881
LUCILLE LEMOINIER	1880
MADAME JULES CHRÉTIEN	1891
MINERVA	1881
M. LOMBARD	1880
SUPASSE VANQUEUR DE PUEBLA	1867

WILLIAM BULL (1828-1902)

Born in Winchester, Hants in 1828. In 1861 he acquired the nursery and stock of John Weeks & Co, Kings Road, Chelsea. He introduced and hybridized very many new Fuchsias listed below, but he was also very interested in orchids and introduced *Caffea liberica*.

ACHILLES	1898	BRITON	1901
ACIS	1880	BRUTUS	1901
ACMON	1880	BUDGET	1901
ADAIR	1888	BULRUSH	1880
ADELA	1869	CALLAO	1876
ADELINE	1862	CALLIOPE	1896
ADMIRATION	1875	CALYPSO	1875
AGRA	1899	CAMEO	1901
ALBERTA	1868	CAMERON	1872
ALFONSO	1875	CANARY BIRD	1873
ALICE	1873	CASILDA	1901
ALLIANCE	1869	CASINO	1897
ALTAIR	1900	CASSIA	1875
AMADEO	1879	CECIL	1898
AMBASSADOR	1861	CERBERUS	1874?
AMBASSADOR	1871	CERES	1896
AMBROSIA	1880	CHAMPION	1870
AMPHION	1872	CHAMPION	1895
ANGELIC	1869	CHARMER	1875
ANITA	1885	CHIEFTAIN	1872
ANNIE LUSTRE	1876	CISSIE	1879
ANOMIA	1875	CLARISSA	1870
ANTONA	1881	CLARICE	1905
ARCHETTE	1872	CLAUDIA	1900
ARIA	1883	COMA	1873
ARPA	1883	COMMANDER	1871
ASPASIA	1900	COMPACT	1874
ASSEMBLY	1869	CORINTH	1872
ATALANTA	1874	CORSAIR	1870
ATHALIE	1878	COUNTESS OF WARWICK	1895
AUTOCRAT	1871	CYPRIS	1905
AZUREA SUPERBA	1879	DACIA	1901
BALTIC	1897	DAMON	1898
BARONESS	1875	DARING	1905
BARONNE BLANCHE EZPELTA	1875	DECIMA	1880
BASILISK	1873?	DELIGHT	1870?
BEACON	1871	DIANA	1901
BEATRICE	1863	DICTATOR	1871
BELLA	1872	DIONE	1873
BELLONA	1896	DISPLAY	1869
BERCERA	1897	DOMINGO	1872
BERENICE	1880	DORCAS	1887?
BLACK PRINCE	1876	DORIS	1896
BLUE KING	1877	DUNOIS	1876
BRAVO	1862	EGERIA	1875
BRENDA	1900?	ELAINE	1901
BRIGADE	1871	ELBA	1897
BRIGHTNESS	1861	ELEGANCE	1898
BRILLIANT	1865	ELEGANS	1866
		ELFIN	1875
		ELFRIDA	1871
		ELSA	1901
		EMBLEM	1869?
		EMPEROR	1867
		EMPRESS	1868?
		EMPRESS OF INDIA	1877
		ENCOUNTER	1868?

ENSIGN	1871?	ICARUS	1899
ERMAN	1900	IDRA	1899
ERNEST	1872	ILIAD	1905
ETHEL	1872	INCOMPARABLE	1861
ETRURIA	1874	INDIAN CHIEF	1876
ETTIE	1863	INNOCENCE	1868
EUGENIA	1900	INSTANCE	1869
EURYDICE	1901	INSTIGATOR	1869
EUSTACE	1872	INTENSITY	1877
EVA	1864	INTERNATIONAL	1862
EXCELSIOR	1895	IONA	1905
FABIUS	1882	IRENE	1872
FAGUS	1905	IRENE	1896
FAIRY	1863	IRIS	1896
FALCON	1900	IRMA	1887
FANE	1897	JANUS	1899
FARA	1883	JESSICA	1871
FASCINATION	1898	JOSEFA	1863
FATMA	1886	JUMNA	1885
FAVOURITE	1895	JUNO	1888
FESTINA	1874	JUNON	1905
FLAMBEAU	1879	LAFAYETTE	1896
FLORA	1887	LAMUS	1881
FLORETTA	1863	LATONA	1897
FORTUNA	1896	LAVINA	1871
FREEDOM	1900	LEDA	1896
FREUND J DURR	1870	LEONARD	1871
GANNET	1887	LEWALD	1872
GAZELLE	1883	LILLAH	1872
GEM	1874	LINA	1872
GEM OF THE SEASON	1862	LINDA	1899
GENEROUS	1870	LOTHAIR	1900
GEORGE FREDERICK	1875	LOUISE	1900
GERARD	1900?	LUCIUS	1897
GERTRUDE	1870	LURLINE	1869
GERTRUDE	1891	LUSTRE	1868
GIANT	1869	LYDIA	1863
GIDOUR	1899	LYRA	1901
GIPSY QUEEN	1865	LYSIAS	1900
GRAPHIE	1901	MAGNATE	1900
GRENADIER	1871	MAID OF HONOUR	1870
HAIDEE	1901	MANDARIN	1872
HALLOWEEN	1901	MANTLE	1871
HANDEL	1905	MAORI CHIEF	1873
HARMONY	1872	MARATHON	1873
HECLA	1901	MARGARET	1863
HECTOR	1868?	MARGUERITE	1865
HECTOR	1898	MARMION	1871
HERALD	1869	MARTIUS	1905
HER MAJESTY	1862	MARVEL	1870
HERO	1862	MATCHLESS	1863
HERON	1886	MAY QUEEN	1869
HIGHLAND CHIEF	1875	MEDINA	1871
HILDA	1872	MEDORA	1901
HOGARTH	1870	MENNON	1870
HUME	1881	MENTO	1899
IANTHE	1872	MENTOR	1873

CORNELISSEN

Nurseryman of Arras, Belgium, responsible for the following introductions:

AMBROISE VERSCHAFFELT	1866
ANGELINA BRAEMT	1868
COMTE DE FLANDRE	1868
COMTESSE DE FLANDRE	1868
CORNELISSEN	1857
DUC DE BRABANT	?
DUC DE CRILLON	1866
DUC DE TREVISE	1859
E.G. HENDERSON	?
EMPEREUR DES FUCHSIAS	1863
F.C. HEINEMANN	?
GÉNÉRAL BORREMANS	1860
GERARD CORNELISSEN	1869
GUSTAVE HEITZ	1866
IMPERATRICE ELIZABETH	1866
JEAN CORNELISSEN	1868?
JEANNE D'ARC	1868
LAURENT PALMAERT	1864
LOUIS DE SMET	1867
MADAME AMBROISE VERSCHAFFELT	1868
MADAME CAMBIER	1866
MADAME CORNELISSEN	1860
MADAME DEPROOST	1867
MADAME PANIS	1866
MARIE CORNELISSEN	1861
M. BRUANT	1862
MONSIEUR ACKERMAN	1868
MONSIEUR CHARLES GAILLY	1868
MONSIEUR LAURENTIUS	?
MONSIEUR MAIL	1865
MONSIEUR TAGLIARUE	1863
MURAT	1859
PRESIDENT MULLER	1866
PRINCE GHIKA	1859
SOUVENIR DE CORNELISSEN	1864
TRIOMPHE DE BRUXELLES	1857
TRIOMPHE DE CORNELISSEN	1861
WONDERFUL	1858

WILLIAM JAMES EPPS (1817-1885)

Nurseryman of Maidstone Kent, noted for fuchsias and Cape heaths. According to contemporary sources, he is believed to have raised the following fuchsias:

ADMIRABLE	1856
BRIDEGROOM	1844
COUNTESS OF CORNWALLIS	1846
DUKE OF WELLINGTON	1844
EPPSII	1843
ESPARTERO	1843
FAIR ROSAMUNDE	1846
FLORENCE	1844

KENTISH HERO	1844
LADY JULIA	1846
MARCHIONESS CORNWALLIS	1846
MARIA	1844
MONARCH	1844
NOVELTY	1852
NYMPH	1845
QUEEN OF THE BEAUTIES	1845
STANDARD OF PERFECTION	1852
WEBBII	1847
WONDERFUL	1856

J HARRISON

Nurseryman of Dereham, responsible for the following introductions:

AMATO	1842
AMULET	1844
ARAGO	?
ARG	?
BEAUTÉ PARFAIT	1847
BLANCHE	1842
CLARA	1844
CLIO	1842
CORINNE	1846
CORNELIA	1846
DESDEMONA	1844
ENCHANTRESS	1842
FAIRY	1842
FLORA	1842
FORMOSA	?
GARLAND	1846
GEM	1842
GOLDFINCH	1844
GREAT EXHIBITION	1862
HARRISONII	1862
MADONNA	1843
MEDORA	?
METEOR	1842
PEARL	1843
PRIMA DONNA	1843
PULCHERRIMA	1842
QUEEN VICTORIA	1845
RECURVA	1845
SPECTABLIS	1842
TROPHY	1862
VENUSTA	1842
VILLAGE MAID	1845
ZENOBIA	1844

EDWARD GEORGE HENDERSON (1782-1876)

He was the eldest son of Andrew Henderson (fl. 1790s - 1840s), founder of the Pine Apple Place Nursery. He also became a nurseryman, of Vine Place, Edgware Road, Paddington, London and later of Wellington Road Nurseries, St Johns Wood. He introduced many new fuchsias from his nurseries, and is believed to have hybridizied the following ones himself:

ALBA COCCINEA	1867
ALWAYS READY	1861
ANNIE	1861
AVALANCHE	1869
CARMINATA ROSEA	1873
CHICAGO	1873
CONFIDENCE	1850
CORA	?
DESIDERATA	?
DON GIOVANNI	1850
FAIR ROSAMOND	1850
FAIRY QUEEN	1875
FULGENS CARMINATA ROSEA	1873
GARIBALDI	1868
GAZELLE	1870
GOLDEN FLEECE	1867
GOLDEN MANTLE	1870
GOLDEN TREASURE	1870
GRAND MASTER	1850
GUARDSMAN	1872
HARVEST HOME	1870
HEATHER BELL	1869
HELIGOLAND	1873
HERMIONE	1861?
IMPROVEMENT	1871
INIMITABLE	1870
INSPECTOR	1874
JOSÉPHINE	1871
KETELEERI	1862
LITTLE GEM	1872
LORD OF THE ISLES	1851
MADAME SONTAG	1851
MIZPAH	1877
MONARCH	1854
NABOB	1871
NOBLESSE	1871
NORFOLK HERO	1866
ORANGE BOVEN	1870
PEARL OF ENGLAND	1850
PREMIER	1853
PRIME MINISTER	1851
PRINCE OF ORANGE	1850
PRINCESS ALEXANDER	1873
RESPLENDENT	1851
ROSALIE	1861
SIMS REEVES	1850
SNOWDROP	1868
TRICOLOURED BEAUTY	1873
WARRIOR QUEEN	1870
WATER NYMPH	1871
WHITE EAGLE	1870
WHITE LADY	1862
WHITE PERFECTION	1872

VICTOR LEMOINE (1823-1911).

Born in the village of Delme near Nancy, Lorraine, France and educated by D A Baumann, Botanist and Gardener at Bolwiller in the Haute Rhine. He worked first for the firms of Van Houtte in Ghent and Meillez in Lille, before eventually establishing his own successful plant-nursery business in Nancy. According to the research undertaken for this book, he is responsible for the introduction of the different cultivars of Fuchsias listed below. He received international recognition for his achievements and died at the age of 88.

ABEL CARRIÈRE	1868
ABBÉ DAVID	1901
ABBÉ FARGES	1901
ABD EL KADIR	1880
A. DE.NEUVILLE	1888
ADOLPHE WELCH	1868
ADRIEN MARIE	1894
AÉROSTAT	1889
AIMÉ MILLET	1891
ALBERT DELPIT	1893
ALBION	1890
ALEXANDRE DUMAS FILS	1895
ALFRED DUMESNIL	1882
ALFRED FOUILLÉE	1898
ALFRED NEYMARCK	1907
ALFRED PICARD	1906
ALFRED RAMBAUD	1896
ALPHAND	1900
ALPHONSE DAUDET	1883?
ALPHONSE KARR	1891
ALSACIEN LORRAIN	1874
AMI HOSTE	1866
AMIRAL AUBE	1891
AMIRAL COURBET	1887
AMIRAL EVANS	1908
AMIRAL MIOT	1886
AMIRAL OLRY	1891
ANDRÉ CARNEGIE	1906
ANDRÉ LENOSTRE	1909
ARMAND GAUTIER	1904
ARTÉMISE	1892
ATHENES	1911
ATROPURPUREA FLORE PLENO	1858
AUGUSTA HOLMES	1903
AUGUSTE FLEMENG	1884
AUGUSTE HARDY	1892
AUGUSTIN THIERRY	1889
BARON DE KETTELER	1901
BARTHOLDII	1887
BAUCIS	1901
BEAUMARCHAIS	1897
BÉRANGER	1865
BÉRANGER	1897
BERTRADE	1906

BLANCHE DE CASTILLE	1900	ED.ANDRÉ	1878
BLANCHETTE	1904	EDMOND ABOUT	1888
BOQUET	1893	EDMOND PERRIER	1904
BRENNUS	1867	EDMOND PERRIER	1912
BULGARIE	1886	ELÉGANT	1893
BUSSIERE	1903	ELIANE	1913
BUZENVAL	1887	ELYSÉE	1887
BYZANCE	1911	ÉMILE BAYARDE	1892
CALCHAS	1911	ÉMILE DE WILDEMAN	1905
CAPITAINE BINGER	1894	EMILE ERCKMANN	1903
CAPITAINE BOYTON	1878	ÉMILE LAURENT	1904
CAPITAINE TILHO	1907	EMILE LEMOINE	1863
CARMEN	1893	ÉMILE RICHEBOURG	1894
CARMEN SYLVA	1898	EMMA CALVÉ	1912
CASTELAR	1899	ENFANTE PRODIGUE	1887
CELINE MONTALAND	1891	ERNEST RENAN	1888
CERVANTES	1889	ESPÉRANCE	1887
CHARLES GARNIER	1900	ÉTIENNE LAMY	1906
CHARLES LAMOUREUX	1900	EUGÈNE DELAPLANCHE	1891
CHARLES SECRÉTAN	1893	EUGÈNE VERCONSIN	1892
CHRISTOPHE COLOMB	1893	FÉLICIEN DAVID	1903
CLAUD DE LORRAIN	1872	FELIX DUBOIS	1894
COLIBRI	1898	FILLE DE L'AIR	1862
COLONEL BORGNIS-DESBORDES	1886	FILLE DES CHAMPS	1887
COLONEL BRANLIÈRES	1908	FIRMIN GÉMIER	1914
COLONEL DE TRENTIAN	1899	FLEURE ROUGE	1885
COLONEL DOMINIÉ	1886	FLEUVE BLEU	1901
COMMANDANT MARCHAND	1899	FLOCON DE NEIGE	1884
COMMANDANT TAILLANT	1874	FLORIAN	1897
COMTE DE MEDICI SPADA	1859	FORMOSE	1885
COMTE LÉON TOLSTOI	1888	FORMOSE	1901
COMTE WITTE	1906	FRANCISQUE SARCEY	1879
CONCILE	1870	FRANÇOIS BOUCHER	1910
CORINTHE	1911	GABRIEL BONVALOT	1899
CORNE D'ABONDANCE	1894?	GAMBETTA	1876
CORNEILLE	1897	GARNIER PAGES	1879
DAUBENTON	1888	GÉNÉRAL CHANZY	1874
DE CHERVILLE	1896	GÉNÉRAL D'AMADE	1908
DE GONCOURT	1896	GÉNÉRAL DODDS	1893
DÉLOS	1911	GÉNÉRAL DRUDE	1908
DÉMOSTHÈNE	1875	GÉNÉRAL FORGEMOL	1882
DÉMOSTHÈNE	1878	GÉNÉRAL GALLIENI	1899
DE MONTALIVET	1879	GENERAL GRANT	1869
DÉPUTÉ BERLET	1881	GÉNÉRAL LAPASSET	1883
DÉPUTÉ TEUTSCH	1874	GÉNÉRAL LEWAL (LEVAL)	1885
DE QUATREFAGES	1892	GÉNÉRAL LYAUTEY	1908
D. FOURNIER	1905	GÉNÉRAL SAUSSIER	1882
DRAME	1887	GÉNÉRAL VOYRON	1901
DR. BEHRING	1902	GEORGES FEYDEAU	1894
DR. BORNET	1912	GEORGES LYON	1907
DR. CREVAUX	1880	GERBE DE CORAIL	1901
DR. GODRON	1878	GRACIEUX	1881
DR. JOHANNSEN	1904	GUILLAUME GRANDIDIER	1904
DR. PRILLIEUX	1890	GUSTAVE DORÉ	1880
DR. TOPINARD	1890	GUSTAVE FLAUBERT	1891
DUC D'AUMALE	1896	GUSTAVE NADAUD	1892
DUCHESSE DE GEROLSTEIN	1868	GUY DE MAUPASSANT	1890

PIERRE JOIGNEAUX	1893
PIERRE LOTI	1889
PIERRE MOUILLEFÉRT	1904
PRESIDENT CARNOT	1888
PRESIDENT GRÉVY	1886
PRESIDENT HUMANN	1868
PRESIDENT PORCHER	1862
PRINCE GEORGES	1899
PRIX NOBEL	1902
PROFESSEUR LIPPMAN	1909
PROFESSEUR ROENTGEN	1902
PROFUSION	1887
RACHILDE	1912
RACINE	1897
RAOUL PUGNO	1910
RAOUL TOCHÉ	1892
ROCHAMBEAU	1903
ROLLA	1913
RONSARD	1897
ROSSINI	1869
ROUGET DE L'ISLE	1903
RUY BLAS	1868
SARAH BERNHARDT	1899
SATRAPE	1912
SCHLIEMANN	1891
SCULPTOR BARTHOLOMÉ	1900
SENATEUR BERLET	1884
SÉVERINE	1911
SOCRATE	1875
SOLFERINO	1860
STATUAIRE DALON	1900
STEPHEN PINCHON	1901
SULLY-PRUDHOMME	1902
TAGLIONI	1868
TAKOU	1901
TALMA	1869
TELEGRAPH	1887
TERPSICHORE	1860
THAIS	1913
THEROIGNE DE MERICOURT	1903
TIENTSIN	1901
TRIPHYLLA HYBRIDA	1895
TWRDY	1868
ULYSSE TRÉLAT	1890
VAN T'HOFF	1902
VERDI	1892
VERA SERGINE	1914
VICTOR HUGO	1897
VICTORIEN SARDOU	1866
VICTORIEN SARDOU	1907
VICTOR MASSÉ	1903
VILLE DE NANCY	1875
VINCENT D'INDY	1910
VIOLLET-LE-DUC	1879
VOILE BLUE	1908
VOIX DU PEUPLE	1874
VOLUNTAIRE	1887

YVES DELAGE	1904
YVONNE DE BRAY	1914
ZAMPA	1882

JAMES LYE (1830-1906)

Born in Market Lavington James Lye commenced work at the age of 12 in the gardens of Clyffe Hall. At 23 he was appointed Head Gardener and from about this time began to concentrate on growing and exhibiting Fuchsias. He became renown for his pyramid and pillar Fuchsias and one finds frequent references to these in gardening revues of the period. He started hybridising in the 1860s and below are listed what contemporary sources indicate were his introductions.

ABUNDANCE *Tru*	1887
ADA BRIGHT	1889
ALICE (MARY) PEARSON	1887
AMY LYE	1901
ANNIE EARLE	1887
ARABELLA IMPROVED	1871
AURORA	1885
AYRSHIRE	1889
BEAUTY OF CLYFFE HALL	1883
BEAUTY OF LAVINGTON	1886
BEAUTY OF SWANLEY	1875
BEAUTY OF THE WEST	1880
BEAUTY OF WILTS	1877
BENJAMIN PEARSON	1887
BLUSHING BRIDE	1877
BOUNTIFUL	1883
BRILLIANT	1901
CECIL GLASS	1887
CHARMING	1877
CLIPPER	1901
C.N. MAY	1888
CONSTANCY	1889
CRIMSON GLOBE	1879
DELICATA	1877
DELIGHT	1889
DIADEM	1886
DUCHESS OF ALBANY	1885
DUCHESS OF FIFE	1892
DUKE OF ALBANY	1885
ECLIPSE	1897
ELEGANCE	1877
ELLEN LYE	1882
EMILY BRIGHT	1886
EMILY DOEL	1880?
EMILY LYE	1878
EMPEROR	1886
FAIR MAID	1889
FAIRY QUEEN	1878
FINAL	1881?
GEM OF LAVINGTON	1888
GEM OF THE WEST	1877

MEILLEZ
Nurseryman, working in Lille, France

W MILLER
Nurseryman, working in Ramsgate.

EXPANSIA	1845	CAMPANULE	1926 Jr
FLORIBUNDUS	1848	CARACAS	1910
GLOBE CELESTE	1846	CARILLON	1913
GLOBE TERRESTE	1846	CARILLON	1926 Jr
GREAT BRITAIN	1846	CASCADE FLEURIE	1938 Jr
JEHU	1854	CELESTINUM	1898
MAGNUN BONUM	1847	CLOCHE BLUE	1934 Jr
MISS PRETTYMAN	1846	COELESTINA	1891
QUEEN VICTORIA	1846	COLONEL ARCHINARD	' 1893
SPLENDISSIMA	1845	COMMANDANT BARATIER	1900
SULTAN	1846	COMTE D'HUGUES	1897
TRIUMPH	1848	COMTE DE MUN	1893
UNIQUE	1845	COMTE DE VERTAMONT	1904
ZEBRINA	1844	COMTE LÉONTIEFF	1898

JOSEPH ROZAIN (1850-1917)

Nurseryman, of Lyons, France. He married the niece of Laurent Boucharlat and worked in the family horticultural business, which he took over in 1884. Two years later his son, Benoit Rozain-Boucharlat was born and he continued the successful family horticultural business until his death in 1943. 1937 the nursery had no less than 366 separate medals and awards both national and international in recognition of its outstanding contribution to horticulture. Joseph Rozain's Fuchsia introductions and those of his son (where evident) are listed below:

A. BERTHOUD	1905	CONTRASTE	1897
ABBÉ GARNIER	1889	COQUELIN	1904
ABBÉ GOURDON	1899	COTE D'AZURE	1912
ABBÉ LEMIRE	1896	CRISTAL	1925 Jr
ABELINE FABRE	1899	DANUBE BLEU	1929 Jr
A. DE LEAU	1887	DEFIANCE	1890
ALGERSIRAS	1907	DE JUSSIEUX	1898
ALSACE	1921 Jr	DE SAINT-HILAIRE	1909
AMBROISE LAUGIER	1906	DEUIL DE L'AMIRAL COURBET	1886
AMIRAL GERVAIS	1892	DE WITTE	1906
AMIRAL REINIER	1893	DIADÈME	1891
ANGELO FERRARIO	1911	DIAMANT	1902
A P VIDAL	1903	DIDON	1885
ARC EN CIEL	1891	DIRECTEUR POYARD	1906
ARLEQUIN	1894	DR. NOEL-MARTIN	1899
ARLEQUIN	1923 Jr	E.CHAPOTON	1895
ASPIRATION	1892	ED. DE CARVALA LUPI	1892
AVANTE GARDE	1920 Jr	ED. FARINA	1903
AZUREA	1888	EDOUARD DE PERRODIL	1910
BACCHUS	1924 Jr	E. JOUBERT	1904
BAHIA	1910	ELDORADO	1888
BELGIQUE	1915	ÉMILE DAVID	1907
BENGALI	1911	ÉMILE SALLE	1893
BERTHENAY	1906	EMPEROR NICOLAS II	1898
BOSSUET	1898	ERICA	1922 Jr
BOU-DENIB	1909	ESMERELDA	1922 Jr
BRANLY	1913	EXPLOSION	1894
BUISSON BLANC	1907	FEMINA	1913
CAMELIA	1928 Jr	FLAMBOYANT	1906
		F. LEMON	1905
		FRANC-NOHAIN	1907
		FRANÇOIS COPPÉE	1903
		FRÉDÉRIC PASSY	1902
		FRÈRE HILDEGRIN	1892
		FRÈRE MARIE-PIERRE	1886
		FRÈRE MICHEL	1890
		FUNCK-BRENTANO	1909
		GASTON CAZALIS	1911
		GAY-LUSSAC	1893
		GÉNÉRAL MERCIER	1900
		GÉNÉRAL NEGRIER	1900
		GERBERT	1907
		GLOIRE DES MARCHES	1894

205

GUY DAUPHINE	1913
H. DUTERAIL	1905
HALLALI	1913
HENRI ETIENNE	1887
HENRI D'ORLÉANS	1898
HÉRISSÉ	1887
ISABELLE	1913
IVOIRE	1934 Jr
JACQUES ROZE	1909
J. ALDRUFEU	1891
JARRY-DESLOGES	1895
J.B. VARRONNE	1885
J. DE LA PERRIÉRE	1908
J. LEJEUNE	1903
JOSEPH ROZAIN	1881
J. MOINS	1902
J. PERINI	1904
JUBILÉ	1888
JULES CHRÉTIEN	1891
JUPITER	1889
JUSSIEUX	1898
KHÉDIVE	1912
KRÜGER	1901
LACORDAIRE	1898
LAMARTINE	1897
L'AVENIR	1882
LE CYGNE	1880
LEONARD DE VINCI	1914
LEO XIII	1885
LE PASCAL	1905
LE ROBUSTE	1903
LIMA	1910
LOUIS FAUÇON	1892
LOUIS TRICON	1905
MADAME A. ROZAIN	1895
MADAME GUIGNARD	1891
MADAME ROSTAING	1894
MADAME ROZAIN	1886
M. LE BORGNE	1899
M. BONFIGLIOLI	1899
MENÉLIK	1899
MÉROPE	1889
M. E. VAUCHER	1892
M. GINDRE	1899
MICHEL ANGE	1914
MIKADO	1912
MINOS	1902
M. LEQUET	1902
M. LUQUET	1902
MME. CHAMBEYRON	1905
MME. DANJOUX	1902
M. RIBOULON	1900
MRS. CHARLES DANIELS	1891
O. BOTTERI	1891
PATRIE	1887
PAUL GAILLARD	1900

P. BRONDEL	1899
PHARAON	1912
POMPIEN	1907
PORT ARTHUR	1895
PORT SAY	1908
P. RADAELLI	1893
P. RESTELLI	1897
PRINCE D'ESSLING	1911
PRINCE GEORGES	1915
PROFUSION	1901
PYTHAGORE	1902
RAOUL D'ALLARD	1902
RENAULT-MORLIERE	1904
RIFLARD	1888
R.P. OLIVER	1898
RUBENS	1899
SAPHIR	1911
S. BOREL	1904
SCIPION	1902
SEMPERFLORENS	1888
SULTAN	1912
TORPILLEUR	1903
TROPHEE	1890
TSAR	1912
ULYSSE BONDON	1908
VAN DYKE	1914
VELASQUEZ	1914
VESTA	1896
VILLE DE LYON	1890
VIRGINAL	1891

JOHN SALTER (1798-1874)

Born in Hammersmith, London, he was by trade a cheesemonger. He established a nursery for the sale of English flowers at Versailles 1838-48. He then founded a nursery at Hammersmith where he specialised in chrysanthemums.

AENEAS	1845
AGATHA	1845
ALBINOS	1844
ALFREDI	1844
ALFRED SALTER	1851
AMADIS	1848
ANDROMEDA	1846
ANDROMEDA NOVA	1848
ARTEMISIA	1847
ATROSANGUINEA	1847
AUDOTI	1843
BAUDUIN	1844
BEAUTÉ PARFAITE	1846
BELLONA	1844?
BIANCA	1844
BRENNUS	1844
CHAUVIERII	1843
COMTE DE BEAULIEU	1846
CONQUEROR	1844

CORENTINI	1845
DIDO	1845
EDWARDSII	1843
ÉTOILE DE VERSAILLES	1848
EULALIE	1848
ÉVELINA	1847
GEANT OF VERSAILLES	1844
GLORIOT	1846
HENGIST	1853
HERCULES	1848
LA CHINOIS	1848
LANSEZEUR	1846
LE CHINOIS	1843
LEMICHEZ	1846
LEVERRIER	1846
MADAME BRAVY	1846
MADAME PELE	1846
MADAME THIBAUT	1847
MISS TALFOURD	1844
PIUS IX	1848
REINE DE FRANCAIS	1844
RÊVE D'AMOUR	1846
RHODERIC DHU	1845
ROSA QUINTAL	1848
SALTERII	1844
SANGUINEA SUPERBA	1842
SPLENDENS	1842
VICTORIA	1842
VULCAIN	1846

GEORGE SMITH (c.1812-1883)

Nurseryman of Liverpool Road, Islington, London and (?) of the Tollington Nursery, Hornsey Road, London. It is unclear from contemporary sources if there were infact two George Smiths active in the same period in London, or they were the same man working in the course of his life in two nurseries. The fuchsia cultivars attributed to G. Smith of Hornsey and/or Islington according to my father's research are as follows:

ADMIRAL BOXER	1856
ADONIS	1857
ALARIC	1859
ALPHA	1851
ALPHA	1872
AVALANCHE	1870
BEAUTY	1853
BELLE ÉTOILE	1851
BRIDESMAID	1863
BUTTERFLY	1860
CHANCELLOR	1859
CONQUEROR	1856
CONSPICUA	1863
CORONET	1855
CRITERION	1860
CYLINDRICA SUPERBA	1844

DANDY	1863
DELICATA	1854
DELIGHT	1873
DIADEM	1865
DICTATOR	1862
DREADNOUGHT	1866
EASTERN BEAUTY	1849
ECLAT	1859
ECLIPSE	1878
ELEGANTISSIMA	1860
EMPRESS	1868
EXCELLENT	1865
FANTASTIC	1865
FASCINATION	1859
FIGARO	1861
GENERAL LEE	1865
GENERAL WILLIAMS	1856
GLOBOSSA GRANDIFLORA	1844
GOLDEN PLOVER	1859
GOVENOR GENERAL	1858
GRAND CROSS	1868
GRAND DUCHESS	1880
GRAND DUKE	1864
GREAT EASTERN	1860
HAMLET	1845
HERCULES	1863
INIMITABLE	1850
JUNIUS	1845
KING OF PURPLES	1861
KOSSUTH	1850
LADY FRANKLIN	1853
LONDON RIVAL	1844
LORD NELSON	1849
LORD WOLSELEY	1883
MAGNUM BONUM	1881
MAMMOTH	1861
MEILLEZI	1854
NEGRO	1860
NIL DESPERANDUM	1852
NIMROD	1855
OMER PASHA	1855
ORION	1850
ORLANDO	1855
ORLANDO	1880
PERICLES	1859
PIONEER	1861
PRESIDENT	1881
PRIMA DONNA	1858
PRINCESS ALICE	1863
PRINCESS OF PRUSSIA	1858
PSYCHE	1851
PURPLE PRINCE	1870
QUEEN OF MAY	1850
QUEEN OF WHITES	1860
RAPPER	1868
SANSPAREIL	1863
SCIPIO	1859

Smith, G. cont.

SENATOR	1860
SIDONIA	1851
SOLFERINO	1860
SOLON	1860
STRIPED UNIQUE	1868
SULTAN	1870
TELEGRAPH	1854
UNIVERSAL	1862
WARRIOR	1868
WHITE UNIQUE	1874

JOHN SMITH
Nurseryman of Dalston, Hackney, London

ACHILLES	1844
ALATA	1843
ALBION	1844
ALICE MAUD	1844?
APOLLO	1843
ARBOREA	1841
ATLAS	1845
AURANTIA	1842
BEAUTY OF DALSTON	1846
BLANDA	1842
BRITANNIA	1842
CAPTIVATION	1848
CARNEA	1841
CHAMPION	1842
CLEOPATRA	1845
COCCINEA VERA	1844
COMPACTA	1842
CONSPICUA	1840
CORONET	1844
DALSTONII	1841
DECORA	1844
DEFIANCE	1843
ECLIPSE	1842
EMINENT	1845
ENCHANTRESS	1846
EXCELSEA	1842
EXIMIA	1846
EXPANSA	1844
GIGANTEA	1843
GRANDIS	1841
HECTOR	1844
HELENA	1845
HEROINE	1845
ILLICIFOLIA	1842
INCARNATA	1844
INVINCIBLE	1841
ISIGNIS	1841
LORD ASHLEY	1845
MAGNET	1845
MAGNIFICA	1841
MAGNIFLORA	1845
MAJESTICA	1843
MIRABLIS	1841

MODESTA	1844
MRS FRY	1845
NEPTUNE	1844
NIMROD	1844
NOBLISSIMA	1844
NONPAREIL	1848
ORION	1848
PARAGON	1843
PRINCEPS	1842
QUEEN VICTORIA	1843
RACEMOSA	1842
RECURVA	1845
REFLEXA	1844
ROBUSTA	1843
SALMONIA	1842
SANGUINEA	1840
SULTANA	1848
TRIUMPHANT	1844
VENUSTA	1845
VERNALIS	1842
VESTA	1844
VICTORY	1843

W H STORY
Nurseryman of Newton Abbott, England

AGNES	1852
ATTRACTION	1851
AURORA	1852
COUNTESS OF BURLINGTON	1856
DANDIE DINMOUNT	1856
DEVONIENSIS	1851
DUPLEX	1850
ELEGANTISSIMA	1849
EMPRESS EUGENIE	1855
FANTOME	1851
FLORENCE NIGHTINGALE	1855
GALANTHIFLORA PLENA	1855
GEM OF WHITEHILL	1856
GLORIOSA SUPERBA	1856
IGNEA	1849
MIRABLIS	1850
MRS STORY	1855
MULTIPLEX	1850
NEWTONIENSIS	1849
PECULIARITY	1852
PERUGINO	1855
PILOT	1856
PRINCE ARTHUR	1851
PULCHERRIMA	1842
QUEEN VICTORIA	1855
RAFFAELLE	1855
RANUNCULAEFLORA	1855
SNOWDROP	1855
SOUTH DEVON	1860
STAR	1856

STRIATA	1849
UNIQUE	1850
WATER NYMPH	1855

J N TWRDY
Nurseryman, working in Brno, Austria

ALABASTER	?
AMALIA	1870
AMOENA	1866
ANASTASIUS GRÜN	1878
ANNA MARIE	1884
ARCHIDUCHESSE MARIE THERESE	1874
BRUNA	1872
CUSTOZZA	1867
DON PEDRO	1872
EUROPA	1872
EXQUISITA	1878
GOLIATH	1866
HÉLÈNE	1876
HERCULE	1874
HERMINE	1879
LOHENGRIN	1873
MADAM KARL SCHICKLER	1872
MADAME LEMOINE	1872
MORAVIA	1873
PIETRO	1872
PRINCESS DESTRICHEN	1866
PSYCHE	1873
SCHNEEPYRAMIDE	1870
SCHWAN	1866
STRIATA INCOMPARIBLE	1868
TRIOMPHE DE BRUNN	1873
VICE ADMIRAL TEGETTHOFF	1867

WILLIAM YOUELL (-1883)
Nurseryman of Royal Nurseries, Great Yarmouth, Norfolk

AGNES	1846
ALICIA	1845
BEAUTY	1844
CONQUEROR	1846
CONSERVATIVE	1844
COUNTESS OF TYRECONNEL	1844
ELEGANS	1844
EXQUISITE	1843
GLOBOSA SPLENDENS	1845
HERO	1845
IRENE	1845
LACONII	1845
LADY ALICE PEEL	1844
LADY RAE REID	1843
LADY SALE	1844
LADY SONDES	1843
LADY WALSINGHAM	1844
LAURA	1846
LINDLEYANA	1844
LORD CLYDE	1859
MAGNIFICIENT	1846
MARCHIONESS OF NORMANBY	1844
MARCHIONESS OF ORMONDE	1843
MEDORA	1845
MODEL	1849
PERFECTION	1849
PRINCE ALBERT	1844
PRINCE OF WALES	1844
PRINCESS LOUISE	1845
PRINCESS ROYAL	1844
QUEEN VICTORIA	1844
SANSPAREIL	1846
SIR GEORGE MACKENZIE	1846
THE PRESIDENT	1849
TRANSPARENS	1843

BIBLIOGRAPHY

Sources are specifically recorded in the text for each named Fuchsia, however, I have also attempted to outline a bibliography for readers. To assimilate this list, I have only had books, papers and articles in my fathers possession, photocopies of various articles and old library borrowing request sheets, so it will be far from complete. I hope, however, that it will provide a useful summary of source materials, and give acknowledgement to other possible sources of information. At this point, I would also like to acknowledge the great help the late Leo Boullemier must have provided my father in sourcing documents. A great many of the photocopied articles in my fathers possession had been sent by Leo Boullemier, often neatly annotated with his own thoughts and observations.

Books & Articles

The Checklist of Species, Hybrids & Cultivars of the Genus Fuchsia	Leo Boullemier
A Practical Treatise on Fuchsias (1883)	Frederick Buss
Victorian Sportsman & Fuchsia Grower	Edward R G Banks of Sholden, Alec Cowan
Dictionary of British And Irish Botanists & Horticulturists	Ray Desmond
A Checklist of Fuchsias	E O Essig
R B Aubin & L M Berger, Fuchsiaphiles 1989	B M Y Fournier
Rozain-Boucharlat- Un Saga D'Horticulture, Fuchsiaphiles 1989-90	B M Y Fournier
Culture of Flowers & Plants	G Glenny
Glenny's Garden Almanac	G Glenny
Glenny's Illustrated Garden Forget Me Not	G Glenny
The Properties of Flowers & Plants	G Glenny
Early Horticultural Catalogues	John H Harvey, Victor Lemoine, Marcel Leanerts
A Revision of the Genus Fuchsia	Munz
Le Fuchsia (4 Editions)	Felix Porcher
Lovely Fuchsias	A G Puttock
The Garden under Glass (1914)	W F Rowlas, Victor Lemoine, Pierre Valck
James Lee & the Vineyard Nursery Hammersmith	E J Wilson
A Fuchsia Survey	W P Wood
The Fuchsia, A Garden History, The Plantsman	J O Wright

19th & Early 20th Century Periodicals & Journals

Botanical Register
Birmingham & Midland Gardeners Magazine
British Fuchsia Society, Early Annuals (1938-)
Cassell's Popular Gardening
Cottage Gardener & Illustrated Horticulture
Cottage Gardener & Country Gentleman
Curtis Botanical Magazine
De Fuchsia, Floralia, Vols IX & X by H Witte
Floral Cabinet & Magazine of Exotic Botany
Floral Annual
Floral Magazine
Floral World & Garden Guide
Flore des Serres et des Jardins de L'Europe
Floralia
Floricultural Cabinet
Floricultural Review & Florists & Gardeners Register
Floricultural Magazine
The Florist
Florist & Pomologist
Florists Journal
Florists Magazine
The Garden
The Garden & Practical Florist
The Fuchsia Book, American Fuchsia Society
Fuchsia Introductions (1 - 4) American Fuchsia Society
Garden Oracle & Economic Year Book

Garden Work for Villa, Suburban Town & Cottage Garden
Gardeners Chronicle
Gardeners Chronicle of Agricultural Gazette
Gardeners Magazine
Gardeners Weekly
Gardeners Record & Amateur Florists Companion
Gardening Illustrated
Gartenflora
Garten Zeitung
Horticultural Journal & Florists Register
Horticultural Register & General Magazine
L'Illustration Horticole
Journal of Horticulture & Cottage Gardener
Journal of Horticulture & Home Farmer
Journal of the Royal Horticultural Society
Loddiges Botanical Cabinet
Midland Florist
Maunds Botanic Garden
Moeller's Deutsche Gaertner Zeitung
Nederlandsch Tuinbouwblad
Paxton's Magazine of Botany
Revue Horticole
Scottish Gardener

Nurserymen's catalogues
Bainbridge & Hewison, York
B & H M Baker, Bourne Brooke Nurseries, Halstead, Essex
Bass & Brown, Sudbury, Suffolk
H A Brown, Chingford, London
Bruant, Poitiers, Catalogue General des Cultures Floriales
W J Bull, Chelsea - New & Choice Fuchsias
H Cannell & Sons. Floral Guide
Des Freres Cels, Chausee du Maine, Paris
J Cocker, Aberdeen, Catalogue of Florists Flowers, Bedding Plants, etc.
R Cooper
Dickson's Seed Warehouse, Chester
Dobbie & Co Florists, Rothesay, Scotland
John Forbes, Buccleuch Nurseries, Hawick
Girling, Stowmarket
Haage & Schmidt, Frankfurt
Joseph Harrison, Downham, Norfolk
Hart & Nicklin, Guildford
Howard & Smith
Thomas Jackson & Sons, Kingston
H J Jones
Kelways, Manual of Horticulture, Longport
J Laing, Forest Hill, S.E.
R B Laird & Sons, Catalogue of Florists Flowers
V Lemoine & Fils
Luccombe & Pince, Exeter
W Miller, Ramsgate
W Rumley, Richmond
Charles Turner's General Catalogue, Slough
James Veitch, Exeter
Vilmorin & Andrieux
H Walton, Burnley
B S Williams, New Plant Catalogue